Lecture Notes in Computer Science 5793

Commenced Publication in 1973
Founding and Former Series Editors:
Gerhard Goos, Juris Hartmanis, and Jan van Leeuwen

T0223388

Pedro M. Ruiz
Jose Joaquin Garcia-Luna-Aceves (Eds.)

Ad-Hoc, Mobile and Wireless Networks

8th International Conference, ADHOC-NOW 2009
Murcia, Spain, September 22-25, 2009
Proceedings

 Springer

Volume Editors

Pedro M. Ruiz
Faculty of Informatics, University of Murcia
Campus de Espinardo, Murcia, Spain
E-mail: pedrom@um.es

Jose Joaquin Garcia-Luna-Aceves
Department of Computer Engineering
University of California at Santa Cruz
317 Engineering 2 Bldg, Santa Cruz, CA 95063, USA
E-mail: jj@cse.ucsc.edu

Library of Congress Control Number: 2009934010

CR Subject Classification (1998): C.2, D.2, K.4.4, K.6.5, E.3, C.2.1

LNCS Sublibrary: SL 5 – Computer Communication Networks
and Telecommunications

ISSN   0302-9743
ISBN-10   3-642-04382-8 Springer Berlin Heidelberg New York
ISBN-13   978-3-642-04382-6 Springer Berlin Heidelberg New York

springer.com

© Springer-Verlag Berlin Heidelberg 2009
Printed in Germany

Typesetting: Camera-ready by author, data conversion by Scientific Publishing Services, Chennai, India
Printed on acid-free paper   SPIN: 12755837   06/3180   5 4 3 2 1 0

Preface

The 8th International Conference on Ad-Hoc Networks and Wireless (ADHOC-NOW 2009) was held September 22–25, 2009 in Murcia, Spain. Since ADHOCNOW started as a workshop in 2002, it has become a well-established and well-known international conference dedicated to wireless and mobile computing. During the last few years it has been held in Toronto, Canada (2002), Montreal, Canada (2003), Vancouver, Canada (2004), Cancun, Mexico (2005), Ottawa, Canada (2006), Morelia, Mexico (2007) and Sophia Antipolis, France (2008). The conference serves as a forum for interesting discussions on ongoing research and new contributions addressing both experimental and theoretical research in the area of ad hoc networks, mesh networks, sensor networks and vehicular networks.

In 2009, we recived 92 submissions from 28 different countries around the globe: Algeria, Australia, Brazil, Canada, China, Egypt, Finland, France, Germany, Greece, India, Iran, Ireland, Italy, Japan, Korea, Luxembourg, Malaysia, Mexico, Norway, Poland, Portugal, Serbia, South Africa, Spain, Tunisia, UK and USA. Of the submitted papers, we selected 24 full papers and 10 short papers for publication in the proceedings and presentation in the conference.

We are grateful to our Technical Program, Organizing and Steering Committees for their support. Without their help, expertise and experience we would not have been able to select such an outstanding technical program. We thank our invited speakers Andrew Campbell from Dartmouth College, Mischa Dohler from the Centre Tecnologic de Telecomunicacions de Catalunya (CTTC) and Silvia Giordano from the University of Applied Science (SUPSI) for accepting our invitation to give keynotes at the conference. We also thank our Local Arrangements Comittee members for their effort and good work at making the conference a success.

July 2009   Pedro M. Ruiz
                                                                J.J. Garcia-Luna-Aceves

Organization

ADHOCNOW 2009 was organized by the department of Information and Communications Engeneering, Univeristy of Murcia.

Executive Committee

Conference Chair	Pedro M. Ruiz (University of Murcia, Spain)
Program Co-chairs	Pedro M. Ruiz (University of Murcia, Spain)
	J.J. Garcia-Luna-Aceves (University of California at Santa Cruz, USA)
Submission Co-chairs	Juan A. Sanchez (University of Murcia, Spain)
	Hannes Frey (University of Paderborn, Germany)
Panel and Demonstrations	Carolina Pinart (Telefónica I+D, Spain)
	Juan A. Sanchez (University of Murcia, Spain)
Workshop Co-chairs	Miguel Labrador (University of South Florida, USA)
	Ivan Stojmenovic (University of Ottawa, Canada)
Publicity Co-chairs	Chun Tung Chou (University of New South Wales, Australia)
	Jaime Lloret (Universidad Politecnica de Valencia, Spain)
Local Organization	Antonio Ruiz-Martinez (University of Murcia, Spain)
	Juan A. Martinez (University of Murcia, Spain)
	Rafael Marin-Perez (University of Murcia, Spain)
	Juan A. Sanchez (University of Murcia, Spain)
	Francisco J. Ros (University of Murcia, Spain)
	Rafael Marin-Lopez (University of Murcia, Spain)
Steering Committee	Evangelos Kranakis (Carleton University, Canada)
	Michel Barbeau (Carleton University, Canada)
	S.S. Ravi (SUNY Albany, USA)

Ioannis Nikolaidis (University of Alberta,
Canada)

Violet R. Syrotiuk (Arizona State University,
USA)

Thomas Kunz (Carleton University, Canada)

Ivan Stojmenovic (University of Ottawa,
Canada)

Program Committee

Nael Abu-Ghazaleh	SUNY Binghamton, USA
Stefano Basagni	Northeastern University, USA
Luciano Bononi	University of Bologna, Italy
Jiannong Cao	Hong Kong Polytechnic University, Hong Kong, SAR China
Juan Carlos Cano	Universidad Politecnica de Valencia, Spain
Jean Carle	University of Lille, France
Arnaud Casteigts	SITE University of Ottawa, Canada
Edgar Chavez	Universidad Michoacana San Nicolas de Hidalgo, Mexico
Chun Tung Chou	University of New South Wales, Australia
Costas Constantinou	University of Birmingham, UK
Sajal Das	University Texas at Arlington, USA
Mischa Dohler	Centre Tecnologic de Telecom. de Catalunya, Spain
Falko Dressler	University of Erlangen, Germany
Vasilis Friderikos	King's College London, UK
Jie Gao	Stony Brook University, USA
Silvia Giordano	University of Applied Science - SUPSI, Switzerland
Xiaohua Jia	City University of Hong Kong, Hong Kong, SAR China
Holger Karl	University of Paderborn, Germany
Ralf Klasing	CNRS, France
Evangelos Kranakis	Carleton University, Canada
Thomas Kunz	Carleton University, Canada
Ivan Lequerica	Telefonica I+D, Spain
Xiang-Yang Li	Illinois Institute of Technology, USA
Xu Li	University of Ottawa, Canada
Weifa Liang	The Australian National University, Australia
Hai Liu	Hong Kong Baptist University, Hong Kong, China SAR
Pietro Manzoni	Universidad Politecnica de Valencia, Spain
Cecilia Mascolo	University of Cambridge, UK
Jelena Misic	University of Manitoba, Canada
Nathalie Mitton	University of Lille, France

Additional Reviewers

Sponsoring Institutions

Ministerio de Ciencia e Innovación through grant TEC2009-06754-E/TEC
Fundación Séneca under Grant 04552/GERM/06
Vicerrectorado de Investigación, University of Murcia

Table of Contents

Regular Papers

TCP over Multi-Hop Wireless Networks: The Impact of MAC Level
Interactions   1
    Adnan Majeed, Saquib Razak, Nael B. Abu-Ghazaleh, and
    Khaled A. Harras

Cooperative Signalling and Its Application in a Power-Controlled MAC
Protocol   16
    Minghao Cui and Violet R. Syrotiuk

Joint Source-Channel-Network Decoding and Blind Estimation of
Correlated Sensors Using Concatenated Zigzag Codes   30
    Javier Del Ser, Mikel Mendicute, Pedro M. Crespo,
    Sergio Gil-Lopez, and Ignacio (Iñaki) Olabarrieta

Challenges for Routing and Search in Dynamic and Self-organizing
Networks   42
    Gerhard Hasslinger and Thomas Kunz

Routing Metric for Interference and Channel Diversity in Multi-Radio
Wireless Mesh Networks   55
    Vinicius C.M. Borges, Daniel Pereira, Marilia Curado, and
    Edmundo Monteiro

Minimum Delay Data Gathering in Radio Networks   69
    Jean-Claude Bermond, Nicolas Nisse, Patricio Reyes, and
    Hervé Rivano

Asymptotic Delay Analysis and Timeout-Based Admission Control for
Ad Hoc Wireless Networks   83
    R. El-Azouzi, S.K. Samanta, E. Sabir, and R. El-Khoury

Statistical Properties of the Delivery Rate for Single-Sink and
Multiple-Sink Sensor Networks   98
    Marco Zuniga, Manfred Hauswirth, and Yang Yang

Application-Driven Analytic Toolbox for WSNs   112
    Jussi Haapola, Flavia Martelli, and Carlos Pomalaza-Ráez

A Diffusion Approximation Analysis of Multilevel Ad Hoc and Sensor
Networks 126
    Jerzy Martyna

Localized Sensor Self-deployment with Coverage Guarantee in Complex
Environment 138
    Xu Li, Nathalie Mitton, Isabelle Ryl, and David Simplot

An Efficient and Scalable Address Autoconfiguration in Mobile Ad Hoc
Networks 152
    Syed Rafiul Hussain, Subrata Saha, and Ashikur Rahman

Towards Fair Leader Election in Wireless Networks.................. 166
    Zbigniew Gołębiewski, Marek Klonowski, Michał Koza, and
    Mirosław Kutyłowski

Auction Aggregation Protocols for Wireless Robot-Robot
Coordination 180
    Ivan Mezei, Veljko Malbasa, and Ivan Stojmenovic

On Minimizing the Maximum Sensor Movement for Barrier Coverage
of a Line Segment.. 194
    J. Czyzowicz, E. Kranakis, D. Krizanc, I. Lambadaris,
    L. Narayanan, J. Opatrny, L. Stacho, J. Urrutia, and M. Yazdani

Mobile Sinks for Information Retrieval from Cluster-Based WSN
Islands 213
    Grammati Pantziou, Aristides Mpitziopoulos, Damianos Gavalas,
    Charalampos Konstantopoulos, and Basilis Mamalis

Secure EPC Gen2 Compliant Radio Frequency Identification 227
    Mike Burmester, Breno de Medeiros, Jorge Munilla, and
    Alberto Peinado

On the Trade-Off between User-Location Privacy and Queried-Location
Privacy in Wireless Sensor Networks 241
    Ryan Vogt, Mario A. Nascimento, and Janelle Harms

SenSearch: GPS and Witness Assisted Tracking for Delay Tolerant
Sensor Networks 255
    Lun Jiang, Jyh-How Huang, Ankur Kamthe, Tao Liu, Ian Freeman,
    John Ledbetter, Shivakant Mishra, Richard Han, and Alberto Cerpa

Monte Carlo Localization of Mobile Sensor Networks Using the Position
Information of Neighbor Nodes 270
    Hamid Mirebrahim and Mehdi Dehghan

Autonomous Transmission Power Adaptation for Multi-Radio
Multi-Channel Wireless Mesh Networks 284
    Thomas O. Olwal, Barend J. van Wyk, Karim Djouani,
    Yskandar Hamam, Patrick Siarry, and Ntsibane Ntlatlapa

A Decentralized Approach to Minimum-Energy Broadcasting in Static
Ad Hoc Networks 298
    Chris Miller and Christian Poellabauer

Heavily Reducing WSNs' Energy Consumption by Employing
Hardware-Based Compression 312
    Grigorios Chrysos and Ioannis Papaefstathiou

Optimal and Fair Transmission Rate Allocation Problem in Multi-hop
Cellular Networks 327
    Cristiana Gomes and Jérôme Galtier

Short Papers

A Topology Management Routing Protocol for Mobile IP Support of
Mobile Ad Hoc Networks 341
    Trung-Dinh Han and Hoon Oh

Implementation and Comparison of AODV and OLSR Routing
Protocols in an Ad-Hoc Network over Bluetooth 347
    Gorka Hernando, José María Cabero, José Luis Jodrá, and
    Susana Pérez

Inside-Out OLSR Scalability Analysis 354
    David Palma and Marilia Curado

Proximal Labeling for Oblivious Routing in Wireless Ad Hoc
Networks 360
    Edgar Chávez, Maia Fraser, and Héctor Tejeda

Proposal and Evaluation of a Caching Scheme for Ad Hoc Networks 366
    F.J. González-Cañete, E. Casilari, and A. Triviño-Cabrera

A Secure Spontaneous Ad-Hoc Network to Share Internet Access 373
    Raquel Lacuesta, Jaime Lloret, Miguel Garcia, and Lourdes Peñalver

A Middleware Family for VANETs 379
    Flávia C. Delicato, Lidia Fuentes, Nadia Gámez, and Paulo F. Pires

Joint IP Address and Public Key Certificate Trust Model for Mobile
Ad Hoc Networks 385
    Abdelhafid Abdelmalek, Mohamed Feham, Zohra Slimane, and
    Abdelmalik Taleb-Ahmed

A Localized Algorithm for Target Monitoring in Wireless Sensor
Networks 391
  Kamrul Islam and Selim G. Akl

A Wireless Sensor Network Architecture for Homeland Security
Application 397
  *António Grilo, Krzysztof Piotrowski, Peter Langendoerfer, and
  Augusto Casaca*

Author Index 403

TCP over Multi-Hop Wireless Networks: The Impact of MAC Level Interactions

Adnan Majeed[1], Saquib Razak[2],
Nael B. Abu-Ghazaleh[1,2], and Khaled A. Harras[2]

[1] State University of New York, Binghamton
{adnan,nael}@cs.binghamton.edu
[2] School of Computer Science, Carnegie Mellon University
{srazak,naelag}@cmu.edu, kharras@cs.cmu.edu

Abstract. In Multi Hop Wireless Networks (MHWNs), nodes act both as end-hosts as well as intermediate routers. When communication occurs, these nodes form chains between different sources and destinations. Researchers have studied how these chains behave, discovering that MAC level interactions play a major role in determining their performance. In this paper, we extend this analysis to study how TCP connections, which involve bidirectional flows, behave over wireless chains. First, we break down and examine the types of chains that occur most frequently in TCP configurations and classify them by the nature of the MAC level interactions that arise in each. We then show that the throughput of TCP over a wireless chain is greatly affected by the type of interactions within the chain. Finally, we show the implications of the MAC level interactions on network performance: specifically, route instability and number of retransmissions.

Keywords: Wireless Mesh Networks, MAC Interactions, TCP.

1 Introduction

Multi-Hop Wireless Networks (MHWNs) have increased in importance and usage at the edge of the Internet over the past several years. Community mesh networks can provide dynamic and extended coverage to urban and metropolitan areas. Sensor networks, another example of MHWNs, have a wide range of applications such as wild life monitoring, detection of potential forest fires, and disaster response scenarios. Mobile Ad-hoc Networks (MANETS), such as vehicular networks, provide connectivity to mobile users where infrastructure is expensive or unavailable.

Nodes in MHWNs route traffic among each other to provide connectivity between nodes that are not within direct transmission range. This sequence of nodes used to communicate between a source and destination is called a *path* or a *chain*, which represents a fundamental communication structure in MHWNs. Understanding chain behavior is critical to designing effective applications and transport layer protocols in MHWNs. Furthermore, insight into the performance

P.M. Ruiz and J.J. Garcia-Luna-Aceves (Eds.): ADHOC-NOW 2009, LNCS 5793, pp. 1–15, 2009.
© Springer-Verlag Berlin Heidelberg 2009

of current protocols on chains is critical to predict performance of MHWNs. Amongst these protocols, TCP is especially important due to its widespread use on the Internet.

Researchers have studied the performance of uni-directional flows [1, 2] as well as bi-directional flows (TCP) [3] over MHWNs. With regards to TCP, Xu et. al. study the behavior of TCP Tahoe, Reno, Sack and Vegas over *a chain* [3]. They only analyze the performance of TCP over a chain where each hop is 200 meters. According to our findings this type of chain accounts for 8.5% of chains that occur; over 90% of the chains that occur are not studied, neither is the performance of TCP over those chains. The performance of TCP over these chains depends on the interference relations between links in the chain; these relations also differentiate between chain types.

In general, links in a chain that do not share a common node can be active simultaneously; these links exhibit different interference interactions. These interactions arise because the state of the channel at the sender, where carrier sense is attempted, is different from that at the receiver. Thus, a sender may sense the channel to be idle, and transmit to a receiver whose channel is occupied, leading to a collision (hidden terminal problem [4]). The collisions caused by these interactions significantly affect chain behavior. Therefore, understanding these interactions and their impact on chain performance is an essential first step towards predicting behavior of MHWNs and the performance of protocols running over these networks.

In this paper we extend this understanding by analyzing how TCP behaves over different types of chains in a MHWN. We first identify the spectrum of chains that occur in a MHWN - all possible types of chains that occur in a network. We then identify the most frequently occurring chains and how often each of these occurs in a random MHWN; we evaluate the performance of TCP over this subset of chains. Finally, we discuss how these chains affect network performance and categorize the chains based this effect.

This analysis leads to insights into the behavior of TCP over MHWNs. Chains that appear identical to routing protocols can behave very differently based on the link interactions they exhibit; routing protocols ought to consider link interactions when picking routes. Furthermore, TCP generates two way traffic (Data and Ack); the overall performance of TCP over a chain depends on how efficiently traffic in both directions is transmitted. Finally, we discuss how the behavior of TCP over different chains affects network performance because of route instability and excessive retransmissions. Being aware of these observations can enable design of protocols that improve network performance.

The remainder of the paper is organized as follows. In Section 2 we discuss related work. In Section 3 we discuss the different types of interactions that occur; we also define naming conventions for chains and present the measured occurrence percentages of the different types of chains. We then evaluate the performance of TCP over the types of chains that occur most frequently in Section 4. In Section 5 we study the effect of chain behavior on network performance. We finally conclude and briefly discuss our future work in Section 6.

2   Related Work

Several researchers have been studying the behavior of chains in MHWNs. Li et al. examine the performance of chains as the number of hops are increased and study the effect of cross-interference between chains [5]. They analyze the effect of MAC 802.11 behavior on the performance of multi-hop chains but do not categorize interference patterns that govern network performance in terms of throughput and bandwidth utilization. Ping et al. present a hop by hop analysis of a multi-hop chain, study the impact of hidden terminals on the throughput chains, and present a quantitative approach towards estimating this throughput [6]. They show that hidden terminals cause packet drops affecting chain throughput and causing route stability.

Razak et al. have studied the effect of MAC interactions on single chains under saturated UDP traffic [1]. They develop a systematic methodology for determining the types of interaction that are possible in chains of 3 and 4 hops and the study the effect of these interactions on chain performance. They further extend their work to analyze chains of n hops. These studies do not consider the effect of TCP traffic on chain performance. TCP introduces several factors like bi-directional traffic, congestion control, round trip time estimations for timeout prediction etc. that are affected by interference interactions within a chain. As we will show in this paper, the types of interactions within chain have a substantial effect on the performance of a network under TCP traffic.

Xu and Saadawi evaluate the performance of TCP over wireless chains. They demonstrate that TCP traffic in a chain has instability problems that degrade chain throughput [3]. They study the effect of various TCP flavors and report a degradation of throughput from 11% in 3-hop chains to 21% in 7-hop chains. In this paper, we show that even within 3 and 4 hop chains, there is throughput degradation of around 25% based on the type of interactions between links of the chain. We also show that the chains Xu and Saadawi consider, represent a small fraction in the spectrum of chains that can occur in bi-directional flows.

3   Chains in a MHWN

In this section we observe all possible interactions under bi-directional flows in a chain. We start by analyzing 3-hop chains, which are the smallest chains with two links that can be simultaneously active. We then analyze chains with four hops. Under normal ratios of carrier sense and communication ranges (carrier sense range more than twice communication range), a four-hop chain is the smallest unit that allows us to analyze links within a chain with hidden terminal interactions. The analysis of three and four hop chains is the basic building block for generalizing this study for arbitrary long chains. This generalization is part of our future work. We first present some general terminology used throughout the paper. Afterwards, we describe the prominent types of link interactions possible in a chain in the presence of bi-directional TCP flows (data and ack). Finally, we determine the types of chains that are possible in a network and calculate occurrence probabilities for each of these chains.

3.1   Terminology

Wireless networks use Carrier Sense Multiple Access (CSMA) protocols to share the wireless medium. IEEE 802.11, which is based on Carrier Sense Multiple Access (CSMA), is the most commonly used channel access protocol in wireless networks. CSMA based protocols avoid simultaneous access to the medium from multiple transmitters by requiring each sender to sense the channel and transmit only after the channel has been idle for a specific amount of time. This method allows only one node to transmit within a Carrier Sense range of a transmitter. The channel is sensed around the sender and not the receiver, it is possible for the state of the channel to be different at the sender and the receiver. Hence packets transmitted by a node that senses the channel to be idle maybe dropped if the medium around the receiver is busy - the *hidden terminal* problem, which causes collisions that are detrimental to the performance of a wireless network.

Signal strength in wireless transmissions attenuates with distance and other environmental factors. A node can successfully receive a packet if the Signal to Interference and Noise Ratio (SINR) of a packet is above a certain threshold. This ability of a receiver to capture packets in the presence of interference from other transmitters is called the *capture effect*.

A chain is a sequence of nodes that forward messages to enable communication between a source and destination that are not within transmission range. Two consecutive nodes in the chain can communicate with each other and can exchange packets with eachother on both directions. We refer to this communication between two nodes as a *flow* and the communication channel is referred to as the *link*. Links that do not share a node can be active simultaneously and can affect each other at the MAC level. The location of the interacting links and the direction of flow on each link defines the interaction. The kind of effect these links have on each other is termed the interaction type.

3.2   Link Interactions

In multi-hop wireless networks, two interfering links can interact in several different ways. Given two source-destination pairs $S1 - D1$ and $S2 - D2$, there exist four secondary links: $S1 - S2$, $S1 - D2$, $S2 - D1$, and $D1 - D2$ that can interfer with each other. Although there can be a large number of combinations for these interactions [7, 8], we discover that a limited number of these interactions are possible between links of chain. We summarize these interactions in Figure 1, and briefly describe each one.

1. Senders Connected (SC): In SC interactions, the sources of the two links are within carrier sense range. Thus, CSMA prevents senders from concurrent transmissions; and no collisions other than those arising when the two senders start transmission at the same time will occur. These collisions are low in probability and we refer to them as synchronized collisions. SC interaction allow equal share of the channel between the senders.

2. Hidden Terminal (HT): In this interaction, the source for one link is a hidden terminal for the destination of the second link but not vice versa.

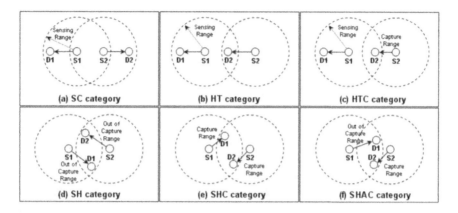

Fig. 1. The dominant types of link interactions observed in a MHWN

Both senders are disconnected and can transmit simultaneously. One destination drops its packets because of interference from the opposite sender. The other destination can successfully receive its packets because it does not experience any interference. In this interaction, one link will always be successful at obtaining maximum throughput, while the second link will experience frequent collisions that will detriment its performance.

3. Hidden Terminal with Capture (HTC): This interaction is similar to HT interaction but the destination that experiences interference is able to capture its packets. Hence whenever the source for this destinations starts transmission first, the link will experience successful packet reception and throughput on this link will not be as severely affected as in HT interaction [9].

4. Symmetric Hidden Terminal (SH): In this interaction, both links experience hidden terminals as both sources interfere with opposite destinations. Both links will experience collisions as the senders transmit concurrently causing throughput to be severely affected.

5. Symmetric Hidden Terminal with Capture (SHC): This interaction is similar to SH interaction except both links are able to capture their packets under interference from opposite sender. In this interaction, every simultaneous transmissions will be successful at one link (the link whose sender starts first) and will fail on the other link. This interaction will suffer from short term unfairness. Overall throughput for both links would be similar to SC interactions except at a cost of much higher number of transmissions.

6. Symmetric Hidden Terminal with Asymmetric Capture (SHAC) This interaction has hidden terminal between both links but only one destination is able to capture its packets. Symmetric interactions occur between links carrying Data traffic in forward direction and links carrying ACK packets back to the source. Because of the geometric restrictions of chains, there are no symmetric interaction between links with uni-directional flows.

3.3   Chain Interactions

We now identify and develop a naming convention for different types of chains, and present their occurrence probabilities in random networks. Figure 2 illustrates the link interactions that we study in three and four hop chains. Each row has an interaction number along with the links in that interaction. The arrows in each row mark which links are considered in that interaction; the arrow direction depicts the flow direction considered. For the TCP flow running on a chain, node 0 is the source and node 3 and node 4 are the destinations for three and four hop chains respectively. Therefore, in the figure, all flows towards the right carry TCP Data packets and all flows towards the left carry TCP Ack packets.

Razak et al. have determined that, between any two links, there can be 10 different interference interaction possible [8]. For a three-hop chain only interactions i1 - i4 apply. With 4 interactions and 10 interaction types for each interaction we can have 10^4 types of chains. In a four-hop chain, the possibilities are even more overwhelming. Four hop chains have 12 interactions, each with 10 possible interaction types; we can have 10^{12} different chains. Fortunately due to geometric limitations, in reality there are only 3 chain types that most commonly occur in three-hop chains and 8 chain types that commonly occur in four-hop chains.

We use the following notation to name these chains: Each chain is represented as F/B/C. F is the prominent interaction between links carrying the forward traffic (data). B is the prominent interaction between links carrying backward traffic (ack), C is the prominent interaction between cross links, i.e. between links

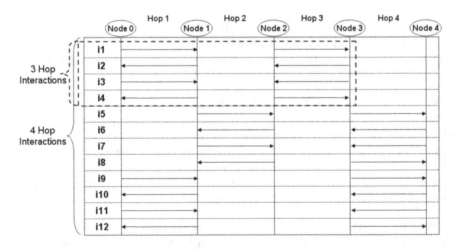

Fig. 2. All the interactions in a three and four hop chain. Each row shows the interaction between two specific links in specific directions.

Table 1. The types of four-hop chains that occur most frequently in a MHWN. The last three columns depict the interaction number of the dominant interaction (refer to Figure 2) in the forward, backward and cross flows, respectively. A dash (-) means that no interaction dominates in that direction. Note that current routing protocols can not differentiate between these chains even though they are significantly different.

Occurrence Percentage	Chain Type Forw/Back/Cross	Dominant Interaction		
		Forward	Backward	Cross
7.3	HT/SC/SHAC	i9	-	i3
3.6	HTC/HTC/SHAC	i9	i10	i7
8.4	HTC/HTC/SHC	i9	i10	i3
32.1	HTC/SC/HTC	i9	-	i11
2.3	SC/HT/HTC	-	i10	i11
1.8	SC/HTC/HTC	-	i10	i11
1.6	SC/SC/SC	-	-	-
37.8	SC/SC/SHC	-	-	i11

carrying forward traffic (data) and backward traffic (ack). A prominent interaction, as used in the above naming, is defined as the interaction number (from Figure 2) that has the most effect on the performance of a chain in a particular direction, forward, backward or cross. Table 1 illustrates the four-hop chains that occur most frequently and states the interaction number of the prominent interaction in the forward, backward and cross flow. The table showing the same information for three hop chains is omitted due to space constraints.

In order to determine commonly occurring interactions and calculate their occurrence probability, we consider a 1500m x 1500m network with 500 nodes, randomly placed with uniform distribution. For routing, we use our implementation of NADV [10], which uses a greedy protocol to pick best next hop at each node. The metric for selecting the hop is the product of link quality and distance traveled towards the destination.

We use this routing protocol to generate all possible three and four hop chains in random networks. We classify the chains according to their type, using the F/B/C convention described above, and study the most frequently occurring chains. Figure 3 shows occurrence probabilities of chain types for three and four hop chains as the carrier sense is varied.

To avoid clutter, we only study a subset of the chains that occur. This subset consists of all chains that have an occurrence probability of over 1.5% in a random network for a realistic carrier sense to transmission range ratio. Most commercial radios set carrier sense range to slightly over twice the transmission range, and this is what we define realistic carrier sense to transmission range ratio to be. As the carrier sense range is increased more pairs of nodes in the network become sender connected until (as depicted in Figure 3(b)) the carrier sense range is high enough to make all nodes in the network sender connected and the only chain type remaining is SC/SC/SC.

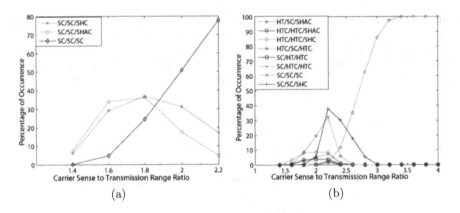

Fig. 3. Occurrences of Different Types of Chains. (a) shows the occurrence probability of 3-hop chains.(b) shows the occurrence probability of 4-hop chains.

4   TCP Evaluation over Chains

In this section we evaluate, via simulation, the behavior of a TCP flow on different chains that occur in a MHWN. We start with three hop chains; the smallest chains that have the interactions we consider. These chains show how TCP behaves when the sources are sender-connected. In general, chains in MHWNs are not limited to three hops; we study four hop chains as well. These give us insight into how TCP behaves over chains in which not all links are sender-connected. This analysis of TCP over three and four hop chains is an important step towards understanding TCP performance over general n-hop chains.

We use network simulator (ns-2 release 2.33) to analyze TCP performance over the most frequently occurring chains identified in section 3. We use FTP at the application layer with TCP Tahoe as the transport layer protocol; all simulation parameters have default values. The simulations use static routes and last 75 seconds each Using static routes ensures that efects of TCP over MHWN are isolated from routing layer effects.

4.1   TCP on Three Hop Chains

This section discusses the performance of TCP over three hop chains. Figure 4(a) illustrates that the SC/SC/SHAC chain has approximately 25% lower throughput compared to the SC/SC/SC and SC/SC/SHC chain. In the SC/SC/SHAC chain links carrying backward flow, i.e. ack traffic, have an SHAC interaction with links carrying forward flow, i.e. data traffic. This interaction causes unfairness towards the forward flow on Hop1. All such cases, where a link carrying backward flow asymmetrically causes drops at a link carrying forward flow, behave similar to each other.

We explain this behavior by a detailed discussion of how the SHAC interaction acts in an SC/SC/SHAC chain. Refer to Figure 2 for the numbers and locations of the nodes and hops used in the following explanation. In the SC/SC/SHAC chain, Hop1 and Hop3 behave as follows. Nodes 0 and 3 can transmit concurrently since they are not sender-connected. When both these nodes transmit concurrently there is a collision at node 1 since it is in capture range with both nodes. However, when node 3 starts transmitting before node 0, node 2 is able to capture the packet [9]; a collision at node 2 occurs only when node 0 starts transmission before node 3. In this interaction, the link between node 0 and node 1 is the *weak* link, i.e. it faces unfairness in terms of collisions. Figure 4(b) shows that this unfairness causes the collision drops for TCP traffic at Hop1 for the SC/SC/SHAC chain to be significantly higher than the other two types of chains. This translates to a high retransmission overhead as depicted in Figure 4(a).

At the TCP layer this effect causes the forward going link to drop packets anytime hops Hop1 and Hop3 are active simultaneously. The repeated TCP drops cause timeouts at the sender and the congestion window is reduced to one. In the mean time, the ack traffic acquires enough channel access to empty the chain of acks, eventually reducing the traffic in the chain. This reduction allows the sender to successfully obtain access to the medium and finally resume transmitting successfully. This phenomenon keeps repeating, causing inefficient use of the medium. This pattern results in the 25 percent lower throughput for the SC/SC/SHAC chain.

In the case of the SC/SC/SHC chain, the SHC interaction is also between Hop1 carrying data traffic and Hop3 carrying ack traffic. However in this case the interaction is symmetric and which ever of nodes 0 and 1 starts transmitting first has a successful transmission. Hence, the collision overhead is much lower at Hop1 in this case causing comparatively better throughput and lower retransmission overhead.

The SC/SC/SC chain is the best in terms of performance and efficiency. It has the lowest overhead since all the sources are sender connected and the medium

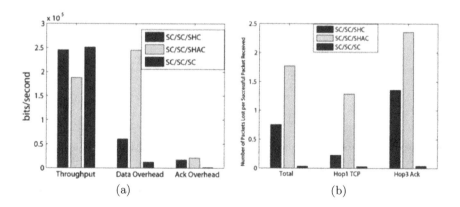

Fig. 4. Performance of Three-Hop Chains. (a) Throughput achieved by each chain and the retransmission overhead of data and ack packets. (b) MAC collisions in each chain and how many of these are data packet drops at Hop1 and ack packet drops at Hop3.

arbitration is synchronized. The only collisions in this case are synchronized collisions. These collisions are caused when two nodes that are sender connected are ready to transmit a packet, sense the medium as idle and then transmit at the same time. Such collisions occur infrequently [11].

We observe that running TCP over chains that are not sender connected, but have symmetric interactions, may give approximately the same throughput as sender connected chains. However, as demonstrated by the higher overhead in Figure 4(a), they generate much more traffic to give the same throughput. This is undesirable due to the effect this behavior can have on other flows in the network. This effect is discussed in more detail in Section 5.

The performance of a chain worsens if the interaction types in the chain are asymmetric in addition to not being sender-connected. These chains have a large number of collisions, leading to excessive retransmissions, leading to further collisions. This translates to a lower throughput for these chains.

4.2 TCP on Four Hop Chains

Chains in MHWN are not limited to three hops; they can be longer. Hence, studying the performance of four hop chains becomes important for a number of reasons. These chains can actually occur in a network, so knowing how they perform is critical to predicting MHWN performance. Furthermore, four hop chains have a variety of interactions that are not sender-connected. Studying TCP behavior over such chains is a critical step towards analyzing TCP behavior over general n-hop chains.

Figure 5(a) presents the throughput of the chains we study. The chains that are not sender-connected and have asymmetric interactions, where the link carrying forward flow is weak, cause severe throughput degradation For all other cases the throughput achieved is comparable. Figure 5(a), however, exhibits that there is a significant difference in retransmission overhead depending on whether the senders are connected or not. Furthermore, the overhead varies significantly

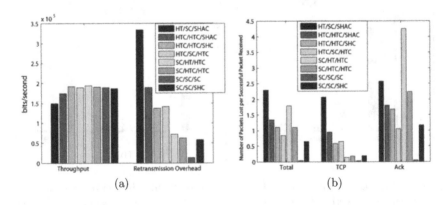

Fig. 5. Performance of Four Hop Chain

based on whether an interaction causes more drops at a link carrying forward flow or the backward flow.

Based on these factors, the chains in a MHWN can be classified into two main classes. Chains (1) where links carrying data flow are the weak links in an interaction and (2) where links carrying ack flow are the weak links in an interaction. Table 2 lists which chains fall in each of these classes. In some chains there are interactions that cause both the data the ack flow to be weak. In such cases, performance of the chain suffers more due to the link carrying data flow being weak. Therefore, these chains are considered in the class (1), described above. We now discuss each of these classes in detail.

1. Chains where the forward going links are at a disadvantage: These chains can be broadly described as having an interaction that causes collisions at an upstream link carrying data packets. The link causing these collisions is a downstream link carrying data or ack packets. The performance of a chain in this category depends on (a) how many such weak links a chain has; and (b) the severity of the interaction.

In Section 4.1 we explained in detail how losses occur in the presence of asymmetric interactions. The same explanation also applies to four-hop chains. If the interaction type is an HT, then the data flow has collisions until all the packets at nodes downstream to this link have been transmitted. After that the data flow can successfully transmit; this pattern keeps repeating. An SHAC is another interaction that causes severe overhead. Anytime the two links that have an SHAC interaction transmit concurrently, the weaker link loses a packet. This degrades performance by causing excessive retransmissions at the weak link. However, with an HTC interaction the weak link starts transmissions before the

Table 2. The macro-effects shown by each chain type. The third and fourth columns state, for each chain type, whether or not there is a link interaction that causes a forward or backward flow to be weak, respectively. The fifth column qualitatively states the amount of interference generated by a chain of each type. The last column qualitatively states the number of route discovery generated due to consecutive collisions of the same MAC packet. Based on how the interference generated and the route instability caused, the chains are grouped into categories.

| Category | Chain Type | Weak Interaction | | Interference | Route |
		Forward	Backward	Generated	Instability
A	HT/SC/SHAC	Yes	Yes	High	Low
	HTC/HTC/SHAC	Yes	Yes	Medium	Low
	HTC/HTC/SHC	Yes	Yes	Medium	Low
	HTC/SC/HTC	Yes	Yes	Medium	Low
B	SC/HT/HTC	No	Yes	Low	High
	SC/HTC/HTC	No	Yes	Low	Medium
C	SC/SC/SC	No	No	Negligible	None
	SC/SC/SHC	No	Yes	Low	Low

stronger link roughly half the time and is successful. The effect of HTC is, hence, not as severe as SHAC or HT.

Among the chains in this class, HT/SC/SHAC behaves the worst in terms of throughput and overhead. This result is intuitive since this chain has two interactions where a link carrying data flow is weak, one HT and one SHAC. The HTC/HTC/SHAC chain has the HT replaced with an HTC interaction resulting in slightly better performance. However, the performance is significantly lower than the other chains.

The HTC/HTC/SHC and HTC/SC/HTC chains are similar to each other and better than both HT/SC/SHAC and HTC/ HTC/SHAC in terms of achieved throughput. The interactions of the links carrying TCP data packets in these two chains are similar. The only difference is that in HTC/SC/HTC Hop1 carrying forward flow is competing with both Hop3 and Hop4 carrying backward flow. However, HTC/HTC/SHC has Hop1 carrying forward flow competing with Hop3 carrying backward flow and Hop2 carrying forward flow competing with Hop4 carrying backward flow. So node0 in an HTC/SC/HTC chain has both node3 and node4 as hidden terminals causing TCP data packet drops while in the HTC/HTC/SHC chain node0 has only one hidden terminal. This difference causes HTC/SC/HTC to have more TCP packet drops at Hop1 resulting in worse performance, in terms of transmission overhead.

2. Chains where the backward going links are at a disadvantage: These chains have interactions that cause collisions at links carrying ack traffic. The collisions could be from other links carrying ack traffic or from links carrying data traffic. The chains that are affected on the most part by this category of interactions are SC/HT/HTC, SC/HTC/HTC and SC/SC/SHC. Qualitatively, the affects caused by HT, HTC and SHC on the ack traffic is the same as what was described above for the case where links carrying TCP packets were at a disadvantage. There are two main differences here however. (1) Ack packets are smaller and hence there is a lower probability (compared to TCP packets) that they will collide with another transmission. However, it is also possible for multiple retransmissions of the same ack packet to collide with a single TCP packet. The smaller size of ack packets causes their transmissions to be shorter and hence retransmissions can be scheduled faster. This effect causes the number of collision drops per delivered packet in the SC/HT/HTC, SC/HTC/HTC and SC/SC/SHC chains (depicted in Figure 5(b)) to be higher than the case where links carrying TCP data packets are at a disadvantage. (2) Due to the much smaller size of the ack packets the overhead of ack collisions is much lower. This is the reason the overhead observed in Figure 5(a) is much lesser for these chains even though the number of ack collisions are close.

The only chain that does not fit in either of these categories is the SC/SC/SC chain. As described in Section 4.1 the transmitters in an SC/SC/SC chains have a complete view of the medium and can arbitrate it in a way to avoid all the affects that cause performance degradation in the other chains.

5 Discussion

This section discusses the impact of chain behavior on a MHWN. We first discuss the interference effect of different chains due to retransmission traffic. We then discuss route instability caused by the behavior of different chains. Table 2 presents the qualitative impact of chain interactions on network interference and route stability. Finally, we categorize chains according to their performance and describe the behavior of each category.

Interference Effects: Figures 4(a) and 5(a) illustrate the retransmission overhead of the chains we analyzed. In the three-hop case, SC/SC/SC gives 25% better throughput, compared to SC/SC/SHAC, using only 5% of the retransmission overhead. Since the overhead is measured in terms of unsuccessful transmissions, this means that by avoiding all of those additional transmissions the SC/SC/SC chain kept the medium busy for a smaller duration – still achieving better performance. The difference is even more pronounced in the four-hop case when comparing SC/SC/SC with HT/SC/SHAC. In this case the HT/SC/SHAC chain has a very high retransmission overhead and a 25% lower throughput. Therefore, in a MHWN limiting connections to use chains that have low retransmission overhead would significantly increase network throughput by facilitating medium reuse. On the other hand, using chains with undesirable interactions greatly increases interference in the network while providing similar or lower throughput to the sender-connected chains.

Route Instability: As mentioned in section 4.1 and 4.2, SHAC and HT interactions affect TCP performance due to numerous collisions. Some routing protocols decide that a route is lost if a certain number of consecutive MAC transmissions lost [12,13]; the routing protocol then initiates route discovery. In the absence of RTS/CTS this number is set to seven. In chains that cause numerous collisions such protocols would initiate route discovery numerous times. Since the route is not lost, the same route will be found every time. Figure 6 shows the number of such route drops in each chain and then breaks up the route drops depending on whether they were caused by TCP data packet collisions or TCP ack packet collisions. Notice that even though ack collisions do not cause significant overhead in terms of bits/second retransmitted, their effect on initiating route discovery is significant. Recall from section 4.2 that due to smaller size collisions of TCP ack packets are significantly higher in number.

Ranking Interactions: Table 2 separates the four-hop chains in categories based on how each chain affects the network. From the table we can see that chains that have interactions where the link carrying data traffic (forward flow) is at a disadvantage generate more retransmission traffic; keeping the medium busy longer. This is due to the high retransmission cost of TCP data packet collisions. The chains in category A are of this type. These links also have interactions where the link carrying ack traffic (backward flow) is at a disadvantage. However, the forward flow being at a disadvantage causes a larger affect and so these chains show relatively lower route instability compared to category B. Category B is the

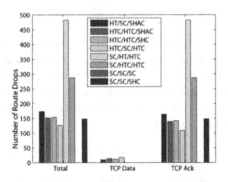

Fig. 6. Route Instability

set of chains that have interactions where the links carrying backward flow are at a disadvantage. This causes a large number of route drops and hence higher route instability.

The attractive category in terms of performance is category C. It has the least amount of interference generated, due to retransmissions, and minimal route instability. From table 1 we see that nearly 40% of the chains in a random network are of this category. Therefore, when a MHWN carries TCP traffic, the link interactions in the forward and backward path both enable efficient communication. Therefore, routing protocols should pick routes that are sender connected in the forward as well as the backward direction. Furthermore, assymetric interactions significantly affect throughput and the routing protocol should, as much as possible, avoid chains with such interactions.

6   Conclusions and Future Work

In this paper, we have demonstrated that wireless chains, that otherwise appear identical to higher layers, can have very different MAC interactions. This difference in MAC interactions between the links of these chains can cause up to 25 percent difference in throughput performance. Furthermore, in some cases, even if the throughput is not affected by these interactions, inefficient chains require a significantly higher number of MAC transmissions to achieve the same throughput. These retransmissions keep the medium busy and degrades throughput of the network. Based on the observed interactions, we have proposed a ranking of the chains in a MHWN. Sender-connected chains provide high throughput with low retransmission overhead and ought to be favored by higher layers.

The analysis and results we have presented in this paper represent a first step towards a better understanding of how chains behave in a general network setting and how performance is affected by cross chain effects. For future work, we plan to extend our analysis to larger n-hop chains. Furthermore, we would like to evaluate and develop routing protocols that exploit this knowledge to improve network performance.

References

1. Razak, S., Abu-Ghazaleh, N.: Self-Interference in Multi-hop wireless chains. In: Coudert, D., Simplot-Ryl, D., Stojmenovic, I. (eds.) ADHOC-NOW 2008. LNCS, vol. 5198, pp. 58–71. Springer, Heidelberg (2008)
2. Razak, S., Kolar, V., Abu-Ghazaleh, N., Harras, K.A.: How do wireless chains behave? the impact of mac interactions. Technical report under arxiv.org: cs.NI arXiv:0903.1002v1 (2009), http://arxiv.org/abs/0903.1002v1
3. Xu, S., Saadawi, T., Lee, M.: On tcp over wireless multi-hop networks. In: Military Communications Conference MILCOM. Communications for Network-Centric Operations: Creating the Information Force, vol. 1, pp. 282–288. IEEE, Los Alamitos (2001)
4. Kleinrock, L., Tobagi, F.: Packet switching in radio channels. IEEE Transactions on Communications (1975) (Part I and Part II)
5. Li, J., Blake, C., DeCouto, D., Lee, H., Morris, R.: Capacity of ad hoc wireless networks. In: MobiCom, pp. 61–69 (2001)
6. Ng, P., Liew, S.: Throughput analysis of 802.11 multi-hop ad hoc networks. IEEE/ACM Trans. Netw. 15(2), 309–322 (2007)
7. Garetto, M., Shi, J., Knightly, E.W.: Modeling media access in embedded two-flow topologies of multi-hop wireless networks. In: MobiCom 2005 (2005)
8. Razak, S., Abu-Ghazaleh, N.B., Kolar, V.: Modeling of two-flow interactions under sinr model in multi-hop wireless networks. In: Proc. LCN, pp. 297–304 (2008)
9. Kochut, A., Vasan, A., Shankar, A.U., Agrawala, A.: Sniffing out the correct physical layer capture model in 802.11b. In: ICNP 2004, pp. 252–261 (2004)
10. Lee, S., Bhattacharjee, B., Banerjee, S.: Efficient geographic routing in multihop wireless networks. In: MobiHoc, pp. 230–241 (2005)
11. Bianchi, G.: Performance analysis of the ieee 802.11 distributed coordination function. IEEE Journal on Selected Areas in Comm. 18(3) (2000)
12. Johnson, D., Maltz, D., Hu, Y.-C.: The dynamic source routing protocol for mobile ad hoc networks (DSR). IETF draft (2003)
13. Perkins, C.E., Royer, E.M.: Ad-hoc on-demand distance vector routing. In: WM-CSA 1999: Proceedings of the Second IEEE Workshop on Mobile Computer Systems and Applications, p. 90. IEEE Computer Society, Los Alamitos (1999)

Cooperative Signalling and Its Application in a Power-Controlled MAC Protocol

Minghao Cui and Violet R. Syrotiuk

School of Computing, Informatics and Decision Systems Engineering
Arizona State University, P.O. Box 878809, Tempe, AZ   85287-8809
{minghao.cui,syrotiuk}@asu.edu

Abstract. In wireless networks utilizing half-duplex transceivers, a mechanism is required to inform a sender of the outcome of its transmission. Traditionally, such feedback comes from the receiver. This approach cannot distinguish between a failure due to a collision at the receiver and a failure due to the receiver moving out of range. To address this problem we propose *cooperative signalling*, where nodes that overhear the transmission provide feedback to the sender in addition to the feedback from the receiver. Cooperating nodes also provide information to the receiver, allowing it to distinguish between failures which, in turn, enables the sender to respond to each outcome differently. We apply cooperative signalling in a *carrier sense multiple access* (CSMA) protocol using transmission power control. In simulation, CSMA/PC achieves substantial improvements in throughput per unit energy compared to IEEE 802.11 in both static and mobile ad hoc networks.

1   Introduction

In wireless networks feedback is essential when the transceiver at each node is *half-duplex*, i.e., it cannot both transmit and receive at the same time. As a result, some strategy is required to inform a sender of the outcome of its transmission. Traditionally, this feedback is provided by the receiver to the sender. Consider the four-way handshake of the IEEE 802.11 distributed coordination function [1], a variant of the *carrier sense multiple access with collision avoidance* (CSMA/CA) *medium access control* (MAC) protocol. A *clear-to-send* (CTS) control packet is fed back to the sender in response to a *request-to-send* (RTS) control packet, and an *acknowledgment* (ACK) control packet is fed back in response to a data packet received without error. When reception fails, the sender obtains no feedback at all. As a result, the sender cannot distinguish between a collision at the receiver and a receiver that has moved out of range.

In this paper, we introduce the idea of *cooperative signalling* where a node that overhears some or all of the handshake provides feedback to the sender in addition to the feedback from the receiver. It also provides information to the receiver allowing it to distinguish between failures which, in turn, enables the sender to respond to each outcome differently.

P.M. Ruiz and J.J. Garcia-Luna-Aceves (Eds.): ADHOC-NOW 2009, LNCS 5793, pp. 16–29, 2009.

Consider a receiver moving away from a sender in a mobile wireless network. Cooperative signalling may allow the sender to detect and report a link failure to the network layer faster than after attempting a fixed number of retransmissions. This could significantly decrease the delay caused by link failures and reduce the energy associated with retransmissions. The potential responsiveness of protocols to more informative signalling may be significant.

In this paper we develop one application of cooperative signalling, in particular its use in a CSMA based MAC protocol for nodes with a half-duplex transceiver capable of transmission *power control* (PC). We assume that the transceiver at each node may be tuned on a per-packet basis to any value in the range $[P_{min}, P_{max}]$, the minimum and the maximum transmission power, respectively.

Cooperative signalling enables CSMA/PC to use a binary search strategy to quickly find the appropriate transmission power, rather than simply follow a predetermined sequence of transmission power levels as in [2,3]. Specifically, cooperative signalling allows CSMA/PC to decide when to increase or to decrease the transmission power. Through simulation, we show that CSMA/PC achieves substantial improvements in throughput per unit energy compared to IEEE 802.11 in both static and mobile ad hoc networks.

The rest of this paper is organized as follows. We discuss related work on cooperation and power control in §2. The idea and a possible implementation of cooperative signalling is described in §3. §4 introduces the CSMA/PC protocol utilizing transmission power control and cooperative signalling. Simulation results comparing CSMA/PC to IEEE 802.11 are presented in §5. Finally, we conclude and propose future work in §6.

2   Related Work

We overview related work on cooperation and power control in the context of medium access control.

Liu et al. [4] propose a cooperative MAC protocol for wireless local area networks. If the direct path between a source and destination has a low signal-to-noise ratio, then using an intermediate cooperating node that relays the packet may be effective. A *cooperative asynchronous multi-channel MAC* (CAM-MAC) protocol is proposed by Luo et al. [5]. In CAM-MAC, the transmitter and receiver obtain channel usage information from idle neighbours (i.e., cooperating nodes) after the handshake; this aids in channel selection.

Transmission power control may be applied at the MAC layer to decrease power consumption. Karn [6] uses a sender to specify its transmission power in the RTS, and the receiver to set the desired transmission power in the CTS. The receiver determines the transmission power based on the required signal-to-noise ratio. The data and ACK packets are then transmitted at the power indicated in the CTS rather than at maximum power. Jung and Vaidya [7] improve this scheme by periodically increasing the transmission power of the data packet to the maximum power to ensure proper reception of the ACK.

Transmission power control may also be applied to increase spectrum reuse. Monks et al. [8] propose the *power control multiple access* (PCMA) protocol, where a control channel is used for carrier sensing. The receiver periodically sends a busy tone on the control channel. A potential sender listens to the busy tone to determine an upper bound on its transmission power so as to not add too much noise to the existing reception. Wu et al. [9] combine busy tones and power control. They use a separate control and data channel together with two busy tone channels, BT_t and BT_r, for transmission and reception respectively. The receiver sends a busy tone BT_r at maximum power. A neighbour can then estimate the channel gain based on the strength of the busy tone and determine whether it is allowed to transmit if its transmission would not add more than a fixed amount of noise; this is similar to PCMA [8]. In addition, the sender saves energy by transmitting the data packets and busy tone BT_t at reduced power based on the power level of the received CTS.

Muqattash and Krunz [10] propose the *power controlled dual channel* (PCDC) protocol in which the RTS and CTS are transmitted on a control channel. The RTS indicates the transmission power used in a new field. The receiver determines the channel gain based on the RTS it receives and computes a required power level for the sender, allowing for a number of future interfering transmissions to take place in its neighbourhood, and puts it in a new field of the CTS. In [11], Muqattash and Krunz devise the *power controlled MAC* (POWMAC) protocol to effectively utilize power control on a single channel. An access window precedes data transmission, during which other neighbouring nodes within the interference range can exchange a handshake if the interference introduced by the new transmission to the on-going communication is below a fixed signal-to-noise ratio; this provides the possibility of concurrent transmission.

3   Cooperative Signalling

Consider Fig. 1, where a circle[1] indicates the transmission range of the node at its center, and an arrow indicates a data transmission. For simplicity, only the transmitter and receiver are shown; *cooperating nodes*, i.e., nodes that overhear some or all of a transmission, are omitted. The figure illustrates types of feedback potentially available to a MAC protocol.

Figure 1(a) shows a transmission received successfully. However, suppose that the feedback transmitted by the receiver is lost. A lost acknowledgment may cause the sender to enter a round of backoff and retransmission. In cooperative signalling, a cooperating node also feeds the acknowledgment back to the sender which may prevent it from entering an unnecessary round of backoff and retransmission.

Now suppose that the sender's transmission fails to reach the receiver. The sender may be able to act if it can obtain the reason for failure. Figure 1(b) and (c) show two reasons for failure. In the first case the receiver is out of the transmission range of the sender, while in the second case there is a collision of packets at one receiver. As we will see, a cooperating node may help the receiver distinguish between these two cases.

---

[1] A circle is used for simplicity.

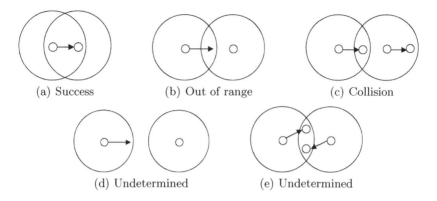

(a) Success   (b) Out of range   (c) Collision

(d) Undetermined   (e) Undetermined

Fig. 1. Types of feedback

There are some situations in which a cooperating node may not help determine a reason for failure. For example, in Fig. 1(d) the receiver is more than twice the transmission range away from the sender; in this case, even a cooperating node cannot help inform the receiver. In Fig. 1(e), there are two concurrent transmissions that result in a collision at two receivers, where both receivers are in range of each sender. Here, cooperating nodes overhear a collision and cannot help.

Although a cooperating node may not always be able to help determine the reason for failure, *in the worst case cooperative signalling degrades into traditional feedback.*

3.1   The Cooperative Signalling Mechanism

Now consider the scenario in Fig. 2(a) in which there is a sender A, its intended receiver B, as well as two cooperating nodes C and D. In traditional feedback, if the sender A transmits a packet to B then the receiver B responds with feedback (if any).

In *cooperative signalling*, a cooperating node provides feedback to the sender in addition to the feedback from the receiver. It also provides information to the receiver that may allow it to distinguish between failures. The receiver's outcome can, in turn, be fed back to the sender with the help of cooperating nodes, enabling the sender to respond to each outcome differently.

To achieve cooperation we introduce a new type of control packet, called a *hint*, sent by cooperating nodes. The hints are very small: they contain a six byte destination address, and one byte to indicate the type of feedback. As well, we introduce new control packets for the receiver to feed back to the sender, in addition to the commonly used feedback of a positive or negative acknowledgment (ACK/NACK).

Consider a two-way handshake, where the sender A in Fig. 2(a) first transmits a data packet to the receiver B. After waiting a *short interframe space* (SIFS) interval [1], cooperating nodes echo a hint with type DATA addressed to node B.

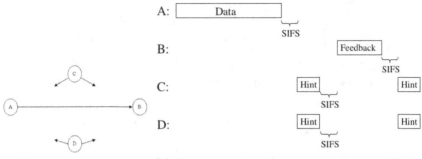

(a) Example scenario   (b) Cooperative signalling in a two-way handshake

Fig. 2. A scenario, and cooperative signalling in a two-way handshake in the scenario

The purpose of this hint is to inform the receiver B that it is the intended recipient of a data transmission and to allow it to determine the appropriate feedback. Cooperating nodes also set their *network allocation vector* (NAV) exactly as is done in IEEE 802.11 [1].

Depending on the outcome of the data packet and of the hint at the receiver B, it takes one of four possible actions:

1. If B receives the data packet correctly then it transmits an ACK to A, i.e., B transmits the traditional feedback response.
2. If B receives the DATA hint but does not receive the corresponding data packet, then it transmits a new *out of range* (OOR) control packet to A. Of course if B is out of the transmission range of A, then A may very well be out of transmission range of B. However, what is important is that any cooperating nodes that overhear the OOR feedback echo it increasing the likelihood that A receives the OOR.
3. If B receives the DATA hint but experiences a collision of the data packet then B transmits a new *collision* (COL) control packet to A. Again, any cooperating nodes that overhear the COL feedback echo it to A.
4. If B cannot decode the packet then it does not respond.

In all cases when feedback is sent by B, it is transmitted after waiting a SIFS interval.

If a cooperating node overhears any feedback (ACK, OOR, or COL) from the receiver it echos a hint to the same destination and with the same type, and then updates its NAV if necessary. The sender A may then determine the outcome of its transmission. Specifically, if A receives either or both of the ACK and ACK hint then its data transmission is successful. If node A receives either or both of the OOR and OOR hint then the receiver is out of the transmission range of A. Finally, if node A receives either or both of the COL and COL hint then its data packet experienced a collision at the receiver. In all other cases, A cannot determine the outcome of its transmission.

Algorithm 1 gives the pseudocode for cooperative signalling executed at a cooperating node; it simply echos a hint that corresponds to the type of packet it overhears to the same destination.

Algorithm 1. Cooperative signalling at a cooperating node

1: **if** overhear packet type T addressed to node N **then**
2:    wait a SIFS interval
3:    transmit a hint of type T addressed to N
4: **end if**

Figure 2(b) illustrates cooperative signalling for the scenario in Fig. 2(a) in which nodes A and B exchange a two-way handshake. Following the transmission of the data packet by A both cooperating nodes C and D transmit a DATA hint to B. They also echo the feedback (e.g., ACK, OOR, or COL) transmitted by B. In this example, both cooperating nodes C and D transmit hints; the signals corresponding to these hints accumulate rather than collide as explained in §3.2.

While the example here has focussed on the operation of cooperative signalling in a two-way handshake, the idea extends naturally to the four-way handshake. Indeed, cooperative signalling is incorporated into the four-way handshake used in the CSMA/PC protocol presented in §4.

3.2   An Implementation of Cooperative Signalling

One possible implementation of cooperative signalling is similar to the *opportunistic large array* (OLA) proposed by Scaglione et al. [12]. In OLA, a receiver accumulates the same signals from multiple nodes transmitting simultaneously. As long as the accumulation of the signals is above a certain signal-to-noise ratio the receiver can successfully decode the signal. At present OLA makes some fairly strong assumptions about synchronization, which we also inherit.

If the network topology is too sparse then there may be no cooperating nodes and cooperative signalling degenerates into traditional feedback. On the other hand, if the traffic load is high in a dense network, then the number of cooperating nodes may need to be limited to alleviate interference among different hints.

Assuming an OLA-based implementation of cooperative signalling, the transmission power for the hints at each cooperating node should be as low as possible to save energy yet minimize interference. The lower bound on transmission power should be such that the summation of the received signal strength of the hints should be greater than the receive threshold. To achieve this, the transmission power for a hint P_{hint} is set to

$$P_{hint} = \frac{\alpha \times p_{min}}{M} \tag{1}$$

where p_{min} is the minimum transmission power required for the hint to reach the receiver, α is a constant greater than one to ensure a transmission power greater than the lower bound, and M is the number of available cooperating nodes.

In the simulation results presented in §5, α is set to 2, and we approximate M by counting the number of available neighbours based on a history of overhearing transmissions.

4   CSMA with Power Control (CSMA/PC)

4.1   Motivation

In CSMA/CA-based protocols, a problem arises from the use of traditional feedback: in the case of the failure of its transmission, the sender must respond *without* feedback. Most protocols assume that the reason for failure is contention.

In contrast, cooperative signalling may provide the outcome of the transmission, allowing the sender to distinguish between a collision at the receiver and a receiver that has moved out of range, and respond appropriately.

For a MAC protocol employing transmission power control:

1. If the packet transmitted by the sender experiences a collision at the receiver then it is likely that contention around the receiver is high. To reduce contention the sender should *decrease* its transmission power.
2. If the receiver has moved out of the transmission range of the sender then contention is likely not the reason for failure. Indeed, in this case, the sender could *increase* its transmission power.

Without knowing the reason for failure, a MAC protocol employing power control cannot tell whether to increase or to decrease its transmission power. Cooperative signalling is one way to provide the information needed to make this decision.

It is worth emphasizing that the application of cooperative signalling is not limited to MAC protocols using transmission power control.

4.2   Fundamental Assumptions

We assume that each node in the network is identically equipped with an omni-directional antenna and a half-duplex transceiver operating on a single channel. We further assume that the transceiver in each node can tune its transmission power to *any* value in the range $[P_{min}, P_{max}]$, the minimum and maximum transmission power, respectively. Finally, we assume that the tuning of a transceiver to a particular transmission power can be accomplished on a per-packet basis and that tuning does not involve any significant cost.

4.3   Overview of CSMA with Power Control

In CSMA/PC we consider a sender s that transmits a series of data packets to a receiver r. Let P_i be the transmission power utilized by s in transmitting the ith data packet.

Initially, the transmission power used by s for the first packet is the maximum power, i.e., $P_1 \leftarrow P_{max}$. The reason we initialize the transmission power this way is because our objective is to minimize hop-count[2] in the multi-hop routing protocol; our objective is *not* to minimize energy usage. (As a side effect we do save energy, but this is not our motivation.)

To transmit the ith data packet, s first senses the channel; if the channel is busy, the node updates its NAV as in IEEE 802.11. If the channel is free, s transmits an RTS at transmission power P_i. If all packets of the four-way handshake are successful then r receives an RTS and replies with a CTS, s receives a CTS and transmits a data packet, and r receives a data packet and replies with an ACK. Responses from r are transmitted using the transmission power P_i embedded in the forward packet.

Each node other than r that overhears a control or data packet follows Algorithm 1 to transmit a cooperative hint of the same type to the intended destination using the transmission power prescribed in (1).

If the sender s does not receive a CTS, then the RTS may have been involved in a collision or the receiver may have moved out of range. In this case, a re-transmission of the RTS by s is required. Similarly, if s does not receive an ACK, a retransmission of the data is required. In both cases, the question is this: at what transmission power should r retransmit?

In CSMA/PC, a *binary search* strategy is used to select the power for the retransmission. In addition to knowing P_{min} and P_{max}, s knows the transmission power P_i used in the failed packet transmission.

If s receives a cooperative hint of type OOR and/or an OOR control packet, then it assumes that r has moved out of range and so the transmission power P_i is increased in order to improve the chance of reception by the receiver. Specifically, the transmission power is set to correspond to the transmission range obtained by bisecting the interval $[Range(P_i), Range(P_{max})]$:

$$P_i \leftarrow Power\left(\frac{Range(P_i) + Range(P_{max})}{2}\right). \tag{2}$$

Here each transmission power naturally corresponds to a unique transmission range. The function $Power(d)$ returns the transmission power required to reach the transmission range d, and the function $Range(p)$ returns the transmission range corresponding to the transmission power p.

If node s receives a cooperative hint of type COL and/or a COL control packet, then it assumes that r is experiencing contention. Therefore, s first retransmits using the current transmission power, P_i, k times. If the packet fails after k retries then the current transmission power is decreased, to the value that corresponds to bisecting the interval $[Range(P_{min}), Range(P_i)]$:

$$P_i \leftarrow Power\left(\frac{Range(P_{min}) + Range(P_i)}{2}\right). \tag{3}$$

---

[2] Power-aware routing is out of scope of this paper; however, this is a challenging cross-layer problem.

A node must experience k consecutive failures before it decides that the current transmission power is too high for the current contention in the network.

Overall, if the packet fails $GlobalRetry$ times, then this packet is dropped and a link failure is reported to the network layer.

The complete CSMA/PC transmitter and receiver protocols executed at the transmitter s and the receiver r, appear in Algorithms 2 and 3, respectively.

Algorithm 2. CSMA/PC transmitter protocol at s

1: **while** there is a data packet to transmit from s to r **do**
2:      **if** packet i has the same destination as packet $i - 1$ **then**
3:          $P_i \leftarrow P_{i-1}$
4:      **else**
5:          $P_i \leftarrow P_{max}$
6:      **end if**
7:      $retry\_count \leftarrow 0$
        RESEND:
8:      **if** there is an active transmission **then**
9:          set the NAV; wait until NAV expires; goto RETRANSMIT
10:     **end if**
11:     send RTS using power level P_i and wait for CTS
12:     **if** a CTS or a CTS hint is received **then**
13:         send DATA using power level P_i and wait for ACK
14:         **if** an ACK or an ACK hint is received **then**
15:             return success
16:         **end if**
17:     **end if**
        RETRANSMIT:
18:     **if** a COL or a COL hint is received **then**
19:         $retry\_count \leftarrow retry\_count + 1$
20:         **if** $retry\_count == k$ **then**
21:             $P_i \leftarrow Power\left(\frac{Range(P_{min}) + Range(P_i)}{2}\right)$
22:             $retry\_count \leftarrow 0$
23:         **end if**
24:     **else**
25:         $P_i \leftarrow Power\left(\frac{Range(P_i) + Range(P_{max})}{2}\right)$
26:         $retry\_count \leftarrow 0$
27:     **end if**
28:     goto RESEND
29: **end while**

An important issue in CSMA/PC is determining the appropriate transmission power for the *next* packet (i.e., packet $i+1$) in the series after a successful packet transmission of packet i. In CSMA/PC, the value of P_{i+1} *depends on the next hop destination of packet $i+1$*. If that destination is the same as that of packet i, then P_{i+1} is initialized to the value of P_i; otherwise the value of P_{i+1} is initialized to P_{max}.

Algorithm 3. CSMA/PC receiver protocol at r

1: **if** receive an RTS or a DATA packet at r from s **then**
2:    send a CTS or an ACK packet to s, respectively
3: **else if** receive a hint at r but no RTS or DATA **then**
4:    send an OOR control packet to s
5: **else if** receive a hint at r but a collision occurs **then**
6:    send a COL control packet to s
7: **end if**

4.4 Discussion

In the binary search strategy proposed we bisect on distance. That is, we select the transmission power that corresponds to bisection of either the interval on the transmission range $[Range(P_i), Range(P_{max})]$ or the transmission range $[Range(P_{min}), Range(P_i)]$. Rather than bisecting on distance, we could instead bisect on power, i.e., bisect either $[P_i, P_{max}]$ or $[P_{min}, P_i]$. We could also bisect on the area corresponding to the transmission range. The difference in these bisection strategies is in the speed of convergence.

There is some transmission overhead associated with the use of the cooperative signalling: the extra hints and the interframe spacing between the hints and the handshake packets. This overhead is relatively low as the hints can be as small as seven bytes (a six byte address plus one byte indicating hint type). We use the same interframe spacing specified for the IEEE 802.11 handshake, with the addition of a SIFS interval before the transmission of each hint. Clearly, the amount of the overhead is relative to the length of the data packets.

5 Simulation Results

We evaluate the CSMA/PC protocol in the **ns-2** network simulator version 2.26 [13], and compare its performance to IEEE 802.11. Table 1 gives the simulation parameters; transmission power is based on the WaveLAN PCMCIA card [14].

Table 1. Simulation parameters

Simulation time	$200\,s$
Traffic type, arrival rate	UDP, $0.5\,Mbps$
Data packet size	$1000\,bytes$
Channel data rate	$1\,Mbps$
Carrier sense threshold	$1.559 \times 10^{-11}\,W$
Receive threshold	$3.652 \times 10^{-10}\,W$
$[P_{min}, P_{max}]$	$[8.5872 \times 10^{-4}, 0.2818]\,W$
$[Range(P_{min}), Range(P_{max})]$	$[40, 250]\,m$
k, α, GlobalRetry	2, 2, 7
p_{min}	$0.2818\,W$

5.1   A Simple Static Topology

We first investigate the simple static topology in Fig. 3. There are three pairs of transmitters and receivers. Each node is $30\,m$ away from the next node. Nodes that are not transmitters or receivers act as cooperating nodes.

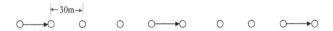

Fig. 3. A simple wireless topology with 3 flows

We evaluate the total throughput, total energy consumption, and the throughput per unit of energy in the network. The total throughput is the total amount of data in bytes that is delivered from the sources to the destinations in the network over the course of the simulation. The total energy consumption is the total amount of energy spent by all the nodes in the network. The throughput per unit of energy is the total throughput divided by the total energy consumption.

Figure 4 shows the total throughput, energy consumption, and throughput per unit of energy in the simple wireless topology using the two protocols. Each point is the average of 20 simulation runs. CSMA/PC outperforms IEEE 802.11

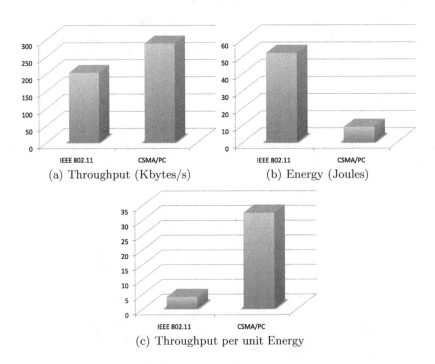

Fig. 4. Results for the static scenario in Figure 3

in all metrics. CSMA/PC delivers roughly 40% more data packets than IEEE 802.11. This gain comes from the potential concurrency in transmissions of multiple flows in the network when power control is used. The energy consumption for CSMA/PC is about 17% that of IEEE 802.11. This is because of the savings in transmission power; see Table 1 for the maximum and minimum transmission power. It is therefore no surprise that in throughput per unit of energy, CSMA/PC shows a great advantage compared to IEEE 802.11.

5.2   A Mobile Wireless Network Scenario

Now we consider a mobile wireless network scenario with 50 mobile nodes randomly deployed in an area of $300\,m \times 300\,m$ square; we use the AODV routing protocol [15]. We randomly choose four source and destination pairs from the 50 nodes. All of the nodes move according to the steady-state initialized random way-point mobility model at $2\,m/s$ with a $2\,s$ pause time. This scenario is designed to simulate occasional link breaks due to nodes moving out of range.

Figure 5 shows the simulation results for the mobile wireless network scenario. Again CSMA/PC outperforms IEEE 802.11 in all metrics. However, the improvement in throughput is very small compared to the static scenario. This is because the flows are well structured and the channel access behaviour is relatively stable in the static scenario; thus, concurrency among flows is established and maintained for a long period of time. In the mobile network scenario, flows

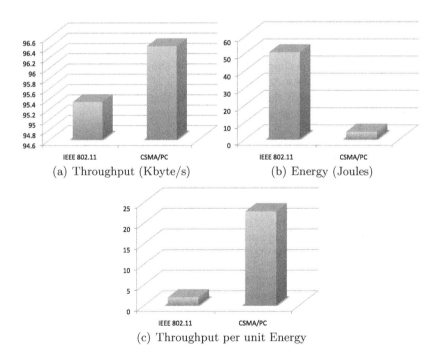

(a) Throughput (Kbyte/s)   (b) Energy (Joules)

(c) Throughput per unit Energy

Fig. 5. Results for the mobile scenario with four flows

are selected and deployed randomly, and due to node mobility, channel access behaviour may change frequently. Thus, concurrency among flows is harder to establish and maintain. However, an improvement in total energy consumption still results in a significant increase in throughput per unit of energy.

5.3 Overhead

In our scenarios, the data packet size was 1000 *bytes*. Since a four-way handshake was employed, a seven byte long hint is transmitted after each control or data packet, as well as introducing additional delay due to the extra SIFS intervals. In this study, the overhead was nearly 3%.

6   Conclusions and Future Work

This paper makes two contributions. We introduce the idea of *cooperative signalling* and then apply it in a CSMA/CA-based protocol utilizing power control. Our simulation results show that CSMA/PC significantly improves all metrics measured in both static and mobile scenarios when compared to IEEE 802.11.

The potential responsiveness of protocols to the more informative feedback provided by cooperative signalling appears worth investigating more. At the MAC layer, incorporating cooperative signalling into collision resolution in the time domain is of interest. Cooperative signalling also opens research directions for higher layer protocols.

A study examining the density and load requirements for effective cooperative signalling is also required. For small data packet sizes where the overhead of cooperation can be high, perhaps such signalling should only be used when the receiver feeds back a response to the sender.

As presented, cooperative signalling assumes that nodes are not malicious. Investigating it in this context could also be of interest.

Acknowledgments

We thank Charles J. Colbourn and Errol L. Lloyd for useful discussions.

This work was supported, in part, by National Science Foundation grant ANI-0240524. Any opinions, findings, conclusions, or recommendations expressed in this paper are those of the authors and do not necessarily reflect the views of NSF.

References

1. IEEE Standards Association: IEEE standard 802.11: W-LAN medium access control & physical layer specifications (1999)
2. Colbourn, C.J., Cui, M., Lloyd, E.L., Syrotiuk, V.R.: A carrier sense multiple access protocol with power backoff (CSMA/PB). Ad Hoc Networks 5(8), 1233–1250 (2007)

3. Yang, X., Vaidya, N.H.: On physical carrier sensing in wireless ad hoc networks. In: Proceedings of IEEE INFOCOM Conference (March 2005)
4. Liu, P., Tao, Z., Panwar, S.: A cooperative MAC protocol for wireless local area networks. In: Proceedings of the IEEE International Conference on Communications (ICC 2005), pp. 2962–2968 (2005)
5. Luo, T., Motani, M., Srinivasan, V.: CAM-MAC: A cooperative asynchronous multi-channel MAC protocol for ad hoc networks. In: Proceedings of the 3rd International Conference on Broadband Communications, Networks, and Systems (BroadNets 2006) (October 2006)
6. Karn, P.: MACA — a new channel access method for packet radio. In: Proceedings of the 9th ARRL/CRRL Amateur Radio Computer Networking Conference, September 1990, pp. 134–140 (1990)
7. Jung, E.S., Vaidya, N.H.: A power control MAC protocol for ad hoc networks. In: Proceedings of the 8th ACM International Conference on Mobile Computing and Networking, September 2002, pp. 36–47 (2002)
8. Monks, J.P., Bharghavan, V., Hwu, W.M.: A power controlled multiple access protocol for wireless packet networks. In: Proceedings of 20th Annual Joint Conference of the IEEE Computer and Communications Societies, April 2001, pp. 219–228 (2001)
9. Wu, S., Tseng, Y., Sheu, J.: Intelligent medium access for mobile ad hoc networks with busy tones and power control. IEEE Journal on Selected Area in Communications 18(9), 1647–1657 (2000)
10. Muqattash, A., Krunz, M.: Power controlled dual channel (PCDC) medium access protocol for wireless ad hoc networks. In: Proceedings of 22nd Annual Joint Conference of the IEEE Computer and Communications Societies, pp. 470–480 (2003)
11. Muqattash, A., Krunz, M.: A single-channel solution for transmission power control in wireless ad hoc networks. In: Proceedings of the Fifth ACM International Symposium on Mobile Ad Hoc Networking and Computing, May 2004, pp. 210–221 (2004)
12. Scaglione, A., Hong, Y.: Opportunistic large arrays: Cooperative transmission in wireless multihop ad hoc networks to reach far distances. IEEE transactions on Signal Processing 51(8), 2082–2092 (2003)
13. ns-2: The network simulator,
    http://nsnam.isi.edu/nsnam/index.php/User_Information
14. NCR Corporation: WaveLAN/PCMCIA card user's guide (version 4.0)
15. Perkins, C., Royer, E.: Ad hoc on-demand distance vector routing. In: Proceedings of the Second IEEE Workshop on Mobile Computing Systems and Applications, February 1999, pp. 90–100 (1999)

Joint Source-Channel-Network Decoding and Blind Estimation of Correlated Sensors Using Concatenated Zigzag Codes

Javier Del Ser[1], Mikel Mendicute[2], Pedro M. Crespo[3],
Sergio Gil-Lopez[1], and Ignacio (Iñaki) Olabarrieta[1]

[1] TECNALIA-Robotiker
TELECOM Unit, 48170 Zamudio, Spain
{jdelser,sgil,iolabarrieta}@robotiker.es
[2] University of Mondragon
20500 Arrasate, Spain
mmendikute@eps.mondragon.edu
[3] CEIT and TECNUN (University of Navarra)
20018 San Sebastian, Spain
pcrespo@ceit.es

Abstract. Focusing on densely deployed wireless sensor networks, this paper presents a novel method for joint source-channel-network coding of distributed correlated sources through multiple access relay channels. In such networks, the role of intermediate sensors as relay nodes permits to achieve enhanced end-to-end error performance and increased spatial diversity in presence of channel fading. This paper addresses this scenario for a two source, single relay architecture by proposing a novel coding approach based on concatenated Zigzag codes, whose low complexity is specially suitable for energy-constrained autonomous systems. Joint decoding and estimation of the parameters defining the correlation between sensors is iteratively performed at the receiver side. Simulation results show that the proposed joint coding scheme attains significant energy gains with respect to traditional routing techniques, specially at high signal to noise ratios.

1 Introduction

Based on the dramatic breakthrough that the concept of network coding entailed in multicast applications through error-free links [1], there is an unquestionable trend within the research community aimed at extending the network coding principle to more involved noisy communication scenarios. One of those communication setups is the multiple access relay channel, where several transmitters forward their information to a single common receiver through a number of intermediate nodes. In these systems, processing the incoming data locally at each intermediate node (i.e. network coding) can provide enhanced end-to-end reliability and diversity in the case of varying wireless channel conditions [2], thus extending the network coding benefits beyond the original noiseless scenarios.

P.M. Ruiz and J.J. Garcia-Luna-Aceves (Eds.): ADHOC-NOW 2009, LNCS 5793, pp. 30–41, 2009.

In this context, although a large part of the related literature in this area has yet been based on independent edges of given finite capacity, the interest in applying network coding to networks where links are subject to channel errors has risen sharply in the last years, originating a plethora of contributions driven at efficiently combining ideas from channel coding and network coding into an unified framework [3]-[7].

One of the main domains of application for network coding is the implementation of new cost-effective transmission schemes for communication over sensor networks [8]. When the node density is sufficiently high in such multiterminal systems, the information transmitted by nearby sensors often appears to be correlated in space and/or time, which should be exploited to achieve lower energy consumption, enhanced end-to-end noise immunity or augmented radio coverage [9,10,11]. Focusing on the particular setup where all sensors convey their information to a common shared receiver, the parameters defining the correlation among senders should be made available (or estimated with sufficient fidelity) at the receiver so as to attain such benefits.

This paper proposes a novel iterative joint source-channel-network decoding method for wireless sensor relay networks. Our work expands earlier network coding schemes applied to non-ideal links by considering estimation and exploitation of the correlation among the data sensors at the receiver. Another key contribution of this paper is the application of concatenated Zigzag codes [12] as a means to reduce the computational complexity with respect to other coding schemes used in relay channels such as Turbo [4,13], LDPC [3], fountain codes [14] or parity forwarding techniques [15]. As shown in [12], the performance of medium-to-high-rate concatenated Zigzag codes in point-to-point scenarios is very close to the corresponding capacity limit (e.g. within 1 dB in the Gaussian case), while requiring dramatically lower encoding and decoding complexity than other capacity-approaching codes.

To be more concise, Figure 1 depicts the communication scenario under consideration. Two binary sources S_1 and S_2 generate correlated information

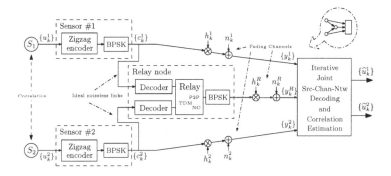

Fig. 1. Block diagram of the considered two-user multiple access communication scenario

modelled by the ergodic process $\{U_k^1, U_k^2\}_{k=1}^{\infty}$. It should be remarked that the majority of related investigations reported so far assume memoryless correlation between the sensors, i.e. $\{U_k^1, U_k^2\}$ is i.i.d. and $Pr(U_k^1 = U_k^2) = p \; \forall k$. However, this paper considers that the correlation between the sources follows a Hidden Markov Model (HMM) as in [16,17], which matches a variety of real application scenarios (e.g. video surveillance). Such information sequences are separately encoded and sent through two independent fading channels to a joint decoder. In addition, a relay node receives and decodes the transmitted signals coming from S_1 and S_2, which are then combined into a new stream to be forwarded to the destination. The joint decoder at the receiver will then iteratively decode, estimate and exploit the correlation between the sources based on the incoming streams from the three channels. Intensive computer simulations show that the proposed network coding approach outperforms traditional routing-based relaying techniques.

This manuscript is organized as follows: in Section 2, the signal and system model for the proposed system is introduced, while Section 3 describes the relaying techniques under consideration. The proposed iterative joint receiver is detailed in Section 4. Section 5 discusses the obtained simulation results and, finally, some concluding remarks are provided in Section 6.

2   System Model

As mentioned in Section 1, Figure 1 depicts the communication scenario under consideration. The binary information outputs of two correlated sensors, represented by the joint random process $\{U_k^1, U_k^2\}_{k=1}^{\infty}$ (to be detailed in Subsection 2.1), are segmented in blocks of length N and separately processed by means of a pair of error-correcting systematic concatenated Zigzag encoders with equal coding rate R_c (information symbols per encoded symbol), yielding codewords $\{c_k^i\}_{k=1}^{N/R_c}$. As introduced in [12], systematic concatenated Zigzag codes are described by a triplet (I, J, K), where $N = I \cdot J$ and $R_c = J/(J+K)$. The parity bits at source S_i are constructed as follows: first, the information input $\{u_k^i\}_{k=1}^{N}$ is arranged as an $I \times J$ matrix $\mathbf{D}^i$ whose $d_{n,j}^i$ element is set to $u_{J(n-1)+j}^i$, with $n \in \{1, \dots, I\}$ and $j \in \{1, \dots, J\}$. Next, a set of K interleaved copies of $\mathbf{D}^i$, denoted as $\{\Psi_k(\mathbf{D}^i)\}_{k=1}^{K}$, is built by first generating $K - 1$ random interleavers of length N, scrambling the sequence $\{u_k^i\}_{k=1}^{N}$ through each of such interleavers and rearranging the interleaved data in the aforementioned matrix form. Observe that no interleaving is made at $k = 1$, i.e. $\Psi_1(\mathbf{D}^i) = \mathbf{D}^i$. Finally, K parity sequences, denoted as $\{p_j^{k,i}\}_{j=1}^{I}$ ($k \in \{1, \dots, K\}$ and $i \in \{1, 2\}$), are recursively computed as

$$p_1^{k,i} = \bigoplus_{j=1}^{J} d_{1,j}^{k,i}, \qquad p_n^{k,i} = \left(\bigoplus_{j=1}^{J} d_{n,j}^{k,i} \right) \oplus p_{n-1}^{k,i}, \quad n = 2, \dots, I, \qquad (1)$$

where $\bigoplus$ denotes modulo-2 sum, and $d_{n,j}^{k,i}$ denotes the (n, j) element of the interleaved matrix $\Psi_k(\mathbf{D}^i)$. Observe that, by properly selecting the (I, J, K) values, fine tuning of the coding rate R_c can be achieved. Also note that the highly structured encoding process is very suitable for low-cost energy-constrained sensor architectures.

Going back to Figure 1, we further assume that the information sequences $\{u_k^i\}_{k=1}^N$ ($i \in \{1,2\}$) are available at the relay with no errors and/or delay, based on the fact that the interest of our work does not hinge on the error propagation at the relay, but on jointly performing decoding, estimation and exploitation of the correlation in an iterative fashion at the receiver. The relay will then combine the incoming streams under a certain strategy (explained below in Section 3), giving rise to an output sequence $\{c_k^R\}_{k=1}^{2N/R_c^*}$, where R_c^* denotes the coding rate at the relay (input symbols per channel symbol).

The links from both sources and from the relay to the receiver are assumed to be independent (by using, for example, orthogonal signalling or sufficiently separated multiple receive antennas) and subject to Rayleigh fading. Let us denote the fading coefficient for source S_i ($i \in \{1,2\}$ and the relay ($i = R$) as h_k^i. The received signal $\{y_k^i\}$ from source $i \in \{1,2,R\}$ will be therefore given by[1]

$$y_k^i = h_k^i \cdot c_k^i + n_k^i, \tag{2}$$

where h_k^i is independently drawn from a Rayleigh distributed random variable satisfying $E[|h_k^i|^2] = 1 \; \forall i$, and n_k^i represents Additive White Gaussian Noise (AWGN) with zero mean and variance $N_0/2$. The overall rate of the system will be $R_S \triangleq R_c R_c^* / (R_c + R_c^*)$. In all cases, perfect Channel State Information (CSI) will be assumed to be available at the receiver.

2.1   Correlation Model for the Sensors

Regarding the generation of the joint binary random process $\{U_k^1, U_k^2\}_{k=1}^\infty$, we consider the general case where (U_i^1, U_i^2) and (U_j^1, U_j^2) ($\forall i, j$ such that $i \neq j$) are not independent, i.e. the correlation among S_1 and S_2 has memory. Furthermore, the symbols $\{U_k^i\}$ are assumed to be i.i.d. and equiprobable, i.e. $Pr(U_k^i = 1) = Pr(U_k^i = 0) = 0.5 \; \forall k$, thus emphasizing that the correlation between both sources is exclusively embedded in the memory of the aforementioned joint random process.

The following model meets such constraints: $\{U_k^1\}$ is a sequence of i.i.d. equiprobable binary random variables, while $\{U_k^2\}$ is symbolwise built as $U_k^2 = U_k^1 \oplus E_k$ where $\{E_k\}$ is a binary stationary random process generated by a Hidden Markov Model (HMM, [18]). The HMM is characterized by the set of parameters $\lambda_{HMM} \triangleq \{S_\lambda, \mathbf{A}, \mathbf{B}, \mathbf{\Pi}\}$, where:

- S_λ is the number of states of the HMM, i.e. $S_k \in \{1, \dots, S_\lambda\} \; \forall k$.
- $\mathbf{A}$ is a $S_\lambda \times S_\lambda$ state transition probability matrix with entries $a_{s',s}$, where $a_{s',s} \triangleq P_{S_k|S_{k-1}}(s|s')$ ($s, s' \in \{1, \dots, S_\lambda\}$), satisfying $\sum_{s=1}^{S_\lambda} a_{s',s} = 1 \; \forall s' \in \{1, \dots, S_\lambda\}$.

---

[1] We implicitly assume that all encoded sequences are BPSK modulated with average energy per channel symbol E_c prior to transmission.

- **B** is a $S_\lambda \times 2$ output distribution probability matrix with entries $b_{s,j}$, where $b_{s,j} \triangleq P_{E_k|S_k}(j|s)$, $j \in \{0,1\}$ and $s \in \{1,\ldots,S_\lambda\}$.
- **Π** is a $S_\lambda \times 1$ initial state probability vector with components π_s, where $\pi_s \triangleq P_{S_1}(s)$, $s \in \{1,\ldots,S_\lambda\}$. If the HMM is stationary, the initial state probability vector **Π** equals the stationary distribution of the chain **Π***, given by **Π*** = **A Π***.

Note that by properly setting λ_{HMM}, the outputs of both sources S_1 and S_2 can be made i.i.d. and equiprobable. On the other hand, the memory defining the correlation between sources is rendered by the entropy rate $\mathcal{H}(E)$ of the underlying HMM output variable, since

$$\mathcal{H}(S_1|S_2) \triangleq \lim_{k\to\infty} \frac{1}{k} H(U_1^1,\ldots,U_k|U_1^2,\ldots,U_k^2) = \lim_{k\to\infty} \frac{1}{k} H(E_1,\ldots,E_k) = \mathcal{H}(E),$$

where $H(\cdot)$ is the standard binary entropy function, and $\mathcal{H}(S_1|S_2)$ denotes the conditional entropy rate of the joint process $\{U_k^1, U_k^2\}$. Observe that the lower $\mathcal{H}(E)$ is, the higher the correlation among the sources will be, since the difference between the entropy rate for source S_i ($\mathcal{H}(S_i) = H(S_i) = 1$) and the conditional entropy rate $\mathcal{H}(S_1|S_2)$ increases accordingly. Therefore, by changing the parameters of the HMM, different correlation levels can be obtained. We refer [16,17,19] for further details on this model.

3 Analyzed Relaying Techniques

As previously mentioned in Section 2, the information coming from sources S_i ($i \in \{1,2\}$), namely, $\{u_k^i\}_{k=1}^N$, is combined at the relay under a certain strategy. Fairness among the compared relaying techniques would require to utilize the same resources (time, energy or bandwidth) for all the considered strategies. To that end, the overall rate of the system will be always kept fixed to a given value by properly selecting the values for the (I, J, K) triplet at all Zigzag encoders. For the sake of clarity, $(I, J, K)_i$ will hereafter denote the (I, J, K) values at Zigzag encoder $i \in \{1, 2, R\}$. In the following we will elaborate on these strategies, first proposed in [4]:

- *Point to Point (P2P) scheme*: No relay is employed in this case. Consequently, each sensor transmits to the central receiver exclusively through two independent parallel fading channels. Neither time nor frequency resources are reserved to the relayed data, which allows allocating a greater amount of Zigzag parity encoded symbols for the distributed sensors. In this case, our simulations utilize $(I, J, K)_{1,2} = (250, 6, 6)$ concatenated Zigzag codes (i.e. $N = 1500$ source symbols), giving rise to an overall coding rate $R_s = R_c = 0.5$. Notice that no spatial diversity gain is expected due to the lack of relay.

- *Time Division Multiplexing (TDM) scheme*: In this second technique, the relay independently encodes the incoming source sequences $\{u_k^i\}_{k=1}^N$ through

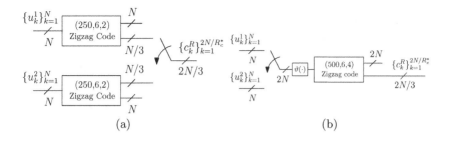

Fig. 2. Schematic diagram of the (a) TDM and (b) NC schemes

two parallel $(I, J, K)_R = (250, 6, 2)$ concatenated Zigzag codes (see Figure 2.a). The resulting parity bits are then multiplexed in time and forwarded to the common destination (i.e. no systematic part is sent to the receiver), yielding $R_c^* = 3$ at the relay site. On the other hand, by selecting $(I, J, K)_{1,2} = (250, 6, 4)$ in the distributed sensors the overall rate is kept fixed to $R_s = 0.5$. Observe that full diversity gain is not achievable in this second technique, since the transmission resources are orthogonally exploited by the sensors.

- *Joint Network-Channel Coding (NC) scheme*: In this third scheme (Figure 2.b), the relay first constructs a $2N \times 1$ sequence $\{u_k^R\}_{k=1}^{2N}$ by alternately multiplexing the source symbols $\{u_k^i\}_{k=1}^N$. Next, the resulting vector is interleaved by means of an randomly generated interleaving function $\vartheta(\cdot)$, and processed through a $(I, J, K)_R = (500, 6, 4)$ concatenated Zigzag code, whose output parity symbols are sent to the common receiver (again, no systematic symbols are transmitted from the relay). Zigzag parameters at the distributed sensors are set to $(I, J, K)_{1,2} = (250, 6, 4)$, yielding $R_c = 0.6$ and thus $R_s = 0.5$. In this case, spatial diversity gain is efficiently exploited thanks to the collaborative sharing of temporal resources, as opposed to the previous TDM scheme.

4   Iterative Receiver

As stated in Section 1, the receiver performs joint source-channel-network decoding, estimation and exploitation of the HMM correlation parameters in an iterative fashion. Following the *Maximum-A-Posteriori* (MAP) criterium, the proposed receiver estimates both source sequences $\{u_k^1\}_{k=1}^N$ and $\{u_k^2\}_{k=1}^N$ as $\{\widehat{u}_k^1\}_{k=1}^N$ and $\{\widehat{u}_k^2\}_{k=1}^N$ under the decision rule

$$(\widehat{u}_k^1, \widehat{u}_k^2) = \arg\max_{u_k^1, u_k^2 \in \{0,1\}} P(u_k^1, u_k^2 | \mathbf{y}^1, \mathbf{y}^2, \mathbf{y}^R), \tag{3}$$

where $\mathbf{y}^i \triangleq \{y_k^i\}$ ($i \in \{1, 2, R\}$), and $k = 1, \dots, N$. Observe that the right-hand conditional probability $P(u_k^1, u_k^2 | \mathbf{y}^1, \mathbf{y}^2, \mathbf{y}^R)$ in the previous expression results proportional to

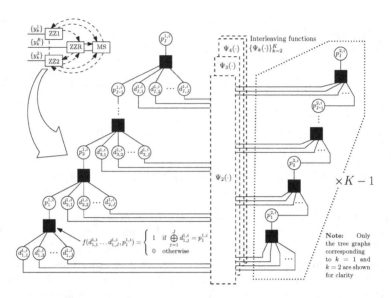

Fig. 3. Factor subgraph representing one of the concatenated Zigzag decoders corresponding to transmitter $i \in \{1, 2, R\}$

$$\sum_{\sim u_k^1, u_k^2} \underbrace{(P(\mathbf{u}^1, \mathbf{u}^2)}_{\text{Source model MS}} \cdot \underbrace{P(\mathbf{c}^R | \mathbf{u}^1, \mathbf{u}^2) P(\mathbf{y}^R | \mathbf{c}^R)}_{\text{ZZR + Channel (Relay)}} \cdot \prod_{i \in \{1,2\}} \underbrace{P(\mathbf{c}^i | \mathbf{u}^i) P(\mathbf{y}^i | \mathbf{c}^i))}_{\text{ZZ}i \text{ + Channel } (i)},$$

where $\mathbf{c}^i \triangleq \{c_k^i\}$ ($i \in \{1, 2, R\}$), and $\sim u_k^1, u_k^2$ denotes that all variables are summed over except u_k^1 and u_k^2. Please observe that an exhaustive MAP search that evaluates the conditional probability of expression (3) for every possible $(\mathbf{u}^1, \mathbf{u}^2)$ combination would render an computational complexity unaffordable for a sensor network with energy-constrained nodes.

Such an issue can be overcome by taking into account the factorization of $P(u_k^1, u_k^2 | \mathbf{y}^1, \mathbf{y}^2, \mathbf{y}^R)$, where the joint conditional distribution breaks down into terms accounting for the utilized concatenated Zigzag codes (ZZ1, ZZ2, ZZR), the fading channels and the multiterminal source model (MS) comprising the output of sources S_1 and S_2. This factorization will be represented by an overall factor graph[2], composed of three tree-like factor subgraphs corresponding to the utilized concatenated Zigzag codes (see Figure 3), and a Trellis-like subgraph describing the statistical structure of the multiterminal source model. Regarding this latter MS subgraph, observe that the generation model for the correlated sensors can be reduced to an equivalent HMM that directly outputs the pair (U_k^1, U_k^2) without any reference to the HMM output variable E_k. Its Trellis diagram would have S_λ states and $4S_\lambda$ branches arising from each state, one for

---

[2] A tacit knowledge on factor graphs and the SPA is assumed in this section (see [20] for a tutorial).

each possible output (U_k^1, U_k^2) combination. The associated branch transition probabilities are easily derived from the set of parameters λ_{HMM} of the original HMM and the marginal probability $P(U_k^1)$. Since we have assumed that $Pr(U_k^1 = q) = 0.5$ for $q \in \{0, 1\}$, the branch transition probabilities of the overall Trellis diagram result in

$$T_k^{MS}(S_{k-1}^{MS} = s', S_k^{MS} = s, U_k^1 = q, U_k^2 = v) \triangleq \begin{cases} a_{s',s} \, b_{s',0} \, 0.5 \text{ if } q = v, \\ a_{s',s} \, b_{s',1} \, 0.5 \text{ if } q \neq v, \end{cases} \quad (4)$$

where $s, s' \in \{1, \ldots, S_\lambda\}$ and $q, v \in \{0, 1\}$. The factor graph representing this Trellis diagram is then attached to the overall factor graph through variable nodes $\{U_k^1\}$ and $\{U_k^2\}$.

The marginalization of the joint conditional probability in expression (3) will be achieved by executing the message-passing Sum-Product Algorithm (SPA, [20]) over the overall factor graph describing the joint receiver. Notice that, since the resulting compound graph of the proposed receiver is cyclic, the SPA algorithm leads to an iterative message passing procedure which is performed, within a given iteration, in the order ZZ1↦ZZ2↦ZZR↦MS.

4.1   Estimation of the Correlation Parameters

Notice in expression (4) that the receiver must estimate in advance the parameters λ_{HMM} defining the correlation between the sensors. To that end, we will adopt the iterative soft-input estimation procedure introduced in [17] for joint source-channel coding and estimation of correlated sources with side information at the decoder. The estimation process is based on a modification of the Baum-Welch Algorithm (BWA) applied to the Trellis diagram that describes the correlation between the sensors. The complete decoding algorithm is summarized as follows:

1. Set the iteration index j to 0, and perform the SPA algorithm over the factor graphs that describe the Zigzag decoders ZZ1, ZZ2 and ZZR without considering any soft *extrinsic* information coming from the MS block.
2. For each $k \in \{1, \ldots, N\}$, obtain a hard estimate $\tilde{u}_k^i$ for u_k^i ($i \in \{1, 2\}$) based on the *a posteriori* information generated in Step 1.
3. Apply the standard BWA [18] on $\tilde{e}_k \triangleq \tilde{u}_k^1 \oplus \tilde{u}_k^2$ to obtain an initial estimate of the HMM parameters at iteration $j = 0$, denoted as $a_{s,s'}^0$, $b_{s,e}^0$ and π_s^0.
4. Set $j = j + 1$. Perform the SPA algorithm over the MS factor graph using, as factor nodes, the functions $T_{k,j}^{MS}(\cdot)$ in expression (4) with HMM parameters $\{a_{s,s'}^{j-1}, b_{s,e}^{j-1}, \pi_s^{j-1}\}$. This will produce the set of *a posteriori* information $\delta_{k,j}^{MS}(u_k^i)$ for each source symbol.
5. Execute the SPA algorithm over the factor graphs ZZ1, ZZ2 and ZZR by the messages $\delta_{k,j}^{MS}(u_k^i)$ as *extrinsic* information coming from the factor graph MS.
6. Reestimate the λ_{HMM} parameters. For sake of brevity, and following the notation in [17], the update rule of the parameters $\{a_{s',s}^j, b^j(s, e), \pi_s^j\}$ at iteration j will be given by

$$a_{s',s}^j = \frac{\sum_{k=1}^N \sum_{\sim s,s'} \alpha_{k-1,j}^{MS}(s) \cdot T_{k,j}^{MS}(s,s',u_k^1,u_k^2,e) \cdot \beta_{k,j}^{MS}(s') \cdot \xi_{k,j}^{MS}(u_k^1) \cdot \xi_{k,j}^{MS}(u_k^2)}{\sum_{k=1}^N \sum_{\sim s} \alpha_{k-1,j}^{MS}(s) \cdot T_{k,j}^{MS}(s,s',u_k^1,u_k^2,e) \cdot \beta_{k,j}^{MS}(s') \cdot \xi_{k,j}^{MS}(u_k^1) \cdot \xi_{k,j}^{MS}(u_k^2)},$$

$$b_{s,e}^j = \frac{\sum_{k=1}^N \sum_{\sim s,e} \alpha_{k-1,j}^{MS}(s) \cdot T_{k,j}^{MS}(s,s',u_k^1,u_k^2,e) \cdot \beta_{k,j}^{MS}(s') \cdot \xi_{k,j}^{MS}(u_k^1) \cdot \xi_{k,j}^{MS}(u_k^2)}{\sum_{k=1}^N \sum_{\sim s} \alpha_{k-1,j}^{MS}(s) \cdot T_{k,j}^{MS}(s,s',u_k^1,u_k^2,e) \cdot \beta_{k,j}^{MS}(s') \cdot \xi_{k,j}^{MS}(u_k^1) \cdot \xi_{k,j}^{MS}(u_k^2)},$$

$$\pi_s^j = \frac{\sum_{\sim s} \alpha_{0,j}^{MS}(s) \cdot T_{1,j}^{MS}(s,s',u_1^1,u_1^2,e) \cdot \beta_{1,j}^{MS}(s') \cdot \xi_{1,j}^{MS}(u_1^1) \cdot \xi_{1,j}^{MS}(u_1^2)}{\sum_{\sim \emptyset} \alpha_{0,j}^{MS}(s) \cdot T_{1,j}^{MS}(s,s',u_1^1,u_1^2,e) \cdot \beta_{1,j}^{MS}(s') \cdot \xi_{1,j}^{MS}(u_1^1) \cdot \xi_{1,j}^{MS}(u_1^2)},$$

with $s,s' \in \{1,\ldots,S_\lambda\}$ and $e \in \{0,1\}$. In such expressions, $\xi_{k,j}^{MS}(u_k^i)$ denotes the *extrinsic* probability of u_k^i coming from ZZ1, ZZ2 and ZZR blocks, $\alpha_{k,j}^{MS}(s)$ and $\beta_{k,j}^{MS}(s)$ are the α and β variables rendered by the SPA in Step 4, and functions $T_{k,j}^{MS}(\cdot)$ are defined as in [17, equation (15)].

7. Go back to Step 4 until the desired maximum number of iterations is reached.

5   Simulation Results

In order to assess the performance of the proposed system, several Monte Carlo computer simulations have been done by considering the transmission of 10^5 different source sequence pairs $\{u_k^1\}$, $\{u_k^2\}$ with $N = 1500$ binary symbols. Regarding the generation model for the correlated sources, two different HMM with $S_\lambda = 2$ states have been used, yielding $\mathcal{H}(S_1|S_2) = \mathcal{H}(S_1) = 1$ (i.e. independent sensors), and $\mathcal{H}(S_1|S_2) = 0.45$ (moderate correlation between the sources). The (I,J,K) parameters of the utilized concatenated Zigzag codes have been specified for each relaying strategy in Section 3. We further consider quasi-static block fading, i.e. the multiplicative factors of all channels are assumed to be constant over a burst of N source symbols. Results are plotted as a function of the ratio between the average energy per source symbol and the noise spectral power density amplitude $E_s/N_0 = E_c/(R_s \cdot N_0)$, where E_c denotes the average energy per BPSK channel symbol. The maximum number of iterations of the SPA algorithm has been set to 20.

The first set of simulation results is shown in Figure 4.a, where the end-to-end Bit Error Rate (BER) is plotted versus E_s/N_0 for the three analyzed relay techniques and the two multiterminal source models under consideration. Perfect knowledge of λ_{HMM} is assumed in this first set of curves. On one hand, notice that, for both independent and correlated source models, the best performance is achieved by using the proposed NC scheme, which at BER=10^{-3} outperforms the P2P technique by 13.4 dB (independent sources) and 10.4 dB (correlated sources). On the other hand, observe the energy gap obtained by iteratively exploiting the correlation between the sensors, which at BER=10^{-3} is equal to 5.5 dB (P2P), 3.6 dB (TDM) and 2.6 dB (NC), approximately.

In order to verify the convergence of the proposed correlation estimator, the second set of curves in Figure 4.b depicts the BER performance versus the iteration index for $\mathcal{H}(S_1|S_2) = 0.45$, the NC relay technique and both perfect knowledge and blind estimation of the HMM parameters. It should be remarked that the estimation of the HMM parameters is done afresh for each input block,

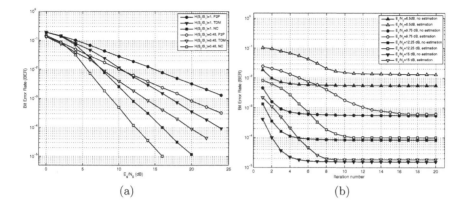

(a)   (b)

Fig. 4. (a) BER versus E_s/N_0 for the $\{P2P, TDM, NC\}$ relay techniques and the two considered source models. (b) BER performance versus iteration index for $\mathcal{H}(S_1|S_2) = 0.45$ and the NC relay scheme with blind estimation of the HMM parameters.

i.e. without relying on any previous estimate. At low E_s/N_0, observe that the proposed estimation algorithm does not converge to the exact parameter set λ_{HMM} for low E_s/N_0 ranges. Also observe that the convergence speed of the proposed algorithm also grows with E_s/N_0.

6 Concluding Remarks

This paper has presented a novel iterative joint source-channel-network decoding scheme for multiple access relay sensor networks based on low-complexity concatenated Zigzag codes. Furthermore, the proposed receiver is able to exploit the existing correlation between the data sensors blindly by incorporating a soft-input correlation estimator to the iterative decoding process. Simulation results have verified, on one hand, that traditional routing techniques are outperformed by relay schemes based on the network coding principle. On the other hand, it has been shown that the exploitation of the correlation between the sensors yields dramatic energy savings with respect to the case where the sensors register statistically independent data. Finally, the performance degradation due to the blind estimation of the correlation parameters has been proven to be negligible, specially at high signal to noise ratios.

Acknowledgments

This work was supported in part by the Spanish Ministry of Science and Innovation through the CONSOLIDER-INGENIO 2010 programme (CSD200800010, *www.comonsens.org*), and by the Basque Government through the *Future Internet* project (ETORTEK programme).

References

1. Ahlswede, R., Cai, N., Li, S.-Y.R., Yeung, R.W.: Network Information Flow. IEEE Transactions on Information Theory 46, 1204–1216 (2000)
2. Tuninetti, D., Fragouli, C.: Processing Along the Way: Forwarding vs. Coding. In: Proceedings of the International Symposium on Information Theory and its Applications (ISITA) (October 2004)
3. Hausl, C., Schreckenbach, F., Oikonomidis, I., Bauch, G.: Iterative Network and Channel Decoding on a Tanner Graph. In: Proceedings of 43rd Allerton Conference on Communication, Control, and Computing (September 2005)
4. Hausl, C., Dupraz, P.: Joint Network-Channel Coding for the Multiple-Access Relay Channel. In: Proceedings of International Workshop on Wireless Ad Hoc and Sensor Neworks (IWWAN) (June 2006)
5. Bao, X., Li, J.: Matching Code-on-graph with Network-on-graph: Adaptive Network Coding for Wireless Relay Networks. In: Proceedings of 43rd Allerton Conference on Communication, Control, and Computing (September 2005)
6. Effros, M., Medard, M., Ho, T., Ray, S., Karger, D., Koetter, R.: Linear Network Codes: A Unified Framework for Source, Channel and Network Coding. In: Proceedings of DIMACS Workshop on Network Information Theory (March 2003)
7. Yeung, R.W., Cai, N.: Network Error Correction, Part I: Basic Concepts and Upper Bounds. Communications in Information and Systems 6(1), 19–36 (2006)
8. Servetto, S.D., Knopp, R., Ephremides, A., Verdu, S., Wicker, S.B.: Guest Editorial: Fundamental Performance Limits of Wireless Sensor Networks. IEEE Journal on Selected Areas in Communications 22, 961–965 (2004)
9. Chou, J., Petrovic, D., Ramchandran, K.: A Distributed and Adaptive Signal Processing Approach to Reducing Energy Consumption in Sensor Networks. In: Proceedings of the Annual Joint Conference of the IEEE Computer and Communications Societies (INFOCOM), March 2003, vol. 2, pp. 1054–1062 (2003)
10. Xiong, Z., Liveris, A.D., Cheng, S.: Distributed Source Coding for Sensor Networks. IEEE Signal Processing Magazine, 80–94 (2004)
11. Jin, J.-Q., Ho, T., Viswanathan, H.: Exploiting Spatial Correlation for Improving Coverage in Sensor Networks. In: Proceedings of IEEE Global Telecommunications Conference (GLOBECOM), November 2007, pp. 1329–1333 (2007)
12. Ping, L., Huang, X., Phamdo, N.: Zigzag Codes and Concatenated Zigzag Codes. IEEE Transactions on Information Theory 47, 800–807 (2001)
13. Del Ser, J., Crespo, P.M., Khalaj, B.H., Gutierrez-Gutierrez, J.: On Combining Distributed Joint Source-Channel-Network Coding and Turbo Equalization in Multiple Access Relay Networks. In: Proceedings of the IEEE International Conference on Wireless and Mobile Computing (WIMOB 2007), October 2007, p. 18 (2007)
14. Pakzad, C.F.P., Shokrollahi, A.: Coding Schemes for Line Networks. In: Proceedings of IEEE International Symposium on Information Theory, September 2005, pp. 1853–1857 (2005)
15. Razaghi, P., Yu, W.: Parity Forwarding for Multiple-Relay Networks. In: Proceedings of IEEE International Symposium on Information Theory, July 2006, pp. 1678–1682 (2006)
16. Zhao, Y., Garcia-Frias, J.: Turbo Codes for Symmetric Compression of Correlated Binary Sources with Hidden Markov Correlation. In: Proceedings of the CTA C&N Symposium (April 2003)

17. Del Ser, J., Crespo, P.M., Galdos, O.: Asymmetric Joint Source-Channel Coding for Correlated Sources with Blind HMM Estimation at the Receiver. Eurasip Journal on Wireless Communications and Networking, Special Issue on Wireless Sensor Networks 4, 483–492 (2005)
18. Rabiner, L.R.: A Tutorial on Hidden Markov Models and Selected Applications on Speech Recognition. Proceedings of the IEEE 77, 257–285 (1989)
19. Del Ser, J., Munoz, A., Crespo, P.M.: Joint Source-Channel Decoding of Correlated Sources over ISI Channels. In: Proceedings of the IEEE Vehicular Technology Conference, vol. 1, May 2005, pp. 625–629 (2005)
20. Kschischang, F.R., Frey, B.J., Loeliger, H.A.: Factor Graphs and the Sum-Product Algorithm. IEEE Transactions on Information Theory 47, 498–519 (2001)

Challenges for Routing and Search in Dynamic and Self-organizing Networks

Gerhard Hasslinger[1] and Thomas Kunz[2]

[1] T-Systems, D-64295 Darmstadt, Germany
gerhard.hasslinger@telekom.de
[2] Department of Systems and Computer Engineering,
Carleton University, Ottawa, Canada
tkunz@sce,carleton.ca

Abstract. Search methods in self-organizing networks usually cannot rely on stable topology from which shortest or otherwise optimized paths through the network are derived. When no reliable search indices or routing tables are available, other methods like flooding or random walks have to be considered to explore the network. These approaches can exploit partial knowledge in the network to reach a destination, but the search effort naturally increases with the lack of precise paths due to network dynamics. This problem is especially relevant for wireless technology with strict limitation on power consumption/ We address the efficiency of random walks and flooding for exploring networks based on case studies evaluated by simulation and transient analysis. In this way, performance tradeoffs are demonstrated when combining shortest path routing with randomized techniques.

Keywords: Self-organizing networks; routing; flooding; random walk.

1 Introduction

Routing and search functions are presently under investigation to cope with challenges in network areas subject to dynamic changes. There are at least three networking scenarios which may lead to increasing dynamics when integrated in future Internet structures

- Peer-to-peer (P2P) and other self-organizing overlays on the IP infrastructure,
- mobile ad hoc networks (MANET) and
- sensor networks.

A search may refer to users, network nodes, information, content or services of any kind residing on network resources based on identifiers like IP addresses or hash values used in P2P networks. Peer-to-peer networks even show developments towards distributed databases with replication schemes for data in order to support reliability, performance of search as well as increased throughput via multi source downloads.

P2P networks contribute a major portion of the Internet traffic since the millennium mostly due to file sharing [13]. Nevertheless, their performance could be

P.M. Ruiz and J.J. Garcia-Luna-Aceves (Eds.): ADHOC-NOW 2009, LNCS 5793, pp. 42–54, 2009.

enhanced by avoiding unnecessary long paths for exchange of content that is also locally available [12] as currently discussed in the IETF ALTO BoF [2]. Although distributed hash tables could be used to optimize search and routing in P2P networks, considerable effort is required for updating those tables with currently valid information under steady churn of peers joining and leaving the network. Therefore popular P2P networks prefer random mechanisms to select sources for distributing information. While early versions of the Gnutella P2P network [29] used flooding, which caused scalability problems even with a limited hop count, random walks proved to be a promising alternative for search in unstructured large scale networks [1][9][10][14] [15][24][30].

For mobile ad hoc networks (MANETs), the dynamic nature of the network topology challenges routing protocols in new ways. For example, it has long been known that node mobility causes unicast routing protocols to perform poorly, as shown in [18][28]. In the case of multicast routing, [19] similarly shows that routing protocol performance suffers with an increase in node mobility. Approaches such as simply flooding all packets in the network can be surprisingly competitive both in the resulting protocol performance and the induced overheads. But even in the absence of node mobility, multihop wireless networks experience highly dynamic topologies, challenging any routing protocol. For example, measurements in existing wireless mesh testbeds show that even static wireless links are highly asymmetrical and have time-varying behaviour due to interference, requiring new routing solutions [8].

In the case of Dynamic Source Routing (DSR) [16], one of the MANET routing protocols standardized by the IETF, a packet delivery ratio of as low as 4% was observed, i.e., only one out of 25 data packets transmitted by a sender was successfully delivered to the intended receiver. One of the main reasons for this poor performance is the fact that shortest-path routing protocols tend to select relatively long-distance hops, which are then subject to interference, similar to the observations in [8]. Even if the routing metric is changed to select more stable links, the problems of sharing a limited bandwidth wireless channel, interference from transmissions in the neighborhood, etc. can still result in relatively poor overall performance [20].

Almost all MANET routing protocols provide parameters to adapt the protocol behavior to the specific characteristics of the network in which they are deployed. For example, protocols that discover neighbors through periodic HELLO messages typically define the periodicity of these messages as a protocol parameter. This way, a larger HELLO interval sending fewer overhead messages can be chosen for relatively static networks. When a node's neighborhood changes at a more rapid pace, a smaller HELLO interval allows a node to learn about these changes faster, albeit at the cost of higher protocol overheads. We have done extensive evaluations of the Optimized Link State Routing (OLSR) protocol [6] and found that tuning these parameters has little influence on the protocol performance, though carefully choosing the appropriate parameter values can reduce protocol overheads [32]. Also, adjusting these control parameters does not increase the accuracy of any state information collected by individual nodes [20].

The IETF has recognized as well that MANET routing protocols such as OLSR and DSR may not meet the routing requirements of low power and lossy networks, charter-ing a new working group in this field [30]. The work starts on requirements, a review and evaluation of existing IETF routing protocols [23] and will develop new protocols if necessary. Our experience, reported in [19] shows that broadcasting/flooding can be superior to routing, as mentioned above. Besides studies showing favourable properties of random walks in large unstructured networks, other investigations proposed random schemes for ad hoc and sensor networks [5][6][8][11][22]. Moreover, it is demonstrated [4] that random walks essentially benefit even from imprecise and only partially valid information in support of a search or when many nodes in the network are able to respond, i.e. when it is sufficient to reach one node of a larger set.

In Section 2 we start with an investigation demonstrating problems for providing consistent updated information on dynamically changing state through routing messages to all nodes of a network. Section 3 discusses search based on flooding, random walks and combined methods. Transient analysis is briefly introduced in Section 4 as an evaluation method for random walk performance and afterwards applied in an example. Section 5 concludes the paper.

2   A Case Study on Imprecise Routing Information

We consider wireless broadcasting nodes placed at different locations spread over an area. We assume that two nodes can directly exchange messages when their distance does not exceed a common transmission range. In this way, the transmission links between nodes and the network topology is determined by the node locations.

The nodes use OLSR [6] to route the messages over multiple hops, including Hello and topology control (TC) messages at default intervals of 2 and 5 seconds, respectively. We consider the queue size of messages that arrived at a node but are not yet forwarded towards the destination as a QoS measure. OLSR is extended to distribute the queue size such that each node is aware of the queue size at all other nodes subject to a delay until routing updates are received between nodes. The queue size information is not used for load balancing. To store the QoS-related state associated with a node, a new field is added to the neighbourhood information base and to the topology information base maintained by the protocol. To populate these fields, the message format of Hello and TC messages were extended as well. Table 1 summarizes the parameters of the modelling and simulation parameters.

In this scenario, we study the absolute difference between the current queue size at a node and the aged information about it, which is available at the other nodes through routing messages at the same time, as a measure for inaccuracy of the routing information state. Figure 1 combines the evaluation of deviations in queue size information with the age of the information at the nodes. The k-th column gives the mean deviation for nodes whose information is aged between k-1 and k seconds or is larger than 21s in the last column.

As can be expected, the deviation is essentially increasing with the traffic load, which varies in the five curves by a factor of 10 from low and medium load up to congestion. Inaccuracy is also increasing with knowledge age, although not monotonically and partly even decreasing for the low load curves. This effect is due to the fact that the paths of messages utilize nodes in the middle of the square area more often than nodes in the outer regions. Thus the nodes in the middle experience higher load and queue variability. But the knowledge age about nodes in the outer regions is larger, while they have a low and less variable queue size. This trade-off causes a tendency to decrease the inaccuracy in spite of larger knowledge age, which becomes apparent especially for the low traffic curves. We analyzed the impact of sending more frequent Hello and TC messages but did not obtain a positive impact on the overall inaccuracy level. In order to reduce knowledge age, we enhanced the routing by a probing scheme. The current state of a node is looked up by a probing message which is triggered by a threshold for the age of information. Probe messages are fully exploited by updating the new status information for all nodes on their paths as well as for nodes which receive the information due to broadcasting in the surrounding of the path.

Table 1. Simulation Parameters

Simulator Parameters	
Network Type	IEEE 802.11
Propagation model	Two-Ray-Ground
Mobility model	Static
Transmission range	250 m
Network topology	50 nodes randomly located in 1 km^2
Traffic model	20 random source-destination pairs, constant messaging intervals: 0.2s, 0.14s, 0.09s, 0.04s, 0.02s for different traffic load levels
Packet size	128 Byte
Queue	for max. 50 packets; Tail-Drop
Simulation time	200s; 50s start phase not evaluated

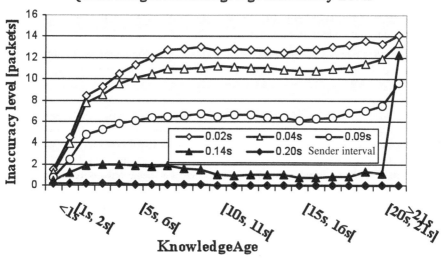

Fig. 1. Inaccuracy in routing information

The probing scheme was able to reduce the mean knowledge age to about half, but in spite of the improvement in knowledge age, probing was unable to reduce the inaccuracy in the queue size estimates. This is also apparent from the results in Figure 1, since the inaccuracy level stays almost constant for knowledge ages of 5 and more. Only for ages below 3 seconds essential improvements of the accuracy are observed.

This case study shows that inaccuracy of routing information can be high in many wireless and mobile communication scenarios. Inaccuracy referring to mobility or high churn instead of queue sizes in a fixed topology will also affect the transport of routing messages which may cause route flapping and loops.

When high dynamics impedes convergence of link state and distance vector routing protocols, then flooding and random walks can be used as well as methods combining flooding, random walks with partial routing knowledge.

3 Flooding and Random Walks Combined in Search

Dynamic overlay networks on the Internet as well as ad hoc networks often rely on self-organizing distributed communication and construction techniques. When there are no central management facilities and search indices available, flooding is a standard method to collect knowledge about the network structure and the content on the nodes. In recent time, random walks have attracted attention as an alternative search method in P2P networks. The efficiency of the method is usually evaluated by simulation studies.

Notations
We denote the topology of a communication network as a graph $G = (V, E)$ with sets V of nodes and E of edges, which are assumed to be undirected. As main characteristics we consider

- the degree $d(a) = |\{k \mid k \in V, (a, k) \in E\}|$ of a node $a \in V$, i.e. the number of edges attached to the node with minimum $d_{min} = \min\{d(a) \mid a \in V\}$, and
- the hop distance h_{ab} between a pair of nodes a, b as the length of a shortest path from a to b, whose maximum is the network diameter $dia = \max\{h_{ab} \mid a,b \in V\}$.

3.1. Flooding

In the simplest case, flooding will spread a request from a node to all its neighbors which repeat it in order to contribute to an exhaustive flood covering the entire network. When the same request is received several times from different neighbors, then only the first receipt is forwarded and later ones are discarded. Wireless networks spread messages through broadcasting over a limited range. Therefore only one message is required per node for flooding, whereas $d(a)$ messages are sent per node in overlay or meshed point-to-point networks. Thus flooding is more competitive in broadcast environments.

In order to reduce the messaging overhead, flooding is usually restricted by a predefined hop limit h [29], which is set with regard to knowledge of the network structure and demands for coverage. Otherwise, a small initial value for h may be stepwise increased if the search radius turns out to be insufficient. Then the next step at first visits all the nodes of the previous step and as another disadvantage, the number of nodes being reached for a larger search radius is not known a priory. It depends on the network topology. In a 2-dimensional grid only $2h^2 + 2h + 1$ nodes are found within a distance of $\leq h$ hops, whereas scale-free networks [14], which proved to be useful to model very large scale social networks as well as Internet connectivity, exhibit small world effects with a diameter of only about 20 being observed in the Internet. Then the number of reachable nodes grows exponentially fast, such that incrementing h to $h+1$ can extend the coverage by a considerable factor, which makes it difficult to execute a fine granular control of the flood. Budget based flood control and other variants to reduce the overhead are discussed in the next section together with random walks.

3.2 Random Walks

Randomized techniques approve to be useful in the construction and exploration of self-organizing networks, when the maintenance of structured indices may be expensive. There are several studies on how randomness can help to manage dynamic networks with minimum overhead while preserving sufficient connectivity [6][9][24][30]. Many of the largest known networks built by humans exhibit properties which are generated by random expansion including the Internet, networks of social relationships, citation indices etc. [4].

Basic random walks
We follow a random walk through the network as a stepwise process, which proceeds from a node to a neighbor at the next hop. A random walk R of length L is denoted by the series $r_0, r_1, r_2, ..., r_L$ of visited nodes, where an edge $(r_{k-1}, r_k) \in E$ is chosen for the k-th hop ($1 \leq k \leq L$). Usually a random walk chooses its next hop with the same probability among all neighbors of the currently visited node

$$\forall\, a, k;\; (a, k) \in E:\; p_{ak} = \Pr(r_{n+1} = k \mid r_n = a) = 1 \,/\, d(a).$$

The corresponding transition matrix $P = (p_{ak})$ determines a random walk as a Markov process, where the network nodes directly correspond to the states of the underlying Markov chain and edges to allowable transitions from a state to another.

In peer-to-peer file sharing networks like Gnutella, eDonkey and BitTorrent, which have gained high popularity as overlays on the Internet, a decomposition into disconnected parts is avoided via random selection of sources for downloading, even if the topology is changing frequently. They establish basic routing functions including Hello messages on the application layer, although this may cause unnecessarily long paths [12][13]. Optimization of P2P traffic engineering is presently discussed in the ALTO BoF [2].

The BubbleStorm P2P approach [24][30] is conceived in order to be highly reliable, such that a simultaneous disappearance of up to 90% of the peering nodes e.g. caused by breakdowns in the underlying transport network still leave the rest of the network intact. This includes a replication scheme for data over subsets of nodes in the network ("data bubbles"). As a consequence, each data item can be found on many nodes in a P2P network in order to improve the reliability and the download

performance. The most popular data is simultaneously requested from many participants, who would experience a bottleneck if the number of source peers with copies
of the data is too small.

The search time for content naturally depends on the number of replicas of data in
the network. In the BubbleStorm approach, the size of a "data bubble" is made larger
than the square root of the network size and the set of nodes included in a data bubble
is almost a random sample among all network nodes. Thus, visiting only a limited
portion of the network nodes is sufficient for most searches [33]. In general, more
complex queries can be handled with randomized search functions in an environment
of a distributed database scheme on an overlay of peer nodes.

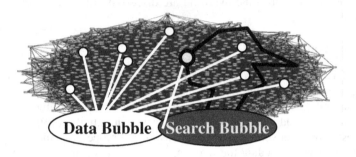

Fig. 2. Bubblestorm: Random search for replicated data

The search by flooding and random walks in P2P networks has been compared and
evaluated in simulation studies [3][10][11][14][24]. The main drawback of a single
random walk is the long delay while it may take some winding route through the
network. Flooding spreads search messages in parallel to all nodes in the neighborhood up to some hop distance d. In graphs with small diameter it is difficult to find an
appropriate search radius d to cover a predefined number of network nodes, which
contributes to the disadvantage of a large messaging overhead. This motivates to
propose new routing schemes for sensor networks [6] or to combine random walks
with flooding [8][9].

Combined variants include

– random walks with an additional flooding step with small radius from all nodes
  being traversed or from the last node,
– starting several random walks in parallel or branching a random walk into multiple paths.

As a rigorous overhead control scheme, the number of messages in a random walk,
flooding or combined search can be limited by a time to live counter, also denoted as
budget controlled search by [9]. When the search is split up in multiple paths being
traversed in parallel, the budget must also be split.

Multiple random walks in parallel
Random walks often can reduce the communication overhead, but they traverse the
hops sequentially and thus usually spend much more time than flooding. Multiple

random walks in parallel may be applied in a compromise between demands for low delay and low overhead. If a random walk is assured a success rate of $\sigma < 1$ within m steps, then k random walks of the same type in parallel each with m steps reduce the failure rate from $1 - \sigma$ to $(1 - \sigma)^k$. Thus a success rate of $\sigma = 90\%$ is improving up to 99.999% when 5 random walkers are combined in parallel. A single walk often achieves this success rate in less than mk steps but even then needs up to k-fold time.

Biased random walks using partial routing information
When we assume that nodes can partly use valid routing information to forward a search or routing request and otherwise forward it to a randomly chosen neighbour, then this leads to biased random walks combining deterministic and random steps [5][11][26][33]. The mean search time of biased random walks usually grows linear with some factor times the hop distance to the destination, where the factor is roughly proportional to the ratio of random to deterministic steps. A bound and a case study for the favourable behaviour is included in the following section.

As a final remark, relevant self-organizing network types are encountered with largely different size from small ad hoc groups to millions of users who are simultaneously active in popular peer-to-peer networks. The performance of the routing and search alternatives depends on and performs differently with the size of the network, where e.g. a basic random walk may be acceptable in small, but too slow in larger networks. For larger networks, self-organization is often combined with a hierarchical structure, e.g. by super nodes in eDonkey and other P2P networks or by backbone nodes which subdivide wireless or sensor networks into different areas assigned to them. Thus hierarchical structuring is a means to limit the size of self-organizing network areas with decisive influence on the search and routing performance.

4. Evaluation: Simulation and Transient Analysis

4.1. Transient Analysis

While flooding overhead can usually be directly expressed in mathematical terms or bounds, random walks are prevalently evaluated using simulation [9][10][24], with results being subject to confidence intervals. The classical transient analysis approach [5][11][15] is also scalable for basic random walks, yielding numerical exact results on the coverage and success probability of a search.

Therefore, the probabilities $p_m^{(R)}(a)$ of a random walk R to enter a network node a at its m-th hop are determined step by step. When the random walk starts at a specific node s, then we have

$$p_0^{(R)}(s) = 1 \quad \text{and} \quad \forall a \neq s: \ p_0^{(R)}(a) = 0$$

as the initial distribution. The transient analysis iteratively computes the distribution of the next hop location. From knowledge of $p_m^{(R)}(a)$, the distribution $p_{m+1}^{(R)}(a)$ for the next step is computed by

$$p_{m+1}^{(R)}(a) = \Sigma_{k:\ (k,\ a)\in E}\ p_m^{(R)}(k)\ q_{ak} ,$$

where $q_{ak} = 1/d(a)$, when each of the neighbors $d(a)$ is chosen with equal probability $1/d(a)$. In order to obtain the probability

$$q_m{}^{(R)}(t) = \Pr(\exists\, j;\, 0 \le j \le m:\, r_j = t\,)$$

that a node t is reached as the target of a random walk search of length m, the previous computation steps are slightly modified, such that the target node is never left as an absorbing state

$$\forall\, a, k;\, (a, k) \in E:\, q_{ak} = 1/d(a) \qquad \text{if } a \ne t;$$

$$\forall\, k;\, (t, k) \in E:\, q_{tk} = 0 \quad \text{if } k \ne t; \qquad q_{tt} = 1;$$

where again $q_{m+1}{}^{(R)}(a) = \Sigma_{k:\,(k,\,a)\in E}\; q_m{}^{(R)}(k)\, q_{ka}$.

The computational per hop complexity of the transient analysis due to those equations is proportional to the number $|E|$ of edges in the network. Therefore the effort to compute $p_m{}^{(R)}(a)$ is linear in the number m of steps and in the number of edges $O(m|E|)$, which makes transient analysis applicable to large scale networks with millions of nodes.

The transient analysis can be extended to cover a set of destination nodes, to include some memory e.g. to avoid a return to the previous node and to variants of multiple random walks.

4.2 A Performance Bound for Biased Random Walks

Assuming that a biased random walk decrements the distance Δ to the target in each step with probability q or increments the distance with probability $p < q$ or stays at the same distance with probability $1 - p - q$, the process of approaching the target becomes a simple birth-death process, as is well known e.g. for analysing M/M/1 queueing systems. Note that for a grid, as used throughut this paper, the distance changes with each step, so $p + q = 1$. However, the model as expressed here is more general and can accommodate scenarios where not every step will result in a change of distance.

The reduction to a 1-dimensional view is appropriate when the random walk has the same behaviour at each node. The same simplification is often applied for modeling user mobility.

The transient behaviour of the birth-and-death process is characterized by a geometrically distributed number of hops until the next change in the distance with parameter $1 - p - q$. In case of 2-dimensional grids, the distance changes in each step,

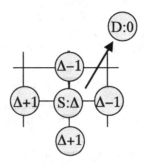

Fig. 3. Hop distances with regard to a destination D in a grid

i.e. $p + q = 1$. Starting at a distance Δ from the target, the distance Δ_m after m steps has a binomial distribution,

$$\Pr\{\Delta_m = \Delta + m - 2k\} = \binom{m}{k} \omega^k (1 - \omega)^{m-k} \qquad \text{for } k = 0, \ldots, m \text{ where } \omega = q/(p+q).$$

If m only counts steps with changes in the distance, the binomial distribution is valid for arbitrary topologies. In principle, the distribution includes negative distances, which are only reachable by previously traversing the target at distance 0. The complete probability mass below 0 indicates that the search was already successful, i.e. state 0 should be an absorbing bound.

When we continue the analysis of the non-truncated birth-death chain, the mean $E(\Delta_m)$ of Δ_m is given by

$$E(\Delta_m) = \Delta - (2\omega - 1)\, m \quad \text{for } E(\Delta_m) \le 0.$$

For $m \ge \lceil \Delta / (2\omega - 1) \rceil$ we can conclude that the target has been reached at least with 50% probability, since a binomial distribution is symmetrical and has most of its probability mass in the negative part when the mean is negative, see Figure 4.

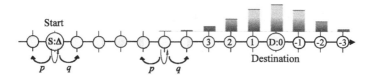

Fig. 4. Linear Markov chain approach for the distance to the target

This gives a clear and simple hint on the number m of steps required for a successful biased random walk. For high success probabilities $1 - 10^{-k}$ we can include the variance $\sigma^2(\Delta_m)$ of the distribution in the analysis via Chebychev's bound

$$\Pr\{\Delta_m > E(\Delta_m) + 10^{k/2}\sigma(\Delta_m)\} \le 10^{-k}.$$

The mean and variance of the binomial distribution

$$E(\Delta_m) = \Delta - (2\omega - 1)\, m \quad \text{and} \quad \sigma^2(\Delta_m) = 4\,\omega(1 - \omega)\, m$$

lead to a bound on $\Pr\{\Delta_m > 0\}$, from which we derive a sufficient number m_{Che} of steps in order to reach the destination with probability $1 - 10^{-k}$:

$$m_{Che} = \left\lceil \frac{\Delta}{2\omega - 1} + \frac{2\omega(1-\omega)10^k}{(2\omega-1)^2}\left(1 + \sqrt{1 + \frac{2\omega - 1}{\omega(1-\omega)}\frac{\Delta}{10^k}}\right)\right\rceil.$$

The result shows that the number of required steps can be bounded by a linear function of the distance Δ, where a constant term is involved depending on the success probability, which becomes very large with increasing k. In this way, a linear behaviour is confirmed in general, although the bound is often not very tight. The linear factor $1/(2\omega - 1)$ in the first term of the latter equation is confirmed as the asymptotical behaviour for all curves in the evaluation example in Figure 5.

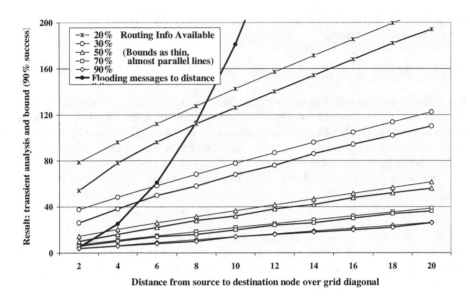

Fig. 5. Biased random walk search time: Bound and transient analysis

Applying the bound to random walks in a planar grid, we obtain

$$q = \Pr\{\Delta_{m+1} = \Delta_m - 1\} = (2+2\rho)/4 \text{ and}$$

$$p = 1 - q = \Pr\{\Delta_{m+1} = \Delta_m + 1\} = (2-2\rho)/4$$

if the current node is not in a line with the target or otherwise $q = (1+3\rho)/4$; $p = (3-3\rho)/4$. We adopt $q = (2+2\rho)/4$, $p = (2-2\rho)/4$. In this way, we get an approximation rather than a bound, which is valid for most of the traversed nodes except for those on both grid lines crossing at the target. Figure 5 compares the evaluations with the transient analysis results for biased random walks on a planar grid. The destination is located in diagonal direction at distances from 2 up to 20 hops. 5 pairs of curves show the number of random walk steps required until the destination is reached with 90% probability, where the fraction of deterministic steps towards the destination supported by valid routing information is varied from 20%, 30%, ..., up to 90%. The upper curve of each pair shows the estimation result due to the previously derived bound, whereas the lower is obtained by transient analysis.

5 Summary and Conclusions

The Internet is extending into dynamic network environments of different type including mobility and churn of nodes. With higher dynamics, link state and distance vector routing is subject to imprecise information base which may cause instability and invalid path selection. Arising problems are illustrated in a case study. With a lack of precise routing information, random walks are proposed and have been investigated in a number of recent studies as a promising alternative to flooding. Methods which combine routing information, flooding and random walks provide flexibility to adapt to different levels of dynamics in a network.

The most efficient way of embedding random steps in routing and search methods depends on the degree of valid up-to-date information and the network type, where mobile networks, low power networks, and peer-to-peer overlays have some similarities but also many different characteristics. In future work, the unique characteristics of these networks and the application of random steps into routing and searching for each network will be refined further.

References

1. Albert, R., Barabasi, A.-L.: Statistical Mechanics of Complex Networks. Rev. Mod. Phys. 74(47), 1–54 (2002)
2. ALTO Application-Layer Traffic Optimization IETF BoF,
   http://www.ietf.org/proceedings/08jul/minutes/alto.txt
3. Avin, C., Krishnamachari, B.: The power of choice in random walks: An empirical study. Computer Networks 52, 44–60 (2008)
4. Barabási, A.-L., Albert, R.: Emergence of scaling in random networks. Science 286, 509–512 (1999)
5. Beraldi, R.: Service discovery in MANET via biased random walks. In: Proc. Autonomics, Rome, Italy (2007)
6. Braginski, D., Estrin, D.: Rumor routing algorithm for sensor networks. In: Proc. WSNA 2002, Atlanta. ACM, New York (2002)
7. Clausen, T., Jacquet, P.: Optimized Link State Routing Protocol (OLSR), IETF, RFC 3626 (2003), http://www.ietf.org/rfc/rfc3626.txt
8. De Couto, D., Aguayo, D., Chambers, B.A., Morris, R.: Performance of Multihop Wireless Networks: Shortest Path is Not Enough. In: Proc. of the First Workshop on Hot Topics in Networking, Princeton, USA (2002)
9. Gkantsidis, C., Mihail, M., Saberi, A.: Hybrid search schemes for unstructured P2P networks. In: Proc. IEEE Infocom (2005)
10. Gkantsidis, C., Mihail, M., Saberi, A.: Random walks in P2P networks: Algorithms and evaluation. Performance Evaluation 63, 241–263 (2006)
11. Hasslinger, G., Kunz, T.: Efficiency of search methods in dynamic wireless networks. In: Cerdà-Alabern, L. (ed.) EuroNGI/EuroFGI 2008. LNCS, vol. 5122, pp. 142–156. Springer, Heidelberg (2008)
12. Hasslinger, G.: Cross-layer aspects of P2P overlays on IP platforms of network providers. In: Proc. IEEE P2P 2008, Aachen, Germany (September 2008) (to appear),
    http://www.p2p08.org
13. Hasslinger, G.: ISP platforms under a heavy peer-to-peer workload. In: Steinmetz, R., Wehrle, K. (eds.) Peer-to-Peer Systems and Applications. LNCS, vol. 3485, pp. 369–381. Springer, Heidelberg (2005)
14. Hasslinger, G., Kempken, S.: Efficiency of random walks for search in different network structures. In: Proc. Valuetools 2007, Nantes, France, ACM digital library (2007)
15. Hasslinger, G., Kempken, S.: Applying random walks in structured and self-organizing networks: Evaluation by transient analysis. PIK journal 31/1, Special issue on self-organizing networks, 17–23 (2008)

16. Johnson, D., Hu, Y., Maltz, D.: The Dynamic Source Routing Protocol (DSR) for Mobile Ad Hoc Networks for IPv4. IETF standardization, RFC 4728 (2007), http://www.ietf.org/rfc/rfc4728.txt
17. Kunz, T.: Energy-efficient Variations of OLSR. In: Proc. of the Internat. Wireless Comm. and Mobile Comp. Conf., Crete, Greece (August 2008)
18. Kunz, T.: On the inadequacy of MANET routing to efficiently use the wireless capacity. In: Proc. IEEE Conf. on Wireless and Mobile Computing, Networking and Comm. (WiMob 2005), Montreal, Canada, pp. 109–116 (2005)
19. Kunz, T.: Multicast vs. broadcast in a MANET. In: Nikolaidis, I., Barbeau, M., Kranakis, E. (eds.) ADHOC-NOW 2004. LNCS, vol. 3158, pp. 14–27. Springer, Heidelberg (2004)
20. Kunz, T., Alhalimi, R.: Load-balanced routing in wireless networks: State information accuracy using OLSR. In: Proc. 3rd IEEE Conf. on Wireless and Mobile Computing, Networking and Communications (WiMob 2007), New York, USA (October 2007)
21. Kunz, T., Hasslinger, G.: Efficiency of search methods in dynamic wireless networks. In: Cerdà-Alabern, L. (ed.) EuroNGI/EuroFGI 2008. LNCS, vol. 5122, pp. 142–156. Springer, Heidelberg (2008)
22. Lima, L., Barros, J.: Random Walks on Sensor Networks. In: Proc. 5th Wireless Optimization Symposium, Limassol, Cyprus (April 2007)
23. Levis, P., Tavakoli, A., Dawson-Haggerty, S.: Overview of existing routing protocols for low power and lossy networks, IETF draft in progress, http://www.ietf.org/internet-drafts/draft-levis-roll-overview-protocols-02.txt
24. Lv, Q., Cao, P., Cohen, E., Li, K., Shenker, S.: Search and replication in unstructured peer-to-peer networks. In: Proc. ACM Supercomputing (2002)
25. MANET - Mobile ad hoc Networks, IETF working group, http://www.ietf.org/html.charters/manet-charter.html
26. Meshkova, E., Riihijärvi, J.J., Petrova, M., Mähönen, P.: A survey on resource discovery mechanisms, peer-to-peer and service discovery frameworks. Computer Networks 52, 2097–2128 (2008)
27. Mian, A.N., Baldoni, R., Beraldi, R.: An efficient biasing strategy for random walk in wireless ad hoc networks. In: Proc. Internat. Wireless Communications and Mobile Computing Conf., Crete, Greece (August 2008)
28. Qian, L., Kunz, T.: Mobility metrics for adaptive routing. In: Proc. 3rd IEEE Conf. on Sensor and Ad Hoc Comm. and Networks, pp. 803–808 (2006)
29. Ripeanu, M., Iamnitchi, A.: Mapping the Gnutella network. IEEE Internet Computing, 50–57 (2002)
30. ROLL: Routing over low power and lossy networks, IETF working group, http://www.ietf.org/html.charters/roll-charter.html
31. Terpstra, W., Kangasharju, J., Leng, C., Buchmann, A.: BubbleStorm: Resilient, probabilistic and exhaustive P2P search. In: Proc. ACM SIGCOMM, Kyoto, Japan, pp. 49–60 (2007)
32. Villanueva-Pena, P., Kunz, T., Dhakal, P.: Extending network knowledge: Making OLSR a Quality of Service conducive protocol. In: Proc. Int. Conf. on Comm. and Mobile Comp., Vancouver, Canada, pp. 103–108 (2006)
33. Zhong, M., Shen, K.: Popularity-biased random walks for P2P search under the square root principle. In: Proc. 5th P2P Workshop, IPTPS (2006)

Routing Metric for Interference and Channel Diversity in Multi-Radio Wireless Mesh Networks

Vinicius C.M. Borges, Daniel Pereira, Marilia Curado, and Edmundo Monteiro

Laboratory of Communications and Telematics
Center for Informatics and Systems of the University of Coimbra
Polo II, 3030-290 Coimbra, Portugal
{vcmartins,dvieira,marilia,edmundo}@dei.uc.pt

Abstract. More than providing a wireless structure for Internet access, Wireless Mesh Networks are being challenged to support diverse kinds of multimedia applications such as Voice over IP and video streaming in publish-subscriber and peer-to-peer service models. In this context, several routing metrics have been proposed to improve the routing performance as well as the network capability to satisfy the requirements of multimedia applications. However, most routing metrics lack the consistent integration of efficient monitoring mechanisms for interference and traffic load characterization in order to support the adequate decisions by the routing algorithms. In this sense, a new routing metric is proposed in this paper, called Metric for INterference and channel Diversity (MIND), that measures network interference and load, based on a passive monitoring mechanism in order to avoid the overhead of active network state information gathering. An evaluation of MIND and relevant existing routing metrics was performed using NS2. The results showed that when path selection is based on MIND, traffic performance is significantly better than with the other metrics.

Keywords: Wireless Mesh networks, interference-aware routing metric, isotonicity, passive monitoring and traffic load estimation.

1 Introduction

Wireless Mesh Networks (WMNs) are multi-hop wireless networks with self-organization capability that provide low cost solutions for ubiquitous Internet access. WMNs comprise Mesh Clients (MCs), Mesh Routers (MRs) and Mesh Gateways (MGs). A set of MRs forms the WMNs backbone that offers connectivity to the Internet for MCs. Usually, MRs are stationary and do not have energy constraints [1]. In addition, MRs can employ Multi-Channel Multiple-Radio (MCMR) capability [1, 2] to achieve an improved performance. With MCMR, each radio is associated with its own MAC and physical layer. Therefore, a MCMR empowered WMN has better potential to scale as the size of the network increases [3].

Quality of Service (QoS) provisioning has become important in WMNs for the support of multimedia applications such as Voice over IP (VoIP) and Video. In

P.M. Ruiz and J.J. Garcia-Luna-Aceves (Eds.): ADHOC-NOW 2009, LNCS 5793, pp. 55–68, 2009.

this context, path selection plays a key role. For this purpose, routing protocols, algorithms and metrics have been developed to enhance WMNs performance [4].

Since several nodes share the wireless medium, a wireless link in WMNs does not have dedicated bandwidth and consequently, neighboring node transmissions may compete for the same bandwidth interfering with transmissions of neighboring links. Therefore, in order to select paths that satisfy requirements for multimedia applications, the routing process must be aware of the link quality and traffic load so that it captures the interference between neighboring nodes and links with heavy traffic. For this reason, the routing metric needs to combine information about interference and load in the wireless link, while avoiding introducing excessive overhead due to the measurement and distribution of this information. In order to gather information from different layers, a cross-layer design is usually employed [5, 6].

There are two interference models that have been studied in the literature, namely, protocol and physical interference models [7]. The protocol interference model determines that a transmission from a node A to a node B is successful if (i) there exists a link between them in the network topology, which is used for the transmission; and (ii) any node C such that $d_{CB} \leq R$ or $d_{CA} \leq R$ is neither transmitting nor receiving in the channel used by A and B. d_{CB} represents the distance between nodes C and B, and R represents the interference range, which for simplicity is assumed to be the same for all the nodes. Therefore, channel assignment algorithms have been adopted in MCMR WMNs in order to assign the available channels to radio interfaces of mesh routers, minimizing the overall interference [8].

The physical interference model captures the interference experienced by wireless links in the WMNs. In this model, a communication between nodes k and l is successful if the Signal to Interference-plus-Noise Ratio ($SINR$) at the receiver l is above a certain threshold which depends on the desired transmission characteristics, such as channel and data rate. Furthermore, the physical model is less restrictive compared to the protocol model, since it only depends on the signal strength values, such as Signal-to-noise ratio (SNR) and SINR, whereas the protocol model uses the concept of transmission range and interference range. It has the advantage of measuring the parameters of the model using on-line data traffic.

In addition, the restricted number of channels available in the IEEE PHY specification [9] does not permit to assign one channel for each wireless link in the WMN (for instance, the simultaneous operation of three non-overlapping channels in the 2.4 GHz band and 12 non-overlapping channels in the 5 GHz band). Therefore, channels are assigned in a repetitive way among the links and therefore, there will be interference among some links. For these reasons, the routing decision helps to reflect the actual link quality if it is based on the physical interference model. Summing up, interference-aware routing metrics are more suitable to WMNs, since they capture the link quality in a more realistic way.

Since many MCs may access the Internet to use multimedia applications provided by external servers, the traffic might mainly flow towards or from the MGs. Thus, the routing metric also needs to consider the traffic load in order to balance the load on the entire WMNs. Furthermore, due to the restricted resources of the wireless networks, it is desirable to use routing metrics that are based on passive monitoring mechanisms. A passive metric should provide a sufficiently accurate link representation that allows a routing algorithm to select high quality paths as well as eliminate the overhead associated with active monitoring techniques. For these reasons, in this paper, a new routing metric based on cross-layer design is presented, called as Metric for INterference and channel Diversity (MIND). MIND is then used by the Optimized Link State Routing (OLSR) protocol [10] for path selection.

This paper is organized as follows. Section 2 describes related work about routing metrics for WMNs. The proposed routing metric is presented in Section 3 as well as the implemented mechanisms in order to satisfy the requirements of the metrics in the WMNs. Section 4 describes the simulation study comparing MIND with relevant existing routing metrics. Finally, Section 5 presents, conclusions and issues to be addresssed in future work.

2   Related Work

This section presents the main routing metrics for Wireless Mesh Networks.

The Expected Transmission Count (ETX) [11] is defined as the expected number of MAC layer transmissions that is needed to successfully deliver a packet through a wireless link. The weight of a route is defined as the total sum of the ETX of all links along the route. This metric takes into account both packet loss ratio and route length. Moreover, ETX is also an isotonic routing metric, which guarantees calculation of minimum weight paths and loop-free routing [12]. If Bellman-Ford or Dijkstra's algorithms are used in hop-by-hop routing, isotonicity is a necessary condition to calculate the minimum weight paths. Nevertheless, ETX does not take into consideration interference and different links that may have different transmission rates.

The Expected Transmission Time (ETT) [13] routing metric improves ETX by considering the differences in link transmission rates. Namely, ETT is defined as the amount of time that is needed to transmit a packet through the link. The weight of a path is the sum of the ETT of all links on this path. This metric is also isotonic. Nevertheless, it has a drawback, since it does not fully capture the intra-flow and inter-flow interference in the network. For example, ETT may result on a route that uses only one channel, although a route with more diversified channels, and thus with less intra-flow interference, is available.

The Weighted Cumulative Expected Transmission Time (WCETT) [14] routing metric was proposed to reduce the number of nodes on the route of a flow that transmit on the same channel. WCETT captures the intra-flow interference of a route since it gives low weight to paths that have more diversified channel assignments on their links and hence lower intra-flow interference. Notwithstanding, it does not consider the effects of the inter-flow interference. Hence, WCETT may route flows to dense areas where there is congestion and may even result in starvation of some nodes due to congestion. Furthermore, WCETT is not isotonic and consequently prevents the use of an efficient loop free routing algorithm to compute minimum weight paths [14].

The Metric of Interference and Channel-switching (MIC) [15] improves WCE-TT by overcoming its non-isotonicity and its inability to capture inter-flow interference. MIC estimates inter-flow interference measuring the number of links that can interfere in the transmission. Namely, MIC does not consider interference in a dynamic way, which is a limitation, since the interference can change over time due to signal strength variations and to the amount of traffic generated by the interfering nodes.

The interference-AWARE (iAWARE) [16] routing metric aims to support the computation of paths that have lower inter-flow and intra-flow interference than MIC, WCETT and ETT. This metric resorts to SNR and SINR to continuously reproduce neighboring interference variations onto routing metrics and therefore, being based on the physical interference model. iAWARE employs a correlation between (SINR/SNR) and ETT, thus, capturing the effects of variation in link loss-ratio, differences in transmission rate, as well as inter-flow and intra-flow interference, in a dynamic way. However, iAWARE is not isotonic. The iAWARE and WCETT non-isotonicity is demonstrated in [15].

Despite the improvement from ETX to iAWARE, all the metrics discussed employ AdHoc probing (i.e., active monitoring) that sends fixed size packet-pairs (e.g., 1000 bytes) in order to estimate the delay [17]. This mechanism causes an excessive overhead and therefore, it might not scale in large or high density networks. In addition, active techniques need to access the medium, which may be difficult if the links are congested. For this reason, Resource Aware Routing for mEsh (RARE) was proposed [18], which uses a passive monitoring technique that combines available bandwidth, signal strength and average contention in the same link cost function. Nevertheless, RARE's performance is equivalent to ETT and there are even some situations where ETT outperforms RARE.

Recently, improvements of the ETX and ETT metrics were proposed, such as Interferer Neighbors Count (INX) [19] and Contention-Aware Transmission Time (CATT) [20]. Similarly to MIC, INX takes into account interference through the number of links that can interfere on link l and their data rates. This metric presents better performance with low load. In addition, CATT captures the influence that the interfering links, in 1 and 2 hop neighbors, can have on the needed time to transmit a packet over link l. Therefore, the use of CATT avoids the congested paths and has better performance than MIC, ETT and ETX. Nonetheless, these metrics still use a probing mechanism and do not consider interference in a realistic way, as explained before.

Table 1 summarizes related work on routing metrics, according to the main requirements, e.g. interference awareness, load awareness, isotonicity and probing mechanism. The analysis of this table shows that existing solutions address only some specific requirements and fail to provide interference and load awareness

Table 1. Related Work on Routing Metrics

Related Work	Interference-Aware	Load-Aware	Isotonic	Passive Monitoring
ETX [11]	No	No	Yes	No
ETT [13]	No	No	Yes	No
WCETT [14]	No	No	No	No
MIC [15]	Yes	No	Yes	No
iAWARE [16]	Yes	No	No	No
RARE [18]	No	No	Yes	Yes
INX [19]	Yes	No	Yes	No
CATT [20]	Yes	Yes	Yes	No

using passive monitoring while achieving isotonicity. For this purpose, a new routing metric is proposed in order to simultaneously address all these aspects.

3   MIND - Metric for INterference and Channel Diversity

This section presents the MIND routing metric. The MIND metric includes two components, one that concerns inter-flow INTERference and LOAD awareness ($INTER\_LOAD$) and the other that captures intra-flow interference, called Channel Switching Cost (CSC). Moreover, MIND employs a virtual network to achieve isotonicity (Virtual nodes will be explained in sub-section 3). Hence, Bellman-Ford or Dijkstra's algorithms can be used to find out the minimum weight paths. $MIND$ is defined as follows:

$$MIND(p) = \sum_{link i \in p}^{n} INTER\_LOAD_i + \sum_{node j \in p}^{m} CSC_j \qquad (1)$$

where n is the number of links and m is the number of nodes of the path p.

As it can be seen in Equation 2, the rationale behind the $INTER\_LOAD$ normalization is that it depicts information about interference and traffic load simultaneously and therefore, this information can be used on the path selection. For this purpose, Interference Ratio (IR) is employed to capture the interference among links based on the physical interference model [16, 21]. Therefore, MIND mainly considers interference whereas using Channel Busy Time (CBT) as a smooth function of multiplicative weighted over IR. Thus, it allows a trade-off between interference and load balancing in which interference has higher weight than traffic load. τ, a configurable parameter, is used to provide a higher weight to interference in the $INTER\_LOAD$ component.

$$INTER\_LOAD_i = ((1 - IR_i) * \tau) * CBT_i \qquad (2)$$

where $0 \leq IR \leq 1$ and $0 \leq CBT \leq 1$.

The IR sub-component depicts the interference based on the ratio between $SINR$ and SNR. Thus, this sub-component takes into consideration interference through the signal strength values which can be measured using commodity wireless cards. It also relies on a passive monitoring technique to capture the $SINR$ and SNR values without additional traffic, in contrast to routing metrics proposed which use special kind of traffic (e.g., probe packets) to measure the degree of interference between links [15, 20]. It is worth noting that when there is no interflow interference (i.e., no interfering neighbors or no traffic generated by interfering neighbors) $SINR$ of link i is equal to the SNR and thus IR_i is 1. In this case, the link i is independent of inter-flow interference and the quality of the link is determined by the intra-flow interference component. A more detailed description about the SNR formulas and $SINR$ is presented in [16]. Equation 3 shows the IR ratio.

$$IR_i = \frac{SINR_i}{SNR_i} \qquad (3)$$

CBT is the most direct and passive metric to measure the channel utilization in wireless networks [6, 22]. Therefore, the estimation of the traffic load is based on CBT, according to Equation 4. The CBT calculation is based on the time that packets spend in a wireless medium for a successful transmission. Namely, it uses a complementary calculation through the idle period. The $IdleTime$ value (Equation 4) considers the backoff times and time that no data keeps the channel busy. Instead of using the current value of a single packet, CBT is smoothed through the CBT average of the last 20 packets (this value is based on an empirical study - the detailed analysis performed is not presented here due to lack of space) in order to improve reliability and reduce the probability of CBT oscillations. The smoothing function is also used in IR values.

$$CBT_i = \frac{TotalTime - IdleTime}{TotalTime} \qquad (4)$$

MIND uses the CSC component to reduce the intra-flow interference. With this approach, paths with consecutive links using the same channel have higher weight than paths that alternate their channel assignments, essentially favoring paths with more diversified channel assignments. Equations 5 describes the CSC component.

$$CSC_j = \begin{cases} w1 \text{ if } CH\left(prev\left(j\right)\right) \neq CH\left(j\right) \\ w2, \text{ if } CH\left(prev\left(j\right)\right) = CH\left(j\right) \end{cases} \qquad (5)$$

where $0 \leq w1 < w2$, $CH(j)$ represents the channel assigned for node i's transmission and $prev(i)$ represents the previous hop of node i along the route p.

MIND is an isotonic interference-aware routing metric that considers the interflow interference in a more realistic way, intra-flow interference based on the local information and traffic load estimation through passive monitoring. The virtual network decomposition is described in the following sub-section.

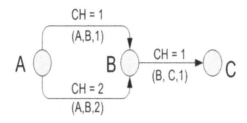

Fig. 1. MIND without Virtual Network [15]

Decomposition of MIND into a Virtual Network: MIND employs a virtual network scheme in order to become isotonic [15]. Figure 1 shows that the non-isotonic behavior of MIND is due to the fact that the additional weight that link $(B, C, 1)$ brings to a path not only depends on link $(B, C, 1)'s$ own status, but it is also related to the channel assignment of the link that precedes link $(B, C, 1)$. Due to the common channel used by links $(A, B, 1)$ and $(B, C, 1)$, adding link $(B, C, 1)$ to path $(A, B, 1)$ introduces a higher cost than adding link $(B, C, 1)$ to path $(A, B, 2)$. Hence, even though $MIND((A, B, 1)) < MIND((A, B, 2))$, $MIND((A, B, 1) \oplus (B, C, 1)) > MIND((A, B, 2) \oplus (B, C, 1))$, where $\oplus$ indicates a link concatenation.

By introducing several virtual nodes to represent these possible channel assignments for the precedent link, MIND can be translated into isotonic weight assignments to the links between these virtual nodes. Namely, for every channel c that a node $A's$ radios are configured to, two virtual nodes $A_i(c)$ and $A_e(c)$ are introduced. $A_i(c)$ represents that node $prev(A)$ transmits to node A on channel c. $A_e(c)$ indicates that node A transmits to its next hop on channel c.

Figure 2 shows an example of the virtual nodes for nodes A, B and C. Links from the ingress virtual nodes to the egress virtual nodes at node A are added and the weights of these links are assigned to capture different CSC costs. In addition, two additional virtual nodes are introduced, A+ and C- that are the start and end points, respectively.

Link $(A_i(c), A_e(c))$ means that node A does not change channels while forwarding packets and hence weight $w2$ is assigned to this link. Similarly, weight $w1$ is assigned to link $(Ai(c), Ae(c1))$, where $c \neq c1$, to represent the low cost of changing channels while forwarding packets. Links between the virtual nodes belonging to different real nodes are used to capture the $INTER\_LOAD$ weight. By building the virtual network from a real network, MIND is essentially decomposed in the real network into weight assignments to the links between virtual nodes. This is because the MIND weight of a real path in a real network can be reconstructed by aggregating all of the weights of the virtual links on the corresponding virtual path. The $INTER\_LOAD$ part of MIND is reflected in the weight of the links between virtual nodes in different real nodes. The CSC costs are captured by routing through different virtual links inside real nodes. Table 2 illustrates the real network mapping into the virtual network.

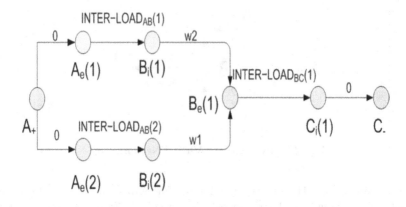

Fig. 2. Virtual Network of MIND

Table 2. Real network mapping to the virtual network

Real Path	Virtual Path	MIND weight
$(A, B, 1) \oplus (B, C, 1)$	$A_e(1) \to B_i(1) \to$ $B_e(1) \to C_i(1)$	$INTER\_LOAD_{AB}(1)$ + $INTER\_LOAD_{BC}(1) + w2$
$(A, B, 2) \oplus (B, C, 1)$	$A_e(2) \to B_i(2) \to$ $B_e(1) \to C_i(1)$	$INTER\_LOAD_{AB}(2)$ + $INTER\_LOAD_{BC}(1) + w1$

The iAWARE and WCETT non-isotonicity is caused by the dependence of the intra-flow interference component that captures the channel assignment of all links in a path. Namely, the weight increment of adding a link l to a path p depends on how many times each channel has appeared in path p. As the length of p increases, the combination of channel assignments can become infinite and therefore, iAWARE and WCETT cannot be decomposed into virtual networks. Moreover, a node usually does not interfere with other nodes that are more than two hops away even if they share the same channel. A detailed description about the WCETT non-isotonicity is described in [15]. Contrarily to these metrics, MIND uses local information to reduce intra-flow interference.

OLSR extension for Virtual Network: CSC needs to be computed in order to correctly implement the virtual network in the OLSR routing protocol. The implementation of the virtual network resorts to two different components, the extension of the information residing in the routing control messages that aggregate hello and topology control messages, and the weight calculation (i.e., $w1$ and $w2$). The control packet is enhanced with information about the previous CSC value and about the arriving interface. Since this information is not available at the routing layer, the calculation of the weights is computed in the forwarding phase of the OLSR routing protocol. Therefore, and following the specified schema by [15], if a control packet is originated from the current node, the CSC is not calculated (i.e., CSC is equal to zero), as any interface chosen will give the lowest CSC value.

On the other hand, if the control packet is destined to the current node, the CSC is not calculated, as it will not be forwarded again. When the node has to forward a control packet not originating from it, it will use the incoming interface to find the best route according to the routing table. If the chosen route corresponds to a different interface, the metric will have a lower penalization than when using the same interface, and the new CSC value will be updated in the packet information. This way, the different states of the virtual network can be reached, depending on the previous and next steps to take, as well as making sure that new packets and packets that have reached their destination will follow the proposed schema.

4   Experimental Results

This section presents the performance evaluation of MIND and compares the results obtained with the CATT, INX, iAWARE, MIC, ETT and ETX routing metrics. To the best of our knowledge the work presented in this paper is the most thorough evaluation of WMNs routing metrics. These metrics were implemented in the OLSR protocol using the NS-2 simulator version 2.31 [23]. Table 3 shows the simulation parameters used [24].

Table 3. Simulation Parameters

Parameter	Value
Network Size	50
Topology Size	$1000m^2$
Transmission Range	250m
Interference Range	500m
Propagation Model	TwoRayGround
CBR Source Data Rate	8Kb/s
Simulation Time	60s
τ	10
Data Channel rate	2Mbps
PHY Specification	802.11 b/g
Antenna	Omnidirectional
Runs	10

The routing metrics were evaluated according to different parameters, such as throughput, delay, loss and jitter and under different loads, in a random topology. Source and destination flows were predefined in the network so that they intersect each other and consequently, cause a higher interference among data flows. All nodes have the same physical configuration. Figures 3 and 4 show

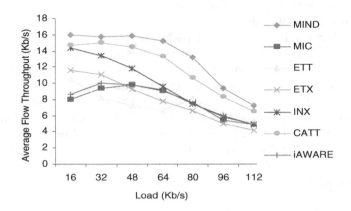

Fig. 3. Throughput

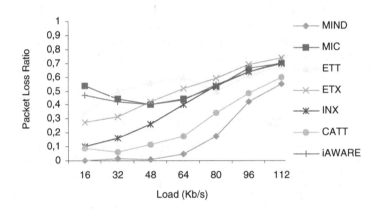

Fig. 4. Packet Loss Ratio

that MIC and iAWARE have worse throughput and loss ratio than ETT, ETX and INX with low loads (16 and 32 Kb/s).

However, the results of MIC and iAWARE improve as the traffic load increases and consequently, MIC and iAWARE have higher throughput and lower loss ratio than ETT, ETX and INX with medium and high loads. iAWARE and MIC have similar results, as expected. However, in some cases, iAWARE has a slight performance improvement over MIC, since iAWARE considers interference in a more realistic way. ETX and INX have better throughput and loss ratio with low loads, and decrease significantly their performance in high loads.

ETT presents an unstable behavior due to the probing technique that over-estimates the link quality. Moreover, ETT does not depend on the traffic load, as was already assessed in [20, 25]. Although MIC and iAWARE rely partially

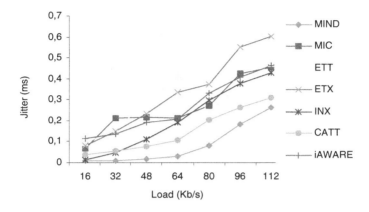

Fig. 5. Jitter

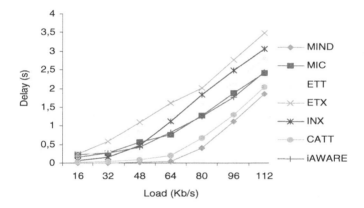

Fig. 6. Delay

on ETT, these metrics employ normalization functions to smooth the ETT values and therefore become more stable. Overall, CATT achieves better results than MIC and iAWARE for all loads, due to the avoidance of congested paths, achieved through the traffic load estimation.

Figures 3, 4, 5 and 6 show that MIND is able to achieve higher throughput, lower loss ratio, lower delay and lower jitter than the remaining metrics for all loads considered. Table 4 shows the MIND performance gain over the other metrics.

MIND has better performance than CATT for all loads and parameters considered. These results are due to the fact that MIND considers interference and traffic load in a more realistic way and uses passive monitoring. The difference of performance between MIND and CATT decreases for high loads (96 and 112 Kb/s), since the wireless medium resources become very scarce and thus, the impact of the routing metric becomes negligible.

Table 4. MIND Performance Gains

Metrics	Throughput	Loss	Delay	Jitter
ETX	67%	192%	241%	297%
ETT	77%	210%	166%	248%
MIC	71%	206%	113%	271%
iAWARE	65%	197%	106%	229%
INX	37%	130%	166%	149%
CATT	11%	52%	26%	79%

There are several characteristics that motivate a better performance of the MIND in all evaluated loads and parameters compared with the other metrics. MIND is an isotonic metric that allows routing algorithms to select minimum weight paths; it takes into consideration interference in a more realistic way through the physical interference model; it has a lower overhead due to lack of probe packets in order to estimate the traffic load; and lastly, it provides better load balancing among paths during the routing process due to the channel busy time component.

5   Conclusions and Future Work

This paper discussed the main aspects needed to design efficient routing metrics for multi-radio WMNs. After the identification of the relevant characteristics which are not provided by existing metrics, a new routing metric was proposed and implemented, called as Metric for INterference and channel Diversity (MIND), this metric considers several aspects that improve the WMNs performance, such as the selection of paths providing reduced inter-flow and intra-flow interference and the avoidance of overhead caused by active probing techniques. In addition, the MIND metric is isotonic which allows its employment with existing routing algorithms to select minimum weight paths and to avoid routing loops. MIND was evaluated in the NS2 simulator, using the OLSR routing protocol.

The results showed that MIND outperformed the most relevant routing metrics for WMNs. It is evidenced that MIND has better performance for all loads in the network and hence, it improves the network scalability. For example, an improvement of 26% and 79% in delay and jitter, respectively, when compared to CATT was obtained.

In the future, new correlations with differents information to improve MIND performance as well as virtual network extensions in order to simplify implementation of this scheme will be investigated.

Acknowledgement

This work was partially funded by FCT (scholarship contract SFRH/BD/44378/2008).

References

[1] Akyldiz, I.F., Wang, X., Wang, W.: Wireless mesh networks: a survey. Computer Networks 47, 445–487 (2005)

[2] Liu, T., Liao, W.: On routing in multichannel wireless mesh networks: Challenges and solutions. IEEE Network 22, 13–18 (2008)

[3] Networks, B.: Capacity of wireless mesh networks - understanding single radio, dual radio and multi-radio wireless mesh networks (2006)

[4] Karrer, R.P., Pescape, A.: 2nd generation wireless mesh networks: Technical, economical and social challenges. Future Generation Communication and Networking 1, 262–267 (2007)

[5] Akyildiz, I., Wang, X.: Cross-layer design in wireless mesh networks. IEEE Transactions on Vehicular Technology 57, 1061–1076 (2008)

[6] Athanasiou, G., Korakis, T., Ercetin, O., Tassiulas, L.: A cross-layer framework for association control in wireless mesh networks. IEEE Transactions on Mobile Computing 8, 65–80 (2009)

[7] Gupta, P., Kumar, P.: The capacity of wireless networks. IEEE Transactions on Information Theory 46, 388–404 (2000)

[8] Crichigno, J., Wu, M.Y., Shu, W.: Protocols and architectures for channel assignment in wireless mesh networks. Ad Hoc Networks 6, 1051–1077 (2008)

[9] : Wireless LAN Medium Access Control (MAC) and Physical Layer (PHY) Specifications. IEEE Standard 802.11 (1999)

[10] Jacquet, P., Mühlethaler, P., Clausen, T., Laouiti, A., Qayyum, A., Viennot, L.: Optimized link state routing protocol for ad hoc networks. In: IEEE INMIC 2001 (2001)

[11] Couto, D.S.J.D., Aguayo, D., Bicket, J., Morris, R.: A high-throughput path metric for multi-hop wireless routing. In: 9th MobiCom 2003, pp. 134–146. ACM, New York (2003)

[12] Sobrinho, J.L.: Algebra and algorithms for qos path computation and hop-by-hop routing in the internet. IEEE/ACM Trans. Netw. 10, 541–550 (2002)

[13] Bicket, J., Aguayo, D., Biswas, S., Morris, R.: Architecture and evaluation of an unplanned 802.11b mesh network. In: 11th MobiCom 2005, pp. 31–42. ACM, New York (2005)

[14] Draves, R., Padhye, J., Zill, B.: Routing in multi-radio, multi-hop wireless mesh networks. In: MobiCom 2004, pp. 114–128. ACM, New York (2004)

[15] Yang, Y., Wang, J., Kravets, R.: Designing routing metrics for mesh networks. In: Proceedings of the IEEE Workshop on Wireless Mesh Networks (WiMesh). IEEE Press, Los Alamitos (2005)

[16] Subramanian, A., Buddhikot, M., Miller, S.: Interference aware routing in multi-radio wireless mesh networks. In: 2nd IEEE Workshop on Wireless Mesh Networks, 2006. WiMesh 2006, pp. 55–63 (2006)

[17] Chen, L.J., Sun, T., Yang, G., Sanadidi, M., Gerla, M.: Ad hoc probe: path capacity probing in wireless ad hoc networks. In: First International Conference on Wireless Internet, 2005. Proceedings, pp. 156–163 (2005)

[18] Kowalik, K., Keegan, B., Davis, M.: Rare - resource aware routing for mesh. In: IEEE ICC 2007, pp. 4931–4936 (2007)

[19] Langar, R., Bouabdallah, N., Boutaba, R.: Mobility-aware clustering algorithms with interference constraints in wireless mesh networks. Comput. Netw. 53, 25–44 (2009)

[20] Genetzakis, M., Siris, V.: A contention-aware routing metric for multi-rate multi-radio mesh networks. In: 5th IEEE SECON 2008, pp. 242–250 (2008)

[21] Neishaboori, A., Kesidis, G.: Sinr-sensitive routing in wireless 802.11 mesh networks. In: IEEE MASS 2008, pp. 623–628 (2008)

[22] Wu, G., Chiueh, T.-c.: Passive and accurate traffic load estimation for infrastructure-mode wireless lan. In: ACM MSWiM 2007, pp. 109–116. ACM, New York (2007)

[23] The network simulator ns-2 (2009), http://www.isi.edu/nsnam/ns

[24] Willkomm, D., Machiraju, S., Bolot, J., Wolisz, A.: Primary user behavior in cellular networks and implications for dynamic spectrum access. IEEE Communications Magazine 47 (2009)

[25] Ramachandran, K.N., Sheriff, I., Belding, E.M., Almeroth, K.C.: Routing stability in static wireless mesh networks. In: Uhlig, S., Papagiannaki, K., Bonaventure, O. (eds.) PAM 2007. LNCS, vol. 4427, pp. 73–82. Springer, Heidelberg (2007)

Minimum Delay Data Gathering in Radio Networks*

Jean-Claude Bermond, Nicolas Nisse, Patricio Reyes**, and Hervé Rivano

Mascotte Project, INRIA–I3S(CNRS/UNSA), Sophia Antipolis, France
Firstname.Lastname@inria.fr

Abstract. The aim of this paper is to design efficient gathering algorithms (data collection) in a Base Station of a wireless multi hop grid network when interferences constraints are present. We suppose the time is slotted and that during one time slot (step) each node can transmit to one of its neighbours at most one data item. Each device is equipped with a half duplex interface; so a node cannot both receive and transmit simultaneously. During a step only non interfering transmissions can be done. In other words, the non interfering calls done during a step will form a matching. The aim is to minimize the number of steps needed to send to the base station a set of messages generated by the nodes, this *completion time* is also denoted *makespan* of the call scheduling. The best known algorithm for *open-grids* was a multiplicative 1.5-approximation algorithm [Revah, Segal 07]. In such topologies, we give a very simple +2 approximation algorithm and then a more involved +1 approximation algorithm. Moreover, our algorithms work when no buffering is allowed in intermediary nodes, i.e., when a node receives a message at some step, it must transmit it during the next step.

Keywords: Sensor Networks, gathering, makespan, grid.

1 Introduction

We address here the challenging problem of gathering information in a Base Station (denoted BS) of a wireless multi hop grid network when interferences constraints are present. This problem is also known as data collection and is particularly important in sensor networks, but also in access networks.

The communication network is modeled by a graph. In this paper we focus on grid topologies as they model well both access networks and also random networks (which approximatively behave like if the nodes were on a grid [1]). We assume that the time is slotted and that during each time slot, or *step*, a transmission that is activated between two neighboring nodes can transport at most one data item (referred in what follows as a message). Each vertex of the grid may have any number of messages to transmit, including none. We also suppose that each device (sensor, station,...) is equipped with an half duplex interface: a node cannot both receive and transmit during a step. As for an example, this is a relevant model of mono-frequency smart antennas radio system: at any step, each device can configure its antenna array to shape a beam and reach

---

* This work is partially supported by Project IST-FET IP AEOLUS, ANR Verso project Ecoscells.
** Supported by CONICYT(Chile)/INRIA.

P.M. Ruiz and J.J. Garcia-Luna-Aceves (Eds.): ADHOC-NOW 2009, LNCS 5793, pp. 69–82, 2009.
© Springer-Verlag Berlin Heidelberg 2009

any of its neighbours without interfering with others. Nevertheless, sending a message prevents a node from receiving another one because, among other causes, of near-far effects. We refer to this model as the *smart-antennas model*.

During any step a set of pairwise non interfering transmissions can be achieved, and such a set form a matching of the grid. Our aim is to design algorithms to do a gathering under such hypotheses, which minimize the minimum number of steps needed to send all messages to BS, this *completion time* is also denoted *makespan* of the call scheduling.

Following the work of Revah and Segal [2], we focus on the specific case of "*open-grid*", that is a grid network with the base station at a corner (say lower-left w.l.g.) and no message is generated by a node on the lower and lefter borders of the grid (line 0 and column 0). As a matter of fact, the case of *closed-grid*, which is by the way similar to having the BS anywhere on the grid, is more complex and cannot be solved to optimality with shortest paths[1]. Even though we know how to adapt our weakest algorithm, the value of the lower-bound in that case is still under active investigation [3].

1.1 Related Work

A lot of authors have studied the gathering problem under various assumptions (see the surveys [4] and [5]).

In [6], the smart antennas model is considered with the extra constraint that non buffering is allowed in intermediary nodes: when a node receives a message at some step, it must transmit it during the next step. In this setting, optimal polynomial-time algorithms are presented for path and tree topologies [6,7]. The work of [6] has been extended to general graphs in [8] and [9] but in the uniform case where each node has exactly one message to transmit. The case of *open-grids* is considered in [2] where a 1.5-approximation algorithm is presented. The gathering problem has also been studied when nodes can both emit and receive a message during the same step. When no buffering is allowed, this kind of routing is known as the hot-potato routing and it is considered in [10,11].

The case of omnidirectional antennas has been extensively studied. In this model, nodes can transmit at any of their neighbours at distance $d_T \geq 1$ but any emission creates some interferences. More precisely, when a node v transmits, any node at distance at most $d_I \geq d_T$ of v cannot receive a message from another node than v during the same step. Moreover, any node has to transmit at least one message and buffering is allowed. In this setting, computing the makespan is NP-hard [12]. A 4-approximation algorithm and lower bounds for general graphs are also provided in [12]. A 4-approximation algorithm has been proposed to handle the online version [13]. In [14], the case of grids is considered when $d_T = 1$: an optimal polynomial-time algorithm is provided when BS stands at the center of the grid. Gathering in grids is also considered within a continuous model in [15].

1.2 Our Results

We focus on the gathering problem in *open-grids*. We provide a very simple algorithm that schedules all messages within a lower bound of the makespan plus two steps, and

---

[1] The authors would like to thanks Prof. Frédéric Guinand who raised this question.

a more involved $+1$ approximation algorithm. As a matter of fact, we prove that our algorithms delay each message by at most 1 or 2 steps (depending on which algorithm) from a given scheduling which would be optimal if there were no interference (hence lower bounding the real makespan). We also provide a linear-time (in the number of vertices of the grid) distributed algorithm for the $+2$–approximation algorithm. Besides, our algorithms need no buffering, which considerably improves on existing algorithms. Our algorithms are presentend in the smart antennas model, even though we conjecture that they can be extended to other distance-based interference model.

One helpful idea is to actually study the related one–to-many personalized broadcast problem in which the BS wants to communicate different data items to some other nodes in the network. Using this framework, protocols may be described easier. Solving the above dissemination problem is equivalent to solve data gathering in sensor networks. Indeed, let T denote the makespan (delay), that is, the largest step used by a personalized broadcast algorithm; a gathering schedule with delay T consists in scheduling a transmission from node y to x during slot t iff the broadcasting algorithm schedules a transmission from node x to y during slot $T - t + 1$, for any t with $1 \leq t \leq T$.

2   Preliminaries

From now on, we consider the equivalent problem of personalized broadcasting where BS has to transmit messages to some destination nodes in the open grid.

2.1   Notations

In the following, we consider a $N \times N$ grid $G = (V, E)$ where vertices are given there natural coordinates. The base station BS, also called *the source*, has coordinates $(0, 0)$, and any vertex v has coordinates (x_v, y_v). A vertex v is *above* (resp., *below*) $w \in V$ if $y_v \geq y_w$ (resp., if $y_v \leq y_w$). Similarly, v is *to the right* (resp., *to the left*) of $w \in V$ if $x_v \geq x_w$ (resp., if $x_v \leq x_w$). Finally, a vertex v is *nearer to the source* than $w \in V$ is $d(v, BS) \leq d(w, BS)$, where $d(u, v)$ denotes the classical distance between nodes u and v.

We consider a set of $M \geq 0$ messages $\mathcal{M}$ that must be sent from the source BS to some destination nodes. Let $dest(m) \in V$ denote the destination of $m \in \mathcal{M}$. A message $m \in \mathcal{M}$ is *lower* (resp., *higher*) than $m' \in \mathcal{M}$ if $dest(m)$ is below (resp., above) $dest(m')$. A message m is *righter* (resp., *lefter*) than m', if $dest(m)$ is to the right (resp., to the left) of $dest(m')$. We use $d(m)$ to denote $d(dest(m), BS)$, and $m \preceq m'$ if $dest(m)$ is nearer to the source than $dest(m')$, that is, if $d(m) \leq d(m')$. We suppose in what follows that the messages are ordered by non increasing distance of their destination nodes, and we note $\mathcal{M} = \{m_1, \cdots, m_M\}$ where $m_i \succeq m_j$ for any $i \leq j \leq M$, so $d(m_1) \geq d(m_2) \geq \cdots \geq d(m_M)$.

$S \odot S'$ denotes the sequence obtained by concatenation of two sequences S and S'.

2.2   Lower Bound

Consider a model whitout interferences, i.e., any node can receive and transmit simultaneously, but where the source can only send one message per step. Whatever be the broadcasting scheme, a message m sent at step $t \geq 1$ will be received at step $t' \geq d(m) + t - 1$. A broadcasting scheme is said *greedy* if, given an ordered sequence S of the messages, the source sends one message per step, in the ordering S, and each message follows a shortest path toward its destination node. Note that, in the model without interferences, if the messages follow shortest paths, a vertex will never receive more than one message per step.

Definition 1. $LB = \max_{i \leq M} d(m_i) + i - 1$.

Lemma 1. *In the model without interferences, when the source emits at most one message per step, a greedy algorithm following the ordered sequence of messages $(m_1, m_2, \cdots, m_M)$ is optimal, with makespan LB.*

Proof. Clearly, sending the messages following the sequence $(m_1, m_2, \cdots, m_M)$ along shortest paths achieves such a makespan. Let us consider an optimal schedule of the messages $(s_1^*, \cdots, s_M^*)$ different from $(m_1, m_2, \cdots, m_M)$ and let $i \geq 1$ be the smallest integer such that $s_i^* \neq m_i = s_j^*$ $(j > i)$. Sending the messages following the sequence $(s_1^*, \cdots, s_{i-1}^*, s_j^*, s_{i+1}^*, \cdots, s_{j-1}^*, s_i^*, s_{j+1}^*, \cdots, s_m^*)$ does not increase the makespan: indeed, only the ith and j^{th} messages differ and $\max\{d(s_j^*) + i - 1, d(s_i^*) + j - 1)\} \leq d(s_j^*) + j - 1)$ because $d(v_i, BS) = d(s_j^*) \geq d(s_i^*)$ and $j > i$. By iterating this process, we get that the ordering of the sequence $(m_1, m_2, \cdots, m_M)$ is also optimal.   □

Corollary 1. *In the smart antennas model, no algorithm can achieve a makespan less than LB.*

3   Personalized Broadcasting Algorithms

In this section, we present a very simple broadcasting scheme that we prove to be sufficient to obtain a good approximation of the optimal makespan. We then refine it to obtain an almost optimal algorithm.

These algorithms use Horizontal-Vertical routing schemes, hence proving that fancier shortest path routing is worthless with respect to the minimum makespan objective.

3.1   Horizontal-Vertical Broadcasting

Given a message whose destination node v has coordinates (x, y), the message is sent *horizontally* to v if it follows the shortest path from BS to v passing through $(x, 0)$. The message is sent *vertically* if it follows the shortest path from BS to v passing through $(0, y)$.

Definition 2. *A Horizontal-Vertical broadcasting scheme, or HV-scheme, takes an ordering S of M as an input and proceeds as follows. A direction, horizontal or vertical, is chosen for the first message. Then, the source sends one message every step in the ordering S, alternating horizontal and vertical messages.*

Let us do some easy remarks about any HV-scheme. Consider two distinct messages sent by the source x time-slots apart. Since these messages follow shortest paths, while the first message has not reached its destination, both messages are separated by a distance at least x. Hence,

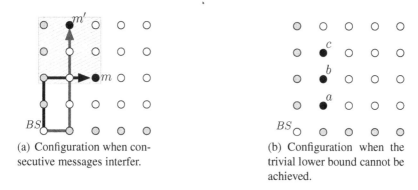

(a) Configuration when consecutive messages interfer.

(b) Configuration when the
trivial lower bound cannot be
achieved.

Fig. 1. Two particular configurations

Fact 1. *In a HV-scheme, only consecutive messages may interfer.*

Let us characterize forbidden and acceptable configurations in HV-scheme. Assume that two messages are sent consecutively. It is possible to guess the respective positions of their destination nodes by knowing whether both messages interfer or not. In Figure 1(a), messages in the grey part are those higher and lefter than the message m. Figure 1(a) illustrates the following Fact.

Fact 2. *Let m, m' be 2 messages sent consecutively by a HV-scheme, with m sent vertically and m' sent horizontally. Messages m and m' interfer if and only if their destinations are distinct and m' is higher and lefter than m.*

Before continuing, let us remark that there exist configurations for which no gathering protocol can achieve better makespan than $LB + 1$. Figure 1(b) represents such a configuration. Indeed, in Figure 1(b), the three destinations a, b and c have coordinates $(1, 1), (1, 2)$ and $(1, 3)$, and $LB = 4$. However, to achieve such a makespan, the first message must be sent to c (because c is at distance 4 from BS) and the second message must be sent to b (because the message start after the first step and must go at distance 3). To avoid collision, the only possibility is to send the first message vertically, and the second one horizontally. But then, the last message cannot reach a before step 5.

3.2 +2 Approximation

Recall that $(m_1, \cdots, m_M)$ denotes the ordered sequence of the messages in the non increasing ordering of the distance to their destinations. In this section, we give the Algorithm $TwoApprox$, depicted in Figure 2, that computes an ordered sequence $\mathcal{S} = (s_1, \cdots, s_m)$ of the messages satisfying the two following properties:

(i) HV-scheme($\mathcal{S}$) broadcasts the messages without collisions, sending the last message vertically, and

(ii) $s_i \in \{m_{i-2}, m_{i-1}, m_i, m_{i+1}, m_{i+2}\}$ for any $i \leq M$, and $s_M \in \{m_{M-1}, m_M\}$

Theorem 1. *Algorithm $TwoApprox$ computes an ordering $\mathcal{S}$ of the messages satisfying properties (i) and (ii) and so HV-scheme($\mathcal{S}$) achieves makespan at most $LB + 2$.*

Input: $\mathcal{M} = \{m_1, \cdots, m_M\}$, the set of messages ordered in non increasing distance order
Output: $(s_1, \cdots, s_M)$ an ordered sequence of $\mathcal{M}$ satisfying (i) and (ii)
begin
    Case $M = 0$ **return** $\emptyset$
    Case $M = 1$ **return** (m_1)
    Case $M \geq 2$
        Let q be the lowest message in $\{m_{M-1}, m_M\}$ and let r be the other one
        if $M = 2$ **return** (q, r)
        else let $\mathcal{O} \odot p = TwoApprox(\{m_1, \cdots, m_{M-2}\})$
            if p is higher than q **return** $\mathcal{O} \odot (p, q, r)$
            else return $\mathcal{O} \odot (m_{M-1}, p, m_M)$
end

Fig. 2. Algorithm $TwoApprox$

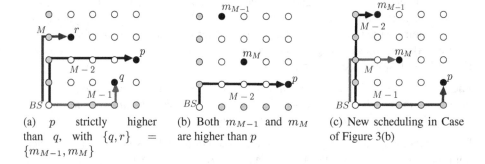

(a) p strictly higher than q, with $\{q, r\} = \{m_{M-1}, m_M\}$

(b) Both m_{M-1} and m_M are higher than p

(c) New scheduling in Case of Figure 3(b)

Fig. 3. $M - 2$ messages have been scheduled, finishing with the one to $p \in \{m_{M-2}, m_{M-3}\}$. When the next two messages must be scheduled, two cases occur according to the position of m_{M-1} and m_M relatively to p. In the figures, an arrow with label i represents the route of the ith message.

Proof. To prove the correctness of Algorithm $TwoApprox$, we proceed by induction on M. If $M \leq 2$, the result holds obviously. Let us assume that the ordering of the sequence computed by $TwoApprox(\{m_1, \cdots, m_{M-2}\})$ satisfies properties (i) and (ii). Let p be the last message of this sequence. By the induction hypothesis, $p \in \{m_{M-3}, m_{M-2}\}$ is sent vertically. Let t be the message before p in this sequence. By Fact 2, p must be higher or lefter than t. The sequence is denoted by $\mathcal{O} \odot p = \mathcal{O}' \odot (t, p)$.

Let q be the lowest message in $\{m_{M-1}, m_M\}$ and let r be the other one. We consider two cases depending on the positions of p, q and r.

a) **Case p is higher than q.** It is sufficient to send q horizontally at step $M - 1$, and r vertically at step M. This case is depicted in Figure 3(a). Indeed, by Fact 1 only

p and q, or q and r may interfer. By Fact 2, there are no interferences. It is easy to check that $\mathcal{O} \odot (p, q, r)$ satisfies (i) and (ii).

b) **Case q and r are higher than p.** Since $q, r \preceq p$ (i.e. q, r closer to BS than p.), they are higher and lefter than p. This case is depicted in Figure 3(b). In this case, instead of sending p at step $M - 2$, the source sends m_{M-1} vertically at step $M - 2$, then p horizontally at step $M - 1$, and then m_M vertically at step M. The transformation is depicted in Figure 3(c). Clearly, $\mathcal{O} \odot (m_{M-1}, p, m_M)$ satisfies (i) and (ii). By Fact 1 only t and m_{M-1}, or m_{M-1} and p, or p and m_M may interfer. Since m_{M-1} is higher and lefter than p that is higher or lefter than t, by Fact 2, m_{M-1} interferes neither with t nor with p. Similarly, m_M is higher and lefter than p and these messages do not interfer.   □

3.3   +1 Approximation

In this section, we give the Algorithm *OneApprox*, depicted in Figure 4, that computes an ordered sequence $\mathcal{S} = (s_1, \cdots, s_m)$ of the messages satisfying:

(i) HV-scheme($\mathcal{S}$) broadcasts the messages without collisions, sending the last message vertically, and

(iii) $s_i \in \{m_{i-1}, m_i, m_{i+1}\}$ for any $i \leq M$ (in particular, either $s_M = m_M$, or $s_M = m_{M-1}$ and $s_{M-1} = m_M$).

An ordered sequence $\mathcal{S} = (s_1, \cdots, s_M)$ of $\mathcal{M}$ satisfying (i) and (iii) is said *valid*. Clearly, for any valid sequence $\mathcal{S}$, HV-scheme($\mathcal{S}$) achieves makespan at most $LB + 1$. To prove that Algorithm *OneApprox* computes a valid ordered sequence of $\mathcal{M}$, we proceed by induction on M. Roughly, starting from a valid ordered sequence of $\{m_1, \cdots, m_{M-2}\}$, the algorithm includes m_{M-1} and m_M in this ordered sequence. Then, either the obtained sequence $\mathcal{S}$ is valid, or it is 1-good, where the notion of i-*goodness* is defined as follows:

Definition 3. *Let $i \in \{1, \cdots, \lfloor M/2 \rfloor - 1\}$. An ordered sequence $\mathcal{S} = (s_1, \cdots, s_M)$ is i-good if*

- $s_{M-2i-1} = m_{M-2i-1}$, $s_{M-2i} = m_{M-2i+1}$ *and* $s_M = m_M$, *and*
- $\mathcal{S}$ *satisfies properties (i) and (iii) but s_{M-2i-2} may interfer with s_{M-2i-1}.*

In the latter case, subprocedure *MakeValid* (see Figure 5) is recursively applied to $\mathcal{S}$ increasing the parameter of goodness until either a valid sequence is obtained or we arrive to an $(\lfloor M/2 \rfloor - 1)$-good sequence. But, by definition, a $(\lfloor M/2 \rfloor - 1)$-good sequence is always valid.

We now detail the execution of Algorithm *OneApprox* on the example depicted in Figure 6. In this example, BS must send 8 messages $\{m_1, \cdots, m_8\}$ to distinct vertices in a 6×6-grid. Algorithm *OneApprox* first computes a valid ordered sequence $(s_1, \cdots, s_6) = (m_1, m_2, m_4, m_3, m_6, m_5)$ of first 6 messages. This scheduling is depicted in Figure 6(a). Then, the positions of m_7, m_8 and $s_6 = m_5$ are compared. In the example, m_8 is the lowest message among m_7 and m_8, and it is higher than s_6. Moreover, $s_6 \neq m_6$. Hence, Algorithm *OneApprox* applies Subprocedure *MakeValid* to

Input: $\mathcal{M} = \{m_1, \cdots, m_M\}$, the set of messages ordered in non increasing distance order

Output: $(s_1, \cdots, s_M)$ an ordered sequence of $\mathcal{M}$ such that $m_i \in \{s_{i-1}, s_i, s_{i+1}\}$ for any $i \leq M$

begin

  Case $M = 0$ **return** $\emptyset$

  Case $M = 1$ **return** (m_1)

  Case $M \geq 2$

    Let q be the lowest message in $\{m_{M-1}, m_M\}$ and let r be the other one

    if $M = 2$ **return** (q, r)

    else let $\mathcal{O} \odot p = OneApprox(\{m_1, \cdots, m_{M-2}\})$

      if p is higher than q **return** $\mathcal{O} \odot (p, q, r)$

      else if $p = m_{M-2}$ **return** $\mathcal{O} \odot (m_{M-1}, p, m_M)$

      else

        /* This last case may occur only if $M > 3$ */

        Let $(s_1, \cdots, s_{M-4}) \odot (m_{M-2}, m_{M-3}) = OneApprox(\{m_1, \cdots, m_{M-2}\})$

        return $MakeValid((s_1, \cdots, s_{M-4}) \odot (m_{M-3}, m_{M-1}, m_{M-2}, m_M), 2)$

end

Fig. 4. Algorithm $OneApprox$

Input: A $(j-1)$-good (see def. 3) sequence $\mathcal{O} = (s_1, \cdots, s_M)$ of a set of messages $\{m_1, \cdots, m_M\}$, and an integer j, $1 < j \leq \lfloor M/2 \rfloor$.

Output: A valid sequence of $\mathcal{M}$

  if s_{M-2j} and s_{M-2j+1} do not interfer

    /* In particular, this case occurs if $M - 2j = 0$ */

    return $\mathcal{O}$

  else if $s_{M-2j} = m_{M-2j}$

    /* In particular, this case occurs if $M - 2j = 1$ */

    return

$(s_1, \cdots, s_{M-2j-2}) \odot (s_{M-2j-1}, s_{M-2j+1}, s_{M-2j}, s_{M-2j+2}) \odot (s_{M-2j+3}, \cdots, s_M)$

  else return

    /* This last case may occur only if $M - 2j \geq 2$ */

    /* Note that, in this case, $s_{M-2j} = m_{M-2j-1}$ and $s_{M-2j-1} = m_{M-2j}$ */

    $MakeValid((s_1, \cdots, s_{M-2j-2}) \odot (s_{M-2j}, s_{M-2j+1}, s_{M-2j-1}, s_{M-2j+2})$

        $\odot (s_{M-2j+3}, \cdots, s_M), j + 1)$

end

Fig. 5. MakeValid

integer $j = 2$ together with the ordered sequence $(s_1, \cdots, s_4) \odot (m_5, m_7, m_6, m_8) = (m_1, m_2, m_4, m_3, m_5, m_7, m_6, m_8)$. The scheduling corresponding to this sequence is depicted in Figure 6(b). It is easy to check that this sequence is 1-good: in particular, it is valid except for the interference between m_3 and m_5. Note that the integer variable j in the input of Subprocedure $MakeValid$ simply indicates that the interference may appear between the $M - 2j^{th}$ and the $M - 2j + 1^{th}$ messages of the given

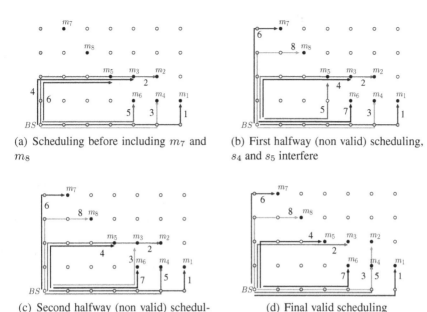

(a) Scheduling before including m_7 and m_8

(b) First halfway (non valid) scheduling, s_4 and s_5 interfere

(c) Second halfway (non valid) scheduling, s_2 and s_3 interfere

(d) Final valid scheduling

Fig. 6. Recursive modifications of the scheduling

sequence. The goal of Subprocedure $MakeValid$ is to locally modify the sequence in order to remove interference between the $M - 2j^{th}$ and the $M - 2j + 1^{th}$ messages. However, a new interference may appear between the $M - 2(j + 1)^{th}$ and the $M - 2(j + 1) + 1^{th}$ messages of the obtained sequence, in which case Subprocedure $MakeValid$ is recall recursively. Such a situation occurs in the example. Indeed, in the sequence $(m_1, m_2, m_4, m_3, m_5, m_7, m_6, m_8)$, m_3 and m_5 interfere and the fourth message of this sequence is not m_4. Then, Subprocedure $MakeValid$ is applied to the sequence $(m_1, m_2) \odot (m_3, m_5, m_4, m_7) \odot (m_6, m_8)$ with $j = 3$. This sequence is depicted in Figure 6(c) and is 2-good since m_2 and m_3 interfer. Note that the second message of this sequence interferes and that this message is actually m_2. Therefore, the next call to Subprocedure $MakeValid$ only exchanges m_2 and m_3 (Case 2 of the subprocedure) and returns the ordered sequence $(m_1, m_3, m_2, m_5, m_4, m_7, m_6, m_8)$. The scheduling corresponding to this sequence is depicted in Figure 6(d) and it is easy to check that it is valid.

Due to lack of space, the proofs of the correctness and time-complexity of algorithms $OneApprox$ and $MakeValid$ are omitted and can be found in [16].

Theorem 2. *Algorithm $OneApprox$ computes an ordering $\mathcal{S}$ of the messages satisfying properties (i) and (iii) and so HV-scheme($\mathcal{S}$) achieves makespan at most $LB + 1$. Moreover, Algorithm $OneApprox$ performs in linear time, with respect to the number of messages.*

4   Distributed Algorithm

We present a synchronous distributed algorithm for the gathering in a N^2-node grid, which is based on the Algorithm $TwoApprox$, for personalized broadcasting presented in section 3.2. This algorithm uses control messages of size $O(\log N)$ bits and it performs in $O(N^2)$ steps (with similar complexity in terms of number of control messages), i.e., its time-complexity is linear in the size of the grid.

4.1   Distributed Model

The network is assumed to be synchronous. Each node has only a local view of the network. However, it has access to the following global information: its position (x, y) in the grid, the position of BS (for sake of simplicity, we assume that BS has coordinates $(0, 0)$), and the size $N \times N$ of the grid (an upper bound on N is sufficient). Finally, any node v has $m(v) \geq 0$ messages that it must send to BS. At every step, a node can send or (exclusive) receive a control message, or *signaling*, of size $O(\log N)$ to (from) one of its neighbours. In the following, for any $i \leq 2N$, $Diag(i)$ denotes the set of vertices at distance i from BS. We refer to $Diag(i)$ as the *diagonal* i. The *central node* $c(2a)$ (resp., $c(2a+1)$) of $Diag(2a)$ (resp., $Diag(2a+1)$) is the node with coordinates (a, a) (resp., $(a + 1, a)$). Finally, let $AntiDiag$ be the set that consists of the vertices $c(i)$ for all $i \leq 2N$. The algorithm consists of four phases that we describe now.

4.2   Basic Description of Distributed Algorithm

Our algorithm aims at giving to any message m its position in the ordering S computed by Algorithm $TwoApprox$ (in terms of personalized broadcasting) and the makespan. This is performed in $Y = O(N^2)$ steps (Y will be specified below) using $O(N^2)$ signalings. Then, with this information, any message can compute its starting time, given that the first message will be sent at step $Y + 1$.

Let us give a rough description of the four phases of the distributed algorithm. First two phases consist in giving to any message m its position in the non increasing order of their distance to BS such that nodes in the same diagonal are ordered up to down (the ordering of messages hosted at a same node is arbitrary). Moreover, each message m_{2a+1} with $a \geq 0$, resp., m_{2a+2}, (actually, the node hosting this message) will learn the position(s) of messages $m_{2a+2}, m_{2a+3}, m_{2a+4}$, resp., $m_{2a+1}, m_{2a+3}, m_{2a+4}$. Then the third phase starts. With the information previously learnt, according to Algorithm $TwoApprox$, message m_1 can decide the ordering in S of the first three messages: s_1, s_2, s_3. Two of these three positions are occupied by m_1 and m_2. The remaining place is occupied by m_3 or m_4 (This comes from the definition of the $TwoApprox$ algorithm). Then, at some step, the message s_{2a+3} is fixed. With this information, we prove that message m_{2a+3} can extend the ordering to s_{2a+4} and s_{2a+5} using the $TwoAlgo$ algorithm. At the end of this phase, any node knows its position in S and BS knows the makespan. During the last phase, BS broadcasts the makespan to any node. With this information, each node can compute its starting time for the gathering process.

4.3   Formal Description of Distributed Algorithm

Phase 1. It is divided into 2 processes executed "almost" simultaneously.

– The first one is executed in parallel by all diagonals. For any $i \leq 2N$, it aims at
collecting some information in $c(i)$, the central node of $Diag(i)$. When this process
ends up at step $i + 5$, $c(i)$ has learnt
   • the number of messages l_i standing in $Diag(i)$ in nodes with greater ordinate
   than $c(i)$,
   • the number of messages r_i standing in $Diag(i)$ in nodes with smaller ordinate
   than $c(i)$,
   • the position(s) of the three messages with greatest ordinate in $Diag(i)$.
  Moreover, at the end of the phase, any node v with coordinates (x, y) in $Diag(i)$
  has learnt the position of the (at most 3) node(s) of $Diag(i)$ hosting the closest 3
  messages that are higher (if $y \geq x$) or lower (if $y \leq x$) than v.
   To do so, two signalings $D1_i$ and $D1'_i$, initiated by nodes $(i, 0)$ and $(0, i)$ respectively, are propagated toward $c(i)$. From $(i, 0)$ (resp., from $(0, i)$), $D1_i$ (resp.,
  $D1'_i$) is transmitted to node $(i, 1)$ and then to $(i - 1, 1)$ (resp., to $(1, i)$ and then to
  $(1, i - 1)$), and so on until reaching $c(i)$. To avoid interferences, $D1_i$ and $D1'_i$ are
  initiated at step 1 by $(i, 0)$ and $(0, i)$ if i is odd. If i is even, $D1_i$ is initiated at step
  5 by $(i, 0)$, and $D1'_i$ is initiated at step 6 by $(0, i)$. It is easy to see how information
  can be aggregated as $D1_i$ and $D1'_i$ go along, in order to obtain the desired information. Moreover, signalings $D1_i$ (resp. $D1'_i$) have size $O(\log N)$ since they contain:
  the number of messages they met, the position(s) of the first three messages they
  met, and the position(s) of the last three messages they met.
– At step 7, a signaling $A1$ is initiated in BS and is propagated along $AntiDiag$
  towards $(N - 1, N - 1)$. When $c(i)$ receives $A1$ at step $i + 6$, it learns the total
  number of messages hosting by nodes in $\bigcup_{j<i} Diag(j)$ and the position(s) of the
  three messages in $\bigcup_{j<i} Diag(j)$ that are further to BS and with greatest ordinate.
  Then, using the information propagated by messages $D1_i$ and $D1'_i$, $c(i)$ updates
  message $A1$ and sends it to $c(i + 1)$ during the next step.
   The signaling $A1$ arrives to $(N - 1, N - 1)$ at step $2N + 5$ which concludes
  this phase.

Phase 2. The second phase is divided into three successive processes.

– At step $2N + 6$, a signaling $A2$ is initiated in $(N - 1, N - 1)$ and is propagated
  along $AntiDiag$ towards $(0, 0)$. When $c(i)$ receives $A2$ at step $4N + 6 - i$, it
  learns the total number of messages M and the position(s) of the three messages in
  $\bigcup_{j>i} Diag(j)$ that are closest to BS and with smallest ordinate.
   Note that after step $4N + 6 - i$, $c(i)$ knows the interval of the positions occupied
  by messages in $Diag(i)$, i.e., from $M - \bigcup_{j \leq i} Diag(j) + 1 = \bigcup_{j>i} Diag(j) + 1$
  to $\bigcup_{j>i} Diag(j) + l_i + r_i + m(c(i))$.

The two last processes ensure that any message m_{2a} (resp., m_{2a+1}) knows its position in the non increasing order of their distance to BS, i.e., its position in the ordered sequence $\mathcal{M}$, and the position(s) of messages $m_{2a+1}, m_{2a+2}, m_{2a+3}$ (resp. m_{2a},
m_{2a+2}, m_{2a+3}).

- At step $4N + 6 - i + 3$ if i is odd and $4N + 6 - i + 5$ if i is even, a signaling $D2_i$ is initiated in $c(i)$ and is propagated toward $(i, 0)$. $D2_i$ transmits: the next position (in $\mathcal{M}$) to be attributed to the messages in $Diag(i)$ with smaller ordinates than $c(i)$, i.e., from $\bigcup_{j>i} Diag(j) + l_i + m(c(i))$ to $\bigcup_{j>i} Diag(j) + l_i + r_i + m(c(i))$ (in such a way that any message lower than $c(i)$ in $Diag(i)$ learns its number in the ordering when it meets the signaling $D2_i$), the position(s) of the last three messages met by this signaling, and the position(s) of the three messages in $\bigcup_{j<i} Diag(j)$ furthest to BS and with greatest ordinates.

- At step $4N + 6 - i + 2$ if i is odd and $4N + 6 - i + 6$ if i is even, a signaling $D2'_i$ is initiated in $c(i)$ and is propagated toward $(0, i)$. $D2'_i$ transmits: the next position (in the ordering) to be attributed to the messages in $Diag(i)$ with greater ordinates than $c(i)$, i.e., from $\bigcup_{j>i} Diag(j)$ to $\bigcup_{j>i} Diag(j) + l_i$ (in such a way that any message higher than $c(i)$ in $Diag(i)$ learns its number in the ordering when it meets the signaling $D2'_i$), the position(s) of the last three messages met by this signaling, and the position(s) of the three messages in $\bigcup_{j<i} Diag(j)$ furthest to BS and with greatest ordinates.

This phase ends at slot $4N + 12$.

Phase 3. Any message will learn its position in the final ordering $\mathcal{S}$.

We define the start of this phase at slot $4N + 13$ after finishing phase 2.

At the beginning of this phase, message m_{2a+1} ($a \geq 0$) knows its position in the ordered sequence $\mathcal{M}$ and the position(s) of m_{2a+2}, m_{2a+3}, and m_{2a+4}.

The procedure starts as follows. Node m_1 knows m_2, m_3, m_4. Using $TwoApprox$ algorithm with input (m_1, m_2, m_3, m_4), it computes the ordering of the first three positions of $\mathcal{S}$. According to the algorithm the possible configurations for the first three messages in $\mathcal{S}$ are (m_1, m_2, m_3), (m_1, m_3, m_2), (m_1, m_2, m_4), (m_2, m_1, m_3), (m_2, m_3, m_1), (m_2, m_1, m_4). Note that, although the algorithm returns also a message for the fourth position, it is not definitive because it could be modified when the next pair of messages (m_5, m_6) is included. The first message s_1 is decided arbitrarily to be vertical.

Then, m_1 computes the current makespan, i.e., $\max_{j \in \{1,2,3\}} d(BS, s_j) + m_j - 1$ and propagates the information to m_2 and m_3. That is, m_1 sends them the ordering of the first three messages (s_1, s_2, s_3) of $\mathcal{S}$ (again, $\{s_1, s_2, s_3\} \subset \{m_1, \cdots, m_4\}$) and the current makespan. The corresponding signaling is sent at step $4N + 13$ to m_3 and at step $4N + 15$ to m_2. The signaling reaches m_3 at step $4N + 12 + t$ where t is the distance between m_1 and m_3.

The process continues iteratively until m_{2a+3} receives a signaling from m_{2a+1} at step $4N + 12 + t$, for $t = \sum_{0 \leq k \leq p} dist(m_{2k+1}, m_{2k+3})$. This signaling contains the positions of messages $s_{2a+1}, s_{2a+2}, s_{2a+3}$, and the current makespan, i.e., the makespan restricted to messages s_1 to s_{2a+3}. At this step, m_{2a+3} must decide which messages will occupy positions s_{2a+4} and s_{2a+5} in $\mathcal{S}$. This decision is taken according to Algorithm $TwoApprox$. Note that, Algorithm $TwoApprox$ requires as input the next pair of messages m_{2a+5}, m_{2a+6} and the message $m^* \in \{m_1, \cdots, m_{2a+4}\}$ whose position in $\mathcal{S}$ has not been decided yet. By property of Algorithm $TwoApprox$, $m^* \in \{m_{2a+3}, m_{2a+4}\}$.

Thus, m_{2a+3} is able to decide which messages will occupy positions s_{2a+4} and s_{2a+5} in $\mathcal{S}$, and then it can update the current makespan. Finally, at step $4N + 12 + t + 1$

(resp., at step $4N + 12 + t + 3$), message m_{2a+3} sends a signaling to m_{2a+5} (resp., to m_{2a+4}). This signaling contains the current makespan, s_{2a+3}, s_{2a+4} and s_{2a+5}. The signaling is received by m_{2a+5} at step $4N + 12 + t + t'$ where t' is the distance between m_{2a+3} and m_{2a+5}.

The end of this phase is upper bounded by step $4N + 12 + 2N^2$.

Phase 4. At the end of previous phase, BS learns the makespan of a HV-scheme realizing the computed ordering and starts broadcasting it to any node at step $4N + 13 + 2N^2$.

This is done thanks to a signaling through $AntiDiag$, and signalings from $c(i)$ to $(i, 0)$ and $(0, i)$ $(i \leq 2N)$ in a similar way as Phase 2. This process ends at step $6N + 19 + 2N^2$.

Defining $Y = 6N + 19 + 2N^2$, each node knows the step when it has to send the message given that the starting step is $Y + 1$. Moreover, the message s_j is sent horizontally or vertically according to the parity of j.

5   Conclusion and Further Works

In this paper, we have presented almost optimal centralized and distributed algorithms for the minimum makespan personalized broadcasting in *open-grid* networks. In these settings, the problem is strictly equivalent to the data gathering problem.

The next step is obviously to provide algorithms for the closed grid case. As a matter of fact, one can check that the lower bound is weaker then and one cannot restrict the routing to shortest paths anymore. The +2–approximation algorithm can be fixed to handle this case even though its actual approximation gap is still under investigation [3].

Besides, one can note that our network model assumes that an optimal MAC layer is available. It would be interesting to investigate on the behaviour of the problems under weaker assumptions, such as faulty transmissions and/or intermittent nodes.

Another direction to investigate is the online version of the problems. It is worth pointing out that, in this case, personalized broadcasting and gathering are no longer equivalent. Last but not least, the time complexity of the gathering problem in (open) grids is an open problem.

References

1. Klasing, R., Lotker, Z., Navarra, A., Pérennes, S.: From balls and bins to points and vertices. In: Deng, X., Du, D.-Z. (eds.) ISAAC 2005. LNCS, vol. 3827, pp. 757–766. Springer, Heidelberg (2005)
2. Revah, Y., Segal, M.: Improved algorithms for data-gathering time in sensor networks ii: Ring, tree and grid topologies. In: Third International Conference on Networking and Services 2007. ICNS, p. 46 (2007)
3. Bermond, J.C., Guinand, F., Nisse, N., Reyes, P., Rivano, H.: Minimum delay data gathering in closed half-duplex grid. On-going work and discussions (June 2009)
4. Bonifaci, V., Klasing, R., Korteweg, P., Stougie, L., Marchetti-Spaccamela, A.: Data Gathering in Wireless Networks. In: Graphs and Algorithms in Communication Networks. Springer, Heidelberg (2009)

5. Gargano, L.: Time optimal gathering in sensor networks. In: Prencipe, G., Zaks, S. (eds.) SIROCCO 2007. LNCS, vol. 4474, pp. 7–10. Springer, Heidelberg (2007)
6. Florens, C., Franceschetti, M., McEliece, R.: Lower bounds on data collection time in sensory networks. IEEE Journal on Selected Areas in Communications 22(6), 1110–1120 (2004)
7. Revah, Y., Segal, M.: Improved bounds for data-gathering time in sensor networks. Computer Communications 31(17), 4026–4034 (2008)
8. Gargano, L., Rescigno, A.A.: Optimally fast data gathering in sensor networks. In: Královič, R., Urzyczyn, P. (eds.) MFCS 2006. LNCS, vol. 4162, pp. 399–411. Springer, Heidelberg (2006)
9. Gargano, L., Rescigno, A.A.: Collision-free path coloring with application to minimum-delay gathering in sensor networks. Discrete Applied Maths (in Press)
10. Busch, C., Herlihy, M., Wattenhofer, R.: Hard-potato routing. In: Proceedings of the thirty-second annual ACM symposium on Theory of computing, Portland, Oregon, United States, pp. 278–285. ACM, New York (2000)
11. Mansour, Y., Patt-Shamir, B.: Many-to-one packet routing on grids. In: Proceedings of the twenty-seventh annual ACM symposium on Theory of computing, Las Vegas, Nevada, United States, pp. 258–267. ACM, New York (1995)
12. Bermond, J.C., Galtier, J., Klasing, R., Morales, N., Pérennes, S.: Hardness and approximation of gathering in static radio networks. Parallel Processing Letters 16(2), 165–183 (2006)
13. Bonifaci, V., Korteweg, P., Marchetti-Spaccamela, A., Stougie, L.: An approximation algorithm for the wireless gathering problem. Operations Research Letters 36(5), 605–608 (2008)
14. Bermond, J.C., Peters, J.: Efficient gathering in radio grids with interference. In: Septièmes Rencontres Francophones sur les Aspects Algorithmiques des Télécommunications (AlgoTel 2005), Presqu'île de Giens, pp. 103–106 (2005)
15. Gomes, C., Pérennes, S., Reyes, P., Rivano, H.: Bandwidth allocation in radio grid networks. In: 10èmes Rencontres Francophones sur les Aspects Algorithmiques de Télécommunications (AlgoTel 2008) (May 2008)
16. Bermond, J.C., Nisse, N., Reyes, P., Rivano, H.: Fast data gathering in radio grid networks. Technical Report RR-6851, INRIA (2009)

Asymptotic Delay Analysis and Timeout-Based Admission Control for Ad Hoc Wireless Networks

R. El-Azouzi[1], S.K. Samanta[1], E. Sabir[1,2], and R. El-Khoury[1]

[1] LIA/CERI, University of Avignon, Agroparc BP 1228, Avignon, France
[2] LIMIARF, University of Mohammed V-Agdal, B.P. 1014 RP, Rabat, Morocco
{rachid.elazouzi,sujit.samanta2,essaid.sabir,
ralph.elkhoury}@univ-avignon.fr

Abstract. In this paper, we present an analytic model for evaluating average packet delay and achievable end-to-end goodput in a collision channel based multihop wireless ad hoc networks. We consider each node operates not only as a host but also as a router, i.e., the packets may have to be forwarded by several intermediate nodes before they reach their destinations. The end-to-end delay of a connection and throughput of this network depend on the number of nodes, the source traffic characteristics, the number of retransmissions at nodes, the forwarding cooperation level and the behavior of the MAC protocol. Our analysis gives expressions for the queue length and the delay in terms of probability generating functions. In addition to address routing and transmission scheduling, we adopt a cross-layer design that allows information sharing across different layers for efficient utilization of network resources, and meeting the end-to-end performance requirements of demanding applications. Furthermore, we propose a packet admission control scheme based on delay timeout mechanism. This guarantees quality of service for multimedia applications such as voice and video streaming. Afterward we conduct extensive simulations in order to verify our analytical results.

Keywords: Wireless ad hoc network, Cross-layer mechanism, MAC protocols, End-to-end delay, G/G/1 queue, Embedded Markov chain.

1 Introduction

An ad hoc wireless network is a collection of wireless nodes that communicate with each other without any established infrastructure or centralized control. Due to the limited transmission range of wireless network interfaces, multiple network "hops" may be needed for one node to exchange data with another across the network. In such a network, the packets may have to be forwarded by several intermediate nodes before they reach their destinations, and therefore each node operates not only as a host but also as a router. Thus each node may be a source, destination and relay (intermediate). Many factors interact with each other to make the communication possible like routing protocol and channel access method. With the emerging of real-time applications in wireless

P.M. Ruiz and J.J. Garcia-Luna-Aceves (Eds.): ADHOC-NOW 2009, LNCS 5793, pp. 83–97, 2009.
© Springer-Verlag Berlin Heidelberg 2009

networks, delay guarantees are increasingly required. In order to provide support for delay sensitive traffic in such network, an accurate evaluation of the distribution of delay is a necessary first step. Knowing the nature of the multihop ad hoc networks, many factors are crucial for the study of the end-to-end (e2e) delay. We cannot study separately the delay generated by a given layer without considering the others. Hence we adopt a cross-layer architecture with its potential synergy of information exchange between different layers, instead of the standard OSI non-communicating layers.

Many studies of packet delay and loss in various network environments have been reported in the literature. It should be pointed out that due to the lack of analytic solutions, many studies of packet delay and loss behavior have been conducted with simulation and experimental approaches. In this work, we provide a framework for cross-layer of delay distribution in the context of wireless ad hoc networks. The analysis takes into account the queueing delays at source and intermediate nodes. The delay of a connection and throughput of this network depend on the number of nodes, the source traffic characteristics, the number of retransmissions at nodes, the forwarding cooperation level and the behavior of the MAC protocol. However the delay is defined as the time taken by a packet to reach the destination after it has left the source. We focus on the asymptotic properties of the delay due to buffering of packets at network layer and random access protocol on MAC layer. The analysis is done using the probability generating function approach which allows us to estimate the distribution of delay at intermediate nodes for all ongoing connections. We assume that time is slotted into fixed length time frames. In any time slot, a node having a packet to be transmitted to one of its neighboring nodes decides with some fixed probability in favor of a transmission attempt. If there is no other transmissions by other nodes those may interfere with the node under consideration, the transmission is successful. As examples of this mechanism, we find Aloha and CSMA type protocols. We consider a parameter that measures the aptitude of a node to forward packets coming from its neighbors. At any instant of time, a node may have two kinds of packets to be transmitted: (1) packets generated by the node itself: data or control packets, and (2) packets from other neighboring nodes those need to be forwarded. To carry these two types of packets, we consider two separate queues handled with a weighted fair queueing (WFQ) discipline.

Many papers in the literature have studied the problem of cooperation in ad hoc networks, see [14, 17]. In [7] and [11], authors worked with the above mentioned system model, and studied the impact of routing, channel access rates and weights of the weighted fair queueing on throughput, stability and fairness properties of the network. Important insights were revealed into various tradeoffs that can be achieved by fine-tuning certain network parameters. The throughput maximization of the multihop wireless networks has been extensively studied in [9] and [12]. However, it is shown that the high throughput in an ad hoc network is achieved at the cost of a high amount of delay. In [8], the authors characterized the delay-throughput tradeoffs in wireless networks with stationary and mobile nodes. These problems have drawn our attention to the relation between the delay characteristic and the throughput. However, most of the related studies do not consider the problem of forwarding. The authors in [13] contributed to quantifying the impact of hidden nodes on the performance of linear wireless networks based on the IEEE 802.11 protocol and taking into consideration the effects of queueing and retransmissions at each node. In [15], authors provided closed form expressions for the queue length in the presence of arbitrary arrival patterns, packet size distributions and finite network load. In [18], using the decomposition approach authors analyzed the e2e delay of wireless multihop networks for two MAC schemes, m-phase TDMA and slotted aloha, and related references therein. They considered the arrival processes to every node are only relayed versions of the original traffic flow generated at the source node. The main contributions in this paper are: (i) The distributed cross-layer scheme proposed here (besides of its novelty and efficiency) is characterized by its high simplicity. It does not need any external information, but a local decision can be taken with the help of routing information from the network layer as well as the MAC layer. (ii) We derive a mathematical framework based on the probability generating function (PGF) approach to estimate the distribution of delay. (iii) In contrast to [7] where average end-to-end goodput is calculated based on approximation, we derive here closed form of the e2e goodput and then conclude the exact value of packet admission rate (the probability that the end-to-end delay of a connection does not exceed the timeout delay). (iv) To get the distribution of delay for each connection, we investigate an important issue for real-time multimedia over multihop ad hoc networks on different layers. Indeed, multimedia packets (streams) encounter variable delay while crossing the multi-hop system, which is mainly due to the variable queueing time in intermediate nodes. In order to play the receiver stream, an application buffers the packets and plays them out after a certain deadline to get again a periodic stream at the application level. Packets arriving after their corresponding delay timeout are lost and then not played out. We furthermore derive a closed form of the end-to-end goodput for a traffic multimedia.

The rest of the paper is organized as follows. In the next section, we introduce the general model framework. We study the distribution of delay in multihop ad hoc networks in Section 3. Based on the conducted survey, we compute the rate of packets arrived before their scheduled playout time in Section 4. In Section 5, we validate the analytical results using a discrete time simulator and carry out extensive numerical examples. Due to the page limit, many details are omitted, we invite the reader to see the technical report [1].

2 Cross-Layer Architecture

We consider a collection of autonomous mobiles able to communicate with other mobiles in their respective direct range. Each one can reach nodes those are outside of its direct range by communicating indirectly through intermediate nodes those forward packets towards the required destination. We assume that nodes use the same channel for transmitting with an omnidirectional antenna. A node j receives successfully a packet incoming from a node i if and only if there is no interference at the node j due to another simultaneous transmission. It also follows that a node cannot receive and transmit at the same time slot because of the use of a single channel. Each node i handles two separated buffers: buffer Q_i carries the own packets of i and buffer F_i carries packets originated from a given source, to be forwarded to neighbors till achieving the final destination. These queues are considered to have infinite storage capacity, packets inside are served with a First-In-First-Out fashion and are managed using Weighted Fair Queueing scheduling; The buffer F_i is selected for transmission with probability

f_i. Since we assume that each node has always packets to send from queue Q_i, then it follows that queue Q_i is selected with probability $1 - \pi_i f_i$, where π_i is the probability that queue F_i has at least one packet. The forwarding capability permits to each node to behave as a router and this allows to relay packets originated from a source s to a destination d. Routing tables that ensure the network reachability and define which neighbors to use to reach any given destination are periodically updated using a proactive routing protocol as OLSR (Optimized Link State Routing). We use throughout this paper the notation $R_{s,d}$ to denote the set of intermediate nodes in a path between a source s and a destination d (s and d not included). The MAC layer protocols play the most important role in a communication chain. Many access and resources reservation methods have been elaborated to ensure performance guarantee. Here, we assume a channel access mechanism only based on a probability to access the network, i.e., when a node i has a packet to transmit, it accesses the channel with a probability $\bar{P}_i$. In IEEE 802.11 Distributed Coordination Function based ad hoc system, the attempt rate is given by [19]

$$\bar{P}_i = \frac{2(1 - 2\gamma)}{(1 - 2\gamma)(CW_{min} + 1) + \gamma CW_{min}(1 - (2\gamma)^m)}, \tag{1}$$

where γ is the conditional collision probability given that a transmission attempt is made, CW is the contention window and $m = log_2(\frac{CW_{max}}{CW_{min}})$ is the maximum of backoff stage. For example, in IEEE 802.11 standard, $\bar{P}_i$ depends on the number of neighbors, on the backoff mechanism and the probability of collision, see Yang et al. [19] for the ad hoc extension of Bianchi [2] results. The problem of hidden or exposed terminal known with the IEEE 802.11 are included implicitly in the value of $\bar{P}_i$. The scheduler of transmission overall the network depends on $\bar{P}_i$. We assume that each node is notified about the success or failure of its transmitted packets. A packet is failure only when there is an interference on the intended receiver, in other terms, when a collision occurs on the receiver. The only source of packet loss is due to collisions. For a reliable communication, we fix a limit number of successive transmissions of a single backlogged packet, after that it will be dropped definitively. We denote $K_{i,s,d}$ the maximum number of successive collisions allowed for a single packet sent from the node i on the path $R_{s,d}$. Unlike the OSI model where layers are clearly separated, we jointly consider network and

Accessing the channel starts by choosing the queue from which a packet would be selected. Then, this packet is moved from the network layer to the MAC layer, where it will be transmitted and retransmitted, if needed, until success or definitive drop. This way, it is clear that the end-to-end QoS (mainly, throughput and delay) depends on several layers as well as the cooperation level f_i of intermediate nodes, i.e., those play relays role.

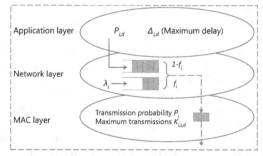

Fig. 1. Proposed cross-layer architecture

MAC layer parameters. This allows communication and information exchange between different layers and henceforth is more powerful, flexible, allows global optimization and in particular permits manipulating cooperation level.

3   Delay Distribution Analysis

For soft real-time applications, which are delay sensitive but loss tolerant, delay distribution is an important quality of service (QoS) measure of interest. In order to effectively support delay-sensitive applications such as video streaming and interactive gaming in an ad hoc wireless network, it is crucial and challenging to develop feasible methodologies and techniques for accurately analyzing, predicting and guaranteeing the end-to-end delay performance over multi-hop wireless networks. Our analysis takes into account the queueing delays at source and intermediate nodes of random access multihop wireless ad hoc networks. However the delay is defined as the time taken by a packet to reach the destination after it has left the source. We aim behind this to determine the distributions of the number of forwarding packets and their sojourn times in the system. We focus our study on the forwarding queue F_i of a given node i. In [7], it has been shown that packets arrive to F_i (i.e. packets received successfully by node i) according to a random arrival process with average λ_i, it can be written as:

$$\lambda_i = \sum_{s,d:i\in R_{s,d}} \lambda_{i,s,d} = \sum_{s,d:i\in R_{s,d}} \frac{(1-\pi_s f_s)P_{s,d}\bar{P}_s}{\bar{L}_s} \prod_{k\in R_{s,i}\cup s}\left[1-(1-P_{k,s,d})^{K_{k,s,d}}\right], (2)$$

where π_s is the probability that queue F_s has at least one packet in the beginning of each cycle and $P_{s,d}$ is the probability that the node s generates a new packet for the destination d. We denote the attempt probability of node s by $\bar{P}_s$ and its corresponding average number of attempts till success or definitive drop by $\bar{L}_s$ [7]. The quantity $P_{k,s,d} = \prod_{j\in j_{k,s,d}\cup N(j_{k,s,d})\backslash k}(1-\bar{P}_j)$ represents the probability that a transmission from node i on route from node s to node d is successful, where $j_{k,s,d}$ is the entry in the set $R_{s,d}$ just after k and $N(j_{k,s,d})$ is the nodes which are neighbors of node $j_{k,s,d}$. We note that λ_i is exactly the aggregate arrival of packets from different paths and different kind of connections to the forwarding buffer F_i of node i. When a packet leaves the network layer that means it stays in the MAC layer (server) for some arbitrary number of slots. One conclude that the forwarding queue F_i constitutes a $G/G/1$ queue that has some special characteristics due to the presence of saturated queue Q_i. Furthermore, we will derive the desired distributions. For the sake of simplicity, in the following, we omit the index i that identify the node i itself to facilitate the notations and the reading, e.g., $F_i \equiv F$. Also, the notations indicating connections identities will be omitted until contraindicate. Each connection $R_{s,d}$ has its own service time which depends on the topology (set of neighbors), the transmission probability of nodes and the limit number of transmissions.

- Let r denote the number of arrival packets to the buffer F during the residual service time of a packet which is picked from buffer Q and seen by an arrival packet to buffer F.
- Let a^F denote the number of arrival packets to the buffer F during a service time of a packet picked from buffer F.

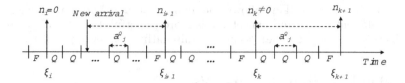

Fig. 2. Departure instances from network layer to MAC layer

- Let a_j^Q denote the number of arrival packets to the buffer F during the jth packet service time of packets picked from buffer Q.

Figure 2 shows the evolution of MAC service in terms of cycles (Q and F transmission cycles), it shows also the departure instants ξ_i of forwarding packets in the two cases of the system (for $n_i = 0$ and $n_i \neq 0$). This leads to the following balance equation of the number of packets in F at departure instants:

$$n_{i+1} = \begin{cases} r + \sum_{j=1}^{m} a_j^Q + a^F, & \text{for} \quad n_i = 0 \\ n_i + \sum_{j=1}^{m} a_j^Q + a^F - 1, & \text{for} \quad n_i \neq 0, \end{cases} \tag{3}$$

where m represents the number of consecutive packets which are from buffer Q take service before the next packet from buffer F. Note here that $m = 0$ denotes that there is no packet which is from buffer Q takes service before the next packet from buffer F except the residual service packet for the case $n_i = 0$. Putting the two cases of n_{i+1} together in one equation, we get

$$n_{i+1} = n_i + rI(n_i) + \sum_{j=1}^{m} a_j^Q + a^F - 1 + I(n_i), \quad \forall i, \tag{4}$$

where $I(n_i)$ is an indicator defined by: $I(n_i) = 0$ if $n_i \neq 0$ and $I(n_i) = 1$ if $n_i = 0$. We now focus on the solution of the difference equation (4) in the domain of the generating functions. First of all, we consider the equality obtained by taking the exponentiation with base z at both sides of (4) and for any i index,

$$z^{n_{i+1}} = z^{n_i + rI(n_i) + \sum_{j=1}^{m} a_j^Q + a^F - 1 + I(n_i)}, \quad \forall i.$$

Then, we multiply both sides for the joint distribution $P_{h_1, h_2, h_3, h_4, h_5} \equiv P\{n_{i+1} = h_1, n_i = h_2, r = h_3, a^F = h_4, \sum_{j=1}^{m} a_j^Q = h_5\}$ and we sum over h_1, h_2, h_3, h_4, h_5. Note that on the left side the summations on h_2, h_3, h_4, h_5 can be exhausted; Whereas on the right side the summation on h_1 can be exhausted. Therefore, we can write:

$$\sum_{h_1=0}^{\infty} z^{h_1} P_{h_1} = \sum z^{h_2 + h_3 I(h_2) + h_5 + h_4 - 1 + I(h_2)} P_{h_2, h_3, h_4, h_5}. \tag{5}$$

Let $P(z)$ denote the PGF at regime of the state probability distribution at the imbedded instants. Then the left side of equation (5) can be written as:

$\sum_{h_1=0}^{\infty} z^{h_1} P_{h_1} = P(z)$. Further, let $A^F(z)$ and $A^Q(z)$ denote the PGF of the number of arrivals at regime during the service time of a packet which are from buffers F and Q, respectively. Also let $R(z)$ denote the PGF of the number of arrivals at regime during the residual service time of a packet from buffer Q. Then the right side of equation (5) can be written as:

$$\sum_{h_2=0}^{\infty}\sum_{h_3=0}^{\infty}\sum_{h_4=0}^{\infty}\sum_{h_5=0}^{\infty} z^{h_2+h_3 I(h_2)+h_5+h_4-1+I(h_2)} P_{h_2,h_3,h_4,h_5}$$

$$= \sum_{h_4=0}^{\infty}\sum_{h_5=0}^{\infty} z^{h_5+h_4}\left[\sum_{h_3=0}^{\infty} z^{h_3} P_{h_3,h_4,h_5} P(h_2=0) + \sum_{h_2=1}^{\infty} z^{h_2-1} P_{h_2,h_4,h_5}\right]$$

$$= \left(P_0 R(z) + \frac{P(z)-P_0}{z}\right)\sum_{h_4=0}^{\infty}\sum_{h_5=0}^{\infty} z^{h_5+h_4} P_{h_4,h_5}. \tag{6}$$

Since $a_j^Q, j \geq 1$ and a^F are independent random variables, the term $\sum_{h_4=0}^{\infty}\sum_{h_5=0}^{\infty} z^{h_4+h_5} P_{h_4,h_5}$ appeared in (6) becomes

$$\sum_{h_4=0}^{\infty}\sum_{h_5=0}^{\infty} z^{h_4+h_5} P_{h_4,h_5} = \sum_{j=0}^{m}\{(1-f)A^Q(z)\}^j f A^F(z). \tag{7}$$

If the number of consecutive packets from buffer Q becomes large enough, i.e., $m \to \infty$ then

$$\sum_{h_4=0}^{\infty}\sum_{h_5=0}^{\infty} z^{h_4+h_5} P_{h_4,h_5} = \frac{f A^F(z)}{1-(1-f)A^Q(z)}. \tag{8}$$

Then the right side of equation (6) can be written as:

$$\left(P_0 R(z) + \frac{P(z)-P_0}{z}\right)\frac{f A^F(z)}{1-(1-f)A^Q(z)}. \tag{9}$$

After some mathematical manipulations, we get the PGF of the number of packet distribution seen by a departure:

$$P(z) = \frac{P_0(zR(z)-1)f A^F(z)}{z-(1-f)z A^Q(z) - f A^F(z)}. \tag{10}$$

For detail derivations of $A^Q(z)$, $A^F(z)$ and $R(z)$, readers refer to technical report [1]. We now turn to the calculation of how long a packet spends in an intermediate node. From queueing theory, there is a relation between the PGF of the number of packets in the buffer and the PGF of waiting time. Considering a First-In-First-Out fashion, it is clear that the packets left behind are precisely those arrived during its stay in the buffer. Due to presence of two queues including one saturated queue, we precise that *the delay including service time cannot be less than two time slots.* Thus, we have

$$P(z|t) = \sum_{n=0}^{t-2} z^n \binom{t-2}{n}\lambda^n(1-\lambda)^{t-2-n} = (1-\lambda+\lambda z)^{t-2}.$$

Denote the total time spent in the system for this customer by the random variable D with distribution

$$P(z) = \sum_{t=2}^{\infty} P(z|t)P(D=t) = \sum_{t=2}^{\infty}(1-\lambda+\lambda z)^{t-2}P(D=t) = \frac{D(1-\lambda+\lambda z)}{(1-\lambda+\lambda z)^2}.$$

Hence, the PGF of the waiting time in the system $D(z) = \sum_{n=2}^{\infty} d_n z^n$ can be written as

$$D(z) = z^2 P\left(\frac{z-1+\lambda}{\lambda}\right). \tag{11}$$

It follows that the end-to-end delay PGF is obtained by $D_{s,d}(z) = \prod_{i \in R_{s,d}} D_i(z)$. The expected waiting time and the variance of waiting time at node i are, respectively, given by

$$D'(1) = 2 + \frac{P'(1)}{\lambda} \quad \text{and} \quad Var[D] = D''(1) + D'(1) - [D'(1)]^2,$$

where $D''(1) = 2 + \frac{4}{\lambda}P'(1) + \frac{1}{\lambda^2}P''(1)$, where $\phi'(1)$ and $\phi''(1)$, respectively, represent the first and second derivative of any PGF $\phi(z)$ at $z = 1$. Since we are interested to derive the end-to-end delay of some given connection, we should not consider time elapsed due to dropped packets. Then, we have to deduct it from the total delay (waiting and service times) at node i. The average number of successful transmissions and the average time spent by dropped packet at source s are, respectively, given by

$$L_{s,s,d}^{succ} = \sum_{k=1}^{\widetilde{K}} k(1-P_{s,s,d})^{k-1}P_{s,s,d}, \quad \text{and} \quad \tau_{i,s,d}^{drop} = \frac{\widetilde{K}(1-P_{i,s,d})^{\widetilde{K}}}{\bar{P}_i}.$$

Finally, the expression of the end-to-end delay of the connection $R_{s,d}$ can be derived by

$$\widehat{D}_{s,d} = \frac{L_{s,s,d}^{succ}}{\bar{P}_s} + \sum_{i \in R_{s,d}}\left(D_i'(1) - \tau_{i,s,d}^{drop}\right). \tag{12}$$

The first term is the average service time at the source s, whereas the term inside symbol sum is exactly the average waiting and service time in intermediate nodes.

4   Application: Playout Delay Control

Due to its vast potential for providing ubiquitous communication, ad hoc and the emerging mesh networking have received overwhelm interest over the last years. Several research works have been done to claim the ability of supporting multimedia applications over ad hoc networks [4] and [16]. In this section, we deal with multimedia streaming (e.g., VoD, TV, ...) over ad hoc networks. Streaming over wireless medium is very challenging due to many factors that cause high error rate. In such interactive multimedia applications, packets loss and connection reliability deterioration are generally caused by delay, jitter (un-expected phase variation) and decoding errors. With a self-managing nodes such as ad hoc networks, the problem becomes more complicated due to the absence of a central entity that monitors the changes in the network. In order to en-able supporting real-time services, some QoS demand should be stochastically fulfilled (e.g., the average goodput should be strictly fulfilled or a maximum de-lay should not be exceeded). This way, the newly designed H.264 video coding standard has been developed such as to support wireless medium [10]. Here, we assume that the ongoing application buffers received packets and plays them out after a given deadline. Henceforth, a packet arriving after the deadline will not be played out. This allows to resolve the problem of variable delay while crossing intermediate nodes but may cause some throughput degradation. Let $\Delta_{s,d}$ be the maximum tolerable delay for connection $R_{s,d}$. Hence, the end-to-end goodput (effective throughput) can be written as $goodput_{s,d} = thp_{s,d} \cdot P(\widehat{D}_{s,d} \leq \Delta_{s,d})$, where $thp_{s,d} = \lambda_{d,s,d}$ (which is given by equation (2) by replacing i by d), and $P(\widehat{D}_{s,d} \leq \Delta_{s,d})$ is the probability that the accumulative delay does not exceed the threshold $\Delta_{s,d}$, we call it *packets admission rate*. Here, we derive an expres-sion of the admission rate, one can note that $P(\widehat{D}_{s,d} \leq \Delta_{s,d}) = \zeta(D_{s,d})$ where $\zeta(\cdot)$ is the Cumulative Distribution Function of the e2e delay. Let $l = |R_{s,d}|$ be the number of intermediate nodes (s and d not included) in route $R_{s,d}$. It is clear that the minimum delay on route $R_{s,d}$ after leaving the source s is $2l$, and hence we have

$$P(\widehat{D}_{s,d} \leq \Delta_{s,d}) = \sum_{j=2l}^{\Delta_{s,d}} P(D_{s,d} = j), \qquad (13)$$

where $P(D_{s,d} = j)$ is the probability that the e2e delay is exactly j slots (con-sidering all l-length partitions of the integer delay j in slots subject to all its parts are greater than or equal to 2). It is given by

$$P(D_{s,d} = j) = \sum_{j_1=2}^{j-2l+2} \sum_{j_2=2}^{j-2l+2-j_1} \cdots \sum_{j_l=2}^{j-2l+2-j_1-j_2\cdots-j_{l-1}} \prod_{i=1}^{l} P(D_{i,s,d} = j_i), \quad j \geq 2l,$$

given that $d_{j_i} = P(D_{i,s,d} = j_i)$ can be calculated by differentiating j_i times the polynomial $D(z) = \sum_{j_i=2}^{\infty} d_{j_i} z^{j_i}$ at $z = 0$, provided by result (11).

Dynamic retransmissions. Giving more priority to packets that arrive near final destination or the ones whom accumulative delay is less than the threshold, could improve the end-to-end goodput. This can be seen as a kind of cross-layer congestion control that can enhance the admission rate and help to support multimedia streams. This motivates us to use the dynamic retransmission scheme first described in [6] by setting a fixed average $\tilde{K}_{s,d}$ of all $K_{i,s,d}$ (for $i \in R_{s,d} \cup s$) values of each connection. For instance, this average $K_{s,d}$ can be the default value of the maximum number of transmissions in a network operating with a static $\tilde{K}_{s,d}$. It will be easy to compare the static case performance and the dynamic one. After some number of iterations, the average queue size (or equivalently the load) of F_i may increase drastically which will induce a huge waiting time (a threshold is to be defined by higher layers). To reduce the appeared huge delay, we integrate the dynamic retransmission scheme jointly with a *reset* technique, i.e., the $K_{i,s,d}$ of the connection that suffers from huge delay is set to its respective $\tilde{K}_{s,d}$. When congestion is bellow some threshold, the node can decide to restart the dynamic retransmission scheme again.

5   Numerical Examples

We now turn to study a typical example of ad hoc networks. We consider an asymmetric static network formed by 11 nodes as shown in Fig. 3. We established five connections (or streams) a, b, c, d and e. Two nodes are neighbors if they are connected with a dashed or solid line. For illustrative purpose, we consider that the time slot duration is $100\mu s^1$ and all nodes are supposed to have the same transmissions limit K per packet. In order to get stability for all nodes, let $\bar{P}_2 = \bar{P}_3 = \bar{P}_7 = \bar{P}_8 = 0.3$, $\bar{P}_4 = \bar{P}_{10} = 0.4$ and $\bar{P}_5 = 0.5$ over all the realized simulations. We present extensive numerical and simulation results to show the accuracy of our method. For that aim, a discrete time simulator that implements the model of Section 2 is used to simulate the former network.

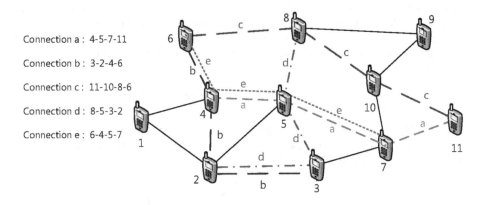

Connection a : 4-5-7-11

Connection b : 3-2-4-6

Connection c : 11-10-8-6

Connection d : 8-5-3-2

Connection e : 6-4-5-7

Fig. 3. The ad hoc network used for simulation and numerical examples

Model validation. All involved nodes are considered to be cooperative and their forwarding probabilities (cooperation levels) are set to $f_i \equiv f = 0.8$. While $\bar{P}_i \equiv \bar{P}$ is varying for all nodes 1, 6, 9 and 11. Figures 4 (a) and (b) show the average end-to-end delay of considered connections, from analytical model as well as simulation results. The analytical results are closed to the simulation results. This is also true in the case where nodes forward to different neighbors on different paths. However, one can see a sharp gap which is perhaps due to the approximation of the number of consecutive Q_i cycles.

Impact of cooperation level f_i. Here, we address a crucial parameter that impacts significantly the end-to-end reliability. We fix here the transmission probabilities as follows $\bar{P}_1 = \bar{P}_6 = \bar{P}_{11} = 0.4$, $\bar{P}_9 = 0.3$. For simplicity and without any loss of generality, we consider same cooperation level for all nodes,

---

[1] In IEEE 802.11b/g and IEEE 802.11a, the slot duration is $20\mu s$ and $8\mu s$, respectively.

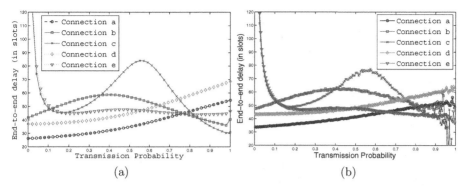

Fig. 4. Analytical (a) and simulation (b) end-to-end delay versus transmission probability for $K = 4$ and $f = 0.8$.

i.e., $f_i \equiv f$. When nodes are altruistic ($f = 1$), the e2e delay is minimized and a maximum throughput can be achieved. But when $0 < f < 1$, we note that above some given threshold (depending on transmissions probability vector) all forwarding buffers become stable. We refer to this region as the system stability region; therein throughput becomes insensitive to the cooperation level, see Fig. 5 (a). At any fixed transmission probability vector, we come out that the end-to-end delay is strictly decreasing with f, see Fig. 5 (b). We note here that connection c outperforms other connections in term of throughput. Analyzing the topology, it is clear that connection c has no common segments with other connections. However, it seems that this connection suffers from relatively high delay compared to other connections. This can be explained by high load of forwarding queues in path c, in particular forwarding queue of relay 10, see Fig. 6. Next, we depict the distribution of the average delay in Fig. 7 (a), when cooperation level is set to 0.7. A similar behavior is observed at $f = 0.99$, but the curve is shifted to the left where probability to have small or average delay becomes greater. The delay distribution is as narrow as the cooperation level

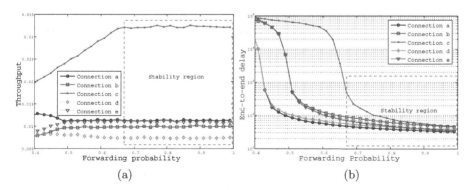

Fig. 5. Average e2e throughput (a) and average e2e delay (b) versus cooperation level for static retransmissions limit $K = 4$, $\bar{P}_1 = \bar{P}_6 = \bar{P}_{11} = 0.4$ and $P_9 = 0.3$.

The figure depicts here the load of forwarding queues versus the cooperation level for static transmissions limit $K = 4$, $\bar{P}_1 = \bar{P}_6 = \bar{P}_{11} = 0.4$ and $P_9 = 0.3$. Giving more weight to F_i decreases the load π_i of node i and henceforth enhances the corresponding stability. The dashed rectangle shows the region where all forwarding queues are stable. In this region, based on QoS requirement, each node can fix its own cooperation level so as to achieve a good throughput/delay tradeoff.

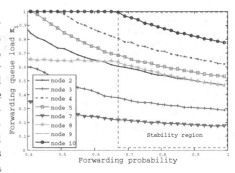

Fig. 6. Forwarding queue load

increases. This imply that the average e2e delay decreases with f whereas the average throughput may remain constant.

Impact of transmissions limit K. Another important factor that impacts e2e performances is the maximum number of transmissions per packet. It is clear that the waiting time does not depend on K whereas the service time depends strongly on it. With $K = \infty$, the throughput is maximized $thp_{s,d} = \frac{(1 - \pi_s f_s) P_{s,d} \bar{P}_s}{\bar{L}_s}$, see eq. (2), corresponding to a huge delay (may goes to infinity due to long service time caused by successive collisions, in particular when neighbor nodes are very aggressive). When $K = 1$, a minimum average throughput is obtained $thp_{s,d} = \frac{(1 - \pi_s f_s) P_{s,d} \bar{P}_s}{\bar{L}_s} \prod_{k \in R_{s,d} \cup s} P_{k,s,d}$, where the delay is optimized. Fig. 8 (a) and Fig. 7 (a) show the distribution of delay with $f = 0.7$ for $K = 1$ and $K = 4$ respectively. One note that the distribution becomes larger when increasing K.

Static transmission Vs. Dynamic transmissions. Consider a step $K' = 2$, i.e., $K_{i,s,d} = K_{j,s,d} + 2$, where node j is just before node i in route $R_{s,d}$. We note that performances are improved since this new scheme gives more chances to packets arrived near the final destination, see Fig. 8 (b). Indeed, the delay distribution of dynamic case is more narrow than static case under same value of parameters. In contrast, a huge delay may be observed at intermediate nodes and the use of reset mechanism becomes crucial. Using this new routing, we achieve a better average delay (resp. throughput) for each connection without changing the average throughput (resp. delay). In extreme cases, a reset technique is introduced to reduce congestion and optimize the e2e performances. This scheme seems to be very interesting for delay-sensitive traffic.

A Throughput/Delay tradeoff. From proposed cross-layer point of view, see Fig. 1, the delay can be written (with some abuse of notation and disregarding other parameters) as $\text{delay}(f, k, \bar{P}) = \text{waiting-time}(f) + \text{service-time}(K, \bar{P})$. Using a dynamic transmission scheme and based on Fig. 5 (a and b), one can find an appropriate tradeoff between the throughput and the delay, so that the average delay will be less than some threshold while keeping the average throughput almost constant. This way, making the system running is such region improves considerably the end-to-end reliability and makes the system able to support

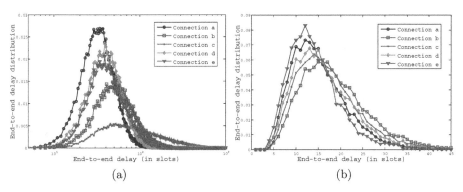

Fig. 7. The cooperation level is set to $f = 0.7$, $\bar{P}_1 = \bar{P}_6 = \bar{P}_{11} = 0.4$ and $P_9 = 0.3$. Figure (a) shows the delay distribution for $K = 4$ (a) and $K = 1$ (b).

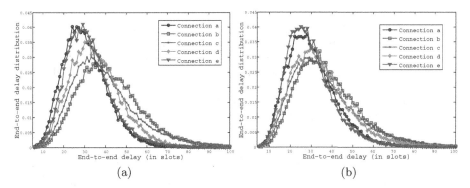

Fig. 8. The cooperation level is set to $f = 0.99$ (altruistic nodes), $\bar{P}_1 = \bar{P}_6 = \bar{P}_{11} = 0.4$ and $P_9 = 0.3$. This figure shows the distribution of e2e delay for static transmissions limit $K = 4$ (a) and dynamic K (with step 2, mean $\tilde{K} = 4$ and reset mechanism) (b).

several classes of services with different QoS requirements, in particular real-time traffic. Another way to get an appropriate tradeoff between throughput and delay is to fully use the information of our cross-layer model. Exploiting the instantaneous length of the forwarding queue, a node can efficiently adjust its cooperation level as well as its maximum number of transmissions per packet.

Delay control for real-time media streaming. Next, we depict the variation of average goodput with respect to transmission probability for all established connections. We consider a service requiring a delay threshold value $\Delta_{s,d} \equiv \Delta = 10$ms (100 time slots). This means that a packet arrives after 100 slots is dropped and not played out. The goodput turns to decrease and vanishes when nodes become very aggressive (transmit at probability close to 1). This situation is similar to the well known prisoners dilemma in game theory. Yet, this control mechanism causes packets drop and therefore the goodput is deteriorated (Fig. 9 a). Next, we depict in Fig. 9 (b) the dropping probability for connections a, b, c, d and e as a function of transmission probability. It represents

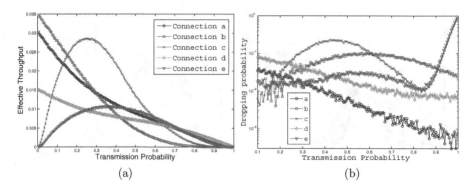

(a)   (b)

Fig. 9. end-to-end goodput (a) and packets dropping probability when cooperation level is set to $f = 0.8$, $K = 4$ and $\bar{P}_1 = \bar{P}_6 = \bar{P}_9 = \bar{P}_{11} \equiv P$ is varying

the amount of packets lost due to delay time-out. When we fix the forwarding probability at $f_i \equiv f = 0.8$ and vary the transmission probability, we note a clear correlation with the corresponding e2e delay. Indeed, when average delay is huge, the dropping probability tends to increase and vice-versa. One can note that the dropping probability may increase when the transmission probability goes to 1. This is not due to a huge delay but because of retransmissions expiration. Whereas for fixed transmission probability vector and variable forwarding probability, we note that the admission probability increases with f.

6   Conclusion

We have presented a framework to derive the end-to-end delay in ad hoc networks taking into account the parameters related to several layers (cross-layer architecture). We have obtained the distribution of the forwarding queue size and then the average delay based on the probability generating function approach. As an application of our results, we have considered the case of real-time traffic which requires delay constraints. By using the delay analysis we calculate the admission rate/loss rate of this traffic. We also used the dynamic retransmission scheme first proposed in [6] to improve end-to-end QoS. Preliminary investigations show good match with our experimental illustrations. A part of future guidelines is to address the choice of cooperation level (forwarding probability and retransmission limit) in a game theoretical perspective and analyze the behavior of the selfish nodes. We are also interested in extending our results for wide Mesh networks as well as heterogeneous systems.

References

1. El-Azouzi, R., Samanta, S.K., Sabir, E., El-Khoury, R.: Asymptotic delay analysis and timeout-based admission control for ad hoc wireless networks. Technical report (2009),
   http://lia.univ-avignon.fr/fileadmin/documents/Users/Intranet/
   chercheurs/sabir/Delay-full.pdf

2. Bianchi, G.: Performance analysis of the IEEE 802.11 distribute coordination function. IEEE Journal on Selected Areas in Communications (2000)
3. Bisnik, N., Abouzeid, A.A.: Queuing network models for delay analysis of multihop wireless ad hoc networks. Ad Hoc Networks 7(1), 79–97 (2009)
4. Bruno, R., Conti, M., Gregori, E.: Mesh Networks: Commodity Multi-hop Ad Hoc Networks. IEEE Communications Magazine, 123–131 (2005)
5. Cooper, R.B.: Introduction to Queueing Theory, 2nd edn. North Holland, Amsterdam (1981)
6. El-Khoury, R., El-Azouzi, R.: Dynamic Retransmission Limit Scheme for Routing in Multi-hop Ad hoc Networks. In: Inter-Perf 2007 Workshop. ACM, Nantes (2007)
7. El-Khoury, R., El-Azouzi, R., Altman, E.: Delay analysis for real-time streaming in multi-hop ad hoc network. In: Proc. WiOpt 2008, Germany (2008)
8. Gamal, A.E., Mammen, J., Prabhakar, B., Shah, D.: Throughput- delay trade-off in wireless networks. In: Proceedings of IEEE INFOCOM. IEEE, Los Alamitos (2004)
9. Grossglauser, M., Tse, D.: Mobility Increases the Capacity of Adhoc Wireless Networks. IEEE/ACM Transactions on Networking 10(4), 477–486 (2002)
10. ITU-T Recommendation H. 264/ISO/IEC 14496-10 (AVC).: Advanced Video Coding for Generic Audiovisual Services (2003)
11. Kherani, A., El-Azouzi, R., Altman, R.: Stability-Throughput Tradeoff and Routing in Multi-Hop Wireless Ad-Hoc Networks. In: Proceeding of Networking Conference, Coimbra, Portugal (2006)
12. Kulkarni, S.R., Viswanath, P.: A deterministic approach to throughput scaling in wireless networks. IEEE Trans. on Information Theory 50(6), 1041–1049 (2004)
13. Ray, S., Starobinski, D., Carruthers, J.B.: Performance of wireless networks with hidden nodes: A queuing-theoretic analysis. Computer Communications 28(10), 1179–1192 (2005)
14. Srinivasan, V., Nuggehalli, P., Chiasserini, C.F., Rao, R.R.: Cooperation in wireless ad hoc networks. In: Proceedings of IEEE INFOCOM, vol. 2, pp. 808–817 (2003)
15. Tickoo, O., Sikdar, B.: A queueing model for finite load IEEE 802.11 random access MAC. In: Proceedings of IEEE ICC, Paris, France, vol. 1, pp. 175–179 (2004)
16. Toh, C.K., Tsai, W.K., Li, V.O.L., Guichai, G.: Transporting Audio over Wireless Ad Hoc Networks: Experiments and New Insights. In: Proceedings of 14th IEEE PIMRC, China, vol. 1, pp. 772–777 (2003)
17. Urpi, A., Bonuccelli, M.A., Giordano, S.: Modeling cooperation in mobile ad hoc networks: a formal description of selfishness. In: Proceedings of WiOpt (2003)
18. Xie, M., Haenggi, M.: Towards an end-to-end delay analysis of wireless multihop networks. Ad Hoc Networks 7, 849–861 (2009)
19. Yang, Y., Hou, J.C., Kung, L.C.: Modeling the effect of transmit power and physical carrier sense in multi-hop Wireless networks. In: Proceedings of INFOCOM (2007)

Statistical Properties of the Delivery Rate for Single-Sink and Multiple-Sink Sensor Networks

Marco Zuniga[1], Manfred Hauswirth[1], and Yang Yang[2]

[1]Digital Enterprise Research Institute,
National University of Ireland, Galway
{marco.zuniga,manfred.hauswirth}@deri.org
[2]Department of Electrical Engineering,
University College London, U.K.
y.yang@ee.ucl.ac.uk

Abstract. In wireless sensor network applications where each node sends a packet to a sink, the stochastic nature of the link affects the delivery rate (total number of packets delivered at the sink).

Based on a simple analytical model, we study the statistical properties of the delivery rate for scenarios without link or transport layer retransmission (*best-effort* routing). For these *best-effort* scenarios, we derive bounds for the expectation and variance of the delivery rate for single-sink and multiple-sink architectures. Our analytical findings are further validated through simulations using a realistic link-layer model.

1 Introduction

A variety of applications envisioned for wireless sensor networks (WSN) share two important characteristics: (a) large scalability and (b) data required from every node (converge-cast). However, in this type of scenarios, the stochastic nature of the wireless link leads to a random behavior of the delivery rate – defined as the total number of packets received at the sink. A simple and well-known solution to overcome this problem is the use of link-layer or transport-layer retransmissions. However, these solutions may cause significant overhead, especially in large scale networks where data needs to travel through several hops. In the absence of retransmissions, it is important to describe the statistical properties of the delivery rate, namely its expectation and variance.

Studying these statistical properties is important because they provide information about the expected quality of service to the user. After deploying a network of n nodes, a user may specify the minimum delivery rate required to run an application and/or the maximum variance that can be tolerated.

Several works have investigated the impact of unreliable links on MAC and routing protocols [2,17,20]. Motivated by these studies, our work advances the understanding of the area by providing an analytical framework to *quantify* the impact of unreliable links on the expectation and variance of the delivery rate.

P.M. Ruiz and J.J. Garcia-Luna-Aceves (Eds.): ADHOC-NOW 2009, LNCS 5793, pp. 98–111, 2009.
© Springer-Verlag Berlin Heidelberg 2009

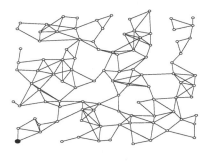

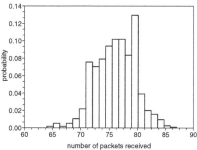

(a) Random Topology with 100 nodes   (b) Delivery Rate: μ=76.1, σ=3.5

Fig. 1. Variability of Delivery Rate. (a) Links have a transmission probability between 0 and 1 [19]. Each node transmits a packet to the sink (bottom-left node). (b) probability distribution of the delivery rate (mean μ and stdev σ).

Figure 1 depicts the motivation for our study. Figure 1 (a) presents a random topology where each link is assigned a realistic transmission probability between 0 and 1 according to the model presented in [19]. The sink is the bottom-left node (black dot) and each node sends a packet to the sink through its most reliable path. Figure 1 (b) depicts the *high variability* of the delivery rate.

In this work, *we propose an analytical framework to estimate the expectation and variance of the delivery rate for single-sink and multiple-sink scenarios.* Our analysis is presented in Section 2 and it is based on an unreliable grid –a grid where nodes transmit to their closest neighbors (up-to 4) with probability p. In Section 3 we provide simulation results that validate our analytical findings. The simulations remove two of the main assumptions made in our analysis: we use random deployments (instead of grids) and individual transmission probabilities for each link (as opposed to the same probability p used in our model). The related work and conclusions are presented in Sections 4 and 5, respectively.

Scope: Our work is focused on applications requiring periodic data gatherings with relaxed delay constraints. Examples of such scenarios are environmental monitoring applications where nodes report the soil moisture of a plantation [3].These scenarios permit the use of TDMA-based algorithms which eliminates MAC collisions. MAC collisions and varying channel conditions are important effects to consider on various scenarios. However, in this work our aim is to focus primarily on the effect of unreliable links.

2   Analysis

In this section we analyze mathematically the impact of unreliable links on the delivery rate. First, we present the model used in our analysis and then, based on this model, we derive the expectation and variance of the delivery rate for single-sink and multiple-sink architectures.

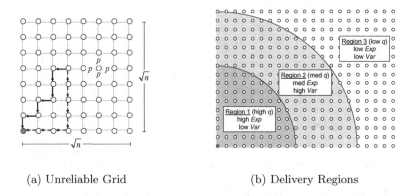

(a) Unreliable Grid   (b) Delivery Regions

Fig. 2. (a) nodes communicate with their neighbors with probability p and send packets to the sink through one of their shortest-paths. (b) the node-sink distance determines the contribution of each node to the expectation and variance of the delivery rate.

2.1   Grid Model and Delivery Regions

For the analysis we consider an unreliable grid of n nodes. We define an unreliable grid as a regular grid where nodes can communicate with their closest neighbors with probability p. With the aim of describing the delivery regions, let us locate a single sink at the bottom-left corner of the network and have each node send a packet through its most reliable path. In a grid, the most reliable path is the shortest path, and most nodes have several shortest-paths towards the sink. For the purposes of our analysis any shortest-path can be chosen. Figure 2 (a) shows an unreliable grid and a node with two possible paths towards the sink.

Let X be a random variable representing the delivery rate (total number of packets received at the sink), and X_i a Bernoulli random variable representing the reception of a packet from node i. That is, $X_i=1$ if the packet from node i is received, and $X_i=0$ if the packet is not received.

X and X_i lead to $X = \sum_{i=1}^{n} X_i$, and we are interested in obtaining $E[X]$ and $Var[X]$. Considering that X_is are mutually independent[1], we obtain:

$$E[X] = E[\sum X_i] = \sum E[X_i] \qquad (1)$$

$$Var[X] = Var[\sum X_i] = \sum Var[X_i] \qquad (2)$$

We observe that each node i contributes independently to the expectation and variance of the delivery rate. This observation allows us to classify nodes into *delivery regions*.

---

[1] The received wireless signal is the sum of many contributions, coming from different locations with random phases [11]. And our focus is on scenarios where the statistical properties of the channel are similar throughout the network.

Delivery Regions. The delivery regions provide the intuition behind the be-havior of the delivery rate of single-sink and multiple-sink architectures. These regions are determined based on the interaction of two phenomena: (a) prop-erties of the expectation and variance of Bernoulli random variables and (b) relation between node-sink distance and packet-delivery probability.

The expectation and variance of a Bernoulli random variable with parameter q are q and $q(1 - q)$, respectively. Hence, the expectation is linear with q, but the variance is concave, with a maxima of 0.25 for $q = 0.5$. Coupling these properties with the fact that in WSN the path-delivery probability decreases with the node-sink distance[2] leads to the regions shown in Figure 2 (b):

Region 1 [high Exp, low Var]. Nodes in this region traverse a small number of hops, and hence, they have a high path-delivery probability q. A high q implies a high expectation and a low variance of the delivery rate.

Region 2 [moderate Exp, high Var]. Compared to region 1, nodes have a lower path-delivery probability ($q = 0.5 \pm \Delta$). Without loss of generality, in this work we assume $\Delta = 0.3$. The lower q implies that nodes contribute moderately to the expectation of the delivery rate but significantly to its variance.

Region 3 [low Exp, low Var]. Nodes in this region have a very low path-delivery probability q and their contribution to both, the expectation and variance of the delivery rate, is minimal.

Clearly, Region 1 provides the best statistical properties for the delivery rate. In this work we analyze the impact of regions 2 and 3 on the delivery rate of single-sink and multiple-sink architectures.

Model. Let $q_i = E[X_i]$ be the path-delivery probability of node i, that is, the probability that node i will deliver a packet to the sink. Then $q_i = p^{h_i}$, where h_i represents the number of hops from node i to the sink s. Denoting (x_i, y_i) and (x_s, y_s) as the coordinates of node i and the sink, the number of hops is given by $h_i = \|x_i - x_s\| + \|y_i - y_s\|$ (Manhattan distance).

Introducing q_i in equations 1 and 2 we obtain:

$$E[X] = \sum p^{h_i} \tag{3}$$

$$Var[X] = \sum p^{h_i}(1 - p^{h_i}) = E[X] - \sum p^{2h_i} \tag{4}$$

The higher the expectation and the lower the variance, the better the delivery rate. This requirement is captured by the coefficient of variation cv:

$$cv[X] = \frac{\sqrt{Var[X]}}{E[X]} \tag{5}$$

In the next subsections we obtain expressions for the expectation, variance and coefficient of variation for single-sink and multiple-sink architectures.

2.2   Single Sink

When considering a single sink, most data gathering studies place the sink at the border of the network (especially at one of the corners). This common -and

---

[2] Longer distances lead to more hops which in turn leads to lower delivery probabilities.

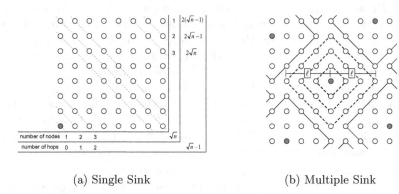

(a) Single Sink   (b) Multiple Sink

Fig. 3. Reasoning followed to obtain the path-delivery probabilities for single-sink and two-tier multiple-sink architectures

to some extent logical- assumption motivated us to investigate the expectation and variance of this scenario.

In order to calculate the expectation and variance of the delivery rate, we require the path-delivery probability for each node. The reasoning to obtain these probabilities is depicted in Figure 3 (a). Nodes on lines parallel to the diagonal have the same path-delivery probability. Hence, recalling that n is the number of nodes and letting $s = \sqrt{n} - 1$, equations 3 and 4 lead to:

$$E[X] = 1 + 2p + 3p^2 + \ldots + 3p^{2s-2} + 2p^{2s-1} + p^{2s}$$
$$= (1 - p^s) \sum_{i=0}^{s} ip^i + (1 + p^s + sp^s) \sum_{i=0}^{s} p^i - 2 \tag{6}$$

$$Var[X] = E[X] - (1 - p^{2s}) \sum_{i=0}^{s} ip^{2i} + (1 + p^{2s} + sp^{2s}) \sum_{i=0}^{s} p^{2i} \tag{7}$$

When $n \to \infty$, we obtain (the derivation is presented in Appendix A):

$$E_{n\to\infty}[X] = \frac{1}{(1-p)^2} \tag{8}$$

$$Var_{n\to\infty}[X] = \frac{1}{(1-p)^2} - \frac{1}{(1-p^2)^2} \tag{9}$$

Table 1. Notation

X	: Random variable representing the Delivery Rate
X_i	: Random variable representing a packet reception from node i
n	: number of nodes in the network (s = $\sqrt{n} - 1$)
p	: link transmission probability
q_i	: path-delivery probability for node i ($q_i = E[X_i]$)

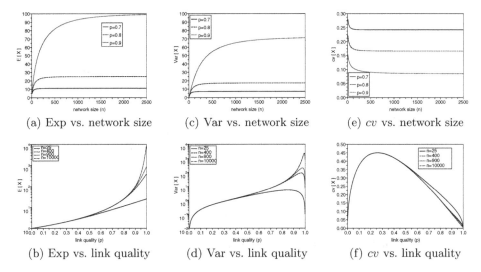

(a) Exp vs. network size   (c) Var vs. network size   (e) cv vs. network size

(b) Exp vs. link quality   (d) Var vs. link quality   (f) cv vs. link quality

Fig. 4. Analytical Expectation, Variance and Coefficient of Variation of the Delivery Rate for Single-Sink Architectures

$$cv_{n \to \infty}[X] = (1 - p)\sqrt{1 - \frac{1}{(1+p)^2}} \qquad (10)$$

Figure 4 depicts $E[X]$, $Var[X]$ and $cv[X]$ with respect to the network size n and the link quality p (equations 6 and 7). This figure, together with equations 8, 9 and 10, will allow us to illustrate the statistical properties of the delivery rate on single-sink architectures.

Limitations of single-sink architectures. The main limitation of single sink architectures is captured in equation 8: unless links are perfect (a highly unrealistic behavior), the delivery rate is bounded.

Several empirical studies have shown [16,15,20] that even at close distances links are not perfect. Instead of having transmission probabilities of 1.0, these links are more likely to have transmission probabilities between 0.95 and 0.98 (good but not perfect). This implies, according to equation 8, that the maximum delivery rate expected for single-sink wireless sensor networks would be on the range [400 pkts (for p=0.95), 2500 pkts (for p=0.98)]. Furthermore, Figure 4 (a) shows that achieving even modest delivery rates require a vast number of nodes. For instance, for an average link quality p=0.9, an expected delivery rate of 75 packets requires deploying around 375 nodes, which implies that the network would be working 80% below its data gathering capacity. Hence, single-sink architectures are reasonable for networks consisting of at most a few hundred of nodes and with good link qualities[3].

---

[3] Notice that not only the delivery rate is affected but the sampling is highly uneven. Areas close to the sink are well covered, while further areas are barely sampled.

Impact of link quality on the stability of the delivery rate. Figure 4 (f) shows that the *cv* is concave with respect to the link quality *p*, which suggest that increasing link quality does not necessarily improve the delivery rate, i.e. increasing the expectation while at the same time reducing the variance.

A simple derivative of equation 10 shows that *cv*=0.45 for *p*=0.26. In realistic deployments, the average link-quality *p* should be significantly higher than 0.3 for the network to work properly, otherwise, the network would be severely disconnected [19]. Hence, for practical purposes, the better the link quality (higher transmit power or higher node density), the better the delivery rate.

Impact of delivery regions on the delivery rate. The impact of the delivery regions is summarized in Figure 4 (e). The coefficient of variation decreases monotonically with the size of the network, which implies that the larger the network the more stable the delivery rate. However, the reduction follows a *diminishing returns* pattern. Initially, for small networks, the *cv* reduces sharply because most nodes are in Region 1 (high Exp and low Var). For medium scale networks, which include regions 1 and 2, the reduction of the *cv* is less pronounced (bending of curves). This is because Region 2 still contributes to the expectation of the delivery rate but at the cost of a high contribution to the variance. Finally, further increasing the size of large networks reduces *cv* minimally due to the negligible impact of Region 3 on the expectation and variance.

Nodes Providing the Maximum Variance. Nodes with path-delivery probability $q=0.5$ provide the maximum variance[4]. When the sink is located at one of the corners of the network, the delivery rate variance is maximized when nodes in the diagonal of the network satisfy $p^{h_d} = 0.5$, where h_d is the number of hops from the sink to the diagonal. Since $h_d = \sqrt{n} - 1$, the variance reaches its maximum when the link probability p is $\exp\left(\frac{\ln 0.5}{\sqrt{n}-1}\right)$. In Figure 4 (d), the values of p that maximize the delivery rate variance are 0.840, 0.964, 0.976 and 0.993, for the respective network sizes.

In our analysis we placed the sink at one of the corners of the network. When the sink is placed at the center of the network, the results for the Exp, Var and *cv* are very similar. These results are not presented due to space constraints.

2.3   Multiple Sinks

Multiple-sink architectures are based on a two-tier hierarchy (two types of nodes). Nodes in the lower-tier have limited resources and their function is mainly to send/relay information to the sinks. Nodes on the upper-tier act as local sinks and form an overlay network with highly reliable communication among them.

In this subsection we investigate in more detail a well-known and intuitive design guideline: multiple-sink architectures provide better delivery rates than single-sink architectures by collecting information from their local areas, but *what is the number of sinks required to provide a particular delivery rate?*

The analysis of two-tier multiple-sink architectures is also based on the unreliable grid. Figure 3 (b) depicts the formation of clusters. In this grid model,

---

[4] Recall, that Bernoulli r.v. with parameter 0.5 have the maximum variance.

sinks are deployed uniformly (equally spaced), and the diameter of the cluster (in number of hops) is 2ℓ. Lower-tier nodes send information to the sink with which they have the most reliable path[5].

The value of ℓ depends on the number of sinks c to be deployed, more sinks implies a lower value of ℓ, and it is given by:

$$\ell \approx \sqrt{\frac{n}{c}}\frac{1}{2} \tag{11}$$

Denoting $E_c[X]$, $Var_c[X]$ and $cv_c[X]$ as the expectation, variance and coefficient of variation of the delivery rate for multiple-sink architectures, we obtain the following bounds (the derivation is presented in Appendix A):

$$E_c[X] > np^\ell \tag{12}$$

$$Var_c[X] < \frac{n}{4} \tag{13}$$

$$cv_c[X] < \frac{1}{2\sqrt{n}p^\ell} \tag{14}$$

Letting E_u be the delivery rate expected by the user, equations 11 and 12 can be used to derive the number of sinks c_u required to guarantee $E_c[x] > E_u$:

$$c_u = \frac{n}{4}(\log_{\frac{E_u}{n}} p)^2 \tag{15}$$

It is important to observe that the expectation of the delivery rate in multi-sink architectures is linear with the number of nodes in the network (equation 12). *This property removes the main limitation of single-sink architectures: the constrained expectation of the delivery rate.* Also, the coefficient of variation $cv_c[X]$ indicates that the larger the network and the better the link quality, the more stable the delivery rate. Furthermore, as $n \to \infty$, the $cv \to 0$, which implies a great stability of the delivery rate for very large networks.

3   Evaluation of Delivery Rate on Realistic Communication Graphs

In this section we validate our analytical insights on more realistic scenarios: (a) we use random deployments and (b) each link is assigned a different transmission probability p.

3.1   Simulation Set Up

We performed simulations using Scilab[6]. As describe in Section 1, we focus on the impact of unreliable links on the delivery rate. In order to capture this single effect, the simulations do not include MAC collisions (TDMA is assumed).

---

[5] Sinks perform constrained floods to determine the most realible path of each node.
[6] Scilab is an open source package similar to Matlab.

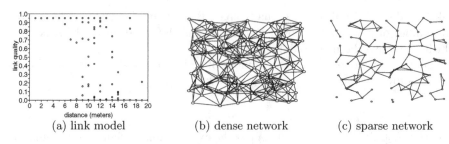

(a) link model   (b) dense network   (c) sparse network

Fig. 5. Link Layer Model. (a) sample of link quality model (based on [19]), (b) sample of a dense (connected) network, (c) sample of a sparse (disconnected) network.

Link Layer Model. We calculate link qualities based on a slightly modified version of the probabilistic model presented in [19]:

$$p(d) = (1 - \frac{1}{2} \exp^{-\frac{\gamma(d)}{2} \frac{1}{0.64}})^{8f} \qquad (16)$$

Where $p(d)$ is the link quality for an internode distance d. f is the number of bits transmitted and $\gamma(d)$ is the signal to noise ratio, which includes the output power and channel parameters. In our simulations, the output power is set to 0 dBm and the channel parameters are 4.0 for both, the path loss exponent and the shadowing variance (f=160 bits).

This model is quite useful but it tends to overestimate the link quality of nodes at close distances by assigning perfect transmission probabilities. Several empirical works [16,15] show that nodes at close distances have high but not perfect transmission probabilities (between 0.95 and 0.98). Denoting p_{model} as the link probability obtained by the above equation and p_{max} as the link quality for close distances, we assign each link an individual probability p_r according to $p_r = \min\{p_{model}, p_{max}\}$. Without loss of generality, we assume $p_{max} = 0.95$. Figure 5 (a) shows samples of p_r for various internode distances, and we can observe that the model resembles the behavior of empirical studies [16,15,19].

Topology. Various network sizes were tested (25, 100, 225, 400, 625 and 900). The network followed a normal-random topology, where nodes are initially deployed on a grid layout with an internode distance of d meters. Then, a normal r.v. with parameters (μ=0,σ=d/4) is used to introduce noise on the x and y coordinates of each node. We tested dense (d=6m) and sparse networks (d=10m). Figures 5 (b) and (c) show network samples (only links with $p_r > 0.1$ are shown). Each tuple (network size n, internode distance d) was evaluated 100 times, and the average expectation and variance of the delivery rate was calculated.

Placement of Sinks. For single-sink architectures the sink is the node closest to the bottom-left corner of the network. For multiple-sink architectures, the area of the network is divided in cells according to the number of sinks, and the node closest to the center of each cell is selected as a sink. On both architectures, nodes send packets through its most reliable path to a sink[7].

---

[7] In future work we will evaluate the performance of local forwarding metrics such as geographic routing.

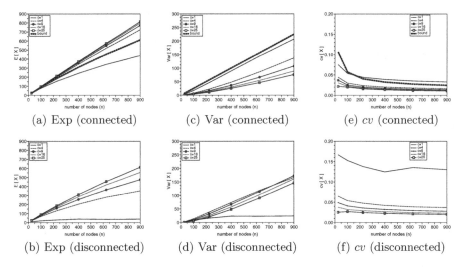

(a) Exp (connected)   (c) Var (connected)   (e) cv (connected)

(b) Exp (disconnected)   (d) Var (disconnected)   (f) cv (disconnected)

Fig. 6. Exp, Var and cv for random deployments. Dense and sparse networks were simulated. c is the number of clusters, $c=1$ is the single sink scenario. The thick-dashed curves in (a), (c) and (e) represent the bounds for multiple-sinks (eqs. 12 13 14).

3.2 Simulation Results

Figure 6 presents the expectation, variance and cv for dense (connected) and sparse (disconnected) networks. In Figures 6 (a), (c) and (e), the thick dashed curves represent the bounds obtained in equations 12, 13 and 14 for multiple-sink architectures. Figure 6 (a) shows that the expected delivery rate of single-sink architectures ($c=1$) reaches a bound around the value predicted by equation 8 (400 for $p_{max}=0.95$). The higher expectation in the simulations is due to the presence of long-good-quality links. Contrary to the analytical model, where nodes communicate only with their immediate neighbors, real deployments have long-good-quality links. These long links reduce the number of hops traversed by packets, which in turn increase the path-reliability and the delivery rate. For multiple-sink architectures ($c > 1$), Figure 6 (a) shows the linear relation between the expected delivery rate and the size of the network (derived in eq. 12). The bounds presented in this figure are for $c=4$ (using eqs. 12 and 11).

Figure 6 (c) shows that the variance of the delivery rate is still increasing linearly for $n=900$. This effect is also due to the better path-reliability caused by long-good links. For a given network size, better path-reliability increases the size of regions 1 and 2, and reduces the size of region 3. Hence, in realistic dense scenarios, the convergence of the variance will be observed for larger networks.

Figure 6 (e) shows that the coefficient of variation of single-sink architectures converges to the value presented in equation 10 (0.043 for $p_{max}=0.95$), and the cv of multiple sinks is below the bound presented in equation 14. *The monotonic reduction of cv validates an important insight provided by the analytical model: the stability of the delivery rate increases as n grows.*

Figures 6 (b) and (d) show that the expectation and variance of sparse (disconnected) networks increase significantly on multiple-sink architectures. Clearly,
the increment in both metrics occurs because more sinks will cover the disconnected parts of a sparse network. Figure 6 (f) shows that despite the increment of
the variance, the coefficient of variation is significantly reduced for multiple-sink
architectures leading to more stable delivery rates.

3.3   Empirical-Based Evaluation

The empirical data was obtained from the authors of [19]. 21 Mica2 motes were
deployed in an outdoor environment forming a chain topology (internode distance = 1m), and 2 power levels were evaluated (-17 and -14 dBm).

Figure 7 (a) depicts the expected delivery $E[X_i]$ and variance $Var[X_i]$ for each
node i in the x axis. The sink is located at position 0. For the high power level,
all nodes have a high path-delivery probability and a low variance. While for the
low power level, the path-delivery probability decreases rapidly with distance
and the last 4 nodes are disconnected.

Figure 7 (b) shows the expectation and variance $(E[X], Var[X])$ of the delivery rate. We emulate single-sink ($c = 1$) and multiple-sink architectures ($c > 1$).
In single-sink, the sink is placed at 0, and in multiple-sinks, the sinks are evenly
distributed. We observe that further increasing the number of sinks in dense
networks does not improve significantly the delivery rate (this behavior is also
observed in the simulations, Figure 6 (a)).

Considering that Region 1 includes nodes with $E[X_i] > 0.8$, the high power
level extends Region 1 beyond 20 meters, while for the low power level it is
limited to 8 meters. This is because in dense networks, adding further sinks
cover closer areas of Region 1, which is an improvement but not a significant
one. In sparse networks, adding more sinks not only covers disconnected nodes
but it also limits the coverage of Regions 2 and 3 (in favor of Region 1). Also, this
evaluation illustrates the trade-off between the output power and the number

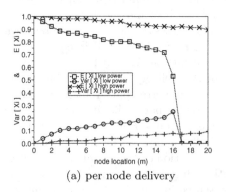
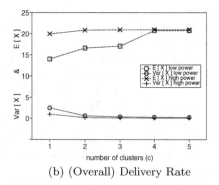

(a) per node delivery   (b) (Overall) Delivery Rate

Fig. 7. Emulation Results. 21 Mica nodes on a chain topology. (a) Exp and Var of
path-delivery per node. (b) Exp and Var of the Delivery Rate.

of sinks required to improve the delivery rate, i.e. increasing the output power by 3dBm significantly reduces the number of sinks required to achieve similar delivery rates.

4   Related Work

The low delivery rate caused by multi-hop routing in wireless networks is a well-known and studied phenomena [4,1]. Most of the solutions include retransmissions at the link and/or transport layers. In the area of mobile ad-hoc networks (MANETS), the focus has been on enhancing traditional transport protocols (TCP) to differentiate between congestion and lossy links in order to improve the end-to-end delivery rate [10,8]. In the area of wireless sensor networks, novel retransmission schemes have been proposed for the link and transport layers [14,13,12]. The trade-off in the proposed mechanisms is to increase the reliability by utilizing energy on retransmissions. *Our work evaluates a different trade-off: assuming no extra energy is utilized in retransmission, we presented the impact of unreliable links on the statistical properties of the delivery rate for single-sink and two-tier multiple-sink architectures.*

An important set of related work pertain the ones investigating the impact of unreliable links on the performance of protocols in wireless sensor networks. Several empirical studies have exposed the unreliable nature of links in wireless sensor networks [16,15,7]. Following these initial studies, several works analyzed the impact of unreliable links on protocols at the link, routing and transport layers [2,17,20]. Similarly to these works, our study contributes to a better understanding of the impact of unreliable links on wireless sensor networks. However, our focus is on the study of a global metric (the delivery rate) and not on the performance of an specific protocol.

Some works have also focused on the impact of unreliable links on the delivery rate, and our study is closer in spirit to these. In [18], the authors provide initial results on the impact of unreliable links on the statistical behavior of the total number of transmission and retransmission required to deliver all packets in a data gathering tree. However, this study is limited and does not provide a model to explain the behavior. Deb *et. al.* [5], proposes a multi-path mechanism to overcome the packet losses due to unreliable links, and on the same line of work the authors of [6] use multi-path techniques to improve the reliability and delay of the delivery rate. Our work does not consider routing alternatives to enhance the delivery rate, we studied the statistical properties of *single-path best-effort* transmissions and analyzed the impact of the architecture (single-sink and multiple-sinks) on the delivery rate.

5   Conclusions and Future Work

We studied the impact of unreliable links on the expectation and variance of delivery rate for *single-path best-effort* forwarding (no retransmissions). Our study shows that single-sink architectures are realistic for data gathering networks consisting of at most a few hundred nodes. For multiple-sink architectures we provide an analytical framework to determine the number of sinks required to satisfy the expectation required by the user. We also show that in multiple-sink architectures: the larger the network the more stable the delivery (but this improvement requires a set of more powerful nodes acting a local sinks).

It is important to remark that two-tier architectures have been argued to be the only feasible option for large scale wireless sensor networks [9]. Our work provides analytical support to that argument.

Current Limitations of Study and Future Work

In this study we assumed the use of local floods to obtain the most reliable path for each node. Local metrics, such as geographic routing, will lead to less reliable paths, and hence, lower delivery rates (our work could be seen as an upper bound of the delivery rate). As part of our future work we plan to evaluate distributed forwarding techniques.

Our work focused on a particular type of WSN applications: periodic data gathering with relaxed delay constraints, such as moisture monitoring [3]. These scenarios permit the use of TDMA schemes, which limit MAC collisions. In future work, we plan to evaluate more dynamic scenarios and evaluate the joint impact of link unreliability and MAC collisions on the delivery rate.

Acknowledgement. This work has been funded in part by an IRCSET Post-doctoral fellow Grant PD200857, SFI Grant No. SFI08CEI1380 and by CONET, the Cooperating Objects Network of Excellence, EU FP7-2007-2-224053.

References

1. Banerjee, S., Misra, A.: Minimum energy paths for reliable communication in multi-hop wireless networks. In: MobiHoc 2002, pp. 146–156 (2002)
2. Biswas, S., Morris, R.: Opportunistic routing in multi-hop wireless networks. SIGCOMM Comput. Commun. Rev. 34(1), 69–74 (2004)
3. Cardell-Oliver, R., Kranz, M., Smettem, K., Mayer, K.: A Reactive Soil Moisture Sensor Network: Design and Field Evaluation. International Journal of Distributed Sensor Networks 1(2), 149–162 (2005)
4. Couto, D., Aguayo, D., Chambers, B., Morris, R.: Performance of multihop wireless networks: shortest path is not enough. In: SIGCOMM Comp. Com. Rev. 2003 (2003)
5. Deb, B., Bhatnagar, S., Nath, B.: ReInForM: reliable information forwarding using multiple paths in sensor networks. In: LCN 2003, pp. 406–415 (2003)
6. Felemban, E., Lee, C., Ekici, E., Boder, R., Vural, S.: Probabilistic QoS guarantee in reliability and timeliness domains in wireless sensor networks. In: INFOCOM 2005 (2005)
7. Ganesan, D., Krishnamachari, B., Woo, A., Culler, D., Estrin, D., Wicker, S.: Complex behavior at scale: An experimental study of low-power wireless sensor networks. UCLA Computer Science Technical Report, 02–0013 (2003)
8. Gerla, M., Tang, K., Bagrodia, R.: TCP performance in wireless multi-hop networks. In: 2nd IEEE Workshop on Mobile Comp. Syst. and App. (1999)
9. Gnawali, O., Jang, K.-Y., Paek, J., Vieira, M., Govindan, R., Greenstein, B., Joki, A., Estrin, D., Kohler, E.: The tenet architecture for tiered sensor networks. In: SenSys 2006, pp. 153–166. ACM, New York (2006)

10. Holland, G., Vaidya, N.: Analysis of TCP Performance over Mobile Ad Hoc Networks. Wireless Networks 8(2), 275–288 (2002)
11. Rappapport, T.S.: Wireless Communications: Principles and Practice
12. Sankarasubramaniam, Y., Akan, O.B., Akyildiz, I.F.: Esrt: event-to-sink reliable transport in wireless sensor networks. In: MobiHoc 2003 (2003)
13. Stann, F., Heidemann, J.: RMST: reliable data transport in sensor networks. In: SNPA 2003, pp. 102–112 (2003)
14. Wan, C.-Y., Campbell, A.T., Krishnamurthy, L.: Psfq: a reliable transport protocol for wireless sensor networks. In: WSNA 2002 (2002)
15. Woo, A., Tong, T., Culler, D.: Taming the underlying challenges of reliable multi-hop routing in sensor networks. In: SenSys 2003 (2003)
16. Zhao, J., Govindan, R.: Understanding packet delivery performance in dense wireless sensor networks. In: SenSys 2003, New York, NY, USA (2003)
17. Zhou, G., He, T., Krishnamurthy, S., Stankovic, J.A.: Models and solutions for radio irregularity in wireless sensor networks. ACM Trans. Sen. Netw. (2006)
18. Zuniga, M., Krishnamachari, B.: Exploring the predictability of network metrics in the presence of unreliable wireless links. In: SenSys 2004, pp. 275–276 (2004)
19. Zuniga, M., Krishnamachari, B.: An analysis of unreliability and asymmetry in low-power wireless links. ACM Trans. Sen. Netw. 3(2), 7 (2007)
20. Zuniga, M., Seada, K., Krishnamachari, B., Helmy, A.: Efficient geographic routing over lossy links in wireless sensor networks. ACM Trans. Sen. Netw. (2008)

Appendix A: Derivation of Expectation and Variance

Single Sink Architectures when $n \to \infty$. From equations 3 and 4 we obtain:

$$E[X] = 1 + 4p + 8p^2 + \ldots + 8p^{2v-1} + 4p^{2v}$$
$$= 1 + \sum_{i=0}^{v} 4ip^i + \sum_{i=1}^{v} 4(v+1-i)p^{v+i} \tag{17}$$

$$Var[X] = \sum_{i=0}^{v} 4ip^i(1-p^i) + \\ \sum_{i=1}^{v} 4(v+1-i)p^{v+i}(1-p^{v+i}) \tag{18}$$

By replacing the known series:

$$\sum_{i=0}^{\infty}(i+1)p^i = \frac{1}{(1-p)^2} \text{ and } \sum_{i=0}^{\infty}(i+1)p^{2i} = \frac{1}{(1-p^2)^2}, \forall p : 0 < p < 1$$

in the above equations, we obtain equations 8, 9 and 10.

Bounds for Multiple-Sink Architectures The number of nodes per cluster n_c is equal to $1 + \sum_{i=1}^{\ell} 4i = 1 + 2\ell(\ell+1)$. Considering the cluster layout presented in Figure 3 (b), we obtain:

$$E_c = \text{num of clusters} \times E[\text{pkts per cluster}] = \frac{n}{n_c}(1 + \sum_{i=1}^{\ell} 4ip^i)$$
$$> \frac{n}{n_c}(1 + \sum_{i=1}^{\ell} 4ip^{\ell}) = n(\frac{1+p^{\ell}2\ell(\ell+1)}{1+2\ell(\ell+1)}) \tag{19}$$
$$> np^{\ell}$$

$$Var_c = \frac{n}{n_c} \sum_{i=1}^{\ell} 4ip^i(1-p^i)$$
$$< \frac{n}{n_c} \sum_{i=1}^{\ell} 4i0.25 = \frac{n}{2}(\frac{\ell(\ell+1)}{1+2\ell(\ell+1)}) \tag{20}$$
$$< \frac{n}{4}$$

$$cv_c < \frac{\sqrt{\frac{n}{4}}}{np^{\ell}} = \frac{1}{2\sqrt{n}p^{\ell}} \tag{21}$$

Application-Driven Analytic Toolbox for WSNs

Jussi Haapola[1], Flavia Martelli[2], and Carlos Pomalaza-Ráez[1]

[1] CWC, University of Oulu, Finland, P.O. Box 4500 FIN-90014, University of Oulu, Finland
{jhaapola,carlos}@ee.oulu.fi
[2] DEIS, University of Bologna V.le Risorgimento, 2 40136 Bologna, Italy
flavia.martelli@studio.unibo.it

Abstract. In this paper we propose a Generic Analytical DesiGn EnvironmenT (GADGET) Toolbox for designing the most suitable MAC protocol for an arbitrary wireless sensor network (WSN) application. Furthermore, a model to weight the metrics in the design and a new single compound metric are proposed. Comparing performance curves produced by a number of metrics make it difficult to evaluate how well a given protocol suits for the purposes of an application. It may also be difficult to estimate, which of the protocols at hand would perform the best with respect to that application. Matching the application with the most appropriate protocols is critical for efficient WSN operation because the sensor nodes are resource constrained by nature. The analytic hierarchy process and a pair-wise weighted comparison of the protocols enable to emphasise application performance requirements and to produce a single performance curve either by combination of competing protocols (fractional) or per protocol (absolute). The former provides suitability of one protocol over others with respect to an application whereas the latter provides also insight on the absolute performance of the protocol.

Keywords: Analytic Hierarchy Process, Single Compound Metric, Medium Access Control, Wireless Sensor Networks.

1 Introduction

Multi-metric evaluation models use a number of performance metrics or parameters and produce either a single compound metric (SCM) or a lower number of metrics using dimension scaling. They can be roughly categorised into two main areas: multi-metric evaluation during design and multi-metric optimisation during run-time. In this paper we are mostly interested in the former.

Although this paper is limited to addressing the physical (PHY) and medium access control (MAC) layers, related work on SCM for wireless networks can only be found from routing. Insights on SCM and metric selection is discussed in [1]. Waharte et al. [2] compare a number of currently used routing metrics and their performance in mesh networks. Hop Count and Blocking Metric [3] are single and easy metrics that fail to take the specific wireless environment into account. They also do not consider congestion. More sophisticated metrics, namely Expected/modified Expected Transmission Count (ETX [4]/mETX [5]), Expected Transmission Time (ETT) [6], and Metric of Interference and Channel Switching (MIC) [7] possess some compound metric characteristics.

P.M. Ruiz and J.J. Garcia-Luna-Aceves (Eds.): ADHOC-NOW 2009, LNCS 5793, pp. 112–125, 2009.
© Springer-Verlag Berlin Heidelberg 2009

The ETX produces hop count and packet loss into a single metric whereas the mETX adds channel variability, and ETT includes link bandwidth to ETX. The maintenance overhead of MIC is prohibitive, but it provides a term to account for channel diversity. The results of [2] indicate that choosing the proper metric can be challenging and depends on the scenario, but more complex metrics provide better fairness of traffic flows.

While most of the fore-mentioned metrics are applied to routing, they are the closest related work existing for SCMs. The model is often based on hop-by-hop basis evaluation [1, 2, 3, 4, 5, 6]. In [8, 9] SCMs in QoS hop-by-hop routing are considered, which achieve significant performance gains over individual metric algorithms. Hop-by-hop methodology implies that potentially all the desired PHY and MAC layer parameters and metrics can be taken into account per hop, i.e. PHY metrics affect MAC metrics in certain ways. MAC metrics produce the per-hop parameter of routing algorithms; other parameters of routing include route discovery performance and route maintenance performance, which may be affected by the MAC or the PHY parameters. These in turn produce the transport data stream parameter, which have connection set up and error recovery as other parameters. It is possible to construct a tree of parameters and their dependencies in this way to represent metrics for a high number of evaluation criteria.

The authors of [10] discuss on granulating data on data sets and present some initial considerations of strategies for integrating multiple metrics. According to [10], many similarity metrics use pair-wise comparisons in the measurement of similarity between data sets. Most notably, a similarity measure would be $v_{a(1,2)} \times sim(a1, a2) \oplus v_{b(1,2)} \times sim(b1, b2) \oplus v_{c(1,2)} \times sim(c1, c2)$, where $\oplus$ indicates some combination operator and $sim(x, y)$ is a measurement of similarity between attribute values x and y. The $v_{z(1,2)}$ represents the weight for each attribute pair, where $z \in \{a, b, c\}$. With pair-wise comparison the parts of metrics that share common characteristics are evaluated with each other. The similarity measure serves as an inspiration for the SCM proposed in this paper with the analytic hierarchy process (AHP) [11]. Pair-wise comparisons are also made in the AHP. The pair-wise comparison allows for both qualitative and subjective evaluation. The technique is slowly being adopted into telecommunications studies [12], but only a few extend to networking. In [13], the authors propose a routing protocol that takes into account delay, bandwidth, security, and loss probability using the AHP principle. The AHP has not been used in WSN evaluations and modelling of application requirements in WSNs is a new area or research entirely.

Taking the application into account produces a linguistic (subjective) scale for making a comparison. The linguistic scale is characterised as one object being from "extremely less important" to "extremely more important" than another object. This linguistic scale should be transitive, i.e. if object $A1$ is "moderately more important" than object $B1$ and object $B1$ is "strongly more important" than object $C1$, then object $A1$ must be more than "strongly more important" than object $C1$. The authors of [14] address the issue. Furthermore, [15] provides a comprehensive study of the available AHP scales and prioritisation methods.

In this paper we propose Generic Analytical DesiGn EnvironmenT (GADGET) toolbox, which in a novel fashion takes into account WSN application requirements in emphasising performance metrics. Further, we propose a new SCM, termed Goodness, to assist in making a decision on the protocols to use with respect to the application in question. We also propose two novel models of comparing the protocol performances with each other. We argue that the method is flexible and does not depend on any particular protocol layer or analysis method.

The rest of the paper is organised as follows. Section 2 provides a description of the GADGET toolbox and presents two ways of producing application dependent evaluation. In Section 3 the application and the sensors used are described while in Section 4 the MAC protocol alternatives are identified. Section 5 presents the results and Section 6 concludes the paper.

2   GADGET

The GADGET toolbox uses the components described in detail in the following subsections. Shortly, the flow of utilising them is as follows. Firstly, the WSN application scenario at hand is analysed and based on the resulting reasoning the sensors and actuators (S&A) available are pair-wise prioritised using e.g., Saaty scale [15] bearing in mind transitivity [14]. Secondly, the S&A are mapped to the available metrics of performance and by using the AHP [11] weights of each of the metrics are derived e.g., by using eigenvalue method [15]. Thirdly, the performances of the protocol alternatives are derived with respect to available metrics. Fourthly, an SCM of each of the protocols is derived using the weights and the metrics either by combination of competing protocols (fractional) or per protocol (absolute).

2.1   Analytic Hierarchy Process

The AHP is a structured technique and helps in tackling decisions that may be complex. The main feature is that rather than prescribing a "correct" decision, the AHP helps in determining one. This rather subtle difference in definition comes from the fact that AHP provides weights of the compared items as a result rather than a definite answer of one item in the group of compared items. Based on mathematics and psychology [11] it has been extensively studied and refined. The AHP provides a comprehensive and rational framework for structuring a problem, for representing and quantifying its elements, for relating those elements to overall goals, and for evaluating alternative solutions. Users of the AHP first decompose their decision problem into a hierarchy of more easily comprehended sub-problems, each of which can be analysed independently.

There are three main levels of hierarchy in the AHP: the overall goal on the top, the available alternatives at the bottom, and the criteria/subcriteria in the middle. The middle part containing the (sub)criteria can span over an arbitrary depth of levels of hierarchy itself. In this work the Goodness is the goal, the cross-layer WSN MAC protocols are the alternatives, and the protocol performances and the available sensors are the criteria and subcriteria, respectively. The AHP hierarchy used in this paper is presented in Fig. 1. The connecting lines in the figure illustrate the dependency of boxes to other ones. The Fig. 1 in fact illustrates the particular application space presented in Sections 3 and 4 of the paper.

The AHP consists of three successive tasks. First, a decision maker performs a linguistic pair-wise comparison of the available criteria. The scale ranges from "extremely less important" (s_{-8}) to "extremely more important" (s_8) using 17 labels with the monotonically increasing label set defined as $S^{AHP} = \{s_{-8}, s_{-7}, \ldots, s_0, \ldots, s_7, s_8\}$. Second, a numerical pair-wise comparison is achieved by selecting a certain numerical scale to quantify the steps. Examples of existing numerical scales are the Saaty scale, where $s_{-8} = 1/9$ and $s_8 = 9$, and the geometrical scale, where s is an exponent in a function. In all scales $s_0 \triangleq 1$. Let us denote $s = s_\alpha \in S^{AHP}$ and $I(s) = \alpha$. Let $D = (d_{ij})_{n \times n}$ be a linguistic pair-wise comparison matrix. If $d_{ij} = s_\alpha$, then $I(d_{ij}) = \alpha$. If $f : S^{AHP} \to R^+$ is a monotonically increasing function, then it is a scale function given $f(s_\alpha) \times f(s_{-\alpha}) = 1$. Then the Saaty scale and the geometrical scale can be presented as

$$f(s) = \begin{cases} I(s) + 1 & \text{if } s \geq s_0, \\ 1/(1 - I(s)) & \text{if } s < s_0 \end{cases} \tag{1}$$

$$f(s) = \left(\sqrt{c}\right)^{I(s)}, \tag{2}$$

respectively, where $c > 1$ is the geometrical scale parameter [15].

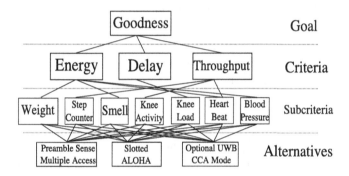

Fig. 1. AHP hierarchy with the considered metrics, the sensors available, and the protocol alternatives of Section 4

Third, a priority vector is derived from the numerical pair-wise comparisons. The two most common prioritisation methods are eigenvalue method and logarithmic least squares method [15]. In this paper the former is used (originally proposed by Saaty), where the principal eigenvector of the numerical pair-wise comparison matrix $A = (a_{ij})_{n \times n}, a_{ij} = f(d_{ij}), i, j \in [1, n]$ is the desired priority vector w. The w can be obtained by solving the linear system

$$Aw = \lambda w, \qquad e^T w = 1, \tag{3}$$

where λ is the eigenvalue of matrix A [15]. Solving the linear system of Eq. (3) provides a matrix of eigenvectors and a diagonal matrix of eigenvalues, where the largest real eigenvalue corresponds to the principal eigenvalue. The principal eigenvector is then the column corresponding to the column of the principal eigenvalue. The w is then normalised by the sum of its elements so that the normalised sum equals to 1.

2.2   Single Compound Metric

The individual metrics used in this paper, namely transmission energy consumption (E_{TX}), throughput (S_t), and delay (D_t) follow the methodology described by the authors in [16], [17] and are not repeated here due to limited space. Furthermore, the individual metrics are not the main focus of the paper. From these metrics an SCM, termed Goodness (G_{ood}), is produced. Inspired by the similarity measure in [10], we propose the Goodness to be defined by

$$G_{ood} = W_e E_{TX}^{norm} + W_S S_t^{norm} + W_d D_t^{norm}, \tag{4}$$

where W_e, W_S, and W_d present the weights of energy, throughput, and delay, respectively and the superscript *norm* indicates "normalised" metric. In Eq. (4) the weights $W_x \in [0,1], x \in \{e, S, d\}$ are normalised so that $\sum W_x = 1$. The weights can be obtained by constructing A with Eq. (1), solving the linear system of Eq. (3), finding its principal eigenvector, and normalising it by the sum of its elements. The normalised elements of the principal eigenvector are now the corresponding weights of each S&A of the application. When each S&A is related to it main metric the sum of their weights with respect to a metric is equal to the weight of the metric. There are two ways of producing the G_{ood}: fractional Goodness (G_{ood}^{frac}) and absolute Goodness (G_{ood}^{abs}).

Fractional Goodness. For the G_{ood}^{frac} the alternatives, i.e. protocols are compared against one another. There is a complication in which a vastly superior or inferior performance of a protocol with any metric could imbalance the weighting set on it. This would cause a bias in the evaluation. As an example of this bias let us consider the following. Two protocols are compared by Eq. (4). A metric, say D_t^{norm} would be now defined as $D_t^{norm} = D_t^{ref}/D_t^{eval}$, where D_t^{ref} and D_t^{eval} are the delays of the reference protocol and of the evaluated protocol, respectively. If D_t^{ref} would be 20 times greater than D_t^{eval} then even with weight $W_d = 0.06$ the Goodness of protocol *eval* would always be greater than protocol *ref* regardless of the 94 % emphasis on other metrics.

To mitigate the bias effect the protocol performances must go through another AHP process at every evaluation point, the normalised offered traffic to the channel (G) in this paper. As an innovation the linguistic (subjective) evaluation is replaced by a qualitative evaluation using the formulas $d_{ij}^E = \frac{E_{TX}^{ref}}{E_{TX}^{eval}}$, $d_{ij}^S = \frac{S_t^{eval}}{S_t^{ref}}$, and $d_{ij}^D = \frac{D_t^{ref}}{D_t^{eval}}$, where $ref = i$ and $eval = j$ in the linguistic pair-wise comparison matrix, D. The superscripts *ref* and *eval* relate to the reference protocol and to the evaluated protocol, respectively. In the second AHP process the numerical scale of Eq. (1) is replaced by the geometric scale of Eq. (2). In addition we perform the mapping

$$a_{ij} = \begin{cases} (\sqrt{c})^{-8} & \text{if } d_{ij} \leq (\sqrt{c})^{-8}, \\ (\sqrt{c})^{8} & \text{if } d_{ij} \geq (\sqrt{c})^{8}, \\ (\sqrt{c})^{I(s)}, & \text{otherwise,} \end{cases} \tag{5}$$

for each d_{ij}^E, d_{ij}^S, and d_{ij}^D where $I(s) = \lfloor \frac{2 \log d_{ij}}{\log c} \rfloor$ if $d_{ij} \geq 1$ and $I(s) = \lceil \frac{2 \log d_{ij}}{\log c} \rceil$ if $d_{ij} < 1$. The scaling factor $c = 1.3$ is used here as it is both reasonable, according to [15], and has sufficient granularity to take into account the relatively small differences in performance. The numerical pair-wise comparison matrices can now be solved by Eq. (3) and the normalised elements of the principal eigenvectors are the corresponding E_{TX}^{norm}, S_t^{norm}, and D_t^{norm} of each of the compared protocols. As a result, the G_{ood} of Eq. (4) is achieved per protocol (G_{ood}^{PSMA}, G_{ood}^{OCM}, and G_{ood}^{SA}) and the E_{TX}^{norm}, S_t^{norm}, and D_t^{norm} represent the fractional weights of the protocols in the metric at a given traffic point so that the $\sum E_{TX}^{norm}$, $\sum S_t^{norm}$, $\sum D_t^{norm}$, and $\sum G_{ood} = 1$ at any traffic point. In the above PSMA, OCM, and SA refer to the WSN MAC protocol alternatives, namely preamble sense multiple access, optional UWB CCA mode, and slotted ALOHA, respectively.

An important observation is that as long as the initial (subjective) linguistic pair-wise comparison holds for the sensor application, the AHP process fully reflects the design criteria for the best protocol, i.e. the weights of the metrics. The value of c affects the results obtained by the geometric scaling and therefore it must be chosen with care. Otherwise, the second AHP process is a fully qualitative process and it depends only on the performances of the compared protocols.

Absolute Goodness. The benefit of G_{ood}^{abs} is that in addition to providing the preference of one protocol solution over another it gives an estimate of the protocols' optimality in the considered scenario. The main drawback of G_{ood}^{abs} is that in order to derive this information an optimal scheme has to be also formulated. The optimal protocol resembles an ideal protocol, but takes into account the constraints produced by the used technology and protocol overhead. As demonstrated later in the paper, deriving the optimal protocol may not be trivial. As a general rule the optimal protocol is modelled by a two-node system using the same physical layer technology and protocol frame formats as the evaluated protocols. A two-node ALOHA system with infinite buffer is in many cases a good starting point for defining the optimal protocol, but the technology may dictate otherwise. Since the optimal (opt) protocol always outperforms the evaluated protocol Eq. (4) can be redefined as

$$G_{ood}^{abs} = W_e \frac{E_{TX}^{opt}}{E_{TX}^{eval}} + W_s \frac{S_t^{eval}}{S_t^{opt}} + W_d \frac{D_t^{opt}}{D_t^{eval}}. \tag{6}$$

The evaluation of the weights for the metrics has been described earlier in the paper. The validity of Eq. (6) can be argued by remembering that $\sum W_x = 1$ and $\frac{E_{TX}^{opt}}{E_{TX}^{eval}}, \frac{S_t^{eval}}{S_t^{opt}}, \frac{D_t^{opt}}{D_t^{eval}} \in [0, 1]$. Therefore, Goodness is always bound in $[0, 1]$ and the individual metrics contribute to it based on the weight assigned on them. The estimate of the evaluated protocols optimality can be perceived from how close to unity, i.e. 1, the G_{ood}^{abs} stays with varying offered traffic loads.

3   Application: Alice in Fitness Centre

The application scenario is taken from the EU FP7 SENSEI project and the scenario is described in detail in [18]. In the scenario, Alice visits a fitness centre in a shopping mall. She is equipped with a body sensor network (BSN) hosting a number of S&A.

Table 1. Numerical pair-wise comparison of S&A

Subcriteria	1°	2°	3°	4°	5°	6°	7°
1° Weight	1	1/3	9	1/3	1/3	1/5	1/5
2° Step Counter	3	1	9	1	1	1/3	1/3
3° Smell	1/9	1/9	1	1/9	1/9	1/9	1/9
4° Knee Activity	3	1	9	1	1	1/3	1/3
5° Knee Load	3	1	9	1	1	1/3	1/3
6° Heart Beat	5	3	9	3	3	1	1
7° Blood Pressure	5	3	9	3	3	1	1

Table 2. S&A main metrics

	1°	2°	3°	4°	5°	6°	7°
Metric	E_{TX}	S_t	E_{TX}	S_t	D_t	$50\% E_{TX}, 50\% S_t$	E_{TX}

During her exercise her BSN is complemented by sensors from the fitness centre and in total the following sensors are used: weight (1°), step counter (2°), smell (3°), knee activity (4°), heart beat (6°), and blood pressure (7°). She also wears a knee load actuator (5°), which purpose is to monitor and actuate the gym equipment state should the stress in her knee exceed a given threshold. Fig. 1 illustrates the hierarchy of sensors, metrics, protocols, and the goal in the application scenario.

Her personal assistant (e.g., PDA or mobile phone) collects the information from the S&A and issues the fitness program. According to the user preferences and quality of service requirements a numerical pair-wise comparison for the S&A is presented in Table 1, where the elements correspond to the elements of A using the Saaty scale of Eq. (1). Table 1 can be also perceived as the numerical pair-wise comparison matrix. It is based on the subjective matrix, D, which must be formulated with care. For the purposes of this paper, Table 1 has been derived with the help of an expert in social sciences, who is also responsible for the development of the scenario in question. The table can be read as follows. A (sub)criteria is always equally important (s_0) to itself, hence the diagonal of Table 1 is all ones. The weight sensor is "moderately less important" (s_{-2}) than step counter sensor in the scenario and hence from Eq. (1): $a_{12} = 1/3$, etc.

Next, the S&A are mapped to the metrics available and they can be found from Table 2. The normalised w ($\tilde{w}(x^o)$), $x \in [1, 7]$ from Table 1 are mapped with Table 2 metrics to produce

$$W_e = \tilde{w}(1^o) + \tilde{w}(3^o) + 0.5\tilde{w}(6^o) + \tilde{w}(7^o), \tag{7}$$

$$W_S = \tilde{w}(2^o) + \tilde{w}(4^o) + 0.5\tilde{w}(6^o), \text{ and} \tag{8}$$

$$W_d = \tilde{w}(5^o). \tag{9}$$

4   MAC Protocol Alternatives

The considered MAC protocols in the scenario operate on top of an impulse radio-ultra wideband (IR-UWB) transceiver as defined by the IEEE 802.15.4a standard. The

GADGET toolbox enables the identification of the most suitable one for the considered application. The authors have provided a detailed description and analysis of the technology and the protocols in [19], [20]. Because derivation of the performance metrics is non-central for this paper and due to limited space the analysis is not repeated here. In fact, the GADGET analysis is not dependent on any particular analysis or simulation method. The MAC protocols are slotted ALOHA (SA), optional ultra wideband clear channel assessment mode (OCM), and preamble sense multiple access (PSMA). The SA functions similarly to its narrowband versions, whereas the OCM multiplexes preamble symbols in the data transmission to enable the detection of IR-UWB transmissions at any time. As with OCM, the PSMA protocol performs a clear channel assessment (CCA) prior to data transmission by performing non-coherent energy collection evaluation.

With probability of detection (P_d) the energy collection technique is able to detect a preamble sequence transmission and determine the channel busy. With probability of false alarm (P_{fa}), the CCA detects the channel busy even if it is idle. These non-trivial probabilities are special characteristics of the IR-UWB environment and significantly affect the protocol performances. Hence they must be made explicit and are defined as

$$P_{fa} = Q\left(\frac{\xi}{\sqrt{4qL_s\sigma_0^4}}\right), \quad P_d = Q\left(\frac{\xi - L_sE_{sb}}{\sqrt{4qL_s\sigma_0^4 + 4\sigma_0^2E_{sb}}}\right), \tag{10}$$

where ξ is the threshold of energy on the channel for deciding the presence of a symbol, q is the time-bandwidth product, L_s is the number of symbols in the preamble, σ_0^2 is the noise variance, and E_{sb} is the energy of the received signal symbol [20]. As only the preamble sequences can be detected using IR-UWB technology, the PSMA protocol must wait after CCA until the next backoff slot before it can transmit. As a consequence The data exchange can last for two backoff slots. The OCM protocol on the other hand enables CCA and data transmission at any time, but with added price in overhead.

Figs. 2, 3, and 4 illustrate the performances of the protocols for average, normalised throughput, transmission delay, and transmission energy consumption. The delay and energy analysis model has been presented in [17] and modelled for IR-UWB environment in [20]. The throughput analysis uses the Poisson process, and the well known $S \triangleq \frac{U}{B+I}$, where U, B, and I represent the useful, the busy, and the idle periods, respectively. In addition, in the analysis Eq. (10) as well as the binary exponential backoff have been taken into account. The purpose of presenting the performance figures in here is to illustrate the difficulty of choosing which protocol would function the best with a given application scenario. The curves in the figures present the performances in very good and very severe non-line of sight (NLOS) channel conditions. In addition, the PSMA throughput, delay, and energy consumption is validated by simulations using OPNET. For the analysis, infinite population Poisson arrival process has been used. For the OPNET simulations a system of 80 nodes using single hop with [min/max/average] SNR of [22/37/28] dB has been used based on channel impulse realisations. The IEEE 802.15.4 super-frame order (SO) and beocon order (BO) are both set as 7. Both analysis and simulations consider a star topology and take into account P_d, P_{fa}, and binary exponential backoff (random uniform backoff for SA).

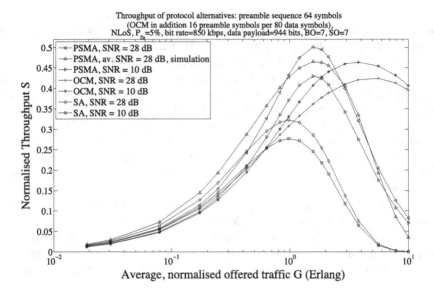

Fig. 2. The throughput of IEEE 802.15.4a compatible MAC protocols with respect to the average normalised offered traffic. The protocols are preamble sense multiple access (PSMA), optional UWB CCA mode (OCM), and slotted ALOHA (SA) with P_d, P_{fa}, and binary exponential backoff (no BEB for SA), indoor non-line of sight environment.

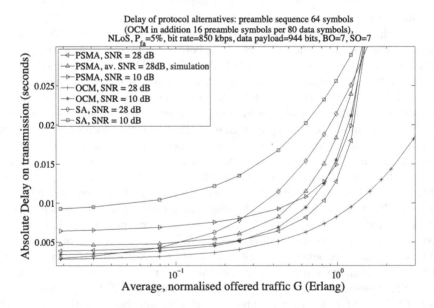

Fig. 3. The transmission delay of IEEE 802.15.4a compatible MAC protocols with respect to the average normalised offered traffic

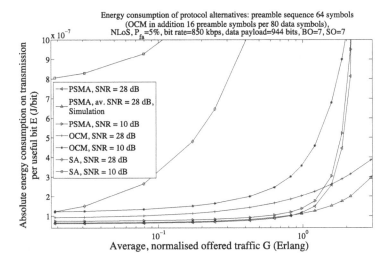

Fig. 4. The transmission energy consumption of IEEE 802.15.4a compatible MAC protocols with respect to the average normalised offered traffic

As can be seen from the Figs. 2, 3, and 4 it is not obvious, which protocol to use in the addressed fitness centre scenario. Moreover, with IR-UWB technology the formulation of the optimal MAC protocol for absolute Goodness is non-trivial, since e.g. a two-node ALOHA system does not always achieve the lowest delay. This is because an unslotted system would require a very long preamble sequence and the OCM would produce a lower delay because of that.

In the case of IEEE 802.15.4a IR-UWB technology an optimal MAC can be defined as follows. The the two-node system would be slotted with slot length equal to the preamble sequence. The slotting ensures coarse synchronisation which enables the usage of short preamble sequences. Since traffic is one directional all generated packets use the same queue and the delay becomes a function of the queue length, which ensures the shortest average queuing and zero contention delay. The energy consumption is only affected by the number of received beacons while queuing as well as the energy spent in the queuing process itself. Naturally, the P_d as well as the protocol overhead have an effect on all of the metrics. The authors recognise that the optimal MAC is quite artificial, but it produces no bias in the absolute Goodness and hence it can be used.

5   Results

With Section 4 metrics, we have all the required information for the GADGET toolbox. The G_{ood}^{frac} of the protocols is presented in Figs. 5 and 6. NLoS (CM2 from the IEEE 802.15.4a channel model) conditions with average received SNR of 28 dB and 10 dB are shown, respectively to illustrate the performances in good and severe channel environments. The higher the fraction of percentage of the protocol at given G, the more likely candidate the protocol is for the scenario. The traffic load offered by Alice's BSN

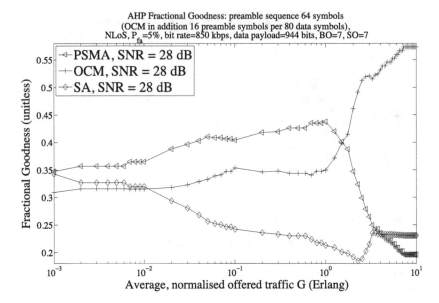

Fig. 5. The G_{ood}^{frac} of IEEE 802.15.4a compatible MAC protocols in the fitness centre scenario with respect to the average normalised offered traffic (PSMA, OCM, and SA) in non-line of sight (NLoS) environment, average SNR = 28 dB

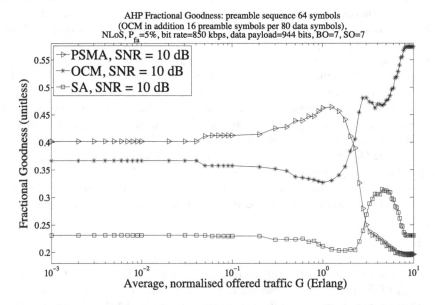

Fig. 6. The G_{ood}^{frac} of IEEE 802.15.4a compatible MAC protocols in the fitness centre scenario with respect to the average normalised offered traffic (PSMA, OCM, and SA) in non-line of sight (NLoS) environment, average SNR = 10 dB

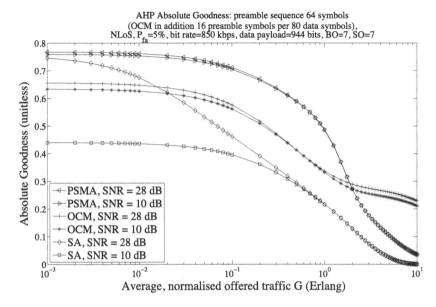

Fig. 7. The G_{ood}^{abs} of IEEE 802.15.4a compatible MAC protocols in the fitness centre scenario with respect to the average normalised offered traffic (PSMA, OCM, and SA) in non-line of sight (NLoS) environment

is less than 0.02 Erlang and Figs. 5 and 6 show that PSMA would be the most suitable protocol for the fitness centre application. The figures also show that the PSMA protocol would still be the best option in the scenario, if a single PAN coordinator would host 50 fitness applications ($G \sim 1$). The difference to OCM is however not so high and does not automatically warrant PSMA's use. This is especially true if Alice's BSN is to be used in other applications requiring very high average offered traffic rates. The fact that PSMA receives the highest fraction in both of the good and the severe channel conditions until the capacity of the channel is exceeded ($G > 1$) hints that the PSMA is quite robust to channel variation. Note that the sum of the fractions of each case at given G is 1.

The results of Eq. (6) are presented in Fig. 7. The figure verifies that both the PSMA and the OCM performances are not significantly affected by the channel conditions when compared to the optimal MAC. The SA however, is severely affected by the propagation environment and therefore cannot be justified for use in the fitness centre scenario where channel variation due to movement is frequent. The Fig. 7 also suggests that the PSMA is less than 25% from the "optimal" MAC with relatively low traffic rates. The OCM provides more stable performance, but suffers from the high protocol overhead produced by its multiplexed preamble symbols and a long CCA period due to the CCA at any time capability.

Since the average offered traffic to the channel produced by the sensors in the scenario is far less than the channel capacity ($G = 1$), 850 kbps, the PSMA protocol would be the most appropriate to use. Since all of the protocols are contention access-based their absolute goodness becomes poor at higher G due to their exponential energy and delay increase.

6 Conclusions

In this paper we have proposed a novel analytical toolbox, termed GADGET, for designing and evaluating MAC protocols with respect to WSN applications. The application is taken into account by the sensors and actuators used and their preference over one another based on user preferences and QoS requirements. Moreover, we have proposed a new single compound metric to help in the decision of the used MAC protocol and presented two methods, fractional and absolute, of deriving the single compound metric. The former enables fair comparison of multiple protocols at once, while the latter also presents a notion of optimality in a given scenario.

The validity of the analysis is dependent on the initial linguistic pair-wise comparison of the sensors; the pair-wise comparisons provide for the weights with which each evaluated performance metric contributes to the Goodness single compound metric. As long as these subjective comparisons reflect the application requirements, the Goodness will reflect the application requirements leading proper conclusions.

Acknowledgment

This paper describes work undertaken in the context of the SENSEI project, Integrating the Physical with the Digital World of the Network of the Future (www.sensei-project.eu). SENSEI is a Large Scale Collaborative Project supported by the European 7th Framework Programme, contract number: 215923. The authors would also like to thank Mr. Fabrice Forest from Université Pierre-Mendèz-France Sciences sociales & humaines for assistance in prioritising the sensors and actuators in the application scenario of the paper.

References

1. Wang, Z., Crowcroft, J.: Quality-of-service routing for supporting multimedia applications. IEEE Journal on Selected Areas in Communications 14(7), 1228–1234 (1996)
2. Waharte, S., Ishibashi, B., Boutaba, R., Meddour, D.: Performance study of wireless mesh networks routing metrics. In: IEEE/ACS International Conference on Computer Systems and Applications (AICCSA), pp. 1100–1106 (2008)
3. Wei, H., Ganguly, S., Izmailov, R., Haas, Z.: Interference-aware ieee 802.16 wimax mesh networks. In: IEEE 61st Vehicular Technology Conference, VTC 2005-Spring, vol. 5, pp. 3102–3106 (2005)
4. De Couto, D., Aguayo, D., Bicket, J., Morris, R.: A high-throughput path metric for multi-hop wireless routing. Wireless Networks 11(4), 419–434 (2005)
5. Koksal, C., Balakrishnan, H.: Quality-aware routing metrics for time-varying wireless mesh networks. IEEE Journal on Selected Areas in Communications 24(11) (November 2006)
6. Draves, R., Padhye, J., Zill, B.: Routing in multi-radio, multi-hop wireless mesh networks. In: 10th annual international conference on Mobile computing and networking, pp. 114–128 (2004)

 7. Jang, Y., Wang, J., Kravets, R.: Designing routing metrics for mesh networks. In: 1st IEEE workshop on wireless mesh networks, WiMesh (2005)
 8. Costa, L., Frida, S., Duarte, O.: Developing scalable protocols for three-metric qos routing. Journal of Computer Networks 39, 713–727 (2002)
 9. Khadivi, P., Samavi, S., Todd, T., Saidi, H.: Multi-constraint qos routing using a new single mixed metric. In: IEEE International Conference on Communications, June 2004, vol. 4, pp. 2042–2046 (2004)
10. Mazlack, L., Coppock, S.: Granulating data on non-scalar attribute values. In: IEEE international conference on Fuzzy Systems (FUZZ-IEEE 2002), May 2002, vol. 2, pp. 944–949 (2002)
11. Saaty, T.: The Analytic Hierarchy Process. McGraw-Hill, New York (1980)
12. Douligeris, C., Pereira, I.: A telecommunications quality study using the analytic hierarchy process. IEEE Journal on Selected Areas in Communications 12(2) (February 1994)
13. Alkahtani, A., Woodward, M., Al-Begain, K.: The analytic hierarchy process applied to best effort qos routing with multiple metrics. In: 5th European IEE Personal Mobile Communications Conference, April 2003, pp. 539–544 (2003)
14. Finan, J., Hurley, W.: Transitive calibration of the ahp verbal scale. European Journal of Operational Research, Theory and Methodology (112), 367–372 (1999)
15. Dong, Y., Xu, Y., Li, H., Dai, M.: A comparative study of the numerical scales and the prioritization methods in ahp. European Journal of Operational Research, Decision Support (128), 229–242 (2008)
16. Haapola, J., Shelby, Z., Pomalaza-Ráez, C., Mähönen, P.: Cross-layer Energy Analysis of Multi-hop Wireless Sensor Networks. In: Proc. of the 2nd European Workshop on Wireless Sensor Networks, pp. 33–44 (2005)
17. Haapola, J., Shelby, Z., Pomalaza-Ráez, C., Mähönen, P.: Multihop Medium Access Control for WSNs: An Energy Analysis Model. EURASIP Journal on Wireless Communications and Networking, Special Issue on Wireles Sensor Networks 2005, 523–540 (2005)
18. SENSEI: D1.1: Sensei scenario portfolio, user and context requirementssensei scenario portfolio, user and context requirements. Technical report, FP7 Contract: 215923 (2008)
19. Haapola, J., Goratti, L., Suliman, I., Rabbachin, A.: Preamble Sense Multiple Access (PSMA) for Impulse Radio UltraWideband Sensor Networks. In: Vassiliadis, S., Wong, S., Hämäläinen, T.D. (eds.) SAMOS 2006. LNCS, vol. 4017, pp. 155–166. Springer, Heidelberg (2006)
20. Haapola, J., Rabbachin, A., Goratti, L., Pomalaza-Ráez, C.: Effect of impulse radio-ultra wideband based on energy collection on mac protocol performance. IEEE Transactions on Vehicular Technology 58(9) (to appear, 2009)

A Diffusion Approximation Analysis of Multilevel Ad Hoc and Sensor Networks

Jerzy Martyna

Institute of Computer Science, Jagiellonian University,
ul. Lojasiewicza 6,
30-348 Cracow, Poland
martyna@softlab.ii.uj.edu.pl

Abstract. In this paper we considered the approximation of a queueing system model of wireless ad hoc and sensor networks. In our model
we admitted an arbitrary distribution for the duration of each M states
that describe the source. Following the Markov Modulated Rate Process
(MMRP) as a source model, we used it to introduce a diffusion approximation for the superposition of such aggregated traffic processes. We
showed that the diffusion approximation of the aggregated traffic from
the Markov modulated sources can illustrate the process of data harvest-
ing by the sensors in different states.

1 Introduction

Wireless ad hoc networks [4] have attracted attention of researchers in the recent
years. These networks are formed in situations where mobile computing devices
require networking applications while a fixed network infrastructure is not available or not preferred to be used. For these networks many basic mechanisms that
enable wireless ad hoc communication have been designed and standarized. To
the most popular examples belong, among others, IEEE 802.11 and Bluetooth
as communication standards.

In a manner similar to ad hoc networks, wireless sensor networks [1] are a particular type of ad hoc network, in which the nodes are 'smart sensors', that is
small devices equipped with advanced sensing functionalities (thermal, pressure,
and so on), a small processor, and a short-range wireless transceiver. These networks have been of the most prosperous research areas in recent years thanks to
its wide spectrum of potential applications, including environment monitoring,
home or industrial automation and control, inventory tracking, etc. Faced to
this trend, large amounts of research being done in the wireless sensor networks
are trying to provide analysis and design methods for better architectures and
protocols [5].

In many practical deployments, nodes in ad hoc and sensor networks can
be rearranged in a hierarchical network topology [11]. This way of introducing
a hierarchy is to identify a virtual *backbone network*. For instance, the first
layer of two-layer sensor network (see Fig. 1) represents all the nodes which are
responsible for the data transmission to the sink. It consists only of clusterhead.

P.M. Ruiz and J.J. Garcia-Luna-Aceves (Eds.): ADHOC-NOW 2009, LNCS 5793, pp. 126–137, 2009.

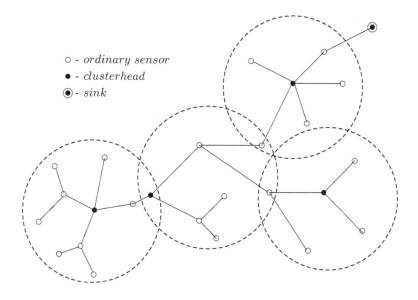

○ - *ordinary sensor*
● - *clusterhead*
◉ - *sink*

Fig. 1. An example of two-layer sensor network

nodes and nodes belonging to the backbone network. The secondary layer is composed of ordinary nodes which collect the information and send it to the clusterheads.

For performance evaluation of these networks a number of queueing networks are proposed. A finite queueing model was proposed in [15] for evaluating the packet blocking probability and MAC queueing delays. A model for a performance evaluation of the closed form expression for the average queueing delay over a single hop in IEEE 802.11 based on wireless networks was presented in [14]. A performance model of wireless networks with hidden nodes was given by Ray et al. [12]. In this model a maximum throughput and collision probability for an elementary four-node network were proposed. Nevertheless, none of these models allows the analysis of more complicated realistic networks in many different situations, such as transmission and data collection, etc.

In this paper, we propose a traffic model for wireless ad hoc and sensor networks which is based on the Markov Modulated Rate Process (MMRP) [3] as a source model. This approach is not restricted to the exponential distribution of interarrival times of packets. Additionally, the diffusion approximation analysis for these networks allows us to replace a discrete number of packets in the aggregated traffic with a continuous variable which, according to the central limit theorem, will be approximately normally distributed under heavy traffic conditions.

We recall that the diffusion approximation was originally introduced as a refinement of the Brownian motion (see W. Feller [2]). At first the application of the diffusion approximation to computer modeling was made by H. Kobayashi

[6], [7]. It was used in the paper [8] for the representation of the ALOHA system. The approximation and analysis of the buffer for the ATM multiplexer by means of the diffusion processes was given also by H. Kobayashi [9]. Studies on the diffusion approximation models of ATM multiplexer with variable input rate had been reported by K. Kobayashi and Y. Takahashi [10].

The rest of the paper is organized as follows. In section 2 we give the diffusion approximation of multilevel ad hoc and sensor networks. Section 3 presents the analysis of aggregated traffic processes. In section 4, we give some numerical results. Finally we present concluding remarks in section 5.

2   The Model Formulation

A multilevel structure in wireless ad hoc and sensor networks is composed of J clusters. In each cluster a dedicated node, the clusterhead, is responsible for aggregating the data of its members and transmits it to the sink node or to other nodes for further relaying. Each cluster has N^j, $j = 1, \ldots, J$, nodes. Let each node be governed by an M-state Markov chain $P = \{p_{lm}\}$; $l, m = 1, \ldots, M$. When a node is in state m, it generates packets at rate R_m [packets/second]. We assume that the duration of state m has a general distribution with the mean α^{-1} and the variance σ_m^2. When the source exists in state l, it moves to state m with probability p_{lm}. Figure 2 shows state transition diagram of a single source. A sample data stream from such source is given in Fig. 3.

Then, an M-dimensional process $\mathbf{n}^j(t)$ can be defined by

$$\mathbf{n}^j(t) = [n_1^j(t), n_2^j(t), \ldots, n_M^j(t)]^T, \quad j = 1, 2, \ldots, J \tag{1}$$

where $n_m^j(t)$ denotes the number of nodes in the state m, $m = 1, \ldots, M$, in

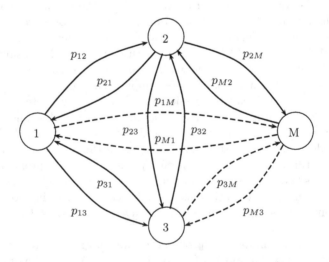

Fig. 2. The state transition diagram for a single source

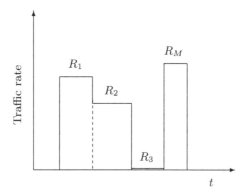

Fig. 3. A sample of packet generation process from a single source

where $n_m^j(t)$ denotes the number of nodes in the state m, $m = 1, \ldots, M$, in the cluster j at time t. Then, we have

$$\sum_{j=1}^{J} \sum_{m=1}^{M} n_m^j(t) = N \tag{2}$$

The traffic rate to the sink of data at time t can be defined as

$$R(t) = \sum_{j=1}^{J} \sum_{m=1}^{M} R_m^j n_m^j(t) \tag{3}$$

The transmission backbone link to the sink of wireless network has a constant capacity C [packets/second]. The change of the memory contents in the sink is given by

$$\frac{dQ(t)}{dt} = \begin{cases} R(t) - C, & \text{if } R(t) > C \text{ or } Q(t) > 0 \\ 0, & \text{otherwise} \end{cases} \tag{4}$$

We assume that a source in state m can be viewed as a packet serviced by one of the N parallel servers at "stations" m with the mean service time α_m^{-1}. Thus, the mean rate of departures of "station" is represented by $\alpha_m n_m$.

There are packet routes after the completion of "service" at "station" l to "station" m with probability p_{lm}^j, $m = 1, \ldots, M$. The arrival process at "station" m, $A_m^j(t)$, is the aggregation of those departures from the "station" which have route ends in "station" m.

Thus, we have

$$A_m^j(t) = \sum_{l=1}^{M} D_{l,m}^j(t), \quad D_m^j(t) = \sum_{i=1}^{M} D_{i,m}^j(t) \tag{5}$$

where $D_{i,m}^j(t)$ represents the counting process of packets which are sent from station l to station m.

Thus, we have an M-dimensional process

$$X^j(t) = [X_1^j(t), X_2^j(t), \ldots, X_M^j(t)]^T \tag{6}$$

which must be a continuous-state Markov process approximation of the discrete-level function $\mathbf{n}^j = [n_1^j(t), n_2^j(t), \ldots, n_M^j(t)]^T$, $j = 1, \ldots, J$. Process $\mathbf{X}^j(t)$ must satisfy the same constraint equation as Eq. (2), namely

$$\sum_{j=1}^{J} \sum_{m=1}^{M} X_m^j(t) = N \tag{7}$$

When $X_m^j(t) = x_m^j$, the mean departure rate can be defined as

$$u_m^{-1}(X_m^j) = \alpha_m^j x_m^j, \quad j = 1, 2, \ldots, J \tag{8}$$

The infinitesimal mean vector $\mathbf{b}(x^j)$ of the vector $\mathbf{X}^j(t)$ is given by

$$\mathbf{b}(X^j) = \begin{bmatrix} b_1(x_1^j) \\ b_2(x_2^j) \\ \vdots \\ b_M(x_M^j) \end{bmatrix} = \begin{bmatrix} -\alpha_1 & \alpha_2 p_{21} & \cdots & \alpha_M p_{M1} \\ \alpha_1 p_{12} & -\alpha_2 & \cdots & \alpha_M p_{M2} \\ \vdots & \vdots & \vdots & \vdots \\ \alpha_1 p_{1M} & \alpha_2 p_{2M} & \cdots & -\alpha_M p_{MM} \end{bmatrix} \begin{bmatrix} x_1^j \\ x_2^j \\ \vdots \\ x_M^j \end{bmatrix} = \beta \cdot \mathbf{x}^j \tag{9}$$

where $\beta = \{\beta_{mm'}\}_{M \times M}$.

Analogously, the infinitesimal covariance matrix $A(\mathbf{x}^j) = \{\alpha_{mm'}(\mathbf{x}^j)\}_{M \times M}$ can be given by

$$\alpha_{mm'}(\mathbf{x}^j) = \sum_{l=1}^{M} \{(c_l(x_l^j) - 1)/u_l(x_l^j)\} p_{lm} p_{lm'} + \{c_m(x_m^j)/u_m(x_m^j)$$

$$+ \sum_{l=1}^{M} (p_{lm}/u_l(x_l^j)\} \delta_{mm'} - (\frac{c_m(x_m^j)}{u_m(x_m^j)}) p_{mm'} - (\frac{c_{m'}(x_{m'}^j)}{u_{m'}(x_{m'}^j)}) p_{mm'} \tag{10}$$

We can see that in the Markov modulated source, we have $p_{m,m'} = 0$ for $m = 1, \ldots, M$. It means that the holding time in one state expires, when the source goes to another state. Then, we have the expression for $\mathcal{A}(x^j)$ as follows

$$\mathcal{A}(x^j) = \sum_{l=1}^{M} \frac{c_l(x_l^j)}{u_l(x_l^j)} \cdot v_l \cdot v_l^T + \mathcal{W}(x^j) \tag{11}$$

where v_l is an M-dimensional column vector whose l-th element is unity and the m-th element $(m \neq l)$ is $-p_{lm}$. We have the column vector v_l as follows

$$v_l = [-p_{l1}, -p_{l2}, \ldots, -p_{lM}]^T \tag{12}$$

Matrix $\mathcal{W}(x^j)$ is given by

$$w_{mm'}(x^j) = \sum_{l=1}^{M} [p_{lm}(\delta_{mm'} - p_{lm'})/u_l(x_l^j)] \tag{13}$$

for $m = 1, \ldots, M, \ m' = 1, \ldots, M$. We note that matrix $\mathcal{W}$ is a non-negative definite.

Now, we can formulate the M-dimensional diffusion process $X^j(t)$ with the help of the stochastic differential equation

$$dX^j(t) = \beta \cdot X^j(t)dt + \sqrt{A(x^j)} \cdot d\mathcal{W}(t), \quad j = 1, 2, \ldots, J \tag{14}$$

where $\mathcal{W}(t)$ is an M-dimensional motion with a zero mean and the covariance matrix function $I\delta(t)$. I is the $M \times M$ identity matrix and $\delta(t)$ is the impulse function.

3 Aggregation of Traffic Processes

Each source at state m can generate packets at constant rate R_m. We can define the aggregated traffic to the sink node at time t as follows

$$R(t) = \sum_{j=1}^{J} \sum_{m=1}^{M} R_m^j X_m^j(t) \tag{15}$$

We can assume that $R_M^j = 0$. It means that a source is always off at state M. Thus, we can only consider processes $X_1^j(t), \ldots, X_{M-1}^j(t)$.

We define $\mathbf{Z}(t) = Q \cdot \mathbf{X}^j(t)$, which implies $Z_1(t), Z_2(t), \ldots, Z_{M-1}(t)$ is orthogonal (hence independent) to Gaussian process. Hence, we obtain

$$
\begin{aligned}
R(t) &= \sum_{j=1}^{J} \sum_{m=1}^{M} R_m^j X_m^j(t) = [R_1^1, R_2^2, \ldots, R_{M-1}^J] \cdot X^j(t) \\
&= [R_1^1, \ldots, R_{M-1}^J] \cdot Q^T \mathbf{Z}(t) \\
&= \sum_{m=1}^{M-1} \sum_{j=1}^{J} R_m'^j Z_m^j(t)
\end{aligned}
\tag{16}
$$

where $R_m^j = \sum_{i=1}^{M-1} R_i^j Q_{mi}^j$. Then, we obtain $R(t)$ as a weighted summation of independent Gaussian processes, whose mean and variance are given as follows

$$\lim_{t \to \infty} E[R(t)] = \sum_{j=1}^{J} \sum_{m=1}^{M-1} R_m^j x_m^\star \tag{17}$$

$$\lim_{t \to \infty} Var[R(t)] = \sum_{j=1}^{J} \sum_{m=1}^{M-1} \lambda_m^j R_m'^{j2} \tag{18}$$

We can define $A(t)$ - the arrival process of all packets obtained through the sink traffic of $R(t)$, namely

$$A(t) \overset{def}{=} \int_0^t R(t)dt = \sum_{j=1}^{J} \sum_{m=1}^{M-1} R_m^j \int_0^t X_m^j(t)dt \tag{19}$$

Let $y^* = (x_1^*, \ldots, x_{m-1}^*)$ be the equilibrium state of process $\mathbf{X}(t)$ such that $\mathbf{b}(x^*) = 0$ and $\mathbf{Y}(t) = [X_1(t), \ldots, X_{M-1}(t)]^T$. Then, $\mathbf{Y}(t)$ satisfies the stochastic differential equation, namely

$$d\mathbf{Y}(t) = \mathcal{B}_1(\mathbf{Y}(t) - \mathbf{y}^*)dt + \sqrt{\mathcal{A}_1}d\mathbf{W}(t) \tag{20}$$

which is a multi-variate Ornstein-Uhlenbeck equation [13].

For a sufficiently large t we obtain the mean and variance of $\int_0^t \mathbf{Y}(t)dt$, namely

$$E[\int_0^t \mathbf{Y}(t)dt] \approx \mathbf{y}^* t + o(t) \tag{21}$$

$$Var[\int_0^t \mathbf{Y}(t)dt] \approx \mathcal{B}_1^{-1}\mathcal{A}_1(\mathcal{B}_1^{-1})^T t + o(t) \tag{22}$$

which implies

$$\lim_{t \to \infty} \frac{E[(A(t)]}{t} \sim \sum_{j=1}^{J} \sum_{m=1}^{M-1} R_m^{jl} x_m^* \tag{23}$$

$$\lim_{t \to \infty} \frac{Var[A(t)]}{t} \sim \sum_{j=1}^{J} \mathcal{R}^j \mathcal{B}_1^{-1} \mathcal{A}_1(\mathcal{B}_1^{-1})^T \tag{24}$$

where $R^j \stackrel{def}{=} [R_1^j, R_2^j, \ldots, R_{M-1}^j]$.

4   A Diffusion Approximation Model for Packet Queue Process

In this section, we derive the steady-state distribution of the diffusion process packet queue process $q(t)$.

In order to discuss the boundary condition and the stationary distribution we approximate the accumulated arrival process $A(t)$ by a diffusion process. The diffusion approximation handles the original process through its first and second order moments in equilibrium, which are given by Eqs. (23) and (24), namely

$$dA(t) = b \cdot dt + \sqrt{a} \cdot dW(t) \tag{25}$$

where $W(t)$ is a standard Wiener process. The coefficient of drift b and the coefficient of diffusion a are given by

$$b = \sum_{j=1}^{J} \sum_{m=1}^{M-1} R_m x_m^* \tag{26}$$

$$a = \sum_{j=1}^{J} \mathcal{R} \mathcal{B}_1^{-1} \mathcal{A}_1 (\mathcal{B}_1^{-1})^T \mathcal{R}^T \tag{27}$$

Thus, from the Eq. (4) the output process $c(t)$ can be approximated by

$$dc(t) = \begin{cases} Cdt, \text{if } Q(t) > 0 \text{ or } R(t) > C, \\ \eta dt, \text{ otherwise} \end{cases} \quad (28)$$

where η is an unknown constant and may be approximated by $E[R \mid R < C]$. Thus, the diffusion process $q(t)$ can satisfies the following stochastic differential equation

$$dq(t) = dA(t) - dc(t) = \begin{cases} (b - C)dt + \sqrt{a}dW(t), & q(t) > 0 \\ (b - \eta)dt + \sqrt{a}dW(t), & q(t) \leq 0. \end{cases} \quad (29)$$

The parameter η can be obtained as

$$\eta = \int_{-\infty}^{C} \frac{r}{\sqrt{2\pi}\sigma_R} exp[-\frac{(r-a)^2}{2\sigma_R^2}]dr / \int_{-\infty}^{C} \frac{1}{\sqrt{2\pi}\sigma_R} exp[-\frac{(r-a)^2}{2\sigma_R}]dr$$
$$\frac{b\Phi(\theta) - \sigma_R\phi(\theta)}{\Phi(\theta)} \quad (30)$$

where $\phi(x) = (1/\sqrt{2\pi})exp[-x^2/2]$, $\Phi(x) = \int_{-\infty}^{x} \phi(u)du$ and $\theta = (C - b)/\sigma_R$.

At $t = 0$ the stationary probability $Prob[q > x]$ is approximated as $Prob[Q > x]$ for $x > 0$ as the Ornstein-Uhlenbeck process [13], namely

$$P[Q > x] \approx B_S exp[-2\frac{C-b}{a}x],$$

where

$$B_S = \frac{e^{-\theta^2}}{\theta\sqrt{2\pi}}, \quad \theta = \frac{C-b}{\sigma_R} \quad (31)$$

H. Kobayashi and Q. Ren [9] also proposed an approximation formula for the model with multiple types of input traffic, namely

$$P[Q > x] \approx B_K exp[-2\frac{C-b}{a}x]$$

where

$$B_K = \frac{1}{\theta^\star\sqrt{2\pi}\sigma_R^2}e^{-\sigma_R^2\theta^{\star 2}/2} = \frac{\phi(\theta)}{\theta}, \quad \theta^\star = \frac{C-b}{\sigma_R^2} \quad (32)$$

By changing the above equation, we obtain

$$B_K = \frac{1}{\theta\sqrt{2\pi}}exp[-\frac{\theta^2}{2}] = \frac{\phi(\theta)}{\theta}, \quad \theta = \frac{C-b}{\sigma_R} \quad (33)$$

5 Numerical Examples

In this section, we give some experimental results to illustrate and verify our model.

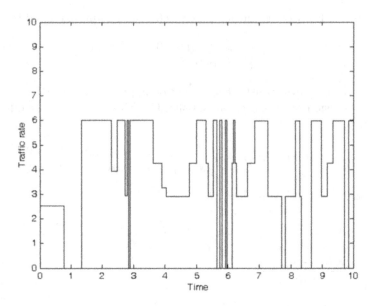

Fig. 4. The traffic process from a single 4-state Markov modulated source for given parameters

We have used 120 independent four-state Markov modulated sources grouped in six clusters. Each source in state m generates packets at rate R_m with the means as follows:

$$\mathbf{P} = \{p_{lm}\}_{4\times4} = \begin{bmatrix} 0 & 3/10 & 1/2 & 1/5 \\ 2/5 & 0 & 2/5 & 1/5 \\ 1/3 & 1/6 & 0 & 1/2 \\ 1/2 & 1/2 & 0 & 0 \end{bmatrix}$$

Let $R_1 = 2.5$, $R_2 = 1.5$, $R_3 = 3.4$, $R_4 = 0$, $\alpha_1 = 1.0$, $\alpha_2 = 0.5$, $\alpha_3 = 1.5$, $\alpha_4 = 2.0$. We assumed that that the burst periods are exponentially distributed with means α_1^{-1}, α_2^{-1}, α_3^{-1}, α_4^{-1}, respectively.

In Fig. 4 we plot a typical packet generation process from a single source as was defined above. The superposition of all traffic streams from all nodes are given in Fig. 5. Figure 6 plots a simulated sample path of the diffusion approximation, with approximates the aggregated traffic stream given in Fig. 5.

Figures 7 gives the probabilities of the buffer overflow of all nodes from simulation and by using diffusion approximation, respectively. In the computation it was assumed that the backbone capacity is equal to 25 [packets/second].

6   Conclusions

In this paper, we have developed a new diffusion approximation for multilevel ad hoc and sensor networks. In our analysis we have treated the traffic stream

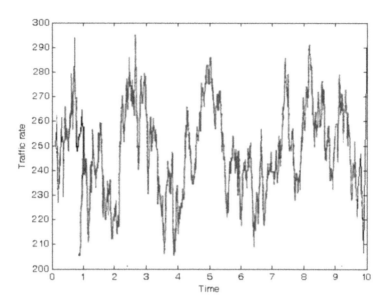

Fig. 5. The aggregated traffic process from all all Markov modulated sources for given parameters

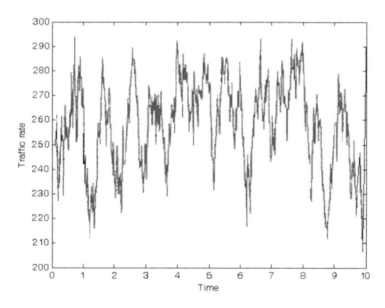

Fig. 6. The diffusion process, which approximates the aggregated traffic process

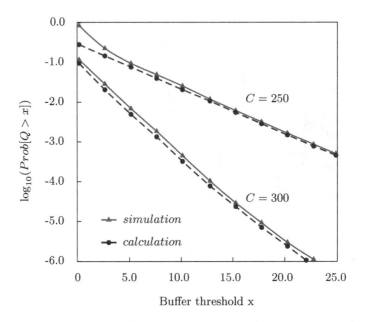

Fig. 7. Simulation results of sink buffer overflow probabilities from the MMRP sources for network with backbone link capacity equal to $C = 250$, $C = 300$ [*packets/second*], respectively

from individual nodes as Markov modulated rate processes. Each of so defined sources has a finite number of states which are described by a discrete Markov chain. Thus, the packets are generated by a source at the constant rate determined by that Markovian state. We used a diffusion approximation for the superposition of such Markov modulated rate processes. This approach is not restricted to the cases with the exponential distribution of the time durations of each state. With the help of the diffusion approximation we aggregated all thus traffic streams defined. Furthermore, the approximation formula provides us with a useful method and estimate the congestion in the buffer of the sink in ad hoc and sensor networks.

It is obvious that this model can be treated for each traffic separately. Thus, a single type of traffic, for instance from a defined cluster or nodes or so-called sleeping nodes, can be viewed individually without the loss of generality.

References

1. Akyildiz, I.F., Su, W., Sankasubramaniam, Y., Cayirci, E.: Wireless Sensor Networks: A Survey. Computer Networks 38, 393–422 (2002)
2. Feller, W.: An Introduction to Probability Theory and Its Applications, vol. II. John Wiley and Sons, Chichester (1966)

3. Heffes, H., Lucatoni, D.M.: A Markov Modulated Characterization of Packetized Voice and Data Traffic and Related Statistical Multiplexer Performance. IEEE J. on Select. Areas in Comm. 4(6), 856–868 (1986)
4. Hekmat, R.: Ad-Hoc Networks: Fundamental Properties and Network Topologies. Springer, Heidelberg (2006)
5. Karl, H., Willig, A.: Protocols and Architectures for Wireless Sensor Networks. John Wiley and Sons, Chichester (2005)
6. Kobayashi, H.: Application of the Diffusion Approximation to Queueing Networks I: Equilibrium Queue Distributions. J. of the ACM 21(2), 316–328 (1974)
7. Kobayashi, H.: Application of the Diffusion Approximation to Queueing Networks II: Nonequilibrium Distributions and Applications to Computer Modeling. J. of the ACM 21(3), 459–469 (1974)
8. Kobayashi, H., Onozato, Y., Huynh, D.: An Approximation Method for Design and Analysis of an ALOHA System. IEEE Trans. on Commun. 25(1), 148–157 (1977)
9. Kobayashi, H.: Steady State Approximation Analysis for ATM Multiplexer by Diffusion Process Without Reflection Barrier. In: Proc. the Symp. on Performance Models for Information Communications Networks, pp. 309–320 (1994)
10. Kobayashi, K., Takahashi, Y.: Steady-State Analysis of ATM Multiplexer with Variable Input Rate Through Diffusion Approximation. Performance Evaluation 23, 163–184 (1995)
11. Kochhal, M., Schwiebert, L., Gupta, S.: Role-Based Hierarchical Self-Organization for Wireless Ad Hoc Sensor Networks. In: Proc. of the 2nd ACM Int. Workshop on Wireless Sensor Networks and Applications (WSNA), San Diego, CA, pp. 98–107 (2003)
12. Ray, S., Starobinski, D., Carruthers, J.B.: Performance of Wireless Networks Networks with Hidden Nodes: A Queueing-theoretic Analysis. Computer Communications 28(10), 1179–1192 (2005)
13. Simonian, A.: Stationary Analysis of a Fluid Queue with Input Rate Varying as an Ornstein-Uhlenbeck Process. SIAM, J. Appl. Math. 51(3), 828–842 (1991)
14. Tickoo, O., Sikdar, B.: A Queueing Model for Finite Load IEEE 802.11 Random Access MAC. In: Proc. of IEEE ICC, Paris, pp. 175–179 (2004)
15. Zeng, G., Zhu, H., Chlamtac, I.: A Novel Queueing Model for 802.11 Wireless LANs. In: Proc. of WNCG Wireless Networking Symposium (2003)

Localized Sensor Self-deployment with Coverage Guarantee in Complex Environment

Xu Li, Nathalie Mitton, Isabelle Ryl, and David Simplot

CNRS/INRIA/Univ. of Lille 1, France
{firstname.lastname}@inria.fr

Abstract. In focused coverage problem, sensors are required to be deployed around a given point of interest (POI) with respect to a priority requirement: an area close to POI has higher priority to be covered than a distant one. A localized sensor self-deployment algorithm, named Greedy-Rotation-Greedy (GRG) [9], has recently been proposed for constructing optimal focused coverage. The previous work assumed obstacle-free environment and focused on theoretical aspects. In this paper, we remove this strong assumption and extend GRG to practical settings. We equip with a novel obstacle "penetration" technique and give it the important obstacle avoidance capability. The new version of GRG is referred to as GRG/OP. Through simulation, we evaluate its performance in comparison with plain GRG.

1 Introduction

Recently, a new sensor self-deployment problem, *focused coverage formation* [9], was brought into attention for dedicated applications. In this problem, mobile sensors are required to surround a given coverage focus, called *point of interest* (POI), while satisfying a priority requirement: an area close to POI is covered with higher priority than a distant one. Focused coverage is measured by *coverage radius*, which is defined as the minimum distance from POI to uncovered areas. Optimal focused coverage has maximized radius. Assuming an obstacle-free environment, a localized algorithm Greedy-Rotation-Greedy (GRG) was presented and analyzed in [9]. It is proven that GRG generates optimal hexagonal focused coverage. Under the same set of assumptions, GRG is optimized to produce optimal circular focused coverage in [10].

In this paper, we extend GRG to a realistic obstacle-prone environment. Inspired by the physical behavior of liquid in a U-tube, we equip GRG with a novel obstacle "penetration" technique without jeopardizing its correctness and localized nature. The resultant version of GRG is referred to as GRG/OP (GRG with Obstacle Penetration). In GRG/OP, sensors around an obstacle simulate a liquid body in a virtual U-tube. They autonomously "flow" to ensure balanced pressure at the tube bottom, *i.e.*, that the top sensors in the two tube arms are at the same deployment layer. A number of rules are designed to handle collision caused by nodal flowing behavior. By GRG/OP, sensors are able to pass around obstacles during self-deployment such that coverage optimality is preserved.

P.M. Ruiz and J.J. Garcia-Luna-Aceves (Eds.): ADHOC-NOW 2009, LNCS 5793, pp. 138–151, 2009.

The remainder of this paper is organized as follows: Section 2 reviews previous related work; Section 3 briefly describes GRG; Sections 4 and 5 present the localized obstacle penetration technique and its implementation; Section 6 evaluates GRG/OP through simulation; Section 7 concludes the paper.

2   Related Work

Previous sensor self-deployment algorithms except GRG [9] were designed for area coverage over a region of interest (ROI) without particular coverage focus. When used for focused coverage formation, they may cause sensors to settle in an arbitrary area in the deployment plan, leading to a coverage radius as bad as 0. In this section, we review some of these relevant work at very short length. An extensive survey can be found in [11].

In [7], sensors are placed in ROI incrementally, *i.e.*, one at a time, to increase coverage based on information gathered from previously deployed sensors. In [4,6,12,8,17], each sensor node computes movement vectors due to its neighbors using their relative position and move according to the vector summation in rounds to maximize coverage. In [5,14], sensors align their sensing ranges with their Voronoi regions in rounds to minimize local uncovered area. In [2], sensors are pushed or pulled to hexagon centers of a hexagonal tiling over ROI. In [3], sensor deployment is modeled as a minimum cost maximum flow problem from source regions to hole regions in ROI. In [13], ROI is partitioned into a grid whose vertices are assigned recursively to sensors using a rooted spanning tree. In [15], the network is assumed dense enough, and sensors are treated as load and balanced among the sub-regions of ROI by multiple rounds of scan.

3   Greedy-Rotation-Greedy in a Nutshell

GRG [9] assumes that there is no physical obstacle in the deployment plane, and requires sensors to know their own locations and the location of POI. Sensors have the same sensing radius r_s and communication radius $r_c \geq \sqrt{3}r_s$. By lower-layer protocols, they have necessary information such as location and movement status of 1-hop neighbors for making protocol decisions. A virtual equilateral triangle tessellation (TT) G_{TT} of edge length $l_e = \sqrt{3}r_s$ is built in the plane with POI as vertex (see Fig. 2). G_{TT} is locally computable to each sensor given a common orientation. Vertices with equal graph distance i to POI form a distance-i hexagon $\mathcal{H}_i$ centered at POI.

GRG translates area coverage problem to vertex coverage problem on G_{TT}. Each sensor first by an alignment rule moves to the closet TT vertex and then acts in the following way: greedily proceed from vertex to vertex toward POI; when blocked, *i.e.*, when greedy next hop is occupied by others, rotate around POI counterclockwise along its residence hexagon to a vertex where greedy advance can resume; if both greedy advance and rotation are blocked, stay put. Greedy advance rules and rotation rules are carefully designed to guarantee progress and termination.

GRG has two variants: GRG-CW and GRG-CV. The former allows Greedy-and-Rotation (G-R) collision and solves it after, while the latter prevents this particular type of node collision by using additional collision avoidance rules. However, notice that GRG (even the -CV version) is not collision free in general, due to initial stochastic node distribution. To solve node collision and ensure coverage maximization, GRG employs a retreat rule, which allows only one node to stay by pushing the others onto the next outer hexagon after a node collision.

GRG does not require fixed network size and allows dynamic node addition and removal. It works regardless of movement asynchrony, network asynchrony, and network disconnectivity. Using merely one-hop neighborhood information, it produces a connected network of TT layout without sensing hole and consequently a maximized area coverage according to [16]. It is the only known localized sensor self-deployment algorithm with such coverage guarantees. GRG yields optimal focused coverage of maximized radius.

4   An Obstacle "Penetration" Technique

In the following, we present a novel localized obstacle "penetration" technique for algorithm GRG. We assume that there is no concave obstacle in the plane. We make this assumption because a concave obstacle can entrap sensors into its pockets (opening against POI) and lead to a partitioned network.

4.1   Virtual U-Tube

A U-tube, as shown in Fig. 1, consists of three parts, *left arm*, *right arm*, and *bottom*. When it is filled with the same type of liquid, the liquid surface in its two arms always remains at the same level so that the pressure (due to gravity) from both sides settles at the bottom. This is simple physics. Our idea of obstacle "penetration" is inspired by this liquid behavior.

We treat POI as center of Gravitation and sensors as liquid molecules. Sensors are attracted to POI. Imagine a virtual U-tube (thus tube for simplicity) wrapping around an obstacle. It has a very small diameter equal to the diameter of a single liquid molecule. The two tube arms point away from POI across a number

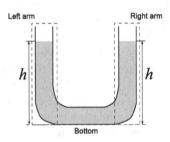

Fig. 1. Water surface remains at the same level in the two arms of a U-tube

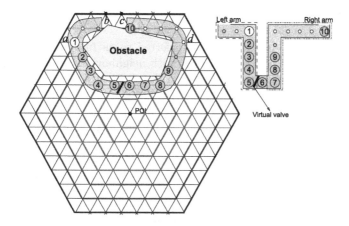

Fig. 2. Virtual U-tube

of hexagon layers, and the height of the tube is measured by the number of those layers. There is a valve between the left arm and the bottom of the tube, which allows liquid (*i.e.*, sensors) to enter the left arm from the bottom and prevents the reverse flow. Figure 2 shows a tube of height 5.

In G_{TT}, a tube is composed of a sequence of vertices, called *tube vertices*. If it contains liquid, then liquid molecules (*i.e.*, sensors) must be located at tube vertices. There are three basic types of tube vertex, *i.e.*, *bottom* vertex, *right-arm* vertex, and *left-arm* vertex, corresponding to the three parts of the tube. A right-arm (left-arm) vertex is a vertex whose rotation next hop (resp., previous hop) is occupied by the obstacle. A bottom vertex is a vertex whose greedy previous hops and only greedy previous hops are occupied by the obstacle. Note that the rightmost and the leftmost bottom vertices are shared by the two tube arms and thus considered arm vertex as well.

In Fig. 2, the three types of tube vertex are shown by solid dots. It is observed that the subgraph of right-arm (left-arm) vertices are not connected. To ensure tube connectivity, we introduce another type of tube vertex, *bridge* vertex. The definitions of bridge vertex for the left arm and for the right arm are symmetric. A right-arm (left-arm) bridge vertex is a vertex who has at least one greedy next hop occupied by the obstacle, and whose rotation next (resp., previous) hop leads to a right-arm (resp., left-arm) vertex. In Fig. 2, bridge vertices are marked by hollow dots. With bridge vertices, the left arm and the right arm each become a connected component; they are finally linked together via bottom vertices.

By the status of neighboring vertices, a node is able to tell the basic tube tole of its residence vertex but not the bridge role. For example, in Fig. 2, there is no difference between vertices a and b (or, c and d) from local view. With one-hop knowledge, a node can only identify potential bridge vertices; to infer exact information, two-hop knowledge is needed. Specifically, a vertex is a left-arm (right-arm) bridge vertex if its rotation previous (resp., next) hop is left-arm (resp., right-arm) vertex or left-arm (resp., right-arm) bridge vertex.

4.2 Fluid-Like Behavior

A node is said to be in a tube, thus referred to as *tube node*, if it is located at a tube vertex. Each node exchanges with neighboring nodes its tube role (if applicable and certain) to enable bridge node self-identification. When two tubes join, tube nodes in the joint part behave with respect to the two tubes separately. Henceforth, we concentrate on the scenario with a single independent tube only. We use term *obstructed* to imply that a node is stopped by an obstacle, and term *blocked* to indicate that a node is stopped by another node.

When a right-arm node, *e.g.*, node 10 in Fig. 2, finds that its rotation is obstructed and it has no unobstructed greedy next hop, it tries to rotate backward to a right-arm vertex with unobstructed greedy next hop. During backward rotation, it may walk through a sequence of bridge vertices, staying at the same hexagon layer. Because it is aware of its presence in the right-arm (by knowing its rotation was obstructed), such a backward rotating node immediately knows that it is a bridge node at each visited bridge vertex. A right-arm bridge node turns itself to *backward_rotation* node as soon as it finds that its right tube neighbor is performing backward rotation.

Backward rotation ensures right-arm nodes to "flow" down to the tube bottom, simulating the behavior (due to gravity) of liquid drops attached on tube side. The tube bottom is considered *open* unless all the bottom nodes' greedy advance is blocked or obstructed. With open bottom, bottom nodes and upcoming right-arm nodes will eventually leak out of the tube, no longer being affected by the obstacle. We only need to handle sealed tube bottom case.

Suppose that the bottom is sealed. As tube nodes keeps flowing into the bottom from the right arm, and bottom nodes rotate to the left, an *effective liquid body* (ELBD) spanning the three parts (*i.e.*, the bottom and the two arms) of the tube will be accumulated. It is a linear sequence of connected tube nodes that are aware of their tube roles without uncertainty. For example, in Fig. 2, ELBD is composed of nodes 2–9; node 1 (which is assumed to arrive by greedy advance) does not belong to ELBD because it is not sure about its tube role. Only nodes that belong to ELBD need to take further action for obstacle avoidance. We focus on these nodes only.

In ELBD, nodes exert pressure on adjacent low-level nodes. Aggregated pressure from the two arms meet through bottom nodes. If it is balanced, no node moves. If it is toward the right arm, no node moves either because of the prevention of the virtual valve, which is naturally realized by bottom nodes' unidirectional rotation. The two cases imply that ELBD's right end node's virtual rotation next hop (on the other side of the obstacle) is currently occupied, and it has to stay still for the time being.

If the pressure biases toward the left arm, then a *pressure adjustment process* starts. In this process, all the ELBD nodes shift their position to the "left" by one hoe. Afterwards, they start to impersonate its left tube neighbor. The left-end node impersonates the right end node. Here, "left" means the clockwise direction along the obstacle if nodal rotation direction is counter-clockwise, or counter-clockwise direction otherwise. Position shifting renders the entire ELBD flow to the left by one position. It appears that the right-end node of the ELBD conducted rotation or greedy advance, "penetrating" the obstacle. Pressure adjustment is performed iteratively until the pressure from the right is no longer larger than that from the left.

For each ELBD node, its position shifting is realized by one of the four types of movement: greedy advance, rotation, backward_rotation, and backward_greedy. *Backward_greedy* is different from retreat (which is also opposite to greedy advance). The former happens only in the left-arm; whereas, the later may take place anywhere and aim for a randomly selected vertex (on adjacent outer hexagon).

5   Implementation

In this section, we show how to implement the obstacle penetration technique without changing the properties of GRG. The implementation includes design of collision avoidance and resolution rules, definition of loop avoidance policies, and development of a pressure adjustment protocol.

5.1   Tube Collision Handling

When a retreat node hits an obstacle, it moves, remaining as retreat node, along the obstacle to the left to find an empty vertex. In case of collision, it is assigned lowest priority to take next deployment step. As such, retreat movement does not affect nodal decision making; thus without jeopardizing correctness, we ignore it in collision avoidance and resolution. We generally refer to tube nodes' movement in the tube as "flowing" behavior. Because collision that does not involve nodal flowing behavior is avoided or resolved by GRG rules, we focus on flowing-related collision, called *tube collision*.

Tube collision needs special treatment because nodal flowing behavior may be invalid in plain GRG and can not be handled by GRG rules. Suppose that a tube node n is flowing to tube vertex v. We examine all possible tube collision that may occur at v by exploring Fig. 3–5. These figures exhaustively list the neighborhood scenarios of v with respect to the obstacle (shaded). Therein, solid arrowed lines stand for node n's flowing movement; broken arrowed lines indicate possible colliding movement (dashed ones for greedy advance and dotted ones for rotation). We define a general rule for tube collision avoidance as follows:

Rule 1 (Tube collision avoidance rule). *When two neighboring nodes, a flowing node n and a non-flowing node m (with respect to the same tube/obstacle), are both aiming at the same tube vertex, n proceeds as usual, while m changes its deployment decision accordingly.*

In collision resolution we no longer need to consider nodal movement locally prevented by the above rule. In Fig. 3–5, it is the movement marked by an "X" sign. Observe that, in Fig. 3(a)–3(c), the flowing behavior of node n is in fact greedy advance. In these case, its resulting tube collision is naturally resolved by

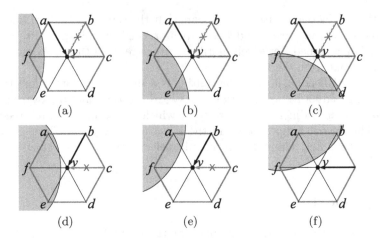

Fig. 3. The neighborhood of right-arm vertex v

regular GRG rules and henceforth out of our consideration as well. It is noticed that no tube collision is possible in Fig. 3(f) and 4(f).

Summarizing, we only need to take care of the following tube collisions, which are not locally prehibitable because colliding nodes are be out of each other's transmission rang:

- Backward_Rotation-and-Greedy (BR-G)
  - Figures 4(c), 5(b), 5(c), where node n comes from vertex f by backward_rotation and collides with a greedy node from vertex b.
- Backward_Rotation-and-Rotation (BR-R)
  - Figures 5(b), 5(c), where node n comes from vertex f by backward_rotation and collides with a rotation node from vertex c.
- Backward_Greedy-and-Greedy (BG-G)
  - Figures 4(a), 4(b), 4(d), 4(e), 5(a), where node n comes from vertex e or d by backward_greedy and collides with a greedy node from a or b.
- Backward_Greedy-and-Rotation (BG-R)
  - Figures 5(a), where node n comes from vertex e by backward_greedy and collides with a rotation node from vertex c.
- Backward_Greedy-and-Backward_Rotation (BR-BG)
  - Figure 6, where v is a joint vertex of two tubes, and node n comes from d by backward_greedy and collides with a backward_rotation node from f.

In the following, we resolve these tube collisions by a number of localized rules. We start with BR-G resolution.

Rule 2 (BR-G rule). *In BR-G, backward_rotation node has higher priority to make deployment decision than greedy node. The latter will retreat if the former decides to stay and it itself can not conduct rotation.*

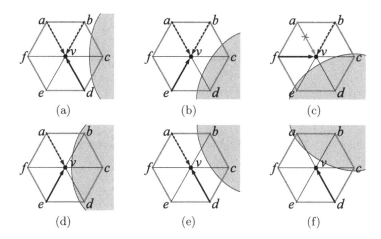

Fig. 4. The neighborhood of left-arm vertex v

Depending on which arm it occurs in, BR-R is resolved in two different, but symmetric, ways. It is not difficult to see that in right-arm BR-R the previous hop of the backward_rotation node can be taken either by a greedy node or by another backward_rotation node. In this case, if the rotation node continues rotating, probably after colliding with a sequence of intermediate backward_rotation nodes and persisting rotation, it will reach either an empty vertex or a vertex occupied by a greedy node. In the former case, right-arm BR-R is resolved; in the later case, G-R collision happens and is then resolved by GRG rules. Justified by this analysis, we define the following rule:

Rule 3 (Right-arm BR-R rule). *In right-arm BR-R, backward_rotation node has higher priority to make deployment decision than rotation node. If the former decides to stay, the latter will keep rotating whether the rotation next hop is occupied or not.*

Symmetric to the situation in right-arm BR-R, in left-arm BR-R the rotation node must have left behind a vertex between its current home vertex and the obstacle. That vertex could be occupied either by a greedy node or by another rotation node. If the backward_rotation node persists backward rotating, it will reach a vertex which is either empty or occupied by a greedy node. In the former case, left-arm BR-R is resolved; in the latter case, BR-G collision occurs and is then resolved by the BR-G rule. Therefore, we define the following rule:

Rule 4 (Left-arm BR-R rule). *In left-arm BR-R, rotation node has higher priority to make deployment decision than backward_rotation node. If the former decides to stay, the latter will keep rotating backward whether the backward_rotation next hop is occupied or not.*

We now proceed to the resolution of BG-related collisions BG-G, BG-R, and BG-BR, which happens only in the left arm. If we view these collisions from a

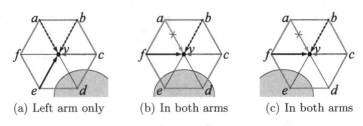

(a) Left arm only   (b) In both arms   (c) In both arms

Fig. 5. The neighborhood of bridge vertex v

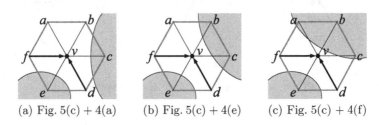

(a) Fig. 5(c) + 4(a)   (b) Fig. 5(c) + 4(e)   (c) Fig. 5(c) + 4(f)

Fig. 6. BR-BG collision at a joint vertex v of two tubes

different angle, they will actually be equivalent or similar respectively to G-R, left-arm BR-R, and right-arm BR-R collision, and therefore be resolved similarly. We define the following rules:

Rule 5 (BG-G rule). *In BG-G, backward_greedy node has higher priority to make deployment decision than greedy node. If the former decides to stay, the latter will retreat.*

Rule 6 (BG-R rule). *In BG-R, rotation node has higher priority to make deployment decision than backward_greedy node. If the former decides to stay, the latter rotates backward whether the backward_rotation next hop is occupied or not.*

Rule 7 (BG-BR rule). *In BG-BR, backward_rotation node has higher priority to make deployment decision than backward_greedy node. If the former decides to stay, the latter rotates whether the rotation next hop is occupied or not.*

5.2   Collision Loop Prevention

Because ELBD is composed of discrete nodes, asynchronous nodal flowing may cause transit empty vertices between ELBD nodes. A *transit empty vertex* is a tube vertex between two consecutive flowing ELBD nodes. It could appear available to adjacent non-tube nodes from their local view. We define *tube intrusion* as the movement (either greedy or rotation) of a non-tube node toward a transit empty vertex. By this definition, tube intrusion never happens in tube bottom. We will investigate every possible tube intrusion scenario in tube arms.

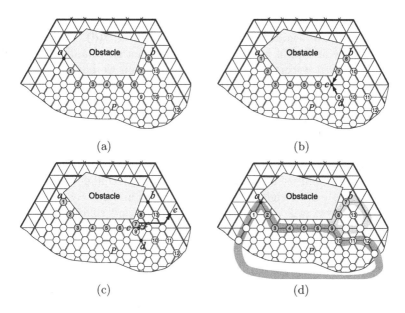

(a)   (b)

(c)   (d)

Fig. 7. Tube intrusion and resulting endless movement

Consider a transit empty vertex v in the left arm. Examine all the possible neighborhood scenarios of v enumerated in Fig. 4. By definition, intrusion is not possible in Fig. 4(d) – 4(f). In Fig. 4(a) – 4(c), intrusion may be only from vertex a, and it is locally prevented by the tube collision avoidance rule (note: there is a node occupying vertex b because, otherwise, v is not a transit empty vertex). We see that tube intrusion will not actually occur in the left arm.

Examine Fig. 3. Assume that the right-arm vertex v is a transit empty vertex. Intrusion is not possible in Fig. 3(f) by definition; in Fig. 3(c) – 3(e), the only possible intrusion (from either b or c) is prevented by the tube collision avoidance rule. In Fig. 3(a) and 3(b), the intrusion from vertex b is prohibited by the tube collision avoidance rule, while that from c is not locally avoidable since the invading node is not neighboring the flowing node n. As we will see below, this intrusion may lead to tube collision loop.

Figure 7, where solid big dots represent ELBD nodes and node ID is for illustrative purpose only, shows an example of tube intrusion and its resulting collision loops. The network configuration before ELBD flows is given in Fig. 7(a). While ELBD is flowing, node 9 invades ELBD by rotation from vertex d to transit empty vertex c, as shown in Fig. 7(b). This intrusion causes a tube collision with flowing node 7, as displayed in Fig. 7(c). After the tube collision, node 9 stays, and node 7 retreats according to GRG. Meanwhile, nodes $10 - 12$ and nodes on the hexagon containing vertices a and b move according to GRG such that the empty vertex d is filled and that tube vertex a becomes empty again. Suppose that node 7 by any chance retreats to vertex e and that node 13 has not made deployment decision yet before node 7 reaches e. By the suspension rule of GRG, node 13 gives way to node 7, which then rotates and greedily advances to vertex b, leading to a configuration in Fig. 7(d). This is the same as Fig. 7(a). The arrival of node 7 at b triggers another round of ELBD flow. Assume it takes place exactly in the same way. Then we have two joint tube collision loops as marked in Fig. 7(d).

Recall that the terminatability of GRG is grounded on the fact that once inner hexagons H_j ($j < i$) are fully occupied, nodes on H_i will never leave H_i (see the proof of Lemma 2 in [9]). This correctness basis is violated in tube intrusion, and for this, collision loop occurs as illustrated in the above example. Since tube intrusion takes place only in the right arm, we require right-arm nodes to flow in a synchronized squirm-like fashion. That is, an ELBD node starts to flow to the left if and only if its right ELBD neighbor has arrived. By this means, no transit empty vertex will appear in the right arm, and collision loop no long exists. Terminatability follows as a result.

5.3   Pressure Adjustment

In the following, we will discuss how to timely capture pressure change in the tube and trigger pressure adjustment. Each tube vertex v is associated with a pressure vector $\kappa(v)$. This vector indicates the pressure that a node located at v would contribute to the left. It is defined as

$$\kappa(v) = \begin{cases} +1 & \text{if } H(v) > H(N_L(v)) \\ 0 & \text{if } H(v) = H(N_L(v)) \\ -1 & \text{if } H(v) < H(N_L(v)), \end{cases}$$

where $N_L(v)$ is the left tube vertex neighbor of v, and $H(v)$ the level of the home hexagon of v. By this definition, a right-arm vertex has non-negative pressure vector, while a left-arm one has non-positive pressure vector.

Denote by $N_R(v)$ the right tube vertex neighbor of v. A tube node at v considers itself the left-end node of ELBD if and only if $\kappa(v) \leq 0$, $N_R(v)$ is not empty, and $N_L(v)$ is empty or occupied by a non-tube node or a node not aware of its own tube role. A tube node sends a *notification message* to the right along the tube if one of the following conditions holds: (1) it just becomes left-end node; (2) it just lost its left-end node status; (3) it remains to be left-end node, but with position change. The message is used to notify the right-end node of ELBD (if applicable) of possible pressure change in the left arm. It may be dropped by a receiver node having no right tube neighbor.

A tube node at v considers itself the right-end node of ELBD if and only if $\kappa(v) \geq 0$, $N_L(v)$ is not empty, and $N_R(v)$ is empty or occupied by a non-tube node or a node not aware of its own tube role. A tube node initiates a *pressure adjustment process* whichever of the following conditions is satisfied: (1) it just becomes right-end node; (2) it remains to be right-end node, but with position change; (3) it remains to be right-end node and just received a notification message. Each of these conditions indicates potential pressure difference between the two tube arms. By acting upon them, timely pressure adjustment is ensured.

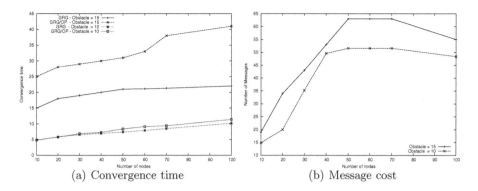

(a) Convergence time   (b) Message cost

Fig. 8. Simulation results

In a pressure adjustment process, the initiator node sends a *pressure message* to the left along the tube, carrying a vector λ equal to its pressure vector (in fact, that of its residence vertex) and other necessary information (*e.g.*, its rotation starting point). After receiving the pressure message, an intermediate tube node increases λ by its own pressure vector, and forwards the updated message to its left tube neighbor. It drops the message if it has no left tube neighbor. The left-end node of ELBD (if applicable) will receive the message and retrieve λ, which implies aggregated pressure from the right. It will also retrieves other embedded information, by which it can impersonate the initiator node.

Apparently, $\lambda = 1$, if the left-end node is at the same level (hexagon layer) as the initiator node; $\lambda < 1$, if it is at a higher level; $\lambda > 0$, otherwise. In the case of $\lambda > 1$, the left-end node sends an *action* message to the right-end node (which may not be the node that initiates the pressure adjustment process) and then flows (to the left by one hop). An intermediate ELBD node flows as soon as it forwards the action message if it is a left-arm node or a bottom node; otherwise, it flows only after its right ELBD neighbor arrives. The right-end node flows immediately after it receives the action message.

6   Simulation Results

We implemented GRG (the -CW variant) and GRG/OP using a custom network simulator with reliable MAC layer; we simulated their execution over a mobile sensor network randomly and uniformly dropped in plane. We fix the dropping area to size 1×1, and take its geographic center as POI. We comparatively study their performance on convergence time, *i.e.*, the number of time units that it takes the network to stabilize. We also study the message cost of GRG/OP for obstacle avoidance. In our simulation, sensors have sensing radius 0.03 and communication radius $0.05 \approx \sqrt{3} \times 0.03$; they may move at different speeds, ranging from $2m.s^{-1}$ to $10m.s^{-1}$ per simulated time unit, for every step.

There is a single obstacle nearby POI, generated in the following way: we first draw a TT graph and choose a vertex as the based of the obstacle; then we grow the obstacle around the base vertex (to ensure a convex shape) till the desired size is reached. We used two different obstacle sizes. One is 10-vertex large, meaning the obstacle occupies 10 vertices; the other is 15-vertex large. We vary the network size from 10 to 100 nodes. By this means, we are able to investigate the impact of node density and obstacle size on algorithm performance. For each simulation setting, we executed GRG and GRG/OP in 50 randomly generated network scenarios and computed average results, which are going to be elaborated below.

In GRG, nodes simply stop when their rotation next hops are obstructed by the obstacle; whereas, in GRG/OP, they pass around the obstacle by simulating fluid behavior in a U-tube. Therefore, we can expect that GRG/OP has larger convergence time then GRG. This expectation is confirmed by Fig. 8(a), where the convergence time curves of GRG are blow their counterparts for GRG/OP. From the figure, we also observe that convergence time is long for scenarios with large-sized obstacle. It is because nodes have to move along a long path to pass around a large obstacle, increasing convergence time.

We ignore communication (used by lower layer protocols) for neighbor information Gossiping. GRG/OP generates messages only for obstacle avoidance, and message transmission takes place only in virtual tube (*i.e.*, along obstacle). The length of a virtual tube depends on the size of the part of the obstacle enclosed by the network. The larger the part, the longer the tube, and thus the higher the message cost. In our simulation, the tube length increases when the obstacle becomes bigger. Consequently the message cost curve for large obstacle is always above that for small obstacle in Fig. 8(b).

When obstacle size is fixed, the larger the network size, the more the obstacle is enclosed by the network, and therefore the longer the tube. This indicates, the message costs of GRG/OP goes up as the network size increases, which can be observed in Fig. 8(b). Notice that after the network size is beyond a threshold, the message cost stabilizes. It is because, when the obstacle is completely included in the network, nodes above it are no longer affected (*i.e.*, no extra message transmission). The threshold value clearly depends on obstacle size. In our simulation it is 40 for small obstacle and 50 for large obstacle.

7   Conclusions

Sensor self-deployment for *focused coverage* is an emerging research issue. The only known solution Greedy-Rotation-Greedy (GRG) [9] was designed for ideal environment with no obstacle. It has limited applicability in practice. In this paper, we removed this assumption by adding a novel obstacle penetration ability to GRG. This version of GRG with Obstacle Penetration (GRG/OP) can be used in realistic obstacle-prone environment. It enables mobile sensors to behave like fluid when obstructed by obstacles, and preserves the optimality of final coverage. We simulated GRG/OP and studied its convergence time and message cost in a single-obstacle environment. In the future, we will test its energy cost for nodal movement and in multi-obstacle scenarios. We notice that GRG/OP can be easily extended for solving area coverage problem if we treat the border of the region of interest (ROI) as obstacle. The point of interest (POI) can be the geographic center of ROI or a collectively computed location, *e.g.*, the location of an elected sensor. This extension will be part of our future work.

References

1. Bai, X., Kumary, S., Xuan, D., Yun, Z., Lai, T.H.: Deploying Wireless Sensors to Achieve Both Coverage and Connectivity. In: Proc. of ACM MobiHoc, pp. 131–142 (2006)
2. Bartolini, N., Calamoneri, T., Fusco, E.G., Massini, A., Silvestri, S.: Snap and Spread: A Self-deployment Algorithm for Mobile Sensor Networks. In: Proc. of IEEE DCOSS, pp. 451–456 (2008)
3. Chellappan, S., Bai, X., Ma, B., Xuan, D.: Sensor networks deployment using flip-based sensors. In: Proc. of IEEE MASS, pp. 291–298 (2005)
4. Garetto, M., Gribaudo, M., Chiasserini, C.-F., Leonardi, E.: A Distributed Sensor Relocation Scheme for Environmental Control. In: Proc. of IEEE MASS, pp. 1–10 (2007)
5. Heo, N., Varshney, P.K.: Energy-Efficient Deployment of Intelligent Mobile Sensor Networks. IEEE Tran. on Systems, Man, and Cybernetics - Part A: Systems and Humans 35(1), 78–92 (2005)
6. Howard, A., Mataric, M.J., Sukhatme, G.S.: Mobile Sensor Network Deployment using Potential Fields: A Distributed, Scalable Solution to the Area Coverage Problem. In: Proc. of DARS, pp. 299–308 (2002)
7. Howard, A., Mataric, M.J., Sukhatme, G.S.: An Incremental Self-Deployment Algorithm for Mobile Sensor Networks. Autonomous Robots 13(2), 113–126 (2002)
8. Poduri, S., Pattern, S., Krishnamachari, B., Sukhatme, G.: Using Local Geometry for Tunable Topology Control in Sensor Networks. IEEE Tran. on Mobile Computing (to appear)
9. Li, X., Frey, H., Santoro, N., Stojmenovic, I.: Focused Coverage by Mobile Sensor Networks. In: Proc. of IEEE MASS (to appear)
10. Li, X., Frey, H., Santoro, N., Stojmenovic, I.: Localized Sensor Self-deployment for Guaranteed Coverage Radius Maximization. In: Proc. of IEEE ICC (to appear)
11. Li, X., Nayak, A., Simplot-Ryl, D., Stojmenovic, I.: Sensor Placement in Sensor and Actuator Networks. In: Wireless Sensor and Actuator Networks: Algorithms and Protocols for Scalable Coordination and Data Communication. Wiley, Chichester (to appear)
12. Ma, M., Yang, Y.: Adaptive Triangular Deployment Algorithm for Unattended Mobile Sensor Networks. IEEE Tran. on Computers 56(7), 946–958 (2007)
13. Mousavi, H., Nayyeri, A., Yazdani, N., Lucas, C.: Energy Conserving Movement-Assisted Deployment of Ad hoc Sensor Networks. IEEE Communications Letters 10(4), 269–271 (2006)
14. Wang, G., Cao, G., La Porta, T.: Movement-Assisted Sensor Deployment. IEEE Tran. on Mobile Computing 5(6), 640–652 (2006)
15. Yang, S., Li, M., Wu, J.: Scan-Based Movement-Assisted Sensor Deployment Methods in Wireless Sensor Networks. IEEE Tran. on Parallel and Distributed Systems 18(8), 1108–1121 (2007)
16. Zhang, H., Hou, J.C.: Maintaining Sensing Coverage and Connectivity in Large Sensor Networks. Ad Hoc & Sensor Wireless Networks 1(1-2), 89–124 (2005)
17. Zou, Y., Chakrabarty, K.: Sensor deployment and target localization in distributed sensor networks. ACM Tran. on Embedded Computing Systems 3(1), 61–91 (2004)

An Efficient and Scalable Address Autoconfiguration in Mobile Ad Hoc Networks

Syed Rafiul Hussain, Subrata Saha, and Ashikur Rahman

Department of Computer Science and Engineering,
Bangladesh University of Engineering and Technology, Dhaka, Bangladesh
rafiulhussain@csebuet.org, subrata@csebuet.org, ashikur@cse.buet.ac.bd

Abstract. Several protocols of address autoconfiguration in the mobile ad hoc network (MANET) are present in the current literature. Although some of these protocols perform decently in sparse and small networks, but exhibit poor performance (e.g., single point of failure, storage limitation, large protocol overhead and so on) when the network is either dense or very large. In this paper, we propose an efficient and scalable address autoconfiguration protocol that automatically configures a network by assigning unique IP address to every node with low overhead and minimal cost. Evenly distributed Duplicate-IP Detection Servers are used to ensure the uniqueness of an IP address during IP address assignment session. In contrast to some other solutions, the proposed protocol does not exhibit any problems pertaining to leader election or centralized server-based solutions. Furthermore, grid based hierarchy is also used for efficient geographic forwarding as well as for selecting Duplicate-IP Detection Servers. Through simulation results we demonstrate scalability, robustness, low latency, fault tolerance and some other important aspects of our protocol.

Keywords: Duplicate Address Detection (DAD), Duplicate-IP Detection Server (DDS), IP Address Autoconfiguration.

1   Introduction

A mobile ad hoc network (MANET) consists of a set of mobile transceivers that communicate via single or multi hop wireless links and function without any predefined infrastructure. A node equipped with such transceiver can join or leave the MANET at its own will. In such predefined infrastructureless environment like MANET, some of the notable challenging issues are routing protocol, power consumption, security and network configuration. Again, network configuration includes IP address autoconfiguration, DNS server setup and so on. Among them, IP address autoconfiguration is more important. It is an inevitable issue not only in mobile ad hoc network but also in all types of network. Nevertheless, with the view to spreading quickly and easily (i.e., like a plug and play device) in situations like battlefields, disastrous areas etc where there is no possibility and time to set up a fixed infrastructure, a very sophisticated issue like large scale *IP Address Autoconfiguration* in MANET should be focused with added emphasis.

P.M. Ruiz and J.J. Garcia-Luna-Aceves (Eds.): ADHOC-NOW 2009, LNCS 5793, pp. 152–165, 2009.

The address autoconfiguration can be defined as the task of automatically assigning conflict-free unique IP address to every constituent node in the MANET without any manual intervention or without using any centralized DHCP [10] server. One of the simple but naïve *non-scalable* solution for autoconfiguration is as follows: suppose there is a special node located in a well known position within the network which stores all the IP addresses assigned in the network. Let us call this special node a *Central Duplicate-IP Detection Server* (CDDS). Any new node requiring an IP address picks up a random IP address and sends a query to this special node (i.e.,CDDS) to verify whether this randomly chosen IP address is already chosen by some other nodes. If the CDDS replies positively (i.e., no node has chosen this IP address so far), then the node may safely assign this IP address to itself. Otherwise, it discards this IP address, chooses another IP address randomly and repeats the same procedure. As this special node is located in a position which is previously known to all other nodes in the network, sending such query using *geographic forwarding* is easy. The problems with this approach are two fold - 1) because there is only one special node which stores all the IP addresses, there is always a chance for a single point of failure; 2) this solution is non-scalable because with the increase of network size, the size of IP address database also grows.

Instead of such a naïve centralized solution, we present a distributed approach of IP address autoconfiguration protocol to automatically configure a large scale MANET. The protocol works with the help of a special service offered by all the nodes called *Duplicate-IP Detection Service*. Any node offering this service is called a *Duplicate-IP Detection Server* (DDS). Instead of storing all the IP addresses in a central database, belonging to a special node, here we distribute this database almost uniformly to all nodes in the network. Without any predesignation or pre-agreement, a node can act as a DDS for other nodes by keeping the information of position, speed and identity (i.e., IP address) of other nodes. Also, for a single node, a group of nodes simultaneously acts as DDSs. With the help of a very simple principle (described in Section III.C) the DDSs are efficiently selected for a particular node. This distributed duplicate-IP detection mechanism, not being centralized, eliminates the risk of single point of failure and yields duplicate-IP detection facility by copying the knowledge of a node at several DDSs. Also different subset of nodes become DDSs for different nodes which ensure load balancing effectively. Every node maintains a table called *Duplicate-IP Detection Table* (DDT). To facilitate scalability, a node's DDT contains information of only those nodes for which it acts as a DDS.

2   Related Works

Prior works on autoconfiguration can be classified into two major groups: *stateful* ([1], [2]) and *stateless* ([3], [6]) address autoconfiguration. In *stateful autoconfiguration* a node acquires its unique IP address either from a centralized node or from one of the nodes of a set of distributed servers which keeps records of disjoint IP address blocks. On the contrary, in *stateless autoconfiguration* nodes do not store any IP address allocation information. A newly joined node randomly picks up an IP address and runs an algorithm called *Duplicate Address Detection (DAD)* [6] within the entire network to ensure that the chosen IP address is unique. Nevertheless, a combination of these two classes, hybrid autoconfiguration [5], can also be mentioned.

For any address autoconfiguration protocol *scalability* is a major challenging issue. But very few works (e.g., [4]) about address autoconfiguration are there in MANET literature which address the scalability issue seriously. The solution of Zeroconf working group [3] uses DAD algorithm. It assigns every node a unique link-local address. Hence, the solution is incompatible to MANET as along with single-hop communications there are also multi-hop communications in MANET. Perkins *et al.* [6] propose a solution where DAD procedure is conducted through broadcasting within the entire network which is non-scalable for growing size of networks. Beside this, their scheme does not describe what will happen if multiple nodes concurrently select the same temporary address during assignment session from the temporary IP address pool (i.e., between 1 to 2047). In MANETconf [1], some preconfigured nodes take the responsibility of assigning IP addresses to newly joined nodes. Here flooding the entire network is also a requirement for each newly joined node which causes the problems like timing delay, network congestion and others. The autoconfiguration proposed by Mohsin *et al.* [2] entails a flaw concerning to the management of departing nodes. IPv6 autoconfiguration [4] which is proposed for large scale MANET has some drawbacks also. This solution uses a modified IPv6 Neighbor Discovery Protocol through the modification of Neighbor Solicitation message to allow a node to broadcast to a pre-defined bounded area (i.e., up to n-hop) instead of single-hop. In addition, it extends [11] to work in multi-hop networks and thus enhances the scalability. But a leader election is required in extending [11] which hinders scalability. Tinghui *et al.* [7], in their Quorum Based Autoconfiguration, propose a two-level hierarchy to configure the MANET. Quorum voting is done to ensure consistency of replicated IP state information which incurs an extra overhead. Yuan *et al.* [8] propose a three-level hierarchy to automatically configure the MANET. But there is no distributed server to efficiently obtain IP address in this scheme. A DAD is also run throughout the entire network. However, in our approach there is no need to run DAD in the entire network. A node just sends query to some selected servers to test uniqueness of the chosen IP.

3   Preliminaries

In this paper we introduce a concept called *Duplicate-IP Detection Service* to ensure uniqueness of an IP address in entire network. But before going into the deep, it is necessary to describe some preliminary issues involved in this protocol:

3.1   Geographic Forwarding

Geographic forwarding is used in our protocol as the basis of routing packets from one node to another. In geographic forwarding, a node knows its

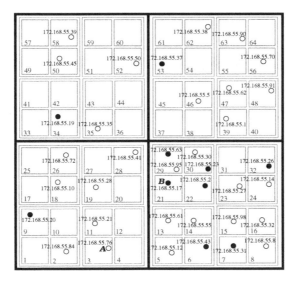

Fig. 1. A DDS example

position i.e., altitude, latitude and longitude from GPS which gives almost correct measurement. Every node then periodically informs its existence to all of its neighbors by broadcasting HELLO messages within one hop. A neighbor node, upon reception of the HELLO message, allocates an entry for the source of the HELLO message into its *Neighbor Allocation Table* (NAT, hereafter) along with the source's IP, position and time of the last HELLO message received from the same source. Now consider a scenario where node A wants to communicate with another node C and has the location information of node C with the help of any location service (e.g., GLS [9]). Before sending a message to node C, node A appends C's IP address and C's current geographic position in the packet header. Then node A looks up its *Neighbor Allocation Table* to find a node B which is geographically closest to node C. If the node C and node B are the same node, then node A sends the packet to node C directly. Otherwise node A forwards the packet to an intermediate node B. This process is then repeated again in node B and in all subsequent nodes until the packet is received by node C.

3.2 The Architecture

To automatically organize *Duplicate-IP Detection Servers* (DDSs), we exploit the architecture proposed for *Grid Location Service* (GLS) [9]. In this architecture the entire network topology is divided into several hierarchical grid structures. The grids are organized with squares of increasing size. The smallest grid is referred to as an Order-1 square. Four such Order-1 squares form an Order-2 square. Similarly, four Order-2 squares make up an Order-3 square and so on. In brief, the **Grid Formulation Rule** is: *Any Order-n (n ≥ 2) square is composed of four Order-(n − 1) squares and any Order-n (n ≥ 1) square is constituent*

Table 1. Grid hierarchy

Hierarchy of squares			
Order-1 square	Constituent parts	Order-1 square	Constituent parts
1	NULL	5	NULL
2	NULL	.	NULL
3	NULL	.	NULL
4	NULL	64	NULL
Order-2 square	Constituent parts	Order-2 square	Constituent parts
A	1, 2, 9, 10	I	33, 34, 41, 42
B	3, 4, 11, 12	J	35, 36, 43, 44
C	5, 6, 13, 14	K	37, 38, 45, 46
D	7, 8, 15, 16	L	39, 40, 47, 48
E	17, 18, 25, 26	M	49, 50, 57, 58
F	19, 20, 27, 28	N	51, 52, 59, 60
G	21, 22, 29, 30	O	53, 54, 61, 62
H	23, 24, 31, 32	P	55, 56, 63, 64
Order-3 square	Constituent parts	Order-3 square	Constituent parts
α	A, B, E, F	γ	I, J, M, N
β	C, D, G, H	δ	K, L, O, P
Order-4 square	Constituent parts		
ξ	α, β, γ, δ		

part of one and only one Order-$(n + i)$ squares, where $i = 1, 2, 3, \ldots$ to ensure no overlap. The rule followed by an Order-n square is that its lower left coordinates must be of the form $(a \cdot 2^{n-1}, b \cdot 2^{n-1})$ for integers a and b. Fig. 1 shows a sample grid hierarchy that follows the above rule.

Fig. 1 depicts the network area up to Order-4 square. Hence, there are four Order-3 squares, each of which in turn contains four Order-2 squares. Again each of such four Order-2 squares contains four Order-1 squares. So, the above mentioned network has 64 Order-1 squares which are numbered from 1 to 64. Among these 64 Order-1 squares, the *1st, 2nd, 9th and 10th* squares form an Order-2 square which is named as A (as listed in Table 1). Thus there are total 16 Order-2 squares which are numbered from A to P as inscribed in Table 1. Among these 16 Order-2 squares A, B, E and F constitute an Order-3 square α (as shown in Table 1). Finally, 4 such Order-3 squares α, β, γ and δ jointly complete the Order-4 square ξ. It is also to be noted that *28th, 29th, 36th and 37st* Order-1 squares or F, G, J and K Order-2 squares cannot form any higher Order-2 and Order-3 square respectively. So, any of such combination of lower Order squares cannot make any higher Order square which violates the **Grid Formulation Rule** given above.

3.3   Selection Process of Duplicate-IP Detection Server

Selection process of DDSs of a node is based on its current IP address and the predetermined grid hierarchy. Here we first describe which nodes are selected as DDSs for a particular node and then how they are selected through HELLO and UPDATE messages. For the grid hierarchy of Fig. 1, at most 10 DDSs can be selected for a node in different Order squares. Of these 10 DDSs, 1 DDS is from the node's own Order-1 square, 3 DDSs are from the node's three peer Order-1 squares, 3 DDSs are from the node's three peer Order-2 squares and 3 DDSs are from the node's three peer Order-3 squares. E.g., in Fig. 1, the different squares from which 10 DDSs (shown as filled circles) are selected for node B are: *21st* Order-1 square; *29th, 30th* and *22nd* peer Order-1 squares; *C, D* and *H* peer Order-2 squares and α, γ and δ peer Order-3 squares. Note also that, if no node is present in a square, then obviously no node in that square is selected as DDS for other nodes. So for node A (in *3rd* Order-1 square) not all 10 DDSs are selected since 2 peer Order-1 squares (*4th and 12th* Order-1 squares) are empty. Now which node in a square is selected as DDS for a particular node follows the principle called **DDS Selection Principle (DSP)**. The principle has 3 cases:

Case (a): In an Order square, that node is selected as DDS whose IP address is least but greater than the IP address of a particular node for which a DDS is going to be selected. If no such node is present in that square go to Case (b).

Case (b): In an Order square, for a particular node one is selected as DDS whose IP address is absolutely least in that square. If no such node is present in that square go to Case (c).

Case (c): In an Order square, the node itself is selected as its own DDS.

Fig. 1 shows the selected DDSs of node B. As there is no other node in its own Order-1 square i.e, in *21st* Order-1 square, node B itself is selected (according to *Case (c)* of DSP) as its own DDS in its Order-1 square. Then, three other DDSs in its three peer Order-1 squares (*29th, 30th and 22nd* Order-1 squares) are also chosen according to the DSP. Therefore, the node B itself and 172.168.55.63 (according to *Case (a)* of DSP) from *29th* Order-1 square, 172.168.55.23 (according to *Case (a)* of DSP) from *30th* Order-1 square and 172.168.55.2 (according to *Case (b)* of DSP) from *22nd* Order-1 square are selected as DDSs of node B in its Order-2 square. Next, 172.168.55.43, 172.168.55.31 and 172.168.55.26 are also chosen as DDSs respectively from *C, D and H* peer Order-2 squares of node B's Order-2 square. In peer Order-2 square C there are 4 nodes with IPs 172.168.55.12, 172.168.55.43, 172.168.55.55 and 172.168.55.61. Under *Case (a)* of DSP 172.168.55.43 is selected as DDS in C Order-2 square for node B. Similarly the other nodes 172.168.55.31 and 172.168.55.26 are selected as DDSs respectively in D and H Order-2 squares for node B under *Case (a)*. Again, 172.168.55.20, 172.168.55.19 and 172.168.55.37 are also picked up (according to *Case (a)*) as DDSs from α, γ and δ Order-3 squares respectively. Similar concept can be extended to determine DDSs at higher Order squares. For illustration and clarity purpose, we show the Fig. 1 only up to Order-4 square.

Now we describe how DDSs are selected efficiently through HELLO messages and geographic forwarding of UPDATE messages with the help of Fig. 1 and Fig. 2(a). In our protocol, only the HELLO message is sufficient to select a DDS in own Order-1 square. But, except the DDS in own Order-1 square of a node, all DDSs from other squares are selected dynamically only when UPDATE messages reach those squares. The most important requirement for nodes B to distribute its current information to the appropriate DDSs in an Order-n square is: *The nodes contained in that square have already distributed their current information throughout that square. As soon as the Order-n DDSs are operating, there is sufficient capability for geographic routing to set up the Order-$(n + 1)$ DDSs.*

Table 2. Partial content stored in node's DDT of Order-2 square G

Node	Content of DDT	Node	Content of DDT
172.168.55.17	172.168.55.17	172.168.55.95	172.168.55.63
172.168.55.2	172.168.55.2	172.168.55.23	172.168.55.30
172.168.55.63	172.168.55.95	172.168.55.30	172.168.55.23

Table 3. Partial content stored in node's DDT of Order-2 square G

Node	Content of DDT
172.168.55.17	172.168.55.17, 172.168.55.2, 172.168.55.95, 172.168.55.63, 172.168.55.30, 172.168.55.23
172.168.55.2	172.168.55.2, 172.168.55.17, 172.168.55.95, 172.168.55.63, 172.168.55.30, 172.168.55.23
172.168.55.63	172.168.55.95, 172.168.55.2, 172.168.55.17, 172.168.55.30, 172.168.55.23
172.168.55.95	172.168.55.63
172.168.55.23	172.168.55.30, 172.168.55.17, 172.168.55.2, 172.168.55.63, 172.168.55.95
172.168.55.30	172.168.55.23

The size of the smallest Order square (Order-1 square) in the grid hierarchy is deliberately chosen in such a way that all the nodes in that square are within their mutual transmission range, i.e., all nodes are able to know all other nodes in their Order-1 square through the periodic HELLO beacons. In Fig. 1 and Fig. 2(a), only node B is present in its own Order-1 square (i.e., 21st Order-1 square). As a result, no HELLO message is received by node B from any node in that 21st Order-1 square. Hence, node B has no information about any other node in that square and thus selects itself as DDS for itself in its Order-1 square. In the mean time, the nodes in other 3 Order-1 peer squares (*29th, 30th and 22nd* squares) also have already known their respective neighbors. Therefore, their DDSs also have been selected there with the help of each others' HELLO messages. DDT of these DDSs will also be updated. At that moment, the partial content of the DDT of each node in the Order-2 square G can be shown as in Table 2.

Under this circumstance, nodes in each Order-1 square of G Order-2 square have already disseminated their current information within their respective Order-1 squares. So after a little while of sending the first few HELLO messages, all nodes send 3 UPDATE messages to their 3 Order-1 peer squares. Node B sends UPDATE messages to *29th, 30th and 22nd* Order-1 squares using geographic forwarding as shown in Fig. 2(a). We call it **Grid Forwarding** because rather than location and IP of the destination node, only location of the destined square's midpoint is written in the destination field of the UPDATE message's packet header. The UPDATE message destined to *29th* peer Order-1 square is first caught by node 172.168.55.95 in that square. Then 172.168.55.95 checks whether it can act as DDS for node B. So it compares node B's IP with its own IP and also with IPs stored in its DDT. It finds that 172.168.55.63 in its DDT is least IP greater than 172.168.55.17 in its (i.e., *29th*) Order-1 square. So it determines 172.168.55.63 is worthwhile (according to *Case (a)* of DSP) to act as DDS

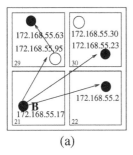 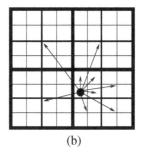

(a)   (b)

Fig. 2. (a) Node B's UPDATE messages to its peer Order-1 squares. (b) 9 UPDATE messages to 9 different Order squares.

for node B and forwards the UPDATE message of node B to 172.168.55.63. After receiving the UPDATE message, 172.168.55.63 also checks its DDT and ensures with its explored knowledge that no other node in its Order-1 square is further least node greater than 172.168.55.17 to become a DDS for node B. Hence, it is selected as the DDS and does not further forward this UPDATE message. On the contrary, node with IP 172.168.55.23 first catches the UPDATE message of node B destined to the *30th* Order-1 square and finds that it is the least node greater than 172.168.55.17. Hence, it acts as a DDS for node B. No further forwarding is also required and it stores node B's information (i.e., IP address, geographic position etc) in its DDT. UPDATE message transmitted for the *22nd* Order-1 square is received by 172.168.55.2 and it selects itself as DDS of node B as no other node is present there. In the same way, each node in the *29th, 30th and 22nd* Order-1 squares also send 3 UPDATE messages to their respective 3 Order-1 peer squares and thus DDSs for them in those squares are also properly selected. So DDT of all nodes in that Order-2 square are updated regularly through the periodic UPDATE messages. The current partial content of DDT of each node in Order-2 square G after sending of the UPDATE messages is shown in Table 3.

Table 3 shows that all nodes have already distributed their current information throughout the Order-2 square G. So when all nodes in an Order-1 square send UPDATE messages to their peer Order-1 squares, all nodes in those squares are able to know the most eligible node for acting as DDS in their Order-2 square (for any other node). In similar way nodes in other Order-2 squares also distribute their current information within their respective squares. However, node B then sends 3 UPDATE messages to its three peer Order-2 squares and subsequently three peer Order-3 squares. Thus DDSs are selected from those squares under the same procedure described above and therefore contents of DDT of them are also updated. So, like node B every node sends total 9 UPDATE messages to 9 different Order squares and hence, 9 DDSs are selected. These maximum 9 DDSs and 1 DDS in own Order-1 square sum up 10 DDSs for each node. A scenario of throwing 9 UPDATE messages of a node is depicted in Fig. 2(b).

4   Autoconfiguration Protocol

The proposed address autoconfiguration protocol assigns a unique IP address to every node in the MANET in two basic steps: 1) *temporary IP assignment* and 2) *real IP assignment*. In the first step a node is assigned with a temporary IP address. In the second step it randomly chooses an IP address for itself. But before allocating this IP address to itself, it needs to ensure that the same IP address is not currently chosen by any other node in the network. To check this duplication, we provide an intelligent mechanism. If the same IP address is already assigned currently to any other node, then there must exist several DDSs in the network for that node (as described in previous section). By consulting all these DDSs for the chosen IP address the possibility of duplication can be very easily avoided. This second step is called *real IP assignment*. As we conduct query to DDSs, an IP is obviously required for a requesting node to get reply from DDSs. Temporary IP assigned in the first step serves this purpose. These two steps are described below in details.

4.1   Temporary IP Assignment

At the very first when the MANET is not initialized, we assume that several nodes simultaneously enter the network and they are connected, i.e., there exists at least one communication path among the nodes. Each Order-1 square is allocated with a predefined disjoint block of IP addresses which we call *temporary IP address pool*. Two Order-1 squares do not have any common IP address in their temporary IP address pool. We also assume that all nodes have prior knowledge of all temporary IP address pools before joining the network.

The necessity of temporary IP address pool is depicted with a suitable example: suppose a MANET has 64 Order-1 squares and its range of temporary IP address is from 1 to 2048. Then every Order-1 square can use (2048/64 =) 32 temporary IP addresses. The *1st* Order-1 square's temporary IP address ranges from 1 to 32, *2nd* Order-1 square's temporary IP addresses ranges from 33 to 64 and so on. Every node must have prior knowledge about this disjoint block of IP address pool to get a temporary IP address before assigning a real IP address. Assigning temporary IP address prior to real IP address assignment is necessary for scalability purpose. If we assign disjoint blocks of real IP to every Order-1 square, there might be a situation where the number of joining nodes in an Order-1 square is greater than the IP address pool explicitly assigned for that Order-1 square. Hence, some of the joining nodes never get real IP address. This is why we assign disjoint block of predefined temporary IP address blocks to every Order-1 square at first place. Once a node acquires a conflict-free real IP address, it releases its temporary IP address. Then its released temporary IP address can be reused by some other newly joined node. This reusability helps in situations where the number of newly joined nodes in an Order-1 square is larger than the number of temporary IP addresses assigned for that particular square. In this case, some joining node may need to wait until one of the nodes of its Order-1 square releases its temporary IP address.

A newly joined node determines its temporary IP address with minimal over-head as described following. When a node joins in the MANET, at first it identi-fies its position using GPS. From its position it can easily calculate the Order-1 square within which it is located. Then it chooses a conflict-free temporary IP address from the temporary IP pool reserved for that Order-1 square. As every node knows all other nodes within its own Order-1 square (the size of an Order-1 square is such that all nodes in that Order-1 square are within their mutual transmission range), choosing of such conflict-free temporary IP address is easy. Therefore, a node randomly picks up an IP address from temporary IP address pool reserved for that square and observes the *Neighbor Allocation Table*. It re-peats the same process in case of conflicts. But conflicts in determining unique temporary IP address may still arise when several newly joined nodes choose the same temporary IP address simultaneously. To prevent such conflicts, every node runs a DAD algorithm within its Order-1 square after choosing temporary IP address. It is done by one-hop broadcasting of DAD message within its own square. If a node finds a DAD message containing the address same as its chosen temporary IP address, it gives up its chosen temporary IP address and randomly chooses another temporary IP address after a random amount of time.

4.2   Real IP Assignment

After resolving temporary IP address, a node randomly chooses a tentative (real) IP address. It then makes queries through QUERY messages to the best nodes (i.e., to DDSs) for the chosen real IP in Order-n (n = 1, 2, 3, ...) peer squares. If an entry is found in the *Duplicate-IP Detection Table* (DDT) of any of those DDSs, the corresponding DDS immediately informs the node using NACK mes-sage. The node then chooses another tentative IP address randomly and the same process is repeated again after a random amount of time. The QUERY messages are sent iteratively. At first, the node sends queries to DDSs in peer Order-1 squares. If IP conflict is detected in any Order-1 square, there is no need to send queries in peer Order-2 squares. In general, when an IP conflict is de-tected in Order-n square, there is no need to send any further query to Order-(n + 1) square or higher Order peer squares. If no conflict is detected in any of the DDSs at any order, no reply is sent to the requesting node. Therefore, if the node receives no NACK message within a timeout interval, it assumes that the tentative IP address is conflict-free and finalizes this IP address as its real IP.

How a query is accomplished is described here with an illustrative example. Suppose a node A in Fig. 1 with temporary IP 172.168.55.76 randomly chooses 172.168.55.17 as its tentative (real) IP address. Note that, node B has already as-signed this IP address 172.168.55.17 to itself and updated all its DDSs, but node A is not aware of this situation yet. After choosing tentative IP address, node A sends QUERY message to its own Order-1 square with the same principle for choos-ing DDSs as described in Section III.C. If no NACK message is received within a predefined time interval, it sends three query messages to its three peer Order-1 squares (i.e., *4th, 11th and 12th* Order-1 squares) and the process is repeated again for higher orders. In our example, no node in the *3rd, 4th, 11th and 12th*

Order-1 squares is currently acting as a DDS for node B and hence, there is no chance of receiving NACK from any node in these squares. After predefined amount of time node A again sends three queries to its three peer Order-2 squares (i.e., A, E and F Order-2 squares). At this point, a node with IP 172.168.55.20, currently acting as a DDS of node B, sends a NACK message to node A using geographic forwarding. If no NACK message is received from the highest Order squares, the node finalizes its chosen tentative IP as its real IP.

Same tentative address may be randomly chosen by several nodes simultaneously or within a *transitive period*. Transitive period is the interval between the time when a node starts its tentative real IP selection process and the time when it finishes updating all of its DDSs in entire MANET with its assigned real IP. Obviously, if there is no mechanism in DDSs to distinguish the same requesting IP from different nodes within this critical time, there must be duplicity of IPs in the network. This unwanted event is easily overcome by creating a REQUEST_QUEUE in every DDS. When a query message for an IP comes to that IP's DDS, it makes an entry in its REQUEST_QUEUE with ⟨ tentative IP, temporary IP, Timeout Count ⟩ tuple. If the server finds an entry already present in its queue with the same tentative but different temporary IP pair, it immediately sends a NACK message to the requesting node and thus avoids duplicate IP address assignment.

A node can depart from the network either gracefully or abruptly (due to mobility or sudden software crash or power failure). So, there is a chance of *"IP address leakage"*. But in our approach it is resolved efficiently without requiring any extra cost. As part of entry update procedure, the UPDATE and HELLO messages are periodically sent by every node in the network. If no HELLO and UPDATE messages are received repeatedly after some predefined time interval from a node, all the neighbor nodes and the DDSs of that particular node remove the entries corresponding to that node. This IP address then can be automatically reused by another newly joined node. Again, when a node moves from one square to another square, depending on a node's new position, a new set of DDSs can be chosen or old DDSs can be updated with its current location and speed. So, there is no need to change the chosen real IP address of a moving node.

5   Simulation

5.1   Simulation Setup

Through simulation we evaluate the performance of our protocol both for static and mobile ad hoc networks. From 100 to 600 nodes are randomly deployed in a fixed area of $1360 \times 1360\ m^2$. The size of an Order-1 square is assumed to be $170 \times 170\ m^2$. For mobile networks each node moves randomly at an average velocity of $25\ ms^{-1}$ without taking any pause time. The transmission range and data rate of a node is $250\ m$ and $2\ Mbps$ respectively. The joining time of all nodes within the network are randomly chosen from 0 to 30 seconds. Each simulation run ends when all nodes are assigned with real IP address. In a 32-bit IP address, the first 8-bit is unique in the network and the rest 24-bits are populated randomly (In Fig. 1 we assume first 24 bits of an IP address as the unique network ID just for simplicity). Under this restriction, first 2048 IP addresses are allocated for temporary IP address pool and the rest are used for real IP addresses.

5.2   Performance Metrics

We analyze the performance of our proposed protocol using the following performance metrics:

a) *Number of Conflicts*: When a node randomly chooses a real IP address, that address may conflict with an already allocated IP address to another node in the network. We define this situation as a *conflict* and count total number of such situations. Note that this conflict is ultimately resolved with the help of DDSs.

b) *Average latency*: Latency is the time interval between the moment when a node joins in the network and the moment when it acquires a non-conflicting real IP address. We sum up such latency for all nodes and find the average.

c) *Average DDT length*: We keep track of the number of entries in each node's *Duplicate-IP Detection Table* (DDT). All nodes' DDT size are summed together to get an average length. For a scalable protocol, the size of DDT should grow very little with the increase in total number of nodes.

d) *Protocol Overhead*: It is defined as a ratio of total size of overhead packets in kilobytes to total number of nodes. For any scalable protocol, this number should be a bounded constant.

e) *Average Packet loss*: Any UPDATE/QUERY packets may get lost due to the limitation of geographic forwarding (i.e. loop-hole) and/or during *transient period* of a node. We count all those losses and take an average.

f) *Average REQUEST_QUEUE length*: This is defined as average number of entries in REQUEST_QUEUE of nodes.

5.3   Simulation Results

At first we show average number of conflicts in Fig. 3(a) for both static and mobile networks. On the average only (roughly) one conflicting situation occurs per node. The number of conflicts increases very slowly as the network size grows. Mobile networks have slightly more conflicting situations than static networks due to mobility.

Fig. 3(b) demonstrates the average latency. On the average, a node needs 8 seconds to 9.5 seconds to acquire a real IP address after joining the network. Also average latency increments very slowly as the number of nodes increases. Dynamic networks exhibits more latency than static networks.

Average DDT length is shown in Fig. 3(c). From the figure it is clearly evident that on the average, a node keeps 7 to 9 entries. In other words, a node acts as DDS for roughly 7 to 9 other nodes in the network. Also the size does not grow too much with the increase in network size. For static networks average DDT length remains almost constant at 8.5 and grows very slowly in dynamic networks. As the protocol is truly scalable such result is quite obvious.

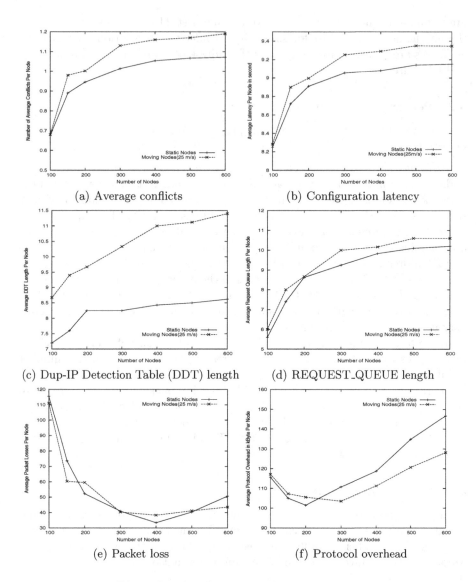

Fig. 3. Results of various performance metrics

Per node storage for REQUEST_QUEUE is shown in Fig. 3(d). The figure indicates highly scalable behavior in memory utilization. The storage requirement
to maintain the protocol is almost same with the increased network size.

Average packet loss per node occurs due to changing identity of nodes and
failure of geographic forwarding because of loop hole. As shown in Fig. 3(e),
average packet loss at the very beginning decrements rapidly as the network is
becoming more denser than the previous one. For further growth of the network,

packet losses per node remains pretty constant and have very little impact on the protocol since the network is now dense enough to prevent loop holes.

Fig. 3(f) shows protocol overhead in KB per node. Protocol overhead grows very little with the network size. In particular, when the number of nodes vary from 300 to 600 nodes, the protocol overhead increases only by 20%.

6   Conclusion

This paper proposes an efficient and scalable autoconfiguration scheme in trusted environment. Distributed DDSs are used to ensure uniqueness of chosen IP addresses. DAD algorithm is run for only one hop to acquire unique temporary IP. Grid based quad tree architecture is used to distribute DDSs evenly across the MANET. Hence, there is no leader election. The protocol is scalable in the following senses: a) No node is a single point of failure or bottleneck—the workload related to address assignment and duplicate IP detection service is distributed evenly over all the nodes in the network. b) The storage and communication cost of address assignment scheme as well as the DDSs size grow as a small valued function of the total number of nodes which also have been verified in section VI.C. Moreover, the protocol handles problems of turning on more than one node concurrently during bootstrapping which is described in section IV.

References

1. Nesargi, S., Prakash, R.: MANETConf: Configuration of a Host in Mobile Ad Hoc Network. In: Proceedings of IEEE Infocom 2002, New York, USA (June 2002)
2. Mohsin, M., Prakash, R.: IP Address Assignment in a Mobile Ad Hoc Network. In: Proceedings of IEEE Milcom 2002, Anaheim, USA (October 2002)
3. Guttman, E., Cheshire, S.: Zero configuration networking group,
   http://www.ietf.org/html.charters/zeroconf-charter.html
   (Cited February 21, 2003)
4. Weniger, K., Zitterbart, M.: IPv6 Autoconfiguration in Large-Scale Mobile Ad-Hoc networks. In: Proceedings of European Wireless 2002, Italy (February 2002)
5. Weniger, K.: PACMAN: Passive Autoconfiguration for Mobile Ad Hoc Networks. Proc. of IEEE Journal on Selected Areas in Communications (JSAC) (March 2005)
6. Perkins, C.E., Malinen, J.T., Wakikawa, R., Royer, E.M., Sun, Y.: IP Address Autoconfiguration for Ad Hoc Networks. Draft-ietf-manet-autoconf-01.txt (2001)
7. Xu, T., Wu, J.: Quorum Based IP Address Autoconfiguration in Mobile Ad Hoc Networks. In: Proceedings of International Conference on Distributed Computing Systems Workshops, ICDCSW 2007 (2007)
8. Sun, Y., Royer, E.M.: Dynamic Address Configuration in Mobile Ad Hoc Networks. In: Proceedings of Wireless Communications & Mobile Computing (2004)
9. Li, J., Jannotti, J., Cuoto, D.D., Karger, D., Morris, R.: A Scalable Location Service for Geographic Ad Hoc Routing. In: Proceedings of the ACM/IEEE Mobicom 2000, pp. 120–130 (2000)
10. Droms, R.: Dynamic Host Configuration Protocol,
    http://www.ietf.org/rfc/rfc2131.txt (Cited March 1997)
11. Thomson, S., Narten, T.: IPv6 Stateless Address Autoconfiguration, IETF RFC 2462 - Standards Track (December 1998)

Towards Fair Leader Election in Wireless Networks*

Zbigniew Gołębiewski[1,2], Marek Klonowski[1],
Michał Koza[1], and Mirosław Kutyłowski[1]

[1] Institute of Mathematics and Computer Science, Wrocław University of Technology
Michal.Koza@pwr.wroc.pl, {klonowski,mirekk}@im.pwr.wroc.pl
[2] Institute of Computer Science, Wrocław University
Zbigniew.Golebiewski@ii.uni.wroc.pl

Abstract. In this paper we consider a leader election problem in ad-hoc single hop radio sensor network with an adversary. The aim of the adversary is to be chosen as a leader. In many scenarios it can be a staring point for performing other attacks and taking control over the whole network.

In our paper we show that in typical and well-known algorithms it is not possible to avoid this threat, i.e. the adversary can always use such strategy, that the node under its control becomes a leader with high probability. This attack is efficient even if the adversary controls very small number of nodes. Moreover, we show that it is not even possible in practice to detect such malicious behaviour.

Our second contribution is a new leader election algorithm that provides, to some extent, immunity against this types of attack. We consider several realistic network models and we design appropriate methods for each of them. We also show that in some scenarios it is not possible to prevent the adversary from becoming the leader.

1 Introduction

Fairness in radio access. One of the key issues in wireless ad hoc networks is granting access to the radio channel. This is difficult, since there is no controlling unit. It is neither known in advance which stations are actually in the network nor which stations wish to transmit. On the other hand, the communication channel is severely limited, so a certain level of fairness of radio channel access should be guaranteed. However, the stations may cheat in order to get a higher share of the radio channel. As we shall see, cheating is quite easy, while detecting unfair behavior is problematic.

It is worth saying that for the wired communication networks the situation is completely different. First, the communication channel in a local network has usually large capacity, so there is no reason for an unfair competition. Second, the network nodes are more or less known and a node offending the rules can be easily excluded from the network. Third, getting access to the network is not that easy as in the case of ad hoc wireless network architecture.

---

* This paper was supported by funds for science in years 2008-2011 from Polish Ministry of Science and Higher Education, grant No. N N206 257335 and Collaborative Project FRONTS within 7th Framework Programme of Comission of European Communities Grant No. 215270.

P.M. Ruiz and J.J. Garcia-Luna-Aceves (Eds.): ADHOC-NOW 2009, LNCS 5793, pp. 166–179, 2009.

Leader election. The problem described so far is a part of a more general issue concerning security of ad hoc networks. In fact, determining the station which can access the radio channel for transmission is a classical problem of *electing a leader*. Indeed it is a basic component of many protocols and it is particularly important for ad hoc environment as a very basic component of self-organization of ad hoc networks. Quite often, the leader is responsible for performing some special tasks in the network (not necessarily as a leader in a literal sense).

Gaining control over the network. Through unfair participation in the leader election protocol an adversary may gain a high degree of control over an ad hoc network. In regular circumstances, if all stations perform exactly the same algorithm and have the same priority to become a leader, then each node has the same probability of winning. If an adversary is controlling some number of nodes and these nodes behave correctly, then the probability that a node controlled by the adversary will become the leader is proportional to the fraction of adversarial nodes in the set of all nodes.

The problem is that even with a single node the adversary may try to gain control over the network. The attack might be extremely simple: a device controlled by the adversary emulates a number of devices behaving correctly. This increases the chances of the adversary since the fraction of adversarial stations is artificially increased. On the other hand, within the standard communication framework it is hard to recognize if two messages come from technically different devices.

To the best of our knowledge, the issue of unfair execution of leader election has been ignored so far – the algorithms are designed under the assumption that all nodes behave honestly. Consequently, they offer no immunity against attacks described above. Moreover, the problem seems to be unsolvable – how can one distinguish between messages sent by two different devices from messages sent by a single device holding all information normally stored by these devices? Of course, with physical measurements in the field and analysis of electromagnetic activity of the stations it would be possible to detect that a single station is pretending several stations. However, these countermeasures are unavailable for ad hoc networks composed of simple devices.

Our goal is to convince that the situation is not that hopeless and that one can achieve some degree of fairness in leader election in ad hoc networks without resorting to advanced equipment. The idea is based on some peculiarities of radio communication. Moreover, it seems that more solutions of this kind are possible.

Different approaches of defense are possible. One can confine oneself to detection of malicious leader election. The other strategy would be to discourage malicious behavior by reducing chances of becoming the leader or by increasing the energy usage of malicious nodes (leading to exhaustion of batteries).

1.1   Previous Work

Leader election algorithms. Due to the application in mind (choosing a station which gets the right to transmit over the shared radio channel) we focus ourselves on single-hop networks, where a message sent by one station can be received by all other stations.

Leader election problem for ad hoc networks has been considered for two cases: for a known number and for an unknown number of participating stations (also called *size of the network*). There are many papers on leader election problem in radio networks with an unknown network size. In a seminal paper [15] Willard presented a leader election protocol for a single-channel, single-hop radio network with collision detection. In average case it requires $\log \log n + o(\log \log n)$ time slots. This algorithm has been improved in papers [6,13,14,1].

Leader election protocols with known number of stations assume that before launching leader election the number of nodes in the network is determined, at least approximately. Usually, the core element of such leader election algorithms is an extremely simple procedure we call in the following *Basic Method* [12].

Unfortunately, the algorithms presented in the literature allow an adversary to influence the protocol so that its station has much better chances to become the leader. This is particularly easy for algorithms with a fine structure, where creating even a few collisions may influence the execution so that many candidates are eliminated. These attacks do not even require creating virtual stations emulated by the malicious station.

Adversary immune algorithms. Constructions of adversary immune algorithms for single hop radio networks were already presented in at least 3 papers. These solutions are focused on an *external adversary* who can merely disrupt communication by creating collisions. That is, it is assumed that the adversary cannot create valid messages, as they are protected by some cryptographic message authentication codes (see for instance [3]). These solutions do not help against an *internal adversary*, who may himself participate in the protocol.

A randomized leader election algorithm running in time $O(\log^3 n)$ with energy cost $O(\log n)$ is presented in [9]. Paper [10] presents a randomized initialization algorithm with runtime $O(n)$ and energy cost $O(\log n)$. Both papers mentioned above assume that the approximate network size is known.

In [11] authors consider aloha protocol with selfish users (the aim of every node is to broadcast its message as quickly as possible) from game theoretic perspective. Considered issues are to some extent similar to our analysis, however it seems to be hard to apply this analysis to our problem.

In [4] authors introduce efficient protocol for reliably exchanging information in a single-hop, multi-channel radio network. Authors model the interference by an adversary that can simultaneously disrupt up to t of the C available channels. At the core of proposed algorithm lies combinatorial function called multi-selector. Considered issues are to some extent similar to our analysis, but the communication model and the problem that we cope with in our paper are different.

Article [8] presents a size approximation algorithm with runtime $O(\log^{2.5} n \cdot \log \log n)$ and energy cost $O(\log \log n \cdot \sqrt{\log n})$. In all these protocols the adversary may use more energy than the protocol participants, namely $\Theta(\log n)$ (some limitation on energy cost by the adversary is necessary, since these tasks cannot succeed if, for instance the adversary jams the whole communication). In the paper [5] authors claim that electing a leader can be delayed for $2\beta + \Omega(\log n)$ rounds assuming that the adversary have only limited broadcast budget (β).

We should also mention about Sybil attack which comes from computer security and p2p studies. The behaviour of Sybil attack is to some extent similar to the attack described in our paper but the computational power and capabilities of devices considered in case of Sybil attack cannot be compared with computational power and capabilities of the sensors in ad-hoc radio networks. Thus the solutions for Sybil attack cannot be transferred to the field of radio sensor networks.

1.2 Paper Contents

Our goal. The main goal of this paper is to analyze possibilities of constructing leader election algorithms immune against an internal adversary trying to become a leader by executing the protocol in an unfair way. So far, we are not looking for ultimate solutions, but for models where such algorithms can be proposed. Thus we are not focused on energy cost or other complexity measures of the algorithms proposed.

Obviously, an adversary can always block a network by transmitting continuously or in a more sophisticated way. However, the goal of the adversary is different: he wishes to become a leader. Thus blocking the network is considered as adversary's defeat. We are trying to construct an algorithm which would elect a leader with probability 1 in the presence of an adversary, who tries to become a leader, but should remain undetected as a malicious party.

Paper organization and contribution. In Sect. 2 we show that the basic method is not immune against an aggressive adversary. Next, in Sect. 3.1 we stress that if adversary can have multiple identities and transmitting stations can listen to the channel, then the adversary can become a leader with probability as close to 1 as he desires. In Sect. 3.2 we show a simple algorithm that provide fairness of leader election in case when the adversary cannot have fake identities, but he can control more than one node in a network. In Sect. 3.3 we show an algorithm that significantly decreases adversary's probability to become a leader on condition that a station can either transmit or listen to the channel at a given moment.

2 Basic Method

2.1 Definition of the Protocol

We assume that the time is divided into slots, stations are synchronized enough to transmit in those slots and within a slot a station of the network can either listen or transmit over the shared radio channel.If more than one station transmits during a single slot, then the messages collide and no message can be reconstructed by the stations monitoring the channel. If the stations are able to recognize that there was a collision, then we talk about *collision detection model*, otherwise it is called *no-collision detection model*.

Below we recall the very basic idea for leader election in such a network (regardless of collision detection issues):

It is easy to see that the probability to elect a leader in a single execution of the loop it is optimal to choose $p = 1/n$ where n is the number of station in the network.

It is obvious that in a network with n stations if all station behave in the same way (transmit with the same probability p) each station x equal chance to become the leader $\Pr(L(x)) = 1/n$. First let us check how the probabilities change, if adversary stations broadcast with a different (greater) probability:

Algorithm 1. A sketch of Basic Method

1: **loop**
2:    **if** decide to send with probability p **then**
3:        send(ID);
4:    **end if**
5:    **if** there is a single transmission **then**
6:        **return** LEADER = transmitted ID;
7:    **end if**
8: **end loop**

Lemma 1. *Let S denote the set of honest stations ($|S| = n$) and Z be the set of stations controlled by the adversary ($|Z| = m$). Let $L(Z)$ denote an event that a node from Z becomes a leader. Let us consider Basic Method with n stations from the set S broadcasting with probability p and m stations from the set Z broadcasting with probability p_z. Then the probability that one of adversarial stations becomes a leader equals $\Pr(L(Z)) = \frac{mp_z(1-p)}{mp_z(1-p)+np(1-p_z)}$, and it grows with p_z reaching 1 for $p_z = 1$ and $p < 1$.*

Proof

$$\Pr(L(Z)) = \sum_{j=1}^{\infty} \Pr(\text{leader from } Z \text{ chosen in round } j \mid \text{some station from } Z$$
$$\text{participates in round } j) \cdot \Pr(\text{some station from } Z \text{ participates in round } j).$$

Note that in this case the total number of stations in a network equals $|S| + |Z| = n + m$. The probability that a leader is chosen in a given round conditioned by the event that a node $z \in Z$ broadcasts in this round equals $\binom{m}{m-1}p_z(1-p_z)^{m-1}(1-p)^n$.
The probability that the leader is not chosen in a given round equals

$$1 - \left(\binom{m}{1}p_z(1-p_z)^{m-1}(1-p)^n + \binom{n}{1}p(1-p)^{n-1}(1-p_z)^m \right)$$

By substituting we get immediately:

$$\Pr(L(Z)) = \sum_{j=1}^{\infty} \left(1 - \left(mp_z(1-p_z)^{m-1}(1-p)^n + np(1-p)^{n-1}(1-p_z)^m\right)\right)^{j-1} \cdots$$
$$\cdot \, mp_z(1-p_z)^{m-1}(1-p)^n = \frac{mp_z(1-p)}{mp_z(1-p)+np(1-p_z)}.$$

2.2 Adversary Detection

As we have seen, an adversary sending aggressively during the execution of Basic Method increases its chances to become the leader. However, in this case the overall behavior of the algorithm changes and one can notice that something goes wrong. We assume that each honest station $s \in S$ transmits with the optimal probability $p = \frac{1}{n}$. Information that stations observe is a sequence of slots with silence (no station transmitting) and collisions followed by one successful transmission containing a message with the leader's ID. Thus the only way they can recognize malicious behavior is to detect that algorithm lasts too long or the ratio between the silent trials and the trials with collisions is far from expectations.

Measuring success time. The expected number of slots used by the algorithm depends only on single trial success probability which equals $P = n\frac{1}{n}\left(1 - \frac{1}{n}\right)^{n-1} = \left(1 - \frac{1}{n}\right)^{n-1}$. Now consider the situation when a single adversary $z \in Z$ is added to the system. It is acting as any other station, except that it transmits with a different probability p_z (depending on its aggressiveness level). Single trial success probability would be $P_z = p_z\left(1 - \frac{1}{n}\right)^{n} + (1-p_z)n\frac{1}{n}\left(1 - \frac{1}{n}\right)^{n-1} = \left(1 - \frac{1}{n}\right)^{n-1}\frac{n-p_z}{n}$. The difference between this two probabilities is $P - P_z = \left(1 - \frac{1}{n}\right)^{n-1} - \left(1 - \frac{1}{n}\right)^{n-1}\frac{n-p_z}{n} = (1-\frac{1}{n})^{n-1}\frac{p_z}{n} < \frac{2}{n}$. For example, in a system with $n = 100$ stations success probability of a single trial is $P \approx 0.3697$. If we add an aggressive adversary always transmitting (i.e. $p_z = 1$), then the success probability in a single trial is $P_z \approx 0.3660$. The difference is insignificant and in both cases we expect the algorithm to terminate after about three rounds.

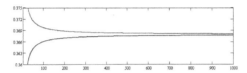

Fig. 1. Trial success probabilities with adversary transmitting with $p_z = 1$ (bottom trace), and without adversary (top trace)

It is interesting to see that if a station $s \in S$ is replaced by an adversarial station $z \in Z$ (so the number of all stations remains unchanged), then the success probability of a single trial equals $P_z = p_z\left(1 - \frac{1}{n}\right)^{n-1} + (1-p_z)(n-1)\frac{1}{n}\left(1 - \frac{1}{n}\right)^{n-2} = \left(1 - \frac{1}{n}\right)^{n-1}$. Surprisingly, the probability does not change! Thereby, we can state the following lemma:

Lemma 2. *In a network performing leader election with Basic Method it is impossible to detect an adversary by examining the time necessary to elect the leader.*

This means that an adversary transmitting with probability $p_z = 1$ (which gives him certainty of becoming leader) will remain undetected.

Measuring silence periods. Previous considerations are relevant for systems with no-collision detection. Indeed, in such a case the only observable information is the number of slots before choosing the leader. Now we analyze Basic Method procedure for the collision detection model, where a station can distinguish between the case when two or more stations transmit and the situation where no station is broadcasting. In such a model one could expect that the presence of an adversary transmitting quite aggressively can be detected by comparing the number of silent time slots and the number of collisions. However, we show that observable effects of algorithm executions with an adversary broadcasting with probability $p_z \gg \frac{1}{n}$ are in practice indistinguishable from the case of no adversary as long as p_z is not too big.

Let us note that the observation gained by all stations can be represented as a pair (T, X), where T is the number of trials before a single station was broadcasting and X is the number of silent slots within the first T slots. So $T - X$ is a number of slots where a conflict has occurred. Let us note that $T \sim \text{Geo}(1 - P_{sORc}) - 1$, where P_{sORc} is a probability of silence or collision, and Geo denotes geometric distribution of a random variable.

Since the stations operate independently, X has a binomial distribution strongly dependent on parameter T, namely $X \sim \mathrm{Bin}(T, P_s)$ for probability P_s representing the probability of silent slot on condition that no station has transmitted or there has been a conflict.

Let us consider two systems, the first one with n nodes, and the second one with n honest stations and one station controlled by the adversary that broadcasts the signal with probability $p_z > 0$. The honest stations in both systems broadcast with probability $\frac{1}{n}$. Let $H = (T, \mathrm{Bin}(T, r))$ and $H^* = (T^*, \mathrm{Bin}(T^*, r^*))$ be a random variable representing the first and the second case, respectively. Below we compare these distributions using the following definition:

Definition 1. *We say that random variables X, Y are (α, δ)-indistinguishable, if there exists a set A such that:* $\Pr[X \in A] \geq \delta, \Pr[Y \in A] \geq \delta$ *and for every $a \in A$ holds* $\frac{1}{\alpha} < \frac{\Pr[X=a]}{\Pr[Y=a]} < \alpha.$

This definition can be regarded as a variant of definition of (α, δ)-privacy used for example in paper [2]. It well reflects the intuition of indistinguishably: two models with probability at least $1 - \delta$ yield the results such that their probabilities can differ at most by a factor of α. We show the following lemma:

Lemma 3. *H^* and H are $(3, 0.3)$-indistinguishable as long as $p_z \leq 0.5$ for appropriate number of stations n in the system.*

Sketch of a proof. Let us compute $L(n, t, l, p_z) = \frac{\Pr[H=(t,l)]}{\Pr[H^*=(t,l)]}$. First, note that $\Pr[H = (t, l)] = \binom{t}{l}(1 - p)^{t-l}p^l(1 - r)r^t$ and $\Pr[H^* = (t, l)] = \binom{t}{l}(1 - p^*)^{t-l}p^{*l}(1 - r^*)(r^*)^t$. We substitute r and $r*$ by appropriate values, namely:

- $r = 1 - \left(1 - \frac{1}{n}\right)^{n-1}$ (probability that the leader is not chosen in a particular trial, if there is no adversary),
- $r^* = 1 - p_z\left(1 - \frac{1}{n}\right)^n - (1 - p_z)\left(1 - \frac{1}{n}\right)^{n-1}$ (probability that the leader is not chosen in particular trial, if there is an adversary station broadcasting with probability p_z),
- $p = \frac{\left(1 - \frac{1}{n}\right)^n}{1 - \left(1 - \frac{1}{n}\right)^{n-1}}$ (probability that the slot is silent on condition that the leader is not chosen in the system without the adversary),
- $p^* = \frac{(1-p_z)\left(1-\frac{1}{n}\right)^n}{1 - p_z\left(1-\frac{1}{n}\right)^n - (1-p_z)\left(1-\frac{1}{n}\right)^{n-1}}$ (probability there is a silent slot on condition that there is an adversary controlling a station broadcasting with probability p_z).

Hence we get:

$$L(n, t, l, p_z) = \frac{n}{n-p_z}\left(\frac{1-\left(\frac{n-1}{n}\right)^{n-1}}{1+(-n+p_z)\frac{(n-1)^{n-1}}{n^n}}\right)^t\left(\frac{(n-1)^{n-1}(n-p_z)-n^n}{(p_z-1)(n^n-n(n-1)^{n-1})}\right)^l$$
$$\cdot\left(1 + \frac{1}{\frac{n}{n-1}-\frac{n^n}{(n-1)^n}}\right)^{t-l} / \left(1 - \frac{(n-1)^n(-1+p_z)}{(n-1)^{n-1}(n-p_z)-n^n}\right)^{t-l}.$$

One can easily see that for any fixed $t, l \geq 0$ and $1 \geq p_z \geq 0$

$$\hat{L}(t, l, p_z) = \lim_{n \to \infty} L(n, t, l, p_z) = (1 - p_z)^{-l} \left(\frac{e-2}{e-2+p_z} \right)^{t-l} .$$

Moreover, one can check that the convergence rate is very fast.

It is important that parameter t has to be small with high probability in both models. The expected value of t tends very quickly to e in both models. Even a rough estimation shows that in both models $t < 6$ with probability at least 0.7. Further investigations show that $1/3 < \hat{L}(t, l, p_z) < 3$ as long as $t < 6$ and $p_z \leq 0.5$. ☐

Lemma 3 says that with probability at least 0.7 in presence of a quite aggressive adversary the algorithm behavior cannot be distinguished from a run of the algorithm without an adversary.

Let us note that the above result cannot be applied to the situation where many consecutive leader elections are performed and the adversary has very aggressive behavior (i.e. when p_z is close to 1). In this case it is possible to apply some statistical tests based on the fact that the number of silent trials is suspiciously low.

3   Models

We will consider three network models differing in a couple of assumptions. In general, we assume collision detection – so stations can distinguish between silence and noise, no knowledge about the size of the network and unlimited adversary's power resources. We do not put any constraints on fair stations either, but algorithms we present do not exceed time complexity $n \log n$. The stations executing leader election procedure have unique IDs which are initially unknown to other participants.

We will show that the ability to simulate multiple fake identities, which is easy without some trusted authority or advanced cryptography, makes an adversary quite powerful. The first model shows that having this ability an adversary can actually completely control the network. The second model shows that without this ability we can construct an algorithm that reduces adversary chances proportionally to the fraction of captured stations in the network. The third model shows how to utilize a standard technical feature to prevent an adversary with a single station from having more identities during a leader election process.

3.1   Model with Full Knowledge and Fake Adversary Identities

We now assume that adversary can have multiple identities, and that transmitting station can monitor the channel state - so everybody has full knowledge about algorithm execution. In this model a single adversary may become the leader with probability as close to 1 as he desires. The most obvious way it can be done is generating an arbitrarily big number of fake identities and then acting according to the algorithm emulating transmissions of fake stations. As the algorithm is symmetric, it gives him success probability $P(L(z)) = \frac{m}{m+n}$, where m is the number of (fake) adversary identities and n is the number of honest stations. The number of stations in the system is unknown, but the adversary can keep track of all stations that managed to transmit their IDs and adjust the amount of own identities. There is no way to detect the malicious activity as each node has full knowledge about the algorithm progress, so there is nothing we could ask the adversary that he would not know. As well, since single station can generate noise, the adversary can do anything that his identities would be able to do, if they would be honest.

3.2   Model with an Adversary Unable to Simulate Fake Identities

In this section we propose an algorithm for a model where adversary controls some number of stations, but his stations cannot have multiple identities. We show that it is possible to construct an algorithm in this model such that:

- probability that adversary's node is chosen as a leader is equal to the fraction of nodes controlled by the adversary in the system,
- time complexity of the algorithm is $O(n \cdot k)$, where k is the number of slots necessary to perform regular leader election (e.g. Basic Method), that would be used as a sub-procedure,
- stations can listen and broadcast at the same time, so we assume that all stations have full knowledge about the algorithm execution.

Let us note that we cannot reduce probability of becoming a leader by the adversary. Indeed, every practical leader election algorithm for ad hoc network assumes symmetric role of stations. Thus, if stations under adversary's control performs the same algorithm as other station, each station has the same probability of becoming a leader.

Verifiable parity game in ad hoc network. The rules of the game are simple: two players $\mathcal{P}_0, \mathcal{P}_1$ play a game. For $i = 0, 1$, player $\mathcal{P}_i$ chooses bit $b_i \in \{0, 1\}$, then they reveal them simultaneously. The winner is $\mathcal{P}_{b_1 + b_2 \mod 2}$. One can easy check that the best strategy for each player is to chose $b_i = 1$ with probability $1/2$. This gives probability of winning the game exactly $1/2$.

We can construct a verifiable parity game for two stations in our model. Verifiable means that all stations may check the correct behavior of the playing stations. The game needs at most three slots:

1st slot. Playing stations broadcast with probability $1/2$. If there is a single transmission the first station wins. Otherwise, if there is a silence or collision (i.e. zero or two stations are broadcasting) the second station becomes the leader.

2nd and 3rd slot. If there was a collision in the the 1st slot, both playing stations are silent in the 2nd and in the 3rd slot. If there was a collision and the first playing station was not broadcasting in the 1st slot, it broadcasts in the 2nd slot. Similarly, if there was a collision in the 1st slot and the second playing station was silent, it broadcast in the 3rd slot. Any transmission in 2nd or 3rg slot means an alarm.

If there was a collision in the first slot and there was no silence in the 2nd and the 3rd slot, all stations stop the procedure and the leader is not chosen. Let us note that the adversary having more than one station is able to force a collision in the first slot. However it is unable to generate silence in the 2nd and the 3rd slot.

Of course the adversary is able to stop the procedure, however it is possible also by generating collisions in all slots.

Algorithm

Algorithm consists of two phases, first we make a list of all stations, then one station is being chosen as leader performing parity games many times. For the sake of simplicity we assume that the number of stations n is a power of 2.

Listing stations. To list all the stations we can use any leader election algorithm (possibly for networks with an unknown number of stations) as a building block (e.g. tournament algorithm [7]). Each chosen station is added to the list and does not participate in this phase anymore. This sub-procedure is repeated until all stations are on the list. After the end of each sub-procedure we introduce a "check slot" in which only stations that are not yet on the list transmit. If there is silence in this slot, then all stations are on the list. The adversary cannot cheat, since it is impossible to force any station to be silent. Cheating in leader election does not help him as well as the first phase lasts as long as needed, so that each station appear the list, and since each station can be added only once.

Parity game verification. For pairs of stations with consecutive numbers from the list the parity game is performed. Looser of each pair is removed from the list. After $n/2$ parity games we have $n/2$ stations on the list. We continue this process until only one station remains on the list and this station is chosen for a leader.

It is easy to check that if the winning station is chosen with probability $1/2$ then each station becomes a leader with probability exactly $1/n$.

3.3   Model with Limited Knowledge and Fake Identities

The assumptions are:

- transmitting station cannot simultaneously listen to the channel - silent stations know the status of the channel, while a transmitting station knows only that it is not silent,
- an adversary can have multiple identities,
- a station can calculate a secure hash function.

In this model will be able to utilize the model property that transmitting station cannot simulateneously listen to the channel. This gives us an advantage over the adversary, since he cannot listen when any of fake stations transmits (while the other fake station should recognize the channel status).

Leader Election Algorithm with Leader Verification

We describe a leader election algorithm with verification against fake participants. It significantly decreases chances of becoming a leader by an aggressive adversary. Adjusting the algorithm parameters will allow to manipulate the trade off between speed and credibility. The algorithm consists of three phases. Initially all stations get listed, one of them is elected as a leader at random and then it is verified against having any fake identities in the set.

Auxiliary procedures. To construct a leader election algorithm with leader verification we need some auxiliary procedures:

Listing the stations. The stations are listed in the same way as for the previous model. The difference is that the adversary can place on the list as many fake identities as he desires. (It would force any symmetric procedure to give him much more chances compared to other stations.)

Riddle. This procedure is the key point for exposing multiple adversary identities on the list. It poses a riddle that with high probability an aggressive adversary cannot answer. The procedure lasts a couple of rounds. It forces a leader (chosen at random from he set of stations) to transmit and thus prevents him from listening. Other stations transmit with such probability so that in each round the leader transmission is jammed with probability 0.5 (it is easy to check that for each station jamming probability shall be $^{n-1}\sqrt{0.5}$ where n is the number of stations on the list). This way each station but the leader (and its fake identities) know exactly when the leader was jammed. Indeed, a silent station can hear if there is noise or single leader transmission, while the transmitting ones know for sure that the leader transmission is jammed (by them) without inspecting the channel. The leader could try to cheat in this round by being silent and trying to listen, but if the other stations hear silence, then it would be evident that the leader was cheating and can be excluded from the list.

Answer Commitment. This procedure gathers answer cryptographic commitments from all the candidates. The commitment should be the result of a one-way function (e.g. a hash function) and it has to depend on station ID and some random value to prevent adversary from guessing the answer or replaying other station commitments.

Answer. This procedure gathers answers from all the candidates. An answer consists of the actual *answer*, station ID and random number used to generate the answer commitment. An *Answer* is a list of riddle trials for which the leader was jammed.

Random Permutation. This procedure produces a random permutation of stations. In asks stations first to send some random number commitment and to reveal these numbers after all commitments are there. Combination of these numbers indicates the permutation.

Algorithm description. Having described all needed procedures we can state the actual algorithm.

First, the list of all stations (including the fake ones) is created. Then the list is reordered using the Random Permutation procedure. The first station on the list is the *leader candidate* who needs to pass verification to become finally the leader.

Next, the riddle is posed. Since a single station can transmit noise, the adversary being the leader candidate could send noise continuously and then easily construct the correct answer. Thus we can demand some minimal number of not jammed transmissions. After the riddle a single alarm slot can be reserved. If any station claims that there were too few single transmissions, it can sound the alarm and restart the riddle

Algorithm 2. Leader Election with verification
1: stations = list_stations()
2: **repeat**
3:      $stations$ =   random_permutation($stations$)
4:      $leader\_candidate = stations[0]$
5:      **if** I am the Leader Candidate **then**
6:          $state =$ CANDIDATE
7:      **end if**
8:      **repeat**
9:          riddle()
10:     **until** not too much noise
11:     answer_commitment()
12:     answer()
13:     remove all nodes that answered wrong from set of candidates
14: **until** all answers were correct

Algorithm 3. Riddle(t) t-number of rounds
1: **for** $i = 1$ to t **do**
2:      **if** $state =$ LEADER **then**
3:          send(ID)
4:      **else**
5:          **if** jam with prob $^{n-}\sqrt[1]{0.5}$ **then**
6:              send(ID)
7:          **else**
8:              listen()
9:          **end if**
10:     **end if**
11: **end for**

procedure. Riddle is then repeated, but without changing the leader candidate. (Changing leader candidate at this step would let the adversary to eliminate any fair leader candidate.)

Next, all stations except for the leader candidate – one after another, send answer commitments. The commitments are necessary as we do not want the solution to be revealed after the first station answers. All stations that did not answer correctly can be removed from the set as suspicious. This procedure is designed to detect other copies of a malicious leader, however let us state clearly that we must not remove the leader candidate in case of any incorrect answer. This would open a way for the adversary to eliminate fair candidates by sacrificing one of its copies.

If any station was removed, stations are re-randomized and another leader candidate is tested. It is very important that if the test fails the set of candidates is not constructed again. This would allow the adversary to restart the whole algorithm every time when the leader is not one of his copies and wait for luck in guessing the riddle. This way adversary can ensure that he is chosen a leader in finite time. After a closer look we will notice that even if there is a lot of adversary's fake identities, once one of them becomes the candidate, with a high probability all its copies with fake identities will be removed, then the set is re-randomized. After reordering the list at most one station on the list is controlled by the adversary, so he has the same chances as the other stations. If a fair station is chosen, the adversary cannot achieve much. He could answer in a wrong way to force re-randomization. However in this case one of his (fake) IDs would be removed from the list of stations.

Time complexity. Let us estimate time complexity of the above algorithm. Phase one is repeating leader election algorithms until each station wins one of them. If for instance we take algorithm described in [7] the first phase has complexity of $O(n \log n)$.

Complexity of posing the riddle is $O(t)$ where t is a security parameter. Gathering answers can be done in linear time. Thus the total time complexity is $O(n \log n)$ as we do not expect t to be greater than $n \log n$.

Fig. 2. Example algorithm 2. execution: the numbers in the top row are step numbers, the numbers in boxes represent stations ID's. In steps $1, 3, 5, 7, 9, 11$ the stations are listed (by means of a standard leader election algorithm). In steps $2, 4, 6, 8, 10, 12$ checks are performed to see, if there are still stations in the system not present on the list: noise (steps $2, 4, 6, 8, 10$) signifies that there are still some unlisted stations; silence (step 12) signifies that all stations are already on the list. After step 12, the list is randomly sorted and first station becomes the candidate (here $ID = 5$). In steps $13 - 17$ the riddle is posed, the answer commitments are gathered in steps $18 - 21$. Stations' answers are revealed in steps $22 - 25$. If all answers are correct, the leader candidate becomes the Leader; if any station answered wrongly it is removed from the list and algorithm goes back to step 13.

4   Conclusions

The presented models show that an internal adversary poses major and realistic threats to ad hoc systems. We showed that ability to emulate virtual stations with fake identities might be a quite big advantage of the adversary.

Presented models prove that it is easy to construct algorithms to completely diminish advantage of adversary that cannot have multiple identities, and that without trying to deprive him of this ability it is completely impossible to limit his chances in any way. Although assuming that the adversary will be unable to have multiple identities is quite unrealistic, it is optimistic to discover that we can utilize other network parameters to defend against such a behaviour. Algorithm with leader verification that we proposed is not merely a theoretical model. It is actually a scheme that is quite suited for implementations. Indeed: It is quite immune against the DoS attacks; It does not stop in case of any alarm reported by any station; It restarts each phase in such a way that it does not give the adversary any advantage. However, it does not help against two cooperating adversaries. Namely, they can cheat during verification since one of them can always listen and inform the other one about the outcome of the riddles. Finding a simple and efficient mechanism that would work in this scenario is an interesting and challenging problem.

References

1. Bordim, J.L., Ito, Y., Nakano, K.: Randomized leader election protocols in noisy radio networks with a single transceiver. In: Guo, M., Yang, L.T., Di Martino, B., Zima, H.P., Dongarra, J., Tang, F. (eds.) ISPA 2006. LNCS, vol. 4330, pp. 246–256. Springer, Heidelberg (2006)

2. Chaudhuri, K., Mishra, N.: When random sampling preserves privacy. In: Dwork, C. (ed.) CRYPTO 2006. LNCS, vol. 4117, pp. 198–213. Springer, Heidelberg (2006)
3. Dolev, S., Gilbert, S., Guerraoui, R., Newport, C.C.: Secure communication over radio channels. In: Bazzi, R.A., Patt-Shamir, B. (eds.) PODC, pp. 105–114. ACM, New York (2008)
4. Gilbert, S., Guerraoui, R., Kowalski, D., Newport, C.: Interference-Resilient Information Exchange. In: IEEE InfoCom 2009 (2009)
5. Gilbert, S., Guerraoui, R., Newport, C.C.: Of malicious motes and suspicious sensors: On the efficiency of malicious interference in wireless networks. In: Shvartsman, M.M.A.A. (ed.) OPODIS 2006. LNCS, vol. 4305, pp. 215–229. Springer, Heidelberg (2006)
6. Hayashi, T., Nakano, K., Olariu, S.: Randomized initialization protocols for packet radio networks. In: IPPS/SPDP, p. 544. IEEE Computer Society, Los Alamitos (1999)
7. Janson, S., Szpankowski, W.: Analysis of an asymmetric leader election algorithm. Electr. J. Comb. 4(1) (1997)
8. Kabarowski, J., Kutyłowski, M., Rutkowski, W.: Adversary immune size approximation of single-hop radio networks. In: Cai, J.-Y., Cooper, S.B., Li, A. (eds.) TAMC 2006. LNCS, vol. 3959, pp. 148–158. Springer, Heidelberg (2006)
9. Kutyłowski, M., Rutkowski, W.: Adversary immune leader election in ad hoc radio networks. In: Di Battista, G., Zwick, U. (eds.) ESA 2003. LNCS, vol. 2832, pp. 397–408. Springer, Heidelberg (2003)
10. Kutyłowski, M., Rutkowski, W.: Secure initialization in single-hop radio networks. In: Castelluccia, C., Hartenstein, H., Paar, C., Westhoff, D. (eds.) ESAS 2004. LNCS, vol. 3313, pp. 31–41. Springer, Heidelberg (2005)
11. MacKenzie, A., Wicker, S.B.: Stability of multipacket slotted aloha with selfish users and perfect information. In: INFOCOM (2003)
12. Metcalfe, R.M., Boggs, D.R.: Ethernet: distributed packet switching for local computer networks. Commun. ACM 19(7), 395–404 (1976)
13. Nakano, K., Olariu, S.: Randomized o (log log n)-round leader election protocols in packet radio networks. In: Chwa, K.-Y., Ibarra, O.H. (eds.) ISAAC 1998. LNCS, vol. 1533, pp. 209–218. Springer, Heidelberg (1998)
14. Nakano, K., Olariu, S.: Randomized leader election protocols in radio networks with no collision detection. In: Lee, D.T., Teng, S.-H. (eds.) ISAAC 2000. LNCS, vol. 1969, pp. 362–373. Springer, Heidelberg (2000)
15. Willard, D.E.: Log-logarithmic selection resolution protocols in a multiple access channel. SIAM J. Comput. 15(2), 468–477 (1986)

Auction Aggregation Protocols for Wireless Robot-Robot Coordination

Ivan Mezei[1], Veljko Malbasa[1], and Ivan Stojmenovic[1,2]

[1] FTN, University of Novi Sad, Serbia
[2] SITE, University of Ottawa, Canada
imezei@uns.ac.rs, malbasa@uns.ac.rs, stojmenovic@gmail.com

Abstract. Robots coordinate among themselves to select one of them to respond to an event reported to one of robots. The goal is to minimize the communication cost of selecting best robot, response time, and cost of performing the task. Existing solutions are either centralized, neglecting communication cost, assuming complete graph, or based on flooding with individual responses to robot decision maker (*simple auction* protocol), ignoring communication cost and response time bound. This article proposes *auction aggregation* protocols for task assignment in multi-hop wireless robot networks. Robot collector leads an auction and initiates response tree construction by transmitting search message. Each robot, after receiving the message, makes decision on whether to retransmit search message, based on the estimated response cost of its robots up to *k*-hops away. Robots wait to receive the bids from its children in the search tree, aggregates responses by selecting the best bid, and forward it back toward the robot collector (auctioning robot). When distance is used as sole cost metrics, traversal aggregation algorithm (*RFT* – routing toward the event with traversal of face containing the event) can be applied and is an optimal solution. Advantage of our auction aggregation over simple auction protocol is shown by simulation results.

Keywords: auction aggregation, robot-robot coordination.

1 Introduction

Multi robot systems (MRS) are well studied in literature [1] and the focal point of majority of MRS related papers are on the coordination and cooperation. The term *networked robotics* emerged recently emphasizing that robots can be connected by wireless medium forming a communication network. There are various applications of networked robots. They can coordinate to perform exploration, mapping, search, reconnaissance, fire prevention tasks or gaming (e.g. robot soccer). According to recent review paper on status of robotics [2], communication between entities is fundamental to both cooperation and coordination and hence the central role of the network. Communication cost for coordination among robots should be minimized for several reasons. Wireless medium is shared, so multiple synchronous messages cause collisions. Mobile robots are energy constrained. Large robot multi-hop networks may

P.M. Ruiz and J.J. Garcia-Luna-Aceves (Eds.): ADHOC-NOW 2009, LNCS 5793, pp. 180–193, 2009.

pose scalability issues and significant delay in making action decisions unless coordination protocols are tailored to the application, energy and time constraints.

Two major topics of robot-robot coordination are communication and task assignment, which are closely interrelated. In this article we only consider a simple task assignment formulation. We assume that an event was reported to one of robots, and a response by one robot is required. Thus the task assignment problem is to *find the best robot to respond to an event and assign task to it*. The input of the problem is information about event (location, response time etc.), and the output is assigned task to the best robot.

Robots are organized into a network that is modeled as the unit disk graph (UDG). All robots have the same transmission radius R, and message sent by one robot is received by all neighboring robots located at distance up to R. Robot receiving the event information needs to decide which robot is the best to respond. To make decision, it initiates message exchange (sending and receiving messages) among robots, following UDG. Normally, messages originate from and converge toward robot decision maker.

Solutions described in this article do not depend on the particular environment served by networked robots. One such environment of interest to us are wireless sensor and robot networks (WSRN), as an extension of MRS. WSRN consist of sensors and robots linked by wireless medium to perform distributed sensing of physical world, processing of sensed data, making decisions and acting upon sensed events (see Fig. 1 and Fig. 2). We will illustrate our problem statement using this scenario. Upon event occurrence (for example, a fire, or the failure of a sensor), sensors detect event and route information to one of robots in the vicinity, which may not be the closest one. The robot that receives report may itself be the best candidate for responding. However, a remote, busy or energy limited robot could receive report.

In Fig. 1, robot *R3* is the closest but event was reported to *R1*. *R1* is decision maker, and consults other robots in its vicinity to find the best responder, which would be robot closest to the event, for example. In Fig. 1, *R1* consults *R4* and *R2*, and decides that *R4* is the best robot to respond. In this example, two more robots exist, *R3* and *R5*, which are disconnected from *R1*. Robot *R3* is really the closest, but was not involved in the process of selecting best responder. In example in Fig. 2, *R3* received report because

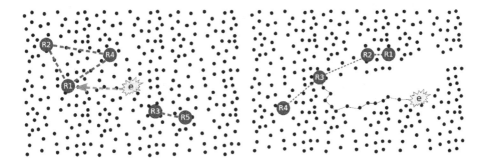

Fig. 1. Area with one event being monitored by sensors and 5 robots

Fig. 2. Sensors not deployed uniformly (or malfunctioning)

there is sensor void area between the event and closest robot *R1*. *R1* is able to act but sensors were not able to report the event directly to it. *R3* initiates bidding process and discovers the nearest robot *R1* that is then assigned to the task.

Most existing solutions referring to multi-robot coordination for single or multiple events, single or multiple robots, single or multiple tasks to each robot etc. are centralized. One of robots, or a central entity, gathers all the information from other robots and makes a decision. Communication cost for gathering information in case of multi-hop robot networks is rarely considered. Indirectly (since no details of communication protocols used are given), a *complete graph* (where each robot is within communication distance to any other robot) is assumed. Centralized solutions usually define coordination problem as an integer linear programming problem. Main advantage of a centralized solution is that, theoretically, optimal solution can be found. However, centralized solution features high computation and communication overhead, lack of scalability and slow responsiveness. Moreover, the actual cost for communicating is ignored, especially for large robot networks. It is further not clear how robots communicate if the graph is not complete one. Centralized solutions also have low fault tolerance if leader is malfunctioning in any way.

Localized and distributed solutions utilize spreading all decision making and planning responsibility among robots. We consider here the *multi-hop* UDG scenarios, where the communication graph is not complete. Robots use only locally available information to make their decision. Good scalability and fault tolerance are the main advantages. Proposed solutions are normally close to optimal one. However, decisions made based on the local information can be sometimes highly suboptimal. We identified only one distributed solution designed for multi-hop scenario, *simple auction* protocol [3], which considers multi-hop UDG model of robot communication. It is flooding based; each robot retransmits received search request exactly once, and responds to auctioneer by separate routing task. For large robot networks, it incurs unacceptable delay in selecting the best robot, although the best responding robot is expected to be near the event.

In this paper, we first propose to limit the robot selection to certain local neighborhood, even for simple auction protocol. We then propose a localized solution, based on market paradigm, called *auction aggregation protocol*. The bidding process is spreading to neighboring robots until no improvement can be envisioned within *k*-hop neighborhood of a robot that analyzes if any more remote robot could provide better service than the best service it is aware of. If not, it stops search process and responds back to its 'parent' robot with best possible recommendation it has. During the bid gathering process, best bids are forwarded back to the auctioneer robot by intermediate robots. The main advantage is that search is limited to some neighborhood and flooding potentially huge robot network is avoided. When the best robot is selected based solely on its distance to the event, the search can be very efficient by simply routing toward the event location, with traversal of face of Gabriel graph containing the event discovering the nearest robot (*RFT – routing with face traversal* algorithm). Simulation data confirm findings and show the performance of our protocol in some scenarios.

2 Literature Review

2.1 Multi-Robot Task Assignment

A taxonomy of *multi-robot task allocation* (MRTA) problems are presented in [4]. In most of the papers task assignment problem is formulated as a variant of integer linear programming problem (e.g. [3], [5]). Mobility is usually not considered (exceptions are [5], [6]). In those centralized formulations optimization objective is either energy consumption minimization, maximization of processing time, utility maximization, total travel distance minimization or residual energy maximization. Although these centralized solutions can be formulated to target our scenario (single event), they either ignore communication cost or assume complete graph.

Communication aspects of task assignment are rarely taken into account. In centralized MRTA [7], communication aspects are modeled by including one term in optimization objective function which represents the number of robot pairs that can communicate (and that should be maximized). Communication protocol is not specified and only single-hop (direct) communication is considered.

Communication efficient multi-robot (CEMR) task scheduling algorithm for heterogeneous MRS is given in [8]. CEMR assumes direct communication between each robot and a central unit, and direct communication among some robot pairs. Each robot reports its status and detected tasks to a central unit, which allocates tasks using an auction-based method with a fitness function (including capability, distance from task, and availability). Robots receive status (including position) of all other robots from the central unit, and can also ask directly help from other nearby robots. The article does not discuss any multi-hop communication protocol. Simulation is made with 6 robots, and the alternative approach is 'broadcasting', which is direct request to all other robots instead to few of them who might be available based on a priori knowledge.

Three decentralized task allocation schemes among unmanned aerial vehicles (UAVs) in destroy targets scenario using negotiation concepts from team theory and game theory are given in [9]. It is acknowledged that full communication between all UAVs poses high communication costs and idea of localized communication (communication among neighbors only) is given as well as necessity for multi-hop communication if agents are out of communication range. However only complete graph is simulated. Multi-hop communication was stated in some scenarios, but there is no discussion of any communication protocol actually applied.

In summary, finding solutions to concrete task assignment scenarios in the presence of robot mobility, when communication cost is not negligible, and communication protocols need to be specified, still remains a research challenge.

2.2 Market-Based Task Assignment and Auctions

For robot-robot coordination, a *market-based* approach [10] is considered. It is based on auctions organized by robot or sink (central unit) collecting the task, the cost of performing tasks by each robot and potential benefit to the team. Robots positioned in local neighborhood participate, but the locality is not pre-determined; it is rather task-dependent. Robots participating in the auction decide on whether or not to 'invite' more robots to the auction, as the invitation themselves cause communication overhead. Auctions as a coordination tool have been used since Contract Net Protocol was published [11] and several similar protocols are used in robotics. One of the well-known auction protocols is MURDOCH [12]. It uses anonymous broadcasting as a means to communicate and has the following five distinct steps: task announcement, metric evaluation, bid submission, auction closing and progress monitoring/contract renewal. However, MURDOCH assumes complete graph among robots, while we use UDG. Similarly, in [13] and [14], local auctions are used as a distributed solution to dynamic MRTA. However, all robots participating in auction can communicate directly to the auctioneer. There are some articles that report improvements of auction algorithms used as solution to MRTA in terms of computational complexity [15], [16], [17].

Survey article [18] summarizes research work done in the field of robot coordination using market-based approach. Auction can be either centralized (for all robots) or localized, where only nearby robots will respond. Market-based approaches have yet to be implemented on teams of more than a few robots [18]. There is no discussion of communication cost for large robot teams, except a simple statement (Table 3 in [18]) that communication cost is proportional to the number of robots.

To the best of our knowledge, bid aggregation in task assignment problem in robot-robot coordination was not considered in literature. We refer here to the aggregation of responses of several robots by an intermediate robot, which then selects the best of them and forwards only that bid to the auctioneer. For example, in [19], robots aggregate information gathered from bids of other robots to improve the decision making process for its own bid, for the map exploration task. Communication issues are not discussed in [19] (only two robots are used in experiments).

2.3 Simple Auction Protocol

We identified only one protocol [3] for single task single robot (called 'actor' in [3]) assignment, which explicitly considers multi-hop scenarios (UDG). It is a localized solution for actor-actor coordination based on 'auction protocol' [3], and is called here a *simple auction* protocol (*SAP*). The request for service is flooded from actor node that collected the report, and each actor responds back (the offer to provide service and the cost of doing it) to it by separate routing task. If blind flooding is used for actor search, each robot retransmits the request upon receiving it for the first time, and ignores it afterwards. This protocol can always find the closest robot to the event, since all robots are consulted. However, the response time can be large if the best robot is near the event, but robot network is large and the response from all robots is gathered before a decision is made.

2.4 Face Traversal

Stateless position based routing with guaranteed delivery was first described in [20]. It was applied in [21] for data storage problem, as follows. Geographic hash table is used to find the location for storing data based on its hashed table. Data is then routed toward 'home' decided by hash table and stored there; in Figure 3, point *E* is the home. However *E* is not an existing node in the network. Routing proceeds with GFG

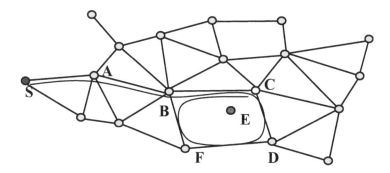

Fig. 3. Face traversal algorithm over Gabriel graph of UDG

(greedy-face-greedy) algorithm [20] from the source *S* toward destination *E*. It will create a loop in the face containing *E*. In Fig. 3, the whole path is *SABCDFB*, and loop *BCDFB* is detected. The closest node in the network to node *E* is the one from the loop. In Fig. 3, it is node *C*, and node *B* can decide it since the closest node to *E* travels together with the message. Face traversal is done using Gabriel graph of UDG. An edge *uv* belongs to Gabriel graph if and only if no other edges is located inside the circle with diameter *uv*. Thus its construction is easy. Fig. 3 shows only Gabriel graph of UDG for clarity. A readable and correct explanation of GFG algorithm can be found in [22].

3   Improved Simple Auction and Auction Aggregation Protocols

For simplicity, in the following sections, we assume that the robot network is connected and the event location is known to the bidding robot (robot collector). Note that in WRSN sensor nodes may be used to connect some robots; however this scenario is not considered here.

In this section we describe five new protocols: *k-SAP, SAAP, k-SAAP, k-AAP* and *RFT*. The first one is an improvement of simple auction protocol (*SAP*). Instead of flooding the whole network, one can search for bids only among robots located up to *k* hops away from bidding robot. This protocol applies limited flooding (only up to *k*-hop neighbors), and it will be designated as *k-SAP*. In example in Fig. 4, *1-SAP* will gather bids from *R2* and *R3* only, and thus the best bid from *R4* is not considered. *2-SAP* will flood from *R1* robots *R2, R4, R3, R8* and *R5. 3-SAP* will consult all the robots.

Another improvement of SAP in terms of communication overhead reduction is the use of *auction aggregation protocol.* Instead of using separate routing tasks, the constructed tree can be used for reporting back. The protocol has tree 'expansion' and tree 'contraction' phases. Tree expansion starts from collecting robot *R1* by creating a tree rooted at *R1* (see Fig. 4). Retransmissions create a response tree. Each node, with retransmission, includes ID of its parent robot in the message, so that robots can locally decide whether or not they are leaves in the created tree. Note that each node selects only one parent, in case of multiple received bids (e.g. *R9* is joined only to *R4*). They become leaves if they do not retransmit the bid or do not hear any other robot listing them as their parent.

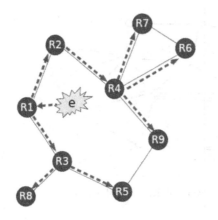

Distances from event to robots:
[e,R1] = 1	[e,R5] = 4
[e,R2] = 2	[e,R6] = 5.5
[e,R3] = 2	[e,R7] = 5
[e,R4] = 0.8	[e,R8] = 4
	[e,R9] = 3.5

Fig. 4. Auction-aggregation protocol for selecting the best robot

Leaf nodes start responding back to parent robots, with the best cost they are aware of. This is in fact auction aggregation and thus reduces number of messages in bidding phase. Each intermediate node waits to hear from all neighbors, which declared it as parent thus becoming a local collector. After hearing, they select the best cost and report further towards the collector. Collector at the end decides which robot is the best to perform the required action, and routes the decision to that robot. In the example in Fig. 4, robots *R5*, *R6*, *R7*, *R8* and *R9* are leaves in created tree, and return their bids to their parent nodes. *R4* returns to its parent *R2* its own bid as the best it is aware of; similarly *R3* also returns its own bid. *R2* returns *R4* as the best bidder. The root node (*R1*) then selects the best bid (in this case from *R4*) from two received offers, and delivers the task to *R4* along created path *R1-R2-R4*. This version of auction aggregation protocol will be designated as *SAAP* (simple auction aggregation protocol). In case of limited flooding (only up to *k*-hop neighbors from the collector), it is called *k-SAAP*. The difference between *k-SAAP* and *k-SAP* (and similarly between *SAP* and *SAAP*) is that individual bids are aggregated at intermediate nodes, instead of routing all of them back to the collector robot.

Providing autonomy in retransmitting decisions to individual robots can further refine the algorithm. In *k-SAAP*, receiving robot will retransmit only if it is at distance <*k* hops from collector. The new *k-AAP* protocol applies *k*-hop neighborhood around current robot. Each robot is assumed to already know the position, cost and availability of all its neighboring robots up to *k* hops away. One simple way is periodic diffusion of its local information (including the status of its (*k-1*)-hop neighbors) to its neighbors ('hello' message), or piggybacking it to data messages. The cost associated with these control messages or piggybacking is not measured in our later simulations.

In our *k*-hop auction aggregation protocol (*k-AAP*), robot that received the bid (and the best learned cost *C* associated with previous senders on the path from the bidding robot to it) will compare *C* and the cost of providing service by all of its *k*-hop neighbors. It will retransmit the message only if at least one of its own *k*-hop neighbors has cost <*C*. Otherwise it will not retransmit, and will start auction aggregation by returning a response message to its parent node on the search path.

k-AAP is a localized algorithm where each robot makes decision on whether or not to retransmit based on *k*-hop knowledge. In the simplest version, *0-AAP* protocol (for *k=0*), receiving robot declares itself as the selected one, corresponding to the use of 0-hop knowledge (no knowledge at all). In the *1-AAP* protocol, collecting robot *R1* will retransmit if any of its first neighbors has lower cost. In the example in Fig. 4, this still results in no transmission from *R1*. In the *k-AAP*, *R1* will retransmit if any of its *k*-hop neighbors has lower cost. In Fig. 4, *R4* is 2-hop neighbor of *R1* with a lower cost, and *R1* then retransmits in *2-AAP* version. *R3* will not retransmit, while *R2* will because *R4* is its 1-hop neighbor. Every retransmitting node will include with the message the lowest cost it is aware of. *R4* will not retransmit.

In the special case when cost metrics equals distance (from given robot to the event), another specialized algorithm may be used. We formalize it as *RFT algorithm* (routing toward the event with face traversal encircling the event). It is in fact algorithmically equivalent to the *face traversal* algorithm described in the literature review. In example in Fig. 4, *RTF* algorithm starts after collecting robot *R1* receives the task. *RTF* routes from *R1*, using robot networks, toward event location *e*. Routing will end by traversing a face containing *e*. In Fig. 4 face is *e-> R1->R2->R4->R9->R5->R3->R1->e*. Upon completing face traversal, the first node on the face (*R1* in Fig. 4) decides the best (closest) robot (*R4* in this example).

4   Simulations and Results

We used MIN-DPA algorithm [23] to generate connected pseudo random unit graphs that represent robot networks. This algorithm aims to distribute node degrees (number of neighbors in UDG) more uniformly while maintaining connectivity, and is very fast (especially for 'sparse' networks) compared to typical algorithm used in literature.

There is always one event at a time that needs response from robots. 2D space being monitored is a square 100m x 100m, and there are *n*=10, 20, 50 or 100 robots. Average number of robot neighbors is *d*=4,5,6,7,8,9 or 10. Robots bid only according to their distance from event. We measured the number of messages per robot, the percentage of optimal (closest robot) assignments, and the average ratio of distance of selected robot to distance of closest robot.

Robot collector can be chosen in several ways. Obviously the comparison and measured metrics greatly depend on the relative distance of selected collector with respect to the closest collector, as provided by particular event reporting mechanism. To avoid dependence on particular anycasting or other algorithm, we used the following randomized selection for our experiments. Collector is chosen probabilistically, according to their distances from the event. Let d_i be the distance of robot i from the event, and let $D = 1/d_1 + 1/d_2 +... +1/d_n$. The probability of selecting robot i as the collector is then $1/(D*d_i)$.

Ten graphs were generated, and 100 random events were selected for each. We compared algorithms described in sections 2 and 3: *SAP, k-SAP, k-SAAP,* and *k-AAP*, for different values of *k*. In *SAP* protocols, the shortest path algorithm was used to report from each robot to collector (that is, hop distance is counted in simulations).

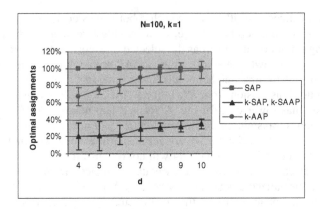

Fig. 5. Percentage of optimal assignments as function of *d*

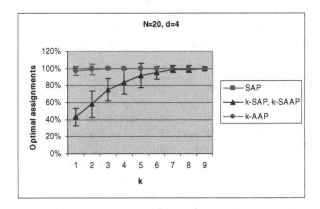

Fig. 6. Percentage of optimal assignments as function of *k*

Using probabilistic collector selection algorithm, collector is the closest robot to the event in 15% of cases on average. Actual values vary from 5 to 27%, in such way that the higher the number of robots the lower the percentage is. The average ratio of distance of collector to the distance of closest robot is 2.42, 3.34, 5.34, 7.72 for N=10, 20, 50 and 100, respectively.

SAP protocol always finds optimal robot (Fig. 5). However, to make the assignment, it takes more messages per robot than for any other protocol. The denser the network, the better SAP performs (Fig. 7). Simulations showed that for k=1, d=4-10, N=20,50, 100, for k-*SAP* and k-*SAAP* protocols, percentage of optimal assignments is in the range between 20% and 70%. Only for small and dense networks it can achieve 100% or for k>8 (Fig. 6). Percentage of optimal assignments is for k-*AAP* in the range between 70% and 100% for the same values of independent variables.

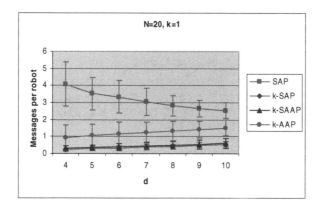

Fig. 7. Average number of messages per robot as function of *d*

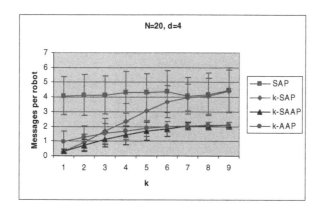

Fig. 8. Average number of messages per robot as function of *k*

For small networks ($N \leq 10$), all protocols show similar behavior in terms of average message per robot needed to make the assignment (around 2 messages per robot is needed). For larger networks ($N > 10$), *k-SAP* and especially *k-SAAP* features communication overhead reduction compared to *SAP* (Fig. 7) for up to 200 times. However, having at the same time lower optimal assignment percentage. It could be improved with larger k-hop values, but with more messages per robot needed. In such cases *k-SAAP* is up to twice better than *k-SAP* (Fig. 8).

For *k-AAP*, optimal (the closest) assignments are always found for $k > 3$. For dense networks it could be found even for $k=1$ (Fig. 5). Simulations showed that *k-AAP* protocol outperforms other protocols and features higher optimal assignments percentage compared to other protocols. For almost the same communication overhead, *k-AAP* is up to 3 times better in terms of percentage of optimal assignments. For example, for $N=20$, $k=2$, *k-SAP*, *k-SAAP* and *k-AAP* needs around 1 message per robot. At the same time, *k-AAP* achieves almost always 100% optimal assignments while *k-SAP* and *k-SAAP* ranges from 60% up to 90% (depending on density of network).

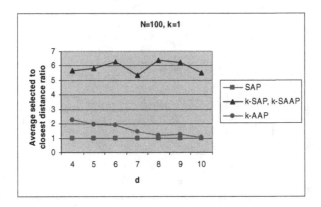

Fig. 9. Average selected to closest distance ratio as function of *d*

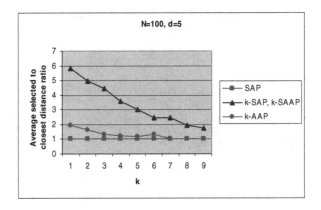

Fig. 10. Average selected to closest distance ratio as function of *k*

Because of localized decisions, *k-SAP* and *k-SAAP* are suboptimal and have higher selected to closest distance (SCD) ratio compared to *SAP* which always selects optimal robot. This is also due to the collector selection function. For larger *N*, there is higher probability of selecting a distant collector, while the restricted locality (low *k*) prevents from finding a nearby robot to act. *k-AAP* protocol has more than twice lower SCD ratio than *k-SAP* and *k-SAAP* (Fig. 9). Fig. 10 shows CSD ratios as function of *k*, for *N=100* and *d=5*. Error bars are not shown on Fig. 9 and Fig. 10 because of high value of standard deviation for SCD that goes up to 10 for this series of simulations (N=100, k=1 and N=100, d=5).

5 Conclusion and Future Work

In this paper we presented auction aggregation protocols as a mean to reduce communication overhead in multi-hop auction based protocols in robot-robot communication for the task assignment. Our protocols were able to find optimal or near optimal robot with significantly reduced communication cost, due to their localized nature.

This paper is the work in progress and there are several possibilities for further improvements. First, more detailed simulations are already in progress. They will include RTF protocol in comparisons. More realistic simulations of *k-AAP* protocol will be accomplished by inclusion of communication overhead measurement that is result of gathering knowledge of the position, cost and availability of all neighboring robots up to *k* hops away.

We used distance as cost metrics in bidding phase. Alternatively, residual energy or energy balancing could be used. As communication cost, average number of messages needed to make assignment is used. Alternatively, total power needed for transmission or load balancing could be applied.

Applying intelligent flooding schemes can further enhance auction aggregation protocols. In addition to criteria for retransmitting search message in particular protocols, an efficient broadcasting can be applied to stop retransmission at node *B* if *B* should not retransmit by neighbor elimination and backbone based broadcasting [24].

Another improvement of aggregation protocols is development of versions that look for the best response within time limits. During flooding, each node adds the best known cost to its message. Whenever a child node retransmits this search message with a better cost than this one, parent node routes such response toward the auctioneer. The response will be blocked along the route by a node that already knows about a better offer. Nodes on the route will also update their best offer information for future service offers. Versions with *k*-hop local knowledge in the search phase can be distinguished.

To improve suboptimality of localized decisions of *k-SAP*, *k-SAAP* and *k-AAP*, especially for large values of *N* and low values of *k*, 1-hop greedy search for better robot could be added after original assignment is proposed. That is, the selected robot, after getting the task, will check if any of its neighbors has lower cost. If so, it can reassign the task, and such search can be repeated by the selected neighbor, until no improvement is possible. *k-SAPG* , *k-SAAPG* and *k-AAPG* protocols will be simulated to find if 1-hop greedy search for better robot will gain better assignments at the cost of small increase of communication overhead.

Acknowledgments

This work is partially financed by the project "Development of systems and instruments for water, oil and gas exploration", pr. num. TR11006, Serbian Federal Ministry of Science and Environmental protection. The work is partially supported by NSERC Strategic Grant STPGP 336406-07 on sensor and actuator networks.

References

1. Parker, L.E.: Multiple Mobile Robot Systems. In: Bruno, S., Oussama, K. (eds.) Springer Handbook of Robotics, pp. 921–941. Springer, Heidelberg (2008)
2. Bekey, G., Yuh, J.: The Status of Robotics. IEEE Robotics & Automation Magazine 15(1), 80–86 (2008)
3. Melodia, T., Pompili, D., Gungor, V.C., Akyildiz, I.F.: Communication and Coordination in Wireless Sensor and Actor Networks. IEEE Transactions on Mobile Computing 6(10), 1116–1129 (2007)

4. Gerkey, B.P., Mataric, M.J.: A formal analysis and taxonomy of task allocation in multi-robot systems. Intl. J. of Robotics Research 23(9), 939–954 (2004)
5. Selvaradjou, K., Dhanaraj, M., SivaRam Murthy, C.: Energy Efficient Assignment of Events in Wireless Sensor and Mobile Actor Networks. In: 14th IEEE International Conference on Networks, vol. 2, pp. 1–6 (2006)
6. Melodia, T., Pompili, D., Akyildiz, I.F.: A Communication Architecture for Mobile Wireless Sensor and Actor Networks. In: Proceedings of the 3rd IEEE SECON 2006, pp. 109–118 (2006)
7. Atay, N., Bayazit, B.: Mixed-Integer Linear Programming Solution to Multi-Robot Task Allocation Problem. Technical report WUCSE-2006-54, Washington University in Sent Louis (2006)
8. Shah, K., Meng, Y.: Communication-Efficient Dynamic Task Scheduling for Heterogeneous Multi-Robot Systems. In: Proc. International Symposium on Computational Intelligence in Robotics and Automation, pp. 230–235 (2007)
9. Sujit, P.B., Sinha, A., Ghose, D.: Team, Game, and Negotiation based Intelligent Autonomous UAV Task Allocation for Wide Area Applications. In: Chahl, J.S., Jain, L.C., Mizutani, A., Sato-Ilic, M. (eds.) Innovations in Intelligent Machines (1), pp. 39–75. Springer, Heidelberg (2007)
10. Tovey, C., Lagoudakis, M.G., Jain, S., Koenig, S.: The Generation of Bidding Rules for Auction-based Robot Coordination. In: Multi-Robot Systems: From Swarms to Intelligent Automata, vol. III, pp. 3–14. Springer, Heidelberg (2005)
11. Smith, R.G.: The Contract Net Protocol: High-Level Communication and Control in a Distributed Problem Solver. IEEE Transactions on Computers C-29(12), 1104–1113 (1981)
12. Gerkey, B.P., Mataric, M.J.: Sold!: Auction methods for multi-robot coordination. IEEE Trans. on Robotics and Automation 18(5), 758–768 (2002)
13. Michael, N., Zavlanos, M., Kumar, V., Pappas, G.J.: Distributed multi-robot task assignment and formation control. In: IEEE International Conference on Robotics and Automation (ICRA 2008), pp. 128–133 (2008)
14. Nanjanath, M., Gini, M.: Auctions for task allocation to robots. In: Proceedings of the 9th International Conference on Intelligent Autonomous Systems, pp. 550–557. IOS Press, Tokyo (2006)
15. Wei, S., Lihua, D., Hao, F., Haiqiang, Z.: Task Allocation for Multi-Robot Cooperative Hunting Behavior Based on Improved Auction Algorithm. In: Proceedings of the 27th Chinese Control Conference, pp. 435–440 (2008)
16. Kishimoto, A., Sturtevant, N.: Optimized Algorithms for Multi-Agent Routing. In: Padgham, L., Parkes, D.C., Müller, J., Parsons, S. (eds.) Proc. of 7th Int. Conf. on Autonomous Agents and Multiagent Systems (AAMAS 2008), pp. 1585–1588 (2008)
17. Zheng, X., Koenig, S., Tovey, C.: Improving Sequential Single-Item Auctions. In: Proceedings of the 2006 IEEE/RSJ International Conference on Intelligent Robots and Systems, pp. 2238–2244 (2006)
18. Dias, M.B., Zlot, R., Kalra, N., Stentz, A.: Market-Based Multirobot Coordination: A Survey and Analysis. Proceedings of the IEEE 94(7), 1257–1270 (2006)
19. Zhang, F., Chen, W., Xi, Y.: Improving Collaboration through Fusion of Bid Information for Market-based Multi-robot Exploration. In: Proceedings of the 2005 IEEE International Conference on Robotics and Automation (ICRA 2005), pp. 1157–1162 (2005)
20. Bose, P., Morin, P., Stojmenovic, I., Urrutia, J.: Routing with guaranteed delivery in ad hoc wireless networks. In: Proc. of 3rd ACM Int. Workshop on Discrete Algorithms and Methods for Mobile Computing and Communications DIAL M99, Seattle, pp. 48–55 (1999)

21. Ratnasamy, S., Karp, B., Yin, L., Yu, F., Estrin, D., Govindan, R., Shenker, S.: GHT: A Geographic Hash Table for Data-Centric Storage in SensorNets. In: Proceedings of the First ACM International Workshop on Wireless Sensor Networks and Applications (WSNA), Atlanta, Georgia, pp. 78–87 (2002)
22. Frey, H., Stojmenovic, I.: On Delivery Guarantees of Face and Combined Greedy-Face Routing Algorithms in Ad Hoc and Sensor Networks. In: 12th ACM Annual Int. Conference on Mobile Computing and Networking MOBICOM, Los Angeles, pp. 390–401 (2006)
23. Atay Onat, F., Stojmenovic, I., Yanikomeroglu, H.: Generating Random Graphs for the Simulation of Wireless Ad Hoc, Actuator, Sensor, and Internet Networks. Pervasive and Mobile Computing (Elsevier) 4(5), 597–615 (2008)
24. Simplot-Ryl, D., Stojmenovic, I., Wu, J.: Energy efficient backbone construction, broadcasting, and area coverage in sensor networks. In: Stojmenovic, I. (ed.) Handbook of Sensor Networks: Algorithms and Architectures, pp. 343–379. Wiley, Chichester (2005)

On Minimizing the Maximum Sensor Movement for Barrier Coverage of a Line Segment

J. Czyzowicz[1,*], E. Kranakis[2,**], D. Krizanc[3], I. Lambadaris[4,**],
L. Narayanan[5,*], J. Opatrny[5,*], L. Stacho[6,*],
J. Urrutia[7,* * *], and M. Yazdani[4,**]

[1] Département d'informatique, Université du Québec en Outaouais,
Gatineau, QC, J8X 3X7, Canada
[2] School of Computer Science, Carleton University, Ottawa, ON, K1S 5B6, Canada
[3] Department of Mathematics and Computer Science, Wesleyan University,
Middletown CT 06459, USA
[4] Department of Systems and Computer Engineering, Carleton University,
Ottawa, ON, K1S 5B6, Canada
[5] Department of Computer Science, Concordia University, Montréal,
QC, H3G 1M8, Canada
[6] Department of Mathematics, Simon Fraser University, 8888 University Drive,
Burnaby, British Columbia, Canada, V5A 1S6
[7] Instituto de Matemáticas, Universidad Nacional Autónoma de México,
Área de la investigación científica, Circuito Exterior, Ciudad Universitaria,
Coyoacán 04510, México, D.F. México

Abstract. We consider n mobile sensors located on a line containing a barrier represented by a finite line segment. Sensors form a wireless sensor network and are able to move within the line. An intruder traversing the barrier can be detected only when it is within the sensing range of at least one sensor. The sensor network establishes barrier coverage of the segment if no intruder can penetrate the barrier from any direction in the plane without being detected. Starting from arbitrary initial positions of sensors on the line we are interested in finding final positions of sensors that establish barrier coverage and minimize the maximum distance traversed by any sensor. We distinguish several variants of the problem, based on (a) whether or not the sensors have identical ranges, (b) whether or not complete coverage is possible and (c) in the case when complete coverage is impossible, whether or not the maximal coverage is required to be contiguous. For the case of n sensors with identical range, when complete coverage is impossible, we give linear time optimal algorithms that achieve maximal coverage, both for the contiguous and non-contiguous case. When complete coverage is possible, we give an $O(n^2)$ algorithm for an optimal solution, a linear time approximation scheme with approximation factor 2, and a $(1 + \epsilon)$ PTAS. When the sensors have unequal ranges we show that a variation of the problem is NP-complete and identify some instances which can be solved with our algorithms for sensors with unequal ranges.

* Supported in part by NSERC grant.
** Supported in part by NSERC and MITACS grants.
* * * Supported in part by CONACYT grant.

P.M. Ruiz and J.J. Garcia-Luna-Aceves (Eds.): ADHOC-NOW 2009, LNCS 5793, pp. 194–212, 2009.

Keywords: Barrier, Coverage, Detection, Intruder, Line Segment, Optimal Movement, Sensors, NP-complete, PTAS.

1   Introduction

Barrier coverage of a region with wireless sensors is an important application area of sensor networks. Barrier coverage is used to detect intruders attempting to penetrate a protected region. Unlike a complete coverage of a region, it does not necessarily protect the interior points of the region, but rather only its perimeter by detecting intruders that either enter or exit the region. In this respect, therefore, barrier coverage can protect a region with much lower cost in comparison to a complete coverage.

In a general setting of the problem we have a predefined geometric planar region with a well defined boundary and a set of sensors forming a wireless sensor network. The sensors are mobile and they can move with constant and identical speeds in any direction in the plane. Each sensor located at x has a pre-set (determined by the manufacturer) *sensing range* r_x such that any other point p in the plane is within the range of the sensor if and only if its Euclidean distance $d(p, x)$ from x is at most r_x (in the sequel we abbreviate sensing range by *range*). The sensors are initially placed in the plane in arbitrary locations either interior or exterior to the region. Starting from these arbitrary initial positions we are interested in calculating final positions of the sensors where they achieve a barrier coverage of the region, i.e., no part of the boundary is outside of the range of all the sensors, and which minimize the maximum distance traveled by any sensor.

The above optimization problem (referred to as *MinMax* in this paper) arises in a natural way in situations when, due to hostile environment, the sensors cannot be placed initially so that they cover the boundary of the region, but each sensor can be instructed to move into a position in which a barrier coverage of the region is achieved. Since the energy required by a sensor to reach its final positions in the boundary is directly proportional to the distance traveled, minimizing the maximum distance traveled by any sensor minimizes the energy spent by any sensor for reaching its final position. Typically each sensor is battery powered, and thus minimizing the energy spent on moving maximizes the energy available for the subsequent barrier surveillance by the sensor network.

In this paper we restrict our study to the a one dimensional version of the barrier coverage problem. More specifically, a barrier is represented by a finite segment of a line (delimited by its two endpoints), the initial positions of the sensors are arbitrary points on the line, and we consider the problem of optimizing sensor movements within a line, while at the same time achieving a coverage of the barrier. We assume that the intruder moves in a two dimensional plane. Thus an *intruder* may traverse the given barrier from any direction in the plane. As before an intruder can be detected only if it is within the range of at least one sensor of the wireless sensor network and the sensor network establishes barrier coverage if no intruder can penetrate the given line segment in any direction without being detected. Although we consider a simplified version of the general barrier problem, it will become apparent in the sequel that it still contains challenging algorithmic questions and interesting solutions that illustrate the complexity of intrusion detection in this setting.

1.1 Notation and Optimization Problems

We now give several preliminary concepts and define more precisely several variants of the barrier coverage problem.

A *barrier* is, without loss of generality, a closed interval $I = [0, L]$ on the real line with pre-defined endpoints 0 and $L > 0$. Consider a set of n points $x_1 \leq x_2 \leq \ldots \leq x_n$ on the real line where x_i represents the initial position of sensor S_i. Let the range of the i-th sensor be denoted by r_i. Then sensor S_i initially covers the closed interval $I(S_i, x_i) = [x_i - r_i, x_i + r_i]$ of length $2r_i$, called the *covering interval* of S_i. It is the set of points of the line (not necessarily in $[0, L]$) which are within the range of the sensor.

We call a *gap* a sub-interval of I none of whose points is within range of any sensor and which cannot be enlarged any further without containing a point within the range of a sensor. Since the ranges of sensors are assumed to be closed intervals, a gap is an open subinterval of $[0, L]$, except when one of the endpoints of the gap is either 0 or L.

The sum of the lengths of all covering intervals is equal to $\sum_{i=1}^{n} 2r_i$ and is denoted by R. Observe that the barrier coverage problem is *feasible* if and only if $R \geq L$, i.e., the sum of the lengths of the covering intervals is at least as large as the length of the interval $[0, L]$.

We investigate how to move the sensors so as to minimize the maximum among the distances traversed by the respective sensors. More formally, if the i-th sensor S_i moves by a distance m_i (a movement to the left will be denoted by $m_i \leq 0$ and movement to the right by $m_i \geq 0$) from its original position x_i, the new position will be $x_i + m_i$ and the new covering interval will be $I(S_i, x_i + m_i)$. Notice that x_i is not assumed to be in the interval $[0, L]$.

If the problem is feasible, i.e., $R \geq L$ then we are interested in studying the following optimization problem.

MinMax optimization problem for $R \geq L$:

$$\text{minimize } \{ \max_{1 \leq i \leq n} |m_i| \} \text{ subject to } [0, L] \subseteq \cup_{i=1}^{n} I(S_i, x_i + m_i). \tag{1}$$

When $R < L$ and thus complete coverage of $[0, L]$ is not feasible, we are interested in a *best effort* solution, i.e., an arrangement of sensors that attains the largest possible coverage while at the same time minimizing the maximum movement of sensors. In particular, we consider two variants of the optimization problem previously defined. We call *contiguous* an arrangement of sensors that attains the largest possible coverage as a contiguous sub-interval of $[0, L]$, and *non-contiguous* an arrangement of sensors that attains the largest possible coverage as a collection of possibly disjoint sub-intervals, while at the same time minimizing the maximum movements of the sensors.

Non-contiguous MinMax optimization problem for $R < L$:

$$\text{minimize } \{ \max_{1 \leq i \leq n} |m_i| \} \text{ subject to } \cup_{i=1}^{n} I(S_i, x_i + m_i) \subseteq [0, L] \text{ and} \qquad (2)$$

$$| \cup_{i=1}^{n} I(S_i, x_i + m_i)| = R.$$

Contiguous MinMax optimization problem for $R < L$:

$$\text{minimize } \{ \max_{1 \leq i \leq n} |m_i| \} \text{ subject to } \cup_{i=1}^{n} I(S_i, x_i + m_i) \subseteq [0, L] \text{ and} \qquad (3)$$

$$| \cup_{i=1}^{n} I(S_i, x_i + m_i)| = R \text{ and}$$

$$\cup_{i=1}^{n} I(S_i, x_i + m_i) \text{ is an interval.}$$

We say that a solution of the MinMax problem is *order preserving* if the final positions of the sensors preserve the original ordering of the sensors, in other words, if two sensors on their way to an optimal location never need to cross paths. The existence of order preserving solutions will be useful in finding efficient algorithms for the Min-Max optimization problems for sensors with identical ranges and also for some more general instances of sensors with non-identical ranges specified below.

Lemma 1 (Order Preservation). *Let $S_1, S_2, \ldots, S_n$ be sensors with ranges $r_1, r_2, \ldots, r_n$ in initial positions $x_1 \leq x_2 \leq \cdots \leq x_n$. If there are no two sensors S_i and S_j, $1 \leq i \neq j \leq n$ such that $x_j - r_j < x_i + r_i$ and $x_j + r_j > x_i + r_i$ then there is an order-preserving optimal solution of any of the three versions of the MinMax optimization problem.*

Proof (Outline). Consider a solution of a MinMax problem in which two consecutive sensors are out of order, i.e., there are sensors S_i and S_j, $i < j$ and the final position of sensor S_j precedes the final position of S_i. It can be easily seen that we can reverse the order of these two sensors so that they cover the same area, or same size area in case $R < L$, without increasing the value of the maximal move in the solution. Thus by a sequence of switches we can obtain an optimal solution that preserves the original order of sensors.

It is easy to see that an order preserving solution does not need to exist when the conditions of Lemma 1 are not satisfied. The hypothesis of Lemma 1 is clearly satisfied when the covering intervals of the sensors form a *proper interval graph*, i.e., an interval graph that has an intersection model in which no interval properly contains another (see [6]), and obviously in the case of sensors with identical ranges. We also note that the special case of the order preservation lemma for sensors with identical ranges was already stated in [2].

1.2 Related Work

In the area of sensor networks, several recent papers considered the problem of deployment of mobile sensors for coverage of a region, see for example [10], [11], and [12]. Unlike the problem considered in this paper, they aim to provide coverage of the inside of a two-dimensional region, and they do not consider the optimization problems stated above. The problem studied in our paper addresses the problem of ensuring efficient border surveillance of a region and intruder detection using a wireless sensor system without covering the inside of the region.

In [9] efficient algorithms are proposed to determine, after sensor deployment, whether a region is barrier covered. It also establishes optimal deployment patterns to achieve barrier coverage when deploying sensors deterministically. In addition, they consider barrier coverage with high probability when sensors are deployed randomly. The problem of local barrier coverage is introduced in [4]. It shows that it is possible for individual sensors to locally determine the existence of local barrier coverage, even when the region of deployment is arbitrarily curved. Techniques for deriving density estimates for achieving barrier coverage and connectivity in thin strips are studied in [1], where sensors are deployed as a barrier to detect moving objects. In all these instances the problem studied concerns *static* optimal sensor deployment patterns and there is no concept of movement of the sensors.

Related to our study is the *Earth Movers Problem* (or EMP) (see [5], [3], [8]). In an ESP problem we have a set of suppliers A which are to move *earth* to the set B of receivers (or holes). The Earth Movers Distance (EMD) of A to B measures the minimum amount of work needed to fill the holes with earth and the aforementioned papers look at optimizations for specific types of motions of the point sets. Results of these papers are not applicable to the optimal movement barrier coverage problem considered in our paper and, despite some similarities, EMP differs from our problem since in barrier coverage there are no fixed destinations, and global coverage should be accomplished with minimizing the maximal distance to final positions.

The most directly related research is the work in [2] where a simpler problem was introduced and studied. Their optimization problem is similar but it differs from our model in that they do not specify the sensor ranges to be employed; unlike in our paper they seek algorithms to move the sensors to equidistant locations on the barrier so as to optimize the efficiency of the barrier coverage regardless of the initial coverage of the sensors. This is generally simpler to accomplish than the problem proposed here. In our work the algorithm is sensitive to the predefined sensor ranges (which are given as input to the problem) thus accomplishing the same barrier coverage task with less movement than may be necessary in [2].

1.3   Results and Outline of the Paper

In this paper we give several efficient algorithms to solve the MinMax optimization problems stated above. We distinguish several interesting variants of the barrier coverage problem, based on (a) whether or not the sensors have identical ranges, (b) whether or not complete coverage is possible and (c) in the case when complete coverage is impossible, whether or not the maximal coverage is required to be contiguous.

Table 1. Results for the MinMax problem assuming the n sensors have identical ranges. L is the length of the barrier and R the sum of length of covering intervals, and C, g are both linear functions of the initial sensor positions and the length of the line segment to be covered.

	coverage	contiguous	non-contiguous
	$R < L$	$O(n)$	$O(n)$
	$R = L$	$O(n)$	n.a.
$R > L$	optimal	$O(n^2)$	n.a.
	2-approximation	$O(n)$	n.a.
	$1 + \epsilon$ approximation	$O\left(n \log \left(\frac{\log(C/g)}{\log(1+\epsilon)}\right)\right)$	n.a.

All our algorithms are centralized: they are given initial positions of sensors and they calculate optimized final positions.

Table 1 summarizes results of the paper for the case of sensors with identical range, say r. In the table n is the number of sensors, $R = 2nr$ is the sum of lengths of covering intervals of all the sensors, and L the length of the barrier to be covered by the sensors. Clearly, the case of sensors with identical range would be very common in practice, since in many sensor networks all sensors are made by the same manufacturer.

When the sensors have unequal ranges, it is an open problem whether or not the MinMax optimization problem is NP-complete in general. However a variation of the MinMax problem whereby one of the sensors is assigned a fixed position is shown to be NP-complete. We also identify some instances of sensors that have unequal ranges which can be solved with our algorithms for sensors with equal ranges.

The paper is organized as follows. Sections 2, 3, 4, and 5 deal with sensors having identical ranges. Section 2 and 3 provide algorithms for the contiguous coverage, Section 5 for non-contiguous coverage and Section 4 approximation algorithms. Section 6 presents two results for sensors with unequal ranges. First, if the sensor coverage intervals satisfy the condition of Lemma 1 then the algorithmic solutions to the MinMax problems previously stated are still valid. Second, we show that a variation of the MinMax problem is NP-complete. The paper concludes with several proposals for extensions as well as related open problems. Due to the page limit some proofs are abridged or omitted.

2 Contiguous MinMax Optimization Problem for $R < L$

To solve the contiguous MinMax optimization problem for $R < L$, we proceed as follows: we first solve the problem of covering an interval of size R on the infinite line while minimizing the maximal movement of any sensor, and then we show how to modify our solution so that the interval covered is a subinterval of $[0, L]$.

Lemma 2. *Let $S_1, S_2, \ldots, S_n$ be n sensors with identical range r located on a line in initial positions $x_1 \leq x_2 \leq \ldots \leq x_n$. There is an $O(n)$ time algorithm that calculates the movements of sensors on the line so that the sensors cover a segment of the line of size $2rn$ and the maximal movement of any sensor is minimized.*

When sensors are in the positions determined by the algorithm of the previous theorem they give a maximal contiguous coverage of a segment of the line with a minimized maximal shift, but they do not necessarily cover the segment $[0, L]$. However, when $R < L$ we can easily modify the solution above to achieve a maximal contiguous coverage of $[0, L]$.

Theorem 1. *Let $S_1, S_2, \ldots, S_n$ be n sensors with identical range r located on a line in initial positions $x_1 < x_2 < \ldots < x_n$ and $R < L$. There is an $O(n)$ time algorithm that solves the MinMax optimization problem of covering a line segment of size R of $[0, L]$ so that the maximal value of the shift of any sensor is minimized.*

3   MinMax Optimization Problem for $R \geq L$

Since the solution to the MinMax problem for $R = L$ consists simply of moving S_i to position $(2i - 1)r$, we discuss below only the case $R > L$. We begin with a lemma that provides sufficient conditions for optimality. We say that a set of sensors $S_i, S_{i+1}, \ldots, S_j$ with $j \geq i$ are *in attached position* if any two consecutive sensors in the sequence are exactly $2r$ distance apart.

Lemma 3. (Sufficient condition for optimality). *Let S be an order preserving solution to the MinMax problem by sensors $S_1, S_2, \ldots, S_n$ of identical range with $R > L$. Let x be the largest shift value of any sensor in this solution. If the solution satisfies one of the following conditions, then x is the largest shift value in any optimal solution to the MinMax problem of this instance:*

(a) $x = 0$.
(b) There exists a pair of sensors S_i and S_j, $i < j$ such that the right shift of S_i is equal to x, the left shift of S_j is equal to x, and sensor $S_i, S_{i+1}, \ldots S_j$ are in attached positions.
(c) There is a sensor S_i whose left shift value is equal to x and all sensors preceding S_i are in attached positions up to position 0.
(d) There is a sensor S_i whose right shift value is equal to x and all sensors following S_i are in attached positions up to position L.

We now give an optimal algorithm to solve the MinMax problem. The key idea is to cover the gaps one by one from left to right, while balancing the cost of covering it from the left versus covering it from the right as much as possible.

Min-max Algorithm
Input: L, n, and $x_1 < x_2 < \ldots < x_n$, the initial positions of sensors $S_1, S_2, \ldots, S_n$ with $R > L$.

Let $rmax$ and $lmax$ be the current maximum right and left shift respectively experienced by any sensor and let $x = max(lmax, rmax)$. Initially $rmax = lmax = 0$. We specify how to cover gap g_i while maintaining as an invariant the disjunction of the conditions (a),(b),(c), or (d) of Lemma 3.

Obviously the invariant (in particular, condition (a)) holds at the start of the algorithm. We only need to consider the situation when there is a gap in the given interval $[0, L]$ that is not covered by any sensor. If the given instance contains a gap starting at 0 and there is no sensor to the left of 0 then this first gap must be covered by shifting to the left sensors of the leftmost group of sensors, (i.e., sensors between this gap and the second gap) in attached position as needed. Then the condition (c) is satisfied at 0 with x equal to the size of the first gap.

Assume one of the conditions (a), (b), or (c) holds just before we cover gap g_i. (We will show that condition (d) can be satisfied only after the last gap.) If $x = 0$ we set inv to be the leftmost sensor. Otherwise, if condition (b) holds then let inv be the rightmost node such that its left shift equals x and such that it is preceded by a node whose left shift equals x, and all intermediate nodes are in attached position. For brevity, we will say that the condition (b) holds at node inv. If condition (c) holds then inv is the rightmost node such that its left shift equals x and all nodes preceding it are in attached position. For brevity, we will say that the condition (c) holds at node inv.

We define $lsurplus(g_i)$ to be the *surplus sensor range* starting at inv up to the node $lnode(g_i)$ and whose right shift would not increase the right shift of sensors past x. Thus $lsurplus(g_i) \leq x$.

Step 1: Move $lnode(g_i)$ to the right by an amount $m = min(lsurplus(g_i), b_i - a_i)$. The nodes to the left of $lnode(g_i)$ follow in attached position as needed.

Observe that the left shift of all nodes in this move cannot increase (and may decrease), and the right shift of any node is at most x, and the invariant (condition (b) or (c)) still holds at node inv. If $m = b_i - a_i$, we have covered gap g_i, and we can move on to the next iteration, that is, to cover gap g_{i+1}.

If instead $m < b_i - a_i$, the gap g_i is not covered completely, and two possibilities exist.

$m = x$: In this case, the right shift of node $lnode(g_i)$ is equal to x. Thus, if moved further to the right, the value of its right shift will exceed x.

$m < x$: In this case, the right shift of node $lnode(g_i)$ is less than x, but all nodes to the left of it are in attached positions up to a node $prev(g_i)$ whose right shift is equal to x.

Step 2: If $lnode(g_i)$ is the rightmost sensor move $lnode(g_i)$ to the right until its range reaches L. The nodes to the left of $lnode(g_i)$ follow in attached position as needed. Clearly, condition (d) holds after this operation at position L. If $lnode(g_i)$ is not the rightmost sensor, we cover the remainder of gap g_i using sensors to the right of the gap g_i as much as possible using left shifts up to x. We move $rnode(g_i)$ to the left by an amount $m' = min(x, b_i - (a_i + m))$, with the nodes between $rnode(g_i)$ and $lnode(g_{i+1})$ (or the leftmost sensor if g_i is the last gap) following in attached position as needed.

Once again, this move preserves the invariant at node inv; no node increases its right shift, and the left shift of nodes does not exceed x. If $m' = b_i - (a_i + m)$, we have covered the gap g_i and we can move on to the next iteration, that is, to cover gap g_{i+1}. Otherwise, $m' = x$ and the gap g_i is not completely covered. Further, the remainder of this gap cannot be covered from the right or left without increasing the shift of some node to more than the value x.

Step 3: Let y be the midpoint of the gap that remains. We now move $lnode(g_i)$ to $m = min(y, 2r(lnode(g_i) - r)$, with nodes to the left of it following in attached position as needed. At the same time, we also move $rnode(g_i)$ to the same position $m + 2r$, with the nodes between $rnode(g_i)$ and $lnode(g_{i+1}$ following in attached position as needed.

Clearly, at this point the gap g_i is covered completely. If $m = y$, then observe that $lmax = rmax$. Indeed in Case 1, the invariant (b) now holds at node $rnode(g_i)$, since $rnode(g_i)$ and $lnode(g_i)$ both now have the maximum value of shift, and trivially all nodes between $rnode(g_i)$ and $lnode(g_i)$ are in attached position. In Case 2, recall that all nodes between $prev(g_i)$ and $lnode(g_i)$ were already in attached position; Step 3 ensures that the maximum right shift and left shift are experienced by $prev(g_i)$ and $rnode(g_i)$ with all nodes in between in attached position. Therefore, condition (b) now holds either at node $rnode(g_i)$ or a node between $rnode(g_i)$ and $lnode(g_{i+1}$ whose left shift is equal to that of $rnode(g_i)$.

If instead $m < y$, it means that the sensor nodes to the left of this point do not have sufficient range to cover the interval $[0, y]$. Indeed, Step 3 results in moving the sensor nodes up to $rnode(g_i)$ in attached position starting at 0, thereby making $lmax > rmax$ but ensuring that invariant (c) holds at node $rnode(g_i)$.

Observe that moving the nodes from the right of the gap g_i may result in creating a new gap, one with no nodes to the right of it. However this can only happen once, and only new gap may be introduced in the course of the algorithm.

Since condition d can hold only after the last gap is covered, the preceding arguments show that the invariant is always maintained by the algorithm.

Theorem 2. *Let $S_1, S_2, \ldots, S_n$ be sensors of identical range in initial positions $x_1 \le x_2 \le \ldots \le x_n$ with $R > L$. The Min-max algorithm specified above solves the MinMax problem of covering of the line segment $[0, L]$ so that the maximal value of the shift of any sensor is minimized in time $O(n^2)$.*

4   Approximation Schemes for the MinMax Problem for $R > L$

In this section we present two approximation algorithms. The first is an $O(n)$ (linear time) algorithm which is 2 times optimal and the second a $1 + \epsilon$ approximation scheme with running time $O\left(n \log\left(\frac{\log(C/g)}{\log(1+\epsilon)}\right)\right)$, where $\epsilon > 0$, g is the length of the largest gap in the original configuration of n sensors on a line segment of length L, and both C, g are linearly dependent on L.

4.1 Linear Time 2-Approximation Scheme

Assume the initial positions of the n sensors create m gaps in the interval $[0, L]$ and that for each sensor i we have $r \le x_i \le L - r$. Since $R > L$, the entire interval can be covered by the n sensors. We need to find a way to move a subset of sensors so that the entire interval is covered, and the maximum movement over all sensors is minimized. We now show a 2-approximation algorithm for this problem.

Theorem 3. *Let* $S_1, S_2, \ldots, S_n$ *be sensors of identical range in initial positions* $x_1 \le x_2 \le \ldots \le x_n$ *with* $R > L$. *There is a linear time 2-optimal approximation scheme for the MinMax optimization problem.*

4.2 $1 + \epsilon$ Approximation Scheme

Theorem 4. *Let* $S_1, S_2, \ldots, S_n$ *be sensors of identical range in initial positions* $x_1 \le x_2 \le \ldots \le x_n$ *with* $R > L$. *There is a polynomial time approximation scheme which for any* $\epsilon > 0$ *gives an arrangement of sensors such that the maximum movement achieved is* $(1 + \epsilon)$ *of the optimal solution in time*

$$O\left(n \log\left(\frac{\log(C/g)}{\log(1 + \epsilon)}\right)\right),$$

where $\epsilon > 0$, *and* C *and* g *are both linear functions of* L *and the initial sensor positions.*

Proof. Let g be half of the length of the largest gap in the original configuration of n sensors divided by 2 on a line segment of length L. It is clear that the value of the MinMax is bounded from above by $C = \max\{L, |x_1|, |L - x_n|\}$, and from below by g, since a sensor must move at least a distance equal to half the largest gap. Now we specify the two steps used in the algorithm.

Step 1. For a given value of M, where $0 < M \le C$, check if you can do coverage making movements that do not exceed the value M. Essentially, this involves using the greedy algorithm to move sensors one by one to cover each gap: first move sensors from the left of the gap and if you run out use sensors from the right of the gap. There are two cases. Either it is possible to do coverage using at most M in which case you set $M \leftarrow M/2$ and iterate or else it is not possible to do coverage using at most M in which case you set $M \leftarrow 2M$ and iterate.

Step 2. Now we can give the $1 + \epsilon$ approximation. Given $\epsilon > 0$ do a binary search to test each of the potential values $g(1+\epsilon), g(1+\epsilon)^2, \ldots, g(1+\epsilon)^k, \ldots$ for M and find the smallest value of k such that $g(1+\epsilon)^k$ is sufficient in Step 1 but $g(1+\epsilon)^{k-1}$

is not. Observe that if M is the optimal value then $g(1+\epsilon)^{k-1} < M \leq g(1+\epsilon)^k$. It follows that

$$k \leq \frac{\log(M/g)}{\log(1+\epsilon)} \leq \frac{\log(C/g)}{\log(1+\epsilon)}.$$

Moreover, it is easy to see that the resulting approximation factor is $1 + \epsilon$ and the running time as desired, which proves the theorem.

5   Algorithm for the Non-contiguous MinMax Problem

As remarked on earlier, this problem only applies for the case $R < L$. We first show how to solve the MinMax problem on the infinite line. Define $le(I)$ and $re(I)$ to be the left endpoint and right endpoint (respectively) of an interval I on the infinite line. As before $I(S_i, x_i) = [x_1 - r, x_1 + r]$ is the covering interval of sensor S_i. We assume that the initial sensor positions x_i are sorted. The solution to the problem is a set of final positions y_i for the sensors. In the non-contiguous case, the sensor ranges corresponding to the final positions coalesce into a *set* of intervals, rather than a single interval as in the contiguous case. In fact, the final positions can be represented as a set of disjoint intervals $L = \{L_1, \ldots L_k\}$. where each L_t corresponds to a set of sensors, the length of each L_t is a multiple of $2r$ and $\Sigma_{t=1}^k |L_t| = 2nr$. As a consequence of the order preservation lemma, the final positions of the sensors can then be derived from the set L quite easily. In particular, to derive the position of sensor S_i, let m be such that $\Sigma_{t=1}^{m-1} |L_t| < 2ri \leq \Sigma_{t=1}^m |L_t|$. Then the final position y_i of sensor S_i will be $le(L_m) + (i - u - 1)2r + r$ where $u = \Sigma_{t=1}^{m-1} |L_t|/(2r)$. We thus can prove the following theorem.

Theorem 5. *Let $S_1, S_2, \ldots, S_n$ be sensors of identical range in initial positions $x_1 \leq x_2 \leq \ldots \leq x_n$ with $R < L$. There is a linear time algorithm for the non-contiguous MinMax optimization problem.*

6   Unequal Sensor Ranges

In this section we look at the barrier coverage problem for sensors with non-identical ranges.

6.1   Algorithms for Sensors with Non-identical Ranges

The results of the previous sections can be easily generalized to some types of instances of sensors with unequal sensor ranges. The key part of the algorithms in Sections 2, 3 and 5 is the existence of a solution of the MinMax problem in which the sensors preserve the initial order. Notice that in the algorithms for the MinMax problem for $R < L$ and for $R > L$, we only used the properties of the order preservation lemma in the solution, and, therefore, these algorithms also can be used to solve the MinMax problems for $R < L$ and $R > L$ for any instance of sensors with unequal ranges satisfying the order preservation lemma.

The appropriate setting for generalizing these results is for the covering intervals of the sensors to satisfy the condition of Lemma 1. In particular, we mention without proof the following theorem which generalizes the results in Sections 2, 3 and 5.

Theorem 6. *Let $S_1, S_2, \ldots, S_n$ be sensors of ranges $r_1, r_2, \ldots, r_n$ in initial positions $x_1 \leq x_2 \leq \ldots \leq x_n$ such that the covering intervals $I(S_1, x_1), I(S_2, x_2), \ldots, I(S_n, x_n)$ satisfy the condition of Lemma 1.*
If $R < L$ then the algorithm from Theorem 1 solves the contiguous MinMax optimization problem in time $O(n)$.
If $R \geq L$ then the algorithm from Theorem 2 solves the MinMax optimization problem in time $O(n^2)$.

6.2   NP Completeness

We now prove an NP-completeness result for sensors with non-identical ranges. We show that a variation of the MinMax problem, where one sensor is assigned a predetermined position, is NP-complete (the sensor with predetermined position could correspond to a sink sensor in practical applications).

Theorem 7 (Case $R > L$). *Consider $n > 1$ sensors $S_1, S_2, \ldots, S_n$ having ranges $r_1, r_2, \ldots, r_n$, respectively, and located in initial positions $x_1 \leq x_2 \leq \ldots \leq x_n$ on a line segment $[0, L]$, Assume further that the final position of sensor S_1 must be equal to a given value z of the segment, and $\sum_{i=1}^{n} 2r_i > L$. The problem of determining for a given k whether there exist final positions of sensors on the line so that the sensors cover the segment $[0, L]$ and the maximum movement of any sensor is at most k is NP-hard.*

Proof. We prove it by reducing the *Partition problem* (see [7][page 47]) into a problem of covering a line segment with sensors such that one sensor must be in a pre-determined final position and the maximum movement of sensors is bounded by a given value. The Partition problem is defined as follows: given a sequence of integers $a_1 \geq a_2 \geq \ldots \geq a_m$, determine whether there exists a set of indices J such that $\sum_{i \in J} a_i = \frac{1}{2} \sum_{i=1}^{m} a_i$.

Let $C = (\sum_{i=1}^{n} a_i)/2$ and consider the barrier coverage problem of segment $I = [0, L]$ where $L = 1 + 4C$, one sensor S_1 of range $1/2$ must be in a pre-determined final position equal to $L/2$, there is one sensor S_{i+1} of range $a_i/2$ for every $1 \leq i \leq m$, located initially in the middle of the line segment. Also, there are two additional sensors S_{m+2}, S_{m+3} of range $(C + a_1)/2$, initially located just outside I so that they cover only points 0 and L of the interval, respectively (see Figure 1).

Now if there is a set of indices J such that $\sum_{i \in J} a_i = (\sum_{i=1}^{n} a_i)/2$, there is a solution to the barrier coverage problem such that for any $i \in J$ the sensor S_{i+1} is moved to the left of the interval covered by S_1 and for any $i \notin J$ the sensor S_{i+1} is moved to the right of the interval covered by S_1. Thus, this way we can cover regions of size C to the left and right of the covering interval of S_1 with

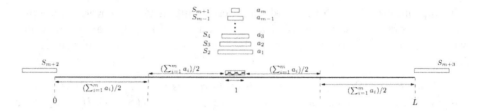

Fig. 1. Arrangement of sensors for proving the NP-completeness of a slightly restricted variation of the MinMax problem when one sensor cannot be moved

all shifts being at most of size C. The two regions at the left and right end of $[0, L]$ can be covered by S_{m+2} and S_{m+3} with shifts being at most C.

If such a partition does not exist, then any distribution of sensors with ranges $a_1/2, a_2/2, \ldots, a_n/2$ to the left and right of S_1 in the predetermined position covers a region of size less that C on one side of the region covered by S_1. Therefore, we have to move one of the sensors at one end of the interval more than C to get a solution. It is easy to observe that ranges of sensors S_{m+2} and S_{m+3} are large enough to have a solution.

Thus if there is an algorithm that can determine if there are movements of sensors on the line so that one sensor is in a predetermined position, the sensors cover the segment $[0, L]$, and the maximum movement of any sensors is at most C, we can determine whether the partition problem has a solution. Clearly, the transformation from the partition problem to the sensor movement problem is polynomial.

Notice that this result also implies NP-completeness of a generalization of the MinMax problem in which the barrier consists of more than one segment.

7   Conclusion and Open Problems

We have studied the barrier coverage problem for a wireless sensor network when the barrier is a finite line segment. In addition to investigating trade-offs and algorithms with improved running time, the following problems are worth investigating and exploring further. First of all for the case of a line segment, considering (a) the problem of barrier k coverage, whereby each intruder should be detected by at least k different sensors, for some fixed $k \geq 1$, (b) the possibility that there are specified zones which do not need (or are not allowed) to be covered by sensors. Another class of problems concerns extensions to higher dimensions. Note that the two dimensional version of the problem is wide open. More specifically it is worth considering the class of problems for other more general geometric barriers, e.g., circular barriers, convex barriers and more generally boundaries of simplex polygons. It is also worth considering other types of sensor movements, e.g., the movement of the sensors towards the globally optimal position on the circular barrier may proceed through the interior of the circle as opposed to only moving on the perimeter. Finally it is worth exploring the case where the relative sensor ranges are bounded, e.g., $b \leq \frac{r_i}{r(S_j)} \leq B$, for all sensors S_i, S_j, for some constants b, B independent of the number of sensors n. The complexity of the general MinMax problem should be answered as well.

References

1. Balister, P., Bollobas, B., Sarkar, A., Kumar, S.: Reliable density estimates for coverage and connectivity in thin strips of finite length. In: Proceedings of the 13th annual ACM international conference on Mobile computing and networking, pp. 75–86 (2007)
2. Bhattacharya, B., Burmester, M., Hu, Y., Kranakis, E., Shi, Q., Wiese, A.: Optimal Movement of Mobile Sensors for Barrier Coverage of a Planar Region. In: Yang, B., Du, D.-Z., Wang, C.A. (eds.) COCOA 2008. LNCS, vol. 5165, pp. 103–115. Springer, Heidelberg (2008)
3. Cabello, S., Giannopoulos, P., Knauer, C., Rote, G.: Matching point sets with respect to the Earth Mover's Distance. Computational Geometry: Theory and Applications 39(2), 118–133 (2008)
4. Chen, A., Kumar, S., Lai, T.H.: Designing localized algorithms for barrier coverage. In: Proceedings of the 13th annual ACM international conference on Mobile computing and networking, pp. 63–74 (2007)
5. Cohen, S.: Finding Color and Shape Patterns in Images. PhD Thesis, Stanford University, Dept. of Computer Science (1999)
6. Fishburn, P.C.: Interval Orders and Interval Graphs. Wiley, New York (1985)
7. Garey, M.R., Johnson, D.S.: Computers and Intractability: A Guide to the Theory of NP-completeness. WH Freeman, San Francisco (1979)
8. Klein, O., Veltkamp, R.C.: Approximation Algorithms for Computing the Earth Mover's Distance Under Transformations. In: Deng, X., Du, D.-Z. (eds.) ISAAC 2005. LNCS, vol. 3827, pp. 1019–1028. Springer, Heidelberg (2005)
9. Kumar, S., Lai, T.H., Arora, A.: Barrier coverage with wireless sensors. Wireless Networks 13(6), 817–834 (2007)
10. Li, X., Frey, H., Santoro, N., Stojmenovic, I.: Localized sensor self-deployment with coverage guarantee. ACM SIGMOBILE Mobile Computing and Communications Review 12(2), 50–52 (2008)
11. Yang, S., Li, M., Wu, J.: Scan-based movement-assisted sensor deployment methods in wireless sensor networks. IEEE Trans. Parallel Distrib. Syst. 18(8), 1108–1121 (2007)
12. Zou, Y., Chakrabarty, K.: A distributed coverage and connectivity-centric technique for selecting active nodes in wireless sensor networks. IEEE Trans. Comput. 54(8), 978–991 (2005)

Appendix

Proof (of Lemma 1). Consider a solution of the MinMax problem in which two consecutive sensors are out of order, i.e., there are sensors S_i and S_j, $i < j$ and the final position of sensor S_j precedes the final position of S_i. It can be easily seen that the reversing of the order of these two sensors cannot increase the value of the maximal move in the solution, and thus by a sequence of switches we can obtain an optimal solution that preserves the original order of sensors.

Proof (of Lemma 2). Let $y_1, y_2, \ldots, y_n$ be positions on the line such that when sensor $S_1, S_2, \ldots, S_n$ move to position $y_1, y_2, \ldots, y_n$ respectively, the sensors cover a contiguous segment of the line of size $2rn$ and the value $\max\{|x_i - y_i| : 1 \leq i \leq n\}$ is minimal among all such possible assignment of values $y_1, y_2, \ldots, y_n$. Notice first that according to Lemma 1, there is an optimal solution to the problem of minimizing the maximal movement of any sensor such that $y_1 < y_2 < \cdots < y_n$. Furthermore, since the sensors cover a contiguous segment of the line, we have $y_i = y_1 + 2(i-1)r$ for $2 \leq i \leq n$ in an optimal solution. Our algorithm determines a solution of this type.

Consider the possibility that the sensors $S_1, S_2, \ldots, S_n$ have moved to positions $y_1 = 0, y_2 = 2r, \ldots, y_n = 2(n-1)r$, respectively on the line, i.e., the sensor S_1 moved to location 0 and the other sensors moved to the subsequent location to the right of it to achieve maximal contiguous coverage. Then the values $-x_1, 2r - x_2, \ldots, 2(n-1)r - x_n$ give the displacements of the sensors, the negative values indicating a shift to the left, positive values indicating a shift to the right on the line and the absolute value of the smallest negative value gives the maximal movement of any sensor to the left, largest positive value gives the maximal movement of any sensor to the right. If the position 0 of sensor S_1 is increased/decreased by c and we shift the positions of other sensors in the same direction by c so that we maintain the maximal contiguous coverage of a line segment then values of all left shifts of sensors are decreased/increased by c, and values of all the right shifts of sensors are increased/decreased by c. Let z_1 be the maximal value and z_2 be the smallest value in the list $x_1, x_2 - 2r, \ldots, x_n - 2(n-1)r$. Thus when we select $c = -(z_1 + z_2)/2$, we achieve a balance between the maximal shift to the right and maximal shift to the left of sensors. Thus any other shift cannot create a smaller maximal shift to the left and to the right. Therefore, $y_i = 2r(i-1) - (z_1 + z_2)/2$ is the position of S_i that minimizes the maximal shift. Clearly, the n values $y_i = 2r(i-1) - (m_1 + m_2)/2$, $1 \leq i \leq n$ can be calculated in $O(n)$ time.

Proof (of Theorem 1). We calculate using the linear time algorithm given in the proof of Lemma 2 the maximal contiguous coverage of a segment of a line, i.e., of size R, which minimizes the maximal move of any sensor. Let c be the position of S_1 in the solution. If $r \leq c \leq r + L - R$, then the sensors already cover a segment of size R of the interval $[0, L]$ and we are done. Otherwise, we consider two cases:

If $c < r$ then the optimal solution of the previous theorem covers a portion of the line to the left of 0. Thus we shift the positions of the sensors to the right by assigning to S_i position $y_i = r + 2r(i-1)$. Clearly, this shift will increase the maximal right shift of sensors and decrease the left shift of sensors, but no other solution can have a smaller right shift.

If $r + L - R < c$ then the optimal solution of the previous theorem covers a portion of the line to the right of L. Thus we shift the positions of the sensors to the left by assigning to S_i position $y_i = L - r - 2r(n-i)$. Clearly, this shift will increase the maximal left shift and decrease the right shift of sensors, but no other solution can have smaller left shift.

Since the modification of the solution obtained by the $O(n)$ algorithm of Lemma 2 requires only $O(n)$ additional operations, the entire algorithm takes linear time.

Proof (of Lemma 3). Let S be a solution of an instance of the MinMax problem with $R > L$ satisfying the condition of the lemma. Let S' be an optimal solution to the same problem with maximum shift less than x. According to the order preservation lemma, we only need to consider S' that preserves the original order of sensors. We have four cases to consider:

Condition (a) is satisfied by S: Obviously no solution could have a maximum shift less than 0.

Condition (b) is satisfied by S: Let p be the position of sensor S_i in solution S. Clearly S' must place S_i in position $p - \epsilon$ for some $\epsilon \geq 0$. If $\epsilon > 0$ then the positions of sensors $S_{i+1}, S_{i+2}, \ldots S_j$ in solution S' must be also shifted to the left by at least ϵ so that there is no gap left in the coverage. However, this implies that the left shift of S_j is at least $x + \epsilon$, contradicting the optimality of S'. Condition (c) is satisfied by S: Clearly if S' places S_i in position $p - \epsilon$ for some $\epsilon \geq 0$ then the left shift of S' is equal to $x + \epsilon$ contradicting the optimality of S'. If S' places S_i in position $p + \epsilon$ for some $\epsilon \geq 0$ then any placement of sensors $S_1, S_2, \ldots S_{i-1}$ in solution S' leaves a gap somewhere between 0 and p. Condition (d) is satisfied: This is symmetric to Case 3.

Proof (of Theorem 2). The optimality of the algorithm follows from Lemma 3. As far as the complexity of the algorithm is concerned, the algorithm needs to cover at most $n + 1$ gaps in $[0, L]$. In order to cover gap g_i, the algorithm must compute the $lsurplus(g_i)$, and adjust the shift values of sensors. This involves a scan of the shift values of the sensors that can be done in linear time. Thus, the time complexity of the algorithm is $O(n^2)$.

Proof (of Theorem 3). Let the i-th gap be $[a_i, b_i]$. Let $lnode(g_i)$ be the index of the sensor node immediately to the left of gap g_i. Observe that $lnode(g_i) + 1$ is the sensor node immediately to the right of the gap g_i. For each gap g_i, we call $lsurplus(g_i)$ to be the *surplus sensor range* between the gap g_{i-1} and gap g_i to cover the gap g_i. Then $lsurplus(g_i) = (lnode(g_i) - lnode(g_{i-1})) * 2r - (b_i - a_i)$. On the other hand, $rsurplus(g_i)$ is defined to be the surplus on the right of the gap g_i to cover the interval $[b_i, L]$. That is, $rsurplus(g_i) = (n - lnode(g_i))2r - (L - b_i)$. Note the asymmetry in the definitions of $lsurplus$ and $rsurplus$.

We define a procedure $RightBlockMove(i, j)$ that puts sensor S_i at position j, then moves sensor S_{i-1} to $i - 2r$ and continues until finding a sensor that would be forced to stay immobile or move left. A precondition for calling the procedure would be that such a sensor indeed exists. The procedure $LeftBlockMove(i, j)$ is defined analogously.

If $lsurplus(g_i) \geq 0$, using procedure $RightBlockMove(lnode(g_i), b_i - r)$, it follows that it is possible to cover the gap g_i with sensors entirely from the left of the gap g_i such that the maximum shift incurred by a sensor is $b_i - a_i$. In fact it is sensor $lnode(g_i)$ that will incur this shift; all other sensors will incur at most this shift. Similarly, if $rsurplus(g_i) \geq 0$, this means that it is possible to cover the interval $[b_i, L]$ using sensors only to the right of the gap g_i.

We now describe our algorithm for MinMax in a recursive manner. We show how to cover gap g_1 and then issue a recursive call to solve a smaller sub-problem.

1. If $lsurplus(g_1) \geq 0$ and $rsurplus(g_1) \geq 0$, then we can use procedure $RightBlockMove(lnode(g_1), b_1 - r)$ to cover the gap g_1 entirely with sensors from the left. Solve recursively the MinMax problem for the interval $[b_1, L]$ using sensors $lnode(g_1) + 1$ to n.

2. If $lsurplus(g_1) < 0$ and $rsurplus(g_1) \geq 0$, cover as much as possible of the gap with sensors from the left. More precisely, sensor node S_i should move to position $(2i - 1)r$. This can be achieved by using the procedure $RightBlockMove(lnode(g_1), j)$ to cover the gap up to position j where $j = (lnode(g_1))2r - r$. Next, use $LeftBlockMove(lnode(g_1) + 1, j)$ to cover the remaining gap using sensors originally on the right of gap g_1. Suppose the rightmost sensor to move left in this procedure was S_k, and the gap immediately after that was g_t. We now recursively solve the MinMax problem on the interval $[x_{k+1} - r, L]$ using sensors $k + 1$ to n. Note that $lsurplus(g_t)$ is recalculated to take into account only sensors to the right of S_k. In other words, we reassign $lnode(g_{t-1}) = k$.

3. Otherwise $lsurplus(g_1) > 0$ and $rsurplus(g_1) < 0$. In this case, some sensors from the left of gap g_1 will have to move to the right of the gap, since there aren't enough sensors on the right of the gap to cover the interval $[b_1, L]$. Let $k = \lceil rsurplus(g_1)/2r \rceil$ and let $j = (n - lnode(g_1) - k)2r$. We move sensors $lnode(g_1) - k + 1$ to $lnode(g_1)$ to the position j. This means the interval $[j, L]$ can be covered exactly by the sensors now in that range using the algorithm for $R = L$ given in this section. Finally we use $RightBlockMove(lnode(g_1) - k, b_1 - r)$ to cover the remaining part of g_1 entirely from the left.

We now argue that this algorithm is 2-optimal. Observe that the sensors that are moved to the right end of a gap in Step 3 are making *necessary moves*; since $rsurplus(g_i) < 0$, it is not possible to cover the interval to the right of g_i using only sensors whose initial positions were greater than b_i. Since the sub-problem will now we solved using the optimal algorithm for $R = L$ given in this section, it is easy to see that the total right shift incurred by these sensors is optimal. For all other sensors, observe that they are moved at most once during the algorithm. We now argue that every such move of a sensor during the algorithm causes a shift that is at most twice the maximum shift produced by the optimal algorithm.

First notice that in Step 1, while considering gap g_i, $RightBlockMove$ always incurs a shift of at most g_i, while $\max\{g_i/2\}$ is a lower bound on the maximal shift incurred by the optimal algorithm. Second, in Step 2, suppose the procedure call $LeftBlockMove(lnode(g_1) + 1, j)$ results in covering the interval $[j, x_{k+1} - r]$ (recall that S_k was the rightmost sensor to move left in the course of the procedure) and results in a maximum left shift of s. We claim that $s/2$ must then be a lower bound for the maximum shift incurred by the optimal algorithm. This is because any decrease in the left shift experienced by sensors covering this interval must come at the expense of an equal increase in right shift of other sensors.

Finally in Step 3, consider the moves made by sensors in the set S' whose initial positions were in the interval $[b_1, L]$. Since the sub-problem is solved optimally, clearly an optimal algorithm for the entire problem could only have improved matters by using more sensors from the left of g_1 to cover the interval $[b_1, L]$. The maximum right shift of sensors in S' cannot be improved this way. Suppose the maximum left shift experienced by sensors in S' in our algorithm is s. Then any decrease in the left shift of sensors in S' in the optimal algorithm must come with a corresponding and equal increase in the right shift of other sensors. This implies that $s/2$ is a lower bound on the maximum shift.

Since the maximum shift incurred by a sensor in our algorithm is always at most twice the maximum shift incurred by sensors in the optimal algorithm, our algorithm is 2-optimal.

Clearly, there are at most $n + 1$ gaps to be considered. Each sensor can be involved in the calculation of $lsurplus(g_i)$ only for one value of i. The value $rsurplus(g_1)$ is calulated at cost $O(n)$ and then it is adjusted for $rsurplus(g_i)$, $i > 1$ with a constant cost. Thus the algorithm is linear.

Proof (of Theorem 5). Next, we describe how to find the set L in an inductive manner. Assume that the optimal solution for the sensors $\{S_1, \ldots, S_i\}$ is given by a set of intervals $\{L_1, L_2, \ldots, L_j\}$ where $j \leq i$. For each L_t, let $ms(L_t)$ be the value of the maximum shift incurred by a sensor in L_t. We now show how to extend the solution to include the sensor S_{i+1}.

If $I(S_{i+1}, x_{i+1})$ does not overlap with L_j, then clearly the sensor S_{i+1} should not move at all, that is, the optimal solution for the set $S_1, \ldots, S_{i+1}$ is the set of intervals $\{L_1, \ldots, L_j, L_{j+1}\}$ with $L_{j+1} = I(S_{i+1}, x_{i+1})$. On the other hand, if $I(S_{i+1}, x_{i+1})$ does overlap with L_j, we need to combine the two intervals L_j and $I(S_{i+1}, x_{i+1})$ to remove the overlap while keeping the maximum shift in the combined solution as small as possible.

We briefly describe how to combine two intervals P and Q assuming $le(P) \leq le(Q) \leq re(P) \leq re(Q)$. The combined interval will be assigned to P. We assume that $ms(P) \geq ms(Q)$. We maintain the invariant that the maximum left shift over all sensors is the same as the maximum right shift over all sensors processed so far. Let the overlap between the two intervals be $c = re(P) - le(Q)$. If $ms(P) - ms(Q) \geq c$, we push Q by c to the right, and attach it to the right end of P. Clearly in this case, the left shift of sensors originally in Q is not increased, and the right shift of such sensors is at most $ms(P)$. Since P is not moved, this does not increase the value of $ms(P)$. If instead $ms(P) - ms(Q) < c$, we push P by $(c - ms(P) + ms(Q))/2$ to the left and Q by $(c + ms(P) - ms(Q))/2$ to the right. It is easy to verify that $ms(P) = (c + ms(P) + ms(Q))/2$, and is in fact the value of the maximum left shift of sensors originally in P as well as the maximum right shift of sensors originally in Q. The case when $ms(P) < ms(Q)$ is similar. The optimality of the combine procedure follows from the maintenance of the invariant and the fact that the two intervals are now exactly adjacent.

We use the above procedure to combine the intervals L_j and $I(S_{i+1}, x_{i+1})$. If the combined interval is disjoint from L_{j-1} we can stop, otherwise, we need to combine again with L_{j-1} repeating as long as necessary.

It remains to analyze the complexity of the algorithm. The combine procedure clearly takes $O(1)$ time, so it comes down to analyzing the number of times the combine procedure is called. We charge the operation $combine(P, Q)$ to the leftmost sensor in Q. Since after the two intervals are merged, that sensor is never again the leftmost sensor in an interval, it is clear that each sensor can be charged at most once. This means the complexity of the algorithm is linear in the number of sensors.

Finally, we outline the algorithm for the case when the final positions of the sensors are required to be within the interval $I = [0, L]$. First we use the algorithm detailed above to solve the problem on the infinite line. If the result falls entirely within I, we are done. Suppose instead that some of the intervals in the output set L lie to the left of the interval I. Then we start with L_1 and push it to the right, attaching it to any interval it encounters, pushing the attached interval, and continuing until $le(L_1) = 0$. If some of the intervals in L lie to the right of the interval I, we do a similar procedure from the rightmost interval in L. The resulting intervals must constitute a valid solution (no overlapping intervals), since $R < L$.

Mobile Sinks for Information Retrieval from Cluster-Based WSN Islands

Grammati Pantziou[1], Aristides Mpitziopoulos[2], Damianos Gavalas[2],
Charalampos Konstantopoulos[3], and Basilis Mamalis[1]

[1] Department of Informatics, Technological Educational Institution of Athens,
Athens, Greece
{pantziou,vmamalis}@teiath.gr
[2] Department of Cultural Informatics, University of the Aegean Mytilene,
Lesvos, Greece
{crmaris,dgavalas}@aegean.gr
[3] Department of Informatics, University of Piraeus Piraeus, Greece
konstant@unipi.gr

Abstract. Mobile sinks (MS) mounted upon urban vehicles with fixed trajectories (e.g. buses) provide the ideal infrastructure to effectively retrieve sensory data from isolated Wireless Sensor Network (WSN) fields. Existing approaches involve either single-hop transfer of data from sensors that lie within the MS's range or heavy involvement of network periphery nodes in data retrieval, processing, buffering and delivering tasks. These nodes run the risk of rapid energy exhaustion resulting in loss of network connectivity. Our proposed protocol aims at minimizing the overall network overhead and energy expenditure associated with the multi-hop data retrieval process while also ensuring balanced energy consumption among network nodes and prolonged network lifetime. This is achieved through building cluster structures consisted of member nodes that route their measured data to their assigned cluster head (CH). CHs perform data filtering upon raw data exploiting potential spatial-temporal data redundancy and forward the filtered information to appropriate end nodes.

1 Introduction

A main reason of energy spending in energy-constrained Wireless Sensor Network (WSN) environments relates with transfers of sensor readings, in raw or processed form, from the sensors to remote sinks. These readings are typically relayed using ad hoc multihop routes in the sensor network. A side-effect of this approach is that the Sensor Nodes (SNs) located close to the sink are heavily used to relay data from all network SNs [4]; hence, their energy is consumed faster, leading to a non-uniform depletion of energy in the network [12]. This results in network disconnections and limited network lifetime. Network lifetime can be extended by reducing data relaying energy spending.

Recent research work in the field WSNs has proved the applicability of mobile elements (submarines, cars, buses, mobile robots, etc) for the retrieval of sensory

P.M. Ruiz and J.J. Garcia-Luna-Aceves (Eds.): ADHOC-NOW 2009, LNCS 5793, pp. 213–226, 2009.
© Springer-Verlag Berlin Heidelberg 2009

data from SNs in comparison with multihop transfers to a centralized element. A Mobile Sink (MS) moving through the network deployment region can collect data from the static SNs over a single hop radio link when approaching within the radio range of the static SNs or with limited hop transfers if static SNs are located further. This naturally avoids long-hop relaying and reduces the energy overhead at SNs near the base station, prolonging the network lifetime [11].

Several WSN applications involve urban areas that need to be monitored with respect to environmental parameters, surveillance, fire detection, etc. In these environments, individual areas are typically covered by isolated 'sensor islands' wherein a number of SNs located in the periphery of the sensor field can be used as 'rendezvous' points so as to collect sensory data from neighbor SNs and deliver them to a MS when the latter approaches within radio range [13].

In this context, the specification of the appropriate number and locations of Rendezvous Nodes (RN) is crucial. The number of RNs should be proportional to the deployment density of SNs. If a small number of RNs is selected, the energy supplies of those SNs and their neighbors will be rapidly depleted. If, on the other hand, a large number of SNs are appointed as RNs, those nodes will attempt to deliver their collected data simultaneously and they will experience a high number of packet collisions and outages [1], which results in buffer overflows.

Herein, we investigate the use of MSs for efficient data collection from urban 'sensor islands'. We argue that the ideal carriers of such MSs are public surface transportation vehicles that repeatedly follow a predefined trajectory with a periodic schedule that may pass along the perimeter of the isolated sensor fields.

Our proposed protocol called MobiCluster aims at minimizing the overall network overhead and energy expenditure associated with the data retrieval process while also ensuring balanced energy consumption among SNs and prolonged network lifetime. This is achieved through building cluster structures consisted of member SNs that route their measured data to their assigned Cluster Head (CH). The CHs perform filtering upon raw data exploiting potential spatial-temporal data redundancy and forward the filtered information to their assigned RNs, typically located in proximity to the MS's trajectory. We also introduce a method for enrolling appropriate SNs as RNs taking into account the deployment pattern and density of SNs.

The remainder of this article is organized as follows: Section 2 reviews related work in the field. Section 3 presents the execution phases of MobiCluster. Section 4 discusses simulation results that compare the performance of Mobi-Cluster against alternative approaches and Section 5 concludes our work.

2   Related Work

Maintaining connectivity and maximizing the network lifetime stand out as critical considerations in WSNs design. Mobile devices can be used as efficient means for addressing these issues. In urban environments, mobile platforms are already

---

[1] The term 'outage' is defined as the fraction of SNs which fail to send their data while remaining within the receiver's transmission range [3].

available in the deployment area, e.g. public buses. With sinks mounted upon mobile platforms, the connectivity problem is tackled using MSs that retrieve information from isolated parts of WSNs. Energy efficiency is ensured by MSs traversing or travelling around a WSN field that moderate the energy consumption of SNs by reducing multihop communication.

Existing approaches exploiting sink mobility for data collection in WSNs mainly differ on the properties of sink mobility as well as the wireless data transfer methods [5]. Several approaches target sparse WSNs deployments that suffer from connectivity problems, wherein an MS visits individually SNs and downloads sensory data over a single-hop wireless transmission; the mobility of MSs can be random [1], predictable (their movement pattern is known beforehand) [3] or controlled (their movement is actively controlled in real time) [5,12]. Rendezvous-based solutions [13] target isolated WSN partitions wherein data are accumulated at designated sensors; these SNs (RNs) buffer collected data until they are relayed to an MS.

Our research targets applications that involve monitoring of isolated urban areas with respect to environmental parameters, surveillance, fire detection, etc. We assume those areas are densely covered by SNs therefore comprising separate urban 'sensor islands'. In such environments, MSs mounted upon city buses that repeatedly follow a predefined trajectory comprise adequate infrastructure for sensory data collection since such vehicles are highly likely to approach the perimeter of the isolated islands.

In this context, the works presented in [2] and [12] are mostly relevant to the research described herein as they assume mobile data collectors with fixed itineraries. In [3], a network access point was mounted on a public bus moving with a periodic schedule. It is assumed that the mobile node comes within direct radio range of all static SNs, i.e. only single-hop data transfers are possible and the majority of the SNs may fail to deliver their cached data (see Figure 1(a)).

In [12], mobile robots are used to collect data from groups of SNs. During a training period, all the WSN edge SNs located within the range of mobile robot routes are appointed as RNs and build paths connected them with the remainder

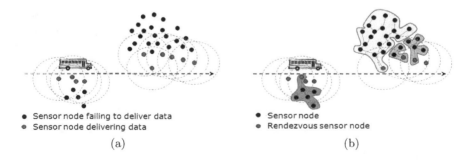

• Sensor node failing to deliver data   • Sensor node
• Sensor node delivering data   • Rendezvous sensor node

(a)   (b)

Fig. 1. (a) SNs delivering or failing to deliver data in [3]; (b) rendezvous SNs and directed diffusion paths in [12]

of SNs. Those paths are used by remote SNs to forward their sensory data to the edge (rendezvous) SNs. Directed Diffusion (DD) [9] is applied upon raw data as they are forwarded from the source to the edge SNs. Similarly to [3], the mobile robots are exclusively used as data collectors. The movement of mobile robots is controllable, which is impractical in realistic urban traffic conditions. Most importantly, no strategy is used to appoint suitable SNs as RNs (all SNs located in proximity to the robot's trajectory are designated as RNs) while selected RNs are typically associated with uneven numbers of SNs (see Figure 1(b)).

Another disadvantage of [12] relates with the use of DD which creates low latency trees from RNs to source SNs. Data from different sources can be opportunistically aggregated at intermediate SNs along the established paths: whenever similar data happens to meet at a branching node in the tree, copies of similar data are replaced by a single message [10]. Also, DD paths are typically prolonged and span large geographical areas, hence they fail to exploit the redundancy inherent in data collected by neighbor source SNs.

Our proposed MobiCluster protocol aims at addressing all the aforementioned problems. We propose the use of vehicles not exclusively engaged to data collection (i.e. urban buses) to carry MSs. MobiCluster ensures delivery of data even through multi-hop transfers from source SNs located far from the MS trajectories. Our focus is on building hierarchical cluster structures comprising neighbor SNs to increase the performance of intra-cluster data filtering and minimize the data relaying overhead (see Figure 2). Cluster-based data aggregation is more effective than DD as it is performed upon data derived from SNs located in a restricted geographical space. Emphasis is given on selecting the appropriate RNs among SNs located in the periphery of the sensor islands (so that they remain within the range of MSs for sufficient time and they buffer data from balanced-sized groups of source SNs).

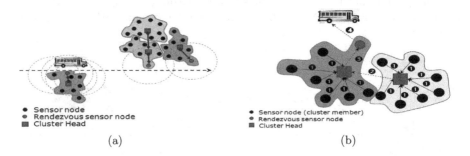

Fig. 2. (a) Rendezvous SNs, cluster structures and data forwarding paths in Mobi-Cluster; (b) sensory data collection and forwarding phases in MobiCluster (numbers indicate the phases time sequence and dotted lines denote inter-cluster traffic and data delivery to the MS)

3   Implementation and Execution Phases of Mobicluster

The execution of MobiCluster is divided in five phases described in the following subsections. The first three phases comprise the setup phase while the last two comprise the steady phase.

3.1   Phase 1: Clustering

Clustering has proven to be an effective approach for organizing the network into a connected hierarchy through partitioning SNs into a number of small groups called clusters. Each cluster has a coordinator, referred to as a CH, and a number of member SNs [7]. The member SNs report their data to the respective CHs. The CHs aggregate the data and send them to a remote processing element through other CHs.

To the best of our knowledge, so far clustering has been proposed for efficiently transferring sensory data to static sinks. However, in the particular context of applications wherein MSs monitor isolated urban sensor islands, clustering also exhibits several advantages:

- For 1-hop clusters, cluster members are located maximum 2-hops away, so high redundancy is likely to exist. Hence, raw sensory data may be effectively filtered by CHs, i.e. the energy-expensive processing of raw data is not performed by RNs.
- The majority of network packet transmissions take place between cluster members and CHs. This results in localization of traffic since data traffic is restricted within clusters and not directly routed to RNs.
- Cluster structures imply a more flexible and scalable network organization: in clustered organizations topology changes are dealt with locally, without affecting the whole network.

The LEACH protocol [7] has been among the first proposals in WSN clustering research. LEACH assigns a fixed probability to every node so as to elect itself as a CH. At the end of the clustering process each node decides whether to become a CH or not. SNs take turns in carrying the role of a CH. In [4] unequal clustering has been proposed.

Our clustering algorithm borrows ideas from the above-mentioned approaches and has been designed based on the following principles: (a) cluster formation is a completely distributed procedure; (b) cluster structures are formed within a single iteration; (c) CHs are reachable in a single hop from their cluster members; (d) since CHs are engaged to data processing tasks and also relaying inter-cluster traffic to RNs, they are elected on the basis of their residual energy supply; (e) since CHs closer to the MS's trajectory are burdened with heavier relay traffic and tend to die faster, an unequal clustering approach is followed which groups the SNs into clusters of unequal size i.e., clusters close to the MS's trajectory include less SNs than the other clusters.

The clustering algorithm is detailed as follows. During an initialization phase, the MS moves along its fixed trajectory broadcasting periodically a BEACON signal to all SNs at a fixed power level. Each sensor can compute the approximate distance to the closest location of the MS based on the largest received signal strength. In the sequel, each node of the network with the same probability p becomes a tentative CH. SNs that fail to become tentative CHs remain in sleeping mode until the final CHs are elected. Each tentative CH executes the final CH election algorithm given below (Algorithm 1):

Algorithm 1. Cluster head election

1: **if** $dist(\nu, MS) < d$ **then**
2:     $\nu.C_{range} = R$
3: **else**
4:     $\nu.C_{range} = R'$
5: **end if**
6: broadcast $Competition\_Msg(\nu.Node\_ID, \nu.E_{residual}, \nu.C_{range})$
7: On receiving a $Competition\_MSG$ from a node u
8: **if** $dist(\nu, u) < max(\nu.C_{range}, u.C_{range})$ **then**
9:     u is added to N_ν
10: **end if**
11: **while** the *"tentative CH competition time"* has not expired **do**
12:     **if** $\forall u \ni N_\nu, \nu.E_{residual} > u.E_{residual}$ **then**
13:        broadcast $Final\_CH\_Msg(\nu.Node\_ID)$
14:        exit
15:     **end if**
16:     **if** a $Final\_CH\_Msg(u.NODE\_ID)$ is received and $u \ni N_\nu$ **then**
17:        broadcast $Final\_CH\_Msg(\nu.Node\_ID)$
18:        exit
19:     **end if**
20:     **if** a $Quit\_Competition\_Msg(u.NODE\_ID)$ is received and $u \ni N_\nu$ **then**
21:        u is removed from N_ν
22:        exit
23:     **end if**
24: **end while**

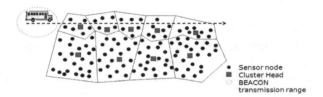

Fig. 3. Unequal cluster formation in MobiCluster

Each tentative CH decides about the value of its competition range (C_{range}). Two different competition ranges R and R' are allowed. These ranges are used to finally create clusters of two different sizes (see Figure 3). No final CH is allowed within the competition range of another final CH. Each tentative CH elects its competition range based on its distance from the MS (lines 1-4 of Algorithm 1). Namely, if the distance of a tentative CH ν from the MS ($dist(\nu, MS)$), is smaller than a predefined distance d, then ν sets its competition range equal to R. Otherwise, it sets its competition range equal to $R' = cR$, where c is a small constant, greater than 1.

Once the tentative CHs have decided about their competition ranges, the approach of Chen et al. [4] is employed for choosing the final CHs. First, each tentative CH ν sends a $Competition\_Msg(\nu.Node\_ID, \nu.E_{residual}, \nu.C_{range})$ announcing its residual energy ($\nu.E_{residual}$) and its competition range ($\nu.C_{range}$). Assuming that the broadcast radius of every control message is R', each tentative CH ν constructs the set N_ν of its "competing neighbors" defined as follows:

$$N_\nu = \{\text{tentative CH } u|\ dist(\nu, u)\ <\ max(\nu.C_{range}, u.C_{range})\}$$

i.e., N_ν contains tentative CHs u such that either u is within the range of ν or ν is within the range of u (lines 7-9 of Algorithm 1). If for each node u that belongs to N_ν, the residual energy of u is smaller than the residual energy of ν then node ν sends a $Final\_CH\_Msg(\nu.Node\_ID)$ message announcing its decision to become a final CH to its "competing neighbors" (lines 12-14). Ties can be solved by choosing the smallest ID SNs [4]. If a tentative CH ν receives from a "competing neighbor" u a $Final\_CH\_Msg(u.Node\_ID)$ message it quits competition by sending a $Quit\_Competition\_Msg(\nu.Node\_ID)$ message (lines 16-18). If a tentative CH ν receives from a "competing neighbor" u a $Quit\_Competition\_Msg(u.Node\_ID)$ message, it removes u from the set N_ν.

Once the final CHs have been elected, sleeping SNs wake up and each CH broadcasts a message to announce its election. Each ordinary (non-CH) node uses the received signal strengths to join to the closest CH.

When the cluster formation finalizes, sensory data collected at CHs from their attached cluster members are forwarded towards the RNs following an inter-cluster overlay graph (see Figure 2(b)). The selected transmission range among CHs may vary to ensure a certain degree of connectivity and to control interference [3].

3.2   Phase 2: RNs Selection

RNs guarantee connectivity of sensor islands with MSs, hence their selection largely determines network lifetime. RNs are selected among candidate SNs typically located in the periphery of the sensor island and lie within the range of travelling sinks. Suitable RNs are those that remain within the MS's range for relatively long time, in relatively short distance from the sink's trajectory and have sufficient energy supplies. In practical deployments, the number of designated RNs introduces an interesting trade-off. A large number of RNs implies that the latter will compete for the wireless channel contention as soon as the mobile robot appears in range, thereby resulting in low data throughput and frequent outages. A small number of RNs implies that each RN is associated with a large group of sensors. Hence RNs will be heavily used during data relays, their energy will be consumed fast and they are likely to experience buffer overflows.

To regulate the number of RNs and prevent either their rapid energy depletion or potential data losses we propose a simple selection model whereby a set of cluster members (in vicinity to the MS's trajectory) from each cluster is enrolled as RNs. RN role may be switched among cluster members when the energy level of a node currently serving as RN drops below a pre-specified threshold. In addition to lying in a short distance from MS trajectories, the best candidates RNs are the SNs with sufficient residual energy that receive a relatively high number of BEACON packets (i.e. they remain long within the sink's range).

In the topology illustrated in Figure 4 for instance, CH #1 selects as RN the one located closest to the MS's trajectory. CH #2 though appoints as RN the one that received the maximum number of BEACON packets (four beacons) as it resides in short distance from a bus stop (we assume that all SNs share the same energy level). In both cases the appointed RNs remain longer within the MS's range than their neighbor SNs. The cluster led by CH #3 represents a case wherein two cluster members (out of mutual transmission range) are designated as RNs. Such clusters are characterized by an expanded front alongside the MS trajectory and MobiCluster protocol promotes the engagement of multiple SNs as RNs so as to share the data buffering and delivery load.

To count the number of received BEACON packets, when a sensor node receives the ith BEACON, it increases a BEACON counter n_b by one, records the receipt time t_i, the signal strength s_i and restarts a 'Connection Dropped Timer' set equal to $3 \cdot T_{beacon}$ (which allows up to two BEACON packets lost due to channel error). The sensor node also keeps record of the receipt time for the first and last received BEACON, T_{first} and T_{last}.

If a BEACON is received at time $t_{i+1} \approx t_i + n \cdot T_{beacon}$ $(n > 1)$ the SN assumes that $n - 1$ BEACON packets have been lost due to channel error or MAC collision and increases n_b by $n-1$. When the 'Connection Dropped Timer' expires the SN assumes that the MS has moved away and the BEACON counter value is finalized.

Then the SN calculates a competence value c_i based on its residual energy, the n_b value and the average signal strength of received BEACON messages (the latter reflects the average distance of the SN from the MS's trajectory). Later on, the SN announces its candidacy to be elected as RN sending to its assigned CH a *RN_Cand* message containing its *node_id*, ci, T_{first} and T_{last}. SNs with relatively high c_i values are likely to be elected as RNs. The algorithm executed by SNs receiving BEACON packets is shown below (Algorithm 2).

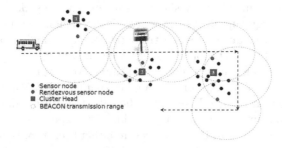

Fig. 4. Selection of RNs in MobiCluster; dashed lines indicate the range of transmitted BEACON packets

Algorithm 2. SNs announcing candidacy for RN

1: initialize $nb = 0, T_{first} = 0, T_{last} = 0$
2: Wait until a BEACON is received
3: record BEACON receipt time t_1 and signal strength s_1
4: $T_{first} = t_1, T_{last} = t_i, n_b = 1$
5: start 'Connection Dropped Timer'
6: **while** 'Connection Dropped Timer' has not expired **do**
7:     wait until next BEACON is received or 'Connection Dropped Timer' is expired
8:     **if** a BEACON i is received **then**
9:         record BEACON receipt time t_i and signal strength s_i
10:         $n_b = n_b + \lceil \frac{t_i - t_{i-1}}{T_{beacon}} \rceil$
11:         $T_{last} = t_i$
12:         reset 'Connection Dropped Timer'
13:     **end if**
14: **end while**
15: compute $C_i = a_1 \cdot \frac{E_{residual}}{E_{max}} + a_2 \cdot n_b + a_3 \cdot \frac{\sum_{i=1}^{n_b} S_i}{n_b}$
16: broadcast $RN\_Cand(node\_id, c_i, T_{first}, T_{last})$

When a CH receives the first RN_Cand message it starts a 'RN Candidacy Timer' set equal to the expected MS itinerary time (i.e. the average time required for a bus to arrive from its departure to its end stop). When this timer expires (the sink has moved away) the CH sorts RN candidates in c_i decreasing order list and excludes those with c_i value below a specified threshold T.

Then, it iterates through the candidates list and for each candidate i it examines whether there exist other candidates j where (i, j) are out of mutual transmission range (this is assumed to be true when $T_{j,first} > T_{i,last}$). In case of multiple alternative RN sets, the CH selects as RNs the SNs of a list based on the following priority criteria: a) select the largest node set; b) in case of a tie (two sets with equal number of SNs) select the set with maximum average c_i value.

Using this simple method, it is guaranteed that RN nodes located within the same cluster will not compete each other in the data delivery phase as each will start delivering its data after the previous ends. Hence the wireless channel is more efficiently used, the number of packet collisions is reduced and data throughput is maximized. In addition the employment of multiple RNs, wherever possible, implies lower demand for data buffering space and fair distribution of the energy expenditure associated with data delivery.

3.3   Phase 3: CHs Attachment to RNs

An important condition for building inter-cluster overlay graphs is that CHs located far from the MS trajectories attach themselves to a RN node so as to address their clusters' data to them. CHs that include a RN as a cluster member advertise that through broadcasting a RN_Attach message to their neighbour CHs. The RN_Attach message includes the RN's CH id and a hops counter (initially set equal to 1). Upon receipt of a RN_Attach message, a CH increases the hops counter by one and forwards it to its neighbours. Duplicate RN_Attach messages (packets with identical CH id value) are dropped. CHs

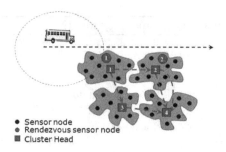

Fig. 5. CHs attachment to RNs

receiving multiple *RN_Attach* messages attach themselves to the RN located minimum hops away to ensure that the inter-cluster transfer of their collected cluster data will incur minimum overhead.

In Figure 5 for instance, CH #1 advertises its attached RN #1 by sending the message *RN_Attach* ($CH = 1, hops = 1$). The message is forwarded to all network's CHs (see dotted red lines) with CH #4 receiving *RN_Attach* (1, 2). At this stage all CHs attach themselves to RN #1. Later on, CH #2 designates a RN within its cluster (RN #2) and announces that through broadcasting a *RN_Attach* message (see dotted blue line). Hence, CH #4 will receive a *RN_Attach* (2, 1) message and will choose to attach to RN #2 located only one hop away.

3.4   Phase 4: Data Aggregation and Forwarding to the RNs

The steady phase of MobiCluster protocol starts with the periodic recording of environmental data from SNs with a T_r period. The data accumulated at individual source SNs are sent to local CHs (intra-cluster communication) with a T_c period (typically T_c is a multiple of T_r). CHs perform data processing to remove data redundancy which is likely to exist since cluster members are located maximum 2 hops away [6]. CHs then forward filtered data towards the cluster where their attached RN belongs to. Alongside the inter-cluster path, a second-level of data filtering may apply.

Upon reaching the end CH, filtered data is forwarded to its local RNs. In the case that multiple RNs exist in that cluster, data are not equally distributed among RNs. Instead, the CH favours the data delivery by the most suitable RNs, i.e. those with highest competence (c_i) value (see subsection 3.2). Data distribution among RNs should ensure that each RN will be able to accommodate its assigned data, that is deliver all its buffered data and not experience an outage. Hence, the CH sorts its RN list in c_i decreasing order and delivers to each RN node RN_i the maximum amount of data d_i it can accommodate, minus an 'outage prevention allowance' amount O. The d_i value is calculated taking into account the RN's data transfer rate r_i and the time interval t_i that RN_i remains within the MS's range. The process is repeated for each RN_i until all data available at the CH are distributed among the RNs.

3.5   Phase 5: Communication between RNs and Mobile Sinks

The last phase of MobiCluster protocol involves the delivery of data buffered to RNs. The communication should start when the connection is available and stop when the connection no longer exists, so that the RN does not continue to transmit data when the MS is no longer receiving it. To address this issue we use an acknowledgment-based protocol between RNs and MSs. The MS, in all subsequent path traversals after the setup phase, periodically broadcasts a POLL packet, announcing its presence and soliciting data as it proceeds along the path. The POLL is transmitted at fixed intervals T_{poll}. This POLL packet is used by RNs to detect when the MS is within range. The RN receiving the POLL starts transmitting data to the MS. The MS acknowledges received data packets to the RN so that the RN realizes that the connection is active and the data was reliably delivered. Once the RN transmits a packet to the MS, it starts two timers:

1. Retransmit Timer: The unacknowledged data packet is retransmitted when this timer expires. These retransmissions overcome the effect of packet losses due to channel errors and MAC layer collisions.
2. Connection Dropped Timer: It has similar function with the 'Connection Dropped Timer' used in the setup phase. The RN ceases packet transfers to the MS if it does not receive a POLL message broadcast from the MS before this timer expires.

The enrollment of specific SNs as RNs is subject to change during the steady phase. Thus, if the energy supply of a RN falls below a threshold, it may request the local CH to engage another node as RN so as to further extend the network's lifetime. To enable RNs substitution, the CHs polls the RN candidate SNs of the setup phase (excluding the retiring RN) to be informed about their current residual energy status and then selects the new RN candidates list.

4   Simulation Results

MobiCluster has been extensively evaluated with respect to several performance parameters. Its performance has been compared against the algorithms presented in [3] and [12] which are the only existing approaches that involve data collection by mobile observers with fixed itineraries. Unless otherwise specified, the parameters used throughout the simulation tests are those shown in Table 1. The simulation results presented herein have been averaged over ten simulation runs (i.e. ten different network topologies). To ensure a fair comparison between MobiCluster and alternative approaches we assume that MSs follow the same mobility model, wherein the MSs repeat the same trajectory in a periodic basis.

Figure 6(a) illustrates the overall number of outages, i.e. the number of data packets cached in RNs, yet, not delivered to the MS due to buffer overflows, packet collisions or the movement of the MS away of the RNs' transmission range. The algorithm of Chakrabarti et al. [3] performs worse since a large percentage of SNs lies away from the sink's range, hence, they fail to delivery their

Table 1. Simulation parameters

Parameter	Value
Simulated plane (m^2)	1000 × 1000
#Sensors	100
Sensors transmission power	4 dBm
Sensors transmission range	100 m
Network transfer rate	250 Kbps
Initial sensors battery lifetime (E_{max})	1000 mJ
Energy required for transmission (per byte with 4 dBm transmit power)	50 nJ
Energy required for reception (per byte)	10 nJ
Energy required for data retrieval from sensors (per byte)	2 nJ
Energy required for data fusion (per byte)	5 nJ
BEACON / POLL broadcast period: T_{beacon}, T_{poll}	10 sec
Mobile sink's itinerary repetition period	250 sec
Probability for a node to become tentative CH (p)	10 %
Bytes transmitted from sensors to CHs every time interval	200
Data fusion coefficient (f)	40%

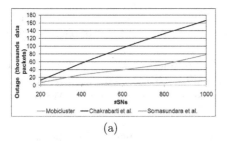
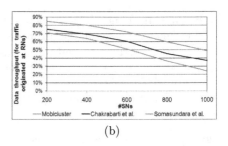

(a)   (b)

Fig. 6. (a) Overall number of outages; (b) network throughput

sensory readings. MobiCluster performs better than [12] because of the more sophisticated selection of RNs which allows them sufficient time to deliver their pre-processed, cashed data. This feature of MobiCluster also justifies its performance gain over alternative methods in terms of network throughput (packets delivered to the MS over those sent from the RNs); those methods employ a large number of RNs without that compete for the contention of the wireless channel contention against other RNs and thus experience a considerable number of packet collisions (see Figure 6(b)). The algorithm of Chakrabarti et al. [3] is shown to perform better than [12], although they involve the same number of RNs (all SNs located within the MS's range), since the latter enables the transmission of sensory data retrieved from all network SNs and thus suffers from higher number of packet collisions.

Figure 7(a) provides an estimate of the total traffic generated throughout the network. MobiCluster outperforms the algorithm of Somasundara et al. mainly due to the improved performance of our cluster-based data fusion method over directed diffusion adopted in [12]. The algorithm presented in [3] incurs lower network overhead as many of the SNs are placed out of the sink's range, thus they do not transmit any packets.

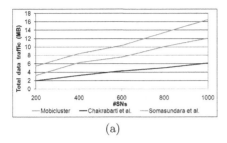 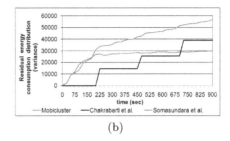

(a)   (b)

Fig. 7. (a) Total generated network traffic; (b) variance of residual energy consumption

Last, MobiCluster ensures more fair distribution (variance) of energy expenditure among SNs (see Figure 7(b)). This is due to its effective data fusion method and the distribution of the data relay overhead among many CHs due to its unequal clustering organization. Besides, the energy-demanding data processing operation is performed by alternating CHs, while initially selected RNs convey their role to other SNs when their energy level decreases below a specified threshold. The abrupt changes in the graph line corresponding to the algorithm of Chakrabarti et al is due to the simultaneous data transmission of a large part of the WSN SNs towards the MS when the latter appears in range.

5   Conclusions

This paper introduced MobiCluster, a protocol that proposes the use of urban buses to carry MSs that retrieve information from isolated parts of WSNs. Mobi-Cluster mainly aims at maximizing connectivity, data throughput and enabling balanced energy expenditure among SNs.

The connectivity objective is addressed by employing MSs to collect data from isolated urban sensor islands and also through prolonging the lifetime of selected peripheral RNs which lie within the range of passing MSs and used to cache and deliver sensory data derived from remote source SNs. Increased data throughput is ensured by regulating the number of RNs for allowing sufficient time to deliver their buffered data and preventing data losses. MobiCluster moves the processing and data transmission burden away from the vital periphery SNs (RNs) and enables balanced energy consumption among SNs through building cluster structures that exploit the high redundancy of data collected from neighbour SNs.

References

1. Anastasi, G., Conti, M., Di Francesco, M.: Data Collection in Sensor Networks with Data Mules: an Integrated Simulation Analysis. In: Proceedings of the IEEE Symposium on Computers and Communications (ISCC 2008), pp. 1096–1102 (2008)

2. Blough, D.M., Santi, P.: Investigating Upper Bounds on Network Lifetime Extension for Cell-Based Energy Conservation Techniques in Stationary Ad Hoc Networks. In: Proceedings of the 8th ACM/IEEE International Conference on Mobile Computing and Networking (MOBICOM 2002), pp. 183–192 (2002)
3. Chakrabarti, A., Sabharwal, A., Aazhang, B.: Using Predictable Observer Mobility for Power Efficient Design of Sensor Networks. In: Zhao, F., Guibas, L.J. (eds.) IPSN 2003. LNCS, vol. 2634, pp. 129–145. Springer, Heidelberg (2003)
4. Chen, G., Li, C., Ye, M., Wu, J.: An Unequal Cluster-Based Routing Protocol in Wireless Sensor Networks. Wireless Networks (2007)
5. Ekici, E., Gu, Y., Bozdag, D.: Mobility-Based Communication in Wireless Sensor Networks. IEEE Communications Magazine 44(7), 56–62 (2006)
6. Hall, D.: Mathematical Techniques in Multisensor Data fusion. Artech House, Boston (1992)
7. Heinzelman, W., Chandrakasan, A., Balakrishnan, H.: An Application-Specific Protocol Architecture for Wireless Microsensor Networks. IEEE Transactions on Wireless Communications 1(4), 660–670 (2002)
8. Hill, J., Szewczyk, R., Woo, A., Hollar, S., Culler, D.E., Pister, K.S.J.: System Architecture Directions for Networked Sensors. Architectural Support for Programming Languages and Operating Systems 35(11), 93–104 (2000)
9. Intanagonwiwat, C., Govindan, R., Estrin, D., John, H., Silva, F.: Directed Diffusion for Wireless Sensor Networking. IEEE/ACM Transactions on Networking 11(1), 2–16 (2003)
10. Luo, H., Liu, Y., Das, S.K.: Routing Correlated Data in Wireless Sensor Networks: A Survey. IEEE Network 21(6), 40–47 (2007)
11. Ma, M., Yang, Y.: Data Gathering in Wireless Sensor Networks with Mobile Collectors. In: Proceedings of the 22nd International Parallel and Distributed Processing Symposium (IPDPS 2008), pp. 1–9 (2008)
12. Somasundara, A.A., Kansal, A., Jea, D.D., Estrin, D., Srivastava, M.B.: Controllably Mobile Infrastructure for Low Energy Embedded Networks. IEEE Transactions on Mobile Computing 5(8), 958–973 (2006)
13. Xing, G., Wang, T., Xie, Z., Jia, W.: Rendezvous Planning in Wireless Sensor Networks with Mobile Elements. IEEE Transactions on Mobile Computing 7(12), 1430–1443 (2008)

Secure EPC Gen2 Compliant Radio Frequency Identification

Mike Burmester[1], Breno de Medeiros[2], Jorge Munilla[3], and Alberto Peinado[3]

[1] Department of Computer Science
Florida State University, Tallahassee, FL 32306, USA
burmester@cs.fsu.edu
[2] Google, Inc.
1600 Amphitheatre, Parkway Mountain View, CA 94043, USA
breno@brenodemedeiros.com
[3] Departamento de Ingeniería de Comunicaciones
Universidad de Málaga, Spain
munilla@ic.uma.es, apeinado@ic.uma.es

Abstract. The increased functionality of EPC Class1 Gen2 (EPCGen2) is making this standard a de facto specification for inexpensive tags in the RFID industry. Recently three EPCGen2 compliant protocols that address security issues were proposed in the literature. In this paper we analyze these protocols and show that they are not secure and subject to replay/impersonation and statistical analysis attacks. We then propose an EPCGen2 compliant RFID protocol that uses the numbers drawn from synchronized pseudorandom number generators (RNG) to provide secure tag identification and session unlinkability. This protocol is optimistic and its security reduces to the (cryptographic) pseudorandomness of the RNGs supported by EPCGen2.

Keywords: EPCGen2 compliance, security, identification, unlinkability.

1 Introduction

Radio Frequency Identification (RFID) is a promising new technology that is widely deployed for supply-chain and inventory management, retail operations and more generally for automatic identification. The advantage of RFID over barcode technology is that it is wireless and does not require direct line-of-sight reading. Furthermore, RFID readers can interrogate tags at greater distances, faster and concurrently.

One of the most important advantages of RFID technology is that tags have read/write capability, allowing stored tag information to be altered dynamically. Typically an RFID system consists of tags, one or more readers, and a back-end server. The communication channel between the reader and the back-end server is assumed to be secure while the wireless channel between the reader and the tag is assumed to be insecure.

P.M. Ruiz and J.J. Garcia-Luna-Aceves (Eds.): ADHOC-NOW 2009, LNCS 5793, pp. 227–240, 2009.
© Springer-Verlag Berlin Heidelberg 2009

To promote the adoption of RFID technology and to support interoperability, EPCGlobal [8] and the International Organization for Standards (ISO) [10] have been actively engaged in defining standards for tags, readers, and the communication protocols. A recently ratified standard is EPC Class 1 Gen 2 (EPCGen2). This defines a platform for the interoperability of RFID protocols, by supporting efficient tag reading, flexible bandwidth use, multiple read/write capabilities and basic reliability guarantees, provided by an on-chip 16-bit Pseudo-random Number Generator (RNG) and a 16-bit Cyclic Redundancy Code (CRC16). EPCGen2 is designed to strike a balance between cost and functionality, with little attention paid to security.

In this paper we are concerned with the security of EPCGen2 compliant protocols. Clearly one has to take into account the additional cost for introducing security into systems with restricted capability. It is important therefore to employ lightweight cryptographic protocols that are compatible with the existing standardized specifications. Several RFID authentication protocols that address security issues using cryptographic mechanisms have been proposed in the literature. Most of these use hash functions [14,19,6,17,7,13], which are beyond the capability of low-cost tags and are not supported by EPCGen2. Some protocols use pseudorandom number generators (RNG) [19,11,3,18,2], a mechanism that is supported by EPCGen2, but these are not optimized for EPCGen2 compliance. One can also use the RNG supported by EPCGen2 as a pseudorandom function (PRF) (as in [2,9]) to link challenge-response flows, however it is not clear if such protocols are vulnerable to *related key* attacks [2].

The research literature for RFID security is extensive. We refrain from a detailed review, and refer the reader to a comprehensive repository available online at [1]. Recently three RFID authentication protocols specifically designed for compliance with EPCGen2 have been proposed [5,15,16]. These combine the CRC-16 of the EPCGen2 standard with its 16-bit RNG to hash, randomize and link protocol flows, and to prevent cloning, impersonation and denial of service attacks. In this paper we analyze these protocols and show that they do not achieve their security goals. One may argue that, because the EPCGen2 standard supports only a very basic RNG, any RFID protocol that complies with this standard is potentially vulnerable, for example to ciphertext-only attacks that exhaust the range of the components of protocol flows. While this is certainly the case, such attacks may be checked by using additional keying material and by constraining the application (e.g., the life-time of tags). We contend that there is scope for securing low cost devices. Obviously, the level of security may not be sufficient for sensitive applications. However there are many low cost applications where there is no alternative.

The rest of this paper is organized as follows. Section 2 introduces the EPCGen2 standard focusing on security issues. Section 3 analyzes three recently proposed EPCGen2 protocols. In Section 4 we propose a novel EPCGen2 compliant protocol that provides tag identification and session unlinkability. In Section 5 we define a security framework for Radio Frequency Identification, and show that our protocol is secure in this framework.

2   The EPCGen2 Standard

EPC Global UHF Class 1 Gen 2, commonly known as the EPCGen2, was approved in 2004, and ratified by ISO as an amendment to the 18000-6 standard in 2006. This standard defines the physical and logical requirements for a passive-backscatter, Interrogator-talks-first (ITF), radio-frequency identification (RFID) system operating in the 860 MHz - 960 MHz frequency range. The EPCGen2 standard defines a protocol with two layers, the physical and the Tag-identification layer, which together specify the physical interactions, the operating procedures and commands, and the collision arbitration scheme used to identify a Tag in a multiple-tag environment.

The system comprises Interrogators, also known as Readers, and Tags. Below we briefly summarize the EPCGen2 requirements.

1. Physical Layer
   - Communications are half-duplex, meaning that Interrogators and Tags cannot talk simultaneously.
   - An Interrogator transmits information to a Tag by modulating an RF signal. Tags are passive, meaning that they receive all of their operating energy from the Interrogator's RF waveform, as well as information.
   - An Interrogator receives information from a Tag by transmitting a continuous wave (CW) RF signal to the Tag; the Tag responds only after being directed to do so by an Interrogator, by modulating the reflection coefficient of its antenna, thereby backscattering a weak signal.
2. Tag memory is logically separated into four distinct banks
   - Reserved memory that contains a 32-bit kill password (KP) to permanently disable the Tag, and a 32-bit access password (AP) used when the Interrogator wants to write/read the memory.
   - EPC memory that contains the parameters of a CRC16 (16 bits), protocol control (PC) bits (16 bits), and an electronic product code EPC that identifies the Tag (32-96 bits).
   - TID memory that contains sufficient information to identify to a Reader the (custom/optional) features of the Tag and tag/vendor specific data.
   - User memory that allows user-specific data storage.
3. Tag-identification layer
   - An Interrogator manages Tag populations using three basic operations: *Select* (the operation of choosing a Tag population), *Inventory* (the operation of identifying Tags) and *Access* (the operation of reading from and/or writing to a Tag).
   - The Interrogator begins an inventory round by transmitting a Query command in one of four sessions. An inventory operates in only one session at a time, and the Interrogator inventories Tags within that session.
   - A random-slotted collision algorithm is used. The Interrogator sends a parameter Q, that is an integer in the range $(0, 15)$; the Tags load a random Q-bit number into a slot counter. Tags decrement this slot counter when they receive a command (QueryRep), and reply to the Interrogator when their counter reaches zero. When the Interrogator detects the reply of a Tag, it requests its PC, EPC, and CRC16.

- Link cover-coding can be used to obscure information during Reader to Tag transmissions. To cover-code data (or a password), an Interrogator first requests a random number from the Tag. Then, the Interrogator performs a bit-wise XOR of the data with this random number, and transmits the result (cover coded or ciphertext) to the Tag.

4. Hardware requirements
   - A 16-bit Pseudo-Random number generator (RNG).
   - A 16-bit Cyclic Redundancy Code.

2.1 The Pseudo-random Number Generator

A pseudorandom number generator (RNG) is a deterministic function that outputs a sequence of numbers that are indistinguishable from random numbers by using as input a random binary string, called *seed*. The length of the random seed must be selected carefully to guarantee that the numbers generated are pseudorandom. The state of the RNG changes each time that a new random number is drawn. Although EPCGen2 does not specify any structure for the RNG, it defines the following randomness criteria.

1. **Probability of RN16**: The probability that a pseudorandom number RN16 drawn from the RNG has value RN is bounded by:

$$0.8/2^{16} < Prob(RN16 = RN) < 1.25/2^{16}.$$

2. **Drawing identical sequences**: For a tag population of up to 10,000 tags, the probability that any two or more tags simultaneously draw the same sequence of RN16s is $< 0.1\%$, regardless of when the tags are energized.

3. **Next-number prediction**: A RN16 drawn from a tag's RNG is not predictable with probability better than 0.025%, given the outcomes of all prior draws.

We refer the reader to the discussion in [2] regarding the strength of EPCGen2 compliant RNGs.

2.2 The 16-Bit Cyclic Redundancy Code

Cyclic Redundancy Codes (CRC) are error-detecting codes that check accidental (non-malicious) errors caused by faults during transmission. To compute the CRC of a bit string $B = (B_0, B_1, \ldots, B_{m-1})$ we first represent it by a polynomial $B(x) = B_0 + B_1 x + \cdots + B_{m-1} x^{m-1}$ over the finite field $GF(2)$, and then compute its remainder: $CRC(B(x)) = (B(x) \cdot x^n) \bmod g(x)$, for an appropriate generator polynomial $g(x)$ of degree n.

EPCGen2 uses the CRC-CCITT generator: $x^{16} + x^{12} + x^5 + 1$, and XORs a fixed bit pattern to the bitstream to be checked. EPCGen2 specifies the Cyclic Redundancy Code CRC16 which, for a 16-bit number B is defined by:

$$CRC(B) = [\, B(x) \cdot x^{16} + \sum_{i=16}^{31} x^i \,] \bmod g(x) = B(x) x^{16} \bmod g(x) + CRC(0),$$

where $CRC(0) = \sum_{16}^{31} x^i \bmod g(x)$ is a fixed polynomial. Since the modulo $g(x)$ operator is a homomorphism, CRC16 inherits strong linearity aspects. More specifically, if P, Q are 16-bit numbers, then

$$CRC(P(x) + Q(x)) = CRC(P(x)) + CRC(Q(x)) + CRC(0). \qquad (1)$$

It follows that the CRC16 of a sequence of numbers can be computed from the CRC16s of the numbers. Consequently CRC16 by itself will not protect data against intentional (malicious) alteration. Its functionality is to support strong error detection particularly with respect to burst errors, not security.

3   Weaknesses in Recently Proposed EPCGen2 Compliant RFID Protocols

In this section we consider three recently proposed EPCGen2 compliant protocols: the Chen-Deng mutual authentication protocol [5], the Quingling-Yiju-Yonghua minimalist mutual authentication protocol [15], and the Sun-Ting authentication protocol [16]. We show that these protocols fall short of their claimed security.

In the protocols below we use the following notation: $\mathcal{S}$ is the back-end server, $\mathcal{R}$ a Reader, $\mathcal{T}$ a tag. We assume that $\mathcal{S}$ and $\mathcal{R}$ are linked with a secure channel, and for simplicity, only consider the case when the authentication is online.

3.1   Analysis of the Chen-Deng Protocol

In the Chen-Deng mutual authentication protocol [5] each tag $\mathcal{T}$ shares three private values with the back-end server $\mathcal{S}$: a key K, a value (incorrectly called nonce) N and an EPC identifier. The tag stores these in non-volatile memory and the server stores them in a database DB. The protocol has three passes:

1. $\mathcal{S} \Rightarrow \mathcal{R} \rightarrow \mathcal{T}$: query, R_r, a random number, and $P = CRC(N \oplus R_r)$.
   $\mathcal{T}$: Check that P is correct. If it is correct,
2. $\mathcal{T} \rightarrow \mathcal{R} \Rightarrow \mathcal{S}$: R_t, a random number, $X = (K \oplus EPC \oplus R_t)$ and $Y = CRC(N \oplus X \oplus R_t)$.
   $\mathcal{S}$: Check that X, Y are correct. If they are correct,
3. $\mathcal{S} \Rightarrow \mathcal{R} \rightarrow \mathcal{T}$: M_{resp}, a response message.

This protocol is clearly subject to a replay attack since the flows from the Reader $\mathcal{R}$ and tag $\mathcal{T}$ use independent randomness (and hence are independent). In fact the adversary needs only one interrogation of $\mathcal{T}$: R_t, $X = (K \oplus EPC \oplus R_t)$ and $Y = CRC(N \oplus X \oplus R_t)$, to impersonate the tag by computing a valid (R_a, X^*, Y^*), for any random number R_a, as: $X^* = X \oplus (R_t \oplus R_a)$, $Y^* = Y$ (Note that new $P^* = P \oplus CRC(R_r \oplus R_a) \oplus CRC(0)$ can be also computed).

3.2 Analysis of the Quingling-Yiju-Yonghua Protocol

The Quingling-Yiju-Yonghua protocol is a challenge-response mutual authentication protocol [15]. Each tag T shares two private 32-bit values with the back-end server S: an access password aPW and a tag identifier $TID = TID_h||TID_l$, where TID_h (TID_l) are the high 16-bits (low 16-bits) of TID. T stores these in non-volatile memory and S stores them in a database DB. The protocol has three passes.

1. $S \Rightarrow R \rightarrow T$: query, and R_r, a 16-bit random number.
2. $T \rightarrow R \Rightarrow S$: R_t, a 16-bit random number, and $M = (M_l||M_h) \oplus aPW$, where $M_l = CRC(TID_l \oplus R_r \oplus R_t)$ and $M_h = CRC(TID_h \oplus R_r \oplus R_t)$.
   S : Check that M is correct. If so, the tag is accepted as the authorized T,
3. $S \Rightarrow R \rightarrow T$: $N = (N_l||N_h) \oplus aPW$, where $N_l = CRC(TID_l \oplus R_t)$ and $N_h = CRC(TID_h \oplus R_t)$.
   T : Check that N is correct. If it is, it accepts that R is an authorized reader.

In this protocol the flows from the tag T and Reader R use combined randomness and are dependent. Therefore one cannot use an identical flow for a replay attack. However, because of the strong linearity aspects of CRC16, it is easy for the adversary to modify the protocol flows from an interrogation of T to get the flow for a replay attack. Suppose that the adversary is given: R_r, R_t and M from a previous successful interrogation; and let R_r^* be the 16-bit random challenge of the Reader for a new interrogation. Then the adversary A can choose any 16-bit random number, R_a, and compute: $A = CRC(R_r \oplus R_r^* \oplus R_a) \oplus CRC(0)$, and send a valid response to S:

$$R_t^* = R_t \oplus R_a \ , \ M^* = M \oplus (A||A),$$

since $M_l^* = M_l \oplus A$ and $M_h^* = M_h \oplus A$, by Equations (1). Therefore the tag T can be cloned after an eavesdropped interrogation. Impersonating the Reader is even simpler: A does not need a previous interrogation. A sends any value R_r^* to an authorized tag T to get M^* from T. Then, A can compute a valid $N^* = M^* \oplus (A'||A')$, where $A' = CRC(R_r^*) \oplus CRC(0)$.

3.3 Analysis of the Sun-Ting Gen2$^+$ Protocol

Gen2$^+$ [16] is a four passes mutual authentication protocol. Each tag shares with the back-end server S a random $(l + 1)$-word string k ($l \leq 127$) called *keypool*. S stores the keypool of each tag T together with its EPC and other identifying data in a database DB. In the protocol T gets identified by revealing information about its keypool, which S uses to locate the tag in DB. The keypool of each tag is updated every 14 successful authentications to prevent cloning attacks. We briefly describe the protocol.

1. $R \rightarrow T$:   query
   T : Draw a 16-bit pseudorandom number, and use the first 14 bits as 7-bit addresses, a and b, to mark a segment $k[a : b]$ of the keypool, and the last

two bits to compute a *check* by XORing the two lsb of the a-th word and the b-th word. If $a \geq b$, the segment $k[a:b]$ contains the words from a to b, otherwise $k[a:b] = k[a:l-1]||k[0:b]$.

2. $\mathcal{T} \rightarrow \mathcal{R} \Rightarrow \mathcal{S}:$ $a, b, check$
   $\mathcal{S}$: First compute *check* for every $k \in DB$, and remove those keypools k with different *check*. Then compute the $CRC(k[a:b])$ of all remaining keypools in the reduced database DB', and finally compute the *central key* ck', whose bits are obtained by taking a majority vote in the corresponding positions of the $CRC(k[a:b])$ in DB' (0 dominates 1).

3. $\mathcal{S} \Rightarrow \mathcal{R} \rightarrow \mathcal{T}:$ ck'
   $\mathcal{T}$: Compute $ck = CRC(k[a:b])$ for the locally stored keypool and compare it with ck': if their Hamming distance is greater than a threshold t (typically $t = 1$) do not respond. Otherwise, send the locally stored EPC.

4. $\mathcal{T} \rightarrow \mathcal{R}:$ nothing or EPC
   $\mathcal{S}$: If there is no response from $\mathcal{T}$ then remove from DB' those keypools k for which the Hamming distance of $CRC(k[a:b])$ from ck' is less or equal to t, and repeat Step 1.

   If the EPC of one of the tags $\mathcal{T}$ in DB is received, then $\mathcal{T}$ is identified, and $\mathcal{R}$ is considered authentic by the tag.

This protocol is clearly subject to replay attacks because only the tag contributes to the randomness of protocol flows. The adversary $\mathcal{A}$ needs to eavesdrop on only one tag interrogation to get the required protocol flows. The protocol is also subject to a more complex statistical attack in which $\mathcal{A}$ first eavesdrops on a number of tag interrogations and then replays the tag flows to the Reader $\mathcal{R}$, changing adaptively the last challenge. This makes it possible for $\mathcal{A}$ to build up gradually sufficient information about the CRC's of the words in a tag's keypool so as to clone the tag. Below we describe the attack in more detail.

1. $\mathcal{A}$ eavesdrops on $m < 14$ successful interrogations of $\mathcal{T}$ (prior to a keypool update). $\mathcal{A}$ stores for every interrogation the values:

$$([a, b, check]_1, ck'_1), ([a, b, check]_2, ck'_2), \ldots, ([a, b, check]_p, ck'_p),$$

where p is the number of challenges or rounds in the interrogation ($p \approx \log(T)/\log(4)$, where T is the total number of tags).

2. $\mathcal{A}$ impersonates $\mathcal{T}$ and replays all but the last of the challenges in each interrogation. The last challenge is replaced by $[x, x, 00]_p$, $0 \leq x \leq l$. $\mathcal{R}$ responds with x' computed by taking a majority vote on the $CRC(k[x:x])$ for all keypools k in the reduced DB'. Note that repeating the first $(p-1)$ rounds guarantees that the target tag is always in DB'. $\mathcal{A}$ repeats this step for each one of the l words of the *keypool*.

3. $\mathcal{A}$ analyzes the collected data. Let n be the number of keypools remaining in DB' after the penultimate round $(p-1)$. $\mathcal{A}$ can compute the CRC16 of the word x in the keypool of $\mathcal{T}$, because of the binary structure of ck': e.g., when $n = 1$ then $ck' = CRC(x)$ and when $n = 2$, ck' is strongly biased with $3/4$ of its bits being 0. The case $n = 2$ is particularly important because it

occurs with high probability ($> 48\%$, for $T = 1000$, $l = 127$, and $t = 1$). Using this information it is now possible to determine $CRC(w)$ of the word w in the keypool of $\mathcal{T}$.

4. $\mathcal{A}$ now impersonates $\mathcal{R}$ to $\mathcal{T}$ and tries to compute a valid ck' for a given $[a, b, check]$. By exploiting the linearity aspects of CRC16, the CRC16 of an interval $k[a : b] = w_a \cdots w_b$ can be computed from the CRC16s of its words:

$$CRC(k[a : b]) = \bigoplus_{i=a}^{b} CRC^{i-a+1}(w_i) \oplus \bigoplus_{1}^{(b-a-1)} CRC^i(0),$$

where CRC^i is CRC iterated i-times. Note also that there is no bound on the number of times that $\mathcal{A}$ can try to compute a valid ck', since the number of challenges in an interrogation is not bounded.

This attack can be modified and enhanced in different ways. For example, $\mathcal{A}$ could use the different tidbit $check$s sent by the tag to guess the values of the lsb of different words, or ask for intervals of different length and combine this with the previous analyzed data. $\mathcal{A}$ could also simplify the attack, by trying to find the CRC of only short block words, and then wait until $\mathcal{T}$ asks for an interval that can be made from these blocks.

4   Gen2Sec: A Secure EPCGen2 Compliant RFID Protocol

We next consider a novel Radio Frequency Identification protocol, Gen2Sec, which only uses the RNG supported by EPCGen2 for security.

4.1   The Protocol

In our protocol each tag $\mathcal{T}$ is identified by drawing consecutive numbers from its RNG. $\mathcal{T}$ draws three numbers, RN_1, RN_2, RN_3, and sends RN_1 to the server $\mathcal{S}$ as a commitment. If $\mathcal{S}$ shares the $RNG(g_{tag})$ with the tag (the algorithm RNG as well as its mutable state g_{tag}), and if both RNGs are synchronized, then $\mathcal{S}$ can also draw these same numbers. It can therefore reply to the tag with the challenge RN_2. $\mathcal{T}$ now sends RN_3 as its response. This third step is also used to keep the RNGs of $\mathcal{S}$ and $\mathcal{T}$ synchronized. One more challenge-response round is needed to deal with replay attacks when these are detected (an $alarm$ triggers this): $\mathcal{S}$ then draws and sends the next number RN_4 as challenge and $\mathcal{T}$ responds by sending RN_5.

Altogether three numbers are drawn when the adversary is passive and five when the adversary is active. The security of the protocol is based on the fact that the random numbers sent by the tag cannot be predicted by the adversary, and consecutive numbers drawn in each interrogation are pseudorandom. Our protocol *identifies tags* (not Readers) and is provably secure. It offers a degree of *privacy* (session unlinkability), as we shall see in the following section.

We now describe the protocol in detail. Each tag $\mathcal{T}$ shares with the back-end server $\mathcal{S}$ an identifier ID_{tag}, its generator (including its mutable state) $RNG(g_{tag})$ and at least one pseudorandom number among the most recent six values extracted from the RNG (which guarantees synchronization as described below). $\mathcal{S}$ stores in a database for each tag a list of seven numbers, ID_{tag} and g_{tag}:

$$DB = \{RN_1^{old}, RN_1^{cur}, RN_1^{next}, RN_2, RN_3, RN_4^{cur}, RN_5^{cur}; ID_{tag}, g_{tag}\}.$$

The lists of DB are doubly indexed by RN_1^{next} and RN_1^{cur} respectively. The tag $\mathcal{T}$ stores in non-volatile memory two pseudorandom numbers, its identifier and g_{tag} (its state):

$$(RN_1, RN_2, ID_{tag}, g_{tag}).$$

To initialize the values of its variables, the tag draws two successive values RN_1, RN_2 from its RNG. $\mathcal{S}$ draws six successive numbers from the RNG of each tag and assigns their values to the variable in the tags lists: RN_1^{cur}, RN_2, RN_3, RN_4^{cur}, RN_5^{cur}, RN_1^{next} (in this order). RN_1^{old} is set to the null value. In the protocol $\mathcal{S}$ uses a *timer* and an *alarm* to manage inventories, thwart man-in-the-middle relay attacks and avoid replay attacks, as well as an *update* function in which: $RN_1^{cur} \leftarrow RN_1^{next}$, and the five values $RN_2, RN_3, RN_4^{cur}, RN_5^{cur}, RN_1^{next}$, are updated by drawing new numbers from $RNG(g_{tag})$.

Gen2Sec Protocol

1. $\mathcal{R} \rightarrow \mathcal{T}$:   query

2. $\mathcal{T} \rightarrow \mathcal{R} \Rightarrow \mathcal{S}$: RN_1
   $\mathcal{S}$: Check in DB
   If $RN_1 = RN_1^{cur}$ for an item in DB then:
        If $RN_1 = RN_1^{old}$ then set $alarm \leftarrow 1$, set $timer$ and broadcast RN_2.
        Else set $RN_1^{old} \leftarrow RN_1$, set $alarm \leftarrow 0$, set $timer$ and broadcast RN_2.
   If $RN_1 = RN_1^{next}$ for an item in DB then $RN^{old} \leftarrow RN_1$, *update*,
        set $alarm \leftarrow 0$, set $timer$ and broadcast RN_2.

3. $\mathcal{S} \Rightarrow \mathcal{R} \rightarrow \mathcal{T}$: RN_2
   $\mathcal{T}$: Check RN_2.
   If RN_2 is valid then draw five successive numbers from $RNG(g_{tag})$, assign them
        to the variables RN_3, RN_4, RN_5 (volatile), RN_1, RN_2, and broadcast RN_3.
   $\mathcal{S}$: On timeout abort.

4. $\mathcal{T} \rightarrow \mathcal{R} \Rightarrow \mathcal{S}$: RN_3
   $\mathcal{S}$: Check RN_3.
   If RN_3 is valid for ID_{tag} then:
        If $alarm = 0$ then *update* and ACCEPT that $\mathcal{T}$ has identifier ID_{tag}.
        Else set $RN_4 \leftarrow RN_4^{cur}$, $RN_5 \leftarrow RN_5^{cur}$, *update*, and broadcast RN_4.
   Else abort.

5. $\mathcal{S} \Rightarrow \mathcal{R} \to \mathcal{T}:$ RN_4

   $\mathcal{T}$: Check RN_4.

   If it is valid then broadcast RN_5.

   $\mathcal{S}$: On timeout abort.

6. $\mathcal{T} \to \mathcal{R} \Rightarrow \mathcal{S}$: RN_5

   $\mathcal{S}$: Check RN_5.

   If RN_5 is valid for ID_{tag} then ACCEPT that $\mathcal{T}$ has identifier ID_{tag}.

   Else abort.

This protocol is *optimistic* in the sense of communication efficiency, because just three flows are necessary to identify a tag $\mathcal{T}$ when the adversary $\mathcal{A}$ is passive. $\mathcal{T}$ sends a commitment in Pass 1, $\mathcal{S}$ sends a challenge in Pass 2, and $\mathcal{T}$ gets identified in Pass 3. $\mathcal{A}$ may try to impersonate $\mathcal{T}$ by obtaining the flows RN_1, RN_2 and RN_3, through an offline man-in-the-middle attack. However this would cause the Server $\mathcal{S}$ to activate the *alarm*. When this happens an additional interrogation is needed (Pass 5 and Pass 6). If $\mathcal{A}$ attempts to replay the numbers RN_1, RN_2, RN_3, RN_4 and RN_5, $\mathcal{A}$ will fail because in the mean time $\mathcal{S}$ and $\mathcal{T}$ will have updated the locally stored values of the pseudorandom numbers.

In the following section we will discuss the security issues of this protocol in a formal framework.

5   A Security Framework for RFID

5.1   RFID Deployments

A typical RFID deployment involves tags $\mathcal{T}$, Readers $\mathcal{R}$ and a back-end Server $\mathcal{S}$. Tags are wireless transponders that typically have no power of their own and respond only when they are in an electromagnetical field, while Readers are transceivers that generate such fields. Readers implement a radio interface to the tags and a high level interface to a back-end server. $\mathcal{S}$ is a trusted entity that processes private tag data. Readers do not store locally any private data.

We adopt the Byzantine threat model. All parties including the adversary $\mathcal{A}$ are modeled as a probabilistic Turing machines. $\mathcal{A}$ controls the delivery schedule of all communication channels, and may eavesdrop into, or modify, their contents and may also instantiate new communication channels and directly interact with honest parties. However the channels that link the Server and authorized Readers are assumed to be secure. Readers do not store any private tag information.

5.2   The UC Framework

The universal composability (UC) framework specifies a particular approach to security proofs for protocols, and guarantees that proofs that follow that approach remain valid if the protocol is, say composed with other protocols (modularity) and under arbitrary concurrent protocol executions (including with itself). The UC framework defines a *real-world simulation*, an *ideal-world simulation*, an *emulation $\mathcal{E}$* that translates protocol runs from the real-world to the ideal-world, and an interactive environment $\mathcal{Z}$ that captures whatever is external to the current protocol execution. The components of a UC security formalization are:

1. A *mathematical model* of real protocol executions in which honest parties (the tags and the Server) correctly execute as specified, and adversarial parties under the control of the adversary $\mathcal{A}$ that can deviate from the protocol in an arbitrary way. $\mathcal{A}$ can interact with the environment $\mathcal{Z}$, in arbitrary ways.
2. An *idealized model* of executions, where the security properties of the protocol depend on the behavior of an *ideal functionality* $\mathcal{F}$. $\mathcal{F}$ controls the ideal-model adversary $\widehat{\mathcal{A}}$ so that it reproduces as faithfully as possible the behavior of $\mathcal{A}$.
3. A proof that, for each adversary $\mathcal{A}$ there is a simulator $\mathcal{E}$ that translates real-world runs in the presence of $\mathcal{A}$ into ideal-world protocol runs in the presence of $\widehat{\mathcal{A}}$ such that, no environment $\mathcal{Z}$ can distinguish whether $\mathcal{A}$ is communicating with a instance of the protocol in the real-world or $\widehat{\mathcal{A}}$ is communicating with $\mathcal{F}$ in the ideal-world.

In the UC framework, the context of a protocol execution is captured by a session identifier *sid*. The *sid* is controlled by the environment Z and reflects external aspects of execution. All parties involved in a protocol execution instance share the same *sid*.

Theorem 1. *Gen2Sec guarantees* availability, tag authentication *and* session unlinkability *in the UC framework provided a cryptographically secure RNG is used.*

Note that the UC simulation approach described here can be readily used to derive a concrete security estimate for Gen2Sec in terms of the estimated probability of breaking the underlying RNG, given an adversarial budget for computation and communication. This makes the approach useful beyond its ability to prove security under traditional assumptions of ideal cryptographic primitives (such as a cryptographically strong RNG) which may not hold for specific instantiations of the scheme.

Proof. We sketch an outline of the proof. First we specify the functionality $\mathcal{F}_{auth}$ of the protocol to capture availability, tag authentication and session unlinkability.

1. Availability requires that the Server and tags be synchronized at all times.
2. Tag authentication requires that the Server can corroborate values produced by the tag in terms of the state of their shared RNG.
3. Session unlinkability requires that: given two tag interrogations $\mathcal{A}$ cannot decide (with probability better than $0.5 +$ negligible) whether these involve the same tag or not, provided that either the first completed successfully, or an intervening interrogation of the tag completed successfully.

The functionality $\mathcal{F}_{auth}$ is illustrated in Figure 1. There are four commands: INITIATE activates the Server and tags, SEND is used to send an output of one

---

Functionality $\mathcal{F}_{\mathsf{auth}}$

$\mathcal{F}_{\mathsf{auth}}$ has session identifier *sid* and only admits commands with the same *sid*.

Upon receiving INITIATE **from** *Server*: Generate a unique subsession identification number s_{ser}. Create a new DB, record and send to $\mathcal{A}$: $\mathtt{flow}(s_{ser}, \cdot, Query)$.

Upon receiving INITIATE **from** *tag*: if $\mathtt{flow}(s_{ser}, \cdot, Query) \in DB$, then generate a unique subsession identification number s_{tag}, select five random numbers: r_1, r_2, r_3, r_4 and r_5 and assign them to the subsession (s_{ser}, s_{tag}). Set $alarm \leftarrow 0$. Send (tag, s_{tag}) to $\mathcal{A}$.

Upon receiving SEND(s_{ser}, s_{tag}) **from** $\mathcal{A}$:

If $\mathtt{flow}(s_{tag}, s_{ser}, r_5) \in DB$ then ACCEPT(tag) and delete all flows of (s_{ser}, s_{tag}) in DB.
ElseIf $\mathtt{flow}(s_{ser}, s_{tag}, r_4) \in DB$ then record and send to $\mathcal{A}$: $\mathtt{flow}(s_{tag}, s_{ser}, r_5)$.
ElseIf $\mathtt{flow}(s_{tag}, s_{ser}, r_3) \in DB$ then:
    If $alarm = 0$ then ACCEPT(tag) and delete all flows of (s_{ser}, s_{tag}) in DB.
    Else record and send to $\mathcal{A}$: $\mathtt{flow}(s_{ser}, s_{tag}, r_4)$.
ElseIf $\mathtt{flow}(s_{ser}, s_{tag}, r_2) \in DB$ then record and send to $\mathcal{A}$: $\mathtt{flow}(s_{tag}, s_{ser}, r_3)$.
ElseIf $\mathtt{flow}(s_{tag}, s_{ser}, r_1) \in DB$ then record and send to $\mathcal{A}$: $\mathtt{flow}(s_{ser}, s_{tag}, r_2)$.
ElseIf $\mathtt{flow}(s_{ser}, \cdot, Query) \in DB$ then record and send to $\mathcal{A}$: $\mathtt{flow}(s_{tag}, s_{ser}, r_1)$.
Else ignore.

Upon receiving REPEAT(s_{ser}, s_{tag}) **from** $\mathcal{A}$:

If $\mathtt{flow}(s_{tag}, s_{ser}, r_3) \in DB$ then ignore.
ElseIf $\mathtt{flow}(s_{tag}, s_{ser}, r_2) \in DB$ then delete all flows of (s_{ser}, s_{tag}) in DB.
    Set $alarm \leftarrow 1$, record and send to $\mathcal{A}$: $\mathtt{flow}(s_{ser}, \cdot, Query)$. SEND$(s_{ser}, s_{tag})$.
ElseIf $\mathtt{flow}(s_{tag}, s_{ser}, r_1) \in DB$ then delete all flows of (s_{ser}, s_{tag}) in DB.
    Record and send to $\mathcal{A}$: $\mathtt{flow}(s_{ser}, \cdot, Query)$.
Else ignore.

Upon receiving message IMPERSONATE(s_{ser}, tag) **from** $\mathcal{A}$: If $\mathtt{flow}(s_{ser}, \cdot, Query) \in DB$ and *tag* is corrupted then ACCEPT(tag).

Fig. 1. The functionality of Gen2Sec

party (tag or Server) to the other (Server or tag) and get their response, REPEAT is used to repeat interrogations that were not completed (the adversary did not send the required flows), and IMPERSONATE is used to impersonate tags. Observe that in both the protocol and $\mathcal{F}_{auth}$, the receiving party of any message or subroutine output is activated next. For more details on security proofs in the UC framework, the reader is referred to [18].

We must show that a real-world adversary $\mathcal{A}$ who can access protocol flows cannot succeed with probability greater than negligible in generating the flows of a "new" interrogation that is accepted by the Server, but *not* accepted in the ideal-world by $\mathcal{F}_{auth}$ (corresponding to an interrogation that is generated in a way not specified by the protocol): if this happens $\mathcal{Z}$ will distinguish real-world from ideal-world executions.

We first emulate real-world actions in the ideal-world. For this purpose we simulate copies $\widehat{\mathcal{A}}$, of the real adversary, $\widehat{Server}$, of the real Server, $\widehat{tag}$, of real tags, and the interactions of the protocol with $\mathcal{Z}$, in particular its invocations of $\mathcal{F}_{auth}$. For our protocol it is straightforward to show that any interrogation in the real-world that is accepted by the Server is also accepted in the ideal-world by the functionality $\mathcal{F}_{auth}$ because:

1. At all times each tag shares at least one number with the Server (availability);
2. If the Server accepts the tag then a fresh flow of numbers must have been used (tag authentication);
3. If for any two interrogations either the first one completed successfully before the second, or an intervening interrogation completed successfully, then the tag will have updated the values it stores (session unlinkability).

This first property holds because the values of the stored numbers are updated by $\mathcal{T}$ and $\mathcal{S}$ with each successful execution. If the previous execution of the protocol was not disrupted then $RN_1^{cur} = RN_1$ (in this case one *update* is needed); otherwise we may get $RN_1^{next} = RN_1$ (two *updates* are needed). Note that the numbers RN_3, RN_4 and RN_5 are used only once. For the second observe that the adversary (e.g., a rogue tag or reader) cannot guess the protocol flows because these are generated by a RNG. There is of course a small failure probability due to "lucky" guessing. The adversary cannot clone a tag because it cannot get access to the seed of the RNG of the tag (which is never revealed). For the last observe that, if the first interrogations completed successfully, or an intervening interrogation completed successfully, then the tag will have updated the values it stores. Finally, in the real world all protocol flows involve pseudorandom numbers whereas in the ideal world we have random numbers: the environment $\mathcal{Z}$ cannot distinguish these because it is a PPT machine.

Observe that there are impersonation attacks in the real-world that are not captured in the ideal-world: if a tag updates its RNG while the Server does not (RN_3 was not delivered) then $\mathcal{A}$ can try to impersonate the tag by re-using the flows RN_1 and RN_3. However it will only succeed with negligible probability in guessing RN_5 in response to the Server's query RN_4. Therefore $\mathcal{Z}$ will not see any difference between the successful instances in real-world and ideal-world. □

Acknowledgement

Research partly supported by the Spanish Ministry of Science and Innovation and the European FEDER Funds, under Project TIN 2008-02236/TSI.

References

1. Avoine, G., http://lasecwww.epfl.ch/~gavoine/rfid/
2. Burmester, M., de Medeiros, B.: The security of EPC Gen2 compliant RFID protocols. In: Bellovin, S.M., Gennaro, R., Keromytis, A.D., Yung, M. (eds.) ACNS 2008. LNCS, vol. 5037, pp. 490–506. Springer, Heidelberg (2008)

3. Burmester, M., de Medeiros, B., Motta, R.: Robust, Anonymous RFID Authentication with Constant Key-Lookup. In: Abe, M., Gligor, V.D. (eds.) ASIACCS, pp. 283–291. ACM, New York (2008); Extended version: J. Applied Cryptography 1(2), 79–90 (2008)
4. Canetti, R.: Universally composable security: A new paradigm for cryptographic protocols. In: Proc. IEEE Symp. on Foundations of Computer Science (FOCS 2001), pp. 136–145. IEEE Press, Los Alamitos (2001)
5. Chen, C.-L., Deng, Y.-Y.: Conformation of EPC Class 1 Generation 2 Standards RFID system with Mutual Authentication and Privacy Protection. In: Engineering Applications of Artificial Intelligence. Elsevier, Amsterdam (in Press), Corrected Proof. doi:10.1016/j.engappai.2008.10.022
6. Dimitriou, T.: A lightweight RFID protocol to protect against traceability and cloning attacks. In: Proc. IEEE Intern. Conf. on Security and Privacy in Communication Networks (SECURECOMM 2005). IEEE Press, Los Alamitos (2005)
7. Dimitriou, T.: A secure and efficient RFID protocol that can make big brother obsolete. In: Proc. Intern. Conf. on Pervasive Computing and Communications (PerCom 2006). IEEE Press, Los Alamitos (2006)
8. EPC Global. EPC Tag Data Standards, http://www.epcglobalinc.orgblock
9. Eun Young Choi, D.H.L., Lim, J.I.: Anti-cloning protocol suitable to Epcglobal Class-1 Generation-2 RFID systems. In: Computer Standards & Interfaces, Elsevier, Amsterdam (in press), Corrected Proof. doi:10:1016/j.csi.2008.11.002
10. ISO/IEC. Standard # (18000) – RFID Air Interface Standard, http://www.hightechaid.com/standards/18000.htm
11. Juels, A.: Minimalist cryptography for low-cost RFID tags. In: Blundo, C., Cimato, S. (eds.) SCN 2004. LNCS, vol. 3352, pp. 149–164. Springer, Heidelberg (2005)
12. Kim, C.H., Avoine, G., Koeune, F., Standaert, F.-X., Pereira, O.: The Swiss-Knife RFID Distance Bounding Protocol. In: Lee, P.J., Cheon, J.H. (eds.) ICISC. LNCS, vol. 5461, pp. 98–115. Springer, Heidelberg (2008)
13. Molnar, D., Soppera, A., Wagner, D.: A scalable, delegatable pseudonym protocol enabling ownership transfer of RFID tags. In: Preneel, B., Tavares, S. (eds.) SAC 2005. LNCS, vol. 3897, pp. 276–290. Springer, Heidelberg (2006)
14. Ohkubo, M., Suzuki, K., Kinoshita, S.: Cryptographic approach to "privacy-friendly" tags. In: Proc. RFID Privacy Workshop (2003)
15. Qingling, C., Yiju, Z., Yonghua, W.: A minimalist mutual authentication protocol for RFID system and ban logic analysis. In: ISECS International Colloquium on Computing, Communication, Control and Management, vol. 2, pp. 449–453 (2008), doi:10.1109/cccm.2008.305
16. Sun, H.-M., Ting, W.-C.: A Gen2-based RFID authentication protocol for security and privacy. IEEE Transactions on Mobile Computing 99, 1 (2009)
17. Tsudik, G.: YA-TRAP: Yet another trivial RFID authentication protocol. In: Proc. IEEE Int. Conf. on Pervasive Computing and Communications (PerCom 2006). IEEE Press, Los Alamitos (2006)
18. van Le, T., Burmester, M., de Medeiros, B.: Universally Composable and Forward-secure RFID Authentication and Authenticated Key Exchange. In: Proc. of the ACM Symp. on Information, Computer, and Communications Security (ASIACCS 2007), pp. 242–252. ACM Press, Singapore (2007)
19. Weis, S., Sarma, S., Rivest, R., Engels, D.: Security and privacy aspects of low-cost radio frequency identification systems. In: Hutter, D., Müller, G., Stephan, W., Ullmann, M. (eds.) Security in Pervasive Computing. LNCS, vol. 2802, pp. 201–212. Springer, Heidelberg (2004)

On the Trade-Off between User-Location Privacy and Queried-Location Privacy in Wireless Sensor Networks

Ryan Vogt, Mario A. Nascimento, and Janelle Harms

Department of Computing Science, University of Alberta, Canada
{vogt,mn,harms}@cs.ualberta.ca

Abstract. By eavesdropping on a user's query in a sensor network, an adversary can deduce both the user's location and his/her area of interest. In many domains it is desirable to guarantee privacy of both places. We propose an effective way to measure how well issuing a disperse set of k queries protects the user's area of interest. However, issuing k queries instead of one facilitates the adversary determining the user's location. To address that issue, we define a quantitative measure of how much information the k queries leak about the user's location. Experiments reveal that how dispersed the k queries are has no effect on the privacy of the user's location. However, smaller k, randomized routing, and non-broadcast transmission improve the user's location privacy. We also show that compromising nodes in the user's network yields no significant advantage to the adversary over an eavesdropping strategy.

1 Introduction

Privacy is an important challenge in many wireless sensor network applications. Consider a sensor network where a user with a portable device interacts with the nodes, for instance, querying a sensor's data at a remote location. As a practical example, the sensor network could be a military one that troops need to query in preparation for an offensive. That query would be received by a nearby node and routed through the sensor network to the location of interest, then processed and returned using one of a large number of previously proposed algorithms. Given an assumed sensitive nature of the information returned by the query, encryption should be used to protect against eavesdropping. Either symmetric encryption or public-key encryption that is sufficiently inexpensive to be performed by a low-power sensor node [1] could be used. However, while cryptography can ensure data confidentiality, encryption alone cannot provide anonymity. By listening to network traffic, using either compromised nodes in the user's sensor network or eavesdropping nodes, an adversary could learn: (a) *where the queried sensor is*, thus providing significant insight into the user's intentions; and (b) *where the query originated*, thus revealing the user's current location. Investigating the *trade-off* between protecting these two locations is the main goal of this paper.

In the context of our aforementioned military scenario, we consider an adversary that wants to learn the user's current location or location of interest. In previous works, a common assumption was the adversary was a mobile single physical agent able to move towards the user. We, on the other hand, assume that the adversary is not a single physical agent; rather, it is virtually present at different points of the network by virtue

P.M. Ruiz and J.J. Garcia-Luna-Aceves (Eds.): ADHOC-NOW 2009, LNCS 5793, pp. 241–254, 2009.
© Springer-Verlag Berlin Heidelberg 2009

of being able to simultaneously eavesdrop on the on-going communication at those points. This "omnipresence" makes our model of an adversary stronger than a single mobile adversary. We also assume that the adversary has complete knowledge of all possible routes that a message could take between two sensors in the user's network (i.e., complete knowledge of the routing tables), as this information could be obtained through eavesdropping on legitimate traffic.

Considering this problem under this threat model, we offer the following contributions. We introduce novel metrics that enable the user to quantitatively evaluate how well he/she can protect the privacy of his/her location of interest by issuing k queries, one directed to the real location of interest and the others directed to $k - 1$ distinct fake locations of interest. This technique for protecting location-of-interest privacy requires no changes, hardware nor software, to an existing sensor network; it is implemented entirely in software on the mobile device interacting with the sensor network, and introduces a multiplicative overhead of factor k in terms of communication in the sensor network. We also discuss in detail the trade-off yielded by the fact that issuing more queries generates more traffic from the user's current location, thus helping an adversary discover that current location. Our experimental results show that how well dispersed the k queries are has no effect on the privacy of the user's current location. Nonetheless, smaller values of k, randomized routing, and non-broadcast transmission between nodes can significantly improve the user's current-location privacy. Finally, we show the surprising result that an adversary who gathers information from compromised nodes in the user's network has no significant advantage over an eavesdropping adversary when broadcast transmission is used.

The remainder of this paper is structured as follows. Section 2 discusses related work on anonymous communication. We then formalize the metrics that we use in Section 3; these metrics define how well the user's location of interest and current location are protected by the k queries issued. Section 4 describes how the fake locations of interest should be chosen. We then present experimental results in Section 5 to illustrate how various parameters affect the user's privacy, before concluding and discussing possible future work in Section 6.

2   Related Work

There are known ways to achieve anonymity of two communication endpoints in some networks. The Tor network implementation of onion routing [2] has the source choose a random route to the destination. The source uses layers of public-key encryption, allowing each host in the route to see only the next host in the route, and none of the data being transmitted. However, this approach demands many public-key cryptography operations that may be too costly or even impossible for some sensor nodes. Finally, Tor does not protect against eavesdropping at communication endpoints, which is a significant threat in a broadcast medium. If an adversary were to overhear a query exiting the Tor network, all privacy about the location being queried would be lost.

Misra and Xue [3] look at anonymity specifically for sensor networks. They show how clusters of nodes can generate and share pseudonyms used as node identities when communicating with a sink. Their work is extended by Ouyang et al. [4] to account for shared keys being compromised. However, these works only look at nodes communicating with a sink, using pseudonyms known only to the endpoints to ensure that eavesdroppers will not know which node is sending information. These schemes are not applicable when nodes need to communicate with each other, as in our scenario.

Ozturk et al. [5] and Kamat et al. [6] examine a problem similar to our user's queries being tracked to their source. However, these papers have a different focus, namely an adversary that moves over time towards a source node that produces a continuous stream of data. They propose a solution called phantom routing, in which each epoch's data is routed in a random directed walk away from the source, before being flooded to the sink. This solution would not be appropriate for our scenario; e.g., a message intercepted during the directed walk phase carries enough information to immediately yield the number of hops and direction to the source of the user's query. A related problem, in which the adversary moves towards the receiver of sensor network traffic over time, is investigated by Jian et al. [7]. While these approaches are useful for protecting privacy in certain situations, they are not applicable to the situation described in this study, in which the adversary does not have to move towards the user's current location or location of interest. In a military scenario, for example, just learning either of these locations could be sufficient for the adversary.

In our work, we rely on obfuscating the user's location of interest by querying k locations, an idea inspired by Sweeney's concept of k-anonymity [8]. The goal then was to allow a data holder (e.g., a hospital) to release personal data to researchers such that no set of data could possibly belong to fewer than k individuals. To our knowledge, no one has investigated the trade-off imposed by preserving the privacy of both the location of interest as well as the user's location, using the notion of k-anonymity.

3   Privacy Metrics

We begin by defining our notation. The sensor network consists of a set $\mathcal{N}$ of nodes, where $|\mathcal{N}| = n$. The user will issue k queries, Q_i, each directed to a location L_i, where $\mathcal{L} = \{L_1, L_2, \ldots, L_k\} \subseteq \mathcal{N}$. One node, $L \in \mathcal{L}$, is the user's real location of interest, and the remaining $k - 1$ nodes are fake locations of interest.

To study how well this k-anonymity scheme preserves the privacy of the user's location of interest (LOI) and current location (CL), we require formal methods to measure the privacy levels that result from any given set of k queries. In the following section, we define the metric used to determine how well the LOI-privacy — and, more specifically, the area in which the LOI lies — is protected. We then define how well the privacy of the current location is protected in Section 3.2.

3.1   Privacy of the Location and Area of Interest

If it is equally probable that any of the k queried nodes is the real LOI, then the adversary cannot learn which of the k nodes queried is the real LOI. Given this assumption (which we revisit in Section 4), what is actually meant when we discuss protecting the privacy of the user's LOI? Consider the two scenarios in Figure 1. In both cases, the user's real LOI is the starred node in the northeast, and $k - 1 = 3$ fake LOIs are chosen to disguise the real LOI. However, in Figure 1(a), all four LOIs are clustered in the east. While an adversary who overhears these queries would not know which node is of interest to the user, it would be obvious that the user is interested in the eastern region of the sensor network. In Figure 1(b), the four LOIs are dispersed throughout the sensor network, obfuscating the area of the network in which the user is interested. We need to define a measure of how dispersed the k LOI choices are. That is, we want to measure how well-protected the privacy of the user's area of interest (AOI) is.

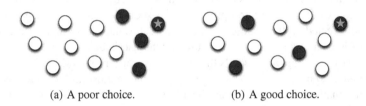

(a) A poor choice.   (b) A good choice.

Fig. 1. A comparison of two choices for $k - 1 = 3$ fake LOIs (dark nodes) given one fixed real LOI (starred node)

To measure how well the set $\mathcal{L}$ of k LOIs preserves the user's AOI-privacy, we define a function $\sigma(\mathcal{L}, \mathcal{N})$ to measure how dispersed the LOIs are over the network $\mathcal{N}$. To allow for comparisons of different methods of choosing the fake LOIs over networks with different topologies, we normalize the score returned by σ. Let $\sigma_{min}(k, \mathcal{N})$ and $\sigma_{max}(k, \mathcal{N})$ be the minimal and maximal values returned by σ, over all $\binom{n}{k}$ possible sets of k LOIs. The normalized measure of AOI-privacy is defined as

$$M_{AOI}(\mathcal{L}, \mathcal{N}) = \begin{cases} 1 & \text{if } \sigma_{min}(k, \mathcal{N}) = \sigma_{max}(k, \mathcal{N}) \\ \dfrac{\sigma(\mathcal{L}, \mathcal{N}) - \sigma_{min}(k, \mathcal{N})}{\sigma_{max}(k, \mathcal{N}) - \sigma_{min}(k, \mathcal{N})} & \text{otherwise.} \end{cases}$$

The function σ must have the property that it returns large values for sets $\mathcal{L}$ with minimal clustering of the LOIs, and small values otherwise. It must also be easy to compute on the user's low-powered, mobile device prior to issuing a query. Next, we discuss some alternatives for σ.

Variance-Based σ. One straightforward approach is to compute a variance-like quantity for the positions of the nodes in $\mathcal{L}$, measuring the squared distance between LOIs:

$$\sigma(\mathcal{L}, \mathcal{N}) = \sum_{i=1}^{k-1} \sum_{j=i+1}^{k} D\left(L_i, L_j\right)^2 \ ,$$

where D is the Euclidean distance between two nodes. However, this definition of σ does not penalize clustering properly. Consider the examples in Figure 2. The choice of fake LOIs in Figure 2(a) has two of the LOIs clustered together. In Figure 2(b) the three LOIs are dispersed evenly. However, the σ value for the first choice is higher.

(a) A choice of LOIs that results in two clusters.

(b) A choice of LOIs that disperses the LOIs across the entire network.

Fig. 2. A comparison of two choices for $k = 3$ LOIs in a five-node sensor network

Union of Circles σ. Another approach is to determine how much overlap exists among the regions around each LOI. Specifically, one can draw a circle of radius r around each LOI and let σ be the area of the union of the k circles. The more clustered the LOIs, the more overlap there would be among the circles, resulting in a smaller area. An example is presented in Figure 3. With k clustered LOIs, shown in Figure 3(a), there is significant overlap among the circles, unlike with the non-clustered choice shown in Figure 3(b).

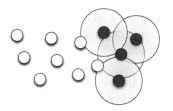
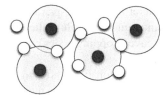

(a) A choice of LOIs with significant overlap among the circles.

(b) A choice of LOIs with minimal overlap among the circles.

Fig. 3. A comparison of two choices for $k = 4$ LOIs in a sensor network, each surrounded by a circle with a fixed, arbitrary radius

One way to choose r is to define d as the maximum distance between any two nodes in $\mathcal{N}$, then set $r = \frac{d}{2}$. This definition ensures that there is no overlap between the regions of the two sensor nodes that are farthest apart, but the regions surrounding any two sensor nodes that are closer together will overlap. While this σ properly penalizes clustering, computing σ is computationally expensive. A Monte Carlo algorithm for computing the area of the union of circles requires a large number of sample points. It may not be practical for the user to run an expensive algorithm to compute the AOI-privacy level of every set of k queries he/she poses. Even more expensive to compute are $\sigma_{min}(k, \mathcal{N})$ and $\sigma_{max}(k, \mathcal{N})$, though these values could be precomputed, provided the sensor network topology does not change.

Sum of Minima σ. Measuring the sum of minimum distances from each LOI to any other LOI penalizes clustering properly and is easy to compute. Formally, let

$$\sigma(\mathcal{L}, \mathcal{N}) = \sum_{i=1}^{k} \min_{j \neq i} \left\{ D\left(L_i, L_j\right) \right\} ,$$

where D is the Euclidean distance between two nodes. That is, the farther away each of the L_i are from each other, the higher the value of σ. Returning to the five-node examples in Figure 2, this σ returns a higher value in the scenario where the LOIs are non-clustered; and, it can be computed quickly, given the location of every node in $\mathcal{L}$.

Considering these three possible σ functions, we use the sum of minima function for the remainder of the paper. We chose this σ since we assume that the user, prior to issuing any set of k queries, will want to precompute the AOI-privacy that will result from the queries using a mobile device with limited processing power. If processing power were not a concern, the union of circles metric could be used instead.

3.2   Privacy of the Current Location

The previous section described a static measurement for how well k queries protected the user's AOI-privacy. How much information these queries leak about the user's current location (CL), on the other hand, cannot be analyzed statically, as that depends on how much information the adversary is able to overhear during the routing of the queries. To determine the CL-privacy that results from a set of queries, we will simulate the user issuing queries while malicious nodes (either compromised nodes in the user's network, or eavesdropping nodes outside the network) attempt to ascertain the origin of those queries.

This section demonstrates how an adversary could use the information captured by malicious nodes to narrow down the possible locations where the user could be. Central to this technique is the concept of a *possible route*. In the sensor network, which we assume to be connected, there must be a routing algorithm capable of routing messages from any source node to any destination node. Consider a route $\mathcal{R} = (N_1, N_2, \ldots, N_l)$, which is a sequence of l nodes. $\mathcal{R}$ is a possible route from N_1 to N_l if it possible that the routing algorithm used in the sensor network could have routed a message from N_1 to N_l along the path $N_1, N_2, \ldots, N_l$.

In this paper, we consider two routing algorithms: fixed shortest-path routing and random shortest-path routing. Both guarantee that any message from N_1 to N_l will arrive in the fewest possible hops. In random shortest-path routing, each node maintains a table indexed by the destination of a message, containing all possible next hops that the message could take to arrive in the fewest hops. When a message arrives at a node N_i destined for node N_l, N_i will look into its table at index N_l, and randomly choose one of the entries as the next hop. In fixed shortest-path routing, each node stores only a single next-hop choice for each possible destination. There is exactly one possible route from N_1 to N_l when fixed shortest-path routing is used, but there can be many possible routes between N_1 and N_l with random shortest-path routing.

Recall that the user uses a mobile device to communicate with a nearby sensor node, in order to route queries through the sensor network to the LOIs. The user sends the k queries, denoted $Q_1, Q_2, \ldots, Q_k$, to the closest sensor node, C. We assume that the mobile device and C communicate using low-power communication. That is, the adversary will only overhear communication between the mobile device and C if C is compromised. We also assume that the adversary knows k — the implication being that if the adversary overhears fewer than k of the user's queries, the adversary knows how many queries were not overheard. Each Q_i takes a route $\mathcal{R}_i$ through the network, starting at C and ending at L_i. Denote $\mathcal{R}_i$ as a sequence of nodes with length l_i, $\mathcal{R}_i = (N_{i,1}, N_{i,2}, \ldots, N_{i,l_i})$, where $N_{i,1} = C$ and $N_{i,l_i} = L_i$. The goal of the adversary is to determine C.

While our k-anonymity scheme can be built over any existing query mechanism, we assume in this paper that query and reply messages are designed to maximize privacy. Specifically, a query message that is being routed from C to L_i cannot contain references to C, nor can a reply; otherwise, the adversary could easily determine C. Query messages contain four pieces of information in addition to the query itself: a unique query identifier for Q_i; the destination L_i (which may be the real location of interest or a fake one); the identifier for the node currently transmitting the query, $N_{i,j}$; and, the next hop in the route, $N_{i,j+1}$. When node $N_{i,j+1}$ receives the query, it remembers the previous node in the route for query Q_i, $N_{i,j}$. Replies to the query message contain only the query identifier for Q_i. When node $N_{i,j+1}$ receives a reply to the query, to be routed back to C, $N_{i,j+1}$ uses its memory to identify $N_{i,j}$ as the next hop in the reply path, and sends the reply to $N_{i,j}$ (without unnecessary information such as the identity of $N_{i,j}$ or $N_{i,j+1}$). However, we assume the worst case: the adversary is able to determine which sensor node is transmitting a reply message if that reply is overheard.

If a query message for query Q_i is overheard, the adversary learns one of the LOIs, L_i. Additionally, the adversary learns one hop that the query took along the route from C to L_i: $N_{i,j}$ and $N_{i,j+1}$, for $1 \leq j < l_i$, where j and l_i are unknown to the adversary. That is, the adversary learns two consecutive elements in the route, but neither their position in the route nor the length of the route. If a reply message for query Q_i is overheard, the adversary learns only a single node that was involved in the route: $N_{i,j}$, for $1 < j \leq l_i$, again with unknown j and l_i.

The adversary can also construct a list of sensor nodes that were certainly not involved in routing Q_i. Because the adversary has complete knowledge of every message that was routed through compromised nodes in the user's sensor network, the adversary knows which compromised nodes were not involved in routing Q_i. An additional consideration for the adversary is that the malicious nodes (either compromised nodes in the user's network, or the adversary's own nodes eavesdropping on the network) could monitor all communication by honest sensor nodes in their communication range. An adversary may conclude that if a malicious node that is monitoring an honest node within its range, H, did not hear H produce any traffic regarding query Q_i, then H must not have been involved in routing Q_i. However, the malicious node may not have heard a message transmitted by H due to interference or a collision. As such, we assume that the adversary will restrict the list of nodes that certainly were not involved with query Q_i to the set of compromised nodes in the sensor network that did not route Q_i.

The key insight for the adversary, having collected information on the routes of the queries, is that if no possible route from a sensor node N to the known destination of Q_i, L_i, is consistent with the known information about Q_i, then N could not have been the origin of the query. Formally, a route $\mathcal{R} = \{N_1, N_2, \ldots N_l\}$ from N to L_i is *consistent* with that information, assuming the destination L_i of Q_i is known, if:

1. $\mathcal{R}$ is a possible route from N to L_i (i.e., $N_1 = N$, $N_l = L_i$, and the routing algorithm could have used this route);

2. For every query message about Q_i overheard by the adversary, sent by $N_{i,j}$ to $N_{i,j+1}$, there is some $k < l$ such that $N_k = N_{i,j}$ and $N_{k+1} = N_{i,j+1}$;
3. For every reply message about Q_i overheard by the adversary, sent by $N_{i,j}$, there is some $k > 1$ such that $N_k = N_{i,j}$; and,
4. No node that is known not to have routed Q_i appears in $\mathcal{R}$.

There is a second insight, about queries for which the adversary does not know the destination. The adversary may still know some information about such a Q_i (e.g., overheard reply messages, or knowledge about compromised nodes that did not route Q_i). Let $\mathcal{D}$ be the set of all possible destinations for the queries with unknown destinations. Specifically, $\mathcal{D}$ is the set of all nodes in N that are not compromised and are not the destination of a query with a known destination. Let $\mathcal{U}$ be the set of queries for which the destination is unknown to the adversary, where $0 \leq |\mathcal{U}| \leq k$. If it is not possible to assign a unique destination from $\mathcal{D}$ to each query in $\mathcal{U}$, in such a way as to ensure that there is a possible route from sensor node N to the destination of each query in $\mathcal{U}$ that is consistent with all of the known information about that query, then N cannot be the origin of the user's queries.

function NARROW-POSSIBLE-CLs
    if the node C with which the user is communicating is compromised **then**
        return $\mathcal{P} = \{C\}$
    $N_{honest} \leftarrow \{N \in \mathcal{N} \mid N$ is not compromised$\}$
    $\mathcal{P} \leftarrow N_{honest}$
    for all queries Q_i for which the destination is known **do**
        for all $p \in \mathcal{P}$ **do**
            if POSSIBLE-CONSISTENT$(p, Q_i) =$ FALSE **then**
                Remove p from $\mathcal{P}$
    $\mathcal{U} \leftarrow \{Q_i \mid L_i$ is unknown$\}$
    if $|\mathcal{U}| > 0$ **then**
        $\mathcal{D} \leftarrow \{N \in N_{honest} \mid N$ is not a destination for any Q_i with known destination$\}$
        for all $p \in \mathcal{P}$ **do**
            foundAssignment $\leftarrow$ FALSE
            for $\mathcal{D}' \leftarrow$ all $\binom{|\mathcal{D}|}{|\mathcal{U}|}$ choices of $|\mathcal{U}|$ destinations from $\mathcal{D}$ **do**
                for all $|\mathcal{D}'|!$ assignments of nodes in $\mathcal{D}'$ as destinations for the queries in $\mathcal{U}$ **do**
                    if POSSIBLE-CONSISTENT$(p, Q) =$ TRUE $\forall\ Q \in \mathcal{U}$ **then**
                        foundAssignment $\leftarrow$ TRUE
            if *foundAssignment* $=$ FALSE **then**
                Remove p from $\mathcal{P}$
    return $\mathcal{P}$

function POSSIBLE-CONSISTENT(src, Q)
    $L \leftarrow$ the destination of query Q
    if $\exists$ a possible route from src to L, consistent with all known information about Q **then**
        return TRUE
    else
        return FALSE

Fig. 4. Pseudocode for finding all possible current locations for the user

In summary, an adversary who eavesdrops on the user's network can overhear nodes that are involved in routing queries; an adversary who is able to compromise nodes in the user's network can also know for certain if those compromised nodes were not involved in routing a particular query. Pseudo-code for the algorithm the adversary can use to narrow down the user's possible current locations is presented in Figure 4. This algorithm will narrow down the possible current locations of the user to $\mathcal{P} \subseteq \mathcal{N}$. Denoting $\mathcal{N}_{honest} = \{N \in \mathcal{N} \mid N$ is not compromised$\}$, it is guaranteed that $1 \leq |\mathcal{P}| \leq |\mathcal{N}_{honest}|$ if $|\mathcal{N}_{honest}| \geq 1$. Normalizing between these two bounds defines the metric for evaluating CL-privacy,

$$
\mathrm{M}_{CL}(\mathcal{P}) = \begin{cases} 0 & \text{if } |\mathcal{P}| = 1 \\ \dfrac{|\mathcal{P}| - 1}{|\mathcal{N}_{honest}| - 1} & \text{otherwise.} \end{cases}
$$

4 Choosing the Fake LOIs

Given the metrics necessary to measure how well a set of k queries preserves the privacy of the user's area of interest (AOI) and current location (CL), we now investigate how the user should choose the $k - 1$ fake locations of interest (LOIs) to query, given one real LOI. Regardless of how the fake LOIs are chosen, recall our assumption that, from the point of view of the adversary, it is equally probable that any of the k queried nodes is the real LOI. Any implementation of k-anonymity for sensor network queries must take into account real-life limitations. For example, if the troops using a military sensor network queried one node at a location of strategic importance, but $k - 1$ nodes at strategically irrelevant positions, the adversary could guess the real LOI with high probability. In this paper we assume a homogeneous environment where each node is equally important.

Another situation that could leak the real LOI is if the user issues multiple queries to the real LOI. Any algorithm used to choose the $k - 1$ fake LOIs based on the real LOI is required to choose the same $k - 1$ fake LOIs each time the user issues a real query. Otherwise, if the user first queries the k nodes in $\mathcal{L}_1$ then later issues queries to the k nodes in $\mathcal{L}_2 \neq \mathcal{L}_1$, and if the adversary can correctly guess that the user was issuing repeat queries to the same node (it is overly optimistic to assume otherwise), the adversary would learn that the real LOI is in $\mathcal{L}_1 \cap \mathcal{L}_2$.

Let F be the choice function that takes the real LOI L and returns a set $\mathcal{L}$ of k LOIs to query, with $L \in \mathcal{L}$. If F is deterministic, repeat queries are of no concern, since $\mathrm{F}(L) = \mathcal{L}$ for each call to $\mathrm{F}(L)$. If F is a random function, taking L and a random seed s_L as parameters (and using a cryptographically secure pseudo-random number generator [9]), the user should encapsulate F in a deterministic function. For example, the user could call $\mathrm{F}'(L) = \mathrm{F}(L, s_L)$, where $s_L = \mathrm{H}(s \circ L)$ is computed using a stored secure seed, s, and cryptographic hash function H, with $\circ$ representing concatenation.

It is not only multiple queries to the real LOI that pose a problem; even a single set of k queries could leak the real LOI. Knowledge of how F works could be sufficient for the adversary to determine the real LOI, given the set $\mathcal{L}$ of all k nodes queried. Consider a deterministic F that takes the real LOI L and returns a list $\mathcal{L}$ that contains L and the $k - 1$ fake LOIs, such that $\sigma(\mathcal{L}, \mathcal{N})$ is maximized over all possible choices of $k - 1$ fake LOIs. This function, which maximizes the user's AOI-privacy, may leak the user's real LOI. Consider the example in Figure 5. If the $k = 3$ nodes illustrated in Figure 5(a) are queried, the adversary would know that the interior LOI is the real LOI. Were the westernmost node the real LOI, the central node and the easternmost node would have been chosen by F as the fake LOIs, as illustrated in Figure 5(b), to maximize σ. Similarly, the easternmost node could not be the real LOI.

(a) The $k = 3$ sensor nodes that were actually queried by the user.

(b) The nodes that would have been chosen as $\mathcal{L}$ were the westernmost node the real LOI.

Fig. 5. An example of the σ-maximizing choice function leaking the real LOI

For F not to leak information in this fashion, F must generate a set $\mathcal{L} \subseteq \mathcal{N}$ that is closed under F. For a deterministic F, this closure requirement means: if $F(L) = \mathcal{L}$ for some $L \in \mathcal{N}$, then $F(L_i) = \mathcal{L}$ for all $L_i \in \mathcal{L}$. For a non-deterministic F, this closure requirement means that there must be no candidate $L \in \mathcal{L}$ that was more likely than the other elements in $\mathcal{L}$ to have generated $\mathcal{L}$. Define $P(F, \mathcal{L}, L_i)$ as the proportion of all seeds in the seed space for which F will generate $\mathcal{L}$, given L_i and a seed as arguments. The closure property necessary for a non-deterministic F is: if $F(L, s) = \mathcal{L}$ for some $L \in \mathcal{N}$ and seed s, then $P(F, \mathcal{L}, L_i) = P(F, \mathcal{L}, L)$ for all $L_i \in \mathcal{L}$. An unbiased random choice of the $k - 1$ fake LOIs — the method of choosing fake LOIs we use for the remainder of this paper — meets this closure requirement. Future work should examine better methods for generating fake LOIs, such as a method that guarantees a minimum AOI-privacy level without leaking the real LOI.

5   Experimental Results

The area-of-interest (AOI) privacy that results from a set of queries to k locations of interest (LOIs), $k - 1$ of which are fake, can be computed by the user before he/she issues the queries. The resulting current-location (CL) privacy, on the other hand, is dependent on how much information the adversary overhears, and cannot be computed by the user. Ideally, the user would like to predict the CL-privacy that will result from his/her queries, based on information that can be known ahead of time.

We first investigated how CL-privacy is correlated with the AOI-privacy of the queries, and also how CL-privacy is correlated with the amount of communication generated by the k queries. As a measure of the communication generated by a set of k queries, we define its *sum of hops* as $\sum_{i=1}^{k} (|\mathcal{R}_i| - 1)$. We simulated a user issuing a set of $k = 3$ queries in a sensor network with 400 nodes, arranged in a 20×20 grid. The nodes communicate over a broadcast medium, using fixed shortest-path routing. The adversary has compromised 10 random nodes in the network, but is guaranteed not to have compromised the node with which the user is directly communicating. We ran 1000 trials in which the user was placed at a random location in the sensor network and queried a random LOI, along with $k - 1 = 2$ fake LOIs chosen at random. In each trial, we recorded the resulting CL-privacy, AOI-privacy, and sum of hops. The results of this experiment are illustrated as scatterplots in Figure 6.

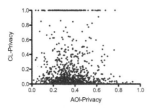 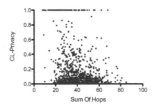

(a) The resulting AOI-privacy and CL-privacy.

(b) The sum of hops metric and the resulting CL-privacy.

Fig. 6. Scatterplots comparing precomputed metrics to the resulting CL-privacy over 1000 trials

These results indicate that the AOI-privacy level from a random selection of $k - 1$ fake LOIs is highly variable, as seen in Figure 6(a). That scatterplot also shows that the user cannot predict the resulting CL-privacy of his/her queries based on the precomputed AOI-privacy. While there is an inverse correlation between these two metrics, it is not a strong correlation ($R^2 = 0.0109$, meaning that only 1.09% of the variance in the CL-privacy can be explained by variations in the AOI-privacy value). From both the value of R^2 and visual inspection of the scatterplot, it is apparent that we cannot fit a function to the graph that could predict CL-privacy based on AOI-privacy. While the correlation between CL-privacy and the sum of hops metric is slightly stronger, as seen in Figure 6(b), it is still not a strong one ($R^2 = 0.0861$).

There is no clear method for predicting the resulting CL-privacy given a set of k queries. However, there are numerous factors that do affect the resulting CL-privacy. In order to investigate the effect of k, we repeated our earlier experiment, but using $k = 2$ and $k = 4$. The results, illustrated in Figure 7(a), show that incrementing k from 2 to 3 and from 3 to 4 did significantly decrease the CL-privacy.[1] A conclusion that can be drawn from this set of experiments is that if the privacy of his/her current location is important, the user should sacrifice some of the privacy of the location of interest (measured as the number of fake LOIs queried).

Until now, we have assumed that fixed shortest-path routing is used; however, the nodes may use random shortest-path routing to prevent messages from being traced back to their source as easily, which we hypothesize will increase CL-privacy. We have also assumed that the nodes communicate over a broadcast medium (e.g., radio). We hypothesize that migrating to a point-to-point (P2P) medium (e.g., optical transmissions) would reduce opportunities for an adversary to intercept traffic, increasing CL-privacy.

---

[1] Significance tests, except where otherwise noted, use Kruskal-Wallis ANOVA with Dunn's multiple comparison test [10], with significant results having $P < 0.001$ and non-significant results having $P \geq 0.05$. This test compares three or more means without assuming Gaussian distribution, then analyzes significance between any desired pairs of means.

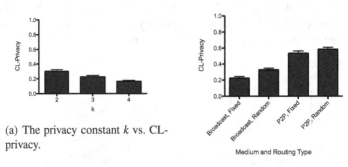

(a) The privacy constant k vs. CL-privacy.

(b) Routing method and transmission type vs. CL-privacy.

Fig. 7. The effect of various parameters on the resulting CL-privacy, with error bars representing the 95% confidence interval around the mean over 1000 trials

We assume that point-to-point transmissions are only heard by the two communicating nodes; so, an adversary would only overhear traffic that involves a compromised node.

Next, we re-ran our previous experiment with $k = 3$, but used either random shortest-path routing, a point-to-point medium, or both. The results of this experiment, illustrated in Figure 7(b) suggest that moving from fixed shortest-path routing to random shortest-path routing, regardless of the transmission medium, significantly increased the resulting CL-privacy. Similarly, moving from a broadcast medium to a point-to-point medium, regardless of the routing algorithm, significantly increased CL-privacy.

To determine which of the two possible changes is more valuable, we performed a two-way ANOVA test. The routing method and transmission medium are not independent changes — the transmission medium used will have an effect on how much the routing method affects the CL-privacy, and vice versa. The choice of transmission medium was more important to the resulting CL-privacy, though. This result means that migrating to a point-to-point transmission system is more important for protecting the user's CL-privacy. However, using random shortest-path routing (which may be an easier change to make, as new hardware might not be required) still helps.

To investigate whether the number and type of malicious nodes would affect the resulting CL-privacy, we re-ran our previous experiment with $k = 3$ using a broadcast medium and fixed shortest-path routing. This time, we varied the number of malicious nodes among 1, 5, 10, 15, and 20; we also changed whether the malicious nodes were compromised sensor nodes in the user's network or eavesdropping nodes deployed randomly within the range of at least one of the user's nodes. The results of this experiment are illustrated in Figure 8. Each increase in the number of compromised nodes significantly decreased CL-privacy, as did each increase in the number of eavesdroppers, i.e., more malicious nodes will result in decreased CL-privacy. Surprisingly, there is no statistically significant difference between any of the five pairs of results with a given number of malicious nodes. That is, there is no significant difference between the resulting CL-privacy when there are ten compromised nodes and when there are ten eavesdropping nodes, and so forth. While there is a small numerical difference between

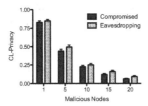

Fig. 8. The effect of compromised nodes and eavesdropping nodes on the resulting CL-privacy, with error bars representing the 95% confidence interval around the mean over 1000 trials

the resulting CL-privacies, based on visual inspection of Figure 8, these statistical results tell us that the extra information gained from compromised nodes, about nodes certainly not involved in routing a query, is not that meaningful overall compared to information about nodes that routed messages. This result does not bode well for a user interested in protecting the privacy of his/her current location; an adversary could deploy eavesdropping nodes, and gain essentially the same amount of information about the user's current location as if the adversary managed to compromise sensor nodes.

6   Conclusions and Future Work

The k-anonymity method for protecting the privacy of a location of interest allows the user to control the trade-off between privacy and communication cost. Both the privacy of the location of interest and the communication cost increase with the number of queries sent, k. We demonstrated a simple metric, based on the sum of minimum distances between queried nodes, that allows a user to know how well his/her selection of k nodes protects the privacy of the area of interest — that is, the area of the sensor network that contains the location of interest. Best of all, this k-anonymity scheme can be implemented over existing query mechanisms in a sensor network, with no need for any changes (hardware or software) to the sensors. This scheme is controlled entirely from the user's mobile device, which interacts with the sensors, and the scheme imposes a multiplicative overhead of factor k to sensor network communications.

However, the adversary can use the traffic generated by the k queries to find the user's current location. There was no clear way for the user to predict, prior to issuing a set of k queries, how much information will be leaked about his/her current location. However, we found factors that, in general, result in higher privacy for the user's current location: lower values for k, random routing approaches, avoiding the use of a broadcast medium, and having fewer malicious nodes available to the adversary. Surprisingly, an adversary that is able to compromise nodes in the user's sensor network does not have a significantly improved ability to locate the user, compared to an adversary who simply scatters eavesdropping nodes that do not participate in the sensor network. This observation provides important insight into the task of securing sensor network communications in sensitive areas.

This paper sheds some light on the trade-off between preserving the privacy of the queried and current locations simultaneously. Future work should examine how the k-anonymity method can be extended to further protect the user's privacy. For example, a user may add random delays in between sending each of his/her k queries into the sensor network. These random delays could make it more difficult for an adversary to know if any queries were not overheard by the malicious nodes.

Another topic for future work is to compare CL-privacy results from networks that use distributed geographic routing to the results in this paper from shortest-path-routing networks. Changing the nature of the adversary could also yield interesting results. Our adversary, for example, only used compromised nodes in the user's sensor network to gain information about what routes queries did or did not take. An active adversary may additionally drop query packets, either as a denial of service attack, or as an effort to make the user re-route queries, generating more traffic. Understanding how different types of adversary could interact with this k-anonymity approach could provide additional insight into privacy in sensor networks.

Acknowledgments

This research has been funded in part by the Natural Sciences and Engineering Research Council of Canada, iCORE and Alberta Advanced Education & Technology, and Alberta Scholarship Programs.

References

1. Lopez, J.: Unleashing public-key cryptography in wireless sensor networks. Journal of Computer Security 14(5), 469–482 (2006)
2. Dingledine, R., Mathewson, N., Syverson, P.: Tor: The second-generation onion router. In: Proceedings of the 13th USENIX Security Symposium, pp. 303–320 (2004)
3. Misra, S., Xue, G.: Efficient anonymity schemes for clustered wireless sensor networks. International Journal of Sensor Networks 1(1/2), 50–63 (2006)
4. Ouyang, Y., Le, Z., Xu, Y., Triandopoulos, N., Zhang, S., Ford, J., Makedon, F.: Providing anonymity in wireless sensor networks. In: Proceedings of the IEEE International Conference on Pervasive Services, pp. 145–148 (2007)
5. Ozturk, C., Zhang, Y., Trappe, W.: Source-location privacy in energy-constrained sensor network routing. In: Proceedings of the 2nd ACM Workshop on Security of Ad Hoc and Sensor Networks, pp. 88–93 (2004)
6. Kamat, P., Zhang, Y., Trappe, W., Ozturk, C.: Enhancing source-location privacy in sensor network routing. In: Proceedings of the 25th IEEE International Conference on Distributed Computing Systems, pp. 599–608 (2005)
7. Jian, Y., Chen, S., Zhang, Z., Zhang, L.: Protecting receiver-location privacy in wireless sensor networks. In: Proceedings of the 26th IEEE International Conference on Computer Communications, May 2007, pp. 1955–1963 (2007)
8. Sweeney, L.: k-anonymity: A model for protecting privacy. International Journal on Uncertainty, Fuzziness and Knowledge-Based Systems 10(5), 557–570 (2002)
9. Blum, L., Blum, M., Shub, M.: A simple unpredictable pseudo-random number generator. SIAM Journal on Computing 15(2), 364–383 (1986)
10. Siegel, S., Castellan Jr., N.J.: Nonparametric Statistics for the Behavioral Sciences, 2nd edn. McGraw-Hill, New York (1988)

SenSearch: GPS and Witness Assisted Tracking for Delay Tolerant Sensor Networks

Lun Jiang[1], Jyh-How Huang[2], Ankur Kamthe[1], Tao Liu[1], Ian Freeman[1],
John Ledbetter[2], Shivakant Mishra[2], Richard Han[2], and Alberto Cerpa[1]

[1] University of California, Merced
[2] University of Colorado, Boulder

Abstract. This paper describes the design, implementation and performance evaluation of SenSearch, an outdoors, GPS assisted personnel tracking system using MICA motes. SenSearch is a mobile wireless ad-hoc network comprised of sensor nodes worn by users. These nodes store and forward information about the location of other nodes in an environment that lacks communication infrastructure. A key feature of SenSearch is that it does not require a continuously connected network for its operation. It is designed for a delay tolerant network that provides only occasional connectivity between nodes. It uses the distributed storage available through multiple nodes and the mobility provided by users to propagate the history of nodes' GPS locations to the processing center. The main contribution of this paper is an extensive, experimental evaluation of the system under controlled as well as uncontrolled environments. The paper discusses in detail the effects of a number of experimental parameters on the performance of the system.

1 Introduction

A delay tolerant sensor network is one in which sensor nodes are mobile and remain disconnected from each other most of the time. These nodes take advantage of occasional connectivity established when two or more nodes[1] wander within close range of one another to transmit data to a base station, which is typically a resource-rich node in a well-connected network, e.g. the Internet. Generally speaking DTNs can be characterized on the basis of the trajectory of the sensor node into open trail and closed trail DTNs. In open trail DTN, a node does not have a specific path and may never come with in close range of a base station. In this case, mobility patterns are unpredictable. Wildlife tracking is an example of this kind of DTN. In closed trail DTN, there are a small number of well-known paths that a node may take and most of the nodes in the system eventually arrive at a base station. Moving patterns are more predictable and nodes usually stay on the path. Hiking and vehicle tracking are examples of this kind of DTN.

---

[1] Node: An object (person, animal) that carries a wireless sensor module capable of communicating with other nodes. This term is used interchangeably along with entity or mote throughout the paper.

P.M. Ruiz and J.J. Garcia-Luna-Aceves (Eds.): ADHOC-NOW 2009, LNCS 5793, pp. 255–269, 2009.

In this paper, we describe the design, implementation and performance evaluation of SenSearch, a GPS and witness-assisted tracking system for hikers in outdoor environments. Our application belongs to close trail DTN , which means the trajectory of the experiment subject is known and it is relatively easy to predict its current position based on prior knowledge. In this system, GPS modules are used to enable a sensor unit to infer its location information. The system uses the concept of witnesses to convey a node's movement and location information to the outside world. This helps overcome the constraint of having a constantly connected network. Different nodes exchange their location data when they encounter each other along the way. This information is subsequently routed to a base station through a series of subsequent data transfers between nodes. This data consists of the history of past locations of a node, and can be used to estimate the location of a missing node using the history information acquired by other nodes. The use of the GPS data drastically reduces the search space, by increasing the accuracy of the system. However, the use of GPS along with the transmission/reception of data in an energy-constrained system also reduces the lifetime of the system. To save energy, SenSearch uses a duty cycling scheme for the GPS and radio units. We discuss in detail the trade-offs between lowered accuracy due to duty recycling and the resulting energy saving in the performance evaluation section of this paper. This paper makes three important contributions:

1. SenSearch is the first sensor-based DTN system designed to locate missing persons and assist in search and rescue in wilderness environment that totally lack communication infrastructure. Using novel coordination strategies and adaptive mechanisms, we drastically improve the lifetime of the system.
2. Two separate implementations of SenSearch on two different computing platforms as well as a simulation in a discrete event simulator are provided. A comparison between the two implementations provides important insights into the effects of the underlying platform on the performance of the system.
3. An extensive performance evaluation of the SenSearch system including experiments in controlled outdoor environments such as a university campus as well as uncontrolled, wilderness environments such as US state and national parks. Overall, a comprehensive analysis of different parameters that affect SenSearch's performance is provided from over 65 different hiking experiments that we performed over a period of seven months in UC Merced campus, Mt. Sanitas and Chautauqua Park in Boulder and Boulder reservoir.

2   Related Work

A large majority of networks [3], [4], [5] used for tracking movements of mobile entities are comprised of hundreds of small, densely distributed wireless sensor nodes deployed in the field. However, it is not well-suited for tracking the movement of entities with random mobility patterns on paths going through large area as it would require a prohibitively large number of nodes to cover all possible locations.

SenSearch is based on CenWits [6], a connection-less sensor-based tracking system using witnesses. CenWits is comprised of mobile nodes that receives its location information periodically from location points and passes it to other nodes during subsequent encounters. This information is then transmitted to access-points distributed at various locations. The improvement of SenSearch compared to CenWits include the followings. Using the state of art low power GPS sensor board with the wireless sensor to improve the accuracy of the system; implementing a group layer protocol to solve and take advantage of the tagging along problem of the human movement. BikeNet [2] is an opportunistic sensor networking system, wherein customized sensor modules and mobile phones are used for real-time and delay tolerant uploading of data. Electronic Shepherd [8] is a low-power, low-bandwidth application for tracking the movement of animals with flock- behavior. It requires a GPRS/GSM or 802.11 network to retrieve data form the sensors. All of the above systems depend on the presence of some communication infrastructure backbone such as location points (CenWits) and cell towers (BikeNet) to convey information to the base station. In many out-door scenarios (or hostile environments), it is not practical to deploy location and access points for information storage and recovery. SenSearch does not need a communication infrastructure as it relies on people carrying data (muling) collected during encounters with other nodes to the base station. Also, we provide real world experimental results in addition to a complete evaluation of the parameters in the design space that was lacking in earlier papers [6].

SenSearch is similar, in intent, to the ZebraNet [7,10], which is designed for the tracking of wild animals. SenSearch differs from ZebraNet in a number of areas. In ZebraNet, hardware comprises of a CPU, a low power radio for short range communication, a long range radio for communication with the base station and a solar cell array along with the Li-Ion batteries. The total weight is around 1,151 grams. The hardware is powered by rechargeable solar cells supplying 13.5 Ampere-hour of energy. On the other hand, SenSearch consists of MICAz sensor nodes powered by 2 AA batteries having a limited battery life of 5.2 Ampere-hour of energy and weigh around 150 grams. SenSearch is intended for use in outdoor activities for human tracking and hence, the weight restrictions are more severe in comparisons to ZebraNet. For SenSearch, it would be impractical to have solar cells to power such a system, because carrying anything larger than a pager would be burdensome. Also, in ZebraNet, the use of high power, long range radios allows for transfer of data to reach the base station even in a single-hop communication. As opposed to that the use of low power, short range 802.15.4 radios in SenSearch which requires the use of a different strategy, relying on the encounter between nodes as the method of forwarding information back to base station. The disconnected nature of SenSearch network denies the possibility of using an muilihop routing protocol, as used by ZebraNet which has a routing path from each node to the base station all the time. These distinct differences in purposes of the applications result in different hardware as well as software infrastructures used between these two projects.

In this paper, the design problems that are unique to systems like SenSearch are highlighted. We propose solutions in the form of two implementations for slightly different hardware platforms and perform extensive performance evaluation on points of interest for system designers.

3   System Description

SenSearch uses Berkeley MICAz motes equipped with an RF transmitter and a GPS receiver to track locations of entities (example: people, animals, etc.) in natural or urban environments in the absence of a communication infrastructure.

Each node has a unique ID. It keeps records of its locations by periodically using the GPS receiver and saving the information in an internal database. Energy savings by duty-cycling the GPS results in decreased accuracy in the sense of the localization of missing entities. Continuously sampling the GPS data increases accuracy but results in prohibitively large power consumption. Each node emits periodic radio beacons to detect the presence of other nodes in its vicinity. When any two nodes are within radio range of each other (encounter), they exchange their databases in response to the radio beacons. An encounter can be classified as successful or missed, depending on whether the nodes are able to exchange their databases when sending periodic radio beacons. The information exchanged in an encounter is propagated among multiple nodes in subsequent encounters during database exchanges. It is possible to estimate the expected position or area of any missing node by examining the history of its past locations from GPS data muled by other nodes. Fig. 1 shows an illustration of the GPS acquisition in hot start mode, radio beacons and data transmission during a node encounter.

3.1   Hardware

Wireless Sensor Module. The MICAz is based on the ATmega128L microcontroller with ChipCon CC2420 radio with a a 250kbps data rate. The MICAz has 4KB of RAM and 512KB of external flash memory.

GPS Module. In the first implementation (*SenSearch-A*), the MTS40CA sensor board was used. It has an 12-channel integrated Leadtek 9546 GPS module with a SiRFstart chipset having position accuracy up to 10m. It has times of 45s, 38s and 8s for cold, warm and hot starts respectively, with a reacquisition time of 0.1s. It draws current of 60mA@3.3V [1]. In the second implementation (*SenSearch-B*), the MTS420CC has a uBlox LEA-4A GPS module with the ANTARIS 4 chipset. It has 16 channels and position accuracy of 3m CEP. It has times of 34s, 33s and 3.5s for cold, warm and hot starts respectively, with a reacquisition time of <1s. It draws current of 35mA@3V.

Power Measurements. In Table 1, we provide the power consumption for the MICAz mote and the MTS420CC sensor board in different modes of operation for the SenSearch-B implementation. We measured the power consumption using the National Instruments ELVIS platform. Each measurement is averaged over 5 different nodes.

Table 1. Factors affecting the power consumption and data transmission of a MICAz mote with a GPS Module

Name	Explanation	Value
P_{CPU}	Base Power (CPU only)	11.04 mW
P_{GPS}	GPS in Hot Start mode	170.07 mW
P_{TX}	Radio in TX state	78.49 mW
P_{RX}	Radio in RX state	74.85 mW
P_{LPL}	Power used by the Radio in LPL Listen state	21.95 mW
$T_{GPS_{HS}}$	Avg. Time for GPS to get coord. in Hot Start mode	3.42 sec
R_{BW}	CC2420 TX bandwidth	250 Kbps
B_{SIZE}	Beacon packet size	120 bits

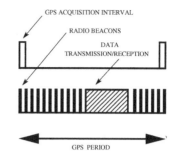

Fig. 1. Nodes have overlapping periods in which they acquire GPS and send radio beacons, even data exchanges with other nodes

3.2 Software Architecture

In the following section, we cover the design decisions and trade-offs specific to each of the SenSearch implementations:

SenSearch-A. MANTIS is a multithreaded embedded OS for wireless sensor networks. The MANTIS implementation is based around actions executed in response to a periodic timer and radio interrupts. When there are no other motes in the radio range and the timer fires, the application layer is triggered. The application layer will then decide if it is time to send a beacon or to take a GPS reading. While sending a radio beacon, the program accesses the network layer. Periodically, we update our GPS position by recording a new reading in our database. Upon getting an interrupt from the radio, the network layer forwards the packet to the application layer which takes actions based on the type of packet (HELLO (beacon), REPLY and DATA. The received database entries replace older entries for each node in the local nodes database. We save a subset of the total received entries in the RAM to avoid the latency of accessing the data from the flash storage module.

SenSearch-B. In *SenSearch-B*, we used the event-based TinyOS operating system for wireless sensor network platforms. The TinyOS (TOS) implementation is based around actions being executed according to a state machine shown in Fig. 2. In the background, the node records GPS information in its database according to the GPS period. At the beginning, the node is in SEND BEACONS state. When a node receives a beacon from another node in its vicinity, it goes into SEND TABLE state. In SEND TABLE state, the node sends its database in response to the beacon. In the last packet, the node transmits an END OF TRANSMISSION flag to signal the switch to DATAMSG TIMEOUT state. The node switches to the RECVING TABLE state when it starts receiving GPS data from the other node. If the other node has moved out of radio range, then the node will wait for a specific period in the DATAMSG TIMEOUT before

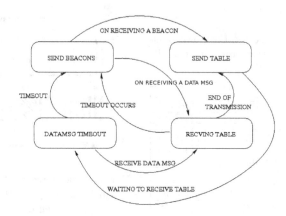

Fig. 2. State Machine for SenSearch-B implementation

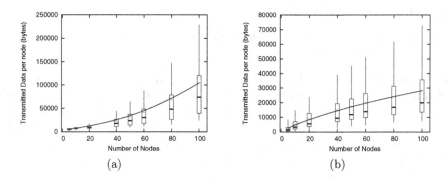

Fig. 3. Amount of data transferred when (a) the system is affected by "tagging along" problem in simulation; (b) "tagging along" problem is averted in simulation by separating nodes by distance greater than radio range

going into SEND BEACONS state again. In the RECVING TABLE state, the received database entries replace older entries for each node in the local node's database. A node can switch from SENDING TABLE or RECVING TABLE state to SEND BEACONS state in case of errors (like packet loss) when its times-out is triggered in the DATAMSG TIMEOUT state.

In order to examine the behavior of different parameters for our implementation, we created a discrete-event simulation environment for SenSearch (See Section 4.2). In the preliminary simulation results, we realized that the nodes transmitted extremely high amounts of data. Nodes in close proximity kept transferring their GPS information databases in response to beacons from one another even though no new information had been recorded since the prior data exchange, leading to high power consumption. This was attributed to the simple encounter-based data transmission which occurs when two or more nodes are in close proximity of each other. This behavior was termed "tagging along of nodes". Figure 3(a) shows the amount of data transmitted as a function of number of nodes in the simulation when nodes tag along with each other. Figure 3(b) shows the reduction in data transmitted when the tagging along is avoided artificially by separating the nodes by distances greater than radio range. Compared to the linear growth in Fig 3(b), Fig 3(a) shows exponential growth of data being exchanged if "tagging along" scenario is not avoided. The "tagging along" effect impairs the system in two ways. First, constantly exchanging beacons and data with the same nodes will reduce the chances of hearing a beacon from a node passing-by. Second, the additional transmission will cost energy and reduce the system life time. The amount of data exchanged via radio can be reduced by comparing times of most recent GPS entry which still results in significant energy consumption. However, this does not eliminate the sending of beacon messages. In SenSearch-B, we take advantage of the occurrence of the "tagging along" scenario by implementing a coordination scheme between nodes which we term as *group layer*. The group layer aims to increase energy savings by adapting radio and GPS usage when nodes "tag along".

Memory Management strategy: Generally, in SenSearch, the encounters between nodes are in the order of a few seconds. The beacon message period is also in the order of seconds (see Table 2). If the beacon arrives at the start of the encounter between nodes, then the data exchange between the two nodes has a greater chance of completion than if the beacon arrives when the two nodes are at the end of the radio range and moving away from each other. Due to this, the size of transmitted GPS database needs to be minimized while not affecting the tracking performance (localization error) of the system. Since, the goal of our system is to narrow the location of a missing node to a relatively small area, and not pin-point its current position, it suffices if we are able to transmit a small number of GPS entries per node. So, we store the latest $MAX\_ENTRIES$ number of entries for every node.

Group Layer Design: From an operational point of view, the group layer is comprised of two node states, leader and member. Initially every node has leader status. The nodes broadcast their leader status and battery voltage periodically at a rate determined by the group leader synchronization period. Other leader nodes. When other leader nodes receive a pre-specified number of group leader synchronization messages and if they have lower battery voltage, they will will respond to the potential new group leader with a request to join its group. When the potential leader node receives a join message, it sends an acknowledgment confirmation message to the group member. When the confirmation from the new leader is received, the leader and the new group member synchronize their GPS entry databases. The group member powers off its GPS module, stops sending beacon messages and listens for group leader update and synchronization messages. Since, the group leader is the only node communicating with other "new" nodes, it sends periodic update messages synchronizing the leader's GPS entry database among its member nodes. The group members respond with a short ACK message with their current battery voltage. In the event that the member node misses a certain number of group leader synchronization messages, the node breaks away from its group leader, reestablishing itself as a group leader. Also, if the group leader finds a member in its group having energy reserves above a certain threshold than its own, it sends out a resign message which will make all the group members independent leaders again. If the nodes still tag along with each other, they will join up as a whole group eventually as described above. The design of group layer follows two important rules: First, all the nodes in a group always have the same GPS entry information, ensuring that there is no loss of the GPS information acquired from encounters. Second, the node with the highest energy reserve serves as the group leader improving the lifetime of the nodes in a group and the system as a whole. Additionally, the *group layer counter* is a parameter which affects the performance of the group layer design. In our implementation, if the group layer counter is set to two, a node needs to receive to at least six group leader synchronization messages i.e., group layer counter times 3, in order to associate with a group leader. A node breaks away from a group, if it misses *group layer counter* number of successive group leader synchronization messages. Thus, the *group layer counter* parameter controls the formation and breakup times for a group. If it is set high, the energy savings from the group layer functionality will be reduced because of the difficulty in forming a group. If it is set low, the group will be constantly breaking up and reforming again.

Adaptive GPS Design: In order to improve the lifetime of the nodes, the power consumption has to be reduced. As seen from Table 1, the GPS module consumes the most power. In the system, if a node does not encounter any other nodes for a long period of time, its old GPS entries are overwritten due to the memory constraints. This indicates that the GPS module is wasting energy by acquiring coordinates too often. In this section, we describe the strategy for GPS period adaptation.

Assuming a Poisson distribution of encounters for a specific node and given a sample of n measured values k_i, we can estimate the value of λ using the maximum likelihood:

$$L(\lambda) = \log \prod_{i=1}^{n} f(k_i | \lambda) = \sum_{i=1}^{n} \log \left(\frac{e^{-\lambda} \lambda^{k_i}}{k_i!} \right) = -n\lambda + \left(\sum_{i=1}^{n} k_i \right) \log \lambda - \sum_{i=1}^{n} \log (k_i!) \tag{1}$$

Solving the equation for the maximum-likelihood estimate of λ,

$$\frac{d}{d\lambda} L(\lambda) = 0 \implies \lambda_{MLE} = \frac{1}{n} \sum_{i=1}^{n} k_i \tag{2}$$

In our case, $k_i = \frac{1}{t_i - t_{i-1}}$ or the inter-arrival frequency. We keep a running average of the encounter frequency, i.e.

$$\lambda_{MLEi} = \frac{n \times \lambda_{MLEi-1} + k_i}{n+1}$$

Because we want at most $MAX\_ENTRIES$ GPS acquisition between two encounters, we dynamically adapt the GPS period to be

$$min\{\frac{1}{\lambda_{MLE} \times MAX\_ENTRIES}, GPS_p\} \tag{3}$$

where GPS_p is the GPS period for a node (refer Table 2).

Table 2. Parameters explored in Experiments for SenSearch.(Note: Values in bold faces are explored in simulation and in experiments whereas values in italics are explored only in simulation.)

Parameter	Values for Experiments
GPS period (GPS_P)	**20, 45, 60**, *90, 180, 300* (sec)
Beacon period (B_P)	**3, 5, 7** (sec)
Number of nodes	**5, 10, 15**, *20, 40, 60, 80, 100*
Group Layer Counter	**2, 4, 8**
max DB size(DB_{SIZE})	**45, 60, 75** (total # GPS entries)

4 Performance Evaluation

4.1 Goals and Objective Functions

Our goals while evaluating the performance of SenSearch are two-fold. First, we want to characterize the behavior of the system based on a specific set of objective functions. Second, we want to understand the relationships between different parameters and their impact on system performance. The parameter space explored is given in Table 2. The objective functions evaluated are:

1. Localization Error: How well can we track the missing entities? What is the localization error based on the information provided by other witnesses?
2. Power Consumption: What is the lifetime of the system? What are the effects of tuning different system parameters?

4.2 Simulation

We built a discrete event simulator in C to understand the effect of different parameters on system performance. For each simulation run, all nodes have the same set of system parameters including GPS period, beacon rate and memory limitation. Nodes have different speeds while traveling along a specified path. We assume a constant radio range of 50 meters in all our simulations.

Through simulations, we investigated the effect of group layer and GPS period adaptation on the power consumption of the system. Figure 4(a) shows power consumption as a function of the number of nodes. In these simulations, the group layer counter is set to 4 and GPS period is set to 45 seconds. Notice that with only group layer enabled, the power consumption reduces from 42mW to 38mW, and with both the group layer and GPS period adaptation enabled, we

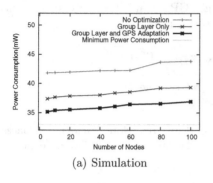 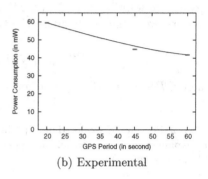

(a) Simulation   (b) Experimental

Fig. 4. (a) Power consumption as a function of number of nodes. (b) Variation of power consumption as a function of the GPS period.

can reduce the power consumption to 36mW. The minimum power consumption is calculated with $P_{CPU}+P_{LPL}$, i.e. 32.99 mW. As the number of nodes increases, the node encounters increase. As a result, the group leaders exchange more beacons with each other and more group messages with the group members, which increases the overall power consumption.

4.3   Experiments

We conducted 12 experiments using the SenSearch-A implementation at the University of Colorado-Boulder (Oct'2007-Mar'2008) and 41 experiments using the SenSearch-B implementation at the University of California-Merced (UCM) (Oct'2007- Mar'2008). We conducted a further 12 experiments after adding the group layer protocol. We performed a number of experiments with SenSearch in real-world environments in Mt. Sanitas near Boulder, and in Boulder Reservoir city park. A typical run involves a hike on a mountain ridge and averages 2 hours round trip time. Different hikers started their hikes at different times with a separation of about twenty minutes. When hikers reached a summit in the middle of their hike, they tended to stay for a while there before returning to the base station. In controlled experiments conducted at the UCM campus, the nodes walk individually or in groups along a path (roughly 1000m) towards each other, starting from opposite ends of the path. From the data dumped at the base station, the localization error, power consumption and memory usage is computed. In both the implementations, we record the ground truth using hand held GPS units at way-points along the path.

4.4   Results

To present our experimental results, we use box-plots [9] instead of displaying the means with error bars. This method improves data visualization by displaying the minimum, first quartile (25%), second quartile (or median, 50%), third quartile (75%) and maximum value of the distribution of data in addition to the mean. In our graphs, we connected the means with a smoothing line to visualize trends in the data.

Localization Error: The localization error is the difference in the real location of a way-point (ground truth) and the estimated position of the same using the data from the SenSearch system relayed back using witnesses. Since, the GPS information recorded by the node is collected periodically, there is uncertainty regarding the location of a node in between two recorded positions. This uncertainty is introduced by the random mobility patterns which includes changes in direction and speed. The GPS hardware error could account for part of the localization error but this was not the case in our experiments. Also, in this paper we are not focusing on the specific algorithms that can be used to calculate the estimated position of the missing node;the goal of our system is to narrow the location of a lost entity to a relatively small area, and not pin-point its current position. For that purpose, we used simple linear extrapolation to estimate an expected position for a node as a function of all the previous GPS records in the database. In order for this simple method to work, we need at the very least two known positions and the corresponding times so we can infer direction and speed of the entity being tracked. Nodes cannot be localized if no data points are received for a specific node, or if only one data point is obtained.

Figs. 5(a) and 5(b) shows the Localization Error (LE) as a function of the GPS period (GPS_P) for SenSearch-A and SenSearch-B, respectively. We see that the LE increases as the GPS period increases. This is attributed to the increase in the number of GPS entries for a node transported to the base station by all other nodes in the system as a function of GPS period. Here, as the GPS period increases, the number of GPS entries at the base station per node decreases. As location information for a node decreases, the localization error increases. Shorter GPS periods results in more location information. With more data points available, we can reduce localization error, as long as past movement behavior of the entity is correlated with future locations. LE values are much greater for the SenSearch-A (Fig. 5(a)) as compared to the SenSearch-B (Fig. 5(b)). This fact can be attributed to the differences in GPS hardware and

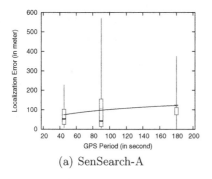

(a) SenSearch-A

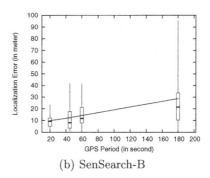

(b) SenSearch-B

Fig. 5. Localization Error (LE) as a function of GPS period

the path followed by the nodes during the controlled experiment. For SenSearch-A, the nodes always walk in a straight line and turn back at the end of the path whereas for SenSearch-B, the nodes walk in a straight line towards each other. For experiments in SenSearch-A, if the nodes do not exchange data on their way back, our linear extrapolation for the expected position does not work and we get inflated errors. This is because the information received at the base station indicates that the node kept moving in a straight line, even though it turned around. In such cases, having contextual knowledge of the terrain and possible paths could significantly improve the quality of the estimation.

Power Consumption: The GPS module is the dominant factor in the power consumption of the system. In addition, in a system with high levels of radio activity, transmissions/receptions/idle listening times account for a majority of the power consumption outside the GPS module. Power consumption would be affected by the amount of transmitted data per node (beacon + database) and the total time the radio and the GPS modules are active. The total power consumption can be expressed as follows:

$$PC = P_{CPU} + \frac{T_{GPS_{HS}} \times P_{GPS}}{GPS_P} + \left(1 - \frac{(T_B + T_{RX} + TTX)}{T_{EXP}}\right) \times P_{LPL}$$
$$+ \frac{T_B}{T_{EXP}} \times P_{TX} + \frac{1}{T_{EXP}} \times (T_{TX} \times P_{TX} + T_{RX} \times P_{RX})$$

(4)

where T_B is the total time spent in sending beacons, T_{TX} and T_{RX} are the total time spent in sending and receiving the GPS entry table, T_{EXP} is the time duration of the experiment. The remaining terms used in this equation are explained in Tables 1 and 2. Each term in Eq. 4 represents power consumed by a different part of the system. The GPS module is the dominant factor in the power consumption of the system. In addition, in a system with high levels of radio activity, transmissions/receptions/idle listening times account for a majority of the power consumption outside the GPS module. Power consumption would be affected by the amount of transmitted data per node (beacon + database) and the total time the radio and the GPS modules are active.

From Figure 4(b) and Eq. 4, we can see that the GPS period is the major factor in the power consumption of the system. As the GPS period increases, the power consumption decreases because the GPS module is active for a lower fraction of time. In the current scheme, and under the range of dynamic conditions tested in our experiments, the GPS period is the dominant factor in power consumption. However, for a system with a longer GPS period, the power consumed in the low power listening mode by the radio becomes dominant. In our experiments, the power consumption remains unaffected by the beacon period and number of nodes in the current scenario.

From Figures 3(a) and 3(b), the difference in data transmission is obvious highlighting the effect of the group layer coordination scheme in improving the lifetime of the system. The group layer counter parameter can lead to significant changes in the way the GPS is utilized, hence affecting the power consumed by each node. As explained earlier, the group layer counter affects the time required for a node to join a group. In Figure 6(a), we see that as we decrease the value of the group

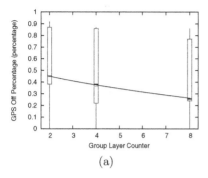 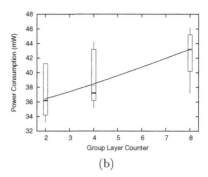

(a)   (b)

Fig. 6. Effects of Group Layer Counter tuning on GPS off percentage and Power Consumption respectively

layer counter, the group member nodes power off their GPS for greater durations of time. Since the GPS module consumes significant energy (see Table 1), powering it off results in significant energy savings. This is demonstrated in Figure 6(b) which shows that power consumption reduces to 36mW when the group layer counter is set to 2. This is a significant saving of 20% compared to power consumption shown in Figure 4(b) (at GPS_p=45s) where no group layer mechanism is implemented. From these results, we conclude that the group layer coordination scheme significantly reduces the energy consumption of the node.

5   Summary and Future Work

It has amply been noted that there is a large gap between building a sensor network system in theoretical realm and a successful, wide-spread deployment of such a system for real-world, every-day use. After creating a working prototype in lab, it has taken us more than seven months, more than 65 outdoor experiments, and a large number of simulation studies to sort out the problems caused by various environmental factors and tune various parameters. The most important contribution of this paper is the lessons learned in a successful deployment of SenSearch in controlled and uncontrolled environmental conditions.

The first lesson is that duty cycling the GPS module is critical for this class of systems. A shorter GPS period enables more data for the missing node to be acquired at the base station. However, increased localization accuracy comes at the cost of higher power consumption and reduction in the system lifetime. It is possible to increase the lifetime of the systems without incurring significant penalties for the localization and tracking of nodes by changing the GPS period adaptively. The balancing point in this trade-off depends on the specific usage of the system and the pre-acquired knowledge of the environment.

The second lesson is that such system must plan for groups of nodes moving together. These groups are typically dynamic in nature with nodes leaving a group and new nodes joining a group at various times. One of the first problems we encountered in our initial experiments was that a significantly large amount of mostly old information got exchanged when nodes moved together, first among the nodes in the group, and then by the rest of the nodes in the system once other witness nodes were encountered. After experimenting with different scenarios, we have implemented a simple optimization that consisted of limiting each pair of node data exchanges to one during a particular GPS period. This simple optimization helped us to significantly reduce the redundant exchange of old information.

The third lesson is that the group structure can be utilized to reduce power consumption. We introduced group layer design along with a tunable parameter, group layer counter. Group layer, along with an adaptive GPS period results in significant power savings. The use of adaptive algorithms similar to the one introduced in this paper can be used to adapt parameters such as GPS entries per node, beacon period and group layer counter.

In the future, we plan to explore more complex methods for localization and tracking than the simple linear fitting methods used in this paper. Furthermore, we would like to continue the exploration of adaptive approaches to tune the other parameters of the system such as those mentioned above. We plan to get further experimental data with a larger number of nodes to verify some of the simulation findings as well as to experiment with the dynamic nature of groups.

References

1. http://www.xbow.com/
2. Eisenman, S.B., Miluzzo, E., Lane, N.D., Peterson, R.A., Ahn, G.-S., Campbell, A.T.: The bikenet mobile sensing system for cyclist experience mapping. In: SenSys 2007: Proceedings of the 5th international conference on Embedded networked sensor systems, pp. 87–101. ACM, New York (2007)
3. Gu, L., Jia, D., Vicaire, P., Yan, T., Luo, L., Tirumala, A., Cao, Q., He, T., Stankovic, J.A., Abdelzaher, T., Krogh, B.H.: Lightweight detection and classification for wireless sensor networks in realistic environments. In: SenSys 2005: Proceedings of the 3rd international conference on embedded networked sensor systems, pp. 205–217. ACM Press, New York (2005)
4. Gupta, R., Das, S.R.: Tracking moving targets in a smart sensor network. In: VTC 2003: Proceedings of 57th IEEE Vehicular Technology Conference, pp. 3035–3039 (2003)
5. He, T., Krishnamurthy, S., Stankovic, J.A., Abdelzaher, T., Luo, L., Stoleru, R., Yan, T., Gu, L., Hui, J., Krogh, B.: Energy-efficient surveillance system using wireless sensor networks. In: MobiSys 2004: Proceedings of the 2nd International Conference on Mobile Systems, Applications, and Services, pp. 270–283. ACM Press, New York (2004)
6. Huang, J.-H., Amjad, S., Mishra, S.: Cenwits: a sensor-based loosely coupled search and rescue system using witnesses. In: SenSys 2005: Proceedings of the 3rd International Conference on Embedded Networked Sensor Systems, pp. 180–191. ACM Press, New York (2005)

7. Juang, P., Oki, H., Wang, Y., Martonosi, M., Peh, L.S., Rubenstein, D.: Energy-efficient computing for wildlife tracking: design tradeoffs and early experiences with zebranet. In: ASPLOS-X: Proceedings of the 10th international conference on Architectural support for programming languages and operating systems, pp. 96–107. ACM Press, New York (2002)
8. Thorstensen, B., Syversen, T., Bjornvold, T.-A., Walseth, T.: Electronic shep- herd: a low-cost, low-bandwidth, wireless network system. In: MobiSys 2004: Proceedings of the 2nd International Conference on Mobile Systems, Applications, and Services, pp. 245–255. ACM Press, New York (2004)
9. Tukey, J.W.: Box-and-whisker plots. In: Exploratory Data Analysis, pp. 39–43 (1977)
10. Zhang, P., Sadler, C.M., Lyon, S.A., Martonosi, M.: Hardware design experiences in zebranet. In: SenSys 2004: Proceedings of the 2nd international conference on Embedded networked sensor systems, pp. 227–238. ACM Press, New York (2004)

Monte Carlo Localization of Mobile Sensor Networks Using the Position Information of Neighbor Nodes[*]

Hamid Mirebrahim and Mehdi Dehghan

Computer Engineering Department, Amirkabir University of Technology, Tehran, Iran
{Hamire,Dehghan}@aut.ac.ir

Abstract. Localization is a fundamental problem in wireless sensor networks. Most existing localization algorithm is designed for static sensor networks. There are a few localization methods for mobile sensor networks. However, Sequential Monte Carlo method (SMC) has been used in localization of mobile sensor networks recently. In this paper, we propose a localization algorithm based on SMC which can improve the location accuracy. A new method is used for sample generation. In that, samples distributes uniformly over the area from which samples are drawn instead of random generation of samples in that area. This can reduces the number of required samples; besides, this new sample generation method enables the algorithm to estimate the maximum location error of each node more accurately. Our algorithm also uses the location estimation of non-anchor neighbor nodes more efficiently than other algorithms. This can improve the localization estimation accuracy highly.

Keywords: Mobile sensor network, Localization, Sequential Monte Carlo method.

1 Introduction

A sensor network is usually a relatively large-scale network of inexpensive, energy-efficient devices [1]. For a node in a WSN, awareness of its location and maybe the location of some other nodes is crucial for a successful operation. As a case in point, routing data in sensor networks requires a fine cooperation among nodes in order to use small amount of energy and to deliver data as fast as possible. A node can choose a proper way to the destination, usually a sink node, if it knows geographic location of itself and its neighbor nodes. Furthermore, most applications of sensor networks need to know position of sensor nodes. For instance, a jungle watching WSN [2] must find out and report the location of a probable fire.

Using GPS[3] devices is the simplest way to determine the location of a sensor node; nevertheless, because of some trait of GPS devices which are in contrary with sensor networks demands, using them in all sensor nodes is not justifiable. These traits include relatively high cost, high weight, and debatable accuracy of GPS equipment in some situations. To overcome GPS Limitations, many localization techniques have developed for sensor networks which don't depend on the GPS

---

[*] This work is partially supported by Iran Telecommunication Research Center (ITRC).

P.M. Ruiz and J.J. Garcia-Luna-Aceves (Eds.): ADHOC-NOW 2009, LNCS 5793, pp. 270–283, 2009.

devices merely. In these localization methods, a few nodes, called anchors or seeds, is equipped with GPS devises and help other nodes to determine their position.

Many algorithms have proposed for localization of static WSNs [4][5]. Nodes in static WSNs do not have movement; in consequences, if a node of these networks could estimate its location once, it won't have to repeat localization process again. Although the majority of deployed WSNs are static nowadays, there are growing number of new sensor network applications which have mobile nodes [6][7]. It is also predictable that the mobile WSNs will be the bigger part of WSNs in the future. Nodes in mobile WSNs may move by external agent like wind, animal's movements, stream of a river, or by internal movement agents like wheels and Continuous track. Mobility has two contrary effects on localization process. In one hand, as previous works [8] indicates, mobility can help localization of static sensor networks. In that, more nodes can get information from mobile anchor nodes. On the other hand, mobile sensor networks may suffer from rapidly changing situation which leads to less validation time for observed information.

This article presents a practical localization algorithm, called USML, based on the sequential Monte Carlo method (SMC) [9] for localization of nodes of a mobile WSN. USML, in overall, improves the accuracy of the previous methods based on SMC, without using additional hardware. In addition, a new method for finding maximum location error of nodes is presented in this paper which improves the previous works.

The rest of this paper is organized as follows. Section 2, describes the previous localization schemes for mobile WSNs. Our proposed method is explained in Section 3. Section 4 illustrates the simulation results and their analyses. Section 5, finally, concludes the paper.

2   Related Work

Monte Carlo Localization (MCL) was the first practical method for localization of mobile WSNs. this section introduces this method and its improved versions briefly. Our method is also an enhanced version of MCL.

2.1   Monte Carlo Localization

Sequential Monte Carlo method had used for localization of mobile robots previously [10]. Hu and Evans adapted this technique for sensor networks and proposed a practical method [11] for localization of mobile sensor networks.

In Sequential Monte Carlo methods, the current state of a system can be obtained by using its current observations and its posterior state. In MCL, the time is divided into discrete intervals. A sensor node moves during a time interval and localizes at the beginning of the next time interval. State of the node i at time t represents by a number of sample positions $L_t^i = \{l_0^i, l_1^i, ..., l_n^i\}$. Each sample has a weight indicating its likelihood to be the real position of the node. When a node needs to estimate its current location, it repeatedly generates new samples and filters them by information obtained from current observations until the sufficient number of samples be generated. Sample generation is based on sample set of the previous location of the node (L_{t-1}^i) and the maximum possible distance which it could travel in the last time interval. This distance can be calculated using the known maximum velocity of nodes (V_{max}). The weight of each sample is then computed based on the current observations. Original implementation of MCL, however, considers an equal weight for all samples. After obtaining the sufficient number of accepted samples for a node, here 50 samples, algorithm announces the Cartesian average of them as the estimated location of the node. MCL, however, assigns a maximum number of attempts for sample generation to avoid the infinite loop in special situations.

Filtering the generated samples is possible by using the information of transmission range of anchors. MCL uses one-hop and two-hop anchors for filtering samples. The one-hop-anchors are those which the node could hear directly. These anchors are supposed to be in the radio range r of the sensor node, r denotes the ideal radio range of nodes and anchors. The two-hop-anchors are those which the node does not hear itself but its one-hop neighbor nodes do. These anchors are assumed to be in the range $2r$ of the node but not within a radius r.

2.2 Monte Carlo Localization Boxed

The main idea of MCB method proposed by Baggio and Langendoen [12] is to limit the area which the samples are drawn in MCL. Unlike the MCL, MCB uses the information obtained from anchor nodes both before and after generation of samples. This can lead to faster and more efficient sample generation; in that, less samples have to reject.

In this method, each node limits its sample generation area by building a box that covers the region where the radio ranges of its one-hop and two-hop heard anchors overlap. In practice, for each one-hop anchor heard, a node builds a square of size $2r$ centered at the anchor position. Similarly, for each two-hop anchor heard, a square of size $4r$ centered at the anchor position is built. The intersection of these squares, a rectangle called "anchor box", would be the new sample generation area.

If a node has some samples in its previous location, the bounding box is built with an additional constraint: for each old sample l_k^i from the L_{t-1}^i, MCB builds an additional square of size $2V_{max}$ centered at the old sample. The circle scribed in each of these boxes indicates the area which the node could travel during the last time interval if it was located on the position of the sample centered in that box.

Adequate numbers of samples is generated in the bounding box and each of which is filtered by observed information similar to MCL, in the hope that the certain number of accepted samples would be found. MCB indicates a lower bound for sampling attempts, confident to its more effective sample generation.

2.4 Other SMC Localization Methods

Some other versions of MCL and MCB have been proposed. Modified version of MCL introduced by the authors of [13] which tries to generate more effective samples by inverting the sampling process used in the original MCL. In that, in this method, first some samples are generated using the information of heard anchors, then they filter by information of its previous location and V_{max}. Another version of MCL designed by authors of [14] to achieve more accuracy by means of flooding location information of anchors to the sensor field. In this method nodes could benefit from information of anchors which are farther than two hops, while the additional communication cost of this method could be considerable. Rudafshani and Datta proposed a method [15] based on MCL to improve the accuracy of Monte Carlo Localization algorithm by using the information of those neighbors which have better location estimation. Wang and Zhu introduced an improved version of MCB [16] which varies the number of generated samples corresponding to observed situation. This leads to indispensable decreasing in the number of generated samples. In [17] the authors proposed an algorithm using position estimation of the non-anchor neighbor nodes to improve location estimation accuracy. In this method, each node uses the estimated location and maximum location error of its non-anchor neighbors to limit its anchor box and to filter samples more accurately in the next time interval. For this purpose, they proposed a method to find the maximum location error of each node, which is described in section 3.2.

3 Our Proposed Method

MCL and MCB have to reject many samples before achieving the desired number of acceptable ones in many cases. The number of these rejected samples may be so high in some situations that these methods limit this number to avoid infinite loops. For MCB, This may happen when the real common area of transmission range of used anchors is so small compare to the area of the anchor box. The real common area is the intersection of actual transmission ranges of heard anchors. All acceptable samples must be located in this small area. We tried to lessen this problem by changing the pattern of sample generation.

Furthermore, nodes can use the estimated location of their neighbors more efficiently. If a node knows the estimated position of its neighbors and possible uncertainty of their estimation, it can consider its neighbors as temporary anchors and improve its position estimation in current iteration.

In this paper, we present a new localization method for mobile WSNs based on MCB. Our algorithm, called USML, improves the accuracy of estimated position of sensor nodes and reduces the average number of sampling attempts by changing the pattern of sample generation. Besides, the different way of sampling in USML helps each sensor node to guess its maximum location error more accurately. It also decreases the localization error by using the information obtained from the non-anchor neighbor nodes more efficiently. Obviously, it burdens more communication cost to the sensor networks. This extra cost is, in fact, the cost of more precise localization.

3.1 Uniform Sampling Monte Carlo Localization

Uniform Sampling Monte Carlo Localization (USML) consist of four steps in processing: initialization phase, sampling phase, filtering and weighting phase and re-sampling phase.

3.1.1 Initialization

In this step anchor box is created using the information of one-hop and two-hop anchors, Similar to MCB method. However, maximum possible movement of nodes in the past time interval does not use in this phase unlike MCB.

3.1.2 Sampling

USML deploys candidate samples over the anchor box uniformly, stead of random sample generation over this area. This guarantee that all part of the anchor box is covered by generated samples. In practice, the known number of candidate samples having pre-calculated positions is generated in such a way that they cover the anchor box uniformly. Figure 2 illustrates an example of uniform candidate samples.

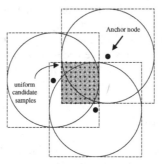

Fig. 1. Uniform samples

The horizontal and the vertical distance of uniform samples can be obtained from following formulas:

$$d_H = \frac{W_{cb}}{\sqrt{N_s \times R}} \tag{1}$$

$$d_V = \frac{L_{cb}}{\sqrt{N_s / R}} \tag{2}$$

where $R = \frac{W_{cb}}{L_{cb}}$

d_H and d_V denote the horizontal and vertical distances between two adjacent samples. W_{cb} and L_{cb} are the width and length of the anchor box. Finally, N_s denotes the desired number of candidate samples for a particular situation. In this paper, We used the following experimental formula for N_s :

$$N_s = \lambda . e^{\mu . V_{max}} \tag{3}$$

In this paper, we set $\lambda = 220$ and $\mu = 0.007$.

In contrary to MCL and MCB, USML does not use L_{t-1}, the sample set of the previous location of the node, in this step. It uses L_{t-1} in the filtering and weighting step, which is described in the next section.

3.1.3 Filtering and Weighting

In this step, each candidate sample is filtered using the information obtained from one-hop and two-hop anchors like previous methods. In that, if distance of a candidate sample, given l_i^k, is more than r to any member of one-hop anchors set (S) or its distance to any member of two-hop anchors set (T) is less than r or more than $2r$, it must reject:

$$filter(l_i^k) = \forall s \in S, d(l_i^k, s) \leq r \wedge \forall s \in T, r < d(l_i^k, s) \leq 2r \qquad (4)$$

Where $d(m, n)$ is the distance between m and n. The position of a candidate sample also must correspond to the maximum possible movement of the node in the past time interval. For a candidate sample, given l_i^k, we define $P(l_i^k)$ as the set of samples which belong to L_{i-1} and their distance to l_i^k is less than V_{max}.

$$P(l_i^k) = \{l_{i-1}^m \in L_{i-1} | d(l_{i-1}^m, l_i^k) \leq V_{max}\} \qquad (5)$$

l_i^k does not reject if $P(l_i^k)$ have at least one member or L_{i-1} be empty. This shows that l_i^k would be the real position of the node in the case that the previous location of the node had been one of the samples in $P(l_i^k)$.

$$filter'(l_i^k) = filter(l_i^k) \wedge (P(l_i^k) \neq \varphi \ or \ L_{i-1} = \varphi) \qquad (6)$$

After finding an acceptable sample, it gets a weight (W_i^k) corresponding to the probability that the sample be located on the real position of the node. Previous Monte Carlo localization methods generate samples randomly; thus, In those algorithms the dense of accepted samples in a given area indicates the probability that the node be located in that area. In contrary, samples positions are calculated priory in USML. They, hence, must give a properly weight. USML assigns the sum of normalized weights of $P(l_i^k)$ members as the weight of l_i^k.

$$W_i^k = \frac{\sum w_{i-1}^m \quad \forall l_{i-1}^m \in P(l_i^k)}{\sum w_{i-1}^j \quad \forall l_{i-1}^j \in L_{i-1}} \qquad (7)$$

This filtering and weighting process repeats for all generated samples. The weighted mean of all accepted samples is the new temporary estimated location of the node at the end of this step. We call this temporary location for node n in iteration i as e_i^n.

Using uniform samples for localization has some indispensible advantages. It can decrease the number of generated samples in comparison to MCL and MCB. Better location estimation is another advantage of uniform sampling. By choosing a proper N_s we can hope that all parts of the real common area be covered by uniform samples. If it merges with precise weighing process, reduction of localization error would be expected. Last but not least, uniform sampling could prepare a ground for better estimation of the maximum possible error of localization, which is discussed in section 3.2.

3.1.4 Re-filtering

Sensor nodes calculate their maximum location error at the beginning of this phase through one of the described methods in section 3.2. Then, each node broadcasts its estimated location and its maximum location error to all of its one-hop neighbor nodes. The nodes re-filter their candidate samples which are not rejected in the previous step by using this new information.

Nodes only use the information of those neighbors which could estimate their location more precisely in previous steps in order to avoid decrease in location accuracy of nodes estimating their location precisely. In other words, nodes use the location information of those neighbors having a smaller maximum location error.

$$U_i^k = \{n \in N_i^k \mid err_i^n \leq err_i^k \}$$ (8)

Where N_i^k is the set of useful neighbors of node k in iteration i, N_i^k is the set of all neighbors of node k in iteration i and err_i^n denotes the estimated maximum location error of node n in i^{th} iteration.

Here, members of N_i^k assumed to be the temporary anchors and the candidate samples filters by location information of these temporary anchors, using the following formula.

$$filter''(l_i^k) = filter'(l_i^k) \wedge d(l_i^k, n) \leq r + err_i^n, \ \forall n \in U_i^k$$ (9)

Finally, the weighted average of all accepted samples is the new estimated location of the node in the current iteration.

3.2 Maximum Location Error

Some WSNs could work better if sensor nodes know the maximum possible error of their position estimation in addition to their estimated location. For instance, a location based routing algorithm can choose a more reliable path if it knows the uncertainty of estimated position of each node.

Authors of [17] calculated the maximum location error of each node in their article. The maximum distance between estimated location of a node and four vertex point of the node's anchor box is selected as the maximum location error of the node in their algorithm.

Uniform sampling enables us to improve the estimation of maximum location error. Let B_i^n denotes the set of accepted samples of node n in i^{th} iteration, which located at the accepted samples' region border. As the samples are uniform, the members of B_i^n can be found easily during the filtering phase by choosing the accepted samples having minimum and maximum x value, in each row of samples. The maximum location error, then, can estimate using the following formula:

$$err_i^n = max_{l_i^k \in B_i^n}\{d(e_i^n, l_i^k)\}$$ (10)

Where err_i^n indicates the maximum possible error of estimated location of node n in i^{th} iteration and e_i^n denotes the temporary estimated location of that node in the mentioned iteration.

4 Evaluation

In this section we compare the performance of USML, MCB, and MCL via study the simulation results. The localization algorithms are implemented by extending the simulator which is created by Hu and Evans[11].

In all simulations, unless stated otherwise, we used a total of 100 regular nodes and 10 anchors. Each anchor is aware of its location independently, for example by means of GPS system. Both nodes and anchors are mobile and they are initially randomly distributed over the area with dimensions of 500×500 meters. The transmission range of both the sensor nodes and anchors is assumed to be a perfect circle. In addition, Time is considered discrete and Nodes move in each time iteration using the random waypoint mobility model [18].

The most important factors for comparing different localization techniques of mobile sensor networks are accuracy and cost. At the one hand, because of limited power source in sensor nodes and repeating nature of localization due to repetitive movement, the amount of energy consumed by localization algorithms must be limited as much as possible. On the other hand, a more precise estimation of location of nodes may lead to decrease in overall used energy by the network. For example, accurate localization may have consequence of finding shorter paths between nodes, which can redound to less energy exhaustion.

4.1 Accuracy

Figure 2 shows the localization error of MCL, MCB and USML for different maximum velocity of nodes and anchors when the transmission ranges of them are 100 meters. The localization error in a time interval is calculated by averaging the distance between estimated location of each node and the real position of the node.

USML outperforms the two other algorithms because of using more information for localization, better dispersion of generated samples and more effective sample weighting. It improves the accuracy of MCB about 20%.

Both MCB and USML show a transitive behavior in very small amounts of V_{max}. This is due to the fact that in low speeds, many nodes could not find their location because they don't hear any anchor node. In addition, other nodes which hear a few anchors may not be able to find appropriate samples because of the large area of their anchor box.

Figure 3 represents the accuracy of the same algorithms for the same network. The only difference is that the transmission range of nodes and anchors are 50 meters. Here, MCB loses most of its advantage compare to MCL regarding to the fact that

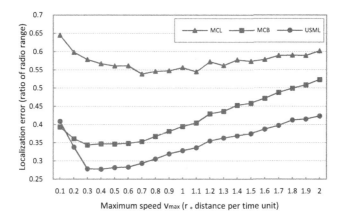

Fig. 2. Localization error ($r=100\ m$)

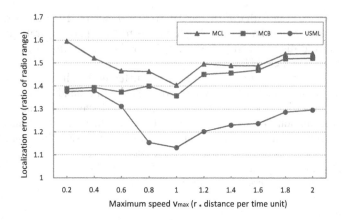

Fig. 3. Localization error ($r=50\ m$)

each node misses many of its one-hop and two-hop anchors and it cannot make a small anchor box. Nevertheless, USML can preserve its relative advantage as it not only depends on anchor nodes.

4.2 Cost

The cost of localization process consists of two major parts: calculation cost and communication cost. MCB and MCL have identical communication cost as they use only information of one-hop and two-hop anchor neighbor nodes. USML has more communication cost because of its re-filtering phase. Each node must send a packet to its neighbors, consist of its temporary estimated location and its maximum location error which calculated using one of the methods presented in section 3.2.

The authors of reference [17] calculated the communication cost of their method which is also true about our algorithm, so we use their notation for comparison the communication cost of algorithms. Suppose that m and n denote the number of anchor nodes and all nodes, including anchor and non-anchor nodes, respectively. s_d Indicates the average number of anchor nodes in a communication range of a node. s_d can be obtained using the following formula:

$$s_d = \frac{m}{s} * \pi r^2 \tag{11}$$

Where s denotes the area of deployment region. MCL and MCB use one-hop and two-hop anchor neighbor nodes for sampling, so their total communication cost is $O(m + n * s_d)$. m and $(n * s_d)$ correspond to the communication cost of finding one-hop and two-hop anchor neighbor nodes respectively. USML uses one-hop non-anchor neighbor nodes in addition to one-hop and two-hop anchor neighbor nodes, so its communication cost is $O(n + n * s_d)$.

The average number of generated samples for a specific set of parameters is the main factor for comparing the calculation cost of SMC localization algorithms. However, it is not completely fair as each algorithm spend a specific amount of energy for generating and filtering a sample. In this paper, we neglect this different and consider the required energy of generating a sample identical for all algorithms. Figure 4 shows the average sampling attempts for each node in mentioned algorithms. The transmission range of nodes is 100 meters. USML can reduce sampling attempt up to 75% compare to MCB.

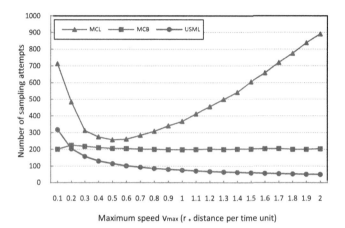

Fig. 4. Sampling attempts

4.3 Anchor Density

Figure 5 shows the localization error of the algorithms for different density of anchor nodes when V_{max} is 60 *m/s*. USML shows the best relative accuracy in low density of anchor nodes compare to other algorithms. The reason is that temporary anchors, useful neighbors of each node, become more valuable in low density of anchor nodes for our algorithm and using them could redress the lack of anchor nodes. In other words, USML is fewer dependants to anchor nodes.

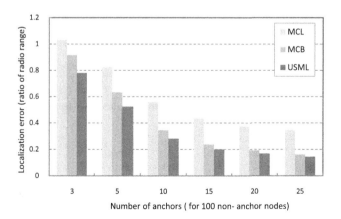

Fig. 5. Influence of anchor density on localization error

4.4 Node Density

Figure 6 shows the average localization error for different density of nodes. The number of anchor nodes is fixed to 10 and only the number of non-anchor nodes is changed. Furthermore, the transmission range of nodes and anchor nodes is considered to be 25 meters in order to intensify the effect of node density on localization accuracy.

MCL and MCB show better behavior when the density of nodes increases. Increasing in density of nodes could help each node to find more neighbor and probably more two-hop anchor nodes. MCL uses the information of two-hop anchor nodes for filtering its generated samples and MCB moreover uses this information for sample generation. As a result, both of these algorithms could improve their location estimation when the node density rises.

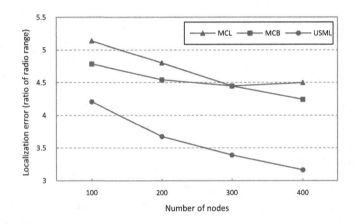

Fig. 6. Influence of node density on localization error

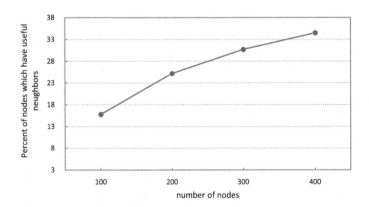

Fig. 7. Influence of node density on percentage of node which could find useful neighbors

This is true about USML too. *USML* also could find more neighbors and re-filter samples more accurately when the node density is higher. Hence, its location estimation improves intensively when the density of nodes increases.

Figure 7 indicates the percentage of nodes which could find at least one useful neighbor. Useful neighbor of a node are those which could estimate their location more precisely than the node. As it is obvious, in a denser network, each node has more neighbors and could find useful neighbor nodes with higher probability.

4.5 Location Error

Figure 8 indicates the localization error of two versions of USML which use different method to estimate maximum location error of nodes. The transmission range of nodes is considered to be 100 meters. The first version which is denoted as v1 uses the previous method of estimating the maximum location error of nodes which is described in [17]. The second version, v2, uses the method of finding the maximum location error based on the border samples, which is describes in section 3.2.

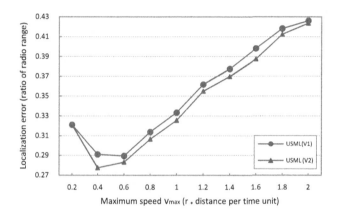

Fig. 8. The accuracy of two versions of USML

Using our method to estimate the maximum location error of nodes led to more accurate localization as the neighbors of a node could find a smaller maximum error and each node could reject more uniform samples.

5 Conclusion

We have presented a new sequential Monte Carlo localization method for mobile sensor networks in this paper. USML, Our proposed method, can reduce the number of generated samples by dispersing them uniformly over the anchor box. The new way of sample generation also led to better localization accuracy. We also proposed a new method to estimate the maximum location error of nodes based on the new sampling method, which is more accurate than the previous method.

USML, besides, decreases uses the estimated location of the non-anchor neighbors and their maximum location error more efficiently compare to previous methods. USML uses more energy for communication than MCL and MCB and, although the new sampling method reduces the number of generated samples in USML, it has more calculation cost as the calculation cost of each sample is higher in this method.

Simulation results indicated that our algorithm can achieve higher location accuracy when the node density is high. Furthermore, nodes can estimate their position more accurately than other methods when there are only a few anchor nodes in the network.

References

1. Yick, J., Mukherjee, B., Ghosal, D.: Computer Networks 52, 2292–2330 (2008)
2. Hefeeda, M., Bagheri, M.: Wireless sensor networks for early detection of forest fires. In: IEEE Internatonal Conference on Mobile Adhoc and Sensor Systems, MASS 2007, October 8-11, pp. 1–6 (2007)
3. Pace, S., Frost, G., Lachow, I., Frelinger, D., Fossum, D., Wassem, D.K., Pinto, M.: GPS history chronology and budgets. In: The global positioning system, pp. 237–270. RAND Corporation (1995)
4. Pandey, S., Agrawal, P.: A Survey on Localization Techniques for Wireless Networks. Journal of the Chinese Institute of Engineers, 1125–1148 (2006)
5. Mo, L., Yunhao, L.: Rendered path: Range-free localization in anisotropic sensor networks with holes. In: Proceedings of the 13th annual ACM international conference on Mobile computing and networking (Mobicom 2007), Montreal, Canada, September, pp. 51–62 (2007)
6. Juang, P., Oki, H., Wang, Y., Martonosi, M., Peh, L.S., Rubenstein, D.: Energy-efficient computing for wildlife tracking: Design tradeoffs and early experiences with ZebraNet. In: Proc. ASPLOS-X, San Jose, pp. 96–107 (2002)
7. Yihan, L., Panwar, S.S., Shiwen, M., Burugupalli, S. Jong ha, L.: A mobile ad hoc bio-sensor network. In: IEEE International Conference on Communications, pp. 1241–1245 (2005)
8. Peng, R., Sichitiu, M.L.: Localization of wireless sensor networks with a mobile beacon. In: First IEEE Conference on Mobile Ad-hoc and Sensor Systems (MASS 2004), Fort Lauderdale, FL, USA (2004)
9. Handschin, J.E.P.: Monte Carlo Techniques for Prediction and Filtering of Non-Linear Stochastic Processes. Automatica 6, 555–563 (1970)
10. Dellaert, F., Fox, D., Burgard, W., Thrun, S.: Monte Carlo Localization for Mobile Robots. In: IEEE International Conference on Robotics and Automation, ICRA (1999)
11. Hu, L., Evans, D.: Localization for mobile sensor networks. In: Tenth International Conference on Mobile Computing and Networking, Philadelphia, Pennsylvania. USA, pp. 45–57 (2004)
12. Baggio, A., Langendoen, K.: Monte Carlo localization for mobile wireless sensor networks. In: Cao, J., Stojmenovic, I., Jia, X., Das, S.K. (eds.) MSN 2006. LNCS, vol. 4325, pp. 317–328. Springer, Heidelberg (2006)
13. Stevens, N., Vivekanadan, E., Wong V.: Dual and mixture Monte Carlo localization. In: Wireless Communications and Networking Conference (2007)

14. Yi, J., Yang, S., Cha, H.: Multi-hop-based Monte Carlo Localization for Mobile Sensor Networks. In: 4th Annual IEEE Communications Society Conference on Sensor, Mesh and Ad-Hoc Communications and Networks, pp. 162–171 (2007)
15. Rudafshani, M., Datta, S.: Localization in wireless sensor networks. In: Proceedings of the 6th International Conference on Information Processing in Sensor Networks (IPSN 2007), Cambridge, Massachusetts, USA, pp. 51–60 (2007)
16. Wang, W., Zhu, Q.: Varying the Sample Number for Monte Carlo Localization in Mobile Sensor Networks. In: Second International Multisymposium on Computer and Computational Sciences, pp. 490–495 (2007)
17. Zhang, S., Cao, J., Chen, L., Chen, D.: Locating Nodes in Mobile Sensor Networks More Accurately and Faster. In: 5th Annual IEEE Sensor, Mesh and Ad Hoc Communications and Networks, pp. 37–45 (2008)
18. Camp, T., Boleng, J., Davies, V.: A Survey of Mobility Models for Ad Hoc Networks Research. Wireless Communications and Mobile Computing 2(5) (2002)

Autonomous Transmission Power Adaptation for Multi-Radio Multi-Channel Wireless Mesh Networks*

Thomas O. Olwal[1,2,3], Barend J. van Wyk[2], Karim Djouani[2,3],
Yskandar Hamam[2], Patrick Siarry[3], and Ntsibane Ntlatlapa[1]

[1] Meraka Institute CSIR,
[2] Tshwane University of Technology,
[3] Paris-12 University
PO. Box 395 Pretoria, South Africa
thomas.olwal@gmail.com, vanwykb@gmail.com, djouani@univ-paris12.fr,
hamama@tut.ac.za, siarry@univ-paris12.fr, nntlatlapa@csir.co.za

Abstract. Multi-Radio Multi-Channel (MRMC) systems are key to power control problems in WMNs. Previous studies have emphasized throughput maximization in such systems as the main design challenge and transmission power control treated as a secondary issue. In this paper, we present an autonomous power adaptation for MRMC WMNs. The transmit power is dynamically adapted by each network interface card (NIC) in response to the locally available energy in a node, queue load, and interference states of a channel. To achieve this, WMN is first represented as a set of Unified Channel Graphs (UCGs). Second, each NIC of a node is tuned to a UCG. Third, a power selection MRMC unification protocol (PMMUP) that coordinates Interaction variables (IV) from different UCGs and Unification variables (UV) from higher layers is proposed. PMMUP coordinates autonomous power optimization by the NICs of a node. The efficacy of the proposed method is investigated through simulations.

Keywords: Multi-Radio Multi-Channel (MRMC), Power Selection Multi-Radio Multi-Channel Unification Protocol (PMMUP), Wireless Mesh Networks (WMNs).

1   Introduction

Wireless Mesh Networks (WMNs) have emerged as a ubiquitous part of modern broadband communication networks [1]. In WMNs, nodes are composed of wireless mesh clients, routers (e.g., mesh points) and gateways. Wireless mesh routers or mesh points (MPs) form a multi-hop wireless network which serves as a backbone to provide Internet access to mesh clients. As a result wireless

---

* This work is supported by Meraka Institute and Tshwane University of Technology, South Africa.

P.M. Ruiz and J.J. Garcia-Luna-Aceves (Eds.): ADHOC-NOW 2009, LNCS 5793, pp. 284–297, 2009.

backbone nodes convey a large amount of traffic generated by wireless clients to a few nodes that act as gateways to the Internet. In order to meet high traffic demands, wireless backbone nodes (e.g., MPs) can be equipped with multiple radios and/or operate on multiple frequency channels [2]. Each radio has a single or multiple orthogonal channels [3]. In this scenario, an MP node has each radio with its own medium access control (MAC) and physical layers [1]. This results in independent communications in these radios. Thus, a single MP node can access mesh client network and route the backbone traffic simultaneously. This brings the advantage of a self-managing and high capacity wireless mesh networking [4]. However, utilizing multiple-radios and channels for each node simultaneously, results in striping related problems [11]. First the use of multiple radios on multiple channels is expensive. In that case one assumes that the number of radios is less than the number of channels. This allows for interface channel switching technique to improve channel utilization. Switching an interface from one channel to another incurs switching delays [8]. Thus, we assume that the frequency of channel switching is low. Second, timeout problems due to packet re-sequencing at the receiver node may become significant. Scalable resolutions of such problems are well known in [11] and [8].

The operation of multi-radio multi-channel (MRMC) WMNs generally requires sustainable energy supply. Substantial deployments of WMNs have recently picked up in rural and remote communities [4]. In applications, electric outlets are not available and nodes must rely on battery power supply for their operations. Due to the nature of topography of the remote communities, mesh networks are expected to deliver packets over long wireless distance ranges. This comes at the expense of additional transmission power consumption. Nodes transmitting with high power shorten network lifetime and as a result network connectivity fails. This phenomenon degrades the robustness of a self-configuring WMN. Moreover injudicious use of transmit power decreases channel reuse in a physical area and increases co-channel interference with neighbouring hosts. This in turn causes severe reduction in network throughput. Therefore besides throughput maximizations [7], transmission power control should be prioritized in such networks [5]. Controlling transmission power would enhance topology control and routing in MRMC WMNs [6].

In this paper we study an autonomous power level adjustment mechanism for MRMC WMN. Radios of an MP adapt transmission powers based on queue arrivals, energy reserves and multiple channel conditions. The optimal power level is changed dynamically after a certain period of time (i.e., slot duration). This work is motivated by the fact that WMN system needs to be dynamic and scalable. That is, it can autonomously adapt to nodes entering the network (i.e., introducing multiple interferences) or those exiting the network due to node failures (i.e., energy depletion), poor connectivity and so forth.

We considered an MRMC system in which each radio or network interface card (NIC) has its own MAC and physical layers. However, all radios of the same MP node were assumed to share common memory, central processor and energy supply modules. In order to make such multi-radio systems work as a single node, we adopted a *virtual* MAC protocol on top of the legacy MAC [1]. The *virtual* MAC coordinates (unifies) the communication in all the radios [8], [9]. This unification protocol hides the complexity of multiple MAC and physical layers from the upper layers. The first Multi-radio unification protocol (MUP) was reported in [8]. MUP discovers neighbours, selects the NIC with the best channel quality based on the round trip time (RTT) and sends data on a pre-assigned channel. MUP then switches channels after sending the data. However, MUP assumes power unconstrained mesh network scenarios. Mesh nodes are plugged into an electric outlet. MUP utilizes only a single selected channel for data transmission.

Our power optimization protocol follows the MUP concept in spirit. Instead we propose the power selection multi-radio multi-channel unification protocol (PMMUP). PMMUP enhances functionalities of the original MUP. Such enhancements include: energy-efficient power selection capability and the utilization of parallel radios or channels to send data traffic simultaneously. Like MUP, the PMMUP requires no additional hardware modification. Thus, the PMMUP complexity is comparative to that of the MUP. It is to be noted that the main motivation behind PMMUP concept is the need for a single MP to access mesh client network and route the backbone traffic simultaneously [1]. The routing functionality of the MP may be of multi-point to multi-point. Therefore, PMMUP manages large scale multi-radio systems with a reduced complexity [18]. In order to achieve this task, PMMUP mainly coordinates local power optimizations at the NICs. While NICs measure dynamic channel conditions. As a result, we have a simple four step power adjustment algorithm. That is, PMMUP *guesses* initial unification variables, NICs *predict* the local channel system states, PMMUP *updates* unification variables and NICs *compute* local optimal transmission power levels for each channel. We assume that each NIC has independent amount of traffic load at its queue and independent dimension of channel states to measure. Therefore each NIC dynamically selects optimal transmission power level asynchronously. We propose a PMMUP algorithm called the Multi-radio multi-channel system Unification Variables Prediction Algorithms (MRSUPA). Through simulations, PMMUP algorithm yielded significant transmission power savings over the MUP [8] and Striping models [11]. MRSUPA presented a better throughput performance than the dynamic channel assignment with power control (DCA-PC) scheme [10]. The MRSUPA algorithm is scalable and practical for multi-radio WMN compared to the single channel methods in [12] and [13].

The rest of this paper is organised as follows. We discuss related work in Section 2. We describe the System model and the PMMUP in Section 3. Section 4 formulates the Problem. In Section 5 we present the MRSUPA algorithm. Section 6 presents simulation results and Section 7 concludes the paper.

2   Related Work

Numerous works have been proposed for multi-channel MAC with power control [5], [9], [10], [13], [15]. The key idea is that data packets are transmitted with proper power control so as to exploit channel reuse. While control packets are transmitted with maximum power in order to warn the neighbouring nodes of future communication activity between the sender and the receiver. However, due to the close vicinity of NICs and neighbouring nodes, we can assume that a sender MP transmits control packets with a probe power level (i.e., a fraction of maximum power). Moreover, achieving this with beam-forming antennas reduces inter-channel interferences and improves neighbour reach-ability with the best channel qualities [17]. Power control approaches using directional antennas are proposed in [5], [16]. This makes it possible for dynamic adjustment of the transmission power for both data and control packets to optimize energy consumption [16]. The use of beam-switched antennas permits interference-limited concurrent transmissions. It also provides a node with the appropriate tradeoffs between throughput and energy consumption. In this paper we assume that the neighbour discovery procedure is achievable via wide switched beam-width antennas and the data packets can be unicast to target receivers using directional antennas [17].

Autonomous dynamic power control mechanisms for single channel wireless networks are well known in [12]-[14]. These mechanisms require each node to adapt the transmission power dynamically in response to the channel interference estimations. Adaptive Kalman filters are often employed to estimate the channel interference conditions [12]. Using adaptive filters in a MRMC system comes with design complexity challenges [18]. In this work we consider parallel optimal asynchronous control of the transmission power levels by the NICs as coordinated by the PMMUP. The optimal controller is based on the linear quadratic methods [18]. Optimal linear quadratic control systems are fast and robust. Parallel algorithms for optimal control of large scale linear systems are well known in [19]. There exist liberal applications of such methods for task assignments in distributed computer networks [20]. To the best of our knowledge, our paper is the first to propose the PMMUP enabled autonomous power adjustment scheme for MRMC WMNs.

3   System Model

3.1   Preliminary

Consider a wireless MRMC multi-hop WMN in Fig. 1, operating under dynamic network conditions. Let us assume that the entire mesh network is virtually divided into L disjoint unified channel graphs (UCGs). A UCG is a set of MP PHYs (interfaces) that are interconnected to each other via a common wireless medium channel. In each UCG there are $\|V\| = N_V$, NICs that connect to each other possibly via multiple hops. This means that each multi-radio MP node can belong to at least one UCG. For simplicity it is assumed that the number of NICs in each MP node is at most the number of available UCGs, i.e., $\|T_A\| \leq \|L_A\|$. Each UCG is a subsystem with NICs as its members. Members of separate UCGs control their transmission powers in parallel [17] through associated PMMUP as the coordinator. PMMUP manages greedy power control behaviours among

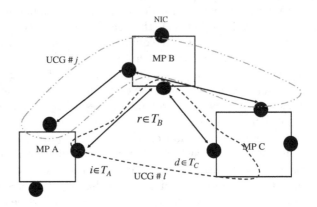

Fig. 1. Multi-Radio Multi-Channel (MRMC) and Multi-hop Wireless Mesh communication system. Two Unified Channel Graphs (UCGs) labeled UCG j and UCG l are shown.

individual NICs [12]. Power resources are dynamically adjusted by each NIC using intra and inter-subsystem (channel) states. In this sequel such states include the signal-to-interference plus noise ratio (SINR) deviation, aggregate interference and link capacity error. Due to the decentralized nature, each MP assumes imperfect knowledge about the global network.

Further we assume that there exists an established logical topology, where some NICs belonging to a certain UCG are *sources* of transmission say $i \in T_A$ while others act as 'voluntary' *relays*, say $r \in T_B$ to *destinations*, say $d \in T_C$. A sequence of connected *logical links* or simply channels $l \in L(i)$ forms a *route* originating from source i . Each asymmetrical physical link may need to be regarded as multiple logical links due to multiple channels. NICs can switch among different free channels at the end of a time slot so that each channel is maximally utilized all the time. Time slot durations are assumed fixed [13]. Each time slot accounts for a power control adjustment mini-slot time, a packet transmission mini-slot time and a guard time interval. For analytical convenience time slots will be normalized to integer units, $t \in \{0, 1, 2, \ldots\}$ [13]. In the duration of a time slot neighbouring nodes transmitting within the same channel cause intra-channel or co-channel interference. In addition, nodes transmitting in different neighbouring channels cause inter-channel or adjacent channel interference due to spatial vicinity [5].

3.2 PMMUP Description

The PMMUP: V-MAC architecture is illustrated in Figure 2. The PMMUP performs neighbour discovery using a fraction of maximum power assigned to NIC, coordinates power selection procedure and sends data. All these activities

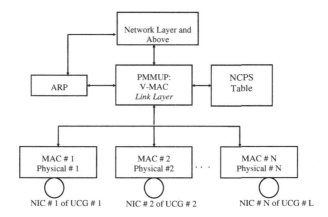

Fig. 2. PMMUP: V-MAC architecture for the WMN

need to happen within the same time slot duration. The coordination variables are stored at the neighbour communication power and states (NCPS) table. The NCPS table is shown in Table 1. Such coordination variable includes battery energy reserves, multiple channel state conditions and higher layer unification variables.

Neighbour Discovery: At start-up, NICs of a node are tuned to orthogonal UCGs [10]. PMMUP initiates communication using an address resolution protocol (ARP) message broadcast over all the interfaces [8]. Each interface sends these messages to neighbours in their corresponding UCGs with a fraction of maximum power as instructed by the PMMUP. Upon receiving the ARP requests, the destination node sends the ARP responses with the MAC addresses of the NICs on which it received the ARP requests. Once the originating host receives the ARP responses it proceeds to communicate with the interface from which it received ARP responses. The PMMUP then classifies neighbours according to the procedure highlighted in [8]. Nodes that support PMMUP are classified as PMMUP enabled nodes otherwise qualified as legacy nodes.

Table 1. Entry in the PMMUP (NCPS) Table

FIELD	DESCRIPTION(NODE,NEIGH)
Neighbour:	IP address of the neighbour host
Class:	Indicates whether *neigh* is PMMUP-enabled or not
MAC list:	MAC address associated with *neigh* NICs
States:	Recent measurements on: Channel Quality, Queue, RTT, and Energy Reserves
TPL:	Recent Transmit power level selected

Power Selection Process: The PMMUP chooses initial probing power and broadcasts to all interfaces. This broadcast power level is vital for neighbour discovery process. We refer to the total probing power over the interfaces as *tot-ProbPow*. The energy residing in a node is referred to as *Energy Reserves*.

If (*tot-ProbPow* > *Energy Reserves* and *Load Queue* = 0 at the NICs) **then do** *Nothing*; /* Conserve Energy*/
else do /*select the transmission power*/
(i) NICs send "ps (power selection) request" message to neighbours using a probe power level. The ps-request message probes for channel state conditions.
(ii) When the neighbouring NICs receive the "ps-request" message they compute the "state information": SINR, Interference, Queue status, and Energy reserves. This information is piggy-backed in the "ps-Ack" message and sent via feedback path to the originating NICs, using probing power level.
(iii) Upon receiving the ps-Ack messages, each sending NIC independently computes the SINR, interference, queue state, energy reserves and RTT, and copies "state information" to the PMMUP. The PMMUP updates the NCPS table and sends the coordination updates including those from upper layers to lower level NICs for power optimization.
(iv) Each NIC runs local power optimization algorithms (See Section 5). Each NIC with DATA in its queue *unicasts* pending traffics to destination neighbour (s) with optimal transmission power. The sending NIC copies the PMMUP with local optimal power information for NCPS table updates.
endif

Other Advantages: PMMUP does not require a global knowledge of the network topology hence it is a scalable protocol. Contents of a neighbourhood topology set are added or subtracted one node at a time. PMMUP utilizes multiple parallel channels. Thus, it has the ability to adapt to switched antenna beams for efficient spectral reuse. That is, neighbour discovery *broadcasts* would require Omni directional beam pattern while data transmissions can be effected using directional beam pattern. PMMUP is located at the Link layer (mid-way the protocol stack) thus; cross-layer information interacts with a reduced latency. The NCPS table is assumed to have a few information to update. Neighbour discovery occurs once throughout the power optimization interval. This reduces memory and computational complexities.

4   Problem Formulation

We derive state transitional models (or, "state information") as functions of the predicted power levels for each transmitter-receiver pairs (users) in every UCG. Let us define the distributed energy-efficient power adjustment law for each user as

$$p_{i,l}(t+1) = \begin{cases} p_{i,l}(t) + f_l(\mathbf{x}) & \forall \mathbf{x} \in \{\mathbf{x}\} \quad \text{if Queue} > 0 \\ 0, & \text{otherwise} \end{cases}, \quad (1)$$

where $f_l(\mathbf{x}) = f_l(\beta_l(t), I_l(t), \Gamma_l(t))$, $\beta_l(t)$, $I_l(t)$ and $\Gamma_l(t)$ as the actual SINR, aggregate network interference and scheduled transmission rate during time slot t. Using Taylor series to obtain first order linear approximations to $f_l(\mathbf{x})$ gives $f_l(\mathbf{x}) \triangleq f(\gamma_l^{ss}, I_l^{ss}, \Lambda_l^{ss}) + \alpha_\beta(\beta_l(t) - \gamma_l^{ss}) + \alpha_I(I_l(t) - I_l^{ss}) + \alpha_\Gamma(\Gamma_l(t) - \Lambda_l^{ss})$ where γ_l^{ss}, I_l^{ss} and Λ_l^{ss} are steady state values of a power adaptation system[18].

Let $\frac{G_{ll}(t+1)}{I_{(i,r),l}(t+1)} = H(t)\frac{m(t)}{n(t)}$ be defined as the predicted effective channel gain with $m(t)$ and $n(t)$ are independent unit mean noise terms with the same variance σ_m^2. Defining the SINR as $\beta_l(t+1) = \frac{p_l(t+1)G_{ll}(t+1)}{I_{(i,r),l}(t+1)}$ and substituting $p_l(t+1)$ we get: $\beta_l(t+1) = [p_l(t) + f_l(\mathbf{x})]H(t)\frac{m(t)}{n(t)}$. Thus the SINR deviation is shown as

$$e_\beta(t+1) = H(t)\frac{m(t)}{n(t)}\alpha_\beta(\beta_l(t) - \gamma_l^{ss})\ H(t)\frac{m(t)}{n(t)}\alpha_I(I_l(t) - I_l^{ss}) +$$
$$H(t)\frac{m(t)}{n(t)}\alpha_\Gamma(\Gamma_l(t) - \Lambda_l^{ss}). \qquad (2)$$

Here, $m(t)$ characterizes the slowly changing shadow-fading and the fast multipath-fading on top of the distance loss [12]. The noise term $n(t)$ models the fluctuation when interfaces increase or decrease their transmission power levels or associated nodes either enter or leave the system.

In a similar way we define the deviation of aggregate interference among the neighbouring interfaces in a UCG as

$$e_I(t+1) = G_{ll}(t)m(t)\alpha_\beta(\beta_l(t) - \gamma_l^{ss})\ G_{ll}(t)m(t)\alpha_I(I_l(t) - I_l^{ss}) +$$
$$G_{ll}(t)m(t)\alpha_\Gamma(\Gamma_l(t) - \Lambda_l^{ss}). \qquad (3)$$

Following similar procedure the deviation of transmission rate for the same link l is written as follows,

$$e_\Gamma(t+1) = \frac{1}{p_l(t)}[\alpha_\beta(\beta_l(t) - \gamma_l^{ss})\ \alpha_I(I_l(t) - I_l^{ss})\ \alpha_\Gamma(\Gamma_l(t) - \Lambda_l^{ss})] +$$
$$\log m(t) - \log n(t). \qquad (4)$$

Let $\mathbf{x}_l \triangleq (\beta_l - \gamma_l^{ss}\ I_l - I_l^{ss}\ \Gamma_l - \Lambda_l^{ss})^T$ be state measurements of a control system. Combining equations (2), (3) and (4) and introducing an input sequence term, we obtain $\mathbf{x}_l(t+1) = \mathbf{A}_l\mathbf{x}_l(t) + \mathbf{B}_l\mathbf{u}_l(t) + \varepsilon_l(t)$ where $\mathbf{A}_l$ is a 3 x 3 coefficient matrix given by $\mathbf{A}_l = \begin{pmatrix} \frac{m}{n}H\alpha_\beta & \frac{m}{n}H\alpha_I & \frac{m}{n}H\alpha_\Gamma \\ mG\alpha_\beta & mG\alpha_I & mG\alpha_\Gamma \\ \frac{\alpha_\beta}{p_l} & \frac{\alpha_I}{p_l} & \frac{\alpha_\Gamma}{p_l} \end{pmatrix}$, and $\mathbf{B}_l\mathbf{u}_l(t) = \begin{bmatrix} u_\beta(t) \\ u_I(t) \\ u_\Gamma(t) \end{bmatrix}$ characterizes the control sequence that needs to be added to $p_l(t+1)$ equation (1) in order to derive network dynamics to steady states. $\mathbf{B}_l$ is assumed to be a 3 x 1 coefficient matrix. The state stochastic shocks term $\varepsilon_l(t)$ is a 3 x

1 random vector with zero mean and covariance matrix, $\Theta_\varepsilon = \mathrm{E}\varepsilon_l(t)\varepsilon_l^T(t) = diag\left(\sigma_\beta^2, \sigma_I^2, \sigma_\Gamma^2\right)$. If we assume that corresponding to a UCG l is the PMMUP user i and $l = i$ then the Multi-radio interaction state space (MRISS) model representation becomes[18]

$$\mathbf{x}_i(t+1) = \mathbf{A}_i(t)\mathbf{x}_i(t) + \mathbf{B}_i(t)\mathbf{u}_i(t) + \mathbf{C}_i(t)\mathbf{y}_i(t) + \varepsilon_i(t), \qquad (5)$$

where $\mathbf{y}_i(t)$, introduced in (5), is a linear combination of states (LCS) from other UCGs available to the ith user. This LCS is defined as

$$\mathbf{y}_i(t) = \sum_{\substack{j=1\\j\neq i}}^{N} \mathbf{L}_{ij}(t)\mathbf{x}_j(t) + \varepsilon_i^y(t), \qquad (6)$$

where $\varepsilon_i^y(t)$ denotes the coordination process shocks with zero mean and covariance matrix $\Theta_\varepsilon = \mathrm{E}\varepsilon_i^y(t)\varepsilon_i^{yT}(t)$, $\mathbf{C}_i(t)$ is considered to be a 3 x 3 identity coefficient matrix and $\mathbf{L}_{ij}(t)$ is the higher level interconnection matrix of states between ith user and jth user. This interconnection matrix needs to be evaluated by the PMMUP. This interconnection matrix needs to be evaluated by the PMMUP. In what follows, we formulate the control problem for each user as the minimization of the following stochastic quadratic cost function subject to the network interaction state equation (5) and coordination states in equation (6):

$$\begin{aligned}
J_i &= E\left[\lim_{t\to\infty}\frac{1}{t}\sum_{\tau=0}^{t-1}\mathbf{x}_i^T(\tau)\mathbf{Q}_i\mathbf{x}_i(\tau) + \mathbf{u}_i^T(\tau)\mathbf{R}_i\mathbf{u}_i\right] \\
&= \lim_{t\to\infty}\frac{1}{t}\sum_{\tau=0}^{t-1}\sum_{\substack{\mathbf{x}_i\in\{\mathbf{x}\}\\\mathbf{u}_i\in\{\mathbf{u}\}}}\left[\mathbf{x}_i^T(\tau)\mathbf{Q}_i\mathbf{x}_i(\tau) + \mathbf{u}_i^T(\tau)\mathbf{R}_i\mathbf{u}_i(\tau)\right]\times \\
&\quad \rho_i(\mathbf{x}_i, \mathbf{u}_i).
\end{aligned} \qquad (7)$$

Here, $\mathbf{Q}_i \in \Re^{3\times3} \geq \mathbf{0}$ is assumed symmetric, positive semi-definite matrix and $\mathbf{R}_i \in \Re^{M\times M} > \mathbf{0}$ is assumed symmetric, positive definite matrix. For brevity, choose $\mathbf{Q}_i$ to be an identity matrix and $\mathbf{R}_i$ to be a matrix of unity entries. The joint probability density function (pdf) $\rho_i(\mathbf{x}_i, \mathbf{u}_i)$ denotes the state occupation measure (SOM). The SOM is defined as $\rho_i(\mathbf{x}_i, \mathbf{u}_i) = \Pr(\mathbf{u}_i|\mathbf{x}_i)\sum_{\mathbf{u}_i\in\{\mathbf{u}_i\}}\rho_i(\mathbf{x}_i, \mathbf{u}_i)$. It gives the steady state probability that the control system is in state $\mathbf{x}_i \in \{\mathbf{x}\}$ and the driving control parameter $\mathbf{u}_i \in \{\mathbf{u}_i\}$ is chosen. Thus, we seek an optimal $\mathbf{u}_i \in \{\mathbf{u}_i\}$ that solves the problem in (7). First, we introduce Lagrange multipliers π_t^i and a state unification (SU) vector ϕ_{t+1}^i to augment the LCS equality in (6) and the MRISS constraint (5) respectively, to the cost function. We then invoke the dynamic programming value function

$$V(\mathbf{x}_t^i) = \min_{\{\mathbf{u}_t^i\}}\left\{\mathbf{x}_t^{iT}\mathbf{Q}_t^i\mathbf{x}_t^i + \mathbf{u}_t^{iT}\mathbf{R}_t^i\mathbf{u}_t^i\right\} +$$

$$\min_{\{\mathbf{u}_t^i\}}\rho E\left[V\left(-\pi_t^T\mathbf{y}_t^i + \pi_t^T\sum_{\substack{j=1\\j\neq i}}\mathbf{L}_t^{ij}\mathbf{x}_t^j + \pi_t^T\varepsilon_t^y\right)\right] +$$

$$\min_{\{\mathbf{u}_t^i\}} \rho \, E \left[V \left(\phi_{t+1}^T \mathbf{A}_t^i \mathbf{x}_t^i + \phi_{t+1}^T \mathbf{B}_t^i \mathbf{u}_t^i + \phi_{t+1}^T \mathbf{C}_t^i \mathbf{y}_t^i + \phi_{t+1}^T \varepsilon_t^x \right) \right]. \tag{8}$$

Differentiating w.r.t. $\mathbf{u}$ and solving in terms of $\mathbf{u}$, with subscripts and super-scripts dropped for notational convinience we have,

$$\mathbf{u}^* = -\mathbf{F}\mathbf{x}, \tag{9}$$

where $\mathbf{F} = \left(\mathbf{R} + \rho \mathbf{B}^T \phi \mathbf{P} \phi^T \mathbf{B} \right)^{-1} \rho \mathbf{B}^T \phi \mathbf{P} \phi^T \mathbf{A}$. Starting from an initial guess of $\mathbf{P}$ matrix in the value function, $\mathbf{P}_k$ is updated to $\mathbf{P}_{k+1}$ according to $\mathbf{P}_{k+1} = \mathbf{Q} + \rho \mathbf{A}^T \mathbf{P}_k \mathbf{A} - \rho^2 \mathbf{A}^T \mathbf{P}_k \mathbf{B} \left(\mathbf{R} + \rho \mathbf{B}^T \mathbf{P}_k \mathbf{B} \right)^{-1} \mathbf{B}^T \mathbf{P}_k \mathbf{A}$.

Hitherto, $\mathbf{y}$ signifies states from other UCGs. ϕ signifies *unification variables* (UV) such as energy reserves and higher layers' information and $\mathbf{x}$ signifies the *interaction variable* (IV) including those states coordinated from other UCGs. Using MRSUPA, each NIC-pair predicts $\mathbf{x}_i$ and ϕ_i locally and autonomously keeping $\mathbf{y}$ fixed [14]. PMMUP assigns NICs the updated $\mathbf{y}$ according to algorithm 1 in Section 5.

5   MRSUPA Algorithm

Table 2. (Algorithm 1: MRSUPA:) Asynchronous Unification Variables Prediction

STEP: CONTROL ACTION TAKEN BY EACH PMMUP USER
Input: ϕ, $\mathbf{y}$, $\mathbf{x}_i$, $\mathbf{A}, \mathbf{B}, \mathbf{C}, \mathbf{Q}$ and $\mathbf{R}$ Output: $\mathbf{u}_i^*$ 1:while $(k \geq 1)$ do   2: for each (user $i \in [1, N]$) do   3:   Predict: $\mathbf{x}_i(k) \leftarrow \mathbf{x}_i(k+1)$; $\phi_i(k) \leftarrow \phi_i(k+1)$;/*from min of Eq. (8)*/   4: if $(\mathbf{x}_i(k+1) \equiv \mathbf{x}_i^*$ && $\phi_i(k+1) \equiv \phi_i^*$ for any $i \neq j, \forall j \in [1,N]$) then   5:   Send converged states to PMMUP;   6: PMMUP Updates: $\mathbf{y}(k) \leftarrow \mathbf{y}(k+1)$;   7: PMMUP Sends Updates to all NICs belonging to the same mesh point;   8: else /*UV do not converge Asynchronously*/ do go to Step 2;   9: end for each.   10:   if $(e(k+1) \leq \varepsilon_{rr}$ a small positive value) then   11:   Compute: $\mathbf{u}_i^* = -\mathbf{F}_{\phi^*} \mathbf{x}_i^*$ /* Local Optimization using Eq.(9)*/   12:   Add: $\mathbf{u}_i^*$ to Equation(1) of Section 4;   13:   else do go to Step 1;   14:   end if   15:end while   Here, $e(k+1) = \|\mathbf{g}(k+1) - \mathbf{g}(k)\|$, $\mathbf{g}(t) = \left[\mathbf{y}_i^T(k) \; \phi_i^T(k)\right]^T$,   and $\mathbf{g}(k+1) = \left[\mathbf{y}_i^T(k+1) \; \phi_i^T(k+1)\right]^T$.

6   Simulation Tests and Results

In our simulations, we used MATLAB version 7.1[21] to implement state information interactions between Link and Physical layers. We assumed 50 stationary wireless nodes randomly located in a 1200 m x 1200 m region. Each node had 4 NICs each tuned to a unique UCG. Thus, each UCG had 50 NICs assumed fully interconnected over a wireless medium. For evaluation purposes, we considered the frequency spectrum of 2412 MHz-2472 MHz. So that in each UCG, frequency carriers are: 2427 MHz, 2442 MHz, 2457 MHz and 2472 MHz. Other simulation specifications were used as illustrated in Table 3 from which design matrices were evaluated.

Fig. 3 shows the simulation when packets were generated by each node and the consumed energy per the transmitted amount of packets were recorded. Time slots of 0.1667% of Simulation time were allowed for at least 60 Monte Carlo Simulation runs for random network configurations. Four non-overlapping UCGs with adjacent power leakage factor of 0.5 were assumed. The results reveal that increasing the amount of generated traffic increases the amount of power needed. At 20 packets per slot, MRSUPA required 28.57% more power than a dynamic channel assignment with power control (DCA-PC) [10], 22.22%, and 66.67% less power than a load sensitive concurrent access protocol (LCAP) based method [16], and MUP without power control [8], respectively. This is due to the autonomy among the NICs, MRSUPA converges fast resulting in a low computational and transmission energy. However, MRSUPA is based on static channel assignments in contrast to the DCA-PC. Switching channels can resolve interference problems [9][10].

For a specific deployment area, the density of users was varied and the average throughput in a UCG was noted as shown in Fig. 4. We calibrated confidence intervals of about 95% plotted along the throughput performance results. When the network density was 2x10-5 , MRSUPA presented superior throughput of 79.17%, 54.17% and 33.33% more over the autonomous interference estimation (AIDPC) based method [12], MUP without power control [8] and DCA-PC [10], respectively. This is because, MRSUPA probes neighbours with a controlled

Table 3. Simulation Specifications

Parameter	Specs.	Parameter	Specification
Bandwidth:	10 MHz	Trx and Interf. Ranges:	240 m and 480 m
Basic rate:	2 Mbps	Probe Power:	Variable[Pmin,Pmax]
Max Link Rate:	54 Mbps	MAC scheme:	Time-Slotted CDMA
Min Trx Power:	10 mW	Slot time:	100 msec
SINR Threshold:	4-10 dB	Offered Load:	12.8,51.2,89.6,128 packets/s
Thermal Noise:	90 dB	Packet and FEC sizes:	1000 bytes and 50 bytes
Max Trx Power:	500 mW	Simulation Time:	60 seconds

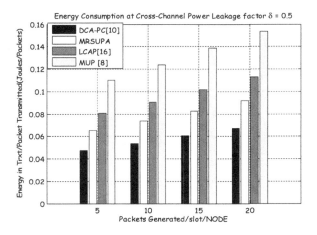

Fig. 3. Energy per transmitted data versus packets generation rate

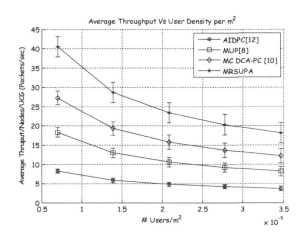

Fig. 4. Average Throughput per UCG versus Users' density

power level and unicasts data packets directionally. This results in a good spatial reuse for throughput enhancement.

Fig. 5 illustrates throughput performance with offered loads using a similar experiment as for Fig. 4. MRSUPA recorded the most superior throughput performance at various loads compared to the related methods. Specifically, at a load of 80 packets/s, MRSUPA yielded 65.38%, 48.08% and 19.23% more throughput than MUP [8], load sensitive striping (LS-striping) [11] and DCA-PC [10], respectively. This is because MRSUPA stripes arriving packets over all the Interfaces resulting in decongested queues. MUP makes use of only one channel and does not take transmission power into account. The LS striping does not

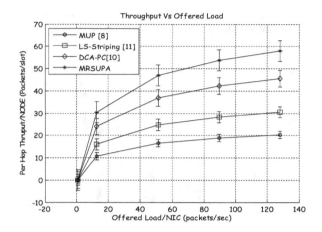

Fig. 5. Per Hop Throughput for every Multi-radio Node versus Offered Load

consider power control. Moreover, MRSUPA autonomously predicts channel state and queue conditions.

7   Conclusions

This paper has demonstrated effectively how to autonomously adapt transmission power in an MRMC WMN. Simulation results showed that using the PMMUP algorithm we can significantly achieve power conservation and throughput improvement for a multi-radio system. However, a scalable joint power control and routing problem with delay constraints in a MRMC WMN forms the basis of our future work.

References

1. Akylidiz, I.F., Wang, X., Wang, W.: Wireless Mesh Networks: a survey. J. Computer Networks 47, 445–487 (2005)
2. O'Hara, B., Petrick, A.: The IEEE 802.11 Handbook: A designer's Companion, 1st edn., 188 pages. IEEE, Los Alamitos (1999)
3. Engim Inc.: Multiple Channel 802.11 Chipset, http://www.engim.com/
4. Ishmael, J., Bury, S., Pezaros, D., Race, N.: Rural community wireless mesh networks. J. IEEE Internet Computing, 22–29 (2008)
5. Ramamurthi, V., Reaz, A., Dixit, S., Mukherjee, B.: Link scheduling and power control in Wireless Mesh Networks with Directional Antennas. In: Proc. ICC 2008, May 19-23, pp. 4835–4839 (2008)
6. Chen, L., Zhang, Q., Li, M., Jia, W.: Joint topology control and routing in IEEE 802.11 based multiradio multichannel mesh networks. IEEE Transactions on Vehicular Technology 56(5), 3123–3136 (2007)

7. Tang, J., Xue, G., Zhang, W.: End-to-end rate allocation in multi-radio wireless networks: cross-layer schemes. In: Proc. 3rd Intl. conf. QShine 2006, Waterloo, August 7-9, vol. 191(5) (2006)
8. Adya, A., Bahl, P., Padhye, J., Wolman, A., Zhou, L.: A Multi-Radio Unification Protocol for IEEE 802.11 Wireless Networks. In: Proc. 1st international conf. Broadband Networks, Broadnets 2004 (2004)
9. So, J., Vaidya, N.H.: Multi-channel MAC for ad hoc networks: handling multi-channel hidden terminals using a single transceiver. In: Proc. ACM Intl. Symposium on Mobil. Ad Hoc Netw. Comp. (MOBIHOC), pp. 222–233 (2004)
10. Tseng, Y.-C., Wu, S.-L., Lin, C.-Y., Shen, J.-P.: A multi-channel MAC protocol with power control for multi-hop ad hoc networks. In: Proc. Distributed Computing Systems Workshop, pp. 419–424 (2001)
11. Adiseshu, H., Parulkar, G., Varghes, G.: A Reliable and Scalable striping protocol. In: Proc. SIGCOMM (August 1996)
12. Sorooshyari, S., Gajic, Z.: Autonomous dynamic power control for wireless networks: user-centric and network-centric consideration. IEEE Trans. Wireless Commun. 7(3), 1004–1015 (2008)
13. Wang, K., Chiasserini, C.F., Proakis, J.G., Rao, R.R.: Joint scheduling and power control supporting multicasting in wireless ad hoc networks. J. Ad Hoc Networks 4, 532–546 (2006)
14. Koskie, S., Gajic, Z.: Optimal SIR-based power control strategies for wireless CDMA networks. J. Inform. And Syst. Sciences 1(1), 1–18 (2007)
15. Poojary, N., Krishnamurthy, S.V., Dao, S.: Medium access control in ad hoc mobile nodes with heterogeneous power capabilities. In: Proc. IEEE ICC, pp. 872–877 (2001)
16. Arora, A., Krunz, M.: Power controlled MAC for ad hoc networks with directional antennas. Elsevier Ad Hoc Networks 5, 145–161 (2007)
17. Winters, J.H., Martin, C.C., Sollenberger, N.R.: Forward Link smart antennas and power control for IS-136. In: Proc. IEEE 48th Vehicle Tech. Conf. 1998, vol. 1, pp. 601–605 (1998)
18. Mahmoud, M.S., Hassan, M.F., Darwish, M.G.: Large Scale Control Systems Theories and Techniques. Dekkar, New York (1985)
19. Gajic, Z., Shen, X.: Parallel algorithms for optimal control of large scale linear systems. Springer, Heidelberg (1993)
20. Abdelwahed, S.S., Hassan, M.F., Sultan, M.A.: Parallel asynchronous algorithms for optimal control of large scale dynamic systems. J. Optimal Control applications and methods 18 (1997)
21. MathWorks Inc.: http://www.mathworks.com/

A Decentralized Approach to Minimum-Energy Broadcasting in Static Ad Hoc Networks

Chris Miller and Christian Poellabauer

Department of Computer Science and Engineering
University of Notre Dame
miller.444@nd.edu, cpoellab@cse.nd.edu

Abstract. Due to the limited resources of most wireless ad hoc and sensor networks, minimizing the cost of commonly used broadcasts is of utmost importance. This has led to work in the minimum energy broadcasting problem. Most solutions require global topology knowledge, however, this information is typically not available in ad hoc applications. Decentralized approaches have been unable to match the energy efficiency of centralized methods. Previous approaches have also relied upon locality information to estimate link cost, which is unreliable. In this paper, we will describe a new distributed approach to the minimum energy broadcasting problem which targets multi-packet broadcast sessions. It constructs a broadcast tree in a distributed fashion using link quality measurements to more accurately estimate link cost. We show by simulation, and confirm through experimentation, that our protocol is capable of constructing a tree that is near to centralized approaches in energy cost.

1 Introduction

Wireless sensor networks and ad hoc networks are a collection of small wireless devices, typically battery powered, that may be static or mobile, and may configure in an ad hoc fashion. Broadcasting is a commonly used feature in wireless networking. It may be used for file distribution, re-tasking, event notification or miscellaneous maintenance. Naive approaches to broadcasting can be extremely costly in terms of network energy usage. It can also result in a high percentage of collisions which could prevent full dissemination. Due to the limited resources of most wireless devices, minimizing the cost of broadcasts is of utmost importance to extending network lifetime.

The minimum energy needed to broadcast a packet to all nodes in a network from a designated source can be found by adjusting the transmission power of each node's radio to achieve a fully connected tree with the minimum transmission cost. This is known as the minimum-energy broadcast tree problem, and it has been shown to be NP-complete [1,2]. Several sub-optimal approximations have been proposed based upon minimum spanning trees [3,2,4], but these have required global knowledge of the topology. In many typical wireless networks, however, there would not be a global knowledge of the topology available at any

P.M. Ruiz and J.J. Garcia-Luna-Aceves (Eds.): ADHOC-NOW 2009, LNCS 5793, pp. 298–311, 2009.
© Springer-Verlag Berlin Heidelberg 2009

centralized node. Distributed and localized approaches have been made [5,6], but these have not been able to match the performance of the centralized approaches. Furthermore, both centralized and de-centralized approaches have used location information for determining the transmission power needed to maintain links. This is not a reliable method of determining link cost, as shown by [7,8]. In this paper, we propose Dynamic Broadcast Incremental Power (DynaBIP), which constructs a broadcast tree in a distributed fashion using only locally available information and that contained within packet headers. No locality information is needed, as DynaBIP uses received signal strength measurements for the estimation of all link costs. Our goals in the design of this protocol are to provide a distributed protocol which can construct a broadcast tree which nears the energy efficiency of centralized approaches, with a minimal overhead which can be amortized over a short broadcast session.

1.1   Related Work

One approach to dynamically generating a broadcast tree in a distributed fashion is to use a modified version of topology control algorithms to reduce forwarders and adjust transmit powers. Cartigny et al. proposed RBOP [9] and LBOP [10] which used a neighbor elimination scheme (NES) for a reduced neighbor set. RBOP used the relative neighborhood graph (RNG) [11] to provide the limited set of neighbors that each node would monitor in the NES to determine if it needed to forward the packet. A node which did forward the packet would adjust its transmission power to the minimum needed to cover the uncovered nodes. LBOP used an identical algorithm, but used the local minimum spanning tree (LMST) [12], which provides a smaller subset. TR-LBOP [13] is built upon LBOP, but it aims for an optimal transmit radius in transmit power selection. These broadcast protocols need only local position information which can be provided by immediate neighbors, however they are not able to provide the same level of energy efficiency as centralized protocols, and all NES schemes will result in some redundant transmissions due to the hidden terminal problem.

   Many approaches to the minimum-energy broadcast problem have been based on minimum spanning trees, such as BIP [3], MLE [4], EWMA [2], and MWIA [14]. These are centralized protocols which require global information of the network topology. Most wireless networks, however, do not have this information available. The most widely referenced solution to the minimum-energy broadcast tree problem is BIP, which has been shown to approximate the optimal solution within a constant ratio [15]. BIP is a centralized protocol which constructs a broadcast tree using a formula similar to Prim's algorithm for constructing a MST. It adds nodes to a tree rooted at the source one by one, but instead of using link cost it uses incremental cost at each step. This modification allows BIP to benefit from the wireless multicast advantage.

   Distributed and localized approaches to BIP have been made. Wieselthier et al. proposed two distributed versions, Dist-BIP-A and Dist-BIP-G [5,16]. In Dist-BIP-A, a source node constructs a BIP tree of its immediate neighbors. It then broadcast its local tree at the power sufficient to reach all of its neighbors. Each node that receives the broadcast will then construct its own local tree, incorporating the tree forwarded in the packet. Dist-BIP-G uses a similar approach, but designates gateway nodes to reduce the number of transmissions in the tree construction process. The tree constructed from these distributed protocols is not able to match the energy efficiency of the centralized protocol, and the overhead cost of the construction may be high.

LBIP [6] is a localized approach to BIP. It uses a similar approach as Dist-BIP, using 2-hop locality information which it has gathered from neighbors. The source node constructs a local BIP tree for its 2-hop neighborhood and includes the local tree with the broadcast of the packet. Nodes which are designated as senders in the tree will construct their own local tree building upon the tree provided. This method allows the broadcast tree to be constructed dynamically for each broadcast, without the setup cost. Simulation results showed LBIP performed close to the efficiency of BIP in dense networks, but the need to incorporate a NES scheme for reliability hindered its ability to match the centralized protocol.

1.2 Contributions

We propose a new distributed protocol, DynaBIP, which uses signal strength measurements to determine link costs, and places the decision process during tree construction on the child nodes. This makes DynaBIP adaptable to any environment, and tree construction is based on a more accurate model of the network, allowing DynaBIP to achieve the full potential of its energy savings. Simulation will show that DynaBIP performs closely to an ideal centralized approach, and these results are supported through experimentation.

2 Dynamic Broadcast Incremental Power

BIP and related protocols provide a good approximation of the minimum-energy broadcast tree. One related requirement, however, is that they all use location information for determining link cost. Location information may be obtained with a GPS device, or by using a localization algorithm, but these can be expensive in energy cost. In addition, there may be additional energy costs associated with propagating the locality information to neighboring nodes, or a centralized node. Of greater concern, though, is the unreliability of computing link cost based on distance. It has been shown that link quality is not consistent with distance [7,8], and that signal propagation can vary widely in different environments. If the degree of pathloss is underestimated, then the calculated transmit powers will be insufficient, and the broadcast tree will become disconnected and incomplete. If the degree of pathloss is overestimated, the calculated transmit powers will be greater than necessary, resulting in reduced energy efficiency and possibly contention.

Distributed implementations of BIP have difficulty approximating the centralized broadcast tree because the nodes constructing local broadcast trees have

limited knowledge of alternate paths to their neighbors. This can result in redundant or inefficient selections, since a node which may designate itself as a
parent is out of immediate range of another potential parent of the child node,
and it is therefore unaware of its actions.

We propose a new distributed approach to this problem to address these issues. Dynamic Broadcast Incremental Power (DynaBIP) performs a distributed
construction of a broadcast tree using received signal strength (RSS) measurements to estimate link costs. It has been shown that RSS measurements have
small variance over short time frames for individual links, and can provide a good
approximation of link quality [8,17,18]. This allows each node to adapt individually to the signal propagation properties of each link. The link cost estimations
are thereby more accurate than can be achieved by path loss calculations, and
adaptable to changes. Construction of the tree is managed by the child nodes,
instead of the parent nodes, to provide a more complete vision of the available
routes. Since child nodes are aware of all potential routes to themselves, they
can determine the optimal path better than a parent node working with partial
information.

2.1   DynaBIP Tree Construction Algorithm

The tree construction of DynaBIP can be completed with a single sweeping
flood across the network. The source node will initiate the tree construction
by broadcasting the first packet. It will include in the header of the packet its
transmit power, P_{src} and the route to this node (a null array for the source).
Each node that receives this broadcast will compare the RSS to the transmit
power, P_{src}, to determine the path loss for this link. If P_i is the initial transmit
power used by node i, the path loss for a link $i \rightarrow j$ may be depicted as

$$PathLoss_{ij} = P_i - RSS \tag{1}$$

Adding this value to the radio receiving threshold needed for the desired SNR
will provide the transmit power necessary to maintain this link. The link cost
can then be represented as

$$C_{ij} = R_{Thresh} + PathLoss_{ij} \tag{2}$$

The link cost, C_{ij}, will be saved in the $Link\_Cost$ table of node j. Each node
will store the route in the header in their $Route\_Cache$, indexed by the sending
node's ID, in this case the source's ID. It will then schedule a rebroadcast of
this packet at a delay proportional to C_{ij} in milliWatts. If it receives another
broadcast of this packet from a closer node (a lower cost link), it will cancel the
previously scheduled rebroadcast, and schedule a new rebroadcast with a delay
proportional to the new link cost. The formula for the delay is

$$ForwardingDelay = \beta \times C_{ij}[mW] \tag{3}$$

where β is the delay multiplier. There is a tradeoff between contention and
latency of tree construction for the multiplier. In our trials, we found that β

values between the range 10 to 100 ms/mW provided a good balance between contention and latency.

The node which has the lowest cost link from the source will rebroadcast first. It will include in its header its transmit power, P_i, the route to this node, which will include only the source node, and the transmit power needed by the source to maintain this link, C_{si}. When the source node overhears this broadcast, it will recognize that is has been selected as the parent for node i. It will update its transmit power for the broadcast session, T_{src}, to the link cost provided in the header, C_{si}. It will also add i to its list of children, and send an acknowledgment to the new child node. Other nodes which overhear the broadcast will store the link cost to the new node, C_{ij}, in their $Link\_Cost$ table, and cache the new route. They will also update T_{src} in their $Transmit\_Power$ table to the link cost value in the header, C_{si}. If C_{ij} has a lower cost than the previous link to the source, or if this is the first copy of the packet it has received, it will schedule a rebroadcast at a delay proportional to the cost of the new link. This process is then repeated by each node that receives a copy of the broadcast.

When a node reaches its scheduled rebroadcast time, it will perform a calculation to determine which link among the nodes currently in the broadcast tree will provide the minimum incremental cost. It does this by scanning through the routing cache. For each entry in the routing cache, it compares the current transmit power of the last hop to the link cost from the last hop in the route to itself. The minimum difference among these entries is the link that will be selected for this node's addition to the broadcast tree. The algorithm for selecting the new link to add at node j is shown in Algorithm 1, where r_i is an entry in the routing cache with last hop node i. The route which provides this minimum incremental cost will then be selected by the node for the next addition. It will set its parent to the last hop node in this route, and will include this route in the packet header, along with the link cost needed by its parent, C_{ij}.

Algorithm 1. Minimum Incremental Cost Link Selection

$minCost \leftarrow \infty$
for all $r_i \in RouteCache$ **do**
  $incrementalCost \leftarrow C_{ij} - T_i$
  if $incrementalCost < minCost$ **then**
    $minCost \leftarrow incrementalCost$
    $parent \leftarrow i$
    $minRoute \leftarrow r_i$
  end if
end for

The proportional delay is what allows DynaBIP to emulate a global incremental power algorithm in the tree construction process. In each case, the link with the minimum additional energy cost will be the node which is added to the tree next. This concept will continue to work over links of varying hop counts. Consider the topology in Figure 1. The source initiates a broadcast at time unit 0. Node B has

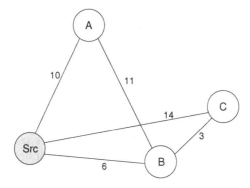

Fig. 1. Example of node selection order of DynaBIP

the lowest link cost, and will schedule a rebroadcast at time unit 6, representing an incremental cost of 6. Node A will schedule its broadcast at time unit 10, and node C at time unit 14. When node B rebroadcasts at time unit 6, node C will cancel its scheduled broadcast at time unit 14, and will reschedule it for time unit 9, since it has a link cost of 3 from node B. Node A will not alter its scheduled rebroadcast time since the link to B is not less than the link to the source. Node C will then be the second node to rebroadcast, with an incremental link cost of 3. Finally, node A will rebroadcast at time unit 10, with an incremental link cost of $C_{SrcA} - C_{SrcB} = 4$. This is the same ordering of adding nodes and links to the broadcast tree as would be observed by the centralized BIP algorithm. The ordering in which nodes are added to the broadcast tree globally may not be precisely by incremental link cost, but locally it is a close approximation.

2.2   Flooding Power Selection

As mentioned in the previous section, the construction of the DynaBIP tree can be completed in a single flood. The cost of tree construction will then be dependent upon the initial transmit power used by the nodes during the flooding phase. The simplest method of implementing the flooding phase of the tree construction is to have each node broadcast at full power. This incurs the highest cost of construction, but requires no information of local topology. As long as the network is fully connected, the broadcast tree will be complete. This method will provide the closest approximation of the BIP broadcast tree for low to medium density networks, since all links will be explored. For high density networks, however, flooding at maximum power can lead to excessive contention and collisions, which could hamper the quality of the broadcast tree and lead to additional construction costs for resends. A lower power may be used for the standard flood method to reduce construction cost and collisions, but without a more intelligent algorithm, full connectivity can not be guaranteed.

The relative neighborhood graph (RNG) [11] provides a fully connected graph with a slightly higher level of redundancy than a MST. By setting the transmit power of each node in the flooding phase to the minimum power needed to cover their RNG neighbors, a near minimal power is used to maintain full connectivity. The slightly higher level of redundancy provided by RNG versus MST leads to a fairly high quality broadcast tree. Though not as optimal as a standard flood in a collision-free environment, it performed very well in comparison to a standard flood in an environment with contention and collisions.

The determination of the RNG neighborhood is performed locally. This requires 2-hop neighborhood information at each node. This information may be maintained using beacon messages, similar to methods used by LBIP [6] and Dist-BIP [5]. Instead of including the location of each of its neighbors, however, nodes will include the link cost to each of its neighbors. As with the tree construction algorithm, our construction of the RNG is based upon energy cost of a link rather than distance.

2.3   Sweep Method

The BIP algorithm includes a method of performing a sweep following the initial construction of the broadcast tree in order to remove redundant links due to the wireless broadcast advantage [3]. The sweep operation may be performed an unlimited number of times, but practice has shown that two iterations is usually sufficient to reach the optimal level. To mimic this operation in a distributed fashion, each node will perform a sweep to determine if an alternate parent may be chosen to reduce transmission cost. After determining a parent and rebroadcasting the initial packet, each node will schedule a sweep operation following a fixed delay period. This delay period will be long enough to allow the initial tree construction process to be completed among its immediate neighborhood. Following this delay, it will perform the same scan of its routing cache as it did during the initial construction phase. If a better parent candidate has increased its transmit power to a level high enough to reach itself, it will select the alternate parent. The previous parent will remove the sending node from its child list, and adjust its transmit power to the minimum needed to cover its remaining children, if any.

2.4   Error Handling

Ensuring that the broadcast tree constructed includes all nodes in the network is an important qualification for our protocol. In order to accomplish this, acknowledgment messages are used. When a node overhears a message that indicates it has been selected as a parent, it will send an acknowledgment packet to the child node to verify that it has added it to its child list. If an Ack from the parent is not received during a short time interval, the packet will be resent. Resends will take place after random delays in order to avoid synchronization of contending nodes. This will ensure that all links are added as expected in case of a dropped packet or collision. An implicit acknowledgment process is also used to ensure that all nodes are included in the construction phase. Each node monitors its RNG neighbors for broadcasts. If any RNG neighbor does not rebroadcast the message, then it may assume this neighbor did not receive a copy of the message, and will resend the message to them. This will ensure that all nodes are included in the tree construction.

3   Results

3.1   Simulation

To evaluate DynaBIP, it was implemented in the Jist/Swans simulation environment [19,20], a scalable wireless ad hoc network simulator based in Java. Swans provides a full representation of the complete network layer model, with accurate representations of a wireless environment, including path loss, environmental noise and collision interference. Each node in the simulation was implemented with an 802.11 radio, with a maximum transmit power of 11 dBm. The environment was modeled using free space path loss with a pathloss exponent of 2 or 4. A fixed field size was used for each simulation, with an increasing number of nodes to provide an increasing density. Each iteration of simulations is performed 100 times, with a differing random node placement for each run. Only trials with a fully connected network topology were included in the results, which primarily affected the trials with node density 50. The results provided are arranged by average node degree. Due to the random placement of nodes in Jist/Swans, the degree of each node can differ drastically from the average node degree. Figure 2 depicts the average node degree for each node density, as well as the minimum and maximum node degree.

For comparison, BIP [3] and LBIP [6] are also implemented in Jist/Swans. BIP provides an optimal benchmark for a distributed solution. The simulations for BIP do not include actual radio transmissions. It is merely a calculation of the BIP tree based on the same topologies as the DynaBIP simulations, assuming that the centralized node in BIP knows the precise energy cost of each link. This implementation of BIP utilizes two sweep operations to provide the minimum cost BIP tree possible. LBIP is provided to allow a comparison to a strong

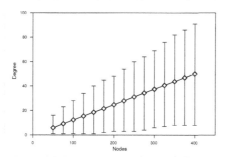

Fig. 2. The average degree of connectivity by node density. The values plotted show the minimum and maximum node degree for each density.

distributed implementation of BIP. LBIP is a localized protocol, so it does not incur the construction cost of a distributed protocol, but provides a good approximation of the energy cost of BIP. The implementation of LBIP uses the NES scheme for RNG neighbors to ensure a fully connected broadcast tree. The primary metrics used to evaluate the protocols are tree construction cost and energy cost of the broadcast tree. As in [6], the energy cost will be represented as EER, the Expended Energy Ratio. EER is the ratio of energy consumed by a protocol in comparison to the energy that would have been consumed by a blind flood. It is defined as

$$EER = \frac{E_{protocol}}{E_{flooding}} \times 100. \tag{4}$$

The graphs in Figure 3 show the total energy cost of the constructed broadcast tree by average node degree, normalized to the cost of BIP. The first graph shows the resulting tree when the environment is modeled with a pathloss exponent of 2, and the second with a pathloss exponent of 4. These results show that Dyna-BIP performs very closely with the centralized BIP protocol. It is important to note here that the results for BIP and LBIP assume that they are able to perfectly estimate the required transmission power to maintain a link based on locality information. Therefore, the plots for BIP and LBIP may be considered ideal results. DynaBIP uses the actual observed link cost, so it will perform consistently regardless of variations in the pathloss properties of the environment. Despite this, DynaBIP still performs very strongly in comparison to the ideal plots of BIP and LBIP.

DynaBIP is designed for session-based broadcast, that is, multi-packet broadcasts. There is an overhead cost associated with the construction phase of Dyna-BIP. In order for DynaBIP to be viable, the construction cost must be small enough that it can be quickly amortized over a small number of packets in order to provide a total energy cost for a broadcast session which is lower than alternatives. This includes all acknowledgment messages and any recovery messages that are necessary, since reliability of tree construction is considered a priority of

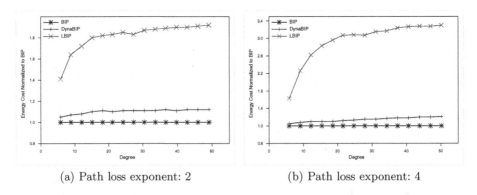

(a) Path loss exponent: 2   (b) Path loss exponent: 4

Fig. 3. Total broadcast tree energy cost normalized to the energy cost of BIP

our protocol. BIP does not require any transmissions for tree construction, since it is computed on a central node, however it will be necessary to disseminate the constructed broadcast tree to the nodes in the network, which may include control messages to ensure reliability. This cost has not been factored into any plot of BIP. LBIP does not have a construction cost because it is a localized protocol which constructs the tree dynamically. Therefore, the broadcast tree cost is the construction cost. As a result, LBIP may provide a more efficient alternative for single packet broadcasts. For session-based broadcast, however, where multiple packets are distributed, the energy savings of a more efficient broadcast tree will provide the best overall savings. Figure 4 shows how the energy cost per packet compares for increasing file sizes. For DynaBIP, this includes the energy cost of construction. The first graph is for a low density network, average node degree 5.85, with a path loss exponent of 4. The second graph is for a high density network with an average node degree of 50.14. As the number of packets in the broadcast increases, the overhead of construction is amortized over more packets, providing a higher level of efficiency per packet.

There are two plots for DynaBIP in Figure 4. The first plot assumes that all packet sizes will be equal, including those in the construction phase. This is not entirely accurate, however, since construction phase packets need only include the header information, which is small. The construction phase also includes acknowledgment and recovery messages, which are also relatively small. This would reduce the impact of the higher transmission cost of the construction phase since only a fraction of the number of bytes would be transmitted. The second plot, DynaBIP-weighted, shows how the session-based broadcast cost would compare if the packets were weighted by their actual packet size, including any network and MAC layer headers. This plot is based on a chunk size of 1000 bytes. The weighted DynaBIP performs close to the efficiency level of centralized BIP after only a few packets, and provides lower total energy cost than LBIP

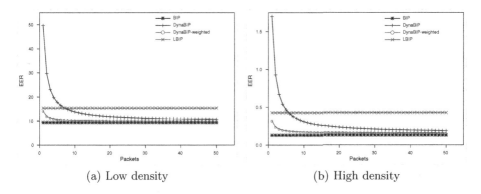

(a) Low density   (b) High density

Fig. 4. Total broadcast session energy cost plotted by number of packets. For DynaBIP, this includes all control messages necessary for tree construction. DynaBIP-weighted is based on a chunk size of 1000 bytes.

after only a single packet. Even under the unweighted DynaBIP plot, the overall energy efficiency of DynaBIP exceeds LBIP after just a handful of packets.

3.2   Experimentation

To further validate the results of the simulation, we implemented DynaBIP on a set of Crossbow Stargate devices [21]. The testbed consisted of 12 SPB400CB gateway devices with 802.11b CompactFlash wireless ethernet cards. The wireless cards have a transmit power range of -10 dBM to 13dBm. We divided the transmit power control range into 64 discrete levels, and for each measured the output transmit power in dBm, and the corresponding current in amperes. A plot of these values is shown in Figure 5.

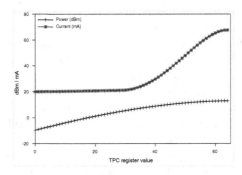

Fig. 5. Plot of radio transmission power in dBm and current in mA for range of values used in transmit power control

The devices were arranged in a residential indoor environment. For each test, a 26 KB file was distributed. The file was divided into 27 chunks, each 1000 bytes, except the last chunk which included the remainder. In order to ensure strong links which minimize packet errors, the transmit power calculation included a 10 dB buffer to provide a SNR of at least 10 dB. Therefore, the equation for link cost estimation from node i to j in decibels is

$$C_{ij} = TransmitPower_i - RSSI_j + Noise_j + 10dB \tag{5}$$

The file distribution tests were run on the Stargate testbed five times, at various times of alternate days. We logged the calculated link cost for all node pairs for each test. As expected, these values varied among the different tests, in some cases significantly. This is due to changes in the environment during each of the test, such as obstacles which have moved, changes in the wireless environment, etc. Also, distance was not a reliable indicator of path cost, and the path cost of each link is typically not reciprocal. As a result, centralized protocols could not perform as optimally as expected in a real environment, because the path cost estimations used in their calculations are not reliable. This can lead to inefficiency or disconnected components.

For each test, the measured link cost for all node pairs was used to determine the broadcast tree that would have been constructed by a centralized BIP algorithm, if it was provided with the actual link cost calculated in the test. This is provided as a comparison to an ideal scenario, since centralized minimum energy broadcast algorithms such as BIP would typically estimate link cost based on distance. A comparison for each of the trials is provided in Table 1.

Table 1. Total Cost of Broadcast Tree

Trial	BIP	Cascade	%Diff
1	82.96	83.37	0.5%
2	108.6	69.53	-36.0%
3	61.8	62.31	0.8%
4	88.08	62.89	-28.6%
5	66.85	62.21	-6.9%
Average	81.66	68.06	-16.6%

This table shows that our distributed approach to the minimum energy broadcast tree solution performed well in comparison to the centralized approach, and actually outperformed BIP on average. This seems suprising, but the reason for this is due to the order of node addition to the tree structure. In BIP, this order is purely based on incremental cost. In our implementation, we emulate this process by delaying the action of nodes based upon the link cost. However, since the cost at the lowest transmit power is 20 mA, we set the delay to be proportional to the difference from 20 mA in the implementation. An unintended but beneficial consequence of this is that nodes which are two-hops downstream select their parent earlier in the process, allowing nodes which are one-hop downstream to use this information in their parent selection process.

To further validate the results of our test, we computed the total energy cost of each file distribution to compare to the efficiency we observed in our simulations. We logged every transmission, along with the size in bytes of the packet and the transmission power. We used this to compute the total energy cost of the distribution, including the tree construction phase and any recovery messages, in milliampere seconds. We also computed the total energy cost that would have resulted from a blind flood, so that we could compute the EER (Expended Energy Ratio) as we did for the simulations. The average degree of connectivity of the tests was around 9. Based on the low density graph in Figure 4, the EER for a broadcast session of 27 packets was about 10.03. Our observed results from the implementation showed an average EER of 9.27, which may be expected from a slightly denser network.

4   Conclusions

Through simulation and experimentation we have shown that DynaBIP is capable of constructing broadcast trees very close in efficiency to an ideal measure of centralized BIP, with an acceptable construction cost that may be amortized over a small number of packets. Our results have shown that DynaBIP provides a closer approximation of BIP for session-based broadcast than LBIP. Most importantly, DynaBIP has shown that it is capable of performing well in comparison to ideal evaluations of centralized BIP and distributed variations, without relying on any information about the environment. Previous approaches depend heavily on their ability to accurately estimate the transmit power necessary to maintain links. If these protocols underestimate this cost, the broadcast trees will become fractured and incomplete. If they overestimate the link cost, the protocols will not provide the level of energy efficiency expected. The strength of DynaBIP is its ability to adjust to the pathloss properties of any environment, even when those properties differ among links in the same network. Also, by placing the decision process of tree construction on the child nodes, rather than the parent nodes, DynaBIP is able to construct a more efficient tree than other distributed algorithms. This is because child nodes have a more complete picture of the routes available to them than their potential parents.

While it was not evaluated in this paper, DynaBIP may be easily tailored to handle different cost metrics in the decision process of tree construction. For instance, there may be a fixed cost associated with any node transmitting due to resources needed to power up the radio, perform processor computations, etc. These costs can easily be factored into the decision process by adding the fixed cost to the estimated link cost. Also, many wireless devices offer only a limited number of discrete power level adjustments. This can be factored into link cost evaluations by providing a ceiling function which rounds the link cost to the next highest power level. For each of these situations, the algorithm will perform the same as before, using the desired adjusted cost metrics. DynaBIP could also be tailored to factor in other desired metrics in the cost decision process, such as remaining battery power. This makes it an easily extendable distributed protocol for achieving minimum-energy cost broadcast trees with multiple decision criteria.

References

1. Liang, W.: Constructing minimum-energy broadcast trees in wireless ad hoc networks. In: Proceedings of the 3rd International Symposium on Mobile Ad Hoc Networking and Computing, pp. 112–122. ACM, New York (2002)
2. Zagalj, M., Hubaux, J.P., Enz, C.C.: Minimum-energy broadcast in all-wireless networks: Np-completeness and distribution issues. In: Proceedings of the 8th Annual International Conference on Mobile Computing and Networking (2002)
3. Wieselthier, J.E., Nguyen, G.D., Ephremides, A.: On the construction of energy-efficient broadcast and multicast trees in wireless networks. In: INFOCOM (2000)
4. Cheng, M.X., Sun, J., Min, M., Du, D.Z.: Energy-efficient broadcast and multicast routing in ad hoc wireless networks. In: Proceedings of IPCCC, pp. 87–94 (2003)
5. Wieselthier, J., Nguyen, G., Ephremides, A.: Distributed algorithms for energy-efficient broadcasting in ad hoc networks. In: Proceedings of MILCOM (2002)

6. Ingelrest, F., Simplot-Ryl, D.: Localized broadcast incremental power protocol for wireless ad hoc networks. In: Proceedings of the 10th IEEE Symposium on Computers and Communications, pp. 28–33. IEEE Computer Society, Los Alamitos (2005)
7. Souryal, M., Klein-Berndt, L., Miller, L., Moayeri, N.: Link assessment in an indoor 802.11 network. In: Proceedings of the IEEE Wireless Communications and Networking Conference (2006)
8. Erdogan, S.Z., Hussain, S.: Using received signal strength variation for energy efficient data dissemination in wireless sensor networks. In: Wagner, R., Revell, N., Pernul, G. (eds.) DEXA 2007. LNCS, vol. 4653. Springer, Heidelberg (2007)
9. Cartigny, J., Simplot, D., Stojmenovic, I.: Localized minimum-energy broadcasting in ad-hoc networks. In: Proceedings of INFOCOM (2003)
10. Cartigny, J., Ingelrest, F., Simplot-Ryl, D., Stojmenovic, I.: Localized lmst and rng based minimum-energy broadcast protocols in ad hoc networks. Ad Hoc Networks 3(1), 1–16 (2005)
11. Toussaint, G.T.: The relative neighbourhood graph of a finite planar set. Pattern Recognition 12(4), 261–268 (1980)
12. Li, N., Hou, J., Sha, L.: Design and analysis of an mst-based topology control algorithm. IEEE Transactions on Wireless Communications 4(3), 1195–1206 (2005)
13. Ingelrest, F., Simplot-Ryl, D., Stojmenovic, I.: Target transmission radius over lmst for energy-efficient broadcast protocol in ad hoc networks. In: Proceedings of the IEEE International Conference on Communications (June 2004)
14. Cheng, M.X., Sun, J., Min, M., Li, Y., Wu, W.: Energy-efficient broadcast and multicast routing in multihop ad hoc wireless networks. Wireless Communications and Mobile Computing 6, 213–223 (2006)
15. Wan, P.J., Calinescu, G., Li, X., Frieder, O.: Minimum-energy broadcast routing in static ad hoc wireless networks. In: Proceedings of INFOCOM, pp. 1162–1171 (2001)
16. Wieselthier, J., Nguyen, G., Ephremides, A.: The energy efficiency of distributed algorithms for broadcasting in ad hoc networks. In: Proceedings of the 5th International Symposium on Wireless Personal Multimedia Communications (2002)
17. Srinivasan, K., Levis, P.: Rssi is under appreciated. In: Proceedings of the 3rd Workshop on Embedded Networked Sensors (May 2006)
18. Reis, C., Mahajan, R., Rodrig, M., Wetherall, D., Zahorjan, J.: Measurement-based models of delivery and interference in static wireless networks. In: Proceedings of the Special Interest Group on Data Communication, pp. 51–62. ACM, New York (2006)
19. Barr, R., Haas, Z.: Jist - java in simulation time / swans - scalable wireless ad hoc network simulator (April 2004), http://jist.ece.cornell.edu
20. Barr, R., Haas, Z.J., van Renesse, R.: Jist: an efficient approach to simulation using virtual machines. Software - Practice and Experience 35(6), 539–576 (2005)
21. Crossbow Technology: Low-power wireless mote solutions overview (2009), http://www.xbow.com/Products/wproductsoverview.aspx

Heavily Reducing WSNs' Energy Consumption by Employing Hardware-Based Compression

Grigorios Chrysos and Ioannis Papaefstathiou

Department of Electronic and Computer Engineering,
Technical University of Crete, Chania,
GR 73100, Greece
chrysos@mhl.tuc.gr, ygp@mhl.tuc.gr

Abstract. Power consumption is a crucial issue for Wireless Sensor Networks (WSNs). The overall energy in the WSN nodes is consumed in three distinct processes: data processing, sensing the surroundings and data transmission. If data compression is applied, the energy consumed for data processing is increased whereas the transmission power consumption is reduced. In this paper we present, for the first time, that one way of significantly reducing the overall energy consumption of a WSN framework is to off-load the compression task to small, very low-cost reconfigurable hardware devices which are connected to the main processor of the WSN nodes. Based on our real-world experiments, this innovative approach can reduce the overall energy consumed by a state-of-the-art WSN by at least 46% and up to 56%!

1 Introduction

Wireless Sensor Networks (WSNs) have been proposed for various applications. Each WSN consists of many interconnected nodes (i.e. motes). The motes communicate with each other wirelessly and their main goals are the sensing of the surroundings, the collection of measurements and the wireless transmission of the data-packets to a central node (sink) of the WSN. The main parts of a typical sensor node are the processing unit, which has limited memory and computational power, the communication unit, which is responsible for sending/receiving packets and the sensing unit for the data collection.

One crucial characteristic of every WSN node is its power consumption. The nodes are powered by batteries which usually can not be recharged or changed. The overall energy in the WSN nodes is consumed in three distinct processes: data processing, sensing the surroundings and data transmission. Experimental measurements have shown that the energy consumed for data processing is considerably less than that consumed by the communication circuits. Therefore, one of the goals of the WSNs designers is to reduce the number of packets, as well their size that are sent over the network, by using data aggregation and/or compression. Various studies, such as the one in [6], demonstrated that the energy for sending/receiving just one bit of information is equal to the energy consumed by hundreds of commands executed in the processing unit. At the same time, the complexity of the data compression and aggregation

P.M. Ruiz and J.J. Garcia-Luna-Aceves (Eds.): ADHOC-NOW 2009, LNCS 5793, pp. 312–326, 2009.

algorithms triggers a significant increase in the processing energy consumption. As a result, a very important question is how the WSN data can be compressed in a way that the energy consumed for data compression is significantly less than that saved by reducing the data transmitted.

Moving to a different sector, Field Programmable Gate Array (FPGA) manufacturers have constructed small low-cost (i.e. less than $5) Complex Programmable Logic Devices (CPLDs) which are programmable logic devices with architectural features of Programmable Logic Arrays (PLAs) and FPGAs. The main characteristics of the CPLDs are their very low energy consumption coupled nowadays with a relative high frequency rate when executing certain data manipulation tasks. On the other hand, the main disadvantage of the CPLDs is their small number of resources allowing them to execute only relatively small, yet very CPU intensive tasks.

In this paper we present, for the first time, that one way of significantly reducing the processing power consumption associated with the compression, is to off-load the compression task to a CPLD. As our real world experimental results clearly demonstrate our CPLD-based approach can reduce the overall energy consumption of a WSN framework by more than 46%.

The rest of this paper is organized as follows: Sections 2 presents the previous work on compression in WSN environments, while Section 3 briefly describes the selected encoding and decoding algorithms. Section 4 presents our implementation, while Section 5 briefly outlines our pioneering platform and Section 6 and 7 demonstrate the performance of our approach when measured in a real-world environment. Finally, Section 8 concludes our work.

2 Related Work

Many schemes have been proposed for the reduction of the data transmitted over WSNs such as the ones presented in [6], [7] and [9]. In particular the techniques utilized for this purpose are mainly three: aggregation, compression and encoding.

Data aggregation techniques [2] are highly coupled with the WSNs' routing protocols. These techniques have great impact on the efficiency of the network and very frequently on the time of life of a WSN. The main methodology followed by such schemes is that the data collected from the neighbor nodes are grouped together so as to create a new unified packet which is finally transmitted over the network[3],[4]; as a result these methods reduce the number of packets that are sent over the WSN. The aggregation algorithms take advantage of the motes placement. This idea led to the implementation of specific algorithms that cluster the nodes in groups in order to reduce the number of transmissions [5].

There are many data compression algorithms presented in the bibliography like BWT, LZE, LZ77, PPM ([6], [7]). The problem with most of the compression algorithms is the size of the memory they occupy. The implementation of each one of them usually requests a large storage area in processing unit's memory which is a severe drawback for the almost memoryless motes.

Moreover, there are certain algorithms, like Huffman encoding [10], in which each character or value that tends to appear frequently has a smaller representation width than the source characters appearing less frequent. In general, encoding algorithms are not very complex and this makes them suitable for WSN applications.

There are numerous research groups that have proposed the use of hardware-assisted data compression in low power embedded systems, such as [11]. Those systems minimize the processing power consumption by compressing the data stored in the memory/cache of the processor; by doing so they reduce the power consumption for the data propagation over the memory bus.

Obviously, our approach is totally different since we are compressing the WSN data in such a way so as to reduce the data-items transmitted. The only work similar to ours is the one by Alippi et al[8]; in this paper the authors propose a simple hardware-assisted scheme for detecting microacoustic emissions generated by formation/organization of cracks and they present a suitable lossless technique for microacoustic event compression. The main differences between this work and our approach are that (a) we have implemented a general purpose compression system that can be applied in numerous WSN environments, (b) our system is based on the most widely used WSN infrastructure, (c) we have performed both real-world experiments and experiments based on widely-used benchmarks that demonstrate the efficiency of our approach. For the system in [8] there are no performance or power consumption results whereas no information is provided regarding the actual WSN environment it can be connected to and more importantly their compression algorithm is application specific.

3 Huffman Algorithm

The data reduction algorithm we have implemented is Huffman encoding, an entropy encoding algorithm used for lossless data compression [10]. The main idea of the algorithm is the variable-length representation of the source data. The length of each source character or value comes from a variable-length code table which is usually filled-in based on the frequency of appearance; each character or value that tends to appear frequently has a smaller representation width than the source characters appearing less frequent. Huffman encoding is a data reduction method that fits to a WSN framework since it is not complicated, which means that it consumes relatively low energy, while as demonstrated in [1], it has a high compression ratio when applied to WSN data. Obviously, this compression scheme can be used together with any other data reduction and aggregation scheme, since Huffman coding just replaces a character with a specific bit-word, based on a table which is "a priori" known by both the sender and the receiver.

3.1 Huffman Encoding Algorithm

The Huffman coding algorithm we have implemented is described in [1]. A crucial part of the Huffman coding is the frequency assigned to each source character and as a result the corresponding width of its encoded representation. Regarding the source characters it should be stressed that the WSN applications, usually measure some natural variables, like light, temperature and humidity.

In our implementation we have taken advantage of two specific features of the WSNs and of the Huffman algorithm. Firstly, we have realized that usually the difference between two successive measurements of the same environmental variable is very small which leads to the fact that the transmission of the difference would need only few bits. Secondly such small values are represented by even fewer bits if Huffman encoding is utilized.

The encoding-table that was used for our implementation and our experiments is shown in Table 1. Those values are used in the baseline JPEG algorithm for compressing and as claimed in [1] their statistical characteristics match those of the WSN data.

The process of compression is described in the flowchart of Figure 1. The new measured value is subtracted from the previous measurement. The result of subtraction, di, according to the formula of Table 1, gives two numbers ni and Si. The next step of the algorithm takes the ni least significant bits of the di value (Ai) and concatenates them with the value of Si ($Si|Ai$). The final result is the encoded data that will be embedded in a data packet which is sent over the network. As demonstrated in the next section, the Huffman compression algorithm is a relatively simple one with very limited memory needs, which makes it suitable for WSNs.

3.2 Huffman Decoding Algorithm

The decompression algorithm follows the reverse process of the compression one. The data packets contain the compressed value of the subtraction between the previous measurement and the new one taken from the source mote. The first step that takes place in decompression is the separation in the incoming data of the two values, Si and Ai. In the second step, the value of ni is generated from the value of Si. Then di is exported from the values of ni and Ai. The last step is the addition of the previous measurement with the new decompressed value. The result is the new measurement that was taken by the source mote.

Table 1. Huffman Variable Length Codes

n_i	s_i	d_i
0	00	0
1	010	-1, +1
2	011	-3, -2, +2, +3
3	100	-7, ..., -4, +4, ..., +7
4	101	-15, ..., -8, +8, ..., +15
5	110	-31, ..., -16, +16, ..., +31
6	1110	-63, ..., -32, +32, ..., +63
7	11110	-127, ..., -64, +64, ..., +127
8	111110	-255, ..., -128, +128, ...,+255
9	1111110	-511, ..., -256, +256, ..., +511
10	11111110	-1023, ..., -512, +512, ..., +1023
11	111111110	-2047, ..., -1024, +1024, ..., +2047
12	1111111110	-4095, ..., -2048, +2048, ..., +4095
13	11111111110	-8191, ..., -4096, +4096, ..., +8191
14	111111111110	-16383, ..., -8192, +8192, ..., +16383
15	1111111111110	-32767,...,-16384,+16384,..., +32767
16	11111111111110	-65535,...,-32768,+32768,..., +65535

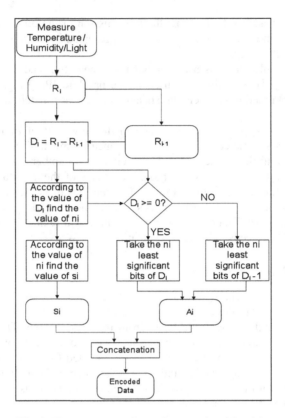

Fig. 1. Flowchart of Huffman Compression Algorithm

4 Hardware Implementation

In order to measure the efficiency of our approach we have implemented the Huffman Compression Scheme in both the processing unit of a standard WSN node and in a CPLD which has been connected to a widely used commercial WSN mote.

4.1 Architecture of Compression System

The block diagram of the proposed compression system is presented in Figure 2. The design consists of four basic modules. The Di module implements the subtraction of the new value, measured by the sensor, from the previous one. The result is sent to the Ni Generation module which creates the value of the *ni* according to Table 1. Using the value of *ni*, the Si generation module creates the first half of the encoded *di.* information and the *Ai* generation module creates the least significant bits of the *di.* Finally, the *Si* and the *Ai* values are concatenated and the result is the encoded information that is sent over the network.

The proposed compression system was fully implemented and fit on a CPLD. The CPLD resources that the design utilizes are described analytically in Table 2.

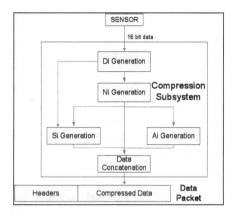

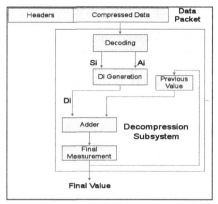

Fig. 2. Compression Subsystem of Huffman Algorithm Implemented with Reconfigurable Logic

Fig. 3. Decompression Subsystem of Huffman Algorithm Implemented with Reconfigurable Logic

Table 2. CPLD Resources for the Compression and Decompression System(Percentage of the Total Available Resources)

Resources	Compression System	Decompression System
Macrocells (256)	101 (40%)	108 (43%)
Registers (256)	42 (17%)	68 (27%)
Pins (118)	42 (36%)	42 (36%)
Function Block Inputs (640)	187 (30%)	305 (48%)

4.2 Architecture of Decompression System

The decompression algorithm has also been implemented in the base mote (sink) which decompresses the data packets that come from the various motes and sends them to a Processing Device or to a remote Storage system.

The block diagram of the decompression system is shown in Figure 3. The compressed data are initially decoded and the two values of Si and Ai are reported. The Di Generation module uses the value of Si and according to the values in Table 1 it produces the ni value. The value of ni is combined with the value of Ai so as to retrieve the di value. The final step is the addition of the decompressed difference (di) with the previous measured values which generate the new value that was measured by the sensor. It is important to stress that our system does not compress the actual measurements of the sensors but the difference between the new measurement and the previous one.

The decompression system was fully implemented in a CPLD and the resource usage is presented in Table 2. As this table clearly demonstrates both a compression and a decompression system can easily fit on a single CPLD.

5   Software Implementation

In order to measure the efficiency of our hardware-based approach when compared with the standard software one, the Huffman Coding algorithm has also been implemented in the "IRIS" mote which is one of the most widely used WSN motes made by Crossbow[14]. In particular for the programming of the sensor nodes we have utilized the PN2 tool and the NesC language. NesC (network embedded systems C) is a component-based, event-driven programming language used to build applications for the TinyOS platform. TinyOS is an operating environment designed to run on embedded devices used in distributed Wireless Sensor Networks. NesC is built as an extension to the C programming language with components "wired" together to run applications on TinyOS. The flow of the implemented program is separated into three distinct parts: the first one takes the data measurement of the physical variables, like temperature, light etc, the second constructs the data packet and the third one is responsible for sending those packets over the network. In order to collect the measurements from the environment we utilized the motes' timers. Each timer sends an interrupt to the CPU periodically (based on a predefined period) and the CPU initiates the collection of the data measurements. Those measurements are then transformed to 16 bit words using an embedded AD converter. The next processing step, is the compression stage where the Huffman compression scheme is applied to the measurements, as described in Section 2.

The final step is the packaging of the data and their transmission. Regarding the data packaging, the standard TinyOS routines use fixed-size packets. In our case, due to the fact that we use Huffman compression, the size of the data depends on the nature of them; as a result we decided to use variable size packets. Since when achieving, the highest possible reduction as the next section clearly demonstrates, each measurement can fit in 1 byte (and an ordinary measurement is 2 bytes long) our variable size packets, in our initial implementation, contain either one or two bytes of data.

6   Proposed Platform and Experimental Setup

The device utilized in our design is one from the Xilinx CoolRunner-II family. The CoolRunner-II CPLD family provides high performance and low power consumption (ultra-low stand-by current) at a very low price. The specific prototyping CPLD board utilized is the Digilent X-Board which includes a very low-cost 256 macrocell CoolRunner-II CPLD device (XC2C256). It provides all essential support circuits for the CoolRunner-II including an on-board USB2 port which was used as a data port for CPLD configuration as well as for user data transfers.

The tool used to implement our hardware design was Xilinx ISE 10.1 while its embedded simulator was used in order to verify the correct operation of our architecture via the process of "Behavioral Simulation". Next, we carried out "Post Fit Simulation" and, for this purpose, we preferred Modesim SE 6.3f . Finally, the CPLD was programmed using the Digilent ExPort.

In order to implement a complete real-world sensor node we connected the X-Board to the Crossbow MDA100 sensor and data acquisition boards [14] which include a precision thermistor, a light sensor/ photocell and provide a general proto-typing area. We have also used a USB PC Interface Board, the Crossbow MIB520 Gateway which provides a USB Interface for data communication and allow the developer to seamlessly program the sensor boards. This board has an in-system processor (ISP) which is an Atmega16L which is used to program the Motes. Code is downloaded to the ISP through the USB port and then the ISP programs the Mote's processor. The actual mote used is the "IRIS" mote which is the newest such mote by Crossbow Technology. It uses the Atmel RF230, IEEE 802.15.4 compliant, ZigBee ready radio frequency transceiver which is integrated with an Atmega1281 micro-controller. These enhancements provide up to three times improved radio range and twice the program memory over the previous generation Motes. The block diagram of IRIS is presented in Figure 4.

One important issue when implementing our reference platform was the I/O problem between the IRIS Mote and the CPLD. Regarding the CPLD connection, the JTAG ports were chosen so as to both import data to the CPLD and to export data to the Mote. To be more specific, J9 and J10 ports of the CPLD, which have 26 and 16 pins respectively, were selected for this purpose. For the Mote connection, after several experiments, it was realized that the fastest available pins are 24 of the ones in the prototyping area; based on a traffic profiling of our applications we decided to use 10 of those pins as an input to the mote and the remaining for the output traffic. As described above, we have a 16-bit input to the CPLD and a 24-bit input to the IRIS Mote, while, the available Mote's high-speed pins are only 24. As a result, a number of the Motes' pins should be used twice for a single Mote-to-CPLD data transfer. In order to efficiently and correctly exchange data between the CPLD and the IRIS

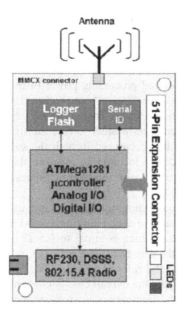

Fig. 4. IRIS Block Diagram

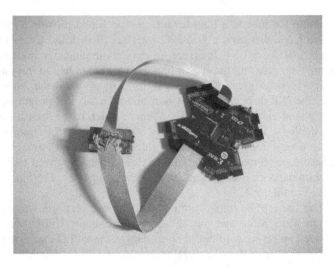

Fig. 5. Our Pioneering Platform

Mote, a simple toggle synchronization protocol was also implemented; in particular a specific output toggle bit get the inverted value of the input toggle bit when the compressed data item is ready. In Figure 5 there is a photo of our platform. It should be noted that the Digilent Board is large because it has a very large prototyping area; we only utilize the Xilinx device which is in the center of the board and which is small enough to fit in an ordinary mote.

6.1 Measurement Framework

The proposed system was evaluated based mainly on two metrics: execution time and energy consumption. All these are critical parameters in WSNs, since it is certainly desirable to increase the limited processing power of the node while also increasing the life time of the battery of the wireless mote by lowering its energy consumption.

Our performance results are based on real-world experiments in which a mixed signal oscilloscope has been used in order to take the speed, energy and power measurements. An extra signal has been used in both the software and the hardware implementation of the application in order to measure the execution time; this signal transits to high when the execution of the specific process starts and then toggles back to low when the process ends.

Furthermore, the energy consumption is calculated using the integral of the measured voltage V_m for the measured execution time period $\Delta\tau$. The result is divided with the reference resistance R_{ref}, which is equal to 0.5 Ω in the experimental topology used, in order to calculate the reference current I_{ref}.

Multiplying the I_{ref} with the reference voltage V_{ref} that is equal to 2.7 V for the Mote and 3.3 V for the CPLD, the overall energy consumption is calculated, based on formula (1) (T is equal to the summary of the time periods $\Delta\tau$).

$$E = I_{ref}V_{ref}, where\ I_{ref} = \frac{\sum_t V_{m,t}\Delta\tau}{R_{ref} * T} \tag{1}$$

7 Compression Ratio Results

Both our software and hardware implementations were tested and evaluated in a real-world environment. In this section, there is a description of the various datasets that were used for the evaluation of the systems and the results of the tests regarding the compression ratio that the algorithm achieves.

7.1 Datasets

It is well known that the efficiency of a certain compression algorithm depends on the nature of the data compressed; for this reason we studied the performance of the proposed compression algorithm when applied to both real-world data, and data which have been widely used as benchmarks for WSNs. Our implementations were tested and evaluated using three different datasets. The first dataset comes from a large number of sensors deployed in the Intel Berkeley Research Lab [12]. The second dataset utilized in the system evaluation was a collection of measurements from the SensorScope framework [13], which is an environmental monitoring network. Finally, the data that were collected from a number of nodes deployed in our laboratory were also utilized in our experiments.

7.2 Compression Ratio

This section presents the compression ratio achieved when the Huffman encoding algorithm is utilized in a number of real-world datasets. As mentioned above, the motes that were used for this work had only two kinds of sensors, thermistors and light sensors. Tables 3 and 4 present the data sizes of the different datasets that were used for the evaluation of the system, the size of the compressed data that were transmitted over the network as well as the compression ratio achieved.

Table 3. Compression Results by Applying Huffman Encoding on Light Data

Data	Light (Intel Labs)		Light (SensorScope)		Light (Lab)	
	Bits	Payload Packet Size (Bytes)	Bits	Payload Packet Size (Bytes)	Bits	Payload Packet Size (Bytes)
Original Size	688736	86092	58624	7328	90864	11358
Compressed Size	150010	48984	13005	3781	21858	5682
Compression Ratio	78.22%	43.10%	77.82%	48.40%	75.94%	49.97%

Table 4. Compression Results by Applying the Huffman Encoding on Temperature Data

Data	Temperature (Intel Labs)		Temperature (SensorScope)	
	Bits	Data Packet Size (Bytes)	Bits	Data Packet Size (Bytes)
Original Size	688736	86092	58624	7328
Compressed Size	195768	52087	14287	3685
Compression Ratio	71.58%	39.50%	75.63%	49.71%

Based on those results, we claim that the Huffman algorithm is very efficient since it achieves a data reduction of more than 70% in all cases. Since there are also certain overheads involved (i.e. the data are sent in byte quantities), the more applicable results are shown in the "Payload Packet Size" columns. These columns demonstrate that when applying Huffman compression the data transmitted over the network (and not including any overhead introduced by the inter-communication mechanism such as the headers of the network packets) is reduced by more than 40%. The next section presents the measured energy gain due to this data reduction.

An important remark for the results presented here is the following: the original size of each light and temperature measurement is 16 bits or 2 bytes; at the same time the shortest datum that can be transmitted is 1 byte (if the value to be transmitted is shorter than 1 byte we zero-pad it so as to create a full byte). As a result the highest compression gain that can be achieved by the proposed framework is 50%. Based on this remark we strongly believe that the results presented in this section are impressive since all the data that were compressed by our innovative system were reduced near to this optimal limit (as the compression ratio achieved is almost 50% in all the cases).

8   Power Consumption Results

8.1   Transmission's Power Consumption

This section presents the energy consumption measurements for the data transmission part. As clearly presented in Section 2.1, where the adopted Huffman encoding scheme is described, the size of the compressed data items varies from 1-4 bytes for each real-world measurement; while the size of the uncompressed data items is always 2 bytes.

At the same time, based on our measurements on the crossbow platform, the energy that is consumed for the transmission of one byte is about 0.339 µJ.

Based on the protocols used in the Crossbow network, the packet length can be up to 29 bytes, where the first 13 bytes are the header of the packet and the rest 1 to 16 bytes contain the actual data transmitted. So the packet size for transmitting one uncompressed measurement is 15 bytes whereas for the compressed ones it can vary from 14 to 17 bytes. Since each mote on the WSN has two sensors (light and thermistor) each packet carries the data collected from two measurements; thus in the uncompressed case the packets are 17 bytes long whereas in the compressed case they vary from 15 – 21 bytes depending on the data compressed (i.e. if the optimal compression is achieved all the packets would be 15 bytes, while in the worst case the data will be extended). Obviously, in all the cases the overhead introduced by the uncompressible header is significant.

If two measurements are placed in a single packet, the measured reduction in the energy consumption, when Huffman Coding is employed, is presented in Table 5. The reduction ratio of the energy consumed for the data transmission is not high since there is a significant transmission overhead due to the long, uncompressible, headers of the packets.

In order to reduce this overhead we have employed a data packing technique: we have placed more than one measurement for each sensor in a packet (one next to the other) and this was done for both the compressed and the uncompressed cases. The results when this data packaging technique is employed are shown in Table 6; as those measurements clearly demonstrate the effectiveness of our approach is significantly increased when the data packaging scheme is employed.

Table 5. Energy Consumed for the Transmission of Packets when only two Measurements are placed in a single packet

Power Transmission	Intel Labs	SensorScope	Lab
	Light and Temperature	Light and Temperature	Light
Uncompressed Data	0.248 J	0.021 J	0.029 J
Compressed Data	0.226 J	0.018 J	0.026 J
Reduction of Power Consumption	8.9%	11.3%	10.3%

Table 6. Energy Consumed fort the Transmission of Packets Containing More Than One Measurements Each (in MJ)

Power Transmission	Intel Labs	SensorScope	Lab
	Light and Temperature	Light and Temperature	Light
Uncompressed Data	105.80	9.01	6.98
Compressed Data	59.52	4.15	3.28
Reduction of Power Consumption	56.25%	46.05%	47%

8.2 Overall Energy Consumption

Tables 6 and 7 present only the actual reduction in the energy consumed by the data transmission process. In order to compress the data, an additional processing task (i.e. the data compression one) is introduced, which obviously increases the energy consumed for the data processing.

This new task will ordinary be executed in the mote's processor; however, within our innovative framework, this task can also be executed in the dedicated reconfigurable hardware unit (CPLD). In order to demonstrate the efficiency of our approach we have measured the energy consumed and the performance achieved when the Huffman coding task was executed in both the CPU of the Mote (which is a standard off-the-shelf low power microcontroller) and the CPLD. We have measured the actual energy consumption for all three datasets and the numbers presented in Table 7 are the average ones (the variance is not significant). As those results clearly demonstrate,

Table 7. Energy Consumed fort the Encoding and Decoding of a Single Data Item

Implementation	Encoding			Decoding		
	CPLD	Processing Unit of node	Reduction Ratio	CPLD	Processing Unit of node	Reduction Ratio
Power Consumption (μJ)	0.0026	0.409	99.36%	0.003	0.463	99.35%
Execution Time (us)	0.022	6.18	280 x	0.025	6.91	275 x

Table 8. Comparison Between the Total Energy Consumed for the Transmission of Packets with Compressed and Uncompressed Data for Both Hardware and Software Approaches (mJ)

	Intel Labs			SensorScope			Lab		
	Light and Temperature			Light and Temperature			Light		
	Transm ission	Comp ression	Total Power Consu mption	Trans mission	Comp ression	Total Power Consu mption	Transm ission	Compr ession	Total Power Consu mption
Uncompressed Data	105.80	0	105.80	9.01	0	9.01	6.98	0	6.98
SW Compression	59.52	35.21	94.73	4.15	2.99	7.14	3.28	1.49	4.77
Total Energy consumption Reduction For SW	10.46%			20.75%			31.66%		
HW Compression	59.52	0.223	94.73	4.15	0.019	7.14	3.28	0.029	4.77
Total Energy consumption Reduction For HW	56.46%			46.27%			47.4%		

our hardware-based approach reduces the energy consumption of the compression task by more than 99%! Moreover, the latency the data suffer due to compression is extremely reduced, by up to 300 times, when the CPLD is utilized.

In Table 8 the overall energy consumption, including the energy consumed by the compression task, is demonstrated for all the datasets. As it is clearly demonstrated the overall energy consumed by the WSN framework is reduced from 46% to 56%, at the cost of a very inexpensive CPLD device. Based on those results we strongly believe that this paper can be a first reference for a new design paradigm for WSN nodes which will include CPLDs for executing the actual compression tasks.

9 Conclusions

This paper presents a new approach for reducing the power consumption of WSNs. The presented approach is based on two facts:

1. Compression can be efficiently applied in WSNs since it reduces the data transmitted and thus the transmission energy

2. When a compression algorithm is implemented in a low power reconfigurable device, its energy consumption is more than 99% lower than that triggered by a software routine executing the same compression algorithm in the processing unit of widely used WSN node.

Based on numerous real-world experiments, executed on our platform, we demonstrate for the first time, that the overall energy consumption of a WSN can be reduced, using a hardware-based compression scheme, by at least 46%. As a result, we claim that the proposed approach doubles the, so important, lifetime of the battery of a WSN, thus increasing significantly its effectiveness at the very low cost of a small reconfigurable device.

References

1. Marcelloni, F., Vecchio, M.: A Simple Algorithm for Data Compression in Wireless Sensor Networks. IEEE Communications Letters 12(6) (2008)
2. Fasolo, E., Rossi, M., Widmer, J., Zorzi, M.: In-Network Aggregation Techniques for Wireless Sensor Networks: A survey. IEEE Wireless Communications (2007)
3. Lee, M., Wong, V.W.S.: LPT for Data Aggregation in Wireless Sensor Networks. In: Proc. of IEEE GLOBECOM (2005)
4. Lee, M., Wong, V.: An energy-efficient spanning tree algorithm for data aggregation in wireless sensor networks. In: Proc. of IEEE PacRim 2005 (2005)
5. Younis, O., Fahmy, S.: HEED: A hybrid, energy-efficient, distributed clustering approach for ad hoc sensor networks. IEEE Transactions on Mobile Computing 3(4), 366–379 (2004)
6. Kimura, N., Latifi, S.: A survey on data compression in wireless sensor networks. Information Technology: Coding and Computing 2, 8–13 (2005)
7. Tang, C., Raghavendra, C.S.: Compression techniques for wireless sensor networks. Wireless sensor networks, 207–231 (2004)

8. Alippi, C., Camplani, R., Galperti, C.: Lossless Compression Techniques in Wireless Sensor Networks: Monitoring Microacoustic Emissions. In: Proc. Of ROSE 2007 - IEEE International Workshop on Robotic and Sensors Environments, Ottawa, Canada (2007)

9. Chen, M., Fowler, M.L.: Data compression trade-offs in sensor net-works. In: Proceedings of SPIE (2004)

10. Huffman, D.: A method for the construction of minimum-redundancy codes. In: Proceedings of the IRE, vol. 40, pp. 1098–1101 (1952)

11. Benini, L., Bruni, D., Macii, A., Macii, E.: Hardware-assisted data compression for energy minimization in systems with embedded processors. In: Proc. of the conference on Design, automation and test in Europe, DATE 2002, Nice, France (2002)

12. http://db.lcs.mit.edu/labdata/labdata.html

13. Schmid, T., Dubois-Ferriere, H., Vetteri, M.: SensorScope: Experiences with a Wireless Building Monitoring Sensor Network. In: Proc. of 2005 Workshop on Real-World Wireless Sensor Networks, RealWSN (2005)

14. Crossbow Technology, http://www.xbow.com

Optimal and Fair Transmission Rate Allocation Problem in Multi-hop Cellular Networks*

Cristiana Gomes[1] and Jérôme Galtier[2]

[1] MASCOTTE Project - INRIA, I3S, CNRS, Univ. Nice Sophia, France
cristiana.gomes@sophia.inria.fr
[2] Orange Labs, Sophia-Antipolis, France
jerome.galtier@orange-ftgroup.com

Abstract. We deal with the rate allocation problem for downlink in a Multi-hop Cellular Network. A mathematical model is provided to assign transmission rates in order to reach an optimal and fair solution. We prove that under some conditions that are often met, the problem can be reduced to a single-hop cellular network problem. The validity of our proof is confirmed experimentally.

1 Introduction

Multihop Cellular Network preserves the benefit of conventional single-hop cellular networks where the service infrastructure is provided by fixed bases, and also incorporates the flexibility of ad-hoc networks where wireless transmissions through mobile stations in multiple hops is allowed [1].

In ad-hoc networks, nodes communicate with each other in a peer-to-peer way and no infrastructure is required. If direct communication is not feasible, the simplest solution is to replace a single long-range link with a chain of short range links by using a series of nodes between the source and the destination: this is known as multi-hop communication [2]. The cooperation between these two networks can be interesting as ad-hoc networks can expand the covered area whitout the high cost of cellular networks infrastructure.

We address in this paper a bottleneck problem that summarizes the situation of many multi-hop cellular networks, as illustrated in Figure 1. In our work, a gateway - or *base station (BS)* - has entire access to the rest of the world and provides this service in a more privileged way to some specific nodes, the *relay nodes* (the white ones in Figure 1). Those nodes are themselves relaying the service to the nodes in the free zone, called the *terminal nodes* (the gray ones in Figure 1). It can happen that nodes in the free zone relay one another to get the final service. In our model, the relay nodes and the gateway form a single-hop cellular network (the critical zone) that constrains the system.

---

* C. Gomes is funded by CAPES, Brazil. This work has been partially supported by European project IST/FET AEOLUS and is part of the CRC CORSO with Orange Labs.

P.M. Ruiz and J.J. Garcia-Luna-Aceves (Eds.): ADHOC-NOW 2009, LNCS 5793, pp. 327–340, 2009.

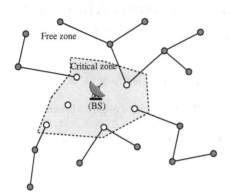

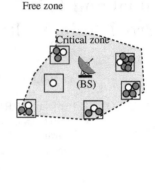

Fig. 1. Multi-hop cellular network

Fig. 2. Multi-hop cellular network reduced in single-hop

Each node has a utility function representing its degree of satisfaction based on the assigned rate transmission. The whole system is governed by the optimization of the sum of utility functions over all the nodes, as in [3,4]. We give a model that allows to transform the multi-hop network (Figure 1) into a single-hop network (Figure 2), by eventually modifying the utility functions on the relay nodes, as depicted in Figure 1.

The rest of this paper is organized as follows. In the next section we discuss the related works. In section 3, we define the problem, the adopted notation and the considered hypotheses. The section 4 shows how the problem can be reduced to a single-hop network. That is how the complete network utility functions can be replaced by a small set of different functions assigned to the relay nodes, in the context of a fair and optimal optimization. We push forward our results in section 5 by applying them to specific cases of fairness.

2 Related Work

This described scenario occurs in multi-hop networks as considered in [1,2]. Indeed, it is observed that often in these networks the bandwidth is constrained specifically by a bottleneck around the gateway [5,6], confirming the fact that it is a representative area. Many real networks deal with this situation. For instance, using UMTS technology for the single-hop network [7,4,8], while the free zone is covered by WiFi or Bluetooth systems.

We show that there exists a set of utility functions that can be assigned to the relay nodes replacing the complete set of utility functions. It is due to the fact that the problem is convex under some conditions that are often met.

Convex optimization techniques are important in engineering applications because a local optimum is also a global optimum in a convex problem. Rigorous optimality conditions and a duality theory also exist to check the solution optimality. Consequently, when a problem is cast into a convex form, the structure of the optimal solution, which often reveals design insights, can often be identified. Furthermore, powerful numerical algorithms exist to solve convex problems efficiently.

We are interested in Pareto-optimal solutions, that is solutions where the utility of an individual cannot be improved without decreasing the utility of one or more other nodes. The fairness is a key issue in wireless networks, since the medium is shared among the nodes. In our problem, it implies that each flow going through a bottleneck receives a fair share of the available bandwidth. Our work admits the generalized fairness criterion as defined in [3] that can assume several criteria (see section 5 for more details), for example, the proportional fairness one.

The proportional fairness has been studied in the context of the Internet flow due the similarity to the congestion control mechanism of the TCP/IP protocols, where each TCP's throughput is adapted as a function of the congestion. The work in [9] addresses the question of how the available bandwidth within the network should be shared between competing streams of elastic traffic[1].

3   Model Definition

We distinguish here three main types of nodes. The BS that is unique in our case, the relay nodes in $\mathcal{R}$ that have a limited link to the BS and the terminal nodes in $\mathcal{T}_r$ that are connected to the BS through an unique relay node r at the single-hop network. Note that multi-hops are allowed as long as connections between terminal nodes are given for free, that is the relay node has bandwidth enough for itself and its relayed terminals. The terminal nodes are considered sparsely distributed around the cell, thus interference is not a problem at the free zone.

We focus on the downlink channel (from the BS to the relay nodes) considering a given fixed bandwidth. Let α_r be the rate of the downlink channel from the BS to relay node r. Let ρ_t be the downlink rate at each node $t \in \mathcal{T}_r$. We consider the following hypotheses.

Hypothesis 1. *All terminal nodes in $\mathcal{T}_r$ use an unique relay node $r \in \mathcal{R}$.*

Hypothesis 2. *We only consider interferences between the relay nodes in $\mathcal{R}$.*

Note that the first hypothesis allows multiple hops and routes in the free zone but imposes to gather all the traffic of an individual node to a unique relay in the critical zone. The second hypothesis means also that the bandwidth is not limited in the free zone.

---

[1] The elastic traffic tolerates packet delays and losses and permits the nodes to adjust their rates in order to fill available bandwidth.

We summarize the important definitions below.

Nodes Set

- BS: node representing the base station. We consider an unique BS.
- $\mathcal{R}$: set of relay nodes, directly connected to the BS by a limited link.
- $\mathcal{T}_r$: set containing the node $r \in \mathcal{R}$ and the set of terminal nodes relayed by r.

Variables

- $p_{b,r}$: power of the signal emitted by the BS to the router r.
- ρ_t: downlink rate for each node $t \in \mathcal{T}_r$.
- α_r: downlink rate for each node $r \in \mathcal{R}$, enough to attend all nodes $t \in \mathcal{T}_r$. $\alpha_r = \sum_{t \in \mathcal{T}_r} \rho_t$.

Utility Functions

- $U_t(\rho_t)$: utility function at the node $t \in \mathcal{T}_r$ representing its degree of satisfaction. This function is non-decreasing with ρ_t.
- $\mathcal{U}_r(\alpha_r)$: cumulative utility function at the node $r \in \mathcal{R}$ representing the maximum degree of satisfaction of the nodes in $\mathcal{T}_r$. Given that the bandwidth is α_r, it is defined $\mathcal{U}_r(\alpha_r) = \max\{\sum_{t \in \mathcal{T}_r} U_t(\rho_t); \sum_{t \in \mathcal{T}_r} \rho_t = \alpha_r\}$.

We deal with the **optimal and fair transmission rate allocation problem** (problem (P)), we have to find a vector of the relay rates α that maximizes $\sum_{r \in \mathcal{R}} \mathcal{U}_r(\alpha_r)$ with a fair sharing among the terminals, guarantying the existence of a vector of transmissions powers $p = (p_{b,1}, p_{b,2}, ..., p_{b,|\mathcal{R}|})$.

In order to model interference in the critical zone, we focus on a commonly used definition of *feasible rates* which depends on both a target γ and a target interference level K. The packet sent by the BS is received by the relay node if the SINR (Signal to Interference plus Noise Ratio) is above a given threshold γ. The constants N_o and $g_{b,r}$ are given considering the network environment. Let N_o be the thermal noise and $g_{b,r}$ is the channel gain between the BS and the relay r. The variables $p_{b,r}$ represent the power of the signal emitted by the BS to the relay r.

A vector of rates $\alpha = (\alpha_1, \alpha_2, ..., \alpha_{|\mathcal{R}|})$ is considered a feasible solution if there exists a vector of transmissions powers $p = (p_{b,1}, p_{b,2}, ..., p_{b,|\mathcal{R}|})$ that satisfies the following conditions for the SINR that a node connected to the BS experiences: $\alpha_r \gamma \leqslant \frac{p_{b,r} g_{b,r}}{N_o + g_{b,r} \sum_{s \neq r} p_{b,s}} = SINR_r, \forall r \in \mathcal{R}$ and $\sum_{r \in \mathcal{R}} p_{b,r} \leqslant K N_o$. A vector of rates α is an *optimal rate allocation* if it is a solution to the following model on variables α and p:

Problem (P')

$$\max \sum_{r \in \mathcal{R}} \mathcal{U}_r(\alpha_r) \tag{1}$$

subject to

$$\alpha_r \gamma \leqslant \frac{p_{b,r} g_{b,r}}{N_o + g_{b,r} \sum_{s \neq r} p_{b,s}}, \forall r \in \mathcal{R} \tag{2}$$

$$\sum_{r \in \mathcal{R}} p_{b,r} \leqslant K N_o. \tag{3}$$

Since utility functions are non-decreasing, an optimal solution verifies:

$$\alpha_r \gamma = \frac{p_{b,r} g_{b,r}}{N_o + g_{b,r} \sum_{s \neq r} p_{b,s}}, \forall r \in \mathcal{R}$$

which gives $p_{b,r} = \frac{\alpha_r \gamma}{g_{b,r}}(N_o + g_{b,r} \sum_{s \neq r} p_{b,s})$, thus

$$p_{b,r} = \frac{\alpha_r \gamma}{g_{b,r}}(N_o + g_{b,r} \sum_{s \in \mathcal{R}} p_{b,s} - g_{b,r} p_{b,r}), \forall r \in \mathcal{R}. \tag{4}$$

Moreover, increasing all the powers by the same factor allows to tighten constraints (3) while relaxing constraints (2). By optimality we have

$$\sum_{r \in \mathcal{R}} p_{b,r} = K N_o$$

which, put into equation (4) gives $p_{b,r} = \frac{\alpha_r \gamma}{g_{b,r}}(N_o(1 + g_{b,r}K) - g_{b,r} p_{b,r})$ and we obtain:

$$p_{b,r} = \frac{\alpha_r \gamma N_o(1 + K g_{b,r})}{g_{b,r}(1 + \alpha_r \gamma)}, \forall r \in \mathcal{R}. \tag{5}$$

Like in [7], we use the substitution $\frac{\alpha_r \gamma(1 + K g_{b,r})}{g_{b,r}(1 + \alpha_r \gamma)} = d_r$. As $\sum_{r \in \mathcal{R}} d_r \leqslant \sum_{r \in \mathcal{R}} \frac{p_{b,r}}{N_o} \leqslant K$, we can say:

$$\alpha_r = \frac{d_r g_{b,r}}{\gamma(1 + g_{b,r}(K - d_r))}, \forall r \in \mathcal{R}.$$

So, we obtain the following equivalent problem on variables d_r:

Problem (P)

$$\max \sum_{r \in \mathcal{R}} U_r \left(\frac{d_r g_{b,r}}{\gamma(1 + g_{b,r}(K - d_r))} \right) \tag{6}$$

subject to

$$\begin{cases} \sum_{r \in \mathcal{R}} d_r \leqslant K \\ d_r \geqslant 0, \forall r \in \mathcal{R}. \end{cases} \tag{7}$$

4   Theoretical Approach with Fairness and Optimality

In this section, the problem is how to define the cumulative utility functions $\mathcal{U}_r(\alpha_r)$ for each relay node $r \in \mathcal{R}$ in a way to represent the utility functions $U_t(\rho_t)$ of all nodes $t \in \mathcal{T}_r$. Moreover, the available bandwidth of each relay node has to be shared with fairness among the nodes in $\mathcal{T}_r$.

Indeed, we prove that there exists a set of utility functions $\mathcal{U}_r(\alpha_r)$ (cumulative functions) that can be assigned to the relay nodes replacing the complete set of utility functions and, it can be expressed analytically in most cases. Moreover, we show that for any fixed available bandwidth α_r at each relay node, if the sum $\sum_{t \in \mathcal{T}_r} U_t(\beta_t \alpha_r)$ is maximized it converges to a fairness equilibrium. Thus, it is always possible to share α_r fairly among the nodes in $\mathcal{T}_r$. The fairness equilibrium point is defined by the utility function adopted. We consider the following technical assumption.

Technical Assumption 1. *The nodes' utility functions $U_t(.)$ are assumed to be strictly increasing concave functions and satisfy the condition $U_t''(x) \leqslant \frac{-1}{x^2}$.*

As said before the particular utility function $\mathcal{U}_r(\alpha_r)$ is defined as follows:

Problem (P_r)

$$\mathcal{U}_r(\alpha_r) = \max \sum_{t \in \mathcal{T}_r} U_t(\rho_t) \tag{8}$$

subject to

$$\alpha_r = \sum_{t \in \mathcal{T}_r} \rho_t, \forall r \in \mathcal{R}. \tag{9}$$

We need the following lemma regarding how the rate α_r assigned to a relay $r \in \mathcal{R}$ can be shared by all terminals it relays. Our objective is that given α_r we can assign a fraction β_t of α_r for each terminal $t \in \mathcal{T}_r$ in a fair way.

Lemma 1. *Given the vector $\rho^* = (\rho_1', ..., \rho_{|\mathcal{T}_r|}')$ being the optimal solution for the problem P_r, we consider a variable $\beta_t' \in [0,1]$, a fixed feasible relay rate α_r and we define $\rho_t' = \alpha_r \beta_t'$. We obtain*

$$U_{t_1}'(\beta_{t_1}' \alpha_r) = U_{t_2}'(\beta_{t_2}' \alpha_r), \forall t_1, t_2 \in \mathcal{T}_r.$$

Proof. Letting $\beta_t = \frac{\rho_t}{\alpha_r}$, we consider the following subproblem with a fixed α_r for a $r \in \mathcal{R}$:

Problem (P_r')

$$\max \sum_{t \in \mathcal{T}_r} U_t(\beta_t \alpha_r) \tag{10}$$

subject to

$$\begin{cases} \beta_t \geqslant 0, \forall t \in \mathcal{T}_r \\ \sum_{t \in \mathcal{T}_r} \beta_t = 1. \end{cases} \tag{11}$$

We can say that it is a local version of the problem P_r, in a way that an optimal solution for P'_r considering the optimal value for $\alpha^*_r = \arg\max_{\alpha_r} \mathcal{U}_r(\alpha_r)$ can be translated into a locally optimal solution for P_r. We can rewrite the constraints as:

$$\begin{cases} -\beta_t \leqslant 0, \forall t \in \mathcal{T}_r \\ \sum_{t \in \mathcal{T}_r} \beta_t \leqslant 1 \\ \sum_{t \in \mathcal{T}_r} -\beta_t \leqslant -1 \end{cases} \quad (12)$$

Based on [10], the Lagrangian of this subproblem can be written as follow:

$$L(\beta) = \sum_{t \in \mathcal{T}_r} U_t(\beta_t \alpha_r) - \sum_{t \in \mathcal{T}_r} \lambda_t (-\beta_t) - \mu \left(\sum_{t \in \mathcal{T}_r} \beta_t - 1 \right) - \nu \left(\sum_{t \in \mathcal{T}_r} -\beta_t + 1 \right)$$

with the lagrange multipliers $\lambda_i \geqslant 0$, $\mu \geqslant 0$ and $\nu \geqslant 0$. As $\beta^* = (\frac{\rho'_t}{\alpha_r}, ..., \frac{\rho'_{|T_r|}}{\alpha_r})$ is necessarily a vector of optimal solutions for the Lagrangian. So it verifies KKT's optimality conditions: $\frac{\partial L}{\partial \beta_t} = 0$ in $\beta^*, \forall t \in \mathcal{T}_r$, which gives

$$\alpha_r U'_t(\beta'_t \alpha_r) + \lambda_t - \mu + \nu = 0, \forall t \in \mathcal{T}_r.$$

Moreover, by KKT complementary slackness conditions $\lambda_t \beta'_t = 0, \forall t \in \mathcal{T}_r$.

Note that under technical assumption 1, we have $U''_t(\rho_t) \to -\infty$ when $\rho_t \to 0_+$ for all t. We can deduce that $U'_t(\rho_t) \to +\infty$ and $U_t(\rho_t) \to -\infty$ when $\rho_t \to 0_+$ for all t, making impossible the case where $\rho_t = 0$. So $\beta_t \neq 0$, that gives $\lambda_t = 0$. Hence $\alpha_r U'_t(\beta'_t \alpha_r) - \mu + \nu = 0, \forall t \in \mathcal{T}_r$. We obtain

$$U'_{t_1}(\beta'_{t_1} \alpha_r) = U'_{t_2}(\beta'_{t_2} \alpha_r), \forall t_1, t_2 \in \mathcal{T}_r$$

As neither $-\mu$ nor ν depends on t, it means that $U'_t(\rho'_t) = C, \forall t \in \mathcal{T}_r$ where C is a constant. ∎

We have then the following theorem regarding the maximum point of the function $\mathcal{U}_r$.

Theorem 1. *The function $\mathcal{U}_r(\alpha_r)$ for each $r \in \mathcal{R}$ is obtained as follows. Let $h_t = (U'_t)^{-1}$ and $h_r = \sum_{t \in \mathcal{T}_r} h_t$, then $\mathcal{U}_r(\alpha_r) = \sum_{t \in \mathcal{T}_r} U_t \circ h_t \circ h_r^{-1}(\alpha_r), \forall r \in \mathcal{R}$.*

Proof. By Technical Assumption 1, we have $U''_t(x) < 0, \forall t \in \mathcal{T}_r$ then $U'_t, \forall t \in \mathcal{T}_r$ are strictly monotonic decreasing functions. So these inverse functions $h_t, \forall t \in \mathcal{T}_r$ exist. We set $h_r = \sum_{t \in \mathcal{T}_r} h_t$. By Lemma 1 and reusing the notation for C, we have

$$h_r(C) = \beta'_1 \alpha_r + ... + \beta'_{|T_r|} \alpha_r = \alpha_r. \quad (13)$$

Now, we can have $\mathcal{U}_r$ expressed by functions U_t. Indeed, we have from equation (13), $C = h_r^{-1}(\alpha_r)$ and $\rho'_t = h_t(C) = h_t \circ h_r^{-1}(\alpha_r)$. We derive $U_t(\rho'_t) = U_t \circ h_t \circ h_r^{-1}(\alpha_r)$ and $\sum_{t \in \mathcal{T}_r} U_t(\rho'_t) = \sum_{t \in \mathcal{T}_r} U_t \circ h_t \circ h_r^{-1}(\alpha_r)$. So, we can consider

$$\mathcal{U}_r(\alpha_r) = \sum_{t \in T_r} U_t \circ h_t \circ h_r^{-1}(\alpha_r), \forall r \in \mathcal{R}.$$

Making $\alpha_r = \alpha_r^*$ we obtain $h_r(C) = \beta_1' \alpha_r^* + ... + \beta_{|T_r|}' \alpha_r^* = \alpha_r^*$ and the solution for P_r' is already optimal for P_r.   ∎

5   Results

In this section we show some results using our model for the problem P. To solve the model, we use a software library for nonlinear optimization of continuous systems, the Interior Point OPTimizer (IPOPT) that is part of the COIN-OR project. We used the modeling environment AMPL (A Mathematical Programming Language).

We show examples of utility functions and their cumulative representations confirming the validity of our proof experimentally. For the sake of simplicity, our examples consider a small network with 5 nodes: 2 relays and 3 terminals, as shown in Figure 3.

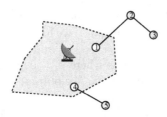

Fig. 3. Example with 5 nodes

We consider the utility functions described below. The graphs in Figures 4, 6 and 8 show the cumulative functions, that is using $\mathcal{U}_r(\alpha_r) = \sum_{t \in T_r} U_t \circ h_t \circ h_r^{-1}(\alpha_r), \forall r \in \mathcal{R}$. Figures in 5, 7 and 9 consider all utility functions and $\mathcal{U}_r(\alpha_r) = \sum_{t \in T_r} U_t(\rho_t)$.

We study the obtained rate ρ_t varying gain $g_{b,r}$ (with fixed target interference level $K = 2$). The graphs below show the evolution of the node rates as we increase the gain of the nodes. We consider the same gain for all relay nodes. Recall that $h_t = (U_t')^{-1}$, $h_r = \sum_{t \in T_r} h_t$ and $\mathcal{U}_r(\alpha_r) = \sum_{t \in T_r} U_t \circ h_t \circ h_r^{-1}(\alpha_r)$. Consider $\rho_t > 0$ and $\rho_t < 1$.

– $U_t(\rho_t) = c_t ln(\rho_t)$

$U_t' = \frac{c_t}{\rho_t} = y_t$, $\rho_t = \frac{c_t}{U_t'} = \frac{c_t}{y_t}$. So, $h_t(y_t) = \rho_t = \frac{c_t}{y_t}$. Consider $x = h_r(y) = \frac{1}{y} \sum_{t \in T_r} c_t$ that implies $y = \frac{1}{x} \sum_{t \in T_r} c_t = h_r^{-1}(x)$. It gives the cumulative utility function:

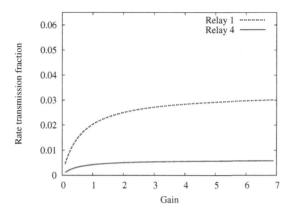

Fig. 4. Aggregated function $\mathcal{U}_r(\alpha_r) = \sum_{t \in \mathcal{T}_r} c_t ln(\alpha_r) + \sum_{t \in \mathcal{T}_r} c_t ln \left(\frac{c_t}{\sum_{t \in \mathcal{T}_r} c_t} \right)$

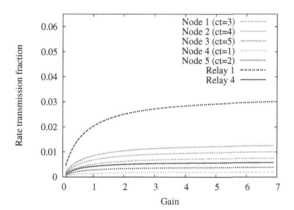

Fig. 5. Considering multi-hop with $\mathcal{U}_r(\alpha_r) = \sum_{t \in \mathcal{T}_r} U_t(\rho_t)$ and $U_t(\rho_t) = c_t ln(\rho_t)$

$\mathcal{U}_r(\alpha_r) = \sum_{t \in \mathcal{T}_r} c_t ln \left(\frac{c_t}{\frac{1}{\alpha_r} \sum_{t \in \mathcal{T}_r} c_t} \right) = \sum_{t \in \mathcal{T}_r} c_t ln(\alpha_r) + \sum_{t \in \mathcal{T}_r} c_t ln \left(\frac{c_t}{\sum_{t \in \mathcal{T}_r} c_t} \right)$.

$- U_t(\rho_t) = c_t \sqrt{\rho_t}$

$U_t'(\rho_t) = -\frac{c_t}{2\sqrt{\rho_t}} = y_t, \; \rho_t = \frac{c_t^2}{4y_t^2}$. So, $h_t(y_t) = \rho_t = \frac{c_t^2}{4y_t^2}$. Consider $x =$

$h_r(y) = \frac{1}{4y^2} \sum_{t \in \mathcal{T}_r} c_t^2$ that implies $y = \frac{1}{2\sqrt{x}} \sqrt{\sum_{t \in \mathcal{T}_r} c_t^2} = h_r^{-1}(x)$. It gives the cumulative utility function:

$\mathcal{U}_r(\alpha_r) = \sum_{t \in \mathcal{T}_r} c_t \sqrt{\frac{c_t^2}{4 \left(\frac{1}{2\sqrt{\alpha_r}} \sqrt{\sum_{t \in \mathcal{T}_r} c_t^2} \right)^2}} = \sqrt{\sum_{t \in \mathcal{T}_r} c_t^2} \sqrt{\alpha_r}$.

$- U_t(\rho_t) = \frac{-c_t}{\rho_t}$

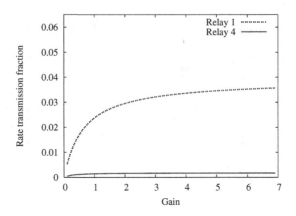

Fig. 6. Aggregated function $\mathcal{U}_r(\alpha_r) = \sqrt{\sum_{t \in \mathcal{T}_r} c_t^2} \sqrt{\alpha_r}$

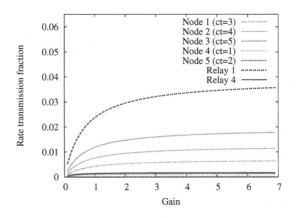

Fig. 7. Considering multi-hop with $\mathcal{U}_r(\alpha_r) = \sum_{t \in \mathcal{T}_r} U_t(\rho_t)$ and $U_t(\rho_t) = c_t \sqrt{\rho_t}$

$U_t'(\rho_t) = \frac{c_t}{\rho_t^{\frac{1}{2}}} = y_t$, $\rho_t = \sqrt{\frac{c_t}{y_t}}$. So, $h_t(y_t) = \rho_t = \sqrt{\frac{c_t}{y_t}}$. Consider $x = h_r(y) = \frac{1}{\sqrt{y}} \sum_{t \in \mathcal{T}_r} \sqrt{c_t}$ that implies $y = \left(\frac{\sum_{t \in \mathcal{T}_r} \sqrt{c_t}}{x}\right)^2 = h_r^{-1}(x)$. It gives the cumulative utility function:

$\mathcal{U}_r(\alpha_r) = \sum_{t \in \mathcal{T}_r} \frac{-c_t}{\sqrt{\frac{c_t}{\left(\frac{\sum_{t \in \mathcal{T}_r} \sqrt{c_t}}{\alpha_r}\right)^2}}} = -\left(\sum_{t \in \mathcal{T}_r} \sqrt{c_t}\right)^2 \frac{1}{\alpha_r}$.

Generalized Fairness Utility Function

Previously we saw some options of utility function respecting technical assumption 1. An interesting function was proposed by [3]:

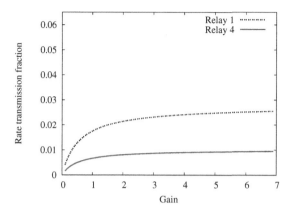

Fig. 8. Aggregated function $\mathcal{U}_r(\alpha_r) = -\left(\sum_{t \in \mathcal{T}_r} \sqrt{c_t}\right)^2 \frac{1}{\alpha_r}$

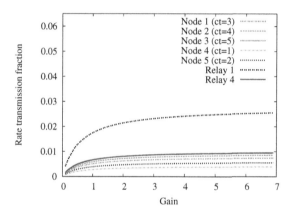

Fig. 9. Considering multi-hop with $\mathcal{U}_r(\alpha_r) = \sum_{t \in \mathcal{T}_r} U_t(\rho_t)$ and $U_t(\rho_t) = \frac{-c_t}{\rho_t}$

$$U_t(\rho_t) = c_t \frac{\rho_t^{1-\kappa}}{1 - \kappa} \tag{14}$$

This function is interesting because it generalizes all the following important cases of fairness:

- The *globally optimal allocation*: when $\kappa = 0$, that is $\max \sum_{t \in \mathcal{T}_r} \rho_t$.
- The *harmonic mean fairness*: when $\kappa = 2$.
- The *MaxMin fairness*: when $\kappa \to \infty$, $\max \min_{t \in \mathcal{T}_r} \rho_t$.
- The *proportional fairness*: when $\kappa \to 1$, $\max \sum_{t \in \mathcal{T}_r} \lim_{\kappa \to 1} \frac{\rho_t^{1-\kappa}}{1-\kappa} =$
$\sum_{t \in \mathcal{T}_r} \lim_{\kappa \to 1} \frac{e^{(1-\kappa)\ln(\rho_t)}}{1-\kappa} \sim \sum_{t \in \mathcal{T}_r} \frac{1+(1-\kappa)\ln(\rho_t)}{1-\kappa}$, that is $\max \sum_{t \in \mathcal{T}_r} \ln(\rho_t)$.
It is equivalent to $\max \prod_{t \in \mathcal{T}_r} \rho_t$ that in a convex framework represents the *Nash Equilibrium*.

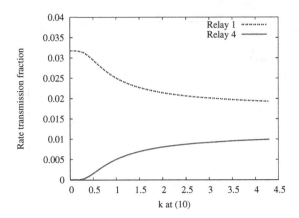

Fig. 10. Cumulative function $\mathcal{U}_r(\alpha_r) = \left(\sum_{t \in \mathcal{T}_r} c_t^{\frac{1}{\kappa}}\right)^\kappa \frac{x^{1-\kappa}}{1-\kappa}$

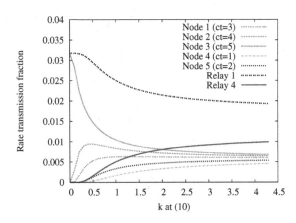

Fig. 11. Considering multi-hop with $\mathcal{U}_r(\alpha_r) = \sum_{t \in \mathcal{T}_r} U_t(\rho_t)$ and $U_t(\rho_t) = c_t \frac{\rho_t^{1-\kappa}}{1-\kappa}$

The previous utility functions are in fact the utility function in (14) with a given κ (respectively $\kappa = 1$, $\kappa = \frac{1}{2}$ and $\kappa = 2$). Considering directly the function $U_t(\rho_t) = c_t \frac{\rho_t^{1-\kappa}}{1-\kappa}$, we have: $U_t'(\rho_t) = c_t \rho_t^{-\kappa} = y_t$, $\rho_t = \frac{y_t}{c_t}^{-\frac{1}{\kappa}}$. So, $h_t(y_t) = \rho_t = \frac{c_t^{\frac{1}{\kappa}}}{y_t}$. Consider $x = h_r(y) = \sum_{t \in \mathcal{T}_r} h_t = \frac{\sum_{t \in \mathcal{T}_r} c_t^{\frac{1}{\kappa}}}{y^{\frac{1}{\kappa}}}$ that implies $h_r^{-1}(x) = \left(\frac{\sum_{t \in \mathcal{T}_r} c_t^{\frac{1}{\kappa}}}{x}\right)^\kappa$. Thus $\mathcal{U}_r(\alpha_r) = \sum_{t \in \mathcal{T}_r} \frac{c_t}{1-\kappa} \left(\frac{c_t^{\frac{1}{\kappa}}}{\frac{\sum_{t \in \mathcal{T}_r} c_t^{\frac{1}{\kappa}}}{x}}\right)^{1-\kappa} =$

$\frac{1}{\left(\sum_{t \in \mathcal{T}_r} c_t^{\frac{1}{\kappa}}\right)^{1-\kappa}} \sum_{t \in \mathcal{T}_r} \frac{c_t}{1-\kappa} c_t^{-\frac{1-\kappa}{\kappa}} x^{1-\kappa}$, therefore we can derive a generalized fairness utility function:

$$\mathcal{U}_r(\alpha_r) = \left(\sum_{t \in \mathcal{T}_r} c_t^{\frac{1}{\kappa}} \right)^{\kappa} \frac{x^{1-\kappa}}{1-\kappa}. \tag{15}$$

We show an example of our problem using the utility function in (14) for all nodes considering different values of κ.

Figures 10 and 11 show the obtained rate ρ_t varying κ (with fixed channel gain $g_{b,r} = 2, \forall r$). Figure 10 shows the rates considering the cumulative function in (15). Figure 11 shows the rates of all the nodes using the utility function in (14), note that each node has a different value for the constant c_t. The figures in this section show that we obtain the same graph for the relay nodes in both approaches as we proved.

6   Conclusion and Perspectives

We have considered in this paper the transmission rate allocation problem for multi-hop cellular networks in a way to reach an optimal and fair solution. We show that it can be reduced to a single-hop problem by only changing the utility functions. We confirm the validity of our proof experimentally.

Reducing multi-hop problems into problems with an unique cell (single-hop) has many advantages for the optimization problem. First we can reuse techniques that were designed basically for the one-cell case [7,4,11]. Second, we can identify bottlenecks, and in particular see if a congestion is due to the particular situation of a relay node, or to the specific utility function of the terminals it relays.

Of course the question on implementing distributed algorithms based on those results remains open. We can wonder if a pricing strategy is achievable. Another question is what kind of intermediate capacity restrictions on the second (or more) hop(s) can be added if we want to keep the same good properties.

References

1. Lin, Y.-D.J., Hsu, Y.-C.: Multihop cellular: A new architecture for wireless communications. In: INFOCOM, pp. 1273–1282 (2000),
   http://citeseer.ist.psu.edu/lin00multihop.html
2. Fitzek, F., Katz, M. (eds.): Cooperation in Wireless Networks: Principles and Applications – Real Egoistic Behavior is to Cooperate! Springer, Heidelberg (2006)
3. Mo, J., Walrand, J.: Fair end-to-end window-based congestion control. IEEE/ACM Transactions on Networking 8, 556–567 (2000)
4. Altman, E., Galtier, J., Touati, C.: Fair power and transmission rate control in wireless networks. In: Proc. of IEEE GlobeCom 2002, Taipei, Taiwan (November 2002)
5. Bermond, J.-C., Galtier, J., Klasing, R., Morales, N., Perennes, S.: Hardness and approximation of gathering in static radio networks. Parallel Processing Letters 16(2), 165–184 (2006)
6. Gomes, C., Pérennes, S., Rivano, H.: Bottleneck analysis for routing and call scheduling in multi-hop wireless networks. In: 4th IEEE Workshop on Broadband Wireless Access (BWA), December 4 (2008)

7. Yun, L., Messerschmitt, D.: Power control for variable QoS on a CDMA channel. In: IEEE MILCOM, vol. 1, pp. 178–182 (1994)
8. Price, J., Javidi, T.: Leveraging downlink for regulation of distributed uplink cdma. In: GLOBECOM (2006)
9. Kelly, F.P., Maulloo, A., Tan, D.: Rate control in communication networks: shadow prices, proportional fairness and stability. Journal of the Operational Research Society, Statistical Laboratory 49, 237–252 (1998)
10. Hiriart-Urruty, J.-B., Lemaréchal, C.: Fundamentals of Convex Analysis. Springer, Heidelberg (2001)
11. Galtier, J.: Adaptive power and transmission rate control in cellular CDMA networks. In: Globecom (2006)

A Topology Management Routing Protocol for Mobile IP Support of Mobile Ad Hoc Networks

Trung-Dinh Han and Hoon Oh*

School of Computer Engineering and Information Technology, University of Ulsan, (680-749) San 29, Mugeo 2-Dong, Nam-gu, Ulsan, South Korea
trungdinhvn@yahoo.com, hoonoh@ulsan.ac.kr

Abstract. Management of wireless multi-hop node mobility is required for global Internet connectivity of ad hoc networks. A new tree-based network topology management approach allows for managing node mobility efficiently and finding the shortest path quickly. Every node maintains topology information that includes the members of a tree being a root itself and the neighbors of each member. Then, a node can find the shortest path for a pair of nodes that belong to its topology information. We present simulation results to show that our approach far outperforms the well-known AODV based approach and works well even with an extremely high mobility of nodes.

Keywords: Mobility Management, Mobile IP, Topology Management.

1 Introduction

Recently, many researchers have addressed the Mobile IP support of Mobile Ad Hoc Networks (MANETs). Broch et al. [4] assume that Internet Gateway(IG) is equipped with two network interface cards. Jonsson et al. [2] focus on when to register with a foreign agent using MIPMANET Cell Switching algorithm, and adopted AODV [1] for MANET routing. In [7], Sun et al. discuss how Mobile IP and AODV can cooperate to discover multi-hop paths. Prashant et al. [6] propose a hybrid scheme for Mobile IP based on AODV. Ruiz et al. [5] focus on developing IG discovery schemes when ADOV is applied. These approaches focus on proposing their mobility management schemes, adopting one of the existing MANET routing protocols; the effectiveness of such that schemes to reduce overhead is limited since they uses an inefficient flooding.

We propose a new approach for mobility management and a new effective routing scheme. We start with our previous work [3], but different in that (1) topology information instead of tree information is managed hierarchically and (2) the shortest path is pursued by calculation based on the topology. Nodes build trees, each of which takes an IG as a root. A tree node manages its topology that consists of the link state for itself and its descendants. For routing, a member can calculate a path for a pair of source and destination that belong to its topology

---

* Corresponding author.

P.M. Ruiz and J.J. Garcia-Luna-Aceves (Eds.): ADHOC-NOW 2009, LNCS 5793, pp. 341–346, 2009.

by applying the shortest path algorithm. If a node fails to find a path, it requests its ancestors, who has more topology information, to do it along the tree path one by one. In this way, we get the initial shortest path. However, the path may not be correct because of the update interval. Thus, we correct the path if a certain link has been broken on the path by sending a route discovery request message along the path. We evaluated our approach against AODV based approach.

Section 2 describes network model with definitions. Section 3 details a topology management and a routing protocol. In Section 4, we evaluate performance by resorting to simulation and followed by conclusion in Section 5.

2   Preliminary

2.1   Network Model

Mobile nodes (MNs) form the trees which stem from an IG. A node is said to be a *member* if it belongs to any tree, and an *orphan* if it does not have a parent.

2.2   Message Definitions

We denote type of control message as CT and version of TMRP as VER.

- IG-Hello(CT, VER): IG broadcasts this periodically.
- MN-Hello(CT, VER, HopToIG): MN sends this to its parent periodically.
- J-REQ(CT, VER, HopToIG): MN sends this to its parent to join.
- CR-REQ(CT, VER): Orphan replies this to its child that sent MN-Hello.
- ILF(CT, VER, Source ID, NextHop): MN sends this to its ancestors to request an immediate update.
- CU-REQ(CT, VER, Node, Neighbor1, Neighbor2, ..., NeighborN): MN sends this to its ancestors periodically.

2.3   Topology Information Base

We define some notations: i.IG is IG to which node i belongs. i.T is set of tree members whose root is node i. i.NS, i.P is set of neighbors and parent of node i, respectively. d(i, j) is distance in hops from i to j and tells HopToIG if j is IG.

Definition 1: i.TIB = (i.G, i.P, d(i, i.IG), where i.G =(i.V, i.E) where i.V = {x, y| y ∈ x.NS, x ∈ i.T} and i.E = {(x, y)| x ∈ i.T, y ∈ x.NS}.

3   Topology Management Routing Protocol (TMRP)

3.1   Topology Establishment

3.1.1   MN-IG Join process

If a MN i receives IG-Hello from an IG and d(i, IG) > 1, it sends J-REQ to join. If it receives ACK from the IG, it becomes a child of the IG. If an IG receives J-REQ, it takes the sender as its child.

3.1.2 MN-MN Join process

When an orphan overhears a MN-Hello from a neighbor member, it sends J-REQ to the neighbor to join. Upon receiving ACK, it becomes a child of the neighbor. A member that receives J-REQ takes the sender as its child. The new child sends CU-REQ to its ancestors immediately.

3.2 Topology Maintenance

3.2.1 Tree-Link Maintenance Process

A mobile member node unicasts MN-Hello to its parent while an IG broadcasts IG-Hello periodically.

Child Maintenance: If a node receives MN-Hello from its child, it updates the child. If it does not receive MN-Hello from a certain child for a specified interval, it deletes the child.

Neighbor Maintenance: A node that overhears MN-Hello from its neighbor updates its neighbor information. If a node does not overhear MN-Hello from a neighbor for a specified interval, it deletes that neighbor.

3.2.2 Parent-Change process

Suppose that a node x overhears MN-Hello or receives IG-Hello from its neighbor y. If $d(x, x.IG) > d(y, y.IG) + 1$, x joins y by initiating the MN-MN Join Process or MN-IG Join Process.

3.2.3 Children-Release process

When a member x fails to send MN-Hello to its parent, it becomes an orphan. If it receives CU-REQ from a child, it replies with CR-REQ to ask it to leave. The child that receives CR-REQ becomes an orphan.

3.3 Path Discovery

3.3.1 Finding Initial Shortest-Path

A node x that wants to have a route to z tries to find the shortest path to z. If it fails, it sends the RC-REQ = (CT, src, dst) message to its parent to request a route calculation. The same procedure continues until a node finds the shortest path to the destination or IG fails to find the shortest path. If a node succeeds, it sends RC-RES = (CT, path, MIPF = 0) to src where path = (src,..., dst). However, if IG fails, it sends RC-RES = (CT, path, MIPF=1) to src where path = (src,..., IG).

3.3.2 Actual Path Discovery

The actual path is explored by exploiting the initial shortest path. The RD-REQ is sent to the destination along the initial shortest path, fixing any broken link by exploring a triangle detour using neighbor information.

3.4 Path Recovery

A node that finds a link failure while sending a data packet initiates the Path Recovery process. It immediately sends ILF to its ancestors to request the TIB

(Definition 1) update. At the same time, it sends R-ERR to source to notify the link failure.

4   Performance Evaluation

We evaluated TMRP protocol using the QualNet 3.9. We used three scenarios - S1, S2, and S3 by distributing one IG and 100 mobile nodes in a square terrain 1000 x 1000(m^2). S1, S2, and S3 have one IG placed at the center, at the top center, and at the top left of the terrain, respectively. The simulation parameters are given in Table 1.

Table 1. Simulation parameters and values

Parameter	Value	Parameter	Value
Mobility Pattern	Random Waypoint	Pause Time	30
Number of Nodes	101 (1 fixed IG included)	Dimension	1000 x 1000
Transmission Range	250m	Wireless Bandwidth	2 Mbps
Traffic Pattern	CBR	Number of Sessions	15 (1 packet/sec.)
Packet Size	512 bytes	Simulation Time	600 seconds

4.1   Evaluation with Different Scenarios

Fig. 2 shows that delivery ratios of TMRP for are in order of S1, S2, and S3. This is closely related to the average size of trees. That is, the higher the depth of tree is, the higher the probability of the change in a tree structure is, increasing control overhead. Control overhead increases as node mobility does as shown in Fig. 1, further degrading delivery ratio.

Fig. 3 and Fig. 4 compare the delay and jitter for the three scenarios. The frequency of path destruction increases as node mobility increases. So, delay time shows a slightly increasing curve with node speed because of the increased number of path recoveries. The gap between different scenarios occurs because the bigger trees cause more topology maintenance overhead. Similarly, if path is broken, delay and jitter tends to increase largely. So, both delay and jitter graphs show the similar curve patterns.

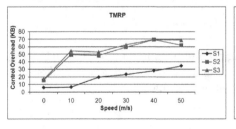 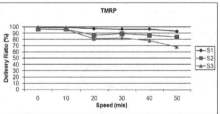

Fig. 1. Control overhead with variation of max-speed (nSessions = 15)   **Fig. 2.** Delivery ratio with variation of max-speed (nSessions = 15)

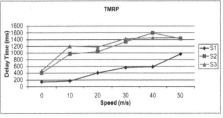
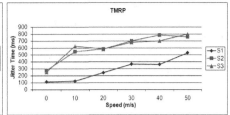

Fig. 3. Delay with variation of max-speed (nSessions = 15)

Fig. 4. Jitter with variation of max-speed (nSessions = 15)

4.2   Comparison with AODVM

We evaluated our approach against the AODV based approach (AODVM)[6] in which AODV is used to explore IG or destination and every mobile node registers with the IG periodically in a reactive manner. In this simulation, the maximum speed of nodes is fixed at 10m/s while the number of sessions is varied from 5 to 45. Fig. 5 shows that control overhead of TMRP is little sensitive to the variation of sessions because number of sessions have nothing to do with link stability. Accordingly, delivery ratio is well sustained over all the ranges.With AODVM, the flooding causes a sharp increase in control overhead, degrading delivery ratio rapidly in Fig. 6. With TMRP, if a path is broken, the packet is

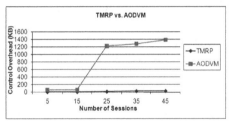
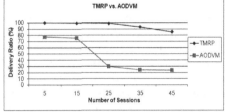

Fig. 5. Control overhead with variation of number of sessions: TMRP vs. AODVM (Speed = 10m/s)

Fig. 6. Delivery ratio with variation of number of sessions: TMRP vs. AODVM (Speed = 10m/s)

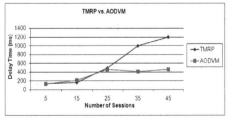
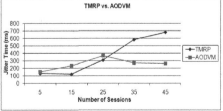

Fig. 7. Delay with variation of sessions: TMRP vs. AODVM (Speed = 10m/s)

Fig. 8. Jitter with variation of sessions: TMRP vs. AODVM (Speed = 10m/s)

kept in a queue and then is salvaged after the broken path is repaired, resulting in the increased delay. On the contrary, delay of AODVM is sustained low because AODVM removes on-processing packets that would experience a big delay if the path were repaired and the packets were salvaged (See Fig. 6). That is why AODVM shows less delay and jitter than TMRP as in Fig. 7 and Fig. 8.

5 Conclusions

In this paper, we proposed the TMRP which comprises a new mobility management method and a new routing scheme specialized to the hybrid networks. In our protocol, every node manages a local network topology that allows for calculating the shortest path for a pair of nodes within the topology. Moreover, mobile nodes do not use flooding for the establishment of a route. The simulation results show that our approach produces outstanding results compared with the AODV based approach.

References

1. Perkins, C.E., Royer, E.M.: Ad-hoc on-demand distance vector routing. In: Second IEEE Workshop on Mobile Computing Systems and Applications, February 1999, pp. 90–100 (1999)
2. Jonsson, D., Alriksson, F., Larsson, T., Johansson, P., Maguire, J.G.: MIPMANET - Mobile IP for Mobile Ad Hoc Networks. In: Proceedings of IEEE/ACM Workshop on Mobile and Ad Hoc Networking and Computing (MobiHoc 2000), Boston, MA, USA, August 2000, pp. 75–85 (2000)
3. Oh, H., Phan, A.T.: A Mobility Management and Routing Protocol using Tree Architecture for Internet Connectivity of Mobile Ad Hoc Networks. In: ICCCN 2007, Hawaii, USA, August 2007, pp. 967–972 (2007)
4. Broch, J., Maltz, D.A., Johnson, D.B.: Supporting Hierarchy and Heterogeneous Interfaces in Multi-Hop Wireless Ad Hoc Networks. In: Proc. Int'l. Symp. Parallel Architecture, Algorithms, and Networks, Perth, Australia, June 1999, pp. 370–375 (1999)
5. Ruiz, P., Gomez-Skarmeta, A.: Enhanced Internet connectivity for hybrid ad hoc networks through adaptive gateway discovery. In: Proceedings of the 29th Annual IEEE International Conference on Local Computer Networks (LCN 2004), pp. 370–377. IEEE Computer Society, Los Alamitos (2004)
6. Prashant, R., Robin, K.: A hybrid approach to Internet connectivity for mobile ad hoc networks. In: Proceeding of IEEE WCNC 2003, vol. 3, pp. 1522–1527. IEEE Computer Society Press, Los Alamitos (2003)
7. Sun, Y., Belding-Royer, E.M., Perkins, C.E.: Internet connectivity for ad hoc mobile networks. International Journal of Wireless Information Networks special issue on Mobile Ad Hoc Networks (MANETs): Standards, Research, and Applications 9(2), 75–88 (2002)

Implementation and Comparison of AODV and OLSR Routing Protocols in an Ad-Hoc Network over Bluetooth

Gorka Hernando[1], José María Cabero[1], José Luis Jodrá[2], and Susana Pérez[1]

[1] Robotiker-Tecnalia Technology Center, Zamudio, 48170, Spain
Tel.: +34 94 6002266; Fax: +34 94 6002299
{ghernando,jmcabero,sperez}@robotiker.es
http://www.robotiker.com/
[2] University of the Basque Country – ETSI, Bilbao, 48004, Spain
Tel.: +34 94 6012000; Fax: +34 94 6012041
joseluis.jodra@ehu.es
http://www.ingeniaritza-bilbao.ehu.es

Abstract. Ad-Hoc networking is one of the most impacting architectures in the development of the Future Internet, where the nodes are expected to be wireless and mobile. Unlike the traditional IP-based and simulation-based approaches inside the Ad-Hoc research field, this work presents a real implementation of proactive (OLSR) and reactive protocols (AODV) over real Bluetooth devices (non-IP approach) in static and dynamic scenarios. Along the paper we point out many handicaps that have been solved in order to make Bluetooth work as supporting technology (the need for a previously established connection to, the lack of broadcast messages, the overhead...). We have carried out a set of experiments to compare the potential and limitations of both protocols.

This work was developed inside the Future Internet project supported by the Basque Government within the ETORTEK Programme and the FuSeN project supported by the Spanish Ministerio de Ciencia e Innovación.

1 Introduction

Ad-Hoc networks are a key field on current research because of their self-configuring properties and short deployment time on several scenarios like natural disasters or short-lived networks. Ad-hoc network routing protocols can be divided into two major routing strategies: proactive and reactive protocols.

Proactive protocols send periodical messages so that each node knows the updated status of the whole topology at every moment and are optimum for delay sensible networks. On the contrary, reactive protocols just send control messages on demand. This implies a higher delay in the connection establishment, but the overhead obtained is better than the one obtained with proactive approaches.

We do not use the Bluetooth Network Encapsulation Protocol (BNEP) [3] to run IP on top, which is what the Future Internet is expecting. We have modified two typical protocols: OLSR (Optimized Link State Routing Protocol) and AODV (Ad-Hoc On Demand Distance Vector Protocol) [4], to adapt them to the new architecture.

P.M. Ruiz and J.J. Garcia-Luna-Aceves (Eds.): ADHOC-NOW 2009, LNCS 5793, pp. 347–353, 2009.

The radio technology chosen for the experiments is Bluetooth [1], a widespread short-medium range radio technology with lower power consumption compared to other radio technologies such as WiFi [2]. There are some obstacles to be solved before using Bluetooth as wireless technology in the Ad-Hoc networking field.

Previous works have presented several algorithms for creating Ad-Hoc networks. [5] proposes a Scatternet formation algorithm to allow multihop data exchanging, but is limited for direct data connections between neighbours. [6] proposes a solution to allow the interconnection of WiFi and Bluetooth devices disguising them into virtual Linux Kernel interfaces, but it can not be implemented on a simple device.

This paper is organised as follows: Sections 2, focused on Bluetooth, and 3, focused on routing protocols, describe the technical solution; Section 4 shows the results of simulations and the comparison; and Section 5 describes main conclusions.

2   Bluetooth Layer

Two main obstacles need to be overcome in order to support the formation of Ad-hoc networks: the need for connection between nodes; and the lack of broadcast messages.

2.1   Data Exchange between Neighbour Devices

Bluetooth provides its own neighbour discovery procedure: Inquiry. This process begins when a device in the Inquiry substate sends Inquiry messages according to a hopping sequence derived by its local device clock. Discoverable devices periodically enter the Inquiry scan substate and send responses when a message is received, so the connection establishment procedure can begin. To consider dynamics, we set up a procedure to check out the network topology by alternating these two substates.

The classic mode of operation on network layer research would have made us use the BNEP for implementing TCP/IP stack. However, this adaptation layer introduces an extra overhead. We propose a non-IP architecture where connections are established by the L2CAP protocol.

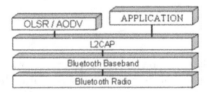

Fig. 1. Protocol architecture

Routing protocols and application services operate at the same level. Hence, it has been necessary to add a new header to distinguish control and data packets.

2.2   Deploying the Ad-Hoc Network on the Link Layer

While routing protocols are based on the exchange of broadcast messages, Bluetooth is a master-slave point to point connection technology where two slave neighbours can not communicate directly, but through their master, instead.

We have developed a Greedy Piconet Establishment procedure where all the nodes try to create an L2CAP connection with all their neighbours so they can communicate directly. Using this method, the number of piconets for the same set of n neighbour nodes will increase from 1 to n-1. Nevertheless, and thanks to the Bluetooth robustness to frequency interference, the network will operate correctly.

Sending broadcast messages is impossible using the standard Bluetooth stack because of the need for synchronization between devices and the point to point connection nature. We propose a simple solution consisting in writing the data to be sent on the UART sequentially; so that the system behaves equal for the routing layer.

Figure 2 depicts the network seen by the link and the network layer. Both are independent, so the master and slave topology is transparent for the routing protocols.

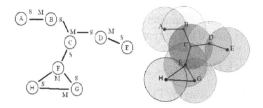

Fig. 2. Network topology for both layers

3 Network Layer

There are some aspects to be considered because of the changes produced by the new physical technology and the memory and processing constraints of the devices used.

3.1 Identifying Devices

Since protocols are defined according to the TCP/IP stack, we must introduce new fields on our headers to identify nodes in the routing layer. We have implemented a static DNS to associate numbers with devices and send just 1 byte of payload.

3.2 Adaptation of the Routing Protocols for Bluetooth

3.2.1 Link Management Modified

Both OLSR and AODV have a discovery algorithm for determining the link relation with their neighbours, differentiating between symmetric and asymmetric links. These considerations do not make sense on Bluetooth; therefore, they have been ruled out.

Protocols permit to define more than one interface per node. All our devices have only one interface, so this message has been discarded in our implementation.

3.2.2 Changes in the Detection of Duplicated Messages

OLSR needs to save in memory too much management information to detect the arrival of duplicated control messages. So, we have completely removed this detection procedure and changed it by one similar to the one used in the AODV routing protocol, which needs much less control information to be saved.

3.2.3 Dispensable Information Removed from Routing Tables

In order to optimize future route discovery strategies, AODV keeps in memory the latest routing info, i.e. latency data. This is too heavy to be supported for our devices. Hence, we decided to discard this information from the routing tables.

Amount of Updates Reduced

OLSR recalculates the routing and the MPR information with each HELLO received. That involves too many processing operations for our devices. Therefore, we compare the old state with the new one, and just update the tables if the state has changed.

4 Definition of Scenarios and Performance Measurements

In this section we explain the characteristics of the Bluetooth devices, the proposed scenarios and the performance measurement.

4.1 Bluetooth Network Devices

Our work was carried out using WT12 [7] Bluetooth modules. WT12 is a Class 2 Bluetooth v2.1 + EDR device with 10 metres of radio coverage, 2-3 Mbps of data exchange throughput, 8 Mb of flash memory, internal clock of 26 MHz and a fully implemented Bluetooth protocol stack.

4.2 Proposed Scenarios and Performance Measurements

4.2.1 Bluetooth Layer Measures

A key parameter for the proper functioning of the network is the efficiency of the neighbour discovery algorithm. On the basis of the results of [8], we have set up a set of experiments consisting of 4 static nodes trying to detect one another.

Table 1. Elapsed time for completing Bluetooth connections

Inquiry Time	2.56 sec	5.12 sec	10.24 sec
Detections (%)	38.1 %	79.1 %	87.5 %

We can conclude that the best Inquiry timer for our network, considering the efficiency in the discovery and the response to the dynamics, is 5.12 seconds.

The next scenarios measure the time needed to establish a link: A – Two nodes connecting each other; B – Three nodes already connected and a new one started.

Table 2. Elapsed time for completing Bluetooth connections

	Scenario A	Scenario B
Connection average value	9.29 s	26.57 s

Noting the mean values of the connection establishment we can conclude that Bluetooth devices behave worse as the number of simultaneous connections increases.

4.2.2 Network Layer Measures

For the network layer measures, we have set up different scenarios: A – four nodes in diamond topology; B – three nodes connected in a semi-diamond topology and a wandering edge node; C – four aligned nodes.

In scenario A we analyze the allowed minimum timer for the HELLO messages and the resulting times to identify the loss of a neighbour on both routing protocols.

Table 3. Allowed minimum Hello Timer value and neighbour loss discovery time

	Hello Value	Neighbour lost identifying
OLSR	8 sec	[24, 32) sec
AODV	2 sec	[6, 8) sec

As we can see in the table, the obtained values for AODV are much better. When an OLSR node receives a HELLO message a lot of operations must be done and the system fails with low timer values due to the capacity constraints. The time threshold to consider information as valid in routing protocols is defined as 3 times its corresponding updating timer. So, the time to identify a lost neighbour in OLSR will be a value between 24 and 32 seconds, too high for a correct functioning of network.

The next parameter to be assessed is the overhead. This experiment has been carried out in scenario B (dynamic topology) and consists of communicating edge nodes, which has to be done through a middle node, i.e. two hops.

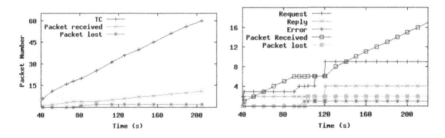

Fig. 3. Introduced overhead for both protocols

We can see that the overhead of AODV is better than the one obtained for OLSR because once the discovery process is completed no more messages are needed.

Another parameter related to the mobility in Ad-Hoc networks is the time needed by the protocols to get readapted to the new topology. This value is dependent on the using Hello Timer (HT). In the table below we show the elapsed time since the node gets out of the radio coverage of the neighbour until the communication is restarted.

We can conclude that OLSR behaves better than AODV against changes in the topology caused by the mobility of the nodes. That is because when a connection is

Table 4. Elapsed time by routing protocols to adapt to the new network topology

Routing protocol	OLSR (HT: 8 sg)	AODV (HT: 2 sg)	AODV (HT: 8 sg)
Elapsed time	27 sec	23 sec	42 sec

lost in AODV the protocol tries first to repair the route and then, if it fails like it happens in our experiment, the source must repeat the route discovery procedure.

Finally, the data exchanging delay will be analyzed. This experiment is carried out in Scenario c. The experiment consists of communicating the edge nodes through the middle nodes, i.e. 3 hops.

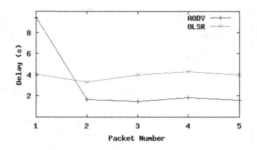

Fig. 4. Network topologies for network measures

AODV gets lower delay times, except when the route has to be discovered, compared to OLSR. This is because OLSR exchanges a great amount of control messages that impact on high processing time.

5 Conclusions

Our work has been focused on the development of Ad-Hoc Networks, a key field of investigation for the construction of the Future Internet. We have implemented some enhanced algorithms to give support to those network topologies using Bluetooth, a widespread wireless technology but limited for this purpose, in a non-IP approach.

Despite the benefits of the proposed algorithms, there are restrictions that make Bluetooth no propitious for high mobility networks due to the need for establishing a previous connection. This process lasts more than 10 seconds for dense networks, and hence, short physical connections will be transparent to the Network layer.

With respect to the performance comparison, we conclude that the reactive protocol AODV behaves much better than the proactive protocol OLSR. On the other hand, the results have been conditioned by the WT12 modules and their constraints.

As future work, the presented solutions will be implemented in our own designed Bluetooth [9] devices, which are not restricted in terms of processing and memory. Another focus is to add the possibility of sending broadcast messages. Some researches have been completed [10], but no optimal solutions have been proposed.

References

1. Bluetooth – Special Group of Interest, `https://www.Bluetooth.org/`
2. Balani, R.: Energy Consumption Analysis for BT, WiFi and Cellular Networks
3. BNEP Specification,
   `http://grouper.ieee.org/groups/802/15/Bluetooth/BNEP.pdf`
4. OLSR: `http://www.ietf.org/rfc/rfc3626.txt`; AODV:
   `http://www.ietf.org/rfc/rfc3561.txt`
5. Cuomo, F., Pugini, A.: A linux based Bluetooth Scatternet formation kit
6. Stuedi, P.: Transparent Heterogeneous Mobile AdHoc Networks
7. WT12 device:
   `http://www.bluegiga.com/WT12_Class_2_Bluetooth_Module`
8. Peterson, B.S., Baldwin, R.O.: BT Inquiry Time Characterization and Selection
9. Cabero, J.M., Unibaso, G., Sanchez, A., Arizaga, I.: The BT Medallion: a Wearable Device for Human MANETs
10. Liang, J., Li, Y., Yu, B.: Performance Analysis and Reliability Improvement of Bluetooth Broadcast Scheme

Inside-Out OLSR Scalability Analysis

David Palma and Marilia Curado

Department of Informatics Engineering
Centre for Informatics and Systems
University of Coimbra (CISUC)
{palma,marilia}@dei.uc.pt

Abstract. The ideal network size for the Optimized Link-State Routing
Protocol (OLSR) was determined taking into account several parameters,
providing concrete and innovative foundations for future clustering solutions much required for Large Scale MANETs. An extensive simulation
study was performed on small scale wireless networks, using the OPNET
Modeler Wireless Suite, considering the OLSR protocol routing scalability. The obtained results revealed a good performance for up to 70 nodes
with moderate node mobility and with no more than 16 traffic flows.

1 Introduction

Ad-hoc networks have increasingly shown their importance in the dissemination of wireless networks. These networks, usually referred to as Mobile Ad-hoc
Networks (MANETs), stand out for being a self-organized, self-administrated
and self-maintained infrastructure independent solution for the deployment of
wireless networks.

Despite all the technological breakthroughs, many important characteristics
of MANETs have to be taken into account [1]. All these aspects are considered by
the existing applications of Ad-hoc networks such as Mesh Networks, Vehicular
Ad-Hoc Networks (VANETs), and for Military and Rescue operations.

The next section presents some of related work on MANETs. In Section 3
simulation results of the OLSR protocol performance are presented. After the
analysis of these results, Section 4 presents the final conclusions, suggesting
how such results could be used to encourage the development of new clustering
solutions for MANETs, extending previous contributions on this area [2][3].

2 Related Work

The performance of the OLSR routing protocol has already been studied by
some existing works. Despite this, no existing contribution provides an extensive
evaluation, handling the variation of the most important parameters.

In [4] a scenario with 50 nodes was analyzed varying the nodes' speed between
0 and 10 m/s and the number of traffic streams between 0 and 100, with a
Constant Bit Rate (CBR) of 64 $bytes/second$. The performed simulations ran

P.M. Ruiz and J.J. Garcia-Luna-Aceves (Eds.): ADHOC-NOW 2009, LNCS 5793, pp. 354–359, 2009.

only for 250 *seconds*, where the streams' duration did not exceed 10 *seconds*, in a field $1000 \cdot 1000$ m^2 while using a pause time between 0 and 5 m/s. This work is limited by the used traffic streams as they are not representative of typical network utilization since 64 *bytes/second* flows should not be typical. Additionally it is not possible to see how the number of nodes influences the performance of the OLSR protocol.

In [5], a higher number of nodes is tested in different field sizes. Scenarios with low and high node density are tested with the nodes' speed varying from 1 to 10 m/s with a pause time of 3 *seconds*. Traffic sources using CBR flows of 32 *byte* packets were used, with a maximum of 10 flows. The simulations ran for an unreasonable short period of time of 60 *seconds*. One important aspect of this work is the variation of the node density in a MANET. However the results are limited by a pause time and amount of traffic generated by each flow which does not seem reasonable for any typical network utilization.

In the results provided by [6], the chosen CBR traffic simulates the background traffic generated by the H.323 ITU signalling standard for IP network audio, with an average session duration of 360 *seconds*. The number of sessions, as well as the number of nodes (up to 1000 nodes), were varied in a terrain field of $2000 \cdot 1200$ m^2, with a node speed uniformly distributed between 0 and 10 m/s and zero pause time.

This work lacks a proper specification of the protocol parameters, has limited duration of the used traffic which represents less than half of the simulation hence providing better results, and has no pause time, rendering an inadequate behaviour of the random waypoint model.

To the best of our knowledge no previous works provide a thorough evaluation of the OLSR protocol.

3   Performance Evaluation

In order to evaluate the OLSR performance several simulations were conducted using the OPNET Modeler Wireless Suite®[7]. With the purpose of analyzing the optimal scenario for the protocol several parameters were varied in different simulation sets. Each one consists of 30 runs with different seed values, in a square area of $1 \cdot 1$ km^2, for 600 seconds. The nodes followed the default random waypoint model, which is usually considered the standard mobility model for MANETs, with a pause time of 50 seconds, suitable for a user behaviour that can correspond to a bus or a semaphore stop. The physical layer of the wireless nodes follows the IEEE 802.11b ($11Mbit/s$) since it is more likely to be found in the majority of the existing devices, transmit power of $0.005W$ and a packet reception power threshold of $-85dBm$ (corresponding to a range of less than $270m$). The OLSR protocol specific parameters are set to default.

3.1   Simulated Scenarios

One of the main purposes of this evaluation is to determine to which extent the OLSR protocol scales in the most different scenarios. For that purpose ten networks with a different number of nodes (10-100) were simulated each with four different node speeds (0, 3, 30 and 120 km/h) and, for each possible scenario, several traffic flows were set (1, 2, 4, 16, 32 and 128), uniformly distributed and with random destinations, having a constant bit rate of $4kbit/s$.

The used speed values represent walking pedestrians and vehicles at different speeds [8].

3.2 OLSR Simulation Analysis Results

In this section the most important parameters are analyzed and all the presented graphs show a 95% confidence interval.

Traffic Delay. The results obtained for the Traffic Delay, presented in Fig. 1, show that static networks tend to suffer a slightly higher delay than networks where nodes are moving, especially in networks with a reduced number of nodes. For networks with mobility a significant increase occurs when the number of nodes increases from 10 to 20, being very similar otherwise, which is consistent with the results obtained in [4]. Afterwards, despite the increasing number of nodes, the obtained delay is maintained. Some of these values are similar to the ones seen in [5] and [6], presenting rather small fluctuations for static networks and slight increase for networks with higher speeds while providing more detailed information. Another aspect that clearly influences the delay in MANET networks using the OLSR protocol is the number of flows.

Traffic Losses. When analyzing the percentage of traffic lost (Fig. 2), the impact of the number of nodes and speed is clearly noticeable. For higher speeds, the amount of losses is higher and rather independent from the number of nodes, except for the scenario with 70 nodes at a speed of 120km/h where a decrease on the losses exists, possibly due to some particular behaviour of the network with the random waypoint model. The best shown results belong to the moderate

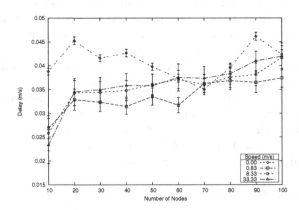

Fig. 1. Average Traffic Delay in seconds for 16 flows

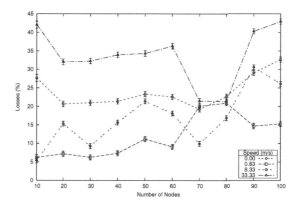

Fig. 2. Average Traffic Losses for 16 Flows

speed network which generally outperforms the static network. This is due to the fact that if the initial topology of the static network is not favourable, many nodes may be unreachable, whereas in the moderate speed network this may be corrected with the nodes' movement without causing too much disruption. It is possible to verify that for higher speeds the number of losses increases significantly, specially for scenarios with a reduced number of flows in which the number of losses increases with speed. Even though [4] does not present a variation of the number of nodes, the results regarding the number of flows and nodes' mobility present a reasonable concordance with our results.

Neighbourhood and MPR Calculations. The number of calculations performed to populate the Multipoint Relay or the Neighbourhood Sets depends mainly on the periodic link sensing performed by every node in the network. These results, as expected, presented a similar behaviour. The study allowed to infer that the number of calculations is closely related with the number of nodes in the network and that increases with a greater number of nodes. It is important to note that for networks with more than 70 nodes, the increase of the number of calculations is substantially higher.

Regarding the nodes' speed impact it becomes clear that, for higher speeds, a higher number of calculations is registered (Fig. 3).

Route Table Calculations. The information contained in the routing table is dependent on the available information of the local link information and topology set. The route table is updated whenever one of these parameters change: the link set, the neighbour set, the 2-hop neighbour set, the topology set and the Multiple Interface Association Base.

The recorded values show that the number of performed calculations, as it would be expected, increases both with the number of nodes in the network and with the speed of the nodes, not being much influenced by the variable number of flows except for the static scenario. The average route table calculations show

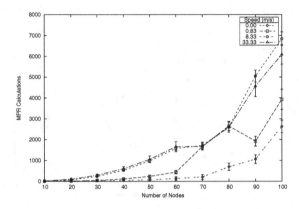

Fig. 3. Average number of MPR Calculations

that for higher speeds such as 30 and 120km/h, the values present an almost linear growth whereas for static nodes or with a low speed, the growth is smoother in networks with less than 70 nodes.

Topology Control Messages. The number of sent TC Messages during each simulation is influenced by the MPR nodes periodic generation of these messages. Additionally, more messages may be generated due to link changes that may occur, forcing their generation before the established interval for that purpose. As it would be expected, the number of TC messages sent increases with a higher number of nodes, and also reveals to be influenced by higher speeds which are more likely to produce topology changes. This behaviour is similar to the one presented in [6] for the registered routing load.

4   Conclusion

The performed analysis of the OLSR routing protocol revealed a robust protocol capable of scaling with good results in networks with up to 70 nodes, preferably with a moderate node speed and where the number of traffic flows is also moderate. Networks with a higher number of nodes could probably be supported, however the amount of protocol specific calculations and the sudden increase of the percentage of losses, indicates that it may not be advisable. This motivates the usage of cluster mechanisms earlier mentioned, as well as improved routing protocols, in order to provide a connection between optimal networks organized in clusters [9].

Existing works on clustering with the OLSR protocol, such as [10], lack an analysis similar to the one presented in this work. In fact, typically, no considerations about the optimal conditions for cluster formation are taken into account. However, we showed that in order to achieve a generic and robust clustering solution, such an analysis is crucial.

The number of performed simulations allowed an analysis of the protocol, however, not only a wider variation of the network size, but also the variation of OLSR specific parameters could improve the study and provide an even deeper analysis. Another interesting aspect would be to perform the same tests in scenarios with different node density. Future work will involve a modification of the OLSR protocol such that it will be capable of performing in a scalable clustered scenario.

Acknowledgement

This work was partially supported by the Portuguese Foundation for Science and Technology (FCT) and by the European projects WEIRD (IP) and CONTENT (FP6). The authors would like to thank the OPNET University Program for the licenses provided for the OPNET Modeler Wireless Suite®.

References

1. Corson, S., Macker, J.: Mobile ad hoc networking (manet): Routing protocol performance issues and evaluation considerations. Request for Comments rfc2501, Internet Engineering Task Force (January 1999)
2. Baccelli, E.: Olsr trees: A simple clustering mechanism for olsr. In: Challenges in Ad Hoc Networking. IFIP International Federation for Information Processing, vol. 197, pp. 265–274. Springer, Boston (2006)
3. Ros, F.J., Ruiz, P.M.: Cluster-based olsr extensions to reduce control overhead in mobile ad hoc networks. In: Proceedings of the 2007 international conference on Wireless communications and mobile computing, pp. 202–207. ACM, New York (2007)
4. Clausen, T., Jacquet, P., Viennot, L.: Comparative study of routing protocols for mobile ad-hoc networks. In: The First Annual Mediterranean Ad Hoc Networking Workshop, MindPass Center for Distributed Systems, Aalborg University and Project Hipercom, INRIA Rocquencourt (September 2002)
5. Ahmed, S., Bilal, M., Farooq, U., Fazl-e-Hadi: Performance analysis of various routing strategies in mobile ad hoc network using qualnet simulator. In: International Conference on Emerging Technologies, 2007. ICET 2007, November 2007, pp. 62–67 (2007)
6. Rasheed, T., Javaid, U., Jerbi, M., Al Agha, K.: Scalable multi-hop ad hoc routing using modified olsr routing protocol. In: IEEE 18th International Symposium on Personal, Indoor and Mobile Radio Communications, 2007, September 2007, pp. 1–6 (2007)
7. Opnet simulator, http://www.opnet.com/
8. 3GPP: Spatial channel model for multiple input multiple output (mimo) simulations. Technical specification group radio access network. Technical Report 7, 3rd Generation Partnership Project (2008)
9. Palma, D., Curado, M.: NODRoP, Nature Optimized Deferred Routing Protocol. In: Infocom, IEEE Conference on Computer Communications S. Workshop (2009)
10. Ge, Y., Lamont, L., Villasenor, L.: Hierarchical olsr - a scalable proactive routing protocol for heterogeneous ad hoc networks. In: IEEE International Conference on Wireless And Mobile Computing, Networking And Communications, 2005 (WiMob 2005), August 2005, vol. 3, pp. 17–23 (2005)

Proximal Labeling for Oblivious Routing in Wireless Ad Hoc Networks

Edgar Chávez[1,2], Maia Fraser[3], and Héctor Tejeda[1]

[1] Universidad Michoacana
[2] CICESE
[3] Instituto Politécnico Nacional

Abstract. For an adhoc network with n nodes, we propose a proactive routing protocol *without* routing tables which uses $O(\log n)$ bits per node for the location service tables. The algorithm is based on 1-dimensional virtual coordinates, which we call labels. The decision of where to forward a packet is oblivious and purely local, depending only on the labels of the immediate neighbours and the label of the destination: the packet is forwarded to the neighbour whose label is closest to that of the destination. The algorithm is based on mapping the network to an ordered list where each node has one or more integer labels. This labeling can be produced by any arbitrary traversal of the network visiting all the nodes, in particular by a depth-first search of a flood tree which gives a $2n$ length traversal. We show experimentally that, in terms of hop number, our routing algorithm is far superior to geographic protocols in randomly generated networks and for sparse networks produces routes of length very close to those of the shortest path.

1   Introduction

An ad hoc wireless network is a network of wireless nodes cooperating among themselves to forward messages without a fixed, centralized infrastructure. Each node in the network has a unique identifier (ID) and can interchange packets only with a subset of the network, the node's neighbors, usually the nodes within radio range but possibly only a subset of these. The network is modeled as a graph of n nodes, where two nodes share an edge if and only if they can communicate directly. The problem of routing consists in discovering a path from source node s to destination node t through a set of intermediate nodes. Each node decides locally to which node(s) to forward the packet. The decision is determined by the routing algorithm based on the ID of the destination node, the local topology (and possibly geometry) of the network, extra information stored in each node about the routes (the routing tables) and information contained in the packet itself.

The many routing protocols which have been proposed since the advent of ad hoc wireless networks may be generally divided into two classes, those which are reactive (i.e., on-demand) and those which are proactive (i.e, pre-calculated). In the former class (see early work by [3], a route is found dynamically whenever it is

P.M. Ruiz and J.J. Garcia-Luna-Aceves (Eds.): ADHOC-NOW 2009, LNCS 5793, pp. 360–365, 2009.
© Springer-Verlag Berlin Heidelberg 2009

needed, that is, for each "data session". In the latter class routes are established and maintained, usually in tables, for some period of time so as to be ready to use when needed. In particular, the Internet Engineering Task Force [2] MANET working group whose aim is the standardization of MANET routing protocols has been considering over a dozen protocols and at this point only two remain, one reactive (called DYMO) and one proactive (called OLSRv2) [7] [2].

In reactive protocols the basic procedure is to flood the network with packets until the destination node is reached; then a functioning route (or routes) is recorded in the intermediate nodes and the data session is started. If multiple nodes are starting sessions (especially short-lived sessions) the recorded routes have to be purged periodically to avoid filling up the memory of the nodes. The entire procedure is not energy efficient.

In proactive protocols the usual approach is to periodically share routing tables so that nodes may obtain knowledge about the entire network and update their tables accordingly - for use by various sessions until the next update. Although this procedure is potentially more energy efficient (given a low enough frequency of update), optimization of the update period is a delicate problem which takes on a critical importance in the design of such protocols (see [7] for a discussion of related statistical techniques and a proposal related to OLSR). Moreover, the mere size of routing tables can become a serious issue since in the basic approach each node u needs to store for each target node t a pair of the form (t, v) where v is the corresponding neighboring node to which packets for t must be forwarded from u. Since memory, as energy, is a scarce resource in MANET's, proactive routing in this usual sense does not scale well.

2   Comparison with Related Work

In this paper we define a routing protocol which is proactive in the sense that topology about the whole network is shared periodically[1] and thus routes are ready for use when needed by sessions. However, the data which is shared and stored in each node is a constant number of labels of size $O(\log n)$, as well as a location service table of order $O(\log n)$. The geographic routing protocol is based on the idea of forwarding the packet trying to reduce the distance to the destination (since it can be measured locally, using only the node coordinates). Although geographic algorithms are reactive in the sense of being on-demand, the topology control algorithms are local and can be thought of as pre-calculated and as well do not have the trial-and-error aspect of reactive algorithms. Moreover, there is the issue of a location service, which we explain below. Thus geographic algorithms constitute somewhat of a gray area between the classes of reactive and proactive protocols and their preferred naming in terms of their geographical aspect becomes appropriate. It is also important to note that geographic routing algorithms only guarantee delivery for certain special subclasses of wireless networks, such as unit disk (UDW) or quasi-unit disk (QUDW) networks (see [9] for a survey of such classes and approaches).

---

[1] i.e., each time a flood-tree is constructed.

Location Service. Routing algorithms based on geographic or virtual coordinates may only be used on their own if destinations are specified by their geographic or virtual coordinates, otherwise, when routing is to a given ID, it is necessary to first translate ID to coordinates. This is the case in most MANET's (that are not sensor networks) and so, in these settings, geographic and virtual coordinate-based protocols need an additional layer, known as a "location service" to translate from the nodes' ID. This extra layer should be designed carefully to avoid a loop in the search procedure.

Energy trade-offs. Neither proactive nor geographic protocols are suitable to handle node mobility without modification. Reactive protocols natively support node mobility but can use a large amount of energy to establish sessions. Static routes can be partially updated when nodes are mobile, but that increases the traffic in the network and the protocol shifts to the reactive spectrum in many senses. For geographic protocols the maintenance of location services increase the demand of energy.

Virtual coordinates. The issue of a location service has also been addressed by Rao in [5], where he proposes a solution based on a distributed hash, similar to ours. However the accompanying routing protocol he proposes is essentially geographic routing based on virtual coordinates and thus involves a much more complicated set-up stage each time that routing updates are made. We show that a simple linked list suffices to establish a temporary routing scheme and show that this scheme performs much better experimentally than even true geographic algorithms.

Metrics for algorithm comparison. For routing algorithms in ad hoc networks, one measure of efficiency is the **packet delivery rate**; i.e. the number of packets actually arriving at the intended destination, another efficiency measure is the **number of hops traversed** by the nodes; or hop distance, which usually gives a measure of the **time for delivery**, and finally the **energy consumption per route** is yet another measure of efficiency. In terms of the latter metric, reactive protocols are typically at a great disadvantage. We focus however on the class of proactive protocols, where energy consumption per route is minimal. Moreover, we are interested only in guaranteed delivery algorithms, since our proposed algorithm has a perfect delivery rate for static networks. As a result, we use hop number as the metric by which to compare algorithms. Moreover, as we propose an algorithm without routing tables, we focus on comparing our algorithm with geographic ones.

Use of position. Both reactive and proactive routing protocols, in the basic version, are blind to the location of the nodes. In other words, the node ID's are related to neither the hop distance nor the reach-ability between nodes. Essentially only the network topology is taken into account in routing, not the geometry. Geographic coordinates, with the advent of geographic protocols, gave a sense of location to the routing algorithms, since closeness in coordinates *is* related to closeness in hop number, and perhaps more importantly, geometry encodes locally – in special classes of networks (planar, UDG, QUDG) – data about the global topology (which allows one to escape from local minima). Virtual coordinates, as introduced in [5] were then an attempt to mimic the above success even without access to true geographic information. In addition, the present paper does not restrict to a subset of allowable edges as most geographic algorithms must (in order to use a face routing derived algorithm on a planar subgraph, see [8] for a thorough discussion of this) but rather greedily uses whichever communication link leads to a node whose label is closest to the destination label.

3   Proximal Labeling

A flood tree is a tree obtained as follows. A root node is selected and it transmits a request message accepting up to a constant number, k, of replies. All the nodes accepted are linked to the root network, and the procedure is repeated recursively until all the nodes in the network are linked to the tree. This is illustrated in Figure 1.

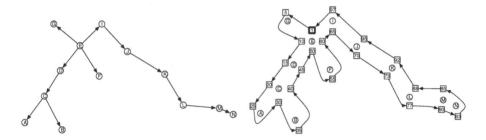

Fig. 1. An initial flood tree example and the linked list obtained by a depth-first traversal of the flood tree. Nodes are labelled $1 \cdots 97$ with gaps.

After the flood tree is built the nodes are labeled in increasing order following a depth-first traversal of tree, leaving gaps between successive labels as shown in Figure 1. The skipping in the labeling procedure allows room for later insertions of new nodes.

3.1   Location Service

Let $I = [i, j]$ and $A = [a, b]$ be intervals of integers, possible node ID's and possible labels (i.e. positions in the list) respectively. We define $H : I \rightarrow A$ a hash function mapping ID's to labels. Once the nodes are ordered and labelled with labels from A, to start a data session it is only necessary to find the label of the target node given its ID. To achieve the above translation, in a preliminary stage each node sends a message containing the pair (ID_u, L_u) to node $H(ID_u)$. In the production state whenever a node wants to send a message to node ID_u, it only needs to ask node $H(ID_u)$ for the corresponding labels[2] $L_u^1, \ldots, L_u^m$, with $m \le k$.

It would be wise to build a certain redundancy into the location service, storing the tuple $(ID_u, L_u^1, \ldots, L_u^m)$ at neighbouring nodes (up to a constant number of hops away) as well.

3.2   Routing Algorithm

Given a label to which one wishes to route, the algorithm simply proceeds in a greedy manner, always forwarding to the neighbor whose label is closest to the destination label. This greedy label-based means of navigating the network is used in two stages for each session: first to reach the node with label $H(ID_u)$ where the labels $(L_u^1, \ldots, L_u^m)$ of the destination node with ID_u are stored, and then to reach the node with a particular label L_u^ℓ from there (keeping same notation as in previous paragraph).

4   Experimental Results

We generated a random set of points in a square region of the plane. We then constructed a communication network by defining two nodes to be in communication if and only if their separation is less than a parameter r. We considered three possible values for r, small, medium and large, corresponding to sparse, medium and dense networks respectively. This correspondence reflects the fact that denser networks are more connected in a unit disk model.

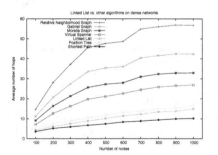 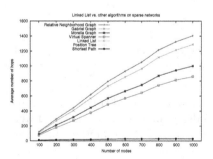

Fig. 2. The proposed algorithm, *Linked Lists*, when compared with geographic algorithms in a **dense network** (left) and **sparse network** (right)

We choose to compare only to geographic protocols because they do not use routing tables. Figures 2 and 2 compare (according to hop number) our algorithm with the face-greedy-face algorithm using four planarization techniques, the Relative Neighborhood Graph, Gabriel Graph, Morelia Graph and Virtual

---

[2] The nodes will have up to k labels, where k is the maximum degree of the flood tree.

Spanner. We also compared with the Position Trees which, although not a geographic protocol, is nevertheless similar to our algorithm in that it guarantees delivery using a tree structure (albeit with labels of size $O(n)$). Both Position Trees and our present proposal are very close to the shortest path. The main differences in these algorithms are the mobility support and the reduced memory usage of our proposal.

5   Conclusions and Future Work

We have presented a proactive routing algorithm based on a compact representation of the route between any two nodes. The algorithm is very competitive, it uses only $O(\log n)$ bits in each node to represent the location service tables and achieves almost the same performance of a $O(n)$ bits per node proactive routing algorithm with full information. We are currently working in node mobility and a fully distributed version of the algorithm.

References

1. Chavez, E., Mitton, N., Tejeda, H.: Routing in Wireless Networks with Position Trees. In: Kranakis, E., Opatrny, J. (eds.) ADHOC-NOW 2007. LNCS, vol. 4686, pp. 32–45. Springer, Heidelberg (2007)
2. Internet Engineering Task Force (IETF) MANET working group documents: http://www.ietf.org/html.charters/manet-charter.html,   and, http://www.ianchak.com/manet/
3. Johnson, D.B.: Scalable and Robust Internetwork Routing for Mobile Hosts. In: Proceedings of the 14th International Conference on Distributed Computing Systems, p. 211. IEEE Computer Society, Poznan (1994)
4. Perkins, C.E., Bhagwat, P.: Highly Dynamic Destination-Sequenced Distance Vector (DSDV) for Mobile Computers. In: Proc. of the SIGCOMM 1994 Conference on Communications Architectures, Protocols and Applications, August 1994, pp. 234–244 (1994)
5. Rao, A., Ratnasamy, S., Papadimitriou, C., Shenker, S., Stoica, I.: Geographic routing without local information. In: MobiCom 2003: Proceedings of the 9th annual international conference on Mobile computing and networking, pp. 96–108. ACM Press, New York (2003)
6. Santosh, V., Kanade, V.: Life (and routing) on the Wireless Manifold, Technical Report, Georgia Tech. (2008)
7. Shaukat, K., Syrotiuk, V.: Statistical Monitoring to Control a Proactive Routing Protocol. In: Kranakis, E., Opatrny, J. (eds.) ADHOC-NOW 2007. LNCS, vol. 4686, pp. 46–58. Springer, Heidelberg (2007)
8. Tejeda, H., Chavez, E., Sanchez, J.A., Ruiz, P.M.: Energy-Efficient Face Routing on the Virtual Spanner. In: Kunz, T., Ravi, S.S. (eds.) ADHOC-NOW 2006. LNCS, vol. 4104, pp. 101–113. Springer, Heidelberg (2006)
9. Urrutia, J.: Local solutions for global problems in wireless networks. Journal of Discrete Algorithms 5, 395–407 (2007)

Proposal and Evaluation of a Caching Scheme for Ad Hoc Networks

F.J. González-Cañete, E. Casilari, and A. Triviño-Cabrera

Dpto. Tecnología Electrónica
University of Málaga
Málaga, Spain
{fgc,ecasilari,atc}@uma.es

Abstract. In this paper, we describe and evaluate the performance of a caching scheme for ad hoc networks. In this proposal the wireless nodes store the documents they request in a local cache and they can also work as a server for the other wireless nodes if they intercept the forwarding requests and serve the documents requested directly using their local cache. On the other hand, the wireless nodes inspect the requests and responses that they forward in order to learn where and how far the documents are located and they use this information to redirect the requests to other nodes that are closer than the original destination of the request. By means of simulations we evaluate the performance of the proposal and demonstrate that they reduce the latency perceived by the nodes.

Keywords: Ad Hoc networks, cache, replacement policy.

1 Introduction

Mobile Ad Hoc Network (MANET) technology brings the opportunity to extend the coverage area of wireless devices so non-connected nodes can communicate through the collaboration of intermediate devices. Initially, this capability made MANETs especially attractive for disaster or battlefield operations where these networks could work without any infrastructure. However, the success of wireless communications has extended the use of MANETs in commercial applications. In these new scenarios, the users require access to external networks, such as the Internet. For this connection, a gateway that provides access to the Internet and to external servers (E.g. HTTP Server) should be available. Nevertheless, the mobility of the MANET may provoke the Gateway to be temporarily unreachable. Web technologies should adapt to this circumstance to operate properly. In this paper, we study how HTTP traffic can be improved in MANETs when web caching is used.

When using web caching, devices store some documents which were previously requested to an HTTP server in their internal cache. Mobile devices in a MANET can benefit from the storage space of other nodes, so that the documents can be served without accessing the HTTP server. With this operation, HTTP requests are satisfied even when the Internet Gateway is not reachable. Furthermore, the traffic generated to

P.M. Ruiz and J.J. Garcia-Luna-Aceves (Eds.): ADHOC-NOW 2009, LNCS 5793, pp. 366–372, 2009.

get the document is reduced as an intermediate node in the route to the server serves it. As a first approach of our study, this work deals with multihop wireless networks composed of static devices.

The rest of this paper is structured as follows. In Section II, the caching scheme is described. Section III details the simulation model and the results of the simulations. Finally, Section IV outlines the main conclusion and suggests possible future work.

2   Caching Scheme Proposed

In this section we present an application level caching scheme for ad hoc networks. In this scheme the network nodes request documents that are located in data servers. Due to the limited capabilities of wireless devices, we assume that the data servers are not part of the MANET but they are accessed through the Internet Gateways. The Internet Gateways are fixed nodes in the MANET as specified in [1].

As in the case of HTTP traffic, the simplest way in which a caching scheme can be implemented is allocating a local cache for node. This cache will store the documents requested by the node once they are received from the data server. The next time the node requires the same document it will be served directly from its local cache. This situation is called a cache hit and it drastically reduces the traffic over the ad hoc network, as well as the energy consumption and the latency to receive the documents.

As the proxies in the HTTP traffic the proxy functionalities can be transferred to the wireless nodes in a similar way to the routing procedures. With this additional task, every node in the path of a request from a node to the data server can respond to this request if it has a valid copy of the requested document in its own local cache.

Figure 1 shows an example of an ad hoc network where *DS* is a data server node, that is, the node that physically stores all the documents. This node is accessed through a Gateway (*GW*). Nodes *1*, *2*, *3* and *4* are user nodes that request documents to *DS*. The connections between the nodes indicate the existing wireless links.

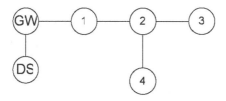

Fig. 1. Example of ad hoc network

In the case that node 2 requests a document *A*, the request will pass through node *1* to *DS* using an ad hoc routing algorithm. The data server will respond with the document using the path from node *1* to 2. Finally the node *2* will store the document *A* in its local cache. If node *3* requests the same document *A* to the *DS* the request will reach node *2* that checks if there is a valid copy of the document *A* in its local cache and, if so, it will respond to node *3* with the document. This interception of the request reduces the number of hops from 6 (*3-2-1-DS-1-2-3*) if there is not an interception, to 2 (*3-2-3*) and consequently the latency perceived by node *3*. This mechanism also saves energy in the nodes and reduces the traffic because terminals do not have to forward the requests and responses. In addition, the interception reduces the possible bottlenecks in the data servers because they do not process all the generated requests. The situation when a node in the path of a request to the DS intercepts the request is called an interception hit.

Aiming at reducing the route length to the serving node we make nodes keep information about the distance (measured as the number of hops) where the served documents can be found. This information is dynamically extracted from the forwarded messages (requests and responses).

To illustrate this procedure, let us suppose that node *4* in Figure 1 requests the document *B* to *DS*. The request will pass through nodes *2* and *1* to *DS* so node *2* knows that node *4* will have the document *B* and that node *4* is one hop away. When the *DS* responds with the document *B* through nodes *1* and *2* to node *4*, node *2* will register that *DS* has the document *A* and it is two hops away. If node *3* requests the same document *B* to *DS*, the request will reach node *2*. In that situation node *2* knows that node *4* and *DS* have the document *B* and they are one and two hops away respectively so node *2* will redirect the request to node *4* because the path to the document is shorter. This redirection of the request reduces the number of hops from 6 (*3-2-1-DS-1-2-3*) if there is not redirection, to 4 (*3-2-4-2-3*). Hence the latency perceived by node *3* is diminished.

Unfortunately, the redirection caching has some drawbacks that have to be considered: the mobility and disconnection of nodes and the replacement of the documents.

In order to decrease the number of redirection misses caused by the replacement of the documents stored in the local caches each node calculates the mean time that the documents are stored in its local cache. In that way, when the redirection information of a document is stored the expiration time of this information will be the minimum between the Time To Live (TTL) of the document and the mean time the documents are stored in the local cache.

3   Simulation Parameters and Performance Evaluation

In this section the simulation model and the performance evaluation of a static multihop ad hoc network are presented. In this work we study the performance of the caching scheme presented in the previous section.

The simulations are based on the network simulator NS-2.33 [3] that is one of the most popular simulators for the researches on ad hoc networks [4]. Table 1 summarizes the main simulation parameters.

In order to quantify the performance of the network we used the next metrics: the delay (defined as the time elapsed between the request of a document and the reception of the response) and the Hit Ratio (defined as the proportion of documents served by the cache). At each node, the local, interception and redirection hit ratio are defined as the proportion of documents served by the local cache, by an intermediate node and by a node after a redirection respectively.

Table 1. Simulation parameters

Parameter	Default	Values
Simulation area (metres)	1000x1000	
Routing algorithm	AODV [2]	
Number of nodes		5x5 – 7x7 – 9x9 grids
Number of servers	2	
Number of Documents	1000	
Number of requests per node	10000	
TTL (s)	2000	500-1000-2000-4000-5000-Infinite
Mean time between requests (s)	10	5-10-50-100
Zipf slope	0.8	0.4-0.6-0.8-1.0
Replacement policy	LRU	
Cache size (documents)	100	25-50-100-200
Warm-up (requests)	2000	
Simulations per point	5	

The figures only show the results of a 5x5 grid network because the 7x7 and 9x9 networks obtain similar results.

Figure 2 represents the delay and hit ratio as a function of the mean time between requests. The use of local caching reduces the delay perceived by the nodes. As the time between requests is increased the mean delay is also increased because of the expiration of the documents in the local caches. This fact causes the reduction of the local cache hit ratio and hence the amount of documents that have to be requested again to the server is increased. The Interception scheme outperforms the local caching and also reduces the delay. Finally, the Redirection does not outperforms the Interception because the Interception hit ratio is very low for all the mean time between requests and it even reaches nearly zero for a request time of 100 seconds. For high loaded networks (a high request rate) the reduction of the delay if the combined caching scheme is adopted is about 30% compared with the scheme without caching, and this difference remains constant even for low loaded networks

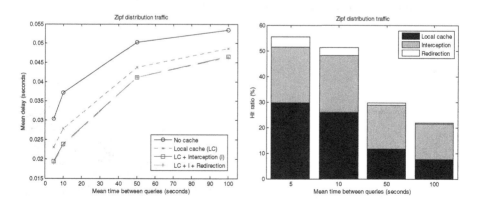

Fig. 2. Delay (left) and Hit ratio (right) as a function of the mean time between requests

(with a low request rate). In very loaded networks with very active the amount of requests served by the local cache or another intermediate cache is about 55%.

Figure 3 shows how the mean TTL of the documents influences on the delay and the hit ratio. As the TTL of the documents increases the time they can be stored in the caches increases and hence they can be useful during more time. As it can be observed from the figure the delay is reduced asymptotically as the TTL increases until the optimal value where the TTL is infinite, that is, the documents do not expire. In the case of infinite TTL the percentage of hits reaches near 60%. This fact causes the reduction of the delay in about 40% compared to the scheme without caching. In the case of short living documents (low TTL) the reduction of the delay is about 20%. The local caching and interception clearly outperform the schema without caching. The Redirection caching obtains a constant and low hit rate for all TTLs and hence practically does not reduce the delay.

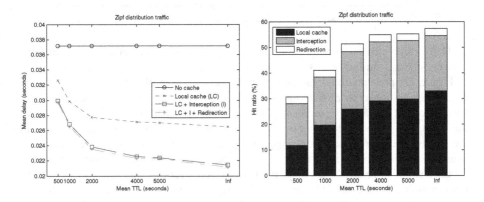

Fig. 3. Delay (left) and Hit ratio (right) as a function of the mean TTL of the documents

Figure 4 compares the delay and hit ratio as we change the slope of the Zipf distribution of the request pattern. As the slope increases the local cache hit is also increased due to the fact that the most popular documents are frequently requested.

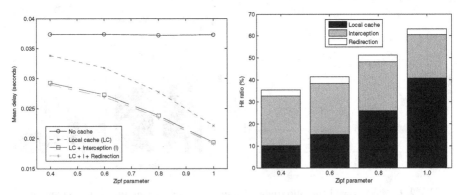

Fig. 4. Delay (left) and Hit ratio (right) as a function of the Zipf parameter

On the other hand the interception hits are decreased as the slope increases because most traffic is served by the local caches. Consequently the delay is widely reduced as the Zipf slope increases following a similar behaviour as the previous studies. The delay is reduced about by 20% and 40% for the 0.4 and 1.0 slope respectively.

Finally Figure 5 shows the delay and hit ratio as a function of the cache size. As in the previous scenarios, the Interception of the requests outperforms the schema without caching. The performance improvement reaches its limit when the cache size is 100 Kbytes as the results obtained for the 200 Kbytes cache size are similar. For a cache of 25 documents the improvement obtained with the Redirection caching is close to zero but the redirection hit ratio increases as the cache size increases. For the 25 documents cache the reduction of the delay is about 20% while for largest caches it is reduced by 35%.

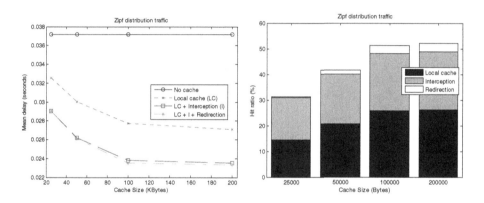

Fig. 5. Delay (left) and Hit ratio (right) as a function of the cache size

4 Conclusions

In this work we have proposed a caching scheme for ad hoc networks. The scheme suggests implementing a local cache at each node of the ad hoc network in order to intercept or redirect the requests by the intermediate nodes from the source to the destination request. In that way the number of hops is reduced, and hence, the delay perceived by the ad hoc nodes. As the number of hops is decreased, the number of forwarding messages also decreases and the power consumption is reduced. We have studied by mean of simulations the influence of the mean time between requests, the effect of the TTL, the influence of the traffic pattern and the cache size.

We can conclude that the use of local caching combined with the use of the interception reduces drastically the delay perceived by the nodes. The reduction of the delay can vary between 20% and 45% depending on the characteristics of the traffic and cache size. The Redirection of the requests obtains poor hit ratios and hence, the reduction of the delay is not significant compared with the Interception caching.

References

1. Wakikawa, R., Malinen, J.T., Perkins, C.E., Nilsson, A., Tuominen, A.J.: Global Connectivity for IPv6 Mobile Ad Hoc Networks, draft-wakikawa-manet-globalv6-05.txt, Internet Draft, Internet Engineering Task Force (2006)
2. Perkins, C.E., Belding-Royer, E.M., Das, S.: Ad Hoc On Demand Distance Vector (AODV) Routing. IETF RFC 3561 (2003)
3. NS-2 Home page: http://isi.edu/nsnam/ns/
4. Kurkowski, S., Camp, T., Colagrosso, M.: MANET Simulation Studies: The Incredibles. ACM's Mobile Computing and Communications Review 9(4), 50–61 (2005)

A Secure Spontaneous Ad-Hoc Network to Share Internet Access

Raquel Lacuesta[1], Jaime Lloret[2], Miguel Garcia[2], and Lourdes Peñalver[2]

[1] University of Zaragoza, Ciudad Escolar s/n, 44003 Teruel, Spain
lacuesta@unizar.es
[2] Polythecnic University of Valencia, Camino de Vera s/n 46022, Valencia, Spain
jlloret@dcom.upv.es, migarpi@posgrado.upv.es,
lourdes@disca.upv.es

Abstract. In this paper, we propose a secure spontaneous ad-hoc network to grant the access of the users to surf the Web. The paper shows the description of our proposal, the procedure of the nodes involved in the system and the designed messages. We also validate the success of our proposal through several simulations and comparisons with a regular architecture. The proposal has been developed with the main objective of improving the communication and integration between different study centers of low resource communities.

Keywords: Spontaneous networks, ad-hoc networks, wireless networks.

1 Introduction

A spontaneous ad-hoc network is type of ad-hoc network that is formed for a certain period of time with no dependence on a central server and without the intervention of an expert user [1]. This network is made up of various independent nodes coming together at the same time and in the same place to be able to communicate with each other. Nodes are free to enter and leave the network and they could be mobile or not. Spontaneous networking happens when neighboring nodes discover each other within a short period of time [2]. Spontaneous networks are basically those which seek to imitate human relationships in order to work together in groups, running on already existing technology. The concept of spontaneous networks was introduced in depth by Laura Marie et al. in paper with reference [3]. Juhani Latvakoski et al. proposed a communication architecture for spontaneous systems in [4], which integrates application-level spontaneous group communication and ad hoc networking together. Victor H. Zarate et al. proposed AWISPA [5], a collaborative learning environment based on wireless spontaneous networks. A spontaneous network enables a group of devices to work together collaboratively at the same time, located very close each other with a minimum interaction.

The model proposed to create spontaneous networks is presented in section 2. Section 3 analyzes the model analytically. The devices procedure of our proposal and the messages designed are shown in section 4. In section 5, the model is validated through a simulation and comparison with a regular architecture. Finally, section 6 summarizes this work and points out the main conclusions.

P.M. Ruiz and J.J. Garcia-Luna-Aceves (Eds.): ADHOC-NOW 2009, LNCS 5793, pp. 373–378, 2009.

2 Secure Spontaneous Network Proposal

If some people wish to form a spontaneous network, they may meet in a physical space at a given moment in order to make use of services provided by other members. The members who make up this community may vary at any specific time (users may join or leave at will). When a device joins the network it must: (i) integrate the device into the network, (ii) discover the services and resources offered by the devices, (iii) access to the services offered by the devices, and (iv) perform collaborative tasks.

If one of the users of the spontaneous network has Internet connection, the connection will be shared. It could be more than one Internet access in the spontaneous network. In this model, a user contributes capabilities, technical resources to access external services and other applications to the system. The following tasks should be performed when a user joins the spontaneous network: (i) Node identification, (ii) Identification between nodes, (iii) Address assignment, and (iv) To join services.

Our approach is based on human relations. The set-up configuration is based on presentation or greeting. In a group of friends, a new individual is introduced to the other members by one of the participants of the meeting. This member already knows the other's presentation data or may obtain it at the moment of presentation. He or she is then responsible for facilitating the new member's integration easily and simply into the group. Consequently, the network management is formed and run by cooperation between nodes, behaving similarly to that in human relations. Thus, the formation of these networks is carried out in two principal phases: the presentation, greeting or pre-identification and the creation of the network and communication.

Any user may be part of the network without having high level of computing knowledge. The user connected to the device will need to input his or her personal information when he/she access the network for the first time. Automatically, a data configuration proposal is generated and the devices available within range are identified. The intervention of the user is limited to select the user among those detected by the device and with which he or she wished to pre-authenticate. Once the device has been selected, the inter-exchange of presentation information can take place automatically between both nodes.

3 Analytical Model

Given the inherent characteristics of a spontaneous network, the network depends on the number of devices, their position and the number of connections between the devices of the network. The nodes could be, or mobile, and they are placed in the network for a limited period time. In our model the devices could leave the network voluntarily or because energy constraints, so we will not take into account the energy of the devices in our analytical model because the spontaneous network may be disappear before the energy of the ad-hoc devices is consumed.

We use the graph theory to define the network. Let $G = (V, S, P, E)$ be a spontaneous network in the time T, where V is a set of devices v_i with $i = \{0, 1,..., n\}$ and $n=|V|$ (number of devices in whole network), S is a set of services offered by the devices of the network, P is the placement function assigned to every element of V, (the placement function assigns to every device i of V and to any time $t \in T$ a set of coordinates $P_i=[x_i,y_i,z_i]$) and E is a set of their connections. The cardinality of V changes along the time because nodes can join or leave the network at will, if the device is mobile, its position P changes along the time and the cardinality of E changes with the creation and deletion of connections.

We can define $N(v_i)$ the neighbourhood of node v_i as it is shown in equation 1.

$$N(v_i) = \bigcup_{v_j \in V, v_j \neq v_i} \left\{ v_j \mid E(v_i, v_j) < tx_{range\_i} \right\} \tag{1}$$

Where tx_{range_i} is the transmission range of v_i. The neighbourhood of a node is the set of nodes which is within its transmission range. Connections allow two-way communication (bidirectional links), so that connected nodes can communicate with each other in either direction, that is, $E(v_i,v_j)=E(v_j,v_i)$.

Let's suppose that at time $t=0$ a device enters the radio coverage area of another device and, therefore, they become neighbours. Let R be the random variable that represents the time when a new node appears in the network. Responsiveness of the discovery process, $F_R(t)$, can be represented by the probability function of the random variable R, which is defined as is shown in equation 2.

$$F_R(t) = P\{R \leq t\} \quad \forall t \geq 0 \tag{2}$$

4 Devices Procedure and Protocol Messages

Our proposal is based in the utilization of two information structures, an identity card (IDC) and a certificate. All devices must have an IDC with a Logical IDentity (LID), the public and private keys of the user (K), the creation date and expiration date, the IP proposed by the user and the information signature.

The first node in the network generates a network key randomly and waits for any new connection. When a new device wants to join the network, it has to exchange its IDC with the first node, so they must start the pre-authentication phase. In the proposed model, bearing in mind the limitations of the devices, we have to secure the start of the network and the addition of new members, and then, we have to provide integrity (by using hash functions), privacy and confidentiality to the network. The connection is performed through a short-range technology, allowing a face to face meeting, so users are known personally.

In order to provide secure connections, we use a model based on the use of the asymmetric infrastructure of public keys, which is mainly used in the distribution and key management processes. The public key is distributed to the other devices, but the private key is stored confidentially. In our model, the authentication is distributed by the trusted devices. Trusted devices will verify the identity of the devices and the validity of the public keys. A device will trust in the identity of another device an in its public key only if it obtained its certificate through a trusted device of the network.

We used a criterion based on human relationships: the trusted networks [6]. When the certificate has been generated, the validity process by the rest of the devices of the network will be based on the trust management process. A public key of other user will not be considered valid by other user until a trusted user recognises that this device is the owner of the key and certify its validity. When a user receives a valid certificate, because it is signed by a trusted device, it signs the key with its private key giving authenticity and integrity to the process. In this process, a user gives trust just to the users that trust when obtains its IDC in the pre-authentication process.

When both devices are pre-authenticated successfully, any information exchanged between them is considered valid. Then, the older device in the network sends to the new one the network key. This key is coded asymmetrically with the public key of the new device and only the new device will be able to decode it with its private key.

An example is shown in figure 1. There are three users: Alice, Bob and Carlos. Alice's key is in the set of keys stored by Bob. Bob has signed it to show their agreement. Moreover, Alice becomes a reliable person for Bob. All keys signed by Alice will be considered valid by Bob. Now, Carlos joins the network and Bob trusts Carlos, but Carlos doesn't trust Bob. Let us suppose that Alice wants to communicate with Carlos, but she doesn't have its public key. Then, she asks Bob Carlos' public key. Bob sends the public key of Carlos signed by him. So, Alice has Carlos' key and can establish a communication with him to share services. But, in this case, Carlos can not initiate any communication with Alice because Carlos doesn't trust Bob, so he has to look for another trusted device to find the public key of Alice.

The data transmission procedure is shown in figure 2.

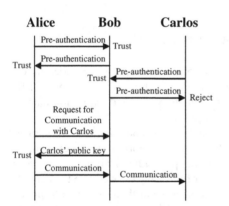

Fig. 1. Devices procedure example

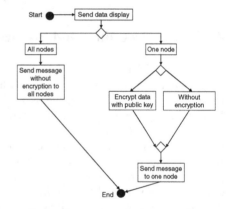

Fig. 2. Data transmission procedure

5   Proposal Validation

5.1   Test Bench

In order to evaluate our proposal we have used the OPNET Modeler simulator. Three spontaneous networks are connected to this IP cloud where there is a web server. We have simulated two scenarios. In the first scenario, nodes make http requests to the web server and only the node that provides Internet access will reply the content. In the second scenario, a regular architecture is simulated: Each http request is sent to the server and it replies with the adequate content.

Each spontaneous ad hoc network is made up of six devices. The nodes in the topology have the following features: 40 MHz processor, a 512 KB memory card, a radio channel of 11 Mbps and 2.4 GHz as the working frequency. We selected AODV as the routing protocol for the spontaneous networks, but it could be changed. The node carrying out the gateway task between the wired IP cloud and the spontaneous ad hoc network has the same characteristics as the other nodes, but an Ethernet interface is added. Each spontaneous network carried out some sort of http request to the server or node connected to Internet. Because of it, we used different type of traffic for each network (predefined by the OPNET simulator): Light browsing, Heavy browsing, and Searching.

5.2 Simulation Measurements

Figure 3 shows the http traffic going through in the IP cloud. We observe the behavior of our architecture and we compare it with the regular architecture. Note that the average http traffic in our proposal is around 430 bytes. It can be compared to the regular architecture which has an average of 1090 bytes, therefore displaying a 61% of improvement. We observed that in our architecture the traffic is more.

In each spontaneous network we have simulated different type of web consultation. In one of them, there is "Light Browsing", in the second one "heavy browsing" and finally, in the third one, it is the "searching" type. In figure 4, we observe the load on the gateway node connected to Internet. All the Web consultations finish at this node. We see that the Web traffic "light browsing" bears little load, only sporadic consultations are carried out. In the case of "heavy browsing" consultations, we see that there is higher http load traffic with peaks at specific time intervals. Finally, the highest load traffic is the "searching" type.

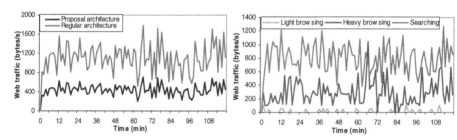

Fig. 3. Http traffic through the IP cloud   **Fig. 4.** Traffic carried our by gateway nodes

In figure 5 we observe the average delivery delay of the Web pages. It can be seen that once the networks converge, the average delivery delay is around 9 seconds in the regular architecture and 3.5 seconds in the proposed spontaneous architecture (improvement of 62%). We can also observe that our architecture is more stable.

In figure 6 we can see the average Web page delivery delay from nodes on our ad hoc spontaneous networks. In this graph we observe that the traffic with the shortest delay is the "searching" type. This is given because when we do a search, the browsers provide information which doesn't consume much bandwidth and so the delay is shorter. With respect to the other two types of traffic, we can see that once the network converges, then the average delay is around 4 seconds. In these cases the delay is longer

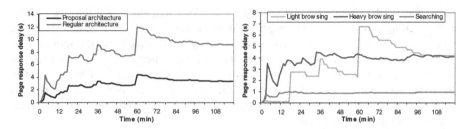

Fig. 5. Average delivery delay   **Fig. 6.** Average Web page delivery delay

because this type of traffic is heavier and therefore there is needed more delivery time to download the full webpage.

6 Conclusions

We have proposed a protocol that allows collaborating in a given time. The resources are provided by the different members of the community. The association between nodes is set up when they are close. In this model all the nodes collaborate for the proper operation and management of the network. The devices don't need to keep all the public keys of the network and the information of all devices inside of it.

In this paper, we have analyzed our proposal analytically and we have shown the device procedure and the protocol messages designed for its proper operation. We have validated the success of our proposal simulating several spontaneous networks connecting to Internet through a gateway node. Now we are extending the protocol to allow the communication with other spontaneous ad hoc network through Internet.

References

1. Preuß, S., Cap, C.H.: Overview of Spontaneous Networking – Evolving Concepts and Technologies. In: The Proceeding of the Workshop on Future Services for Networked Devices (FuSeNetD), Heidelberg, Germany (1999)
2. Gallo, S., Galluccio, L., Morabito, G., Palazzo, S.: Rapid and Energy Efficient Neighbor Discovery for Spontaneous Networks. In: 7th ACM Int. symposium on modeling, analysis and simulation of wireless and mobile systems, Venice, Italy, October 04 - 06 (2004)
3. Feeney, L.M., Ahlgren, B., Westerlund, A.: Spontaneous Networking: An Application-oriented Approach to Ad-hoc Networking. IEEE Communications Magazine 39(6), 176–181 (2001)
4. Latvakoski, J., Pakkala, D., Pääkkönen, P.: A Communication Architecture for Spontaneous Systems. IEEE Wireless Communications (June 2004)
5. Zarate Silva, V.H., De Cruz Salgado, E.I., Quintana, F.R.: AWISPA: An Awareness Framework for Collaborative Spontaneous Networks. In: 36th Annual Frontiers in Education Conference, October 27-31, pp. 1–6 (2006)
6. Stajano, F., Anderson, R.: The resurrecting duckling security issues for ad-hoc wireless networks. In: Malcolm, J.A., Christianson, B., Crispo, B., Roe, M. (eds.) Security Protocols 1999. LNCS, vol. 1796. Springer, Heidelberg (2000)

A Middleware Family for VANETs*

Flávia C. Delicato[1], Lidia Fuentes[2], Nadia Gámez[2], and Paulo F. Pires[1]

[1] Federal University of Rio Grande do Norte
{flavia.delicato,paulo.pires}@dimap.ufrn.br
[2] Dpto de Lenguajes y Ciencias de la Comunicacion, Universidad de Málaga
{lff,nadia}@lcc.uma.es

Abstract. Vehicular Ad-hoc Networks are an important application domain of ubiquitous computing and Wireless Sensor Networks are a key technology for enabling such applications. The development of ubiquitous applications poses challenges as dealing with the low-level programming abstractions and the heterogeneity of hardware and software. Middleware facilitates application development by hiding the heterogeneity and complexity of the underlying hardware and software. We argue that a single middleware is not able to meet the heterogeneity of ubiquitous systems, and propose a Software Product Line approach to design a middleware family. The family is customized according to constraints imposed by three viewpoints: device, network and application. We customize the family considering the variability of the VANETs domain.

Keywords: VANETs, WSNs, Middleware, Software Product Line.

1 Introduction

Ubiquitous computing consists of environments instrumented by sensors that collaborate with other devices to provide user-centric services in a seamless and transparent way. Wireless sensor networks (WSNs) are an important component of ubiquitous systems and refer to the set of sensor nodes linked by a wireless medium that are able to perform distributed sensing and convey useful information to control stations [1]. The first generation of WSNs adopted an application-specific design, with the goal to achieve energy efficiency. WSN systems were designed from scratch, as monolithic software built to a target platform, operating system (OS), and addressing requirements of one single application. Such design principles generated a strong coupling solution, in which one single image of code including the application, the network protocol, and the OS is deployed in the nodes before the WSN installation. Application developers had to know network and protocol specificities and build programs by using the low level abstractions provided by the sensor OS or directly over the hardware. Moreover, once the application code was deployed, if a significant change was required, a new image must be loaded. Such approach was energy efficient but produced WSNs that are rigid, inflexible, and tied to a single application.

Several changes characterize the new generation of WSNs. We can mention the build of WSNs following a modular architecture, and the trend in designing WSNs for

---
*This work has been supported by Spanish *Ministerio de Ciencia e Innovación* Project TIN2008-01942, the European Commission STREP Project AMPLE IST-033710, and by the Brazilian *National Council for Scientific and Technological Development* (CNPq).

P.M. Ruiz and J.J. Garcia-Luna-Aceves (Eds.): ADHOC-NOW 2009, LNCS 5793, pp. 379–384, 2009.

different applications instead of building WSN tailored to a single one. Besides, since application developers are rarely experts in computer networks, a middleware layer was considered as required to allow easy and fast development, hiding the heterogeneity and the low level features of WSNs and offering a set of generic services and a high level interface to applications. The middleware avoids the direct handling of low level sensor hardware or communication protocols. However, considering the highly heterogeneous requirements of ubiquitous systems in terms of devices, hardware and applications, we argue that a single middleware is not able to suitable meet all these needs. To tackle this problem, we proposed in previous works to adopt a Software Product Line (SPL) approach to design a middleware family for ubiquitous systems [3] and later on, we specialized this family to WSNs [4].

Software Product Line Engineering (SPLE) is an approach for creating a diversity of similar software products at low cost, in short time, and with high quality [5]. Following such approach, we built a Feature Model encompassing the variabilities present in scenarios of ubiquitous computing and WSNs, which were divided in device-driven, network-driven, and application-driven, corresponding to three viewpoints: (i) the physical devices vendor; (ii) the network expert and (iii) application domain expert. We argue that these three views need different skills to be developed, but there is a strong dependency among them, for instance, a network protocol is more suitable to a specific application, which in its turn requires the use of a given type of sensor. In this work we address an important domain of ubiquitous computing that are the Vehicular Ad-hoc Networks (VANETs) using the SPL Feature Model, along with the definition of dependences among features, and the SPL configuration process to guide decisions and to automatically generate a complete and correct image to be loaded in the nodes.

2   Motivational Case Study

We will illustrate the variability present in ubiquitous computing using the domain of VANETs. An intelligent transportation system is composed of autonomous vehicles that can operate with minimum help from the driver [7]. They are equipped with several sensors, such as acoustic, accelerometers, temperature, on board computer and a GPS. Form the VANET literature we identified services that a generic middleware should provide to facilitate the build and execution of a VANET application. One of the main difficulties on VANETs is the communication, since the infrastructure is not fixed (the network topology is dynamic) and the existence of a base station is not enforced. Also, different radio technologies can be used (Wi-Fi, UMTS, etc.). Furthermore, the wireless medium and the multihop routing make the security an important issue. Regarding these characteristics we can infer that two main services the middleware should provide to VANET applications are Communication (and all the services related with this task) and Security. Regarding communication, since there is no fixed infrastructure to host centralised services, disconnection is the norm and communicating nodes are often anonymous. To address this, a loosely coupled, asynchronous, anonymous and fully decentralised communication model is required [8]. Furthermore, routing in VANETs is a challenging issue because of frequent topological changes [8], so a Data Delivery service that manages the strategies and protocols involved in the conveyance of data is useful. Coordination and Topology Control services are needed to manage the collaboration among nodes and to solve the rapid changes in the link topology because of the relative fast movement of vehicles and the frequent disconnections. Data Fusion service is required to accommodate for the limited bandwidth of the wireless medium [9]. Context-Awareness refers to the ability of detect changes in the environment and react accordingly. In VANETs, timely event delivery and capacities for handling the QoS of the event channels are crucial for fail safety, so QoS Management and Fault Tolerance are required.

Using our approach of a SPL-based middleware family, VANET applications will benefit from a highly-optimized and custom middleware, which will offer appropriate services consistent with device configuration and resource constraints.

3 SPL-Based Build of a Middleware

Product Line Software Engineering (PLSE) is an effective way to exploit commonality and manage variability among a family of products from a domain perspective [10]. The analysis of such domain is often achieved by using a feature-oriented approach, where commonalities and variabilities are analyzed in terms of features. A feature is any prominent concept that is visible to various stakeholders [10]. The features can be organized into a Feature Model that represents all possible products of a SPL. Commonalities are modelled as mandatory features and variabilities are modelled as variable features, classified as alternative or optional. Furthermore, for each variable feature, a feature dependency analysis identifies types of dependencies between features. PLSE is comprised of two phases: Domain Engineering (DE) and Application Engineering (AE). DE deals with the creation of the infrastructure which will enable the construction of specific systems within the family of products. AE concerns with the engineering of specific products using the infrastructure created at the DE. In the DE phase, we accomplished a domain analysis and produced the Feature Model (FM). Then, in the AE phase, a custom configuration of a middleware variant is generated considering requirements and constraints of the application, network and the device.

We identify three viewpoints reflecting the stakeholders: the builder of devices, the network expert, and the application expert. So, we divided our FM in three features (Fig. 1.a): **Device Driven**, **Network Driven** and **Applications Driven Features**.

Device Driven Features concern hardware properties of devices. A device is characterized by its **Type,** classified into: **High Capacity Devices**, **Sensors**, **Location Devices** and **Consumer Electronics**. We emphasize **Sensors**, which are essential components of VANETs. **Sensors** (Fig. 1.b) can be classified according to their internal components, which are **Microcontroller, Transceiver, Power Unit, Sensing Units, Mobility** and optionally **External Memory, Voice Circuit, RFID**. The figure also depicts examples of **Categories** of nodes, as **Mote, Smart Dust** or **Sun Spot**. The **Role** feature denotes the responsibility of a node and influences the middleware configuration process: **Ordinary Nodes, Cluster-Head** and **Sinks**. Other feature that influences the selection of the correct implementation of middleware services is the **Operating System**. The Device Type and OS influence which **Development Technologies** are available to build the embedded software. The **Development Technology** captures the variability of the available APIs and programming languages for every version of each distribution of an OS. The last mandatory feature is the **Radio Technologies** that can be used in the device, as **ZigBee** or **Bluetooth**.

The middleware services (Fig. 1.c.) are classified as basic (mandatory for the whole family) and extra (optional). Basic services are: **discovery**, **location**, **communication** and **data delivery**. The **discovery** service enables nodes to advertise and know the

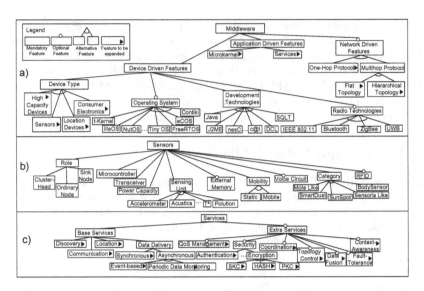

Fig. 1. a) Middleware Feature Model. b) Sensors sub-features. c) Services sub-features.

sensing capabilities of their neighbors and allows applications to submit a description of their sensing requirements. The **location** service is critical to VANETs in case of a GPS fail and it allows a node to know its own geographical position. The **data delivery** service delivers the network generated data to the application. The **communication** service [11] includes a proxy responsible to interact with applications and XML drivers for communicating with the underlying network protocols and devices.

Besides, we identify the need for the following extra services: **coordination, data fusion, security, QoS management, fault tolerance,** and **context-awareness**. **Coordination** encompasses generic operations to create and manage groups of collaborating sensors. **Data fusion** is the process of combining/aggregating raw data generated by individual sensors. The **security** service provides functionalities of cryptography, authentication, authorization and intrusion detection. **Quality of Service management** is an advanced feature of WSN middleware [12] in charge of balancing conflicting requirements demanded by applications. **Fault tolerance** is an important issue in WSNs. Sensors directly interact with the environment and are subject to a variety of forces that can produce fail. Since many ubiquitous applications are safety critical it is crucial to manage fails. Finally, the **Context-Awareness** Service provides awareness of changes in the execution context and adaptability of the middleware to deal with these changes.

At the *Domain Engineering* phase, besides the **FM** the Software Architect must design the Product Line Architecture (PLA) of the middleware considering all the possible **Middleware Components** and their connections that realize the FM. The PLA contains all components required for implementing any product from the SPL family. The link between a FM and the PLA is rarely a trivial one-to-one mapping. For instance, the feature that represents the OS will probably influence all components: considering that TinyOS is selected, we must ensure that the TinyOS compliant version (i.e using nesC development technology) of each component is used to build the product. SPL tools (VML [14]) support the definition of **Feature Mappings**. Then, at

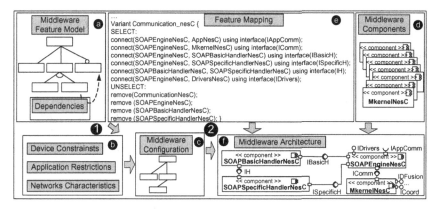

Fig. 2. Process instantiating a specific middleware product of the family

the *Application Engineering* phase, we can divide the configuration process of a family of middleware for ubiquitous system in two steps. First (label 1 in Fig. 2), the *specification* of a middleware configuration and second (label 2), the generation of a *concrete* middleware architecture fulfilling the specification previously defined.

In the first step, the FM (tag (a)) can be specified using the fmp2rsm tool [15]. Besides the FM, **Dependencies** between features must be defined, which are articulated in terms of logical expressions and can be reduced to *usage* and *mutual exclusion* dependencies. A usage dependency is formulated as, "if one feature is selected, then another feature has to be also selected", and mutual exclusion as, "if one feature is selected, another feature must not be selected". The specification of these constraints is crucial to avoid ill-formed configurations of products. To specify dependencies and check their correction, the same tool used to create the FM can be used.

In the ubiquitous system domain, the target device has several resource restrictions that will limit the size of the middleware version to be generated. The applications that will use this middleware configuration impose their needs as input restrictions. Also, the network characteristics influence the final configuration of the middleware. These constraints (tag (b)) are expressed in different XML documents:

Device Constraints: This document specifies the device profile, including its category, computational resources, and sensing units.

Application Restrictions: Applications may require a subset of the available services, so we express them in this file. Considering the resource limitations of devices of ubiquitous systems, only those services will be part of a specific middleware configuration. This file also includes QoS requirements of the application.

Network Characteristics: This document specifies details of MAC and network layer protocols, used to manage the send of messages and the multihop routing including the QoS parameters they fulfil. For instance, some protocols are more energy efficient, others are fault-tolerant and others address time critical requirement.

Finally, using the **Middleware Feature Model** along with **Dependencies,** and the three XML documents, the configuration process automatically selects which features will be in the final well-formed **Middleware Configuration** (tag (c)).

In the second step, to generate the concrete middleware architecture, the configuration process will choose, from the set of **Middleware Components** that implements the possible variations of the family, only those that are compliant with the reduced FM. So, we have to obtain the specific **Middleware Architecture** (tag (f)) that corresponds to the desired configuration using the **Middleware Configuration** (tag (c)), the **Middleware Components** (tag (d)) and the **Feature Mapping** (tag (e)). SPL tools, such as VML, are able to automatically generate the specific architecture. Fig.3 (tag (e)) shows the mapping for the **Communication nesC feature** (version nesC of the Communication service) in VML syntax. As a result, components that will compose the specific middleware, plus their appropriate instantiation, initialisation, configuration and compilation files are automatically obtained.

4 Conclusions

The adoption of an SPL engineering approach for the development of middleware platforms for VANETs applications requires a considerable investment for creating the domain-engineering infrastructure considering the definition of the Feature Model and the Product Line Architecture. However, since the development effort of specific middleware platforms is drastically reduced (practically only a configuration is required), as soon as more and more middleware platforms are instantiated, the construction of the SPL will become cost-effective and generate increasing benefits.

References

1. Akyildiz, I.F., et al.: Wireless Sensor and Actor Networks: Research Challenges. Ad Hoc Networks Journal (Elsevier) 2(4), 351–367 (2004)
2. Fuentes, L., Gámez, N., Sánchez, P.: Managing Variability of Ambient Intelligence Middleware. Int. J. of Ambient Computing and Intelligence (IJACI) 1(1), 64–74 (2009)
3. Delicato, F., Fuentes, L., Gámez, N., Pires, P.: Variabilities of Wireless and Actuators Sensor Network Middleware for Ambient Assisted Living. In: Proc. of IWAAL (to appear, 2009)
4. Pohl, K., et al.: Software Product Line Engineering – Foundations, Principles, and Technique. Springer, Heidelberg (2005)
5. Sivaharan, T., et al.: Cooperating sentient vehicles for next generation automobiles. In: MobiSys, WAMES 2004 (2004)
6. Dikaiakos, M., et al.: Location-aware Services over Vehicular Ad-Hoc Networks using Car-to-Car Communication. IEEE Journal On Selected Areas In Communications 25(8) (2007)
7. Kwanwoo, L., et al.: Concepts and guidelines of feature modeling for product line software egnineering. In: Gacek, C. (ed.) ICSR 2002. LNCS, vol. 2319, pp. 62–77. Springer, Heidelberg (2002)
8. Delicato, F.C., et al.: Reflective Middleware for Wireless Sensor Networks. In: Procs. of the 20th ACM Symposium on Applied Computing, Santa Fe, USA (March 2005)
9. Wang, M., et al.: Middleware for wireless sensor networks: A survey. Journal of Computer Science And Technology 23(3), 305–326 (2008)
10. Loughran, N., et al.: Language Support for Managing Variability in Architectural Models. In: Pautasso, C., Tanter, É. (eds.) SC 2008. LNCS, vol. 4954, pp. 36–51. Springer, Heidelberg (2008)
11. Czarnecki, K., et al.: Fmp and fmp2rsm: eclipse plug-ins for modeling features using model templates. In: OOPSLA Companion 2005, pp. 200–201 (2005)

Joint IP Address and Public Key Certificate Trust Model for Mobile Ad Hoc Networks

Abdelhafid Abdelmalek[1,2], Mohamed Feham[1],
Zohra Slimane[1], and Abdelmalik Taleb-Ahmed[2]

[1] STIC Laboratory University of Tlemcen Algeria
[2] LAMIH Laboratory University of Valenciennes France
{a_abdelmalek,m_feham,z_slimani}@mail.univ-tlemcen.dz,
abdelmalik.Taleb-Ahmed@univ-valenciennes.fr

Abstract. This paper focuses on the autoconfiguration security problem in MANETs. We propose a new fully distributed IPv6 autoconfiguration scheme providing both security and robustness. Our solution introduces a new trust model based on a new concept of joint IP address and public key certificate, exploiting recently published Discrete Logarithm based threshold cryptographic tools. The proposed scheme solves all limitations of earlier approaches and seems to be a perfect solution for MANETs under strong advarsarial model.

1 Introduction

Throughout the last decade, several schemes have been proposed for automatic IP address assignment in standalone Mobile Ad hoc Networks (refer to [1,2] for a survey). However, much less attention has been given to security in the design of such schemes. This lack of security opens the possibility of many real threats, leading to serious attacks in potentially hostile environments, such as IP Spoofing Attack, Exhaustion Address Space Attack, Conflict Address Attack, ... [3,4,5]. Few papers have tackled this problem without however bringing satisfactory solutions. A detailed analysis of these proposals is provided in our previous work [5]. In this paper, we introduce a new robust and secure stateful IP address autoconfiguration protocol for standalone MANETs named TCSAP (Threshold Cryptography based Secure Autoconfiguration Protocol). The most important contributions of this work are the design of a new threshold concept based mechanism in providing the autoconfiguration service functionality, and the introduction of a new trust model based on joint IP address and public key certificate. The remainder of the paper is organized as follows. In section 2, we present our system model. Section 3 is devoted to the design of our protocol TCSAP. Finally, section 4 concludes the paper.

2 Threshold IP Address Assignment Scheme

In this work, we adopt the Fully Distributed CA model [6] in conjunction with threshold cryptography. In the remainder of the paper, we assume that the

P.M. Ruiz and J.J. Garcia-Luna-Aceves (Eds.): ADHOC-NOW 2009, LNCS 5793, pp. 385–390, 2009.
© Springer-Verlag Berlin Heidelberg 2009

threshold cryptosystem is implemented by a DPKI (Distributed Public Key Infrastructure) module including all necessary components. This being, we develop also on the basis of threshold concept a fully distributed stateful autoconfiguration scheme for standalone networks inspired from MANETconf [7]. The IP Address for a newly arrived node is assigned by a subset of at least k nodes. Each valid IP address in the network must be signed by the On-line Certification Authority. In our scheme the coalition of the k nodes which have assigned this IP address should produce also a threshold signature for this same address resulting in an 'On-line Joint IP address and Public Key Certificate' in which both the IP address and the public key are tied to node's identity.

2.1   Maintained State Information

- Free IP Address Table (FAT): contains the lowest free address of each IP Address Block. An IP Address Block is a consecutive range of IP addresses. The Address Space is divided into a fixed number (say M) of disjoint IP Address Blocks with equal sizes (Fig. 1).
- Pending IP Address Table (PAT): contains any assigned IP address which is not registered yet.
- Registered IP Address Table (RAT): contains registered IP addresses.
- Requester Counter (RC): maintained for each node to which an IP address has been assigned but not registered yet. It is incremented for each new request.

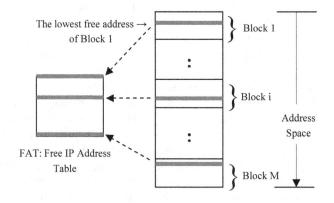

Fig. 1. FAT: Free IP Address Table. The Address Space is divided into M blocks. Only the lowest free address of each block is maintained in the FAT.

2.2   IP Address Assignment

A new node will be assigned randomly one of the lowest free addresses contained in the FAT . We impose to the new joining node to obtain its IP address from at least k nodes. We use for this purpose the threshold signature provided in the DPKI and the new concept of joint certificate defined above. After having received a signed IP Address, the newly aarrived node must broadcast a signed registration message to all nodes in order to participate actively in the network. Any assigned IP address which is not registered yet is removed from the FAT and kept in the PAT. If the registration message is received the IP address is removed from the PAT and put in the RAT.

3   Protocol Specification

This section presents the functional components of our secure autoconfiguration protocol called TCSAP (Threshold Cryptography based Secure Autoconfiguration Protocol (Fig. 2). We first define node's states and then we will describe the procedure for each functional block.

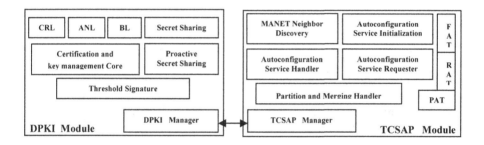

Fig. 2. Functional Blocks of TCSAP and DPKI modules

3.1   Node's States

- Non Configured node: any not already registered node.
- Configured node: any registered node within the MANET.
- Node with Configuration in Progress: any Non Configured node which has initiated an autoconfiguration process that is not finished yet.

3.2   MANET Neighbors Discovery Protocol

MANET Neighbors Discovery protocol allows a node to discover its one-hop neighbors by exchanging periodically signed Discovery messages. The signature here is done according to the node's Off-line public key certificate. The MANET Neighbors Discovery protocol is executed automatically by a node on boots/reboots when his state is Non Configured. The *DiscoveryRequest* message used by a Non Configured node to discover its one-hop neighbors must contain the originator's Off-line public key certificate and its signature. The response to this message will depend on the state of each recipient:

1. Case 1: state Non Configured. The receiving node (say P_i) saves the originator's data in a one-hop Neighbors List $(N_L)_i$, and replies by a *DiscoveryReply*
   message. The requester stores in its cache during a fixed time interval all its
   one-hop neighbors and their associated data, checks the neighbors lists intersection F_N (Founding Nodes): $F_N = \bigcap_{P_i \in H}(N_L)_i$, where H is the set of
   all one-hop neighbors including the requester node itself. If $|F_N| \geq k$ then
   the requester executes the Autoconfiguration Service Initialization protocol,
   otherwise it clears its cache before performing the next MANET Neighbor
   Discovery.
2. Case 2: state Configured. The recipient replies by a *DiscoveryWelcome*
   message. When the requester receives the *DiscoveryWelcome* message, it
   concludes that a MANET is already established and has to start an Autoconfiguration Service Requesting.
3. Case 3: state Configuration in Progress. In this state, the node will discard
   all MANET Discovery messages.

3.3   Autoconfiguration Service Initialization Protocol

We initialize the MANET by at least k neighbor nodes. When a Not Configured
node has discover a number equal or greater than k neighbors belonging to the
same neighborhood (see 3.2 : case1) , it starts the Autoconfiguration Service
Initialization. The founding neighbors have to jointly perform this initialization. Site-local addresses are used to achieve nodes networking and MANETs
membership (Fig. 3).

Site-Local Prefix		Subnet	Host-ID
1111 1110 11	38 bits : Subprefix	16 bits	64 bits

Fig. 3. IPv6 site-local address

The Autoconfiguration Service Initialization is carried out in three phases:

Phase1. Selection of the network prefix and self IP address assignment: In this
phase, first the founding neighbor nodes have to select the sub-prefix (38 bits)
and the subnet (16 bits). Then, they have to set up their Host-ID (64 bits).

a. Selection of sub-prefix and subnet: Let us set $N_{sp} = 2^{38}$ and $N_{sn} = 2^{16}$. The
first node finding the threshold subset F_N of the Founding neighbors, informs
others nodes belonging to F_N by broadcasting a signed *InitStart* message including the list of these nodes. Each $P_i \in F_N$ chooses randomly $\alpha_i \in Z_{N_{sp}}$ and
$\beta_i \in Z_{N_{sn}}$, and broadcasts them in a signed *InitAck* message. After receiving all
values α_i and β_i, each $P_i \in F_N$ computes:

$$subprefix = \sum_{P_i \in F_N} \alpha_i mod(N_{sp}) \quad , \quad subnet = \sum_{P_i \in F_N} \beta_i mod(N_{sn})$$

b. Host –ID setup: The Host-ID space is divided into M blocks according to (2.2). Founding nodes ($P_i \in F_N$) are classified in an ascending order according to their identities. Each node $P_i \in F_N$ will assign itself the lowest value in the block corresponding to its order in the classification.

Phase2. Creation of the On-line Certification Authority: When the above phase is finished, the TCSAP Manager calls the DPKI Manager to start the secret sharing protocol after which the On-line Certification Authority is created and its public key is signed.

Phase3. Signing the 'On-line Joint IP address and Public Key Certificate' for each founding node: In this phase, each node $P_i \in F_N$ must get its 'On-line Joint IP address and Public Key Certificate' signed by at least k founding nodes. At this level, each node checks the correctness of the self-assigned Host-ID before performing its partial threshold signature.

3.4   Autoconfiguration of a New Joining Node

Research of the closest servers: A new joining node which has received a valid *DiscoveryWelcome* message as reply to its MANET *DiscoveryRequest* message starts automatically the Autoconfiguration Service Requesting. First, it assigns itself a link-local address formed by pre-pending the well known local prefix FE80::0/64 to the Host-ID of the IP address contained in any received *DiscoveryWelcome* message. Then, it broadcasts to all nodes in a predefined radius r_k a *ConfigRequest* message including its 'Off-line Public Key Certificate' and its signature. Any receiver of the message checks the signature validity and the Requester Counter (RC). If the requester has already reached the limit of the authorized attempts for the Autoconfiguration Service Requesting, it is declared as malicious and the message is discarded. Otherwise, the recipient sends a *ConfigReply* message including the On-line Certification Authority's public key, a list of the lowest free Host-ID of each block in its FAT, the received HopLimit, its 'Off-line Public Key Certificate', and its signature. If the total received reply messages by the new joining node are less than the threshold k then it repeats the Autoconfiguration Service Requesting using a higher HopLimit value. Otherwise, it starts the Coalition selection and the On-line certificate requesting phase.

Coalition selection and On-line certificate requesting: First, the requester selects among the closest responding nodes a coalition of at least k nodes according to the received HopLimit values appearing in the *ConfigReply* messages. Then, it chooses randomly a lowest free Host-ID common to all the members of the selected coalition. Finally, it broadcasts these members a *CertificateRequest* message.

Verification and signature of the requested On-line certificate: Each member in the coalition checks in its CRL and BL tables if no member of the coalition is malicious nor his public key is revoked. Then, it starts the threshold signature protocol providing an 'On-line Joint IP address and Public Key Certificate' for the requester. The member of the coalition with the lowest IP address will act as the combiner of the partial signatures replying to the requester by a *CertificateReply* message.

Registration: The new joining node, after receiving its 'On-line Joint IP address and Public Key Certificate', verifies its validity and proceeds to registration. This registration is indispensable for a node to be considered as member of the MANET. The registration message must include the new node's 'On-line Joint IP address and Public Key Certificate' and the signature of the whole IPv6 packet. This affirms that the message has been sent to all nodes.

4   Conclusion

In this paper, we have proposed a new fully distributed IPv6 autoconfiguration scheme for MANETs providing both security and robustness. We have introduced a new concept of joint certificate based trust model and developed our framework upon recently published threshold cryptographic tools. Our solution overcomes all limitations of the previously proposed approaches and is nicely suitable for spontaneous standalone MANETs under strong adversarial model. From an efficiency point of view, a performance evaluation of our protocol might be interesting for future research activities.

References

1. Bernardos, C., Calderon, M., Moustafa, H.: Survey of IP address autoconfiguration mechanisms for MANETs, draft-bernardos-manet-autoconf-survey-03 (April 2008)
2. Baccelli, E. (ed.): Address Autoconfiguration for MANET: Terminology and Problem Statement, draft-ietf-autoconf-statement-04 (February 2008)
3. Mohsin, M., Prakash, R.: IP Address Assignment in a Mobile Ad Hoc Network. In: IEEE Milcom (2002)
4. Wang, P., Reeves, D.S., Ning, P.: Secure Address Autoconfiguration for Mobile Ad Hoc Networks. In: MOBIQUITOUS 2005, pp. 519–522 (2005)
5. Abdelmalek, A., Feham, M., Taleb-Ahmed, A.: On Recent Security Enhancements to Autoconfiguration Protocols for MANETs: Real Threats and Requirements. IJC-SNS 9(4), 401–407 (2009)
6. Kong, J., Zerfos, P., Luo, H., Lu, S., Zhang, L.: Providing Robust and Ubiquitous Security Support for MANET. In: IEEE International Conference on Network Protocols, November 2001, pp. 251–260 (2001)
7. Nesargi, S., Prakash, R.: MANETconf: Configuration of Hosts in a Mobile Ad Hoc Network. In: IEEE INFOCOM 2002 (June 2002)

A Localized Algorithm for Target Monitoring in Wireless Sensor Networks

Kamrul Islam and Selim G. Akl

School of Computing, Queen's University,
Kingston, Ontario, Canada K7L 3N6
{islam,akl}@cs.queensu.ca

Abstract. We consider the following target monitoring problem: Given a set of stationary targets $T = \{t_1, \cdots, t_m\}$ and a set $V = \{v_1, \cdots, v_n\}$ of sensors, the target monitoring problem asks for generating a family of subsets of sensors $V_1, \cdots, V_s$ called the *monitoring sets*, such that each V_i monitors all targets. In doing so, the objective of this problem is to maximize $z = s/k$, where $k = \max_{v_j \in V} |\{i : v_j \in V_i\}|$. Maximizing z has direct impact in prolonging the lifetime of sensor networks. For this problem, we present a simple *localized* algorithm which requires each node to know only its 2-hop neighborhood. Nodes do not need to know their geographic positions. It is shown that the algorithm achieves an optimum result in special cases. We prove that the size of a monitoring set is at most a constant times the size of a minimum monitoring set when the number of targets is a constant. We present extensive simulation results to evaluate the performance of the algorithm.

1 Introduction

In this paper, we study the *target monitoring problem*. Given a set of stationary targets $T = \{t_1, \cdots, t_m\}$ and a set $V = \{v_1, \cdots, v_n\}$ of sensors, the target monitoring problem asks for generating a set of subsets of sensors $V_1, V_2, \cdots, V_s$ called the *monitoring sets* such that each V_i monitors all targets. The idea is that only one such set is *active* (only active sensors monitor the targets) for any certain period of time and after that time period another set becomes active and so on, thus providing continuous monitoring. The objective of this problem is to maximize $z = s/k$, where $k = \max_{u \in V} |\{i : u \in V_i\}|$. Considering each i ($1 \leq i \leq s$) as a round, we activate the sensors in V_i in round i to monitor all targets, while keeping $V \setminus V_i$ in the energy-efficient *sleep* mode. We use 'sensor' and 'node' interchangeably in what follows. We define an algorithm as p-localized if each node u is allowed to exchange messages with its neighbors which are at most $p-$hops away and take decisions accordingly based on this information. To solve the target monitoring problem, we propose a 2-localized algorithm. Furthermore, the nodes do not need to know their geographic positions. They only need to know the ids and the connectivity information of their 2-hop neighborhood.

The rest of the paper is organized as follows. In Section 2 we describe related work. In Section 3 we provide definitions and assumptions that are used throughout the paper. The localized algorithm is presented in Section 4 and a

P.M. Ruiz and J.J. Garcia-Luna-Aceves (Eds.): ADHOC-NOW 2009, LNCS 5793, pp. 391–396, 2009.
© Springer-Verlag Berlin Heidelberg 2009

theoretical analysis of the algorithm follows in Section 5. Experimental results are presented in Section 6. We conclude in Section 7.

2   Related Work

Coverage (also called *monitoring*) has been one of the important topics in sensor networks and has received a lot of attention during the past several years [2,3,4,5,6,7]. The main goal of almost all the research on average is to devise scheduling algorithms such that individual sensors in the network are assigned *rounds* which indicate to them during which rounds they will be active and during which rounds they will be in the sleep mode. When a set of sensors monitors a certain area or a target, it is generally possible to monitor the area or the target by a *small* subset of them. So, it is redundant to make all the sensors active at the same for the monitoring instead of using the small subset. This observation leads researchers to devise efficient algorithms such that at any time only a few sensors are set as active to monitor the area or the targets. A recent result related to our problem is described in [1], where the authors consider the *monitoring schedule* problem: Given a set of sensors and a set of targets it is required to find a partition of the sensor set such that each part can monitor all targets. Each part of the partition is used for one unit of time and the goal is to maximize the number of parts in the partition. They present a randomized distributed algorithm which generates at least $(1 - \epsilon) * opt$ parts, with high probability, where *opt* is the maximum number of parts in the partition and $0 < \epsilon < 1$. However, they make the assumption that the sensors must know their geographic positions. The authors also show that by modifying their algorithm they can find a constant approximation factor for the problem and the sensors do not need to know their geographic positions. Our work is related to theirs in the sense that we maximize the number of parts while trying to reduce the use of the same nodes in these parts. Besides, ours is a deterministic algorithm as opposed to their randomized one and we exclude the assumption that the sensors know their positions.

3   Definitions and Problem Formulation

The sensor network is modelled as a graph $G = (V, E)$, where V denotes the sensors and E represents the links $(u, v) \in E$ between $u, v \in V$ if they are within their transmission range, TR. A sensor monitors a target that falls within its sensing range, SR. For a node u, $N(u)$ defines its neighborhood, i.e., $N(u) = \{v | (u, v) \in E, u \neq v\}$ and $N[u] = N(u) \cup \{u\}$. By $N_f(u)$ we mean the set of nodes which are at most f hops away from u. We use $N(u) = N_1(u)$. Let $T(u)$ represent the set of targets monitored by u. For u and $t \in T(u)$, let $T_t(u)$ represent the set of sensors in $N_2[u]$ that monitors the target t (i.e., $T_t(u) = \{t | t \in T(u) \cap T(v), v \in N_2[u]\}$). Node u maintains an ordered pair at each round i (initially $i = 1$), $p_i(u) = \prec (ct_i(u), id(u)) \succ$, where $ct_i(u)$ (also called the *counter*) denotes the number of monitoring sets in which u has already

---

Input: A connected graph $G = (V, E)$ and a set of targets T s. t. each target is monitored by at least one sensor.

Output: A set of subsets of sensors $V_1, \cdots, V_s$ s.t. each V_i monitors all targets in T.

1: $i = 1$, send $p_i(u)$, $T(u)$ to $v \in N_2(u)$ and receive $p_i(v)$, $T(v)$
2: Compute $T_a(u) = \{a | a \in T(u) \cap T(v), v \in N_2(u)\}$, $\forall a \in T(u)$
3: **For** round i, compute $r(T_a(u))$, $\forall a \in T(u)$
4:     **If** $\exists a \in T(u)$ s.t. $r(T_a(u)) < r(T_a(v))$, $v \in N_2(u)$ **Then**
5:         u becomes active **Endif**
6:         $i = i + 1$, **If** u is active **Then** $ct_i(u) = ct_{i-1}(u) + 1$ **Endif**
7:     **If** $ct_i(u) \neq ct_{i-1}(u)$ **Then** Send $p_i(u)$ to $v \in N_2(u)$ **Endif**
8:     Receive $p_i(v)$ from $v \in N_2(u)$
9: **Endfor**

Fig. 1. A 2-Localized algorithm for the target monitoring problem

participated. Initially, $ct_1(u) = 0$ and then for $i > 1$, $ct_i(u) = ct_{i-1}(u) + 1$ if u participates in the monitoring set V_{i-1} in round $i - 1$. The rank $r(X(u))$ of u w.r.t X is the index of u in the lexicographically sorted nodes of X.

We formulate the target monitoring problem in the following way. Given a set of targets $T = \{t_1, \cdots, t_m\}$ and a set sensors $V = \{v_1, \cdots, v_n\}$ (both) randomly and uniformly deployed in the plane such that for each target there is at least one sensor that monitors it, we would like to find a family $\mathcal{V}$ of subsets $V_1, \cdots, V_s$ such that

i) $\forall i$, V_i monitors all targets in T,
ii) $z = s/k$ is maximized, where $k = \max_{v_j \in V} |\{i : v_j \in V_i\}|$.

4   The Algorithm

We present a 2-localized algorithm for the target monitoring problem (assuming now $TR = SR$). Our algorithm works in rounds and at round $i = 1$, node u first forms $T(u)$. Then u sends $T(u)$ and an ordered pair $p_i(u) = \prec (ct_i(u), id(u)) \succ$ to $v \in N_2(u)$ and receives $T(v)$ and $p_i(v)$ from $v \in N_2(u)$. After obtaining $T(v)$ and $p_i(v)$, u forms $T_a(u)$ for each target $a \in T(u)$. Then for each set $T_a(u)$, u computes its rank $r(T_a(u))$ in that round. If u is the smallest ranked node in any set $T_a(u)$, then it becomes active to monitor a, otherwise it goes into the sleep mode. All active nodes in round i are represented by V_i which monitor all the targets. If u becomes active in round i only then its counter is incremented $(ct_{i+1}(u) = ct_i(u) + 1)$. Node u then sends $p_{i+1}(u) = \prec (ct_{i+1}(u), id(u)) \succ$ to, and receives $p_{i+1}(v)$ from $v \in N_2(u)$ and a new round $i+1$ starts. The algorithm is given in Figure 1.

4.1   A Problem with Locality

For a subset X_t of nodes that monitor the same target t in some round, it is supposed that the nodes will be in close proximity (due to the spatial correlation). However, the nodes in X_t, although they monitor the same target, can have arbitrarily long hop distance between each other, while the Euclidean distance maybe slightly more than their transmission range. We call this situation the *Locality Effect*, where the monitoring nodes for a certain target do not know about each other about their monitoring.

5   Theoretical Analysis

In this section we give an overview of the theoretical analysis of the algorithm. Consider a target $t \in T$ and let X_t be the set of sensors that monitors it in some round. For a node $u \in X_t$, u knows only whether other nodes, which are within its 2-hop neighborhood (i.e., $N_2[u]$), can monitor t and therefore chooses exactly one among $N_2([u])$ for the monitoring. However, due to the locality effect there can be two nodes $u, v \in X_t$ such that $v \notin N_2(u)$, both u and v monitor t and u does not have any clue about v. We would like to determine an upper bound on how many sensors can monitor a target while none of them is aware of the other. We show that at any round at most five sensors can simultaneously monitor a target, none of which is within the 2-hop neighborhood of the other.

Lemma 1. *For any target $t \in T$, at most five sensors are set as active.*

Proof. Let X_t be the set of sensors that monitors a target $t \in T$ in some round. Suppose for the sake of contradiction that $|X_t| > 5$ and no two nodes $u, v \in X_t$ are within the 2-hop neighborhood of the other. As t is monitored by all sensors in X_t, the Euclidean distance between t and any node $w \in X_t$ must be at most SR. Consider a disk D centered at t with radius equal to SR. Therefore, all the nodes in X_t must be within the disk D. Since $|X_t| > 5$ and nodes of X_t are in D, there will be at least two nodes $u', v' \in X_t$ whose Euclidean distance must be smaller than TR (since $SR = TR$, we can consider TR the radius of D instead of SR). Then u' and v' are direct neighbors to each other, a contradiction.   □

Then we derive the corollary from the above lemma.

Corollary 1. *If V_i^* denotes the minimal set of sensors monitoring targets at round i then $|V_i| \leq 5m|V_i^*|$, where $m = |T|$ is the number of targets given.*   □

An implication of the above corollary is that if we have a constant number of targets ($|T| = m \leq c$, c is a constant) then we have i.e., $|V_i| \leq 5c|V_i^*|$. So the size of any monitoring set is at most a constant times the size of the minimal monitoring set. Now we show how the algorithm performs towards maximizing the value of $z = s/k$. Denote by z_{opt} the optimal value of z and $z_{opt} > 0$, i.e., $z_{opt} \geq z = s/k$ for all possible values of s and k. If z_{alg} denotes the value of z obtained by the algorithm then we have the following lemma. (Due to the space limitation, please see all the proofs and details in [8]).

Lemma 2. $z_{opt} \leq |X_p|$ *and* $z_{alg} \geq 1$. *Hence* z_{opt} *is at most* $|X_p|$ *times the value of* z_{alg}.   □

For the following results we assume that the transmission range of a sensor is twice its sensing range, $TR = 2 * SR$.

Lemma 3. *With $TR = 2 * SR$, for any target $t \in T$, exactly one sensor is set as active.* □

We obtain the following corollary from the above lemma.

Corollary 2. *If V_i^* denotes the minimal set of sensors monitoring targets at round i then $|V_i| \leq m * |V_i^*|$, where $m = |T|$ is the number of targets.* □

Now we show that the algorithm obtains the optimal result for maximizing z in special cases. Let $X_1, X_2, \cdots, X_m$ be the subsets of sensors that monitor the targets $t_1, t_2, \cdots, t_m$ respectively in some round, where $X_i \subseteq V$. If $X_i \cap X_j = \phi$, $i \neq j$ then we have the following.

Lemma 4. *With the above assumption and $TR = 2 * SR$, we have $z_{alg} = z_{opt}$.* □

6   Simulation

We conducted extensive simulations on random networks to study the performance of the algorithm. We provide and analyze experimental results regarding (i) maximizing $z = s/k$ and (ii) the size of monitoring sets $|V_i|$. We distribute a set of $m \in \{10, 20, 30, 40, 50\}$ targets randomly in a field of 400m x 400m. Then we generate a random graph G by placing $n \in \{100, 200, 300, 400, 500\}$ nodes uniformly and randomly.

Experiments are done using our own simulator in Java. Setting both SR and TR to 60m, we apply the algorithm with $n = 100$, $m = 10$ and compute the minimum cardinality set X_p and generate $V_1, V_2, \cdots, V_{|X_p|}$. In the experiments, we set $z_{opt} = s/k = |X_p|/1$, since the optimal algorithm can generate at most $|X_p|$ monitoring sets. For z_{alg} we derive the maximum frequency k of a node in X_p in these monitoring sets and obtain $z_{alg} = |X_p|/k$. We generate 100 random graphs successively with the same number ($m = 10$) of randomly distributed targets and for each graph we compute the size of the minimum cardinality set $|X_p|$, maximum frequency k of a node in the monitoring sets and hence obtain z_{opt} and z_{alg}. Finally we obtain the average values of z_{opt} and z_{alg}. Keeping $m = 10$, we increment the value of n by 100 each time and repeat the whole procedure until $n = 500$. For each pair of $m \in \{20, 30, 40, 50\}$ and $n = \{200, 300, 400, 500\}$, we run the above experiment 100 times and find the averages of the z_{opt} and z_{alg}. The results are plotted in Figure 2, where the x-axis shows the number of targets in the field and the y-axis represents the average values of z_{opt} and z_{alg}.

7   Conclusions

In this paper, we have presented a simple 2-localized algorithm to compute a family of monitoring sets such that each set monitors all the targets. We provide

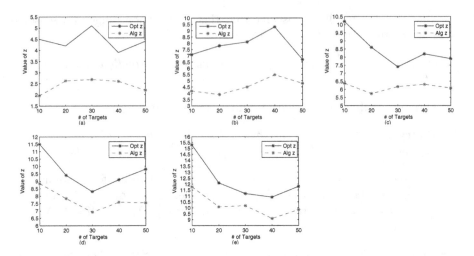

Fig. 2. Average z values (optimal z_{opt} values by solid lines and z_{alg} by dashed lines) for (a) 100 (b) 200 (c) 300 (d) and (e) 500 sensors.

theoretical results about the size of monitoring sets, determine bounds on the value of $z(z = s/k)$ when the transmission range is equal to and twice the sensing range. Although the worst-case bound we prove is not appealing (this is because of the fact that the nodes only have very limited information about the topology of the network), we believe it can be improved if nodes have more knowledge about the global topology. We provide simulation results that show much better results than the theoretical bound established in the paper.

References

1. Calines, G., Ellis, R.: Monitoring Schedules for Randomly Deployed Sensor Networks. In: Proc. Dial-POMC (2008)
2. Cardei, M., Du, D.: Improving Wireless Sensor Network Lifetime through Power Aware Organization. ACM Wireless Networks 11(3), 333–340 (2005)
3. Cardei, M., Wu, J.: Energy-Efficient Coverage Problems in Wireless Ad Hoc Sensor Networks. Computer Communications Journal 29(4), 413–420 (2006)
4. Carle, J., Simplot-Ryl, D.: Energy Efficient Area Monitoring by Sensor Networks. IEEE Computer 37(2), 40–46 (2004)
5. Li, X., Wan, P., Frieder, O.: Coverage Problems in Wireless Ad-hoc Sensor Networks. IEEE Transactions for Computers 52(6), 753–763 (2003)
6. Heinzelman, W., Chandrakasan, A., Balakrishnan, H.: Energy-efficient Communication Protocol for Wireless Microsensor Networks. In: Proc. HICSS 2000 (2000)
7. Wang, X., Xing, G., Zhang, Y., Lu, C., Pless, R., Gill, C.: Integrated Coverage and Connectivity Configuration for Energy Conservation in WSNs. In: Proc. CENSS 2003 (2003)
8. Islam, K., Akl, S.: Target Monitoring in Wireless Sensor Networks: A Localized Approach. Journal Ad Hoc and Sensor Wireless Networks (to appear)

A Wireless Sensor Network Architecture for Homeland Security Application

António Grilo[1], Krzysztof Piotrowski[2], Peter Langendoerfer[2], and Augusto Casaca[1]

[1] INESC-ID/IST, Rua Alves Redol, N° 9,
1000-029 Lisboa, Portugal
antonio.grilo@inesc.pt
augusto.casaca@inesc.pt
[2] IHP, Im Technologiepark 25,
D-15236 Frankfurt (Oder), Germany
piotrowski@ihp-microelectronics.com
langendoerfer@ihp-microelectronics.com

Abstract. This paper introduces an innovative wireless sensor network architecture, which has intrinsic reliability and can therefore be used for some components of homeland security applications such as intrusion detection. The proposed architecture includes a set of communication protocols in the different layers of the model. DTSN is a transport protocol used for reliable data transfer and DSDV is a routing protocol. The distributed and reactive data storage is realized using the tinyDSM middleware. The architecture provides also security features such as data secrecy and integrity. The cipher means used for this are ECC and SkipJack which have been developed for wireless sensor networks. Our homeland security architecture has been implemented as a demonstrator using 15 MicaZ motes equipped with acoustic and passive infra red sensors. This paper provides insight into the architecture and presents the main lessons learnt from a prototype demonstrator.

Keywords: Wireless Sensor Networks, Homeland Security, Distributed Shared Memory, Reliable Transport, Routing.

1 Introduction

Homeland Security (HS) and, more specifically, perimeter or area surveillance for intrusion detection is an important Wireless Sensor Network (WSN) application. In such scenarios, WSNs can be promptly deployed with low cost and with little or no supporting communication infra-structure. They can also be removed and reused elsewhere very rapidly.

When securing sensitive areas or accesses to high risk events, an easy to deploy self-configured self-healing WSN constitutes a valuable asset to a police force, allowing a more flexible and responsive deployment of its security teams, avoiding scattering of the force due to the needs to constantly patrol all the accesses into the target area. Due to its reduced costs, the WSN can also be deployed as a complement

P.M. Ruiz and J.J. Garcia-Luna-Aceves (Eds.): ADHOC-NOW 2009, LNCS 5793, pp. 397–402, 2009.

to police teams, to secure accesses where penetration is considered difficult and improbable in order to prevent unpredictable course-of-actions by a smart attacker.

Fig. 1 shows the envisioned intrusion detection scenario for the WSN deployment. The data issued by the deployed sensors can henceforth be permanently monitored by a few agents in a Command and Control Centre (C2C), which receives the intrusion alerts issued by the sensors nearly in real-time. Police agents may also be equipped with mobile devices such as laptops or Personal Digital Assistants (PDAs) that allow direct connectivity to the WSN, and thus, acting as mobile sink nodes.

For the sake of scalability, a real WSN solution should necessarily be deployed in a multi-tier topology. In the depicted example, a two-tier WSN is presented, which includes building and underground low-power short-range low-bandwidth WSN islands connected to a remotely located C2C, by means of a long-range high bandwidth technology (e.g. IEEE 802.11 or CDMA450). In each WSN island, sink nodes constitute the interface to the WSN.

In order to fulfill the functional requirements of the intrusion detection application as well as non functional issues such as being easy to use, a flexible WSN architecture was defined based on the components of the UbiSec&Sens toolbox [1].

The rest of this paper summarizes the research results obtained in the UbiSec&Sens project. Section 2 presents the WSN protocol architecture of UbiSec&Sens. Then, section 3 describes the demonstrator used in the project that was a proof of concept of the main ideas introduced. The paper concludes with lessons learned from a prototype demonstrator.

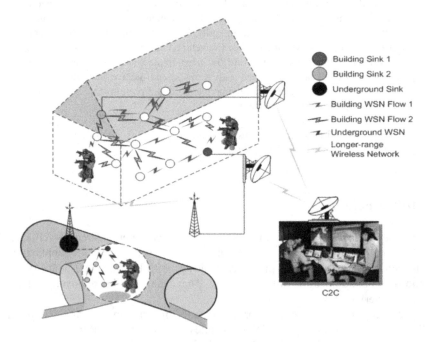

Fig. 1. Envisioned HS-WSN scenario

2 Protocol Architecture

The overall system architecture, whose principles result from the discussed requirements, can be mapped into three distinct layers: application layer (high-level functionality and user interface), protocol layer (message communication protocols) and target system layer (cryptographic primitives and operating system).

The application layer contains a distributed shared memory middleware called tinyDSM [2], which was developed in the UbiSec&Sens project. TinyDSM is a robust data storage due to its inherent replication means. It includes also an event mechanism that allows the definition of thresholds and, for each, the actions that need to be executed in case the threshold is passed. With these properties the data handling system ensures a significant level of dependability and provides a real time detection of alarms.

The protocol layer supports the local distribution of tinyDSM replication messages and also the distribution of event messages. A WSN-optimized version of the Destination-Sequenced Distance-Vector Routing (DSDV) protocol [3] is used for routing and the Distributed Transport for wireless Sensor Networks (DTSN) transport protocol [4] ensures reliable data transport on top of the routing. DSDV is an existing protocol which was adapted in the project and DSTN is a novel approach for transport, which was conceived in UbiSec&Sens.

The target system layer provides services such as memory management, which is used both by tinyDSM and the communication protocols. It also supports security mechanisms used by the application and the middleware by providing implementations of cryptographic means. The latter are essential prerequisites for ensuring data secrecy, data integrity and to enforce proper authentication and authorization, for example, in case the thresholds defined in the application need to be changed after the network deployment.

The architecture of the proposed system is shown in Fig. 2. The cryptographic means for sensor nodes have been developed within the UbiSec&Sens project. The target platform in the project uses mica motes and runs the tinyOS 2.x operating system.

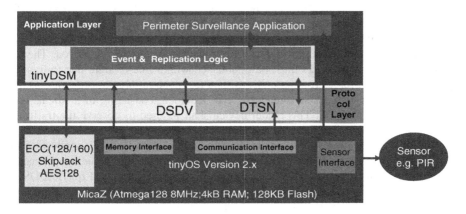

Fig. 2. System Architecture

The tinyDSM interfaces all other components. These interfaces are closely related to the target platform. All the interfaces are fixed in advance and are completely independent of the application running on top of the system. The interface between the data handling system and the application itself, however, is not fixed. The basic primitives for this interaction need to be predefined, but their current number, format and semantics are defined by the application programmer. The security requirements as well as the attacker model for the WSN have been investigated and listed already in the previous section. In order to counter these threats, the WSN includes the following mechanisms:

1. Issuing of "keep-alive" messages from the sensor nodes to the monitoring station, in order to allow the permanent status monitoring of each sensor node, detecting any malfunctions (which might be cause by an attack).
2. Guaranteed delivery of alarm messages based on the DTSN transport protocol, in order to counter temporary jamming attacks.
3. Inclusion of sequence numbers in the middleware messages, preventing replay attacks.
4. Inclusion of integrity-check and authentication mechanisms within the middleware messages (based on symmetric or asymmetric cryptography).
5. Encryption of "keep-alive" and alarm messages, preventing the attacker from correctly interpreting the "keep-alive" and alarm messages, being then unable to distinguish them.
6. Avoidance of periodicity of message generation, to avoid any attempt of analysis of the traffic patterns by an attacker.

3 Proof of Concept

The UbiSec&Sens HS-WSN demonstrator includes only a part of the overall concept, namely the sensor node island with 15 MicaZ sensor nodes equipped with intrusion detection sensors and a MicaZ sink node connected with the C2C in the periphery of the island. An IEEE 802.15.4 short-range radio interface supports communications between sensor nodes and the sink node. The latter constitutes the interface to the external monitoring systems, i.e., the C2C or police agent portable devices.

The demonstrator setting is now deployed at the INOV premises, comprising two rooms interconnected by a corridor, where sensor nodes are also deployed. The fact that all communication links must be established within line-of-sight due to transmit power constraints, forces routing paths to span from one to three hops from sensor to sink and vice-versa. A passive reader is also included, consisting of a MicaZ node connected to a laptop PC. This reader device shall be used to observe the traffic for protocol analysis purposes, as well as to test the security of the HS-WSN.

The GUI application runs both on the C2C and the reader device, allowing the demonstration of several functionalities: HS-WSN operation, including permanent monitoring of node status, alarm detection and issuing the tinyDSM queries; DSDV and DTSN message snooping; routing and application-level security. Configuration parameters such as the IP address and ports used by the tinyDSM proxy, serial port numbers, sensor node status timers, sensor node deployment locations and other attributes can all be set by editing initialization XML files.

Based on these settings, the functional demonstration of the WSN included several aspects. The basic functionalities like the monitoring of the node states, the alert generation and reception, the issuing and processing of tinyDSM queries and DTSN and DSDV protocol analysis were of main concern. However, the security related part proved the applicability of our architecture in such scenario. It included the demonstration of the security mechanisms by attempting to sneak into the WSN on protocol or middleware layer using a device with diverse level of knowledge about the secret keys. This demonstration has shown the node authentication and message integrity and encryption mechanisms on the middleware layer and the packet integrity and node authentication mechanisms of the DSDV protocol.

Regarding the performance evaluation of the demonstrator, the experiments have shown that in the setting described above all alarm messages were delivered within 500 milliseconds when symmetric cryptography was used (integrity check in DSDV, plus encryption and message authentication in tinyDSM). Since the query mechanism did not employ DTSN, the performance of query procedures turned out to be significantly worse than that of the alarm procedure with an average delay of 2 seconds being observed.

In fact, the delay introduced by the security means may be significant. In case of asymmetric cryptography mechanisms, the signature generation/verification and message encryption/decryption need about 2 seconds each for the 128 or 160 bit Elliptic Curve Cryptography. Additional message size overhead causes the asymmetric crypto to be less attractive than the symmetric cryptography (SkipJack, AES-128) where the delay is a matter of milliseconds.

4 Conclusion

This paper presented a WSN architecture, which is capable of satisfying the reliability, robustness and security requirements for intrusion detection. The set-up of a demonstrator allowed us to take also some preliminary conclusions for this type of approach. The physical data rate of 250 kbps featured by the IEEE 802.15.4 constitutes a significant scalability limitation. The low data rate implies that there must be a trade-off between the alarm transmission delay and query reliability, the detection of node failure/damage (generation frequency of the keep-alive messages) and the size of the WSN island. In our experiments, it was concluded that with a WSN island of 15 sensor nodes, the keep-alive message generation rate had to be set once every 6 seconds in order to guarantee an acceptable success rate for query requests due to the sink to nodes traffic. An option here would be an application of distributed keep-alive mechanism. Such a mechanism couples nodes in pairs or small groups where the partner nodes are responsible for monitoring each other states. In case a node is not active the other one generates an alert. Such a solution would reduce the multi-hop traffic to the exceptional situations only. One other issue with the communication is the bandwidth limitation caused by normal traffic in the same frequency band or by a jamming device controlled by an attacker. During our experiments we noticed that standard WLAN traffic can cause our alive and event messages to time out.

The availability of a location service would greatly improve the security of the system, preventing an attacker from changing the position of sensor nodes. Given the already mentioned limitations of indoor location systems, it would at least be useful to have logical topology information available at the sink node in order to detect node movement based on logical topology changes, although this would add to the communications overhead of the WSN.

Acknowledgements. The work described in this paper is based on results of IST FP6 project UbiSec&Sens. UbiSec&Sens receives research funding from the European Community's Sixth Framework Program. Apart from this, the European Commission has no responsibility for the content of this paper. The information in this document is provided as is and no guarantee or warranty is given that the information is fit for any particular purpose. The user thereof uses the information at its sole risk and liability.

References

1. UbiSec&Sens Project, http://www.ist-ubisecsens.org/
2. Piotrowski, K., Langendoerfer, P., Peter, S.: TinyDSM: A highly reliable cooperative data storage for Wireless Sensor Networks. In: Proceedings of International Symposium on Collaborative Technologies and Systems 2009, Baltimore, Maryland, USA, pp. 225–232 (2009)
3. Perkins, C., Bhagwat, P.: Highly Destination-Sequenced Dynamic Distance Vector Routing (DSDV) for Mobile Computers. In: Proceedings of the ACM SIGCOMM 1994, London, UK, pp. 234–244 (1994)
4. Marchi, B., Grilo, A., Nunes, M.: DTSN – Distributed Transport for Sensor Networks. In: Proc. IEEE Symposium on Computers and Communications (ISCC 2007), Aveiro, Portugal (2007)

Author Index

Abdelmalek, Abdelhafid 385
Abu-Ghazaleh, Nael B. 1
Akl, Selim G. 391

Bermond, Jean-Claude 69
Borges, Vinicius C.M. 55
Burmester, Mike 227

Cabero, José María 347
Casaca, Augusto 397
Casilari, E. 366
Cerpa, Alberto 255
Chávez, Edgar 360
Chrysos, Grigorios 312
Crespo, Pedro M. 30
Cui, Minghao 16
Curado, Marilia 55, 354
Czyzowicz, J. 194

Dehghan, Mehdi 270
Delicato, Flávia C. 379
Del Ser, Javier 30
de Medeiros, Breno 227
Djouani, Karim 284

El-Azouzi, R. 83
El-Khoury, R. 83

Feham, Mohamed 385
Fraser, Maia 360
Freeman, Ian 255
Fuentes, Lidia 379

Galtier, Jérôme 327
Gámez, Nadia 379
Garcia, Miguel 373
Gavalas, Damianos 213
Gil-Lopez, Sergio 30
Gomes, Cristiana 327
González-Cañete, F.J. 366
Gołębiewski, Zbigniew 166
Grilo, António 397

Haapola, Jussi 112
Hamam, Yskandar 284

Han, Richard 255
Han, Trung-Dinh 341
Harms, Janelle 241
Harras, Khaled A. 1
Hasslinger, Gerhard 42
Hauswirth, Manfred 98
Hernando, Gorka 347
Huang, Jyh-How 255
Hussain, Syed Rafiul 152

Islam, Kamrul 391

Jiang, Lun 255
Jodrá, José Luis 347

Kamthe, Ankur 255
Klonowski, Marek 166
Konstantopoulos, Charalampos 213
Koza, Michał 166
Kranakis, E. 194
Krizanc, D. 194
Kunz, Thomas 42
Kutyłowski, Mirosław 166

Lacuesta, Raquel 373
Lambadaris, I. 194
Langendoerfer, Peter 397
Ledbetter, John 255
Li, Xu 138
Liu, Tao 255
Lloret, Jaime 373

Majeed, Adnan 1
Malbasa, Veljko 180
Mamalis, Basilis 213
Martelli, Flavia 112
Martyna, Jerzy 126
Mendicute, Mikel 30
Mezei, Ivan 180
Miller, Chris 298
Mirebrahim, Hamid 270
Mishra, Shivakant 255
Mitton, Nathalie 138
Monteiro, Edmundo 55
Mpitziopoulos, Aristides 213
Munilla, Jorge 227

Narayanan, L.   194
Nascimento, Mario A.   241
Nisse, Nicolas   69
Ntlatlapa, Ntsibane   284

Oh, Hoon   341
Olabarrieta, Ignacio (Iñaki)   30
Olwal, Thomas O.   284
Opatrny, J.   194

Palma, David   354
Pantziou, Grammati   213
Papaefstathiou, Ioannis   312
Peinado, Alberto   227
Peñalver, Lourdes   373
Pereira, Daniel   55
Pérez, Susana   347
Piotrowski, Krzysztof   397
Pires, Paulo F.   379
Poellabauer, Christian   298
Pomalaza-Ráez, Carlos   112

Rahman, Ashikur   152
Razak, Saquib   1
Reyes, Patricio   69

Rivano, Hervé   69
Ryl, Isabelle   138

Sabir, E.   83
Saha, Subrata   152
Samanta, S.K.   83
Siarry, Patrick   284
Simplot, David   138
Slimane, Zohra   385
Stacho, L.   194
Stojmenovic, Ivan   180
Syrotiuk, Violet R.   16

Taleb-Ahmed, Abdelmalik   385
Tejeda, Héctor   360
Triviño-Cabrera, A.   366

Urrutia, J.   194

van Wyk, Barend J.   284
Vogt, Ryan   241

Yang, Yang   98
Yazdani, M.   194

Zuniga, Marco   98